FIVE THOUSAND CONCERTS

FIVE THOUSAND CONCERTS

A Commemorative History of the Utah Symphony

Conrad B. Harrison

**Utah Symphony
Society**

We are indebted to
JOSEPH ROSENBLATT
whose generous gift made the
publication of this history possible.

Library of Congress Catalog Card Number: 86-51389
ISBN Number: 0-916095-15-0

Cover Photo: *Maurice Abravanel and The Utah Symphony at Herod Atticus Amphitheatre, Athens, Greece.*

PREFACE

This book tells the remarkable story of the genesis, development, and establishment of the Utah Symphony. Commissioned by the symphony administration as a commemorative history, it is a journey through the rejection and acceptance, frustration and triumph that led to the orchestra's Five Thousandth Concert at the Salt Lake Tabernacle in Salt Lake City on the first day of February 1986.

It all began years ago with an orchestra that started and restarted a half-dozen times before the permanent Utah Symphony emerged from a make-work music project in the great depression of the 1930s. It struggled through the years of World War II, sacrificed to stay alive at mid-century, then progressed through an incredible part-time operation to become a world-class orchestra. The unrelenting persistence of dedicated leaders consistently won the day.

In preparing the history, I found it incomplete without the recognition of early efforts to perform symphonic masterpieces. Consequently, they are herewith recorded in their pioneer setting. Not only do they set the stage for symphony orchestra development in Utah since 1935, but they lend credibility, as well, to a concern for the cultural arts that came here with the pioneers in 1847. In those sporadic endeavors of early instrumentalists, we also find the beginnings of the regional character and spirit that are unique to the music of the Utah Symphony. Moreover, the administrative experiences of the period provided devotees with an early insight into the facts of symphony life—the constant struggle to obtain funds to survive.

Ties between the pioneer and modern eras of music-making are further defined in the personnel involved. Fewer than sixteen of the musicians in early orchestras, some of them dating back to 1902, performed in the Utah State Symphony Orchestra (later the Utah Symphony) inaugural concert in 1940. Arthur P. Freber was successively the concertmaster in 1913 and the concertmaster in 1940, and Reginald Beales was concertmaster in the last of the "pioneer" ensembles in 1927, conductor of the WPA Orchestra in the 1930s, and the second violin principal in 1940. Such a bridge cannot be ignored. Nor can we ignore the responsibility that emanates from the old adage "An institution that does not honor its past has no future."

The successes and failures, the starts and stops of the early orchestras also give added emphasis to the outstanding contributions of those who promoted and organized the Utah Symphony. Such crusaders as Gail Martin, Glenn Walker Wallace, Reginald Beales, and Fred E. Smith did something others had tried and failed to do: they established a permanent orchestra.

It remained for two giants in Utah symphony history to scale the heights with the orchestra. The incredible Maestro Maurice Abravanel breathed musical excellence into the ensemble from the time he took over in 1947. For thirty-two years he was all things to the Utah Symphony. He built it musically, fought for its causes, sacrificed for survival, and, as a father figure, earned the complete confidence and trust of his players. And though he was offered every inducement to move to sunnier climes, Maurice stayed on, a dedicated music director and conductor determined to mold into reality a virtuoso instrument.

"Big Mo," as Abravanel was affectionately called by the musicians, had been building for nearly twenty years when Wendell J. Ashton came on board and began supplying fuel for "the big machine." A raw recruit with absolutely no interest in symphony music, Wendell nonetheless threw all his amazing fund-raising and promotion skills into the search for money— food for the symphony to grow on. He promoted international travel to build prestige and to sell the home folk on the greatness of their orchestra as an asset to community, state, and region. The result has been obvious.

Along with the commission to compile a history of the Utah Symphony, this author was given a challenge to produce a work that would be "factual, fair, and fascinating." Only the reader can say whether or not the book is fascinating, although every effort has been made to make it so.

How factual and fair the contents are can be measured only by the greater effort that went into these two charges—the long hours of research, interviews, conversations, and double-checking over a period far too short for a work of this magnitude. It leaves us grateful and in debt to so many sources of information.

Acknowledgements are due those who graciously gave of their time for interviews and telephone conversations and those who made available important information and documents. Among the most helpful was Herold L. (Huck) Gregory, manager and executive director of the symphony for twenty-nine years and a strong and stable influence through the orchestra's greatest building and growth period. Without his assistance, the book would not have been possible. His recorded minutes of all board, executive, and other committee meetings, together with his daily documentation of operations and proceedings in well-organized files, and the printed symphony programs, brochures, and other publications for the period were at our disposal.

Among those interviewed were former Utah Symphony presidents Glenn Walker Wallace, J. Allan Crockett, Wendell J. Ashton, and Stephen W. Swaner; present chairman of the board, Jon Huntsman; music directors Maurice Abravanel, Varujan Kojian, and Joseph Silverstein; and former associate conductor Ardean Watts. Other musicians to furnish valuable information were Reginald Beales, Kenneth Kuchler, Don Peterson, Dorothy and David Freed, and Sheldon Hyde.

The long list of helpful contacts also includes former governors J. Bracken Lee and Calvin L. Rampton, former United States senator Frank E. Moss, former state senator Mitchell Melich, Obert C. Tanner, Donald P. Lloyd, Willam Christensen, Lowell M. Durham, John M. and M. Walker Wallace, Jack Goodman, Mrs. T. Bowring Woodbury, Mrs. Maxine Bleak Hill, a former symphony development director Ray L. White, Ruby Stringham Garrett, and John Talmage.

For the Ogden section we are indebted to Mrs. Harmon (Gwen) Williams and Jean Pell, and for the Utah Symphony Guild chapter much is owed to Beverly Johnson, Blanche Freed, Margaret Beecher, Helen Lloyd, and Mary Muir.

Our appreciation goes to members of the symphony staff, in addition to Huck Gregory, for their pleasant cooperation and assistance. Carleen Landes was particularly helpful in verifying information about people, places, and dates. While extremely busy in her role as the symphony's artistic manager, she was always available and willing to assist with the research. Another helpful contributor to the story was orchestra manager and consultant Shirl Swenson. Information on financial and fund-raising matters, for which we are most grateful, was supplied by accounting manager Douglas Neiswender and former development director Edward F. John.

Much of the book's readability can be credited to a conscientious editor, Jack Lyon. To Ireva Noren we give thanks for transcribing the interview tapes and typing the manuscript. Finally, we are indebted to the noted historian Leonard J. Arrington; Dr. Burtis R. Evans, chairman of the symphony's history committee, and Jack Goodman, versatile writer, for reading the manuscript and offering suggestions.

My thanks goes to the staff at the main branch of the Salt Lake City Public Library, with special gratitude to those accommodating people in the Special Collections and Periodicals area in the sub-basement where I spent many long hours poring over microfilms of newspapers printed as far back as the 1860s. Realizing that experiences are either forgotten or blown out of proportion when they are not recorded, it became necessary, in order to get the facts, to secure information where it had been written down. Consequently, the *Deseret Evening News,* the *Salt Lake Tribune,* the *Salt Lake Telegram,* and the *Salt Lake Herald-Republican* were constant companions. Excerpts from the *New York Times* were also employed in the research.

While this author's "Pioneer Symphony," a history of early orchestral efforts in Utah published in the printed symphony programs in 1949-50 and updated in 1958-59, offered a quick opening for the history, it was first thoroughly checked for inaccuracies. Helpful in this respect, in addition to the newspaper files, were minutes, located in the symphony office, of those early orchestra organization meetings. These included Salt Lake Symphony and Philharmonic board meeting proceedings from 1914 through 1922, minutes of the Utah Symphony from its organization on April 8, 1940, to September 14, 1943, and minutes of Utah State Institute of Fine Arts board meetings from its organization meeting on June 12, 1937, to December 31, 1958. We would add to these a 1959 thesis by Deane Wakley Brown at Brigham Young University on the "Growth and Development of Utah Professional Symphonic Orchestras Prior to 1940."

Among other research aides were the files of J. Allan Crockett and Maurice Abravanel, the Utah Arts Council, the Utah Historical Society, and the following published books: *The Study of the History of Music*, by Edward Dickinson; *Golden Encyclopedia of Music*, by Norman Lloyd; *Harvard Brief Dictionary of Music*, by Willi Apel and Ralph T. Daniel; *Everyman's Dictionary of Music*, by Eric Blom; *The Columbia Encyclopedia; The International Cyclopedia of Music and Musicians*, edited by Oscar Thompson; *History of Salt Lake City* by Edward W. Tullidge; *Music in the Southwest*, by Howard Swan; *Utah Since Statehood, Historical and Biographical*, by Noble Warrum; *Merchants and Miners, the Walker Brothers and Their Bank*, by Jonathan Bliss; *Bicentennial Center for the Arts*, by Obert C. Tanner; *Symphony Conductors of the U.S.A.*, by Hope Stoddard; *Notes without Music: an Autobiography*, by Darius Milhaud; and *History of the San Francisco Symphony Orchestra*, by David Schneider.

INTRODUCTION

The orchestra, already performing in the opera houses of Europe, became a symphony orchestra when the classical symphony form was born near the end of the seventeenth century. With that event it took on its most important dimension and since has become the most powerful, most expressive, and the greatest of all musical instruments.

The origin of the symphony goes back to the Italian three-movement overture played by the opera orchestra and popularized by Alessandro Scarlatti (1660-1725). The pieces, with their fast-slow-fast movements, were presented as a "Symphony before the Opera," perhaps in the 1690s while Scarlatti was court conductor at Naples.

As the symphony became dissociated from the opera for concert performance, a fourth movement was sometimes added. But it was not until the first of the great symphonists, Franz Joseph Haydn, composed the thirty-first of his 104 symphonies in 1765 that the four-movement form became standard.

Haydn, Mozart, and Beethoven developed the symphony through a ninety-five year period from the birth of Haydn in 1732 to the death of Beethoven in 1827, with the first great symphonies being attributed to the genius of Mozart. All three composed in the classical form, but it was Beethoven who provided a clean break with his magnificent "Eroica" Symphony No. 3 in E Flat. With this work came new challenges for the instrumental ensemble in the field of dynamics, created to heighten dramatic intensity and increase expressiveness. From then on there was no turning back as symphonic works steadily increased the demands on the orchestra.

Germany was the first to show a strong interest in the production of symphony music, responding with orchestras in as many as eight cities by the middle of the eighteenth century. Most famous was the Electoral orchestra of Mannheim with its forty to fifty professional musicians.

Still in existence from that group is the Leipzig Gewandhaus-Orchester, organized in 1743, a full seventy years before the founding of the London Philharmonic in 1813. The Paris Conservatory Orchestra was organized in 1828 and the Vienna Philharmonic in 1842.

The first symphony orchestra in the United States, the New York Philharmonic Symphony, also appeared in 1842, the Society being organized in April and the orchestra performing its first concert the following December 7.

Five years later the Mormon pioneers secured a foothold in the Salt Lake Valley of the Rocky Mountains, and in another forty-five years the Territory of Utah heard its first symphony concert in the Salt Lake Theatre on May 17, 1892.

Several abortive attempts to create a permanent symphony orchestra followed that first concert, leaving in their wake an interrupted march of futility. Strangely enough, it took the depression years of the 1930s and their resulting make-work projects to provide the beginnings of the Utah State Symphony Orchestra, first heard on May 8, 1940. With that, the long parade of frustrating intervals was over, and the symphony was in Utah to stay.

CONTENTS

Preface   v

Introduction   xi

PART ONE: PIONEER SYMPHONY   1

1   The Beginning 3
2   Rhapsodies and Reversals......................... 15
3   The Philharmonic 27
4   End of an Era 41

PART TWO: WPA ORCHESTRA   57

5   Beating the Depression 59
6   The Launching Pad 65
     *Photos:*A Period of Transition 79

PART THREE: MAJOR SYMPHONY   89

7   A State Orchestra 91
8   A Home for the Symphony 123
9   Professional Blueprint........................... 131
     *Photos:*Conductors and Composers 144
10   Enter Abravanel 149
11   Crisis on the Hill 167
12   Part-Time Operation............................ 181

*Photos:*A Sampling of Soloists 186

13 Spit and Baling Wire 195

14 An Era of Recordings 217

*Photos:*Where History was Made 229

15 Mountain West by Bus 239

16 Coming of Age 247

*Photos:*Reaching Beyond the Borders 275

17 International Orchestra 285

*Photos:*Behind the Scenes 301

18 The Symphony Guild 307

19 New Home for the Symphony 317

*Photos:*A Few of the Orchestra's Benefactors 328

20 The Maestro Retires 333

21 The Kojian Years 349

22 Ahead with Silverstein 377

*Photos:*Historic Milestones 402

Index   403

PART ONE

PIONEER SYMPHONY

CHAPTER 1

THE BEGINNING

Five thousand concerts and forty-six years after its first performance at Kingsbury Hall on the University of Utah campus in 1940, the Utah Symphony has played its way to national and international acclaim—a leader among this nation's thirty major orchestras.

Joseph Silverstein, now the fourth music director and conductor in the long pull to the top, says the job was done by Maurice Abravanel with "spit, baling wire, and mirrors." "Incredible!" he exclaims with regard to his predecessor and his thirty-two years at the helm.

The story of those Abravanel years, with the seven before and seven after, represents the principal history of the symphony orchestra in Utah. Through those forty-six seasons the Utah Symphony has found a permanency that eluded musicians and the rest of the cultural community for forty-eight years, going back to 1892.

That bygone era remains as an important segment of a long symphony experience and stands as a collection of events and challenges much like those since 1940. It is a part of an overall history of cultural growth in Utah and Salt Lake City that is little different from that to be found in the sagas of the nation's older and larger music centers. In this western setting the story contains perhaps more and longer periods of inactivity during the struggle for permanency, but the fundamental problems of musical, artistic, and financial growth have been much the same.

As with other orchestras, there has been with the Utah Symphony a battle for existence. From that battle has come a foundation molded from a determination, perseverance, courage, sweat, and loyalty that outlasted and turned aside frustration, discouragement, criticism, disrespect, belittlement, and pettiness along the way.

There has come, too, a Utah "spirit," a regional character and local personality to distinguish the Utah Symphony from so many of the world's great and more famous orchestras. Such a spirit has evolved from the presence of as many "home" musicians as possible in the ensemble and a policy of playing before audiences throughout the entire state of Utah and the surrounding region.

Early production of instrumental music in the Salt Lake Valley quite naturally was the exclusive property of local musicians, all of them pioneer immigrants, who, other than those in the Nauvoo Band, perhaps, had never before played together. Maybe that is why it took forty-five years after the settling of the Valley to produce the first symphony concert in the area.

It was to be expected that the pioneer members of The Church of Jesus Christ of Latter-day Saints would bring their music with them. They were a people always with music and were a factor in its production wherever they traveled or congregated. As Howard Swan observes in his book *Music in the Southwest*, "Wherever he lived the Mormon and his music were inseparable companions. Thus, any history of the Mormon church is complete only if the story of its music is included."

A band organized from the ranks of the Nauvoo Legion of the Illinois Militia led the Saints on their march across Iowa to Winter Quarters, Nebraska, from their mob-pillaged and burned homes in Nauvoo in 1846. That same band was reorganized in 1850, three years after the Mormons moved west, and began playing regular concerts in the Bowery on Temple Square. It also furnished music for pioneer celebrations, dances, and some worship services, its principal duty being to raise the spirits of the pioneer settlers.

As Salt Lake City grew with the influx of Latter-day Saint converts and other immigrants, the number of musicians, particularly those playing instruments, increased proportionately. Writing in New York in 1857, after visiting the Mormon sanctuary, John Hyde said it appeared to him that "almost every third man was a fiddler."

Interest in the symphony and other larger forms of music for the instrumental ensemble became evident as early as 1855 in a letter directed to the LDS British publication the *Millennial Star* and picked up in the *Deseret Evening News* of March 1. Signed by Jonathan Grimshaw, secretary to an organization called the "Deseret Philharmonic Society," which claimed some fifty members, the letter was one of appeal for music.

"I wish through you," it states, "to inform our brethren and sisters preparing to come from Europe and the Eastern States, and who feel an interest in the objects of this Society, as to what kind of music we are most in want of, so that it may be a little guide to them in their selection, which they can donate or loan to the Society on their arrival here.

"We are much in want of the Oratorios of Handel, Haydn, Mendelssohn, etc., and new works of merit, the whole with full orchestral accompaniments in separate parts, and as much as possible with singing copies in separate parts. We also want the best Overtures, Symphonies and Dancing Music for a full orchestra. . . ."

The letter apparently brought some results, some of them most likely coming through a number of well-schooled and talented men drawn from London and other European centers.

One of them, Charles J. Thomas, arrived from England just before The Church of Jesus Christ of Latter-day Saints completed and opened the Salt Lake Theatre on the corner of State Street and First South in 1862, an event that was to have a marked effect on orchestral development on the local scene. Until that time the old Social Hall, built in 1852 and dedicated on New Year's Day in 1853, had been the entertainment center.

Thomas had been associated with several orchestras in England, and his experience gained for him the directorship of both the Salt Lake Theatre orchestra and the Tabernacle Choir. He made such an impression that it prompted Edward W. Tullidge to record in his *History of Salt Lake City* that "the advent of C. J. Thomas marks an epoch in the musical history of the city."

The theater orchestra of twenty men, many of whom had no previous musical training, made its debut at the dedication of the Salt Lake Theatre on Saturday night, March 8, 1862. Its first duty apparently was to accompany soloist William C. Dunbar and a choir in "The Star Spangled Banner."

In the beginning, the musicians played without compensation, either for rehearsal or performance. As may be expected, the players soon objected to that arrangement, and the first labor negotiations between instrumentalists and management in the new territory was recorded. An ultimatum of "no pay, no play" from the musicians initiated the proceedings.

In remembering his days in the old Salt Lake Theatre, George D. Pyper, who for many years managed the historic institution, tells of that early orchestra and its first experience in "collective bargaining." It is very much the same story repeated some years ago by Henry Giles, a pianist with the group, to David W. Evans, a Salt Lake advertising executive who held some rich memories of his own concerning the years in which his father played in the first symphony orchestra of the 1890s.

The elderly Mr. Giles stopped Mr. Evans on the street one day to reminisce about the latter's grandfather of the same name, David W. Evans, second violin player, a shoemaker by trade, who was crippled, and the one player brave enough to confront Brigham Young about the grievance.

A move had been made to negotiate "for higher wage scales," and since the theater was Church-owned and operated, President Young himself appeared to discuss the matter with the musicians.

The meeting started out in the "Green Room" of the theater and then was moved to the stage to accommodate the group of musicians, actors, and stage personnel on hand. The Mormon leader told the musicians that their calling to the orchestra was much the same as that of any other unpaid calling in the Church. Then, starting at one end of the group and directing his question to each player individually, he asked if he would continue to play without pay. All agreed until President Young came to Mr. Evans.

"Well now, President Young," said the violinist, "it seems since the stage hands and other employees at the theater are paid for their services, we should get something also."

"All right, Brother Evans," returned the president, "I have no objections. We'll pay."

John S. Lindsay, writing in *The Mormons and the Theatre*, expands on the incident, reporting that the musicians had already received some compensation of sorts. "Two performances had been gotten up as benefits," he said, "one for the ladies of the company and other for the gentlemen—the two nights' receipts were aggregated and divided up among the company according to their respective merits or worth to the management."

Even this was not a cash arrangement, however, with one-third paid in cash and the remaining two-thirds to be received in store orders and tithing-office pay.

In the confrontation between Evans and the president, Lindsay states that the violinist charged that it was not fair to be paid in the manner being followed because of the demands upon his time and the work he was required to miss.

In the end, other players, encouraged by their colleague's spunk, entered the bargaining procedure, and a settlement was reached providing a wage scale of from fifteen to twenty dollars a week—again "one-third in cash and the other two-thirds in store orders and tithing-office pay."

The incidents surrounding the first labor negotiations involving musicians in Utah quite likely occurred soon after George Careless, a brilliant composer and conductor, became director of the Salt Lake Theatre orchestra and the Tabernacle Choir in 1865. Mr. Thomas had moved to St. George, and Mr. Careless, then only twenty-six, was appointed his successor. The young Mormon convert had studied at the Royal Academy of London and had achieved much success in England before bringing his unusual talents to Salt Lake City in 1864.

George Careless was responsible for changing the status of the Salt Lake Theatre orchestra from a group of twenty unpaid volunteers to a professional ensemble of seven paid musicians. His suggestion to reduce the number of players and pay them won the consent of President Young and probably came as an aftermath of the collective bargaining session.

Ambitious as well as capable, Mr. Careless was named conductor of the "Handel and Haydn Society," which later changed its name to the Philharmonic Society, and he directed the first performance of Handel's "Messiah" in the Rocky Mountains at the Salt Lake Theatre in 1875 with a choir of two hundred and a "full orchestra." Tullidge records the organization of a "Careless Orchestra" in March of 1879 and notes that the conductor, in 1885, "succeeded in organizing the largest local orchestra brought together in this city, consisting of 45 members."

In the meantime, another event that was to have an effect on orchestral music in the city occurred with the opening in 1882 of the elegant Walker Opera House. It stood at or near the site of the present Capitol Theatre on West Second South and was built by the Walker Brothers of early mining and banking fame and the ancestral family of Glenn Walker Wallace, a figure in the formation of a permanent symphony orchestra in Utah nearly sixty years later.

The main attraction at the opening of the new music center on June 5, 1882, was the "Careless Orchestra," which performed in concert and accompanied several solo numbers. Soon after the opening, the opera house developed its own orchestra, and until the building burned down on July 3, 1890, it vied with the Salt Lake Theatre for attention as the cultural showplace of the day.

Undoubtedly members of those orchestras under George Careless later played in Utah's first symphony concert at the Salt Lake Theatre in May 17, 1892, the performance taking place after a long period of planning and preparation. The *Deseret Evening News* reported on March 5, 1888 — four years before the musicians reached the concert stage—the organization of the Salt Lake Symphony Orchestra Association "with the intention of producing some the works of the great composers." C. J. Thomas, who had returned to the Salt Lake Theatre orchestra podium in 1871, became the first president, with Ebeneezer Beesley as vice-president, J. A. Evans as secretary and treasurer, and Anton Pedersen as conductor.

Said the *News*, "The Salt Lake Symphony Orchestra is the name under which a majority of the orchestral musicians of this city have organized themselves.... The movement seems to meet with the approval of all classes of musicians, and the membership includes both professionals and amateurs. The organization is the largest and most complete of the class ever effected in this city."

One more in an impressive list of musical masters to come from Europe to the Salt Lake Valley, Professor Pedersen was obviously a leading force in the 1892 presentation. Since his arrival in 1875, he had gained the respect of the entire community for his musical achievements on a wide front, particularly as a conductor and organizer.

So outstanding was Pedersen's contribution that it prompted John D. Spencer, in a biographical sketch, to conclude, "As one of the pioneer musicians and instructors, his influence has permeated almost every nook and corner of the state and there are few musicians in Utah who do not owe something either directly or indirectly to Anton Pedersen."

It was, indeed, an appropriate observation. The gifted musician not only had initiated Utah's first symphony concert, but had won national honors with his bands and had organized and conducted, with great praise for their performances, the Orpheus and Norwegian male glee clubs and a women's orchestra. His fame as a composer and organist was widely known, and his versatility as an instrumentalist was remarkable. He was an accomplished performer on the piano, baritone horn, viola, violin, and clarinet.

Pedersen also organized and conducted the Walker Opera House orchestra and directed all music affairs at the All Hallows

College, a Catholic school for young men, which operated on
East Second South in Salt Lake City from 1889 to 1918.

A "Gentile" who was greatly respected in a Latter-day Saint
stronghold, Pedersen came to the Mormon mountainland from
the fjords of Norway. He was born and christened Anton Freber
in the little town of Skien, south of Christiania (now Oslo), in
1855. Soon after that his father died, and young Anton eventually took the name of a stepfather named Pedersen. Later,
however, he chose to preserve the name of Freber by per-
suading his own son to adopt the name of Arthur Pedersen
Freber.

From the Spencer story we learn that Pedersen exhibited
unmistakable music talent as a boy. His leanings in that
direction, however, "did not receive the whole-hearted support
of his stepfather, who was a hotel proprietor and land owner
and thought that would be a more profitable field for him to
devote his energies."

Young Anton nevertheless received a thorough musical
training in Skien and became organist in one of the churches
before going to Christiania at the age of seventeen to continue
his studies. There he mastered the violin, piano, and "Wald-
horn" and soon was playing and studying under Edvard Grieg
and Johan Svendsen. He struck up a friendship with another
noted Norwegian composer, Christian Sinding, and the pair
lived together until Pedersen, at the age of twenty, left Norway
for Utah.

The young musician found it most difficult to create an
outlet for his musical talents in the new country, and his trying
experiences in those early days might have driven him back
home had it not been for the one obsession that drew him to
Salt Lake City. That was his love for Mary Olive Larsen, a comely
young Norwegian convert to The Church of Jesus Christ of
Latter-day Saints.

Gleanings from the family history imply that the love of
Anton and Mary Olive for each other was mutually desperate,
and it didn't take much urging on the part of the girl to get
Anton to come to the Beehive country. They were married
within a year after his arrival.

Pedersen's active interest in band music seemed to find a springboard with his membership in Croxall's Band. Not long afterward, in 1882, following the opening of the Walker Opera House, the *Salt Lake Herald* and *Deseret Evening News* noted the organization of a new "Opera House Orchestra and Silver Band under Mr. Pedersen."

This brought on some published statements by concerned parties, indicating some contention over musicians' leaving Mark Croxall's band and the George Careless orchestra to form the new organizations. Apparently the competition for instrumentalists to perform in the growing number of bands and orchestras on the local scene was becoming rather heated.

The published comments of musicians created such a fuss that it prompted one anonymous writer to ridicule the affair in a poetic contribution entitled "Blood on the Music Moon" and subtitled "Sweet Harmony as a Mighty Provocation of Wrath and Jealousy." Its closing entreaty was most appropriate: "Let us have peace."

Apparently "peace" came, and the new orchestra built up an enthusiastic following. In reporting the presentation of "Esmeralda" on January 12, 1883, the press found the execution of the musicians to be "exceedingly beautiful" and handled with "care, study, great ability and abundant taste."

On July 3, 1890, the opera house burned to the ground. It was never rebuilt. Years later the Orpheum Theatre, now the Capitol, was erected on almost the same spot on Second South.

The band organized at the same time as the opera house orchestra, grew into the Knights of Pythias Band, pride of the city in the '90s. Later Pedersen brought into prominence the Utah State Band, and on June 12, 1906, he introduced his "Ladies Orchestra" of ten performers.

So occupied was Anton with his prize-winning bands and other activities that he was out of the symphony picture from 1892 to 1913, when he became conductor of the Salt Lake Philharmonic. Spencer refers to the opening concert of that orchestra on April 6, 1913, as "one of the professor's greatest successes" and suggests the strain of the unusual effort as the cause of a collapse that resulted in his death six weeks later on May 18 at the age of 58.

Pedersen used members of his defunct Walker Opera House orchestra as a nucleus for the 1892 Salt Lake Symphony. Only two members of the original Salt Lake Theatre Orchestra of 1862, violinist Ebeneezer Beesley and trumpet player C. J. Thomas, were among the thirty-three players to perform on the night of May 17, 1892. Two of those on the roster, "Mr. and Mrs. Prof. Hartman," were specialists with the zither.

The concertmaster for the occasion was Willard E. Weihe, an accomplished Norwegian violinist and popular recitalist. Born in 1856 in Christiania, he followed his fellow countryman Anton Pedersen to Utah and conducted the Salt Lake Theatre orchestra briefly, beginning in 1885.

By the time the symphony orchestra began rehearsals two months before its performance in 1892, A. S. Zimmerman had replaced Thomas as president, and George Spohr had become the secretary. Each added strong support to the project, with particular credit extended to Spohr for bringing the body of musicians together. "He has been untiring in his efforts both to get the needed instruments as well as the performers," the *Deseret Evening News* reported. Apparently he had some help from the "Choral Society," which "aided also by loaning money to procure timpanis and trumpets," while offering encouragement toward forming an instrumental ensemble to support its choral efforts.

With the orchestra hard at work on its forthcoming concert, the *News* sent a reporter to a rehearsal at the Social Hall, popular gathering place for the Saints, now long since replaced by the marker on State Street at the west entrance to Social Hall Avenue. He was obviously impressed.

"Unusual strains of music have often of late been heard by people near old Social Hall," said his story in the March 30 edition. "On entering the place a few evenings ago, our reporter was almost lifted off his feet and landed in the dear old Music Hall of Boston. An orchestra of nearly forty men in rows surrounded a conductor's stand, and to complete the picture a magnificent harp towered up in the center.... The *News* long ago devotedly wished that someone might be found who would make of instrumentalists what Professor Evan Stephens [then conductor of the Tabernacle Choir] was making of vocalists—a strong, magnificent organization who labored to improve themselves in a body for art as well as individual benefit. Here, it seems, was the man in the person of Prof. Anton Pedersen, wielding the baton over a fine body of instrumentalists....

"This orchestra is a decided and most important step in our musical advancement, and as such, deserves recognition. With continued perseverance it means that we shall have the finest orchestra west of Chicago."

The writer apparently missed the feminine touch supplied by Mrs. J. Bell at the "magnificent harp" and Mrs. Hartman with her zither, but he caught the vision of a permanent symphony orchestra—a vision to be held and repeated by music reporters and critics until the goal was reached nearly a half century later.

Only two true symphonic works—the Andante and Allegro movements from Beethoven's First Symphony and the Schubert "Unfinished" Symphony—were played at the May 17, 1892, concert. The remainder of the evening, with the exception of the opening "Wander-Ziel Lustspiel," by Keler, and closing selections from "Nanon," by Moses, was given over to vocal and instrumental solos. The programming was after the pattern of the times, with the long list of soloists including Frances Lincoln, George D. Pyper, H. S. Goddard, and R. C. Easton, vocalists; Adolph Saxe, saxophone; William C. Clive, violin; and Walter Simms, clarinet.

Considerable attention was given the concert by the newspapers. The *Salt Lake Tribune* made quite a point of the apparent youthfulness of the personnel. It accepted the orchestra as "an organization for the younger generation of Salt Lake's musicians," adding that "the claims of this juvenile company of musicians have been modest—they have made no pretense of rivaling the efforts of more mature brethren nor of startling the profession with remarkable results."

Both the *Tribune* and the *Salt Lake Herald* said that the listeners were surprised at what they heard, the *Herald* observing that people "had mainly conceived the idea that it was a band composed more or less of amateurs, who should be encouraged and patronized, but who could not be expected to furnish entertainment for a musical audience.

"When the orchestra, therefore, nearly thirty strong and including several instruments seldom seen in local organizations, plunged boldly into Beethoven and Schubert symphonies and executed them with truth, boldness, vigor and correctness, it began to dawn on music lovers that probably the long waited for local orchestra was here at last, and that the Choral Society and Choir no longer need repine over the lack of instrumental adjuncts."

The *News* praised the efforts of the "young musical organization," noting that it was "more than a company of amateurs" that played the symphonies "with much precision and even at times, elegantly." The reviewer concluded that "the rendition indicated sufficiently what may be expected when the orchestra has had time to develop into maturity."

On the financial side, the association may have collected enough to pay its expenses, with a few dollars to spare. The *Herald* reported the audience to be a "very good one, and the orchestra probably cleared $200 on its initial effort." According to advertisements, the house was scaled from a low of twenty-five cents to a high of one dollar for parquette seats.

Pedersen's players did not become the "long waited for" orchestra the community had hoped for. They disbanded and became more interested in theater orchestras, bands, and other pursuits. Consequently, it was ten years before another Salt Lake Symphony tried to establish itself. The period of dormancy was long, but the 1892 orchestra had furnished a beginning for the sound of symphony in the west.

CHAPTER 2

RHAPSODIES AND REVERSALS

T he young look so evident in the first Salt Lake Symphony Orchestra of 1892 was still very much in evidence at the 1902 revival. One needed to look no farther than the podium, where Arthur Shepherd, only twenty-two years of age, was at the controls.

After a dry spell of more than ten years, perhaps some youthful initiative was needed to get symphony music back on the local stage. Shepherd, a remarkably talented musician from the Mormon settlement of Paris, Idaho, was anxious to make his mark and had put together an orchestra of thirty-three members. It was the same number that had played under Professor Pedersen in 1892, but fewer than a half dozen were repeats from the first ensemble.

He had also enlisted some strong support, the most significant coming in the form of full backing from the Salt Lake Theatre as the sole sponsor and underwriter of the event. Two days before the concert, the *Deseret Evening News* reported in its Saturday, November 22, edition that the "Salt Lake Theatre management has taken the matter in hand and is paying every musician for rehearsals as well as for the performance."

Theatre manager George D. Pyper apparently expected the project to pay for itself at the box office. A new surge of good feeling and rising spirits had come to the valley with Utah's admission to statehood on January 4, 1896, and concerts of all kinds seemed to be growing in popularity. The November 24, 1902, symphony offering was but the first in a big Thanksgiving week schedule for music lovers.

Two attractions were billed for Thanksgiving Day, one of them a concert version of Giuseppe Verdi's "Il Trovatore" by the Tabernacle Choir and soloists at the Tabernacle. The other was a concert and minstrel show by the popular John Held Band at the Salt Lake Theatre.

Young Shepherd made his second appearance of the week in the opera production, this time at the piano in sharing accompaniment with organist J. J. McClellan. Evan Stephens conducted the choir in a performance the press found to be disappointing. The *Salt Lake Tribune* chided singers who were apparently more interested in celebrating the holiday than in performing. "Choir members who were absent, and the gaps in the rows of benches told the tale, did not treat their conductor fairly," the reviewer stated. He noted that the choir was at one-third its regular strength and that "the men especially were, oh, so weak."

Except for a letdown at the symphony box office, it was a good week for Shepherd. His first home appearance with the Salt Lake Symphony Orchestra was a distinct success, and his piano accompaniments, with those of McClellan at the organ, were hailed as "the features" of the opera production at the Tabernacle.

The symphony concert was a triumph in every category but the ticket-window receipts. The audience was reportedly "a handsome one, but not what the strong merits of the attraction justified." As a result, the theater wound up with a deficit of $200 to $300—a rather disappointing return for three months of toil on the part of Shepherd and Pyper.

For his initial program, the young conductor catered to the listeners with music very much like that served up at modern "pops" concerts. As in 1892, the one symphony to be played in its entirety was Schubert's "Unfinished." Other orchestral fare included the Overture to Nicolai's "Merry Wives of Windsor," two Norwegian Dances by Grieg, the "Ronde d'amour" by Westerhout, and a minuet by Boccherini.

So roundly was the tuneful "Ronde" applauded that it had to be repeated, the *Tribune* noting that "a rule which the management tried to observe of not responding to encores had to be broken in this instance."

In the opinion of the *News*, the "real ambitious effort of the orchestra" was contained in its performance of the closing Schubert symphony. It was "most admirably executed," added the reviewer, "and though it lasted fifteen minutes, it was followed by a breathlessness that told that this highest form of musical expression was thoroughly appreciated by the audience."

As usual, the sonority of the string section drew special attention. George E. Skelton was outstanding as concertmaster, a position he filled throughout Shepherd's stay with the baton. He was among the "seasoned musicians" who, under "the inspiration of Mr. Shepherd played, as a rule, with precision of confidence, a confidence amply justified," according to the *Tribune*.

Soloists for the evening included a mezzo-soprano, Lottie Levy; Baritone Charles Kent; and a distinguished harpist with the touring Royal Italian Band then in the area, Signor Setaro.

Alluding to the financial deficit, the *News* said that the "deep impression" created by Shepherd and his players "only needs following up in an intelligent manner to have the orchestra placed on a footing that will make it a stable and permanent institution."

But symphony production again stopped, this time for a two-year period, and did not resume until its supporters had built a reserve fund and scheduled a concert for December 6, 1904, at the Salt Lake Theatre. By that time Shepherd had attained considerable stature in his profession, which was not surprising considering his background.

Before the remarkable young musician took over the Salt Lake Symphony in 1902 at the age of twenty-two, he had already

compiled an amazing set of credentials, which included ten
years as a student, teacher, composer, concert pianist, and
conductor. He was only twelve years old when he left his home
on the shores of Bear Lake to enter the New England Conservatory of Music in Boston. There he studied with George
Chadwick and other notable music masters for five years. He
graduated in 1897 and settled in Salt Lake City as a music
teacher and composer. His first major success in composition
came just before his conducting debut in Salt Lake in 1902 when
his "Overture Joyeuse" won the Paderewski prize.

The first of three brothers to have a distinct influence on
early symphony development in Utah before it gave way to the
Federal Music Project in the 1930s, Arthur conducted the Salt
Lake Symphony Orchestra in eleven concerts over a period of
five years. He returned to the New England Conservatory in 1908
as a member of the faculty, then went to Cleveland to become
assistant conductor of the Cleveland Orchestra and professor of
music at Western Reserve University. He returned once more to
the podium in Salt Lake City on December 10, 1952, as guest
conductor of the Utah Symphony in one of his latest compositions, "Horizons"—Four Western Pieces for Orchestra. Not long
afterward he died in Cleveland, where he had found his real
niche as a leader in American music.

Shepherd faced an orchestra of forty players for the 1904
symphony renewal and went to the Mendelssohn "Scotch"
Symphony No. 3 in A Minor for the featured work. Westerhout's
"Ronde" and one of the Norwegian Dances by Grieg were again
on the program, along with the Johann Strauss "Southern
Roses" waltz, a work called "The Two Hussars," and Elgar's
"Pomp and Circumstance." Solo numbers by Baritone Goddard
and Flutist W. J. Flashman rounded out the evening.

In reviewing the affair, the *Deseret Evening News* apparently was unaware of the 1892 or the 1902 concerts. "Salt Lake
experienced its first symphony concert last night," began the
News review. "Other orchestra concerts we have had, but
probably none before in which a symphony was made the
feature of the program."

Reference also was made to "the bassoon in the hands of

Mr. Evans" as a "new acquisition" of the orchestra. Yet this instrument, in the same hands, had drawn mention in the *News's* coverage of the 1892 symphony inaugural.

On the other hand, the *Salt Lake Tribune* treated the concert as if it were one in a series, stating that the Mendelssohn symphony was "the real gem of the orchestra numbers and was splendidly rendered." It also noted the "untiring efforts" of the director, whose aim "first, last and all the time has been to raise the musical standard of the city by making the great majority of persons familiar with the best in music."

Both the musical content and the length of the program were obvious concerns of concert producers for many years. Newspapers seldom, if ever, made mention of the starting time of an evening event, either in advance publicity or advertisements. That was because Salt Lake City was strictly an "8:30 town." Everyone knew that was the time the curtain went up, and they expected to be on their way home within an hour and a half later.

In promoting the orchestra's second appearance under Shepherd, the *News* assured the potential audience that the Mendelssohn would be "the only heavy number of the night" and that "seven lighter and shorter numbers, and encores, including solo specials, were of such length as to bring down the curtain before 10 o'clock."

Afterward, the *Tribune* noted that "the program lasted an hour and a half." The *News* carried the matter to greater lengths by suggesting that "a special word of praise ought to be said for the length of the program," since the audience "was dismissed at 9:50." Whoever the writer was, his comments had the same ring as those reported in the *News* two years earlier. This time he said that the Mendelssohn symphony "lasted just 19 minutes and a half' and was "followed with that breathless attention so flattering to every musician whose heart is in his work."

A most important change to take place in the Salt Lake Symphony between its 1902 and 1904 concerts was in the organization and its accomplishments. The Rev. Elmer I.

Goshen, pastor of the First Congregational Church, had taken over as president, John D. Spencer had become the manager, and H. G. Whitney was the symphony treasurer. They headed a board that was anxious to place the association on stable financial ground and had started a drive for a substantial reserve fund. Contributions were still well short of the $5,000 goal, but the sizeable amount so far collected was heartening.

Following the concert, Goshen told the press he was highly encouraged over the praises heaped upon the conductor and his players, "although the receipts were not all we could have hoped for." Spencer added that while the orchestra would have to "dig into the reserve fund," it was "not discouraged."

"It takes time to let the public know what a first class organization they have in their midst," he said. "We shall not stop until the fund is $4,000 or $5,000."

Whitney's records showed collections of approximately $2,000 from contributors before the concert. The funds were invested in "dividend paying stocks," a practice that Spencer said would be followed as long as the money came in. Some of these results were noted in the Whitney financial statement of May 16, 1905, showing $35 in "sugar stock" dividends among receipts totaling $2,764.72.

Also among the receipts were such items as $2,185 from subscribers to the reserve fund, $37.80 "donated by members of the orchestra," and $488.47 as "part of the proceeds from the concerts." There was also a payment of $18.45 on a French horn the orchestra apparently had purchased for L. P. Christensen at a cost of $54.75 in an effort to build up that section.

A cash balance of $14.52 remained after expenditures of $2,750.20, but these included $997.50 for the sugar stock from which came the dividends. And since Whitney reported that the stock purchased at $9.97-1/2 had increased to $10.50 per share, it actually represented $1,050 on the asset side of the ledger. Other costs included $1,231.10 for concerts, transportation, and so on; $54.75 for the French horn; and $200 to the conductor, "half of same being donated to the reserve fund by him." Shepherd and Spencer had been given set salaries by the board of $200 each.

There were few concerts that came off without a financial loss. One of the rare occasions was that of October 12, 1906, when box-office receipts, including $18 for eighteen tickets sold but not used, totaled $585 against expenses of $584.55, leaving a balance of 45 cents. Forty-eight musicians received $287 for the concert, with $23.50 extra going to Robert Sauer, the Brigham Young University bandmaster and composer of "When It's Springtime in the Rockies," for travel from Provo to play the bassoon.

For its final performance under Shepherd's baton, the orchestra, for the first time, moved from the Salt Lake Theatre to the stage of the Orpheum Theatre. Held on a Sunday night, February 2, 1908, the event drew perhaps the largest crowd to hear a symphony concert in the city to that time. Rumor had spread that Shepherd was leaving and that the orchestra was "not apt to be heard again for some time," and, in Spencer's words, the audience crowded "the Orpheum above and below the stairs." It was a financial success, grossing $731 against expenses of $703 for a $28 profit.

The highlight of the program was what may have been the first local performance of the Tchaikovsky Piano Concerto in B-flat Minor, with Elizabeth Eggleston as soloist. Other orchestral numbers included the Liszt "Les Preludes," Weber's "Invitation to the Dance," and the Prelude to Humperdinck's "Hansel and Gretel."

Shepherd's departure for Boston left the symphony without a conductor, but the association was still well organized with Goshen still functioning as president, Whitney as secretary and treasurer, and Spencer as manager. Dr. John T. White, George D. Pyper, and Joseph Geoghan were members of the board.

Secured to take over the baton was J. J. (John Jasper) McClellan, a thirty-four year-old native of Payson who was then the Salt Lake Tabernacle organist. He was well prepared for his new assignment, having founded and conducted the University of Michigan Symphony Orchestra during his years of study at the Ann Arbor institution. While there he also won recognition as a composer, arranger, and pianist, and as a promoter of

American music. His "Mass for Orchestra and Choir" was performed at the Michigan school on Easter, 1896, before he returned to Utah after five years of intense musical study and preparation.

McClellan visited Europe in 1899 and studied a year in Berlin. He then returned to Salt Lake City to become Tabernacle organist, initiating free organ recitals for tourists and traveling extensively as a concert artist. He once headed the University of Utah Department of Music, where he taught in various fields and conducted some student performances.

Not only did the orchestra have a new conductor when it performed its first concert under McClellan on Sunday, November 29, 1908, but it had a new concert hall as well. The program was presented in the new Colonial Theatre, later the Victory,located between Main and State Streets on Third South. Also new were the starting time of the performance—4:00 P.M.—and the size of the ensemble, now up to sixty or more.

What had not changed, however, was the general financial picture. By that time, and even during much of the Shepherd period, things were back on a "pay-as-you-go" basis. Gone was the reserve fund and apparently the desire to keep one going. The sugar stock was perhaps still around, but dividends from it were insignificant in the meeting of deficits. McClellan's first concert wound up $181 in the hole, and not until his eighth and final appearance on April 6, 1911, did the box office finish out of the red with a profit of $120.

With reserve funds virtually nonexistent, the role of loyal contributors who wanted to keep the orchestra going and symphony music alive was to pick up the losses as they occurred with each concert. These deficits added up to $1,478 during McClellan's stay, while available figures show deficits in five of the last seven Shepherd performances amounting to $1,393.

Evidently many in the community did not realize that public support of a symphony orchestra was something more than buying tickets to concerts, but there were those who were willing to acquaint them with the facts. Prior to McClellan's second concert, the *News* music writer warned in his column,

"Whether or not this concert of the Salt Lake City Symphony will close the season depends entirely upon the patronage. Experience has shown that a successful concert with close upon sixty performers cannot be given for less than $750 and of course it is a royal turnout that nets that much at the box office.

"Therefore the orchestra is prepared for a deficiency for each event and the number of concerts each season depends upon the extent of the deficit and the generosity of the subscribers."

Through such reminders the public was becoming more and more aware of the symphony orchestra's position as a business, that it was not a retail entity designed to show a balance between income and outgo. Rather, as today, it must be treated as an institutional asset in which fees cannot be expected to pay all the costs. If there is one thing the early orchestras of Utah did for the Utah symphony production down the line, it was to help establish the financial facts of life as they dealt with this mightiest of musical media.

Finance, however, was a matter McClellan was not thinking about when he stepped in front of the Salt Lake Symphony to open its new season. He had performed as soloist with the orchestra on March 20, 1905, in the Grieg Piano Concerto, but now he was the conductor and faced a new challenge. He knew his handling of the players and the makeup of his program would be compared to that of his predecessor. The press had said so in viewing the concert as "considerable of an experiment."

The result undoubtedly was pleasing to the new conductor. The *Deseret Evening News* was quick to note that "the verdict rendered at the close was an enthusiastic one."

"The turnout was one of the largest and most brilliant to which the orchestra ever played," the writer continued, "and the expressions of gratification were general and genuine. Mr. McClellan raised his baton over sixty-two musicians, most of them trained men, but quite a number of advanced students. The unusual effects of so many ladies in the string section was especially pleasing.

"All continue to show decided advancement, and Prof.

McClellan is entitled to credit for having trained them especially in precision and attack; the work of the strings was
thoroughly noticeable in this regard."

Length of the program was again considered to be a
"feature which was greatly appreciated," since the "entertainment.... lasted just an hour and a half, and sent the
audience away wishing for more instead of wearied with what it
had had."

A heralded young Salt Lake pianist, Spencer Clawson, Jr.,
who had just returned form an extended course of study in
Vienna, joined the orchestra as soloist in the first movement of
the Beethoven "Emperor" Concerto. The other "heavy" number
of the evening was the fourth movement of the Mendelssohn
"Italian" Symphony.

Clawson drew nothing but superlatives for his performance, with one reviewer being particularly impressed with the
fact that "the number required twenty minutes in rendering,
but was given entirely by memory."

For his second program, McClellan centered on a young
newcomer to the community, a basso right off the Metropolitan
Opera stage in New York City. Little did he know what a role the
young singer would fill in Utah's later symphony history.

Fred E. Smith, who was to become the first president of the
Utah State Symphony Orchestra Association in 1940, was new to
Salt Lake City's banking business when he first became
acquainted with the symphony business on January 17, 1909.
An economics and business graduate of New York's Alleghany
College, where he had excelled as a vocalist in student
appearances, Smith had signed with the Met and started a
career on the opera stage. He had become a regular performer
in minor roles when he gave up his singing profession to accept
a new life, eventually becoming a top executive with First
Security Bank of Utah.

With the orchestra, Smith performed "In diesen heil 'gen
Hallen" from "The Magic Flute" by Mozart. He impressed the
News music writer with his "full, rich bass voice," and he was
given "a big recall when he rendered in equally artistic style a
song from Verdi."

Among other soloists to perform under McClellan were violinist Willard E. Weihe, the concertmaster in the 1892 inaugural concert, and vocalists Alfred Best and Florence Jepperson, who later, as Florence Jepperson Madsen, scored many successes as a conductor, teacher, and composer at Brigham Young University.

The Colonial Theatre continued as the concert hall until December 29, 1910, when Sunday programs were abandoned and the orchestra returned to the Salt Lake Theatre for its final two performances on the regular season schedule.

Rehearsals throughout the Shepherd and McClellan years were held at various halls wherever space was available. Two of the better locations were the Odeon Ballroom just east of Main Street on North Temple and the Christensen Dancing Academy at 137 East First South.

While both were important to the history of their time, the dancing school was of particular interest in the Utah Symphony's connection with the ballet. It perhaps could be called the forerunner of the University Theatre Ballet, which has now evolved into Ballet West.

The academy was founded and operated by four brothers, one of whom, Christian Christensen, was the father and first teacher of Willam F. Christensen, founder and director of ballet production in the Mountain West, beginning at the University of Utah in the 1950s. While teaching and helping to operate the academy, Christian Christensen also played the violin in the symphony orchestra.

The orchestra made one last appearance under McClellan, playing a group of "pops" numbers in a special concert with several other attractions at the Tabernacle on April 6, 1911. Under the management of Fred C. Graham, for many years the local impressario, the program also included the Tabernacle Choir under Stephens and Pedersen's Orpheus Club male chorus.

Featured soloist for the evening was Alexander Heinemann, a German lieder singer who was brought in by Graham at a fee of $300 against a total orchestra payroll of $180.

McClellan accompanied both the choir and the chorus at

the Tabernacle organ in addition to conducting the symphony for the last time. Other than the usual financial difficulties, which again might have been overcome, he had run into two personnel problems that were insurmountable. One involved the musicians union, the other his competition for players.

The federation had laid down an ultimatum. It wanted only union musicians in the orchestra, claiming that the amateur players were no longer needed. The instrumentalists also demanded a raise in salary. This, of course, would have put the entire ensemble under a full and higher union pay scale. To meet these demands, the symphony board, looking at an $800 deficit and knowing that higher ticket prices would not be tolerated, faced a financial burden it was not willing to carry.

And to compound the difficulty for McClellan, certain leaders of other orchestras in the city had forbidden their players to perform with the symphony, threatening to discharge any who did not conform. Since this would rob the symphony's ensemble of some indispensable instrumentalists, any such action would be devastating.

It had been a real struggle for the Salt Lake Symphony Orchestra Association to keep symphony music alive for nine years. So fragile was its financial base, concert after concert, that now, in the light of these threats on the part of the city's instrumental music fraternity, there was nothing left for it to do but fold.

CHAPTER 3

THE PHILHARMONIC

With the forced demise of the Salt Lake Symphony Orchestra in the spring of 1911, the valley went into a period of symphonic drought that did not end until April 6, 1913, exactly two years later.

The organization had disbanded completely, and it showed no inclination toward a restart. The Reverend Goshen and his board had apparently lost all hope of securing the necessary cooperation of the musicians and turned their attention to other pursuits.

In order to get back on the symphony stage, it was necessary for the players themselves to make all the moves and to take over operation of the new society from top to bottom. They renamed the orchestra the Salt Lake Philharmonic and elected Charles L. Berry, a master bassoonist with the group, dating back to the 1902 revival, as president. Violinist Fred Midgley became vice-president, and Clarence J. Hawkins, the clarinet principal, began a long and faithful service as secretary-treasurer.

Professor Pedersen was persuaded to return to the podium for the first time since giving Utah its initial symphony performance back in 1892. He faced a seasoned orchestra, with

the personnel very much the same as that which had closed the
1910-11 season under McClellan.

In the interim the players had kept in tune performing in
the local theater orchestra pits. Many of them were in a large
and popular ensemble conducted by McClellan at the American Theatre, a favorite movie house of the time located on the
east side of Main Street between Second and Third South. This
group played mainly for the movies and on occasion was
presented in special selections between shows.

It is said that the famous keyboard master Paderewski, in
one of his rare appearances in the city, played at the American
and was miffed at being presented in a "common moving
picture hall."

The local newspapers devoted considerable space to
publicizing the revival of symphony programs, beginning on
March 9 with a statement prepared by the conductor. For the
press he said, "Decision to make a public appearance has come
about as a result of numerous requests from lovers of good
music in our principal centers. Especially have leading educa-
tors throughout the state importuned officers of the organization to give a concert, or a series of them. Although the body has
been in existence for a long time there has been no effort to
make a public appearance, the members having gone into it for
no other purpose than to benefit themselves artistically and to
make for higher musical standards."

He went on to indicate that the coming concert was
decidedly a labor of love so far as the players were concerned, as
"no one connected with the orchestra is to receive any
pecuniary benefit from the proceeds."

Professor Pedersen assured his readers that he had been
"complimented by the orchestra in his selection to serve for a
second term as director," and that his "tenure of directorship
holds only so long as the musicians are satisfied with his
service."

Shortly before the April 6 concert, the *Salt Lake Herald-
Republican* music writer, De Sokotum, gave a large part of his
Sunday column to the philharmonic, informing his readers that
the players had banded together for their own musical

enjoyment. He reported that there was no intention on the part of the new orchestra to give public concerts but that it had been prevailed upon to make its music available to all. Much of the listener pressure, he said, had grown out of a rehearsal in front of LDS University students at the school's Barratt Hall between North Temple and South Temple on Main Street.

The *Salt Lake Tribune* emphasized the contribution of the performers, stating that "not one, from Director Anton Pedersen on down, will receive a dollar for services, whether the concert is or is not a financial success."

If the orchestra intended to wipe the slate clean, it seemed to have accomplished its purpose. To complete the change, which now included the name, organization, and conductor, the philharmonic moved to a new concert hall. The Empress Theatre had been made available without charge by the manager, C. N. Sutton, through the courtesy of the owners, Sullivan and Considine. This popular concert and movie house became known as the Paramount and, later, as the Uptown, it was demolished to make way for the ZCMI Center on Main Street.

Presented on the Sunday of LDS general conference, the concert started at 5:00 P.M., and "while the auditors did not tax the capacity of the house," as the *Tribune* reported, "there were yet more than 500 who listened."

It was with this program that Charles Shepherd began an association with the orchestra that was to last through his successful term as conductor in the 1920s. A brother of the noted composer-conductor, Arthur Shepherd, "Charley" appeared at the piano in a performance of the Grieg Piano Concerto. He also displayed a measure of versatility by joining the bassoon section for the remaining numbers.

Appropriate, to say the least, was the programming of Schubert's "Unfinished" Symphony to open the performance. It had been the featured work on Pedersen's first concert twenty-one years before at the Salt Lake Theatre and had become a favorite in the symphony's repertoire. The conductor added Rhapsodie in F Major, by Hallen, and two Wagner works, the Prelude to "Lohengrin" and the "Tannhauser" Overture.

The event was ignored by the *Deseret Evening News* because of a policy against the mention of "Sunday amusements," but the other newspapers covered it well and were most complimentary in their reviews. Writers credited Professor Pedersen for the "unqualified success" of the opening concert on the new series. They added that "none questioned his ability to instruct" and that "his interest in the work has been unflagging from the inception of the orchestra, when a public performance was not considered."

It was Professor Pedersen's last concert. He died six weeks later, and his son and concertmaster, Arthur P. Freber, was elected to succeed him on the podium.

With the ice broken by the April 6 performance, the philharmonic members began planning for the 1913-14 season and scheduled three Sunday concerts at the Empress, with the first on December 14. Freber, only twenty-six at the time, lost no time in getting the orchestra ready for the most ambitious symphony program yet attempted on the local stage. After opening with the Overture from Mendelssohn's Incidental Music to "A Midsummer Night's Dream" and "Farandole" from Bizet's "L'Arlesienne" Suite No. 2, he scheduled the Saint-Saens Cello Concerto, with the cello principal, Otto King, as soloist, and the first Utah performance of the complete Fifth Symphony by Beethoven.

While well-prepared for the assignment, the young conductor faced one of the most challenging experiences of his career. He was born in Salt Lake City in 1887 and had received considerable attention as a child prodigy and budding young virtuoso on the violin when he went to New York to study in 1906. Within a year he had joined the violin section of the New York Philharmonic-Symphony Orchestra and for the next four years performed under Wassily Safonoff and Gustav Mahler.

Freber was on leave from his position in New York when he accepted the concertmaster's seat with the Salt Lake Philharmonic. With the death of his father, he resigned from the New York orchestra to become the conductor in Utah. The last forty years of a most productive career were devoted to advancing the cause of music in his home state.

Freber was a master of orchestral routine and excelled as a teacher, succeeding his father as director of music at All Hallows College and later joining the music faculty at the University of Utah, where he conducted the student symphony orchestra for many years. Throughout the first thirty-eight years of Salt Lake Oratorio Society productions under Squire Coop and others, Freber was the guiding force in the orchestral preparations. After completing this task, he served as concert-master for the performances.

Perhaps his most notable role, however, was the one he performed as conductor of the Salt Lake Philharmonic. Through four seasons he led the orchestra in ten concerts, significantly raising program standards with his discriminating selection of numbers while steadily improving the quality of ensemble production.

Freber never lacked confidence in the ability of his orchestra to play the major works with distinction. After presenting Beethoven's Fifth Symphony in its entirety, he immediately programmed the great master's "Eroica" Symphony No. 3, also played for the first time in its complete form, as the principal work at the next concert on April 5. Other "firsts" in his final repertoire included "The Great" C-Major Symphony by Schubert and the "Pastorale" Sixth Symphony by Beethoven, the latter performed on the final program presented by the philharmonic with Freber as the conductor on April 22, 1917.

Another phase of Freber's programming took notice of new compositions by Utah musicians, including his own efforts in that regard. He was perhaps the first conductor to recognize such writings, beginning with the premiere of a "Festival Overture" which was dedicated to the philharmonic by B. Cecil Gates, a grandson of Brigham Young and one of the West's leading composers in his day.

The new work opened the concert of February 20, 1916, and on the next program, April 9, Freber included a "Characteristic Suite" for Orchestra, conducted by its composer W. J. Flashman, flute principal of local symphony orchestras since

1902. The conductor premiered his own work, "Suite For Orchestra," during the farewell concert in 1917.

Meanwhile, Freber's ambitions to upgrade the material being presented to philharmonic listeners eventually ran afoul of the unwritten rules governing the length of programs. Hawkins's minutes of a board of trustees' meeting on April 1, 1916, were devoted almost entirely to the subject. The minutes noted: "On account of the last concert running so late, the length of concerts [was] thoroughly discussed and it was decided that one hour and fifteen minutes should be the maximum amount of time for the best good of all concerned...."

"Mr. [I. B.] Evans and Mrs. [F. C.] Schramm appointed to see Mr. Freber and urge every cut possible in the coming concert to bring the program within the hour and fifteen minute limit."

The program accused of "running so late" was the one that opened with the Gates Overture and included the Schubert "Unfinished" Symphony, the "Scenes Pittoresques" by Massenet, the Beethoven Piano Concerto No. 5 ("Emperor"), and the "Procession of the Sardar" from Ippolitov-Ivanov's "Caucasian Sketches."

There was no mention as to how well Freber met the time limit at the following concert on April 9. It was the program that contained the Schubert C Major Symphony and Flashman's orchestral suite. Other selections included the Wagner "Tannhauser" Overture and two vocal numbers by one of the local soprano favorites of the time, Mrs. Della Daynes Hills.

The appearance of Mrs. Hills was not an isolated offering among philharmonic programs. While Freber was building the symphonic repertoire, he went along with the board in presenting outstanding local vocalists and instrumentalists in solo performances, not only as an artistic supplement, but for box-office reasons as well.

For its Easter Sunday concert on April 4, 1915, at the Salt Lake Theatre, the orchestra presented two sisters of the conductor, Mrs. Renata Freber Walsh, soprano, and Mrs. Sigrid Pedersen Carl, soprano, in the second-act duet from Puccini's "Madame Butterfly." Among other vocalists to appear at various times were Edna Cohn, Florence Jepperson, Mrs. Agatha Berkhoel-Siegel, and Tenor Alfred Best.

For the February 20 program in 1916 that ran "too late," the noted Ogden pianist, teacher, and longtime director of the Ogden Tabernacle Choir, Lester Hinchliff, was at the piano in a highly praised performance of the Beethoven "Emperor" Concerto.

Just one year later, on March 4, 1917, the beloved Salt Lake City pianist, Becky Almond, then but a mere girl, made her debut on the symphony stage, performing the Liszt "Hungarian Fantasy" with the orchestra. She was later to appear many times with succeeding symphony ensembles and to play a most important role in the founding of the present Utah Symphony Guild, all of which will be dealt with in later chapters.

It was for the concert featuring the Freber-Pedersen sisters that the Philharmonic moved to the Salt Lake Theatre to stay. Exactly why the move from the rent-free Empress was made is not clear, but the local newspapers made quite a point of the "special privilege" extended by The Church of Jesus Christ of Latter-day Saints in allowing the orchestra to use the Salt Lake Theatre for a Sunday afternoon concert. It was contained, in fact, in an article titled "Philharmonic Gets Special Privilege." The article said: "It was made known yesterday that for the first time since the Salt Lake Theatre was built by Brigham Young, a Sunday concert with paid admissions would be held there. This unusual departure from the precedent established by Brigham Young is a special honor paid to the Salt Lake Philharmonic Orchestra, which will give its spring concert there Easter Sunday at the usual time. There have been many lectures, etc., given gratis at the old playhouse, but Easter Sunday will be the first time that any individuals will have bought a ticket for entrance there on Sunday.

"The Salt Lake Philharmonic has shed a great deal of dignity on the musical status of the city, and this great honor is but another demonstration of its value to the community. The annual spring concert has always been held in the Empress Theatre, which has been an admirable place for such affairs, being centrally located, with good acoustics, etc., but this is the first time that the concert date has fallen on Easter Sunday. These two interesting facts concerning the concert will add a great deal to the other fine features arranged by the committee. Arthur Freber will be the conductor."

The spring concert a year later, as indicated by the *Salt Lake Tribune*, apparently ran into some competition with beautiful April sunshine and a Pacific Coast League baseball game at Majestic Park between the Salt Lake Saints and Oakland. There was little doubt, however, as to which group of local performers came out best. Errors were blamed for the Saints' dropping a 6-3 fiasco, while the musicians scored a resounding triumph in a *Tribune*-heralded "best program given this season." More to the point, the writer added: "It is also gratifying to note that the attendance was larger than any previous concert, a condition that is a credit to both musicians and the music-loving public of Salt Lake. And this in spite of the fact that the day was ideal for baseball—and many there are who do 'perceive a divided duty' when the choice is presented between a classic concert and the music of the 'diamond.'"

Less than three weeks later, on April 27, the Philharmonic Association presented Walter Damrosch and the New York Symphony Orchestra, with the renowned Josef Hofmann at the piano, in concert at the Richards Street Auditorium. The pianist was featured in Anton Rubinstein's Concerto in G and was cited for his brilliance and dexterity.

The crowd that gathered in the spacious hall—later the Auditorium Garage (demolished well before its space was taken up by the Crossroads Center and the Marriott Hotel)—paid $2,039.50 to hear the concert. In noting the amount in a meeting of the association's board of trustees on May 5, 1916, Secretary Hawkins noted the "orchestra's (presumably the philharmonic's) share" to be $509.80 "with an additional $25 received from the programs."

So successful was the venture with the touring New York Symphony that the philharmonic not only rescheduled Damrosch and his orchestra the following season, but signed the great Madame Ernestine Schumann-Heink for a solo recital as well. Both concerts were presented in the Salt Lake Tabernacle, with the revered contralto performing the evening of January 25, and the orchestra, with the violin virtuoso Efrem Zimbalist as soloist in the Bruch G Minor Concerto, on May 1. As might be expected, the two events added much to the Philharmonic Society's stature in the community.

The musicians continued to run the affairs of the philharmonic until the middle of the 1914-15 season, when Royal W. Daynes of what was then the Consolidated Daynes Music Company was elected president. Stepping down into the vice-president position was C. G. Berry, the bassoonist, who had served as president; Hawkins continued as secretary-treasurer. The board of trustees was made up of Daynes and Berry and five instrumentalists—Hawkins from the clarinet section; Charles Shepherd, bassoon; Irving Snow, cello; Ralph Baker, trombone; and a veteran on the bass fiddle, Fred Beesley.

It was a well-seasoned orchestra of forty-three to forty-six members that faced Freber for each concert, although in one instance—the March 4, 1917, performance—the number of players reached fifty-three. George Groneman, a symphony violinist from 1902 on through the WPA Orchestra days into the Utah State Symphony in the 1940s, succeeded Freber as concertmaster. He later relinquished the first chair to Morris Andrews, who alternated with Claude Sweeten through the spring of 1917, when World War I forced a temporary halt to operations.

Sam Bruckner, who played second flute to Flashman, and violinist Adolph Brox, for many years a popular dance-band leader in the community, were the librarians. Among other well-remembered players on the roster were Oge Jorgensen, cellist; Thorval Jorgensen, violinist; Dell Beesley and Dow Young, timpanists; Frank Asper, the late Tabernacle organist, who played the celeste and the flute; and LeRoy Midgley, clarinetist.

Further efforts to draw the community into the operation of the philharmonic association was evident as the orchestra moved toward its 1915-16 season. The minutes of a board of trustees meeting on August 31 contained a record of the unanimous election of Mrs. F. C. Schramm as president, with Mr. Daynes taking over as treasurer. Not until two meetings later, on September 24, did the board receive Mrs. Schramm's acceptance, beginning her four years of devoted service to the philharmonic and its purposes.

Will Rees of the string bass section was eventually named vice-president, and Isaac B. Evans became a lay member of the board. The association began selling memberships at an annual fee of $10 and was almost able to meet expenses in that way. Although the players received no pay for the opening concert of the new association in 1913, they worked hard to improve that situation and gathered all the outside support possible. It should be realized that each member of the orchestra was a member of the association and paid all assessments voted by the board.

At the end of the first season, the organization was $50.43 in debt for "hall rent" and other costs. Since the Empress Theatre reportedly came free, the hall expenses may have been for rehearsal space or utility costs. The practice sessions were held at various places, including the Christensen Ballet School (which had moved into the Templeton Building on South Temple and Main, where the Kennecott Building now stands) and the Consolidated Music Hall. Later on the Pantages Theatre, now the Utah, on Main Street, was made available for morning rehearsals each day but Wednesday, provided that the orchestra pay for the lights. This kind of charge may have accounted for the hall expenses.

Mrs. Schramm, of course, faced the usual challenge of raising funds to secure the philharmonic as a viable institution in the community. She was apparently an immediate success— with the help of her board and other musicians—as noted in three sources of information, the first being the printed program from the opening concert on December 12, 1915, which contained the following notes:

"The real standard of a city's culture in music is based largely upon the size and efficiency of its symphony orchestra.

"It requires moral and financial support to develop and maintain size and efficiency.

"The Philharmonic was organized in May, 1912, by about forty of the leading instrumentalists of the city for the purpose of studying and producing only the best of musical literature. . . .

"So far the orchestra has been maintained principally by its members, who, besides giving most of their time, have paid out in individual assessments, over $500 in cash, for music rentals and other necessary expenses.

"The conductor and a board of seven trustees are elected annually by a majority vote of the acting members. A membership committee is constantly on the lookout for suitable members of ability.

"When the orchestra incorporated last spring a patron membership was included to guarantee the financial side of a series of concerts each season.

"Patron memberships cost $10 a season and entitle the member to the amount in tickets to any or all concerts with a choice of seats, before the public sale, and the privilege of attending final rehearsals before any concert."

Hardly six weeks later a letter dated January 22, 1916, and signed by Mrs Schramm and Mr. Freber, was sent to prospective new players, including Arnold Higgins, a violinist. He apparently liked the contents and joined the orchestra. His letter of invitation included the following information:

"The Orchestra incorporated last March and since then we have secured enough patrons and subscriptions to assure the financial success of three concerts this season. . . . The only assessment this year being the annual membership (in the orchestra) of only $1.00.

"We are enlarging our memberships at present and have room for four more violins, therefore we wish to extend you an invitation to become a member. Letters are being sent to other violinists of the city, and due consideration will be given the earliest replies.

"The next concert will be given Sunday afternoon, Feb. 20, at 4:45 in the Salt Lake Theatre. Regular rehearsals are held every Tuesday morning at ten o'clock at the Consolidated Music Hall, at which each member is expected to be present.

Members receive no remuneration for rehearsals, but receive $5.00 for each concert."

The printed program for the final concert of the season on April 9 enlarged upon the favorable financial situation of the Philharmonic. It noted: "The present season is memorable in many ways for the Salt Lake Philharmonic Orchestra. For the first time in its history it has not had to assess its members in order to pay the expenses of its concerts. It has played to the largest audiences ever assembled to hear an orchestra in Salt Lake City. And the patrons' support has been so loyal that the Orchestra could for the first time since its organization, plan for a season's work without fear of loss. For all this the Orchestra wishes to thank its many friends and patrons.

"It will surprise many persons to know that the Philharmonic is only four years old. . . . Nine concerts, including the one given today, have been given; eight in Salt Lake City, and one in Provo.

"The Philharmonic is ambitious to become the best symphony orchestra in the west; and this ambition is within reach if Salt Lake City will support it as splendidly in the future as during the past season. Consistent with the financial support which it receives from the public, the Philharmonic will increase the number of its members and the number of its concerts each season.

"The Orchestra plans to give at least three concerts during the season 1916-17. Patron memberships will be sold at once, and no effort will be spared to make next season the most brilliant in the Philharmonic's history."

The Provo concert mentioned was presented at the Columbia Theatre on March 19, 1915, with forty-five players making the trip by special train. It was the first out-of-town performance by a symphony orchestra based in Salt Lake City. Such trips later on by bus were to carry the WPA Orchestra and Utah Symphony to every corner of the state.

As promised in the program comments, the 1916-17 season proved to be the best ever, but much of the momentum gained was to be lost in the three-year lapse in public concerts to follow.

Almost to the final concert in 1917, neither the war clouds that hung so heavily over Europe in the philharmonic's early years nor the resulting storms of World War I had seemed to generate much concern locally, or, for that matter, nationally. But when the United States declared war on Germany on April 6, the complacency ended, and although not felt immediately, the event was to have a telling effect upon the operations of the Salt Lake Philharmonic in the months and years ahead. Not until January 25, 1920, did the orchestra return to the concert stage.

CHAPTER 4

END OF AN ERA

Had it not been for the participation of the United States in World War I, it is unlikely that there would have been a three-year interruption in regular performances of the Salt Lake Philharmonic Orchestra between 1917 and 1920.

Despite the unrest caused by the resulting military draft and the depressed financial situation, the players continued with their rehearsals, while the orchestra's executive organization met regularly in an effort to keep the philharmonic alive. Full seasons and some individual concerts were planned, but the ever-changing conditions forced repeated cancellations.

One of the first instrumentalists to leave the fold was the devoted secretary and clarinetist, Clarence Hawkins, who became bandmaster of the Utah Artillery Regiment and accompanied the unit to its station in San Diego. His minutes and those of his successor, Fred Beesley, provide a running account of the activities, which included a number of interesting organizational changes.

Noted first was the appearance of Charles L. Shepherd as conductor of the rehearsals. Freber had resigned, apparently because of his heavy load as conductor of the University

Musical Society and other duties in his new position with the University of Utah Music Department. Squire Coop also had declined an offer to take over the baton. Freber did agree, however, to sit in as concertmaster, but he gave that up in the spring of 1918.

While the philharmonic was without any sort of regular schedule of concerts, it did make two appearances in early 1918, both with the Tabernacle Choir at the Salt Lake Tabernacle. The first one, on February 22, was particularly significant. The other found a local symphony in a rare collaboration with the choir, this time in a performance of Mendelssohn's "Elijah" on April 5.

The Washington Birthday concert might well have been called a benefit for the philharmonic. All proceeds from the house, scaled at 50 cents for adults and 15 cents for children under high-school age, went to the orchestra. The hall was donated by the LDS Church, and everyone on the program performed without pay.

The *Salt Lake Tribune* estimated the crowd for the 11:00 A.M. program at "more than 2,000" and reported that the listeners found an "opportunity to express their appreciation " to the orchestra and to "put it on a solid financial basis" as well.

Under its new conductor, the philharmonic performed the Mendelssohn "Scotch" Symphony and short works of Goldmark and Elgar. The choir presented several selections, and the two organizations joined in a mighty finale, "The Star Spangled Banner," under the direction of the choir director, A. C. (Tony) Lund. This may well have been the first joint symphony— Tabernacle Choir performance.

Governor Simon Bamberger spoke briefly, and Professor Thomas Giles of the participating University of Utah Music Department read a highly pertinent statement by Dr. John A. Widtsoe. The university president was scheduled to speak on "The Educational Value of a Symphony Orchestra to the Community" but was unable to attend. His conclusion was prophetic: "It will be most fitting if in this city, the center of the intermountain west, there should be maintained, under municipal or individual support, in cooperation with the whole community, an orchestra of rank and grade and quality to be set side by side with the greatest musical organizations of the land."

Little did Dr. Widtsoe know how long it would take to reach that goal or the many directions and sources from which the support would come, but most important was the fact that the "fitting" moment would arrive.

In the summer of 1918 Shepherd's position as conductor was made official. He was elected by the board of trustees upon recommendation of a committee consisting of Freber, Beesley, and the Reverend Elmer I. Goshen, the new president of the orchestra. Shepherd had expressed to the committee his "willingness to act as conductor for the coming season, provided that he be not drafted into Army service or that nothing now unforeseen should come up." This was typical of the uncertainty of the times, and it became somewhat of a forecast for the board action found in Beesley's minutes of a special meeting on August 17: "On account of Chas. L. Shepherd having been called to the colors and George Groneman having temporarily left the city it became necessary to fill the vacancies of conductor and concertmaster, if it were thought wise to proceed with concert work for the coming season. The general opinion was that, on account of the impending draft which would take many of our members up to forty-five years of age, we suspend concert work until conditions are more favorable for concert work. A motion to that effect was made by C. G. Berry, seconded by Miss [Marian] Cannon and carried unanimously."

But that didn't stop the players from rehearsing on occasion, or the association from trying to set up performances. The ensemble felt ready and anxious to get back to the concert stage.

Meanwhile, the business organization of the philharmonic had come in for some changes. The return of Reverend Goshen as president had resulted from some maneuvering brought on by apparent "misunderstandings" between the orchestra and the local Musical Arts Society. This was the organization Goshen joined after leaving the old Salt Lake Symphony back in 1911.

One of the most widely known clergymen in Utah, Goshen had come to Utah at the age of twenty-seven and from 1899 to 1902 was with the Congregational Church in Ogden. He then moved to Salt Lake City as pastor of the First Congregational Church. His activities in the cause against drug and alcohol abuse were legendary, as was his "habit cure" for addicts. He is credited with helping to initiate the Boy Scout movement in the area, and besides his strong support of music organizations, he found time to serve as a director and vice-president of the Salt Lake baseball club in the Pacific Coast League.

While with the Musical Arts Society, Goshen kept an eye on the symphony organization and responded with aid for orchestra endeavors. Conflicts arose at times, perhaps over dates of events sponsored by the two groups, as well as in other matters, and the minutes of the philharmonic indicated the need of an "amicable settlement."

The resignation of Mrs. Schramm as president was accepted on May 10, 1918, with the board adding a vote of thanks for "her arduous labors during the time of her presidency." At the same meeting Shepherd suggested that a member of the Musical Arts Society be elected to the board, and he was appointed to consult with Goshen on the matter.

A month later Shepherd advised the board that he had been given "assurance that if Mr. Goshen were elected President of our Board, he would go before all the local organizations and endeavor to get their members to patronize our concerts and thus make our organization a financial success." Within a week Goshen had been elected president, with P. C. Stevens as vice-president and Beesley as secretary-treasurer.

The first business at the following joint session of the board and the members of the orchestra was to elect Mrs. Schramm an honorary member as an expression of appreciation for her leadership. Also at this meeting Shepherd was officially elected conductor, but he soon was serving in absentia; he was inducted into military service six weeks later.

With the signing of the Armistice on November 11, 1918, however, the new conductor was soon back on board, and the philharmonic hoped to make an early concert appearance. As

the season wore on, the hopes waned. The last of them vanished when the civic organizations whose assistance Goshen
had sought said they were committed to other projects for the
season and were unable to support a proposed Arbor Day
concert in the spring of 1919.

Shortly after that, Goshen announced plans to present
three concerts during the next season, with the deficits, "if any"
to be "taken care of." Not until the following January 25, 1920,
however, was the first performance given at the Salt Lake
Theatre.

When Shepherd stepped to the podium to open the concert with the Overture to Nicolai's "Merry Wives of Windsor," he
faced an ensemble of fifty-three players, including his brother,
Albert, in the violin section. Eddie Fitzpatrick was the concertmaster, having replaced Groneman, who nevertheless was
present for the season inaugural. The harpist, Lydia White
Boothby, received special mention from the newspapers as a
"former member of the Boston Symphony Orchestra."

The major work was the Liszt Piano Concerto No. 1 in E-flat,
with Sybella Clayton Bassett as soloist. Other numbers on the
program included the "Peer Gynt" Suite, two Norwegian dances
by Grieg, two Hungarian Dances by Brahms, and two Slavonic
Dances by Dvorak.

For the second concert on March 28, Shepherd programmed the Schubert "Unfinished" Symphony, certainly the
most-played work by all the city's early symphony groups, and
the Tchaikovsky "Nutcracker Suite" in its first local performance.

In the closing performance of the season on May 16, Albert
Shepherd made his debut as soloist with the philharmonic,
performing the Bruch Violin Concerto in G Minor. He later
became the third of three Shepherd brothers—Arthur, Charley
and Bert—to conduct symphonic works in the Salt Lake Valley.
They directed a total of twenty-three concerts, and each of them
appeared as soloist on various occasions. They were also
among six brothers (the others being Nathaniel, Ralph, and
Septimus) who served their country in World War I.

The three concerts of 1920 were financially disappointing
perhaps because of a slow revival of the arts in the post-war

period, and the hoped-for momentum failed to materialize. As a result, there was another lapse of nearly two years before the philharmonic returned to the concert schedule.

These lapses, as noted here and in preceding seasons, were not entirely the fault of finances. Although the lack of money may have been the deciding factor in this case, many musicians, also, were without a driving zeal for making symphony music. They had regular employment in the theatre orchestra pits, and a number of them had additional assignments in the several, and very popular, martial bands in the area. On the other hand, the symphony played only two, and sometimes three concerts a season.

Sheldon (Shelly) Hyde, a trumpet player and for thirty-three years personnel manager with the Utah Symphony, remembers this as being the situation with his father, Orson Hyde, one of the top trumpet men of the period. Orson played in the Salt Lake Theatre orchestra and in the brass bands of John Held and others, while Shelly himself started out in Held's Boy Scout band. "Most of the playing was done in the bands," he recalls, "They played in the parks and for the parades and all the whoop-de-do."

But it was the theater work that produced problems for symphony conductors. It had driven the philharmonic under McClellan out of business in 1911, and the absence of a few players, mostly strings, from symphony concerts because of theater assignments was a rule rather than an exception from that time through the 1920s. Since the symphony required more rehearsals than the other instrumental group activities, these also became a concern. At their meetings the loyal orchestra members were constantly seeking ways to increase attendance at rehearsals and issuing warnings of dismissal for those "who show by indifferent attendance that they are not appreciative of their honor."

During the 1920-22 interim, the McCune School of Music became established at Second North and Main Street and formed a small orchestra that performed symphonic works. The school had actually grown out of the music department started by B. Cecil Gates and Guy C. Wilson at the old LDS

University and was quartered for some time in the historic "Gardo House" at State and South Temple Streets.

In April of 1920 it moved to the home from which it took its name, the McCune Mansion. Mr. and Mrs. Alfred W. McCune had given the property to the LDS Church as a residence for its president, but the leader at that time, Heber J. Grant, determined it could be put to more beneficial use as a music conservatory.

As director of the school, Gates conducted the orchestra until 1925, when it was taken over by a member of the philharmonic, Frank W. Asper, who went on to expose young musicians to orchestral classics in some one hundred concerts over a period of thirty years.

When the philharmonic, on February 26, 1922, broke a silence of nearly two years, the players were in a hall entirely new to symphony concerts. They had moved to the Wilkes Theatre, later the Lyric and now the Promised Valley Playhouse on State Street, for a series of two performances.

Shepherd still had an orchestra of fifty-three musicians, now including Arthur Freber, who, at the insistence of the organization, had returned as concertmaster. Conductor and ensemble impressed critics with a program highlighted by a performance of the Tchaikovsky Piano Concerto in B-flat Minor with Mrs. Bassett again at the keyboard.

After noting the concert as the initial one in the philharmonic's "seventh season," the music critic of the *Deseret News* wrote: "The assertion will not be challenged by anyone who was present that yesterday's performance, on the part of conductor, orchestra and soloist, has never been surpassed in local accomplishment and seldom equalled."

The second concert, on Easter Sunday, April 16, drew particular attention to the local premiere of the "Petite Suite" by Debussy. Of more than passing interest was the following parenthesized note beneath the listing of the work on the printed program: "Complete music and score presented to the Salt Lake Philharmonic Orchestra by Mrs. Glenn Walker Wallace."

It was the first mention of Mrs. Wallace in connection with the symphony in Salt Lake City. Soon after, she began a most significant role as a benefactor and leading figure, both then and eighteen years later, in the further development of the orchestra's organizational structure.

At this time the organization was still very much in the hands of the Reverend Goshen, with major assistance from Shepherd Lawrence Clayton, the new secretary. Clayton served from the beginning of 1920 through 1924, and his minutes provide a detailed account of the philharmonic's struggle to reactivate its concert schedule and to solve its problems involving personnel and the music federation.

One interesting paragraph appears in Clayton's minutes covering a meeting of the orchestra at Christensen's Dancing Studio on November 29, 1921. Concerned about the difficulty in securing sufficient players with so many men performing in theater orchestras, Shepherd made a pitch for the female instrumentalists in the city. The minutes tell the story: "Mr. Shepherd asked for an expression of the members relative to the employment of lady musicians for the orchestra so long as it should be necessary. Mr. Goshen asked for a show of hands on this proposition and a large majority were in favor of it. Some members spoke of the awkwardness of asking ladies to fill places without an assurance of a permanent position. It was then pointed out by other members that in many of the leading orchestras throughout the country a few ladies occupied permanent positions. It was thereupon moved by Fred Beesley and seconded by Mr. Moritz Bruckner that the conductor be authorized to employ lady musicians if necessary. Motion carried unanimously."

Mrs. Boothby with her harp, apparently occupied a special niche in the ensemble. She had been there for several seasons, and she remained the only woman on the payroll until 1923, when Helen Hunter Riser and Beth Walton were added to the cello section.

In the same set of minutes Clayton called attention to the founding of the Utah Federation of Music Clubs as a branch of the national federation with Mrs. Bassett, pianist and strong supporter of the philharmonic, as the first president. As might be expected, the new society became a loyal ally of the orchestra.

Two months later Shepherd suggested public rehearsals before each concert to which the school children of the city would be invited at a "nominal price, probably ten cents." The board approved such performances providing that expenses were "moderate" and that the players could be prevailed upon to perform at the fee paid for rehearsals. At a meeting of the orchestra two weeks later, the musicians not only accepted the idea, but agreed to play the public dress rehearsals free. They then accepted a reduced pay schedule of $7.50 for concerts and $1.50 for all other rehearsals.

By this time the philharmonic was settled in the Christensen Dancing Hall for rehearsals and business meetings at a cost of $20 a month, as arranged by Shepherd several weeks before the February concert in 1922. An ambitious financing plan also had been put forward whereby "a permanent body of unlimited guarantors numbering at least one hundred" would be gathered to support the organization. This group was to be held together by "a strictly legal contract providing against withdrawal from the obligation of guarantor except a specified notice of one year," according to Clayton's minutes of March 10. In order to protect against "unwarranted or unwise expenditures," the guarantors would choose their own committee, which in turn would appoint a business manager "to have complete charge of the business and financial transactions of the orchestra."

To accomplish all this, it was necessary to amend the articles of incorporation, a draft of which was finally adopted at a meeting the following October 2 at the home of Mrs. John M. (Glenn) Wallace that required five full typewritten pages of minutes.

More important, however, was the complete reorganization of the association with Mrs. Wallace as president. With her on the board of trustees were P. C. Stevens, the vice-president; the secretary, Clayton; the concertmaster, Freber, from the orchestra; Lloyd Weeter; Mrs. Bassett; and Edward P. Kimball, who already was becoming a force for music in the community and who later, for many years, was Tabernacle organist.

The influence of the new president was soon to become evident. After engineering an amendment to the constitution to allow the election of as many as six vice-presidents and an expanded board, she took the lead in securing a strong cast of supporters. In addition to Stevens, the vice-presidents included John C. Howard, Alex E. Eberhardt, and Fred E. Smith, prominent in the fields of business, industry, and banking.

Although the season produced only two concerts, both in 1923, it was a historic one in the annals of symphony production in Utah. Twice the orchestra basked in the famed acoustics of the Salt Lake Tabernacle, once with a crowd of two thousand school children in February and once, in April, with an even larger audience for the first full-blown regular symphony concert performance by a local orchestra in the great hall.

The innovative concert for the youngsters presented somewhat of a challenge for the musicians, as it required back-to-back performances at two different locations. After playing in the late afternoon for the students, the instrumentalists packed up and hurried to the Orpheum Theatre for the season-opener at 8:15 P.M.

In advance of the two-fold event, the *Salt Lake Tribune* of February 25 announced: "A new element in the work of the orchestra this year will be the school children's concert to be given tomorrow afternoon at the Tabernacle.... Only a nominal charge will be made for tickets by the local symphony organization and the concert will begin at 4:15 o'clock so as to enable all children who have classes late in the afternoon to reach the Tabernacle in time for the opening number."

It would be difficult to calculate the true value of this start in the building of "future audiences," which remains so important in the operations of the Utah Symphony today. More directly, the timely effort provided a forerunner for the heavily attended Saturday morning "youth concerts" in the Tabernacle under sponsorship of the Associated Food Stores in the 1950s and '60s.

There was no extra concert for the young people in connection with the April 12 event at the Tabernacle. Most of the attention was on the guest artist, an opera diva by the name of Alice Gentle, who blew into town with a great deal of fanfare. She immediately won the hearts of her interviewers and the orchestra. She told the *Deseret News* on the day of the concert: "I never rehearsed with an orchestra so easily before in my life. Charles Shepherd and the orchestra members are to be complimented for their work."

The printed program for the concert informed the listeners that the use of the Tabernacle was "through courtesy of the presidency of the L. D. S. Church and the Tabernacle Choir," thus marking one more milestone in the ever-present encouragement and support of the Church of Jesus Christ of Latter-day Saints in the development of the symphony orchestra and its music. As to be noted later, the famous hall was to be the donated home of the Utah Symphony for thirty-two years.

Miss Gentle also apparently won the hearts of her big audience as well, with two operatic arias with orchestra and a group of songs with Mrs. Bassett at the piano. It was a format to be followed in a brilliant symphony series with guest artists at the Tabernacle a year later. Her services very likely had been secured by the local entrepreneur of the day, Fred C. Graham, whose management was listed under the notation about availability of the Tabernacle.

William E. Bassett, a local baritone of note, had been the soloist in the February concert, in which the major orchestral work was the MacDowell Suite for Orchestra. This American composition and the Tchaikovsky "Pathetique" Symphony No. 6, presented in April, were both newcomers to the local symphony repertoire.

While the season closed on a high note musically, it finished on a sour note financially. The enthusiasm of the fall failed to carry through the following spring, and the promising organization disbanded. Planned support, such as the proposed board of guarantors, did not produce the needed funds to handle a deficit, and there appeared signs that the orchestra might again close shop.

The situation gave rise to lengthy but interesting commentary by Mr. Kimball on the question "Shall We Have An Orchestra?" in the *Deseret News* music section of April 21, just nine days after the season closed. He obviously retained some hopes for a guarantor plan and for the establishment of a permanent symphony.

Mr. Kimball first wrote of the value of the symphony orchestra as a music educator, as an uplifting and inspiring cultural unit, and as a medium for performance of great compositions. The gifted artist also gave weight to the professional status of musicians and their right to proper remuneration for their efforts. Then he added: "The musician has proved time and time again that he will sacrifice for the establishment of an orchestra. What is needed is a guarantor's fund which will make it possible for the musician, without whom symphony concerts cannot be given in this town or any other, to make music free of financial worries.

"The public has no more right to expect these men and women to go on making this sacrifice than it has to expect others to do the same in all other lines.

"If 50 men, public spirited and forward-looking as they always are in this city, could be made to see the matter in this light and subscribe $100 each right now, the difficulties in the way of the Salt Lake Philharmonic Orchestra for the best season they have ever given us would be removed and Salt Lake could look forward to the best season of orchestra music in 1923-24 it has ever heard. This year's deficit is small, but is large enough to discourage the men in any effort for next season. Now, all together Salt Lake business men, SHALL WE HAVE AN ORCHESTRA?"

Whether or not Edward Kimball's column was the direct cause, the response of the business community was amazing. By the end of the year the Benevolent Protective Order of Elks had rounded up five other civic and service clubs in a joint display of muscle behind the symphony.

The *Salt Lake Tribune*, on January 13, 1924, enthusiastically greeted the "movement initiated by the Salt Lake Elks Lodge for the reorganization of the symphony orchestra" in which "virtually every civic and business community organization and club in the city" was involved. The Reverend Goshen's try for the same support six years before had finally borne fruit.

A board of forty-five delegates from the six clubs formed the organization, with B. T. Pyper of the Commercial Club (forerunner of the Chamber of Commerce) as manager. Chairman of the executive committee was George Jay Martin, a representative of the Rotary Club, with Lawrence Clayton, already with the symphony and most certainly a figure in the Elks Club action, representing the BPOE as secretary. R. N. Young of Kiwanis was the treasurer, and E. Hugh Miller, Lions Club, and J. A. Greenwald, Exchange Club, were other committee members.

Besides coming up with financial assistance and organizational initiative, the Elks turned over the spacious facilities of their new building on South Temple Street to the orchestra as a rehearsal hall.

With the outlook now as promising as it had ever been, the organization reinstated its former name — the Salt Lake Symphony Orchestra — after thirteen years as the Salt Lake Philharmonic and increased the personnel to a new high of fifty-seven players. Freber remained as concertmaster, and Reginald Beales and Emery Epperson, both of them links with the permanent symphony of the '40s, were newcomers in the violin section. There they joined Ben Bullough, a violinist who was to figure strongly as a union representative in a financial crisis of the Utah Symphony twenty-six years later. He had come on board in 1923.

Adding brilliance to the bright new season was an impressive list of guest artists. Mischa Levitzki, one of the great keyboard virtuosos of the day, was in the wings on the night of February 4 when Shepherd and the orchestra greeted a crowd of thirty-five hundred on Temple Square with the Nicolai "Merry Wives of Windsor" Overture and the Beethoven Second Symphony. The celebrated pianist then joined the ensemble in the Liszt Piano Concerto No. 1 in E-flat and added a solo group, including his own Valse in A Major.

Emma Lucy Gates, Utah's supreme opera diva of the early Twentieth Century's "Golden Age of Opera," came on stage with the symphony on April 7. Her impressive "mastery of techniques" and lucid coloratura quality won repeated curtain calls for her renditions of the "Polonaise" from Thomas's "Mignon" and, as an encore, the Strauss "Blue Danube" with the orchestra. Shepherd was at the piano for her solo group, which became an added source for the superlatives of the *Deseret*

News critic, who wrote: "Miss Gates reached the high E-flat without appreciable effort several times, and the grace and ease with which she soared through the firmament of the ledger lines was a source of wonder and delight to the house."

Mr. Shepherd and the symphony came away with a good share of the honors, particularly for their performance of the Tchaikovsky "Nutcracker Suite." They received an ovation, and Frank Asper drew special mention for his delightful treatment of the "Dance of the Sugar Plum Fairy" on the celeste.

It was a brilliant homecoming for the soloist. This grand-daughter of Brigham Young, with her brother, B. Cecil Gates, provided many great evenings of opera throughout the region with their own company in touring productions of the popular operatic masterpieces. Later in private life as Mrs. A. E. Bowen, she continued for many years as a performer and teacher, and as a loyal benefactress to Utah music.

A second performance by the orchestra of the Debussy "Petite Suite" under Mr. Shepherd preceded the introduction of a sensational young American baritone, Lawrence Tibbett, on May 26. Fresh from his Metropolitan audition a month before, he stunned the Tabernacle audience with his performances of "Eri Tu" from Verdi's "Masked Ball" and "Evening Star" from "Tannhauser." He then added a solo group with Mrs. Bassett at the piano.

Whatever happened to the "business" organization that supported the Salt Lake Symphony Orchestra in 1923-24 is only vaguely perceptible. With the approach of a new season, the forty-five member board of club delegates was gone. The Elks Lodge still entertained the orchestra's rehearsals, but a new set of officers and board members was now on line and, unbe-known to the musicians and their audience, the end of an era in symphony production was in sight.

Even with the lights about to go out, there was strong support for Mr. Shepherd and the players. L. S. Cates, the general manager of Utah Copper Company, was the new presi-dent, and his assistant general manager, D. D. Moffat, was vice-president. E. T. (Ted) Brown, prominent in the laundry business, was secretary, and B. T. Pyper, the only carryover from the previous season's operating staff, remained as manager for the first concert. He was then replaced by C. M. Brown.

For its final season the Salt Lake Symphony returned to the Salt Lake Theatre, where an orchestra of only thirty-five players performed under Mr. Shepherd on February 24, 1925. Theatre orchestras around the city still took precedence over the symphony for some players, and at least two members of the violin section were playing elsewhere.

Albert Shepherd, the soloist for the evening, left his seat in the first violin section long enough to join his colleagues in a performance of the popular "Introduction and Rondo Cappriccioso" by Saint-Saens. Mozart's Symphony No. 39 in E-flat was the major work of the evening.

The orchestra was back up to forty players when it brought down the curtain on thirty-three years of interrupted symphony playing in the valley in the final concert on April 21, with the Baroness Elspeth Von Rhoden, a soprano, as soloist.

Certainly it was most appropriate and perhaps more than coincidental that Shepherd programmed the Schubert "Unfinished" Symphony for what proved to be the farewell concert. The popular work had also been the principal composition on that first program in the same Salt Lake Theatre in 1892.

The reviews were most complimentary, and the newspapers offered every encouragement for a continuance of symphony concerts. In his report on the front page of the *Deseret News* local section on April 22, "H. G." finished with the following: "It is to be hoped that the good work will be carried forward and that next season will see an ever increasing interest and patronage."

It is quite likely that the writer, whose initials were at the end of the review, was H. G. Whitney, the treasurer of the old Salt Lake Symphony twenty years before and who, besides being business manager of the *Deseret News* at this time, was conductor of the Eighteenth Ward choir in the old chapel and adjoining Whitney Hall on A Street. The chapel now stands restored on Third North across from the State Capitol.

H. G.'s hopes were not to be realized, however, and the players were free to turn all their attention to theatre orchestra work until the "talking pictures" arrived. The Salt Lake Symphony disbanded, and Charles Shepherd left for two years in Europe. His brother, Albert, made one futile attempt to revive interest in 1927, but it died after a single concert by a Salt Lake Orchestral Society ensemble at the Salt Lake Theatre on May 18.

This small string orchestra of twenty-three players performed works of Vivaldi, Handel, Grieg, and Beethoven, the latter represented by his Piano Concerto No. 3 in C Minor with William Peterson, a Logan-born artist on the University of Utah faculty, as soloist.

There seemed to be no problem with engaging women musicians in this organization. Eleven of them were on the roster, including seven young violinists, most of whom may have been students of the conductor. Beales offered experience in the concertmaster's chair. Thorvald Jorgensen, Kenneth Roylance, and Adine Bradley made up the viola section. All were known symphony players, as were the cellists, Beth Nelson, Robert Fisher, Helen Riser, and Oscar Heppley and the bass duo, Val Jorgensen and Chris Jesperson.

Bradley, an extremely versatile and skilled musician, played the harp in the Utah Symphony and was organist at the Cathedral of the Madeleine for a number of years. Heppley later became chairman of the Utah State Institute of Fine Arts, from which position he figured in Utah Symphony affairs, while Jesperson appeared in a new role after playing the French horn in symphony orchestras dating back to 1902.

It had been the plan of the society to build a permanent orchestra from the small group, but Bert Shepherd joined his brother Charley in Europe for further study and concert work, and the effort died.

Thus the age of the early symphony orchestra came to a close. In 1927, still inside the prosperous "Roaring '20s," a break between this period and the beginnings of permanency eight years later had become a reality. It was clearly the end of an era.

PART TWO

WPA
ORCHESTRA

CHAPTER 5

BEATING THE DEPRESSION

Had there been any thought of following up on the Salt Lake Orchestral Society's plan for a permanent organization, following its lone concert in 1927, it would have vanished in 1929.

In the summer of that year thunderclouds had darkened the nation's economy, and a precarious uncertainty settled over the high-riding stock market. A steady decline in the Dow-Jones average began to develop, and on "Black Thursday," August 24, the market crashed. From then on into the 1930s an age of prosperity deteriorated into a deep depression.

With the sinking economy came widespread unemployment to be felt by musicians everywhere. Their problem was compounded by the coming of "talking pictures," which idled those who had depended so much on their nightly work in the theater orchestras.

Forced to seek work in other occupations, many musicians found the lines of job seekers to be long and unproductive, and they joined the growing numbers of unemployed on relief. They were looking for a spot to land when a Christmas gift in the form of a Federal Music Project under the Works Progress Administration was delivered in December of 1935.

The bearer of the glad tidings was Dr. Bruno David Ussher, western region director of the project. A prominent music critic, writer, and lecturer in Los Angeles, Ussher was a product of the Leipzig Conservatory and Oxford University and was the selection of the national director, Nikolai Sokoloff, noted Russian-American conductor and violinist.

Franklin Delano Roosevelt had replaced Herbert Hoover in the White House early in 1933, and the new president found support for the "New Deal," his plan to pull America up by its bootstraps. The Works Progress Administration, which touched millions of unemployed from coast to coast, was an element of that plan. Criticized as it was, the make-work scheme provided a refuge of sorts for the unemployed, both skilled and unskilled, in every work category, including the arts.

In setting up a WPA music project for Utah, Ussher selected Reginald Beales, master violinist of the McCune School of Music and Art faculty, and concertmaster in the last local symphonic effort of the 1920s, as its director.

Beales had been summoned to the office of Darrell J. Greenwell, WPA administrator for Utah, at the state capitol. There he met the regional music director and, following an interview, received the assignment. "The idea was to recruit indigent musicians registered on public relief rolls and put them to work in gainful employment," the Utah violinist recalls. "The arts received priority in this [WPA] program, and the pay for these employees was $96 per month."

Meanwhile, as Ussher took occasion to examine the Daughters of Utah Pioneers exhibits, then located on the lower floor of the capitol, he obviously became impressed with Utah's musical background. In the display of musical instruments brought to the Salt Lake Valley by early settlers, he found impetus for a tribute to pioneer efforts. In Gail Martin's music column in the December 21 *Deseret News* announcing Beales's appointment, the director was quoted as saying: "One thing I believe is significant of Utah. Your Capitol is the only one in which I have seen any musical instruments. Your exhibit of pianos and other instruments brought here across the plains by the pioneers shows that they had the right spirit. They believed in music. They believed in self-sacrifice for music. With such a spirit we can do much. They were pioneers. In the same sense we are pioneers, seeking to build for music a more spacious and beautiful edifice for the sponsorship of music."

On December 22, the *Salt Lake Tribune* saw the new project as a means for "employment of professional musicians from family relief rolls." It emphasized the "statewide" scope of the plan, which was to include "an orchestra, two trios and a piano team," as well as a "librarian and a piano tuner."

Perhaps as pleased as anyone with Dr. Ussher's timely and heartening appearance was Leroy J. Robertson, head of the Brigham Young University Music Department in Provo. Mr. Robertson was destined to become a giant among Utah composers. His concerns about the absence of a professional orchestra to tie musicians of the region to their home soil was evident in a brief news note alongside Martin's December 21 column.

Robertson, whose symphonic creations were later to be brought to life by the Utah Symphony, took his cue from Dr. Basil Cameron, then conductor of the Seattle Symphony Orchestra. An invited guest on the Provo campus, Cameron had suggested that Salt Lake City should sponsor a symphony orchestra. Robertson was quick to follow up. He wrote: "Utah is being drained of highly skilled musicians to feed the symphony orchestras of the [Pacific] coast and other centers. Several Utahns are affiliated with Portland, San Francisco and Los Angeles orchestras. Such an organization [as suggested by Cameron] is needed not only to keep Utah musical talent at home, but to fill the need of a state impoverished in fine orchestra music."

Although extremely modest in design, the beginnings of such a move were at hand, and the gathering of players from the relief rolls was soon under way. Not all were to be hired from this source, however, as Beales was given full authority to employ one nonrelief professional on a "full salary" for every ten "relief" players. The object was to provide additional training for the less skilled players as a means of upgrading the ensemble.

The music project director was well-qualified for his new position, and his training and skill soon became evident. Starting as a boy in England, he had prepared well and was an accomplished violinist when the Beales family immigrated to Utah in 1914 as converts to The Church of Jesus Christ of Latter-day Saints.

Within a few years after arriving in Salt Lake City, young Reggie was off to fill a Church mission in West Virginia. Hardly had he returned home when he took his violin to New York City, never intending to stay in Utah but hoping to make his mark in one of the metropolitan music centers. After a period of study and performing in theater orchestras, he returned in 1925 for a visit and was hired to lead a small orchestra at the Capitol Theatre, playing solos and concerts between the silent movies.

A year later Beales again was studying and working in New York City. He soon realized, however, that his heart had stayed with a young maiden in Salt Lake City. He returned home, married his sweetheart, and decided to stay when an offer came to take over the students in the Willard Weihe violin school. Weihe had died after an illustrious career dating back to 1892, when he was concertmaster in the first Salt Lake Symphony.

Eventually Beales took his teaching career to the McCune School, which led to his position with the Federal Music Project and an orchestra that was to evolve into the Utah Symphony.

To get the program under way, the director was handed a list of five players who had all the elements of an interesting modern-day combo. Although the exact makeup of the group is indefinite, at least three were well-remembered regulars—violinist William N. Morris, pianist Elsie Ahearn, and a clarinetist, Roy L. Allen. The trap drummer was either Homer L. Sanderson or Ernie Jones, and the fifth member was either Leroy P. Midgley, a former symphony clarinetist, or a trombone player by the name of Bernard C. Done. All became associated with the federal project, but a tricky Beales memory changed the lineup at interviews given some years apart.

Whatever the makeup, it was not an awesome assemblage that greeted the conductor, but it was the seed from which developed a permanent symphonic presence in Utah.

The original five players gathered with their director for a historic beginning in a little room at the Beesley Music Company on Main Street soon after the project was authorized. Within a few weeks, Beales was forced to find larger quarters for his charges. He had rummaged through the relief rolls to find other players and in due time was rehearsing an ensemble of twenty pieces in the unoccupied old Elks Club Building at 59 South State Street.

Perhaps typical of those to take advantage of the opening offered by the WPA music project was Theron Reynolds, a young bass player in a Provo school orchestra who would one day become the principal in the bass section of the Utah Symphony. The Reynolds family was apparently being supported at the time by an out-of-work father on the relief rolls at $84 a month. By removing Mr. Reynolds from the relief status and placing Theron in the WPA orchestra, the family received a raise of $12 a month, and Beales acquired a much-needed bass player.

It was a matter of pride for the musicians to be gainfully employed in their chosen profession, and they claimed a substantial measure of respect for their earnest efforts even though those so hired were generally regarded as "relief" players. Much less fortunate were the needy employed as outdoor laborers under the WPA program and derided as "leaf-rakers" and "shovel-leaners." Nothing was more applicable to this decade of hard times than the popular theme song of the day, "Brother, Can You Spare a Dime?"

Realizing the limitations of his small and somewhat inexperienced group, Beales selected music that was light but not entirely without substance. He found scores where he could, unearthing some pieces once used by theater orchestras and drawing on music used by earlier symphonies.

A discarded batch of music from the old American Theatre became useful to the conductor. Left over from the silent movie days, much of it was cross-orchestrated and became a boon to Beales in fitting music to the incomplete instrumentation of his ensemble. Since it was not easy to find players with instruments to fit the regular orchestral scoring, it became necessary to make some substitutions, particularly in the winds and brasses. For instance, it was not unusual to hear a trumpet playing the French horn part, or for the bassoon part to be played by a bass clarinet.

At least four short works, all fitted to the instrumentation, were in the repertoire when Beales returned to the state capitol with his players to face their first public audience on Sunday, March 1, 1936. The occasion was the opening ceremonies of the thirty-fourth annual exhibit of Utah art sponsored by the State Art Institute in conjunction with the WPA Arts Project.

For their part on the afternoon program in the marble rotunda, the musicians performed a Schubert "Minuet," the "Intermezzo" from Saint-Saens' "L"Arlesienne" Suite No. 2, selections from "Cavalleria Rusticana" by Mascagni, and Godard's "On The Mountain." The music was repeated in the evening, and the orchestra was heard again at the exhibit in double performances the following two Sundays.

Advance publicity concerning the debut performance noted that the orchestra of "about 20 musicians" had been rehearsing the "last six weeks" and that it was now "open for engagements." On the following Monday, the *Deseret News* reported that the ensemble had created a "deep impression by the excellence of its work, attained with but three weeks of practice."

Little matter how many daily rehearsals were required to get into playing form, Beales' new Utah State Sinfonietta, as he chose to call his little WPA unit, had become a significant contributor to music in Utah. More important, it offered a promise for the future of symphony development statewide.

CHAPTER 6

THE LAUNCHING PAD

Although perhaps lacking the proportion or rating of a symphony orchestra, the Utah State Sinfonietta nevertheless became the launching pad for the permanent professional orchestra that followed. It was, indeed, the genesis of the present-day Utah Symphony.

By the very fact that it was started as a means for musicians to meet and beat the depression, that it grew into a statewide concert attraction, and that it provided the base for a firmly planted symphony orchestra, the Federal Music Project's sinfonietta must be counted among the more remarkable developments in Utah music history.

Here was an orchestra that in less than five years would travel thousands of miles by bus to play nearly eleven hundred concerts in every school district and corner of the state. It began in mediocrity and seldom so much as approached a virtuoso level, but through perseverance at daily rehearsals and by augmenting the personnel with professionals on occasions, it surprised and pleased many listeners. As Beales says, "We were able to do some rather decent things in those days." The final payoff was to be found not only in critical acclaim, but in acceptance of the sinfonietta as the nucleus for a Utah State Symphony Orchestra that was soon to take form.

While the sinfonietta's first appearance came in the brief recitals at the capitol art exhibit, it was not until May 11, a Monday night, at the Assembly Hall on Temple Square that the WPA orchestra first appeared in a formal public concert.

Two months of preparation had upgraded production considerably, and the confidence exhibited by the musicians in their ability to handle a symphonic score was the highlight of the evening. As a vehicle, Beales had brought out the Bruch G Minor Violin Concerto, winning some honors himself for a "musicianly interpretation" of the solo score and presenting the new assistant conductor-director of the music project, Rudolph Hainke, at the podium.

In the following thirteen months, the WPA orchestra played 139 concerts, 49 of which were formal programs. The other 90 performances were on assembly programs before school audiences in Salt Lake City and the outlying areas. The bus trips had begun, and the sinfonietta had established a pace unheard of in previous orchestral endeavors.

Although the number of concerts presented by this ensemble would later become even more amazing, there were already enough to draw some stunning comparisons some years later from Deane Wakley Brown in his thesis on pre-1940 symphony efforts in Utah. He counted up all the professional symphony concerts that had been performed in the state under Pedersen, the Shepherds, McClellan, and Freber and marveled at his findings: "This makes a total of forty-four concerts, over a period of twenty-two years of actual concert playing up to the WPA, or two a year for each year the orchestra was active. Now think of an organization which in thirteen months had played '139 concerts, 49 being formal programs.' It staggers the imagination! If this report is correct, they played more (actually three times more!) concerts in this short space of time than all of the other orchestras did in twenty-two years."

As a matter of fact, the orchestra had barely warmed to its task. Playing three, sometimes even as many as four concerts a day as they toured the state, the players hardly had time to put away their instruments between performances. Between times they were at home base in Salt Lake City, where in the *Deseret*

News of December 16, 1939, Gail Martin reported: "This thoroughly drilled group of musicians has in the last four years played a total of 348 concerts in the Salt Lake City Schools alone to an audience of 113,750! The pupils look upon the Utah Music Project Orchestra as 'their orchestra.'"

Once Beales had secured nearly all the "relief" players he could find, he became more selective, both as to the instrument and its player. George Groneman appeared out of the past to assume his old position as concertmaster. Robert Fisher was the lone cellist and Reynolds the only bass fiddler.

With a great oboe career with the Utah Symphony ahead of him, Louis Booth was persuaded by Beales to leave his job as a shoe clerk on Salt Lake City's Main Street and join the sinfonietta. He became the only double reed player in the group and joined the McCune School faculty about the time the WPA orchestra was making its bow in March of 1935.

There was no bassoon in the ensemble, but a bass clarinet was in the hands of Robert Shelton. Earl Bush played the French horn, and Clyde White and John Omanson the trumpets. Roland Warner, flutist, and two viola players, Alfred Press (whose career spanned from 1913 under Freber to the 1940s) and Charles Josie, had taken seats in the orchestra. In addition to Morris from the original combo and Groneman, the section of ten violins included such future symphony fiddlers as Fred Kalt, Heber Christensen, Thomas Clyde Jones, and Milton N. Austin. Others were Sylvia Kennah, Hazel Ransom, William Lawson, and Joseph William Reece.

All members of the charter combo were still on board, the only change being in Elsie Ahearn's instrument. She had taken up the harmonium as a more adaptable piece than the piano for the traveling ensemble.

Although funded by the federal government, the WPA orchestra was completely Utah-nourished in character. Beales seemingly never lost sight of that important "home" quality, using as many qualified local artists as he could find to perform with his all-Utah contingent and performing every orchestral score by a homegrown composer he could get his hands on.

More than thirty vocalists and instrumentalists, both amateur and professional, student and virtuoso, appeared as soloists with the orchestra in nearly every available hall, no matter
how large or how small. It was not uncommon for the group to
play at the Tabernacle or Assembly Hall on Temple Square or at
Kingsbury hall on the University of Utah campus one night and
a small all-purpose schoolroom or LDS Chapel the next. Even
the Chamber of Commerce meeting room was once the site of a
performance.

Memory Grove at the head of City Creek Canyon was a
favorite spot on Sunday evenings in the summer, beginning in
1937, with light, popular music being the regular fare. Typical
was the closing concert of that first summer series on September 5 with Jessie Evans (later Mrs. Joseph Fielding Smith) as
soloist. Famous for her deep and resonant contralto voice, she
joined the orchestra in selections from the "Bohemian Girl" and
added the usual solo group. Orchestral works included the
"Blue Danube," by Strauss and "Slavic Rhapsody," by Friedman.

Following the sinfonietta from place to place, a listener
might find Becky Almond, Helen Budge (Folland), Martha
Coleman, or Mr. Hainke at the piano. Or he could catch the
Beales violin, the Fisher cello, or the Booth oboe for variety. Next
he might hear the solo voice of Margaret Stewart Hewlett, Rose
N. Sheranian, Beulah Huish Sadleir, Lela Bixby, Richard P. Condie, David Seegmiller, Ruth Jensen Clawson, Marguerite Sinclair, or John Parrish from a long list of local singers.

Young performers were often on Beales's programs. Shirley
Anne Thompson, a thirteen-year-old violin sensation, was given
the solo spot at one performance, and on three different occasions a brilliant young piano student of Mable Borg Jenkins by
the name of Grant Johannesen starred in concertos by Liszt,
Chopin, and Rachmaninoff.

Through this modest beginning Grant Johannesen played
his way into the array of nationally and internationally acclaimed concert artists, a station he has maintained and added
upon for more than thirty-five years. Before yielding to the
insistence of Robert Casadesus that he further his studies in
New York City with this noted French master and Egon Petri,
the Salt Lake youth had already tested his skills.

In his first appearance with Beales and the sinfonietta, he performed the Chopin Concerto No. 2 in F Minor (a work with which he has maintained a close identity) in his home Emerson LDS Ward chapel. Later, on January 3, 1939, he played the Liszt Concerto No. 1 at the Eighteenth Ward, where he shared the evening with Soprano Dorothy Kimball and the orchestra. In another fourteen months, on March 17, 1940, he was back with the sinfonietta for a performance of two movements of the Rachmaninoff Piano Concerto No. 2 in C Minor.

Seldom was a performance of the orchestra missed by local critics when certain soloists were on the program. Becky Almond played the Liszt "Hungarian Rhapsody" with the WPA players at the Lincoln Junior High School on October 5, 1937, and Gail Martin was impressed with the "glittering runs, massive chords, strongly contrasted passages — all brilliantly evoked" by the pianist. The same kind of praise was given Frances Winton Champ, an accomplished Logan pianist, for the "heights of expression" reached with the sinfonietta in the Grieg Piano Concerto at the Assembly hall on January 20, 1939. A full two years earlier, on January 15, 1937, the concert at the Chamber of Commerce had given exposure to the "glistening" keyboard talents of Helen Budge in the Beethoven Piano Concerto No. 3 in C Minor.

It is evident that Beales wanted to give Utah musicians a chance to be heard at home, but he was also eager to give exposure to writings of composers in the state. Manuscripts from Tracy Y. Cannon, Lorin Wheelwright, Seldon Heaps, Maurine Dewsnup, and Armont Willardsen were among the Utah works performed. The list also included a "Pastoral" by Beales and the "Scherzo" movement from a symphony by B. Cecil Gates.

The compositions were almost always present in the music carried by the players as they boarded the bus bound for school assemblies and evening concerts throughout the state. They were not always pleasant trips. Winter took its toll on the vintage buses, and more than once the musicians had to find their way through the snow to temporary shelter while repairs were made.

But most of the days were good days. There was a dedication in the efforts of all to build symphony audiences for the future, and the performers found cooperation most everywhere they went. So delighted were the residents of St. George, for instance, after a day of concerts at the schools and the tabernacle in their town, that they provided room and board.

Such a trip contributed to a report at the end of 1938 showing that the sinfonietta had played 167 concerts to a total audience of 70,518 with programs made available to communities at a distance of 300 miles "for as little as $25."

Another report on February 10, 1940, recounts 250 miles of travel for the month of January, during which the "Utah Music Project Orchestra played 12 concerts to go with performances at the Civic Center, Barratt Hall and the Neighborhood House in Salt Lake City. To date, the orchestra has played 892 concerts, most recently in Logan, Bear River, Box Elder, Park City and Heber."

A significant note in the report was the placing of sponsorship with both the Utah State Institute of Fine Arts and the Works Progress Administration. It was a welding of organizations that was to bring the sinfonietta more fully into its role as the base for symphonic development in the entire region.

Almost from the first gathering of the WPA unit, the thought of turning it into a permanent symphony orchestra was foremost in the collective minds of the music community. On October 5, 1937, the day after Becky Almond's dazzling performance with the ensemble before an audience of 350 in the 1,000-seat Lincoln Junior High School auditorium, the *Salt Lake Tribune* observed: "By the size and enthusiasm of the audience that listened is indicated the ever-widening appreciation of the place this organization fills in the community, such manifestation of its cultural value as might serve to suggest the desirability of giving this organization a permanent standing."

That evening in the *Deseret News*, Gail Martin elaborated further: "The manner in which this orchestra of 30 instrumentalists, directed by Reginald Beales, performed undoubtedly made everyone wish that this orchestra could be made permanent....

"Some enterprising group in the city and the state—should shoulder the responsibility of making this project permanent. Federal and state governments, assisted by private citizens, should see to it that Utah's first permanent orchestra does not languish."

It was the same old plea, but this time Martin knew that the groundwork had been laid and that an opening existed for such a cooperative venture. As the capitol building and legislative reporter as well as the music editor for the *News*, he had been present and a probable participant early that year when Utah's lawmakers were prevailed upon to give state support to all the arts under a thirty-eight-year-old art institute statute.

Up to that time the Utah Art Institute, founded through the efforts of Alice Merrill Horne in 1899, could legally embrace only the visual arts, and little thought had been given to making the situation otherwise. But with the three major categories of music, art, and literature under one roof in the Federal Arts Project, the need to provide the same coverage for the full realm of cultural arts on the state level was evident.

Under the revised statute the expanded organization functioned as the Utah State Institute of Fine Arts. Passed on March 10, 1937, and signed into law by Governor Henry H. Blood, Senate Bill 52 provided for the appointment of a governing board of thirteen members representing music, drama, dance, painting, sculptory, architecture, writing, the crafts, and business.

Most important to future symphony endeavors and the development of the arts in general were two provisions in the new law destined to provide a means for public funding as a permanent policy. The first specifically empowered the institute to cooperate with the federal government in the sponsorship of the arts, setting the stage for participation in what has become today's National Endowment for the Arts. The other permitted establishment of a symphony orchestra, or any other arts unit, as a division of the institute, to which state funds could be allocated.

To the credit of its sponsors and a strong faction from the cultural community, the legislation passed with little or no

opposition. One of the first to endorse the cause was Stanley N.
Child, president of the existing institute and a prominent
builder who later became a leader in the state Senate. Guiding
the bill through the two legislative bodies were Mrs. A. C. Lund,
who introduced the bill in the Senate, and Rep. Thelma Garff, an
effective sponsor of the measure in the House.

Perhaps no one was more interested in the successful
outcome of the effort than the state's directors of federal music,
art, and writing projects. Beales, Elzy J. Bird, and Maurice Howe
lobbied long and hard alongside others whose identity may be
found among those appointed to the institute board.

Once the revised institute law had taken effect May 11 and
the governor had appointed seven men and six women to
direct the new state agency, the board lost little time at its first
meeting in recognizing the WPA's three pronged arts program.
In response to a letter from Beales, the board's first official
business, after the election of officers, took the form of a
unanimous agreement to sponsor the federal projects in Utah.

The Saturday afternoon session in the Governor's Board
Room at the State Capitol on June 12 was convened by the
temporary chairman, Gail Martin. He was promptly elected
permanent chairman, with Dean W. H. Leary of the University of
Utah Law School as treasurer and Judy Farnsworth Lund as
secretary. The three officers and Tracy Y. Cannon, Mrs. A. L.
Beeley, Caroline Parry, and Mrs. John M. Wallace were named to
the executive committee. Other members of the board included
Mrs. F. P. Champ, Logan; LeConte Stewart, noted Kaysville
artist; Maude May Babcock, revered in dramatics at the University of Utah; Leslie J. Hodgson, Ogden architect; W. W. Clyde,
Springville contractor; and Harrison R. Merrill, Brigham Young
University luminary.

With the organization now in place, fund-raising to provide
state support for the federal arts projects became an immediate
objective. At its second meeting on September 2, the board, at
the request of the WPA music unit, agreed to support a ticket
sale for an October concert of the Utah State Sinfonietta. Apparently the effort was not the rousing success hoped for, producing an audience of only 350 at the Lincoln Junior High School.

A professional fund-raising venture was considered but was soon rejected in favor of getting the job done by selling memberships to the institute. A campaign for this purpose was eventually initiated at an art conference in connection with the annual exhibit at the capitol the following March 5, 1938. The price schedule listed subscribing memberships at $5, contributing memberships at $10, and life memberships at $100, with annual dues at $2.50.

As a climax to the conference, the sinfonietta, augmented to forty pieces, scaled new heights in moving to the Salt Lake Tabernacle for a concert with Alexander Schreiner as guest soloist in Guilmant's Concerto for Organ and Orchestra. Schreiner was then on the music staff at the University of California at Los Angeles and a few years away from becoming Tabernacle organist and eventually official organist for the Utah Symphony.

More than usual attention was focused on the orchestra since it had been singled out by Sokoloff the previous September as one of the outstanding units in the entire Federal Music Project. Also, the concert marked quite a jump for the players, who were appearing for the first time in the acoustically awesome Tabernacle. They came away with a good share of the honors, however, producing a tone that *Deseret News* critic Martin found to be "amply rich and full" for the big hall. He also acclaimed Schreiner for his "dazzling technical mastery" and in reference to the event as a whole noted: "The success of this concert, the demonstration that the Utah State Sinfonietta deserves a high place in the esteem of the community, should furnish a cue for more programs of this type, projecting the idea of a 'Utah audience for Utah artists.'"

Beales astutely chose this great moment to premiere his composition "Pastoral," and followed it with another American work, the "Angelus" from Henry Hadley's Third Symphony. Completing the program were the Debussy "Petite Suite" and, as an opener, the overture to Gluck's "Iphigenie en Aulide."

At its next meeting on May 7, 1938, the institute board learned it had netted $550 from its efforts at the art conference. It was also greeted by a warning from Dr. Sokoloff, through the

chairman, Martin, that unless something was done "to cooperate with the Federal Music Project operating in Utah," government support might be withdrawn. Immediate approval was
given to a proposal by Sokoloff and Beales "to augment the
orchestra" in order to build up the "weak spots."

School districts in the state became the first object of a
plan to strengthen the sinfonietta. In a letter authorized by the
board, they were asked to contribute to a sponsor's fund in
amounts from $100 to $2,000, "based on size and funds
available," with hopes of securing $10,000 to hire "six or seven
non-relief musicians, and employ artists" to appear with the
orchestra. What success, if any, the appeal may have known was
never made a part of the institute's available records. In the
years ahead, however, school concerts throughout the state
were to provide a source of revenue for the Utah Symphony
from individual schools, the districts, and later through appropriations from state funds for education.

After nearly two years at the old Elks Club building, the
sinfonietta had found another rehearsal hall on the upper floor
of a two-story structure at 323 South State Street, and the
institute took over the orchestra's former space for a Utah state
art center.

To help with the financing of the project, a benefit concert
by the Utah State Sinfonietta, again augmented for the occasion,
was presented at Kingsbury Hall under the institute sponsorship. E. Robert Schmitz, nationally acclaimed pianist and a
popular recitalist in Utah, joined Beales and the orchestra as
soloist in Listz's First Piano Concerto.

In addition to being a benefit for the new art center, Martin
said that the concert carried the added significance of being
"part of the Utah State Institute of Fine Arts' desire to attract a
new audience to concerts of symphonic music and to develop
opportunities for Utah musicians to be heard at home." After
the concert he wrote: "One of the encouraging features last
night was the rapt attention evident among student members
in the audience during the playing of the Haydn ("London")
Symphony, music that relies on its charm, neither on drama or
emotional appeal. Music appreciation plainly has traveled a

long way. Such manifestation alone proved the worth of the concert, and the need of providing regular musical programs of this type at a low cost of admission as part of the community's cultural and recreational facilities."

When the Utah Legislature convened for its 1939 session, two years after creating the new institute of fine arts, it gave the agency a two-year appropriation of $8,000. Before that, the biennial allocation had been $200, although Governor Blood had supplemented the 1937 and 1939 funds with a grant of $2,500 to help finance the new art center. He had placed the new $8,000 appropriation in his budget, and Martin hailed March 9, 1939, the day the appropriations bill was passed by the legislature as "one of the most important dates in Utah history." In his weekly column he wrote: "Utah is fortunate, indeed, in having a chief executive possessing the integrity, dedicated leadership and acumen of Governor Blood. It is doubly blessed that its governor is a man of culture, who believes that the arts should have their place in the sun along with the material things."

The real worth of the increased appropriation to the state's art program was not to surface until the end of the year when the Federal Arts Project budget was slashed by nearly 75 percent. It was not an entirely unexpected move, as America was riding out of the depression on the wings of an economic surge that developed when most of the European countries went to war against Germany in September 1939. Orders from the warring nations for goods and supplies were like a shot of adrenalin to America's languishing industries. The factories were humming and people were going back to work. The WPA was being phased out.

New money, mainly from private contributions, was needed to keep symphony music alive, and those most sensitive to the situation obviously felt the best way to obtain it was to build an organization for the establishment of a permanent orchestra. Since it still had some government funding and was steadily occupied, the Utah State Sinfonietta was a natural base for initiatory operations. And because it had become a sponsor of the WPA unit and was a legitimate receiver of state funds, the

Utah State Institute of Fine Arts offered a solid and ready-built foundation for the operating structure.

Some members of the institute board, among them Chairman Martin and Mrs. Wallace, had for some time exhibited an intense interest in the founding of a permanent symphony, and at its meeting on February 3, 1940, the board discussed the "possible formation of a Symphony Orchestra Association" as a means of stimulating an institute membership drive.

Beales, hoping to see his ensemble grow into a larger unit with broad support, but not so concerned with the organization concept at that time as with getting money to keep the symphony movement going, attended a WPA orchestra concert in San Diego, conducted by Sokoloff. Noting its success as a benefit for the music in that city, he came back with hopes of duplicating the idea in Utah.

A loyal supporter of the sinfonietta, Mrs. Burtis F. Robbins, had offered Beales $100 to help finance such a concert and the conductor had the idea this money, combined with available WPA and state funds, would provide needed backing for his project. His proposals along this line to Martin, Fred E. Smith, Mrs. Wallace and others perhaps were integrated into plans for a concert that spring, but in the meantime the new symphony organization was taking shape.

On March 18 at a dinner marking the forty-first anniversary of the fine arts institute at the Hotel Newhouse, Smith appeared as spokesman for the potential organizers and put a key in the symphony lock with his paper on "A Permanent Orchestra as a Utah Asset." Dr. Adam S. Bennion was keynote speaker for the event, and Governor Blood spoke briefly while presenting a pin to Alice Merrill Horne, and paying tribute to her as founder of the institute.

But it was Smith's disclosure of the impending new symphony association that stirred up the audience. He declared that the formation of a Utah state symphony orchestra as a department of the institute in cooperation with the music projects division of the WPA was "both possible and entirely practical." He then added: "The wholehearted cooperation of the musicians union has been assured and we plan to bring a great conductor or guest conductors here to handle the initial concerts. It is our desire to make this a statewide project. I have the pledge that a number of our leaders in civic and business life will be associated in this movement, including Dr. Adam S. Bennion, Gail Martin, D. D. Moffat, Charles L. Smith, W. J. O'Connor and George M. Gadsby."

Even Gabriel's trumpet couldn't have sounded sweeter to Utah symphony fans than the good news heralded by Smith. Moreover, as the listeners were soon to know, the organization of the Utah State Symphony Orchestra was less than a month away.

Before that event was to take place, however, the institute board on March 29, 1940, moved with positive and prompt dispatch to facilitate the momentous step to follow. Most significant was the adoption of a set of "Rules and Regulations Establishing and Governing a Department to be known as the 'Utah State Symphony Orchestra Association,'" formulated by Martin and destined to guide operations of the organization for years to come.

Also approved was the appointment of Fred E. Smith to the institute board to fill a vacancy caused by the resignation of LeConte Stewart.

These actions came after a report by Chairman Martin on the progress of the proposed orchestra society, in which he estimated costs of the first concert at $1,100. With this the board launched into a discussion on available guest conductors for such an event, but the list of prospects was not included in the minutes.

Meanwhile, the "Utah WPA Symphony Orchestra," as Beales' ensemble was now being called by the press, was moving ahead under an art institute campaign designed to develop "Utah talent in all the arts." The board had appointed Allen H. Tibbals, a local attorney and avid arts patron, as chairman of a committee to seek out talent for an "opportunity program," and his group arranged a concert at the art center on March 30, 1940, at which William Douglas, a Wellsville violinist just returned from study in the east, and the pianist, Hainke, appeared as soloists. Douglas, a principal in the Utah Sym-

phony's second violin section in later years, was heard in the
Beethoven G Major Romance, and Hainke played the Beethoven
Third Piano Concerto.

Nine days later on April 8, 1940, a historical first meeting of
the combined art institute board and the Utah State Symphony
Orchestra Association convened in the Utah Power and Light
Company board room in the Kearns Building on Main Street
with Fred E. Smith as temporary chairman. After hearing an
opinion from Assistant Attorney General John D. Rice establishing legality of the proposed orchestra's affiliation with the art
institute, the rules and regulations, as approved by the institute,
were adopted.

The document, as set forth by Martin, called for a board of
twenty-five members, including the thirteen members of the
institute's directing body and twelve others to be appointed by
the president of the orchestra association.

In a move obviously authorized beforehand, the temporary
chairman announced appointment of a group of twelve consist-
ing of Dr. Adam S. Bennion, D. D. Moffat, George M. Gadsby, W. J.
O'Connor, Charles L. Smith, Earl J. Glade, Sidney Fox, Lorin F.
Wheelwright, Mrs. Burtis F. Robbins, W. Jack Thomas, John F.
Fitzpatrick, and Mrs. Samuel J. Carter.

Fred E. Smith was then elected president of the association
with Dr. Bennion as first vice-president, Mrs. Wallace as second
vice-president, and Martin as third vice-president. Oscar R.
Heppley of the institute board was named treasurer, and
Donald B. Goodall, who had been installed as executive secretary of the institute and director of the art center, became
secretary of the association. Other members of the executive
board were Fitzpatrick, O'Connor, and Tracy Y. Cannon.

Indicative of the cooperation of the musician's union
Smith had mentioned three weeks before, was a letter to the
board from the Salt Lake Federated Musicians that "established
special rehearsal and wage consideration for augmentation of
the Federal Music Project for special symphony concerts."

As was to be the case for several years, it was thus set forth
that the new orchestra would actually exist as an augmented
Utah state (WPA) sinfonietta.

Top: *Newly formed Utah Symphony at site of its first concert in Kingsbury Hall on May 8, 1940, under Hans Heniot.*
Bottom: *Predecessor of Utah Symphony was the WPA Orchestra organized during the depression.*

DESERET NEWS

New director of Utah State Symphony, Hans Heniot (right), is welcomed to Salt Lake City by Mrs. John M. (Glenn) Wallace, Utah Symphony Board vice president, and Reginald Beales, assistant director and principal second violinist, April 14, 1940.

Top Left: *Fred E. Smith, Salt Lake banker and former basso with the Metropolitan Opera was a founder and president of the Utah Symphony from its beginning in 1940 to 1948.*
Top Right: *An important figure in early Utah Symphony history, Gail Martin was one of its founders, served as its first manager, chairman of the Utah State Institute of Fine Arts, and music editor of the Deseret News.*
Bottom Left: *Sir Thomas Beecham, one of the earliest guest conductors of the Utah Symphony.*
Bottom Right: *Dr. Lowell M. Durham (portrait by Alvin Gittens), Utah Symphony program annotator 1946 to present; music critic; U of U music professor.*

COLUMBIA RECORDS

Top Left: *Becky Almond performed as piano soloist with Utah Symphony later became first president of Utah Symphony Guild.*
Top Right: *Gail Plummer, best known for his long years as manager of Kingsbury Hall, was manager of the Utah Symphony for two seasons: 1944-45 and 1945-46.*
Bottom Left: *Werner Janssen was music director and conductor of Utah Symphony during its first season in Salt Lake Tabernacle, 1946-47.*

1952-53 photo of Maurice Abravanel and Utah Symphony in Salt Lake Tabernacle.

Top: *Newly appointed Utah Symphony Music Director Maurice Abravanel demonstrates conducting technique for Utah Governor J. Bracken Lee.*
Bottom: *Soloists (l. to r.) Harold H. Bennett, Rachel Connors and Blanche Christensen rehearse with Maurice Abravanel (at piano) for one of Utah Symphony's early orchestral-choral presentations.*

Top: *Utah Symphony pianist and piano soloist, Reid Nibley (seated), woodshedding with (standing, l. to r.) Don Watts, baritone; Jean Preston, soprano; and Percy Kalt, violinist, for upcoming concert.*

Bottom: *Four ardent advocates of the Utah Symphony and distinguished performers in their own right are pictured here contemplating a J. S. Bach score. (Seated, l-r) Ruth Jensen Clawson, Emma Lucy Gates Bowen, Annette Richardson Dinwoodey, and (standing) Virginia Freeze Barker Clark.*

Top: *Having previously collaborated on several successful Summer Festival productions at the U Stadium, Maurice Abravanel and Willam Christensen again joined forces to produce the "Nutcracker" in December 1955, thus forging a symphony-ballet relationship that has existed for three decades.* Bottom: *Utah Symphony musicians have provided music for Utah Opera Company productions such as "Die Fledermaus," 1983.*

Maurice Abravanel speaks to capacity audience at one of some sixty Saturday morning AG-Foodtown children's concerts in the Salt Lake Tabernacle.

PART THREE

MAJOR SYMPHONY

A STATE ORCHESTRA

There was no more crucial period in the development of Utah's symphony orchestra than the 1940s. These were the years of the transition from a WPA sinfonietta into the Utah State Symphony Orchestra and of the struggle to give the orchestra the status of a permanent, professional instrument.

That the orchestra survived at all is incredible. It began during the worst of depressions, and it grew into modest symphony proportions through another season of adversity, World War II.

Moreover, the embryo collection of players was scorned as a "relief" outfit of little substance, and the augmented ensemble that emerged from the make-work music project had little credibility as a true symphonic performer. Yet it survived while some established orchestras of long standing in metropolitan centers were forced to cease operations.

Undoubtedly the careful use of available funds had much to do with the survival of the Utah State Symphony Orchestra, but there were other important factors, as well. The underlying support of the Utah State Institute of Fine Arts and the Federal Music Project, for instance, was an essential element in the successful course of the new organization.

At least as significant as any of the other components, however, was the contribution of certain individuals within those agencies and on the sidelines who recognized the opportunity to found an orchestra from all these ingredients. Fortunately, they were convinced that under the conditions it would have a better-than-even chance of hanging on. They possessed a dogged determination to keep the musicians playing and proved it on several occasions. After all, some had seen early endeavors come to naught, and they knew that if the venture failed this time, there would be no tomorrow.

There is no question that some members of the fine arts institute board, such as Gail Martin and Mrs. John Wallace, had the WPA unit in mind as a basis for a Utah state symphony orchestra and were among those most eager to get the project going. At the same time, from his position as conductor of the federal program, Beales could see, and exploited as best he could, the possibilities of turning his little ensemble into a permanent symphony.

Another force in organizing and promoting the new symphony association, once he came into the picture, was its first president, Fred E. Smith. With his musical background and executive experience as president of the Eccles corporation's First Security Trust Company in the Newhouse Building at Exchange Place and Main Street, he proved himself a strong leader over a critical eight-year period.

Other members of the art institute board to figure strongly in the formation of the symphony were some closely associated with Martin and Mrs. Wallace on the executive committee. Tracy Y. Cannon, a prominent teacher and composer and chairman of the General Music Committee of The Church of Jesus Christ of Latter-day Saints, was engaged in the institute's sponsorship of the WPA orchestra. Among others were Dean W. H. Leary, Judy Farnsworth Lund, and Caroline Parry.

As a leader in initiating the new organization, Martin's contributions were well-documented. His recognition of the need for a permanent orchestra is found often in his writing as the *Deseret News* music editor, and his participation in the expansion and operation of the art institute is shown in minutes of board meetings and in biennial reports he prepared as chairman. He was secretary of the old board for two years before the scope of institute operations was broadened in 1937. Then he served as chairman for the next four years. The very fact that he authored the governing rules and regulations of the symphony as a department of the art institute—a document that guided operations of the symphony for many years—attests to his role as one of the true initiators of the movement.

A native of Chicago, where he was born on April 29, 1889, Gail came to Utah in the 1920s. After a stay in Ogden, during which he married Minnie Miller of Salt Lake City in 1929, he taught school in Nevada until he joined the editorial staff at the *Deseret News* in the mid 1930s. Aesthetically inclined and possessed with a boundless energy, Martin was soon covering the entire realm of the arts as well as handling a full-time reporting assignment for his newspaper. With his dedication to music and art, it was not surprising to find him a charter member and later president of the Salt Lake Civic Music Association, or to be so deeply involved in the art institute and the development of symphony music.

An equally strong personality, talented and well-schooled in music and the arts, Frances Glenn Walker Wallace not only was involved in the founding of the Utah Symphony but has been identified with the development of cultural arts in Utah for sixty years. No one among the organizational leaders made a more significant contribution to the orchestra than did she during the crucial decade of the 1940s and the two years following. As a benefactress, an influence for support, and, during one critical period, an administrator, she served tirelessly through the birth and early life of the symphony.

Glenn Wallace's self-assurance and interest in music and the ballet came as a natural consequence of her breeding and education. The product of an enterprising father and an aristocratic mother, she used both of these virtues to good advantage while taking from her involvement in music and ballet the stimulation and vigor so vital to her existence.

A devoted mother, Angelena Hague Walker, saw to it that Glenn received an education at the exclusive Windsor School in

Boston, from which she graduated about the time her father, Matt Walker, last of the famous Walker Brothers, died in 1916. She was an accomplished singer and pianist and was acquainted with dance through her exposure to concert and stage productions in eastern centers. She was then prepared by her mother for her emergence as a debutante in 1917 and came on home a beautiful and skilled heiress to the Walker fortune.

Three years later Glenn married John M. Wallace, creating a union that has wended its way with marked impression through the banking and cultural arts history of Utah for sixty-five years.

Glenn was still in her mid-twenties when she climbed into the symphony arena for the first time in the fall of 1922 to give Charlie Shepherd a boost with his Salt Lake Philharmonic. As will be recalled, the young devotee was elected president of the supporting organization and used her influence to gather around her in the endeavor a prominent group of businessmen, industrialists, and professional people. She had the support of her husband, who was listed as secretary of the board, and such other leaders as E. O. Howard, president of Walker Bank; Fred Smith; Alex Eberhardt; John C. Howard; H. F. Diche; Lloyd Wheeter; and Clarence Bamberger.

The venture lasted only six months, after which a new group stepped in, but Glenn had her start. She could see little hope at the time for a permanent orchestra and decided to bide her time. Her son, Walker, recalls hearing his mother discuss with Shepherd at a later date the possible establishment of an on-going symphony and how the conductor discouraged it with this remark: "Good God, Glenn, there isn't a bassoon player in the whole state of Utah."

Obviously bassoonists were hard to find and had a lot to do with putting together an orchestra of symphonic proportions. When 1940 rolled around, however, there were two such instruments on hand for the all-important venture that resulted in the foundation of a permanent symphony ensemble.

Mrs. Wallace was ready for it, along with other believers, and her influence is seen, as in 1922, down the roll of eminent individuals she helped to enlist in the new symphony cause.

When Fred Smith, as one of the founders, reentered the picture to become an effective organizer and administrator, Glenn was one who encouraged him to accept the presidency of the new management team.

After its expansion in 1937, the art institute took a good deal of Glenn's attention. She was an active participant in organizing benefit concerts and other functions, often enlisting the services of the Junior League in symphony concert promotions. Only while caring for an ailing mother during the spring of 1939 did she curtail her activities. Angelena Walker had the devoted attention of her daughter through her last days, and it was not until several months after her death on June 9 that Glenn again joined the symphony crusade.

Somewhat unnoticed, meanwhile, was her musicianship, maintained through the years and held largely for informal music gatherings at the Wallace home. Reginald Beales was particularly impressed with her skills during the days of the conversion of his sinfonietta into a symphony orchestra, remembering her as a "very fine pianist in informal chamber performances of sonatas by Grieg, Faure, and other masters."

At the symphony organization meeting on April 8, 1940, Mrs. Wallace confidently looked ahead in suggesting the consideration of summer concerts in the University of Utah stadium. Although the board was looking first toward a trial performance at Kingsbury Hall on May 8, one month away, the idea for summer stadium events was to catch on as a significant and popular segment in the schedule of the new orchestra.

Sensing the very essence of time in its immediate planning, the executive board met one day later, on April 9, and selected a promising Chicago musician, Hans Heniot, as guest conductor for the inaugural. Various committees were also named, and a proposed ninety-minute program of five selections was received from Heniot for board consideration.

The young conductor was chosen on the recommendation of Dr. Earl Vincent Moore, who had replaced Sokoloff as director of the Federal Music Project of the WPA, Erich Leinsdorff, then a conductor at the Metropolitan Opera; and Horace Johnson, director of the WPA music project in New York.

Not entirely new to the community, Heniot had appeared as accompanist for his brother-in-law, the noted basso Alexander Kipnis, in a concert at Kingsbury Hall in November 1939. He came from a distinguished line of musicians, his grandfather having come to America with Antonin Dvorak to remain as a music instructor. His father, Heniot Levy, was a noted pianist and teacher in Chicago.

Before coming to Utah, Heniot had conducted in Vienna, Buenos Aires, Moscow, and Berlin, and had won the Paderewski $1,000 prize for orchestral composition. In this country he conducted the New York Federal Orchestra on four occasions and the Illinois Symphony Orchestra of Chicago.

Upon his arrival in Salt Lake City, the ambitious young musician found a challenging task laid out for him. At the beginning of the new symphony campaign, Fred Smith had made it clear that the "objectives of the association are to use the state's musical talent to perform symphonic music in a highly professional manner."

To meet this challenge, Heniot faced the task of whipping an assemblage of fifty-two players into shape in the short time of nineteen days. He also faced a program that now included the Beethoven Seventh Symphony, which the symphony board had substituted for the Dvorak "New World" Symphony originally proposed. The rest of his program remained intact and included the Handel "Water Music," the "Moldau" by Smetana, the Johann Strauss "Emperor" Waltz, and "Finlandia" by Sibelius.

By April 27, 1940, the conductor was enthusiastic about the prospects, and in an interview with Gail Martin, he "earnestly commended" the work of Reginald Beales and praised his players: "I have been amazed at the players' willingness to work, and their desire to overcome technical difficulties. No pains are too great for them to take. I have never seen such enthusiasm any place. I don't believe in leaving anything to chance. Every detail must be worked out again and again so that nervousness, excitement will not upset the performance."

In a more direct acknowledgment of Beales's invaluable contribution to the symphony as a conductor, founder, and player, Martin, in his music column on May 4, 1940, paid this tribute: "His own musicians state that it would be almost impossible to find a more competent, sympathetic or patient director than Mr. Beales. His one pride has been developing and unifying talent. For years he has been working quietly to develop a permanent symphony orchestra. Now that his goal is in sight, he has proved his sincerity by extending fullest cooperation to Hans Heniot..., taking the first chair with the second violins in order to bring the organization to its fullest strength."

It was truly an all-Utah orchestra, and, despite implications that there was no connection between this organization and those of the past, there were a number of players who had reason to feel otherwise. No fewer than sixteen of the fifty-two musicians had played in those early days, three of them in the 1902-1908 period. George Groneman had the distinction of playing under every conductor from Arthur Shepherd through Reginald Beales, occupying the concertmaster's chair in several orchestras and throughout the existence of the WPA sinfonietta. The other two members who had been around since the Arthur Shepherd days were cellists Oge Jorgensen and Albert Press.

Arthur Freber was back in his old concertmaster role, and Beales was first chair in the second violin section. LeRoy Midgley, a fixture in the woodwind section from 1913 through the WPA period, had the solo clarinet; and Roland Warner, out of the 1920s and another sinfonietta graduate, was first-chair flute. Also leading their departments were four other WPA players, Theron Reynolds, bass; Ernie Jones, tympani; Louis W. Booth, oboe; and Robert Fisher, cello.

Fortunately for Heniot, the usually critical bassoon situation proved to be about the least of his worries. Howard Bleak, a talented young local student, had paced his studies well and was ready to move into the principal chair alongside Gayle Irvine, another new Salt Lake bassoonist.

There was no doubt the federal funding of the orchestra's WPA nucleus and the modicum of financial support from the state through the fine arts institute were the real attractions in putting the symphony association together and setting up the trial concert. Even with such favorable footing to start with, however, the impressive group of founders left nothing to chance. The board scaled the house from a top of $1.50 for the better seats to 50 cents in the upper balcony and pulled in Nelson W. Aldrich and several associates from the business community to lead the ticket sales, while Mrs. Wallace chaired a patron's committee. The combined results of the overall effort netted a profit of $1,350.

Just as encouraging was an overwhelming vote from the audience to make the orchestra permanent, this in response to a questionnaire distributed at the door. It was the kind of answer to be expected in light of indicators that had preceded the launching of the trial balloon. Early in March, for instance, the *Salt Lake Tribune*, in announcing a performance of the scherzo movement from a Cecil Gates symphony, prophetically referred to the WPA orchestra as the "Utah State Symphony Orchestra." A week later, just before Smith's first announcement, an editorial in the same newspaper noted the art institute's forty-first anniversary and praised its operation of the Art Center, declaring: "This is not only a worthy movement but very timely.... Art supplies a healthy outlet for human energy, impulses and restlessness. It adds to the total of worthy achievements which are landmarks set by advancing civilization. The Utah State Institute of Fine Arts is doing more for future generations and the cause of peace than can be realized or appreciated, however much we try."

Adding further to the favorable climate for cultural undertakings were these sentiments and encouragements in a brochure issued by the orchestra promoters prior to the May 8 concert: "The symphony orchestra supplies the foundation for all musical development. A permanent organization is needed to give the community's talent a chance for growth. A symphony orchestra is needed as the basis for the production of opera, oratorio and all forms of musical expression. A symphony orchestra is needed for enjoyment and for cultural stimulus."

The brochure credited the cooperative efforts of federal,

state, and local governments with reducing costs, noting particularly that the Utah WPA Music Program was spending about $35,000 (later to be refigured at $60,000) annually to maintain an orchestra. It pointed out: "This can be used as a nucleus for productions. More rehearsal time, daily over considerable periods, is available."

Nothing could have been more encouraging to the symphony faithful than the concert reviews. Eva Hollis in the *Salt Lake Tribune* declared that the performance "gave impressive testimony that Utah has at home the talent to provide symphonic music of the finest calibre, and also that the people of Utah have that whole-hearted interest needed to sustain such an organization." Impressed with Heniot's interpretations, she said they revealed "smoothness and finish and emotional subtlety," adding that the Beethoven Seventh Symphony was conducted with "imaginative detail and richness of color." The reviewer concluded that it was "a cherished evening of music" that will "mark a highpoint in Utah's musical attainments."

At the *Deseret News*, Gail Martin had left his post between the time his column appeared in the previous Saturday edition and the concert night to devote his time to the symphony and the Works Progress Administration. Staff writer John Talmage covered the event and called Heniot's performance the "outstanding feature" of the concert, reporting that he conducted in "remarkable fashion without once referring to a written note of music." He added that "much of the excellence of the musical presentation was directly due to the skill of the conductor in bringing out the best efforts of his men."

Talmage also mentioned a brief greeting by symphony vice-president Adam S. Bennion, who remarked: "Tonight we are making history! The appearance of our own symphony orchestra gives us a metropolitan atmosphere which we have not had before. I feel nearer to New York tonight than I have in a long, long time."

While noting that one of the chief merits of the program was the "familiarity of the music," the reporter found the last half "particularly timely in light of recent world history, presenting outstanding works by composers [Strauss, Smetana, and Sibelius] of Austria, Czechoslovakia and Finland, small countries recently wiped out or divided through the aggressiveness of major powers."

With such a successful start as a springboard, the executive board of the symphony association at its meeting on June 6 quickly disposed of Fred Smith's subject for discussion: "Does the Symphony Orchestra Association want to open an orchestra concert season for 1940-41?" An affirmative approach seemed to be a foregone conclusion, and the only question was the number of concerts to be presented. Board member W. J. O'connor, head man with American Smelting and Refining Company, suggested that a financial campaign be started at once. The group then accepted Gail Martin's motion to recommend that the board of directors proceed with plans for a 1940-41 season. That left one final important decision, to recommend on the initiation of Mrs. Wallace that Heniot be retained as conductor.

Although the issue raised over employing an "outside" conductor in preference to local artists was not to be finally resolved until the end of the season, it was for all intents and purposes disposed of at a board meeting on June 11, 1940. Mrs. Beeley raised the question at that time, only to find strong support for Heniot, who at the next meeting of the executive board on June 26 was authorized to begin rehearsals at a salary of $200 a month. The matter was brought up again by Mrs. Robbins, a strong backer of Beales at a July 1 meeting, but it was quickly explained by Smith that Heniot's selection had been unanimous. As a result, the season proceeded with Beales as assistant conductor and second violin principal.

Acceptance of an outline presented by Smith for a five-concert season with a budget of $10,585 was a mere formality. The list of proposed expenditures included $2,500 for Heniot, $4,500 for the augmentation of the orchestra through employment of forty union musicians to raise the membership to sixty-five or seventy pieces (it wound up at sixty-seven), and $1,000 for guest artists.

In the meantime, an important longtime source of revenues was established on the recommendation of Mrs.

Wallace that memorial funds be sought for the support of the orchestra. She then got the movement underway by creating two endowments, one in the name of her mother and the other for a revered sister, Lena Hague.

In his report to the fine arts institute at the end of the season, Smith referred to the enterprise of Mrs. Wallace in building up a memorial fund of $400 for the advancement of the orchestra. In addition to making note of the special fund, the institute board made certain it was placed in a separate bank deposit away from the general fund, there to grow with an accumulation of other interest-bearing memorials from the McCornick and Steiner families and others to appear later.

The first full season of the new symphony association was summed up well by Gail Martin in the twenty-first biennial report of the Utah State Institute of Fine Arts to Governor Herbert B. Maw on January 25, 1941. In a section on "The Music Project," he wrote: "No more brilliant proof of the manner in which the state's cultural resources can be mobilized for the inspiration of the community exists than the growth of the Utah State Symphony Orchestra from the WPA Music Project. With many premonitions, the association decided to give a test program on May 8 (1940).

"Doubts arose on all sides. Musicians said that the personnel did not exist in Utah for the manning of a first-class orchestra. If the musicians could be found, it was contended, the public would not pay for their music.

"Under the leadership of Fred E. Smith, president, the association decided to make at least one try....

"No more thrilling victory for Utah music has ever been scored. Those who came to scoff went away to praise.... WPA musicians covered themselves with glory. The largest profit, $1,350, ever made from a symphonic program by local musicians encouraged officers and directors to continue their work for a permanent orchestra.

"In August a membership campaign was launched. In spite of the Hitler Blitzkrieg, and the most intense competition of counter-attractions, an audience of 1,400 persons and a budget of nearly $10,000 was assured, the most outstanding accomplishment on behalf of local musicians in the history of Utah.

"Nor should the record of the WPA Orchestra, directed by Reginald Beales, State director, be overlooked. The success of the larger orchestra has been based upon the nucleus WPA Orchestra. Since its beginning in January, 1935, the WPA Orchestra has given 1,012 concerts to 348,075 listeners. In 1940 alone, 52,244 persons were played to during the course of 131 concerts. Schools have been supplied with free concerts and an enduring foundation laid for a wider and more ample support of music."

There was little about this incredible record and the favorable position of the new Utah State Symphony Orchestra that Martin had not envisioned back at the beginning of the Federal Arts Project. He had been involved with the art institute board for six years, and as its chairman at this time, he had not missed the opportunity to establish a symphony.

In addition to his roles with the art institute and the orchestra association, Martin was now managing the symphony. The WPA was furnishing a business and administrative staff and the service of thirty-four musicians, while the state agency supplied headquarters and rehearsal space at the picturesque Utah State Art Center at 59 South State Street.

More than two hundred workers were drawn into the campaign leading to the opening season, with season ticket memberships sought at prices of $10, $5, $3.50, and $2.50. On a larger scale, subscribers in various categories and memorial funds were also solicited. As the first concert date of October 8, 1940, arrived, Fred Smith reported: "The membership campaign was probably the most intensive ever waged for the development of local music resources. In many ways the results were most gratifying. A total of 1,250 members were enrolled, and a budget of nearly $10,000 assured, the largest ever raised for a local orchestra. About 85 percent of this is to be expended right here on our own musicians."

Heniot had induced his brother-in-law, Alexander Kipnis, the Metropolitan Opera basso, to return as a soloist at a fee of $700 for the inaugural concert. Artist and orchestra drew an audience of 1,613, including 1,459 paid admissions and "154 passes." Two other soloists presented during the season, the Polish violinist Henri Temianka, and Webster Aitken, an American pianist of note, received a total of $450 between them.

To bring the orchestra up to sixty-seven members, Heniot was authorized to employ thirty-three players at association expense, including a French horn principal, Bertram Haigh, imported from Denver at a cost of $65 a concert. As specified in the agreement with the musicians' federation, all of these players were to be union musicians paid on a scale of $10 for a concert and two rehearsals, or $20 for a performance and six rehearsals. A special rate of $3.50 was granted for young people's concerts, not including rehearsals.

The overall arrangement resulted in a total cost of $3,664 to augment the orchestra for the full season, as recorded in the financial statements of the treasurer, Oscar Heppley, at the end of the five-concert series. The statements showed a cash balance for the first season's operation of $927. Included in this net income figure was a profit of $281 realized from the three young people's concerts, for which the Granite School District paid $500 for two performances and South High School $300 for one. The orchestra payroll for these concerts was $479.

But while the young association was enjoying rare solvency on the financial front, it found itself confronted with problems in orchestral operations. If the venture was to be a lasting success, the two-level status of players—the WPA nucleus and the augmenting section—would have to be eliminated and the ensemble welded into a single, firmly controlled unit. Also, there was still some opposition to Heniot's appointment to be dealt with.

Both issues were resolved at a rather lengthy session of the board on March 20, near the close of the 1940-41 season, with the two decisions having much to do with setting a professional course for the orchestra.

At the obvious request of Gail Martin, the question "Should the Symphony association become official sponsor of the Utah Music Project, WPA, in order to control the full time of the WPA nucleus orchestra?" had been brought before the board by Fred

Smith. Such control, he said, would include "orchestra tours, school concerts, rehearsal time, and services outside the regular symphony series."

Since the forming of the symphony orchestra twelve months before, the WPA group had continued to present free concerts, mainly in the schools, throughout the state. This was causing problems for Martin and Heniot in controlling work schedules and the use of federal funds. Martin's plan was to eliminate the split in musical functions and present the full symphony in school concerts at a small cost to the students. He believed it "impossible to give free and paid concerts during the same season and continue to maintain the high musical and box office standards desired for the orchestra."

Some concern was expressed by Mrs. Robbins over depriving schools of the valuable free concerts furnished by the smaller orchestra, but Martin insisted that because of the insignificance of the fee, few children would be excluded.

At this point Mrs. Robbins once more questioned the "necessity" of hiring a conductor from outside the state at the exclusion of local artists. Her move spurred a lively defense of Heniot by members of the board, all of whom had received a letter from Beales requesting consideration for the post.

Earl J. Glade credited the combining of players under a "director from outside Utah" with making possible such an orchestra in the state and said he believed that "no local director could at present assemble such support." Mrs. Samuel J. Carter expressed concern over opposition in light of the success experienced and emphasized the need to retain an "experienced and talented conductor." Charles L. Smith then expressed doubt that financing could be secured "unless an outside conductor were employed." Others followed the same line, which resulted in the renewal of Heniot's contract and the acceptance of Martin's plan for orchestral consolidation.

For Heniot, it was the high point in a career of nearly six years with the orchestra, and for Beales it was the end of his association with the young organization he had helped to build. The WPA director found the situation to be the most unhappy he had ever experienced. The problem was that he would not have expected to displace imported conductors of proven artistic credentials, but to lose out to one he felt was no more qualified than himself was a bitter disappointment. As later may be observed, his feelings were to gain a measure of credibility in developments involving the upgrading of orchestral quality through later changes at the podium.

With his situation so intolerable, Beales vacated his chair in the orchestra and on June 27, 1941, announced his resignation as state director of the federal music project. From then on he devoted himself to teaching and concertizing.

In the meantime, the orchestra's board of directors moved quickly on Martin's plan to integrate the WPA players into the general operations and sponsorship of the symphony association. In doing so, it accepted full responsibility for operation of the WPA Music Project, a function delegated by the Utah State Institution of Fine Arts. However, the symphony association was to regulate operations of the WPA unit only "insofar as federal rules and regulations permit." It was also to provide, as nearly as possible, 25 percent financial sponsorship for the federal project, "which is expending about $60,000 of federal funds each fiscal year."

The new program brought an end to problems between the musicians' union and the federal "relief" players. Beales had experienced considerable trouble with the union, which had insisted that his sinfonietta members should join the local federation. He had held that such participation was not necessary. Now the players were on a professional level, and all members of the symphony belonged to a union that was cooperating to keep the movement alive.

In connection with the new plan, John F. Fitzpatrick, board member and publisher of the *Salt Lake Tribune*, drew unanimous support for his motion that in the "interest of improved efficiency and better morale," the expenditure of $30 be authorized for "reclassifying" the WPA music project by the employment division. The money was paid to three judges for auditioning musicians and rating them in two classifications: (1) those entitled to the professional and technical rating for a salary of $94.90 a month, and (2) those entitled to the skilled classification for a salary of $89.70 a month.

Fitzpatrick was also responsible for the only amendment to the Martin plan. The action permitted the functioning of a program advisory committee appointed by Fred Smith, thus denying the conductor full authority to choose the music to be played at each concert. Designed to meet apparent dissatisfaction with the programming, this move grew out of a discussion regarding selection of works with "more consistently popular appeal." The committee, consisting of Smith, Mrs. Wallace, Tracy Y. Cannon, and Gail Martin, was to advise and consult with Heniot on programs for the season. It was a prerogative to be assumed by the board throughout Heniot's remaining four seasons on the podium.

Riding on the momentum carried over from the successful 1940-41 season, the association headed into the new campaign with great expectations. The newly organized Women's Symphony Committee, a forerunner of the Symphony Guild, became important. Headed by Mrs. Martin C. Lindem, president, and Mrs. Fred Smith, Mrs. J. A. Hale, Mrs. Arthur P. (Virginia) Freber, and Mrs. Charles W. Yard, vice-presidents, the committee gave new impetus to a drive that produced 1,665 season ticket subscribers, a 20 percent increase over the previous year.

Orchestra personnel now totaled sixty-five, increasing the cost for augmentation by more than $1,300. Among new acquisitions were Max Dalby as clarinet principal, harpist Grace Louise Webb, and Kenneth Kuchler in the first violin section.

For Kuchler it was the beginning of a long service with the orchestra, a tenure that has progressed through forty-five seasons (with a season or two off for military service) and continues to lengthen as he remains an accomplished and dependable assistant concertmaster. The "dean" of the present symphony, as its earliest performer, Ken has won his share of points along the way, serving for a season or so as concertmaster and for many years in the chair he occupies as this history is being compiled. In addition, he distinguished himself during a term as conductor of the Westminster College

Symphony Orchestra and as an able performer in some formidable chamber music ensembles.

The establishment of the orchestra became more secure than ever before with the success of its second season. The symphony presented thirteen concerts, including five on the subscription series at Kingsbury Hall and the remaining on tours of the state, north and south. Two performances at Ogden sponsored by the Rotary Club on November 26, 1941, prompted the *Ogden Standard Examiner* to report: "Utah at last has a symphony orchestra of which we can be proud.... The program last night would have been a credit to any symphony orchestra anywhere." A crowd of fifteen hundred children heard the afternoon concert and a thousand adults attended at night.

Kuchler smiles as he notes the evening's program, one of his first, which led off with the Tchaikovsky "Nutcracker Suite." It marked his introduction to music he was to play a great many times in "Nutcracker Ballet" productions, beginning in 1955 with Willam Christensen's University of Utah ballet company.

Among other cities to hear the symphony were Cedar City, St. George, Parowan, Beaver, and Price. Tours by this full symphony orchestra were later to blanket the state of Utah and the intermountain region.

It was an ambitious season for the orchestra, which performed the Tchaikovsky "Pathetique" Symphony on the first program and the Brahms First Symphony on October 29, 1941. For the second concert, the popular two-piano team of Frey and Braggiotti was also brought in at a fee of $350 to perform the Gershwin "Rhapsody in Blue" with the symphony. The two middle movements of the Beethoven "Eroica" Symphony were on the Ogden program, and the Mozart Symphony No. 40 in G Minor headlined the third concert at Kingsbury Hall. Orrea Pernel, British violinist, was secured at a cost of $200 to perform the Lalo "Symphonie Espagnole" in the season finale.

On December 7, 1941, Japan attacked Pearl Harbor, and the United States was thrown into war. By the end of the season, Heniot was in uniform and was stationed at the Kearns Army Air Force Replacement Center as a technical sergeant and conductor of the band. Fortunately, however, he remained available to the Utah State Symphony Orchestra and conducted two "Sunset Concerts" at the University of Utah Stadium.

Alec Templeton, the heralded blind pianist, appeared as soloist on July 14, 1942, at a fee of $1,000 and drew an audience of more than 7,000, including 5,004 paying ticketholders, and as guests, 2,000 service men. A month later Frey and Braggiotti returned as soloist, this time receiving $400 for another performance of the "Rhapsody in Blue" before a crowd of 4,500, with 3,612 paying customers.

An appropriation of $2,500 from Salt Lake County and strong support at the box office with its bargain prices of 25 cents to one dollar left the association in the black for its first summer series. And since the 1941-42 regular season had shown a cash surplus of $634, thanks to a response from a $12.50 assessment levied on the guarantors, the symphony faced its third season in sound financial condition. Not included in the surplus, incidentally, was a still-intact memorial fund now up to $550.

Wartime restrictions on travel and other activities through the rationing of gasoline and other items under the OPA (Office of Price Administration) had a rather strange effect on the operations of the Utah State Symphony Orchestra Association. Instead of putting on the brakes and waiting out the tough times ahead, the officers and management speeded up the action and found support at every turn.

More than two hundred volunteers came into the campaign behind a directing force headed by George M. Gadsby, president and general manager of Utah Power and Light Company, and including Mrs. Lindem, president of the symphony's women's committee; Judge J. Allan Crockett, president of the men's committee; Mrs. Robert S. Fisher, secretary; and Gail Martin. They brought in 1,554 season ticket subscribers, three-fourths of Kingsbury Hall's capacity, and increased the number of guarantors to fifty.

To enhance its artistic potential, the orchestra added players at strategic points and was increased to seventy-two members. Five guest conductors were then signed on the recommendation of Mrs. Wallace's talent committee. Britain's great showman of the baton, Sir Thomas Beecham, former conductor of the London Philharmonic, opened the season on September 29 for a fee of $500. Appearing for lesser amounts were conductors Jose Echaniz, Albert Coates, Christos Vrionides, and James Sample, the last named being the assistant conductor of the San Francisco Symphony under Pierre Monteux.

Newcomers to the 1942-43 player roster included three young musicians who in this year's 5,000th concert will be observing forty-third anniversaries since joining the Utah Symphony. For the season opener Frances Johnson (Darger) joined the second violin section, and Don Peterson, a senior at Provo High School, entered the French horn section behind Harold Bawden. Both were to be off the roster later on, Peterson for military reasons; but Dorothy Trimble (Freed), who joined the viola section at midseason, has been a fixture ever since. Now the assistant principal among the violas, Mrs. Freed is credited with the longest continuous record of service and the most years of membership in the present ensemble.

Dorothy had been playing in the viola section of the McCune School Orchestra during the 1942-43 season with Bill and Lorna Hogensen, who were also members of the symphony. They suggested that she talk with Bob Fisher, the symphony personnel manager, who in turn invited her to sit in on a rehearsal. "So I did," she remembers, "and we played the Liszt 'Les Preludes' among other things. At the end of the rehearsal he said, 'OK, you can come. We rehearse Tuesday and Friday nights and Sunday afternoons.' The salary was $12.50 a week."

When she joined the symphony, Dorothy was very much aware of the presence of Thorvald Jorgensen, the viola principal. An uncle of Paul Jorgensen, currently in the symphony's viola section, he had played with the first violins in the 1920s as one of the three Jorgensens in the ensemble. Oge Jorgensen, Paul's father, was the cello principal, and Val Jorgensen was the first-chair bass.

With the beginning of the season, Max Dalby had left for the service, and John Reed assumed the first chair in the clarinet section. Still on hand, however, was Howard Bleak, who had been joined by bassoonists Grant Baker and Paul Wooston. Bleak was bringing more than a little distinction to the section with his registered Heckel bassoon. Don Peterson recalls the amazement expressed by the visiting conductors at finding such an accomplished bassoonist and instrument so far off the beaten path. He was forced to miss the November 24 concert under Coates because of his army duties, and when Jules Seder was imported from Los Angeles to perform the important bassoon role in the Tchaikovsky F Minor Fifth Symphony, the publicized substitute found the comparison a bit costly to his reputation.

Bleak's schedule was illustrative of the arrangements worked out by servicemen in the orchestra who were able to continue playing. Stationed at Fort Warren near Cheyenne, 450 miles away in Wyoming, he missed few subscription concerts at Kingsbury Hall while in uniform. Drum major of the army post's marching band and a performer on the baritone horn in the concert band, he arranged to begin his week end leaves on Friday evening. After kissing his wife, Maxine, good-bye, he boarded a bus for Salt Lake City, arriving there in time to rehearse during the day. After the Saturday night concert he was back on the bus in time to reach the barracks before the bugler sounded taps on Sunday.

In the major change of players in the orchestra line-up, William M. Hardiman replaced Arthur P. Freber as concertmaster, heading a string choir that now numbered forty-three musicians. It marked the end of a long career for Freber, dating back to the old Salt Lake Philharmonic in 1913. Except for four seasons as conductor in that era of symphonic production, he had always occupied the concertmaster's chair.

Changes had also taken place in the organization and general operations of the association, principal among which was a move affecting the status of the manager, Gail Martin. He had become WPA War Services supervisor early in the year and was thus disqualified from serving as a member of a sponsoring board. With his resignation from the art institute board, he was replaced as chairman by Oscar R. Heppley, while his unexpired term as a member of the board was filled by Judge Crockett. Martin remained close to both the institute and symphony operations, however, staying on as manager of the orchestra and serving as secretary of the art agency board. As he had been since the beginning, he was a strong force in keeping the orchestra movement alive, all of which was evident in his documented plans and subsequent direction of operations for each regular and summer season.

In tune with the times, the Art Center on State Street had become the War Services Center, where the symphony rehearsed two evenings a week under Sergeant Heniot. While efforts to secure a deferment for the conductor had been turned down by the draft board, his services as a rehearsal director gained approval of the commanding officer at Kearns.

The season itself was war services oriented, with the national anthem opening each program and the various military branches honored at specific concerts under the orchestra's season slogan: "Music is a weapon and a defense against fear and defeat." United States Navy Day, for instance, was observed in connection with the Echaniz concert on October 27, 1942, and Zimmerman's "Song of the Navy" was performed in honor of the midshipmen.

Contributions to purchase tickets for servicemen along with the presentation of released season tickets to the military was the order of the day.

Musically, it was a good season, starting off with an exciting performance under the Beecham baton. With only two rehearsals, the knighted Briton quickly brought a spontaneous cheer from the audience with his vigorous dispatch of the "Star Spangled Banner." He went on with a typically Beecham program, highlighted by a sparkling rendition of the Mendelssohn "Italian" Symphony and including the "Intermezzo" and "Serenade" from Delius's "Hassan" and the Beecham arrangement of Handel's "The Faithful Shepherd."

Called upon to bring out Dr. Adam S. Bennion for a presentation during intermission, Sir Thomas displayed what Eva Hollis of the *Salt Lake Tribune* described as a "sense of humor quite unexpected in an Englishman." Unfortunately, she left us without his punch line, but she did put her own to an appraisal of the performance. It was her opinion that "under his baton, the orchestra, whose personnel has altered considerably since last season, with much new talent added, performed with technical facility, and an honesty and vitality that bespoke good musical equipment and responsiveness."

Dr. Bennion's role as a symphony association officer was to present a platinum watch to Sergeant Heniot for his valuable contributions as a conductor and "caretaker," a point emphasized by Vernon J. LeeMaster in the *Deseret News*. In his assessment of the concert, LeeMaster concluded that "our little town was one step closer to having a first class symphony orchestra."

By the time the season reached its final concert on March 30, 1943, the orchestra was down to sixty-five members. Sample was on the podium to conduct his first of several important assignments with the Utah organization. As a guest on the evening's program was the Belgian String Quartet, performing with the symphony in Marcel Poot's Concerto for String Quartet and Orchestra. Other than the interest created by a combination entirely new to this area, the presentation commanded little attention. More notable was the presence in the quartet of cellist Joseph Wetzels, who returned a few years later to become the principal in the Utah Symphony's cello section under Maurice Abravanel.

On the financial and managerial fronts, meanwhile, some disturbing setbacks caused the symphony board to pause where it had gone so boldly ahead the year before. In December, 1942, the Utah State Institute of Fine Arts officers and directors were notified by Ruby S. Garrett, state director of the WPA Service Division, that WPA assistance would be discontinued on January 1, 1943. The source for funding administrative costs of the War Services Center and a thirty-man nucleus for the orchestra, not to mention the main employment of its manager, had dried up. Chairman Oscar Heppley and the board were quick to recognize the heavy burden imposed on the art institute if the War Services Center and the symphony were to go on operating. The center closed soon after the close of the year, but the symphony clung to its goal.

Noting the closing of the Art (War Services) Center and the near impossibility of promoting a season of summer concerts, Martin submitted his resignation as executive secretary of the institute and manager of the orchestra, effective June 30, 1943. It didn't seem to take, however, as he continued to manage the symphony through another season and remained as secretary of the two boards until his death in April 1952.

Despite the end of federal funding through discontinuance of the WPA program, the orchestra forces found themselves in a favorable financial condition with respect to plans for a Sunset Concert series in the summer of 1943. Salt Lake County had again appropriated $2,500 for a summer program, the orchestra's memorial fund was up to $860, and the bank balance was $572, thanks to guarantor payments totaling $500.

Prospects for the winter season ahead, however, were not so bright. With the draft now reaching into the ranks of married men with children, it appeared that many musicians would soon be inducted into the armed services, leaving the board with a task of rounding up sufficient personnel in addition to providing adequate funds. Faced with these and other discouraging factors, such as the closing of the Art Center, where operations had been based for four years, and the loss of an administrative staff to carry on its promotional activities, the board decided in June to postpone a decision on the 1943-44 season.

The summer series of two concerts started off so triumphantly on August 3, however, that the association decided at a meeting two days later to proceed with plans for a six-concert winter season.

A pretty seventeen-year-old soprano, Patrice Munsel, winner of the Metropolitan Opera auditions a few months before, was largely responsible for the brighter outlook on the symphony front. The young new star, singing arias and light popular works with the symphony under Sample, drew an audience of more than nine thousand to the Tuesday evening show in the stadium. The box-office draw of $5,300 after taxes was within $700 of meeting all expenses for the two-concert series.

Another success came on August 24, 1943. A large crowd

gave its approval to music under the stars with an all-military trio of artists in an "Armed Forces Night" concert. A young baritone, Lawrence Whisonant (later known on the concert stage as Lawrence Winters), and Captain Joe Jordan, composer-accompanist, from Fort Huachuca, Arizona, were flown in to appear with the orchestra under Sergeant Heniot, on leave from Kearns for the evening.

With prospects so improved over the situation two months before, the orchestra board disregarded symphony closures in some parts of the country and adopted an ambitious $19,500 budget for the season. The Detroit Symphony had been the latest to discontinue public concerts, announcing to the press that it was blaming the war for the interruption in operations.

Sir Thomas Beecham was re-engaged to kick off the series, once again providing a lively evening with a variety program featuring Mozart "Haffner" Symphony and Delius's "On Hearing the First Cuckoo in Spring." Others on the guest list were Coates, Nicolai Malko, and Horace Britt, who brought with him the other members of the Britt String Trio—Viola Wasterlain, violinist, and Conrad Held, violist—as soloists. They performed the Mozart Symphonie Concertante for Violin, Viola, and Orchestra on a program prolonged by a repeat, at the demand of an excited audience, of the French Military March from Saint-Saens' "Algerian Suite."

When the Ballet Russe appeared in November, 1943, symphony president Fred Smith made a point of the orchestra's ability to "give the community something it had never before had—a ballet presented with full orchestral accompaniment." It was an experience greatly appreciated by the near-capacity audience, and perhaps even more by thirty members of the local symphony, who picked up an extra evening's work. They combined with the ballet company's touring twenty-man ensemble to perform Copland's "Rodeo," the "Polovetsian Dances" from Borodin's "Prince Igor," and the Chopin Piano Concerto No. 1 with pianist Rachel Chapman at a spinet in the impoverished orchestra pit.

Since the so-called "pit" was at floor level, the first row of seats went unsold to accommodate the fifty players. Such an arrangement remained the rule for ballet at Kingsbury Hall until Willam Christensen, the founder of professional ballet production in Utah, prevailed upon University of Utah administrators to sink a pit in front of the stage for the "Nutcracker" inaugural in 1955.

For the season finale, Heniot's role again went beyond that of a rehearsal conductor as he took over the baton and once more joined the guest soloist in supplying a military flavor for the main course. The brilliant young pianist, Private First Class Leonard Pennario, on leave from Gore Field in Great Falls, Montana, shared honors with the Kearns sergeant and his forces in a performance of the Tchaikovsky Piano Concerto No. 1 in B-flat Minor.

Heniot was given even greater leeway during the summer. He rehearsed the orchestra and conducted all three sunset concerts at the stadium, beginning with a Fourth of July serving of "pops" specialties, solo ballet, and fireworks. Performing on an improvised dance floor, Monna Montes, the premiere ballerina of the Metropolitan Opera, fascinated the big crowd with pirouettes and arabesques while characterizing the "Six Wives of Henry VIII" in the novel setting.

One month later, a promoted Pennario, now wearing corporal stripes, was flown in from the air ferry command post in Great Falls for another guest appearance with Heniot and the orchestra. Well prepared for his ambitious assignment, the pianist twice brought the multitude to their feet with the performances of the Gershwin "Rhapsody in Blue" and the Grieg Concerto.

A third concert on August 29, 1944, presented Baritone Igor Gorin in several arias with the orchestra and a solo group accompanied by William Peterson at the piano. The orchestral highlight was the "Nutcracker Suite," in which attention was drawn to Becky Almond at the celeste.

Although the summer series showed a deficit at the box office, the annual Salt Lake County contribution of $2,500 and a carry-over from the other donations kept the association in the black as it looked ahead to 1944-45. Gail Plummer, manager of Kingsbury Hall and a new member of the fine arts institute board, had distinguished himself in handling managerial duties for the summer series and was engaged as permanent manager after the Gorin concert.

Gail Martin, meanwhile, had accepted a position as public relations director at Hill Air Force Base and was forced to resign as manager of the symphony. However, "in recognition of his long service to the development of the state's artistic resources," as stated in the art institute board minutes of September 29, 1943, he was reinstated on the board to fill a vacancy caused by the resignation of Ranch S. Kimball, and he was made a life member of the institute.

Anticipating a balance of $6,000 in available resources to cover an estimated deficit of $1,450 for 1944-45, Plummer proposed an innovative plan of presenting pairs of concerts and was given the go-ahead by the board. He immediately signed the Ballet Russe to open the season in a return engagement November 3 and 4. Pianist Andor Foldes, violinist Mischa Elman, and the nationally acclaimed Salt Lake pianist, Grant Johannesen, were engaged to perform in pairs of concerts under Heniot. Guest conductors Nicolai Malko and Jose Echaniz completed the guest list as directors of two other sets of performances in the six-event subscription series.

Heniot was employed at a salary of $3,000 to rehearse the orchestra and conduct three pairs of concerts, but it was to be his last season with the organization. While he had filled a role and served faithfully through an important period of Utah Symphony development, noticeable deficiencies in production standards were drawing criticism from many directions.

In the eyes of many, Heniot may have suffered by comparison with the more accomplished baton masters who appeared in guest performances, but to his leading players, in the words of Don Peterson, he was "just not a very good conductor." At the close of the summer series, this author, in the music column he had inherited from Gail Martin as music editor of the *Deseret News,* commented on a lack of progress in the quality of symphony production: "The general quality of numbers presented by Mr. Heniot and the orchestra this summer is hardly enough to insure outstanding winter concerts." Among responses was one from oboist Louis Booth, stating that so long as Heniot remained, "it is my sincere opinion and that of other musicians that the orchestra is doomed to a very mediocre career."

In defense of the conductor, violinist Alice Fox agreed that Heniot was not the "most capable of conductors," but she said that he did the best he could "under the conditions," including constant changes and two two-hour rehearsals a week.

While the season had its share of successes both on the stage and at the box office, the conductor found his position growing more and more insecure. He had support from a loyal board of directors, but his role in symphony history was running out, and the situation worsened to a point where he was forced to resign in the fall of 1945. Dissension in the orchestra and his failure as a musician to gain the respect of so many players, including the most skilled members of the ensemble, was more than Heniot could overcome. It was not the last time the musicians would wield such influence in bringing about a change at the podium.

There were some dates in Heniot's final season to be etched into the symphony's records, the first being November 28, 1944, when Foldes appeared as soloist. The event was an exciting premiere of the "Rhapsody for Piano and Orchestra" by Utah's eminent composer Leroy J. Robertson, who conducted both the first performance and the repeat on the following night. Not until the following January 26 did the art institute board approve an award of $350 to Robertson in recognition of the new work.

Another rising star in Utah's music firmament, Grant Johannesen, took center stage on March 6 and 7, 1945, to perform with Heniot and the orchestra as guest soloist in the Chopin Piano Concerto No. 2 in F Minor. It was Grant's first of many appearances with the Utah Symphony over a forty-year period, including a fortieth anniversary performance of the Chopin F Minor Concerto in 1985 at Symphony Hall under Joseph Silverstein, only the fourth conductor and music director since founding of the orchestra.

By now the course of the Utah State Symphony Orchestra

was no longer in doubt. With its future mapped out ahead, a new pride in artistic excellence was emerging to give credibility to the desired conductorial change. Funding was becoming more secure as a result of state and county appropriations, plus the support of guarantors and donors, thus providing for more orchestral services and a growth in the payroll. In January, 1945, Oscar Heppley and Gail Martin secured approval of the art institute board to set aside more than five thousand dollars from the agency's unexpended allocation and a "restricted fund account" for the use of the orchestra. Specifically, the funds were designated for keeping the symphony in rehearsal during the months of April, May, and June, and for a postseason series of school concerts in Salt Lake, Provo, Ogden, and Logan.

The summer of 1945 found the orchestra in performance at the stadium on four separate occasions, one of them a historic Sunday evening concert with the Salt Lake Tabernacle Choir in the closing event of the "Days of '47" celebration on July 29. A rarity in the history of both organizations, the collaboration was their only one in the first thirty-six years of the Utah Symphony's existence. Not until the Bi-Centennial year of American independence in 1976 was there to be another alliance of the two internationally distinguished Utah music institutions.

Under the baton of the choir's conductor, J. Spencer Cornwall, the combined company was heard in a performance of Haydn's oratorio, "The Creation," before a crowd of more than 10,000 in the hilltop bowl. Although shortened somewhat to make room for a "pops" section by the orchestra under Heniot, the oratorio drew critical acclaim for the 450 participants, including soloists Fern Sayre, a Van Nuys, California, soprano; tenor Richard P. Condie, the choir's assistant conductor; and Austin Seager, Ogden basso.

America had celebrated the end of military hostilities in Europe with the formal surrender of Germany on V-E Day, May 8, 1945; and its full attention was now on the Pacific and the war with Japan. Thus the entertainment of servicemen was still very much a consideration of the symphony association in preparing the regular Sunset Concert series.

Alec Templeton returned as guest soloist for one of the

popular summer evening productions, with soprano Florence George and the harmonica specialist Larry Adler joining Heniot and the orchestra for the other two.

When fighting in the Pacific ended on V-J Day, August 14, 1945, and the Japanese officially surrendered on September 2, 1945, the symphony was facing a 1945-46 season without a conductor. In what seemed to be an almost routine process, however, the association signed its oft-employed guest conductor and consultant, James Sample, as music director and principal conductor for a six-concert subscription series.

When the new conductor began rehearsals for the first pair of concerts on October 26 and 27, 1945, he was immediately confronted with vacancies in some very important chairs. The concertmaster, Mr. Hardiman, had left to concertize with his wife, pianist Frances Osborne Hardiman; and the principal cellist and personnel manager, Robert Fisher, had taken a position in the cello section of the San Francisco Symphony.

Mischa Poznanski was secured to replace Hardiman, and the new cello principal was a reliable local musician, Joseph C. Clive. Ross Beckstead, a violinist, took over as personnel manager and player representative on union matters.

Sample conducted the first three pairs of concerts, presenting the sensational opera diva soprano Dusolina Giannini as guest soloist in the opener. An all-orchestra program was presented on November 16 and 17, and harpsichordist Alice Ehlers was featured in concerts on December 6 and 7. Milton Forstat was the conductor and Claudio Arrau was at the piano in January, 1946; Nicolai Malko was the baton guest in February; and Jean de Rimanoczy conducted in late March, with Gorin as a vocal guest. The Ballet Russe was no longer on the schedule, but the symphony arranged an extra paid service for half its members by bringing in the San Carlo Opera in early March with a touring ensemble of twenty players. As had once been the case with ballet, opera buffs were treated to something new in hearing a professional opera company on the local stage with a full orchestra providing support for the singers.

Kingsbury Hall had become the established concert hall of the region, housing the symphony concerts, presentations of the Salt Lake Civic Music Association, the University of Utah Lecture and Artists Series, and almost any other musical event that came along. Only an occasional major event was presented at the Salt Lake Tabernacle. Neither hall was available for regular concert rehearsals, and the symphony was hard pressed to find a home for its practice sessions. The Art Center on State Street had long since closed, and the players found themselves shifting from churches to the Utah Power and Light Company auditorium and back again, with a jaunt to some other available space in between.

Consequently a topic under discussion at the time—the need of a civic auditorium to cover the city's requirements in many fields of entertainment—found a most interested participant in the music public.

More than twenty years before today's Salt Palace reached the planning stage, there was talk about building a 10,000-seat arena to house exhibits, sports, music, dance, traveling shows, and whatever else would draw an audience. On this basis, however, there was little unity of support. The feeling of the music-minded, for instance, was expressed quite well in related comments in *Deseret News* music columns dating from September 9, 1944, to September 22, 1945: "A 'Symphony Hall' with a seating capacity of 3,000 to 4,000 would be better suited to Salt Lake's present and future music needs than a 10,000-seat civic auditorium. The city is one of the most music-minded centers in the country and its future demands a suitable concert hall.

"A huge athletic or sports palace is not the answer to the concert hall question."

The final answer to that important question was still more than thirty years down the road when the orchestra association in 1946 decided to take a giant step on its way toward establishing a major symphony. In progress at the time was the last of the symphony's Sunset Concert seasons, a series of three "pops" productions under the direction of Vladimir Bakaleinikoff. Appearing with the noted Russian guest conductor in the summer performances were Larry Adler and his harmonica, baritone Joseph James, and the popular composer-pianist Percy Grainger.

In the midst of these activities, Fred Smith and the board set the stage for their greatest challenge. They resolved to implement a blueprint for a permanent professional orchestra prepared months before by James Sample under board authorization. Then, to give the plan a better chance of succeeding, they assigned to a committee of three the task of securing a home for the Utah Symphony in the historic Salt Lake Mormon Tabernacle.

CHAPTER 8

A HOME FOR
THE SYMPHONY

Symphony president Fred
Smith chose industrialist Morris Rosenblatt and Judge J. Allan
Crockett to accompany him on the Tabernacle assignment.
Late in September of 1946 the three-man committee secured an
audience with President J. Reuben Clark, Jr., first counselor to
President George Albert Smith in the First Presidency of The
Church of Jesus Christ of Latter-day Saints.

The meeting in the Church leader's office at 47 East South
Temple was a cordial affair and produced a most generous
solution to the orchestra's concert-hall problems. The visiting
delegation not only wanted to rent the great Tabernacle for
symphony performances, but they also had in mind a monetary
contribution from the Church, little expecting the two requests
to be met in a single gift of such lasting benefit.

Judge Crockett, then sitting on Utah's Third District Court
bench, has a vivid recollection of the meeting. He recalls the
concern of President Clark, himself a product of the law profession and former U. S. Ambassador to Mexico, for the position of
his guests in their tough job of trying to diplomatically represent and secure funds from all sides of the community, particularly Mormon and "Gentile."

"We know you have to carry water on both shoulders," the
Church official said as he shunted aside as "unrealistic" any
thought of the committee's first gathering from other religious
sects funds to be matched by the Church.

Instead, he went directly to the matter at hand and on behalf of the First Presidency proposed that the Tabernacle be made available for symphony concerts at a nominal fee, with the Church to return an equivalent amount as a contribution to the symphony.

The delegation immediately and gratefully accepted the offer, and the Salt Lake Mormon Tabernacle became a home for the Utah Symphony free of charge for the next thirty-three years, except for the 1962-63 season, when the building underwent extensive renovation. For that season, the orchestra moved to the Highland High School auditorium, where it found a most cooperative host but paid an unreimbursed rental fee and the costs of stage management and equipment handling.

Under the final arrangements at the Tabernacle, the LDS Church not only provided free use of the hall and its facilities for the symphony's dress rehearsals and concerts, but it also contributed the services of an electrician and eventually a crew to erect a temporary platform over the rostrum. Later it made the great sound chamber available for recording sessions under the same conditions.

Perhaps the feelings of the symphony committee were best expressed in this letter written to President Clark by Judge Crockett on October 1, 1946: "It is one thing to speak a perfunctory thank-you for an interview; quite another, after a period of time for reflection and consideration, to express an abiding sense of appreciation.

"May I, in this letter, express my appreciation for your cordial reception and your understanding attitude of the problem we presented to you in connection with the development of the Utah Symphony. You not only bespoke your interest and desire to be helpful, but followed it up by giving substantial help to this enterprise, which should have many far-reaching good effects.

"We are aware of a number of obstacles which it was necessary for the Church Presidency to overcome in determining upon this course. It is my earnest hope that this decision will prove to have been a wise one, and that in lending your support to the development of the symphony orchestra, you will have placed another important stone in the structure of culture, beauty and happiness which the Church has ever sought to build for its people.

"I hope you will find it convenient to express for me the same sentiments of appreciation in like measure to President [George Albert] Smith and President [David O.] McKay."

While it would be impossible to place a dollar value on the Church's unprecedented contribution, suffice it to say that it was by any standard a substantial and important gift spanning a third of a century of the symphony's growth.

There were many benefits to be realized in the orchestra's move to the Tabernacle in addition to the substantial savings in rental and staging costs. The size of the hall, for instance, with its seating capacity of 4,772, based on reserved ticket sales, permitted a schedule of single performances, again reducing production costs. Not included in the house count were the 400 seats in the choir loft, which the members of the Tabernacle Choir were permitted to use free of charge for symphony concerts, and a small section near the orchestra for the general authorities of the Church. Whenever the orchestra programmed a choral work, requiring its own occupancy of the choir seats, the Tabernacle Choir singers were given tickets in the main hall. It was a small price to pay the permanent occupants of the auditorium for its use.

The spectacular acoustics inside the famous domed roof proved another boon to the orchestra in its new location, although the players had a few difficulties in adjusting to the almost uncontrollable production of sound.

In an auditorium with interior measurements of 132 feet in width, 232 feet in length, and a ceiling height of 64 feet, there were bound to be some problems with acoustics. When the Saints gathered for the first meeting in the structure in 1867, it was a reverberative nightmare. The building was far from complete at that stage, however, containing no permanent seats or gallery and only a small part of the original organ.

In the ensuing years, designers and architects responded with some amazing improvements, and by the dedication of the Tabernacle on October 9, 1875, the acoustics were not only acceptable, but, for most of the hall, incomparable. Installed on their stage behind the rostrum, the Tabernacle Choir and organ have become identified with the great sound chamber that projects their music as almost no other hall in the world can do. But with the visiting orchestras, platformed over the rostrum, the production of sound is anther matter. Players have often complained that the lack of resistance to their tones creates the impression that they are performing alone. For the instrumental soloist, the echoes from an empty hall are often a serious distraction.

The phenomenon re-calls one of maestro Maurice Abravanel's favorite anecdotes involving his longtime friend from New York's Broadway, Oscar Levant, in his first visit to the historic Mormon structure. As he tested the keyboard to start a dress rehearsal with the orchestra, Levant was besieged with echoes. The notes seemed to come back as fast as he struck them. With a look of dismay, he turned to Abravanel and asked, "Do people play here?"

The Maestro assured him that when the hall was full of people everything would be all right, and during the next break he followed the pianist backstage. Still somewhat distraught and known to be a nervous chain-smoker, Levant lit up a cigarette and found Abravanel descending on him. "Put it out, put it out, you don't smoke in here," he was told. "What's the matter, Maurice," asked Oscar, snuffing out the cigarette, "is it a church or something?"

Touring musical groups such as the Philadelphia Orchestra in its performance at the Tabernacle on May 5, 1936, under Leopold Stokowski, have expressed concern over the quality of their production in the big hall. Stokowski was in his final season as music director of the famous orchestra at the time, yet he found it necessary to have his staff monitor the sound throughout the rehearsal. In later years, the Boston Symphony, the New York Philharmonic, and other leading orchestras from the United States and Europe have visited the Tabernacle and maneuvered through—and benefited from—its acoustical peculiarities.

With audiences, however, it has been another story. While there are less favorable areas for the discriminating listener, the majority of seats in the Tabernacle offer a sound that is unmatched, even in the new Symphony Hall, for exceptional acoustics. The orchestral output is, with rare exception, at a standard that should allay the fears of the musicians.

An example of the dichotomy will be found in the Utah Symphony's list of recordings. When Seymour Solomon of Vanguard Records heard the Utah Symphony, the University of Utah Chorus, and soloists in a subscription performance of Honegger's "King David" in the Tabernacle, he threw up his hands and insisted that symphony manager Herold Gregory find another hall in which to record the work. From what he had heard, the technician-executive was convinced it would be "impossible" to use the Tabernacle for the project. He told Gregory,"The sound is everywhere." The symphony manager reminded him of the great recordings already produced there by the Tabernacle Choir and told him not to worry. After the recording session, Solomon felt much better about the result. Later, when the recording was nominated for the Grande Prix du Disque in Paris he was, of course, completely satisfied.

By the time the venerable Tabernacle marked its centennial in 1967, the demands upon its facilities had reached a point where Church authorities became concerned about the effects of heavy use on the building. They began to give more importance to preserving this unique treasure that by then had become one of the world's foremost tourist attractions. Steps needed to be taken to reduce wear and tear.

It was another ten years before the orchestra was to move to a new home, receiving through that time the continued support of the Church and noting its backing of civic projects, as well. When construction of the Salt Palace complex was proposed, the Church made available through a fifty-year lease at one dollar a year most of the land on which the facility, and later the Symphony Hall, were constructed.

Contributions of the Church to symphony presentations and projects, sometimes on foreign soil, came in various shapes and patterns, quite often in the form of a substantial monetary donation. There had been such a donation when the Utah Symphony received an invitation to perform at the Athens Festival in Greece and other European music capitals in 1966.

The Church through its business entities contributed its "tithe," or ten percent of the estimated $150,000 subsidy to make the tour possible.

In the same year, the Ford Foundation invited the symphony to participate in an endowment grant program under which the orchestra would receive a $1 million endowment grant (plus $500,000 in non-matching funds) if the local organization would raise an additional $1 million in matching funds. Again, the Church contributed its "tithe" in the amount of $100,000 over a five-year period.

Still another $100,000 contribution came in 1980, this to be added to an endowment fund of $200,000 established by Obert C. Tanner, local philanthropist and patron of the arts, to provide the basis of a retirement program for symphony musicians and staff members. With no such program yet available to the players and other employees, Tanner contributed the $200,000 with the idea of using the earnings of the fund to benefit the instrumentalists and staff.

On numerous occasions over the years, the LDS Church and Utah Symphony have exchanged cooperative efforts for the good of each other. When the symphony experienced a lag in ticket sales for its performance in Vienna in 1966, the orchestra made available seats at a cost of only one dollar to the local LDS mission president. His missionaries were thus enabled to invite at reasonable cost many friends and members while at the same time helping to fill the hall. On still another occasion, during its 1971 South American tour, the symphony invited LDS missionaries to distribute souvenir programs to arriving patrons, providing aide for the orchestra and valuable exposure for the Church.

Most Utah cultural organizations, unless labeled otherwise, are quite naturally identified with the western cradle of Mormon culture, and the Utah Symphony is a prime example. Once it moves beyond the state's borders, whether on concert tours, recordings, or broadcasts, in the eyes of many it becomes the "Mormon" orchestra. Because of this association and out of respect for its longstanding relationship with the LDS Church, the symphony's administrative board and staff have emphasized to all an obligation to project an image of dignity.

During the 1966 European tour, maestro Maurice Abravanel often found it appropriate in his curtain speeches to state that while he was not a Mormon, he had come to admire the members of the Mormon faith. He and the orchestra would then perform the "Pastorale" from the "Book of Mormon Oratorio" by Leroy Robertson.

Perhaps Abravanel's own statement best illustrates the importance of the mutual cooperation and respect between the Church and the symphony. As he has often said, "Whatever we do, it should always be a two-way street that benefits both sides."

PROFESSIONAL BLUEPRINT

Once the Utah Symphony organization decided to upgrade its orchestra to a full-time professional unit, the future of symphony production in the Beehive State took on an entirely new perspective. In one enormous stride the orchestra moved to a higher plateau, and the base for a major symphony was established from its new professional blueprint.

The bold move presented an entirely new concept in symphony operations for the Mountain West, requiring a budget for the 1946-47 season three times larger than any President Fred Smith and his board had ever tackled before. And never before had their role as fund-raisers been so clearly outlined, facing, as they did, the challenge of covering an anticipated deficit of $50,000 a season.

With the same kind of courage and determination it took to adopt and support such a fiscal program, the board on may 13, 1946, organized a drive to collect $150,000 for a "Symphony Progress Fund" designed to cover operating deficits for three years. Board member George C. Hatch, a Salt Lake radio executive, accepted the assignment as general chairman, and a statewide "Utah Symphony Orchestra Council" of seventy members was enlisted in the campaign.

To kick off the drive, Hatch and his committee arranged a banquet for the state's symphony patrons and business community in the Lafayette Ballroom of the Hotel Utah with Olin Downes, music editor and critic of the *New York Times*, as guest speaker. The distinguished visitor gave impetus to the crusade by outlining the great possibilities and opportunity for achievement facing the Utah Symphony, particularly in light of the fact that few orchestras of distinction had survived west of the Mississippi.

The campaign for funds was well on its way before the symphony administrators began implementing the plan outlined in conductor-consultant James Sample's blueprint for excellence, as modified somewhat to fit the funding.

As far back as December 3, 1945, the board had heard Sample's outline for a new professional operation, and two days later it had unanimously agreed that the plan should be put into action if proper and adequate financing could be assured.

The stage had been set for the presentation by board president Smith, whose paper entitled "The Utah Symphony— a Memorial to the Mormon Pioneers" was regarded as "a review and a forecast." Once more the Smith leadership was evident as he set a strong course for the organization with his observations and objectives: "Six seasons of concerts given by the Utah State Orchestra Association have demonstrated beyond a shadow of doubt that there exists in Salt Lake City an expanding demand for symphonic music.

"From a budget of $10,000 annually (not including the Federal WPA Music Project) expenditures have risen to nearly $60,000; the number of concerts has grown from five single programs to seven pairs of concerts.... Season ticket holders have risen from 1,200 to nearly 2,000.... The steady growth in attendance at concerts and in revenues accruing from performances testifies that the orchestra from the first has not faltered in building toward a permanent, professional orchestra."

Smith then outlined six objectives of such an orchestra, the first looking to the immediate future and tied to the title of his statement and the others providing much of the base from which the symphony has grown:

"First — An effort should be made to utilize plans for the 1947 Centennial Celebration to dedicate a permanent and living memorial to the Mormon Pioneers in the form of a permanent orchestra and to make the year 1947 the first in a series of annual musical festivals. The tradition and cultural background for this type of memorial are a part of Utah's history and living. What more eloquent testimonial to the pioneers could be created than a permanent Utah symphony?

"Second—Building of this orchestra would make Salt Lake City and Utah the cultural center of the Intermountain West. Music festivals given each summer would help to draw tourist travel to the city.

"Third—The Utah Symphony should be maintained to serve the entire state. By its tours and its concerts in the schools, the appreciation of music would be vitally fostered.

"Fourth—The Utah Symphony would supply employment and training for native musicians in orchestral, choral and operatic performances.

"Fifth—Entertainment of quality would be available to citizens at a reasonable cost.

"Sixth—Support of an orchestra from year to year which commanded respect for its significant achievements would accomplish much for the state in the way of public relations and favorable publicity."

It was a statement of considerable foresight, and while one or two of the objectives were to be sidetracked briefly along the way, all were eventually fulfilled.

Taking his cue from the symphony president, James Sample then came forth with his ambitious blueprint, much of which was to be erased in the final application. For the most part, however, it offered a basic form of operation.

Speaking as an "outsider, with no ax to grind," Sample stressed the fact that the symphony orchestra is a nucleus of all musical activities, around which revolve the opera, choral works, chamber music, young people's concerts, radio programs, and tours.

He noted that Utah "has not yet a first-class orchestra." He pointed out the drawbacks in rehearsal schedules, the fact that most players were unable to devote needed time to rehearsal because of other employment and activities, and to the small pay schedule and lack of incentive. He then emphasized the necessity of providing "key" performers on higher musical levels to provide a nucleus for artistry and needed training in orchestra routine.

The consultant's proposal included an orchestra of sixty-one players under the premise that "60 really capable instrumentalists will possess a fuller and richer tone than ninety mediocre performers." It also contained twelve pairs of subscription concerts, including two operas with local chorus and guest artists, ten or more young people's concerts, ten radio performances, twenty or more appearances on statewide tours, and six to eight summer concerts.

For the "Memorial Orchestra," Sample suggested a full-time music director and employment of the orchestra on the basis of a twenty-six week season. His plan called for a budget of $135,000, with a deficit "under the most favorable conditions" of less than $25,000.

Not until September, 1946, did the organization sign a conductor and begin the new operation, finally scheduling a season that opened in November. By that time the orchestra had not only its new conductor and music director, but a new name; a new location for its concerts; a new manager; a new professional format with nineteen imported musicians, including a new concertmaster; and a new Main Street office.

The new name had come on May 23, 1946, in connection with organization of the fund drive, the board voting to change the title from the Utah State Symphony Orchestra to the Utah Symphony. Not until September 24, 1946, when the move was ratified by the Utah State Institute of Fine Arts board, however, did the new name become official.

While the speculation about appointment of a new conductor had included such names as Sample, Bakaleinikoff, Rimanoczy, and Richard Burgin, assistant conductor of the Boston Symphony, there was no real action until Werner Janssen entered the picture on September 11, 1946. As conductor of his own Janssen Symphony Orchestra in Hollywood, he appeared as a guest of honor at a joint luncheon of the Salt Lake Advertising Club and the Chamber of Commerce. He had come to Salt Lake City in connection with the world premiere of a ten-minute musical film, "Toccata and Fugue." The venture featured a performance by the Janssen orchestra of Lucien Cailliett's orchestration of the Bach Toccata and Fugue in D Minor coordinated with a photographic spectacular of Bryce Canyon National Park.

As a result of contacts made during the visit, the orchestra officials on September 19 signed Janssen to a three-year contract at a salary of $6,500 the first year. He was to receive $10,000 for a second season, with the fee for the third season to be agreed upon between the conductor; his manager, Arthur Judson; and the symphony board.

Since the contract called for ten pairs of concerts, it was obvious that Fred Smith and his committee had not yet met with President J. Reuben Clark, Jr., about using the Salt Lake Tabernacle. Other interesting terms included a 1947 summer season from July 6 to August 9, consisting "essentially of five appearances per week directing the orchestra with the Centennial music-drama and not to exceed four other concerts to be arranged during said period," all of which was precluded by later plans of the Utah Centennial Commission. A historical first production of the Centennial music-drama "Promised Valley" pre-empted the symphony summer-season proposals but gave the orchestra's musicians some substantial summer work.

Although he was to hold the position of music director and conductor for only one season, at the time of his signing Janssen was considered a prize acquisition for the Utah Symphony. An American conductor of no little accomplishment, he had the distinction of being the first native-born New Yorker to conduct the Philharmonic — Symphony Orchestra of New York. He had graduated form Dartmouth College in 1921, and in 1930 he was awarded the Prix de Rome. After that he remained in Europe for four years and received recognition for his abilities with the baton in a measure unusual for an American musician. He appeared as guest conductor of many European orchestras, among them the Berlin Philharmonic and the Helsingfors Municipal Orchestra.

Janssen's wife was the noted movie actress Ann Harding; she accompanied him to Salt Lake City to be feted in a royal welcome banquet at the Hotel Utah. During the season the actress occasionally made the trip to Utah for her husband's conducting assignments, and the couple seemed to lend a certain amount of Hollywood glamour and showmanship to the atmosphere of several concerts.

Hardly had the new conductor unpacked his baton when he ran head-on into personnel problems. Given a free hand in the selection of his players, he announced plans to import twenty-five musicians and was greeted by the circulation of petitions against the replacement of local players by "imports." In the end, the new leader was able to insert nineteen "outsiders" into the lineup. Pressures were brought to reinstate some local instrumentalists who failed to come up to audition standards, but Janssen's decisions were upheld by the board on grounds that overall quality of the orchestra must be improved if the objectives were to be reached. If and when that objective could be reached with an all-Utah orchestra, it would be done.

Some musicians, largely those who had been able to follow other pursuits while performing under previous conditions, were unable to accept positions that called for daily "full-time" morning and afternoon rehearsals. Out of seventy-two auditions, forty-nine local musicians accepted jobs, with thirty-nine hired full-time and ten others on a part-time basis. Salaries of full-time players were set at "not less than $50 per week."

It was also late in September, 1946, that a change took place in the management of the symphony. Upon recommendation of Janssen, the board hired Ruth Cowan, a veteran in executive work for concert bureaus and later with the USO in the Los Angeles area, as manager. She was installed in the new office at the Art Institute board room at 125 South Main Street just in time to become involved in the season ticket drive.

In a brochure promoting the forthcoming season, Fred Smith pushed the drive along by calling the public's attention to the opportunities available. He wrote: "The Utah Symphony enters its seventh season as a truly great orchestra that represents and belongs to the people of Utah. Through the generosity of the Church of Jesus Christ of Latter-day Saints the Mormon Tabernacle is now the new home of the Utah Symphony, making possible a brilliant season within the price range of all families. Your purchase of season tickets will help assure an ever greater Utah Symphony."

Season tickets for nine subscription concerts were scaled form $8.40 to $15.00.

Although he virtually "commuted" between Los Angeles and Salt Lake City, Janssen made quite a success of the sixty-eight-piece orchestra's first season as a permanent, professional unit. In all, the symphony made forty-four appearances from November, 1946, through April, 1947, including nine subscription concerts in the Tabernacle, twenty-eight performances throughout the state under Utah's 1947 Centennial Commission sponsorship, five youth concerts at the Tabernacle and Capitol Theater, one coast-to-coast broadcast over CBS, and an appearance at the coronation of the Utah Centennial queen at the State Capitol.

When the season opened at the Tabernacle on November 16, 1946, Otis Igelman, formerly with the Los Angeles Philharmonic, made his debut as concertmaster. Few local musicians were retained as principals, among them Ross Beckstead in the second violin section; Lorna Hogensen, viola; Louis Booth, oboe; and Grace Louise Webb, harp.

With Igelman among the imports were Joseph Coppin, the new cello principal, and his brother John, second chair in the second violins. Other new first-chair performers included Russell Brodine, bass; Albert Klingler, clarinet; Arthur Hoberman, flute; Morris Wade, French horn; Ralph French, trumpet; and Lorn Steinberger, trombone. Health problems had forced Howard Bleak to leave, and Gloria Solloway was the new first bassoonist. Taking over the timpani for the first time was Walter Rothaar.

The opener was a gala event, with "black tie" very much the order of attire in the coveted "B" section seats on the left side of the main body of the Tabernacle. The all-orchestra program was enthusiastically received, with an impressive performance of the Brahms First Symphony drawing particular attention from the critics.

It was the first of four programs on the subscription series to present Janssen and his orchestra without solo assistance at the box office, and the success of these concerts was a notable part of the season. A crowd of 4,100 attended the second performance, which included the Sibelius Second Symphony and "Till Eulenspeigel." by Richard Strauss. An all-Tchaikovsky evening included the "Nutcracker Suite," "Romeo and Juliet." and the Fifth Symphony. The fourth all-orchestra concert was the season finale near Easter on March 29, 1947, and Janssen appropriately programmed the oft-played Schubert "Unfinished" Symphony, the Rimsky-Korsakoff "Russian Easter" Overture, the Prelude and Love-Death from Wagner's "Tristan and Isolde," and the Bach-Respighi "Passacaglia."

The five other concerts brought on a variety of guest performers. Violinist Yehudi Menuhin was soloist in the Mendelssohn Violin Concert on a December 14, 1946, program that included the Brahms Fourth Symphony. William Primrose, the premiere violist of the day, performed the Handel Viola Concerto between the Borodin Symphony No. 2 and the Respighi "Pines of Rome" on January 18, 1947.

Early in February, the famous motion picture star Edward Arnold came from Hollywood to narrate a performance of the "Genesis" Suite, a biblical work commissioned by Janssen and composed by several contemporary writers, among them Stravinsky, Toch, Tansman, Milhaud, Korngold, Schoenberg, and Castelnuovo-Tedesco. The rare event stirred considerable interest and caused Dr. Lowell M. Durham, in his review of the work in the *Salt Lake Tribune*, to comment "It was well that we had the opportunity of hearing such a variety of modern composers. Had we waited to hear isolated offerings of each, it might have taken years. Hearing all, even in one dose, was an opportunity, regardless of one's musical allergies."

Utah musicians took over the guest artist roles on two occasions, with Salt Lake Tabernacle organist Alexander Schreiner and composer Leigh Harline sharing the honors on February 22, 1947, and Grant Johannesen making his biennial appearance in the Rachmaninoff Second Piano Concerto on March 8. Schreiner was heard at the great Tabernacle organ in

Marcel Dupre's Concerto in E Minor for Organ and Orchestra. It provided an interesting contrast to the Beethoven Fifth Symphony, with Janssen at the helm, and Harline's timely "Centennial Suite," with the composer conducting. A former Utahn who had won fame as a composer and conductor of music for moving pictures, Harline had created the work through a commission from Janssen in 1941.

Three days before the Johannesen concert, the Utah Symphony on March 5 was heard in a nationwide broadcast over the Columbia Broadcasting System originating over KSL Radio. The one-hour evening program was an interesting potpourri, very much in the "pops" format. Richard L. Evans, internationally known for his "spoken word" on weekly CBS broadcasts of the Mormon Tabernacle Choir, narrated two portions of the "Genesis" Suite as the major offering. Other works included the Prelude to Act 3 of Wagner's "Lohengrin," the Scherzo from Mendelssohn's Incidental Music to "A Midsummer Night's Dream," selections from Dvorak's "New World" Symphony and Janssen's arrangements of Debussy's "Clair de Lune," and "Music George Washington Knew," a medley of American folk songs.

Meanwhile, the statewide tours sponsored by the Utah Centennial Commission kept Janssen and the orchestra on the road for weeks at a time. In two weeks during February, they played twenty concerts, including twelve in a jaunt through southwestern Utah as far south as St. George. The next week they were in northern Utah for eight performances.

It all started in January, 1947, with concerts at the Heber City and Logan Tabernacles followed by the first of a series of five youth concerts on Saturday mornings in Salt Lake City. A trip to Vernal on February 3 commanded thirty-six inches of space over five columns, with a photo of Janssen, in the Sunday *New York Times* of February 23. Written by Jack Goodman, a versatile and prolific writer with a flair for the arts, the music section feature carried the headline: "An Orchestra Pays a Visit to the Back Country," with the subhead reading, "Utah Symphony, Led by Janssen, Brings Living Music to Remote Towns."

Goodman came from New York City to make his home in Utah and has spent much of his life writing about the state. He made the trip to Vernal with Janssen and the symphony and found something to write home about. His impressions tell the story of an important segment of that first season of full-time operations of the Utah orchestra. They bear excerpting:

"Vernal, Utah—'Golly, the music they play is certainly pretty, and they all play together so well,' reported Genevieve Taylor on hearing her first concert by a symphony orchestra. Dark-eyed, pigtailed and pretty, 12-year-old Genny is an Indian girl, one of 1,250 youngsters of assorted ages brought recently by school-bus to this tiny town for one of a pair of concerts given by the pioneering Utah Symphony Orchestra.

"Judged by the rousing applause at the young people's and adult concerts, Werner Janssen's notion of bringing good music to the back country is a happy one. Certainly the 'New World' Symphony, major work presented in Vernal's white-steepled Mormon Tabernacle, has never been performed before a more colorful or more responsive audience. Sheepherders, oil-well riggers and cowpunchers turned out by the truckload, and a number of Indians flocked to town to represent the race from which Dvorak allegedly borrowed a theme or two....

"As for the younger generation, it is true that several printed programs were turned into paper aeroplanes during the children's concert, but most of the town heads squired by Superintendent Avard Rigby of the Uintah School District listened as attentively to music of the masters as do their juvenile counterparts at Saturday morning Carnegie Hall sessions....

"Although this concert was to have been a Utah project, children from Artesia, Colorado, some forty miles away, were cordially invited—and came in droves. . . .

"The only complaint heard following the evening event came from a cowhand who asserted, 'They should've played at the movie house. These Tabernacle seats are too hard.'

"This Vernal visit. . . . was planned because Conductor Werner Janssen wishes to bring his new orchestra to communities off the usual concert track....

"With perhaps 3,500 persons attending each Salt Lake concert, many of them season subscribers, our orchestra would obviously fall short of what I felt was its major goal—bringing good music to those who need it most,' says Mr. Janssen.

"The orchestra will travel 1,800 miles on its tours.... traveling by bus in barnstorming jazz-band style.... Each week, between Salt Lake concerts, the sixty-eight musicians take to the high road, often bucking forty-inch snowdrifts on the overnight jaunts. Since few towns visited have motel accommodations for the entire orchestra, tourist cabins and private homes are utilized. An instrument truck precedes the pair of buses in which the musicians travel, and only one program has been delayed thus far because of hazardous roads.

"Native Utahns in the orchestra, such as violinist Frances Johnson, agree with outlanders such as Concertmaster Otis Igelman.... that the small town series is a highlight in their careers....

"Finally, there's Jimmy Munson, who drives the lead bus.... Said Jimmy: 'Mr. Janssen dragged me into the first concert, found me a seat and made me listen. Since then I've sat in on them all. And since they play the same music at all the concerts, I guess I must really like the stuff.'"

These were not the first of the trips for the Utah orchestra into the hinterlands, of course, nor would they be the last, but they were the first of symphonic proportions.

They wound up late in March, 1947, and the final Salt Lake youth concert on April 2 at the Tabernacle, with Met Soprano Mimi Benzell as guest soloist, was the last for Janssen with the Utah Symphony.

Accustomed to working with seasoned players in Los Angeles, the commuting conductor obviously was not given to training inexperienced musicians. Thus he was not too happy with his personnel in Utah and attempted to have the orchestra board give him six more "imports" and bring the quota up to his original request of twenty-five.

When this was refused, Janssen exercised a clause in his contract that permitted him to cancel after one season. He then accepted a position with the Portland Symphony Orchestra and took with him most of the imports, the main exception being Igelman, who became concertmaster with the Detroit Symphony Orchestra.

In a letter to symphony president Fred Smith on March 31, 1947, Janssen had written: "A symphony orchestra, to interest me, cannot stand still: it must continue to progress, and we can go forward from this point only if the essential possibilities for advancement are present in the personnel. This would mean 25 imports next year (six more than now), and I understand the union requires a minimum of 45 local musicians.

"Salt Lake City is a wonderful place for music—and the magnificent attendance and warm appreciation of its audiences indicate a glorious future for a worthy orchestra—but I cannot regard it as fair to the city or to myself to struggle into another season under the same handicaps that proved too great a strain this year.

"As far as I am concerned my heart is here, but I cannot undertake it again unless 25 imports are assured this time in addition to the 45 local musicians."

For the Utah Symphony, the decision of its board of directors to hold firm on the number of imported players was most fortunate. Had the door been thrown open, one of the orchestra's greatest assets in the years ahead might never have been realized. Nothing was to bring the ensemble more attention and critical acclaim than its regional character and homespun quality. This "home" atmosphere was to be quickly recognized and for thirty-two years encouraged by Maurice Abravanel.

Dave Freed became a part of this unique spirit when he joined the symphony in 1956 and became the cello principal. He married Dorothy Trimble, who had been in the viola section for thirteen years when Dave came on board, and found a permanent home in the community. No longer with the orchestra, Dave is one among past and present local players who will attest to the spirit of the Utah Symphony. He says, "There are very, very few symphony orchestras with the unique regional character to be found in the Utah Symphony."

Janssen's resignation was received with no resistance from the symphony board, which not only opposed his personnel demands but had developed concerns over his status as a "visiting" conductor. He was dividing his time between Los Angeles and Salt Lake City and seemed little interested in becoming a part of Utah's music structure.

While he had served his purpose, Janssen showed little regard for the overall problems involved with symphony operations, nor did he display much interest in his players. Dorothy Freed remembers that "he never talked to us—he didn't say so much as 'hello', 'good morning,' or anything."

By the time Janssen had moved on to Portland, the symphony's administrative organization was planning the 1947-48 season with most of its attention, as usual, on finances. Only a little over $91,000 of the Symphony Progress Fund goal of $150,000 had been collected, and the lack of the remaining portion for the three-year plan was later to return to haunt the board and orchestra.

There was plenty of money on hand to cover the $48,705 deficit remaining from the budget of $120,730, but trouble loomed ahead for a season in which expenditures were expected to reach $130,000. While the Utah Symphony had reached and exceeded the $100,000 minimum expenditure level fixed for a "major" ranking, there was no assurance it could be maintained.

Nevertheless, the board went ahead with determination and fixed its sights on two necessary and important acquisitions, adequate funding and, with much thought to past experience, a master conductor with an interest in building for the future.

Top Left: *Although engaged for only one season, Maurice Abravanel remained as Utah Symphony music director and conductor for 32 years, 1947-1979.*
Top Right: *Varujan Kojian succeeded Abravanel as music director and conductor, 1980-1983.*
Bottom Left: *Joseph Silverstein, current Utah Symphony music director and conductor, assumed the reins in 1983.*
Bottom Right: *Pierre Monteux, celebrated French conductor and erstwhile music director of Paris, Boston and San Francisco orchestras, guest conducted Utah Symphony on two occasions.*

Top Left: *Stanislaw Skrowaczewski guest conducted Utah Symphony's gala opening Symphony Hall concerts, Sept. 14-15, 1979, and first Tanner Gift of Music concert with Tabernacle Choir in 1983.*
Top Right: *Boston Pops Conductor Arthur Fiedler guest conducted Salt Lake, Ogden and Logan concerts of Utah Symphony.*
Bottom Left: *Henry Mancini, Oscar-winning composer-arranger, was Utah Symphony guest conductor on several occasions.*
Bottom Right: *Comedian-turned-conductor Danny Kaye conducted two hilarious benefit concerts of Utah Symphony.*

ROLF W. KAY

Assistant and associate conductors of the Utah Symphony have been as follows:
Top Left: *David Austin Shand, 1952-1965.*
Top Right: *Ardean Watts, 1968-1979.*
Bottom Left: *Robert Henderson, 1979-1982.*
Bottom Right: *Charles Ketcham, 1982-1986.*

Performances of orchestral-choral masterpieces have been a hallmark of the Utah Symphony over the years. Shown here are choral directors for such presentations:

Top Left: *Jerold Ottley, director, Salt Lake Mormon Tabernacle Choir, and guest conductor of Utah Symphony concerts and recordings, 1975 to present.*

Top Right: *Newell B. Weight, director, Utah Symphony Chorus and its predecessors, 1962-1982.*

Bottom Left: *John Marlowe Nielson, founder, U of U Civic Chorale (1950) and co-director, Utah Chorale, 1963-1975.*

Bottom Right: *Ed Thompson, director, Utah Symphony Chorus, 1982 to present.*

Top Left: *Dr. Leroy Robertson was considered Utah's premier composer. His "Trilogy" won the coveted Reichhold Award as the best composition entered in a Western Hemisphere competition. Robertson's works have been performed frequently on Utah Symphony programs.*

Top Right: *Composer/Conductor Guenther Schuller (left) and Maurice Abravanel. Schuller has guest conducted the Utah Symphony on a number of occasions.*

Bottom Left: *The distinguished American composer, Aaron Copland (r.), guest conducted the Utah Symphony in a 1976 program of his own works. He is shown here with his longstanding friend, Maurice Abravanel.*

Bottom Right: *Dr. Crawford Gates (r.), prolific Utah composer of renown, is congratulated by Morris Rosenblatt, industrialist, philanthropist and long-time symphony supporter.*

CHAPTER 10

ENTER ABRAVANEL

When President Fred Smith and the Utah Symphony board went after a new conductor in 1947, they found, by some stroke of good fortune, not only what the orchestra needed at the moment, but just what it was going to need in the continuous battle for its very life as a major symphony organization. Maurice Abravanel had been fighting for music ever since he was a youngster, and he was prepared and equipped for the job, on and off the podium.

Ordinarily, an orchestra conductor of such skill and opportunities as this experienced cosmopolite might have chucked the local symphony's financial storms and moved on to milder climes. But he had loyalty, tenacity, and honesty as well as music in his temperament, and he remained to finish the job he had taken on.

As in the founding of the symphony seven years before, selection of the new conductor was a team effort, this time involving the executive committee and eventually the full board. The executive committee took on the initial task of reducing an impressive list of forty applicants compiled within a month after Janssen's resignation on March 31.

At first because of his place in the alphabetical order and later because of his credentials, Abravanel's name seemed to come out on top of each list of survivors. His chief competition down to the final decision was Walter Hendl, then assistant conductor of the New York Philharmonic and highly recommended by Fritz Reiner, at that time conductor of the Pittsburgh Symphony Orchestra.

Others to receive serious consideration included George Sebastian, associate conductor of the Chicago Civic Opera; Jaques Rachmilovich, conductor of the Santa Monica Symphony; Valter Poole, associate under Karl Krueger at Detroit and a former guest conductor in Utah; Wilfred Pelletier, founder and director of the Quebec Conservatory of Music; Guy Fraser Harrison, associate conductor of the Rochester Philharmonic; and Hans Lange, conductor of the Friends of Music Orchestra in Toledo, Ohio who carried a recommendation from Arturo Toscanini.

Favored by some women on the board were two female conductors, Ann Kullmer and Antonia Brico. Kullmer had her own thirty-piece all-women orchestra in New York City and later became the first woman to conduct the Paris Conservatory Orchestra. Brico, a native of Holland, founded the New York Women's Symphony and at the time was conducting in Denver.

There was some support for Stanley Chapple of the St. Louis Philharmonic and Berkshire Festival faculty, who was recommended by Serge Koussevitzky, and for David Van Vactor of the Kansas City Orchestra. Smallens, Sample, and Burgin were given early attention, while twenty-five-year-old Lukas Foss (then Boston Symphony pianist), Jascha Horenstein (noted Russo-German conductor), and Nikolai Malko also received consideration. Early in May, symphony manager Ruth Cowan told the press that she and Mrs. Wallace and President Smith would be looking over candidates in the East. All three first went to New York City, where the two women visited with Abravanel.

Abravanel had made his move for the Utah job when he read in the *New York Times* that Werner Janssen was leaving Salt Lake City for Portland, Oregon. Abravanel was conducting Kurt Weill's "Street Scene" on Broadway and had just returned from Australia, where he had scored a brilliant success with a "pick-up" orchestra. Once more he had proved to himself that he could make an orchestra play well, and he was now looking for a chance to do the same thing in a permanent position. Salt Lake City offered that opportunity.

The versatile conductor went to his manager, the same Arthur Judson who had handled the move of another client, Janssen, to Utah, and asked if he knew anyone in Salt Lake City. Abravanel recounts the exchange that followed:

Judson: "You can't go to Salt Lake."

Abravanel: "Why not?"

Judson: "It's an impossible situation. There are the Mormons and the non-Mormons, and they don't speak to each other, and I won't let you go to Salt Lake. This is absolutely out of the question."

Abravanel (insisting on a symphony career with his own orchestra): "Look, I have conducted Kurt Weill because I love him, but this is now the time to get away from that. I would really like to think about it."

With his charge holding firm, the agent sent his picture and resume to Utah along with a number of other prospects in his camp. In the course of putting the package together, however, Judson's office personnel attached Abravanel's picture to the resume of Frieder Weissmann, another candidate for the Utah Symphony position, and vice versa. This created an interesting situation a few weeks later when Miss Cowan and Mrs. Wallace stepped off the elevator at the Ritz Hotel to be greeted by Abravanel while expecting someone who looked like Weissmann.

During this visit, the two women attended a performance of "Street Scene," which Abravanel was conducting eight times a week on Broadway. They were invited to a recording session the next morning, but Miss Cowan alone attended. Maurice conducted an album of Debussy and Ravel for Columbia Records with Baritone Martial Singher as soloist, impressing the Utah Symphony manager with his authoritative direction of difficult music the orchestra had never played before. It was the last time he was to discuss the Utah position with anyone until he visited Salt Lake City in June. By then he had conducted the San Francisco Symphony Orchestra in a performance over the

"Standard Hour" radio broadcast, a continuing program of symphonic music sponsored by the Standard Oil Company of California.

In the meantime, the symphony president, Fred Smith, also visited New York City. He had learned of some interest there about Rachmilovich, and when he found the great Toscanini listening intently to a recording by the Santa Monica Symphony conductor in the office of RCA Victor's Samuel Shotzinoff, he was duly impressed.

Both Abravanel and Rachmilovich were among candidates interviewed on the scene in Salt Lake City. Each had his partisans on the board, but Abravanel was committed, perhaps much more than any other candidate, to building with local musicians. Before leaving New York City for the interview, he had refused a tempting offer to take over the Radio City Music Hall Orchestra at a salary of $30,000 a year because of his obsession to develop his own symphony orchestra. The position eventually went to Alexander Smallens, another candidate for the Utah Symphony and a conductor of Ballet Theater.

One story that went the rounds had to do with the possible consideration of Leonard Bernstein as music director and conductor of the Utah Symphony.

The brilliant young composer-conductor, just twenty-eight at the time, was in the midst of a three-year whirl at the helm of the New York (WPA) Symphony, without pay. It seems he was also a frequent visitor at favorite night spots in Greenwich Village, and that one of those haunts was a club operated by Max Gordon, a jazz entrepreneur and a brother of Rabbi Sam Gordon of Salt Lake City.

Through his brother, Max had become acquainted with a number of prominent Salt Lake City residents and was aware of the vacancy on the Utah Symphony podium. He is said to have suggested to Fred Smith and Morris Rosenblatt that they drop by his club and talk to his talented young friend Bernstein about the position.

As the story goes, the interview took place, and the two Utah Symphony officers finally wrote off the prospective candidate as "too young and inexperienced."

With the return of the traveling officers, the board moved into final elimination sessions. One rating sheet from the files of Judge Crockett lists ten candidates after first establishing the fact that "viewing the conductors from the list of forty applicants from the point of view of other national orchestras and their choice, and from personal interviews, the following names merit first attention." The list then included Abravanel, Hendl, Pelletier, Harrison, Poole, Lange, Van Vactor, Chapple, Smallens, and Kullmer. It was noted, also, that "Houston is using guest conductors next season, following which their permanent conductor will be chosen. Guest conductors will be Abravanel, Hendl, Hans Schweiger and Frieder Weissmann."

Judge Crockett recalls that one of Abravanel's strong supporters was Morris Rosenblatt, who was interested not only in the conductor's musical ability but in his ancestral background going back to the Spanish Inquisition of 1517 as well. Some new backing for Rachmilovich and Sebastian was also in evidence, as these two candidates were with Abravanel, Hendl, and Poole on the list of five accepted by the executive committee on May 24. This group was reduced by the executive committee to include Abravanel, Hendl, and Sebastian, and by June 11 only Abravanel and Hendl were left. It was then decided by the committee members present (Smith, Mrs. Wallace, Martin, Heppley, and Rosenblatt) to present Abravanel's name to the board for final consideration.

At the board meeting on June 16, however, both the names of Abravanel and Hendl came in for a "serious discussion" before it was decided to offer Abravanel a one-year contract with a one-year operation, this on a motion by Mrs. Martin C. Lindem and a second by Judge H. M. Schiller. Abravanel signed the next day.

Hendl later went to Dallas to succeed Antal Dorati, after which he joined Reiner as an associate conductor of the Chicago Symphony Orchestra.

When Fred Smith announced the signing of Abravanel on June 17, he told the *Salt Lake Tribune* that the new conductor "was selected by the board after reviewing more than 60 applicants" and that "many of the applicants possessed the highest of qualifications, indicating that the Utah Symphony is gaining a worldwide reputation."

At the same time, Abravanel made it clear that he intended to build the Utah Symphony with Utah musicians and gave the assurance that he would stay on and complete the task he had undertaken. It was not until thirty-two years later, after giving Utah an internationally acclaimed major symphony, that he retired.

When he took over, Abravanel said he could see no reason for importing players if "someone just as good is available here." This was an interesting contrast to the position taken by Janssen less than three months before when he resigned because the board could not assure him twenty-five imported musicians.

In an interview with Donald M. Everett in the *Tribune* on June 19, the new conductor said that "true orchestra building lies in developing the musicians of the orchestra." He said he was a strong believer in the use of resident musicians, and he added that any musician "willing to work and eager to improve, who would take pride in the orchestra and the community, would prove valuable to the orchestra."

Abravanel soon referred to the Utah Symphony as "my first orchestra," then remembered: "The closest I ever came to having my own orchestra before was during my stay in Australia. We built the orchestra because a newspaper wanted it, and it was my greatest thrill to see the ensemble grow from one concert to the next. This is when music is worthwhile."

The arrival of Abravanel marked the first time for the symphony to become identified with one individual. In return, the conductor expressed a great pride in being identified with Salt Lake City. It was a pride that grew as city and state established and maintained "major" status on the symphony front. "There is no reason," he said, "for a city to be artistically provincial simply because it does not have as many opportunities as the so-called sophisticated cities."

In September 1947, three months after signing his contract, Abravanel doubled his worth to the community and the symphony when he married Lucy Carasso of Paris, his invaluable silent partner for thirty-eight years. A vivacious lady, she was a pillar of support to her husband and a quiet but effective champion of the orchestra, especially through her efforts in helping establish and nurture the Utah Symphony Guild. Completing the family of four were her two boys, Roger and Pierre.

Abravanel was a mature and experienced forty-four years of age when he accepted his post as music director and conductor of the Utah Symphony. It was something he had long sought in his schooling and travels, and he greeted the new assignment much as a bright-eyed boy would a model airplane—he knew he could make it fly.

Such confidence, along with the high level of musicianship to go with it, soon won the respect of the orchestra. Local players particularly were happy with the goals of their new conductor and were quick to see his worth and to take pride in the new standard of musical integrity he built into the ensemble.

From the beginning it was also evident that Abravanel did not intend to confine his energies to the podium. He and Lucy became immersed in the community, first acquiring a home and then taking their places as interested, tax-paying citizens. Thus established, the maestro soon became the orchestra's foremost public relations asset with his straightforward manner and good sense. His extemporaneous remarks at the last concert of the financially critical 1948-49 season stopped the show. He simply restated his faith in the orchestra and the people in the face of serious troubles, and the speech brought the crowd of four thousand to its feet, cheering. As one subscriber remarked, "They probably could have paid the bill if they'd passed the hat after that speech."

In his early years in Salt Lake City, Abravanel was both chagrined and hurt because "people who should be helping the orchestra were stabbing us in the back." He was referring to the battle for financial existence in 1948-49, in which he was given little or no chance to bear arms. He merely went without pay for six weeks and kept the orchestra playing without a payroll. Moreover, he turned down a $25,000 a year offer from the Houston Symphony to stay with his objective, weathering storm after storm because of his loyalty and affection for Utah and Salt Lake City. As he has often repeated: "After traveling in this world as much as I have, and after living under so many different conditions, it is only natural to place a value—a monetary, paycheck value— on the air you breathe, the water you drink, your surroundings and the friends you have around you. It is worth much to me to live in Salt Lake City."

The maestro also applauded the respect exhibited by Utahns for good music, once making it a point in connection with the response of a critic to his guest appearance at a large southern city after he had moved to Salt Lake City. He was disturbed by the critic's use of the word "soporific" in reference to the Brahms Second Symphony and said he could not understand people who could call that great work "soporific".

"But when I see listeners moved to tears by the music of the masters—Beethoven's "Missa," his Seventh Symphony—I know then why I love Utah and Salt Lake City," he said. "At least they do not call Brahms soporific."

There were other reasons Abravanel stayed with the Utah Symphony, one of them being the loyalty of his musicians and their willingness to work for the good of the ensemble. "They proved several times that they would go through fire for me," he states.

It was all the result of a relationship between the conductor and players that is extremely rare among major symphonies. In many instances, it was a closeness that existed even beyond retirement, both his and the musicians.

Perhaps Abravanel's reliance upon Utah talent is best explained by the trials and growth that led him to Utah in the first place. He was very much a "self-made" musician, preferring in his early days to rely upon his obvious talents, only to find on his own that they were no substitute for hard work. Aiding his search for excellence were the teachings and influence of such music masters as Bruno Walter, Kurt Weill, and Wilhelm Furtwaengler.

Because he was born in Salonika, Greece, Abravanel has been honored by Salt Lake Helenics and Greeks in Athens and in his "home town." Except for these occasions, however, he is without Greek connections, since Salonika was under Turkish rule at the time of his birth and his parents came from a Spanish-Portuguese-Jewish line that settled in Greece after the Spanish Inquisition of 1517. One of his ancestors, Don Isaac Abravanel, was chancellor to Ferdinand and Isabella and is said to have had a great deal to do with financing the war against the Moors and the expedition of Columbus to America in 1492.

Born on January 6, 1903, Maurice did not get into music until after his father, Edouard Abravanel, retired from the pharmacy business in 1909 and moved his wife, Rachel Bitty, and four children to Lausanne on Lake Geneva in Switzerland.

At the age of six, Maurice began studying music on his own; at the age of twelve, he was playing the piano and composing. So adept did he become by the time he was fifteen that the manager of the Municipal Theater in Lausanne put him to work arranging music and performing for the shows. At the age of sixteen, he conducted for the first time before an ensemble he had gathered at the University of Lausanne to perform his own orchestration of the Moliere-Lully "Le Bourgeois Gentilhomme" and an Offenbach operetta.

By this time his father was becoming concerned over Maurice's deepening interest in music, and since he was convinced that there was no future in such a profession, he sent his son to Zurich to study medicine. The longer he stayed, however, the more he found that his medical classes only interfered with his music, so he informed his father by letter that he was leaving medicine because he could not live without music.

Unable to do anything about it, Papa Abravanel decided to send Maurice to Berlin, where at nineteen he met Kurt Weill, the master pupil of Busoni and Humperdinck, and began a study of harmony, counterpoint, and other fundamentals of music. Within a year or so, however, money became a problem, and the young musician, now without an allowance of any kind, was destitute. Hungry and willing to accept any offer, he followed a suggestion of Weill's and sought a job in an opera house. Fortunately, he was just in time to catch on at the Mecklenburg-Strelitz Theater, some sixty miles northwest of Berlin, as a volunteer coach.

This position led to his first experience as a paid conductor, a goal he reached after a strange set of circumstances. Performing as a substitute in the chorus and orchestra, or in other spots as needed, he found himself shut out of conducting by four baton men ahead of him. When the theater burned to the ground in 1924, however, the four directors lost their jobs, and the thirty-six players, hired for life by the state, approached Abravanel as a body and asked him to conduct a series of three "pops" concerts a week.

After accepting the position, Maurice learned to his surprise that the instrumentalists were paid by the year and wanted no rehearsals. It was a challenge that became a benefit as Maurice told the men, "If you don't need rehearsals, then I don't either!" He went on to conduct more than twenty concerts without rehearsal, and he said that he "learned more about conducting in these concerts than at any other time." Since each concert was a "first," he was forced to make his directions clear and understandable.

His next position was at Zwickau, first as chorus master and then as conductor. He recalls that the manager "thought I was a great guy when I went through 'Carmen' in twenty minutes less time than the previous conductor, so he gave me the job."

Two years of conducting all the operas in the standard repertoire at Zwickau were followed by two years as music director at Altenburg. He then went on to Kassel as conductor and music director before getting a guest conducting opportunity at the Berlin State Opera. There he received an ovation that resulted in several more assignments. He was well in line for a permanent position with the company, but by then he had his eye on Paris.

Among those to hear Abravanel conduct at the Berlin State Opera was the great Bruno Walter, who recommended Maurice as a guest conductor at the Paris Grand Opera. Walter was already scheduled to appear in the same role, and the result threw the two conductors together for several seasons. The influence of that association was to affect the entire career of Abravanel as he drew heavily on the experience, skill, and knowledge of the master musician.

During his stay in Paris, Abravanel added to his experience with guest appearances in 1933 and 1934 before Pierre Monteaux's Paris Symphony Orchestra. He was also conductor and music director for George Balanchine's Ballets in 1933 with an opportunity to direct new ballets and new scores.

With no steady job in Paris and the field beginning to become somewhat crowded with musicians pouring out of Nazi Germany, Maurice heeded a call in 1934 to conduct a season with the British National Opera Company, a wing of Covent Garden, in Melbourne and Sydney, Australia. He remained "down under," building and directing symphony and opera, until 1936, when he was offered a Metropolitan Opera contract on the recommendation of Wilhelm Furtwaengler.

His acceptance put him on American soil for the first time, and he soon took out his citizenship papers, sensing a national loyalty he had found in no other place.

Director Rudolph Bing kept Abravanel busy for two years at the "Met". During one period, Maurice set an all-time record of directing five operas in seven performances in nine days. Of the experience Abravanel recalls: "Most strange was the fact that I received rave reviews during the nine days— one writer [Pitt Sanborn of the *New York Telegram*] said it was not Flagstad, Melchior and Hoffman, but the conducting that made the 'Lohengrin' production great, with the right tempo for the first time in 20 years—and then was panned after that. I guess I was conducting too often and someone didn't like it."

After two seasons at the Met, Abravanel was looking for a change and took up with his friend Kurt Weill, who had just arrived in America. Weill was adapting his genius to the Broadway musical, and Maurice agreed to conduct a series of new shows, beginning with "Knickerbocker Holiday." He was also on the opening night stand for "One Touch of Venus," starring Mary Martin and Kenny Baker; "Lady in the Dark"; "Seven Lively Arts"; "Day Before Spring"; and "Street Scene."

Throughout this period and between his hits on Broadway, a restless Abravanel kept on the move, hoping and hunting for a place to make a home with "his orchestra." He conducted concerts in Montreal, New York's Lewisohn Stadium, and Chicago's Grant Park. There was a season of opera in Mexico City, and another at the Chicago Civic Opera; Abravanel even went back to Australia for a season of symphony concerts in Sydney. The latter experience perhaps gave him more of a feel for what he really wanted than most of his other stops, and not long after, the Utah Symphony came into his sights. He zeroed in, and the result is now an incredible chapter in the history of America's major symphony orchestras.

Abravanel arrived during Utah's busy Centennial summer, and while he was planning his first season with his new organization, he took note of some significant developments. One of them involved the state's foremost native-born composer, Leroy J. Robertson, whose "Rhapsody for Piano and Orchestra" had received its premiere with the Utah Symphony three years before and who now was headed for international prominence with his symphonic masterpiece "Trilogy." Another concerned the Pioneer Centennial-inspired musical "Promised Valley" and its composer, Crawford Gates.

During the summer, Robertson had finished the "Trilogy" and submitted it for consideration in the Henry Reichhold Symphony of the Americas competition. The manuscript had been lying incomplete for eight years until friends encouraged Robertson to seek the first prize of $25,000 offered by the Detroit industrialist.

Open to native-born composers of the Western hemisphere, the competition drew four hundred scores from seventeen different countries. Such was the challenge presented to a panel of judges that included Karl Krueger, then music director of the Detroit Symphony; composers Roy Harris, Eric Delamarter, and Herbert Elwell; and Donald M. Swarthout, dean of the College of Fine Arts at the University of Kansas.

On the weekly ABC radio network "Sunday Evening Hour" out of Detroit, on November 3 Robertson was declared the winner for his "Trilogy" and received the largest cash award ever given in a symphonic competition.

It was not the first award for Robertson, however. He had won the $300 Endicot Prize in 1923 at the New England Conservatory in Boston, where he studied with George Chadwick. Later he worked with Ernest Bloch in New York, Hugo Leichten-

tritt in Berlin, and Arnold Schoenberg and Ernst Toch in Los
Angeles. In 1944, he won the New York Music Critics Circle
Award for his String Quartet in E Minor.

Robertson and Abravanel struck up a close association,
and the composer not long afterward moved from his position
at Brigham Young University in Provo to become head of the
music department at the University of Utah. One of the prime
reasons for accepting the new assignment, he once said, was to
be close to the Utah Symphony, which later moved to the
University campus as a teaching tool in rehearsals through
arrangement with the school administration.

Abravanel was anxious to perform the "Trilogy" but held
up when the Detroit Symphony Orchestra delayed the world
premiere until December 11. The new conductor, impressed
with Robertson's music, selected his "Punch and Judy" Overture for a first performance in the second concert of the season.

Another "first" for the orchestra and Utah music came out
of the lighter score by Crawford Gates from the summer musical. The energetic young composer, a student of Robertson,
arranged a symphonic suite from his tuneful "Promised Valley"
music. Commissioned by the Utah Centennial Commission, the
music was written to a book and lyrics by Arnold Sundgaard.

The keen interest exhibited by Abravanel in Utah's music
and its musicians was all a part of his genuine desire to build
into the Utah Symphony its own home character. Thus he put a
high priority upon his promises to hire local players.

Instead of increasing the number of imported players, as
Janssen had wanted to do, Abravanel actually cut the number
from nineteen to seventeen and increased the number of Utah
musicians in first chairs. Leonard Posner was brought in to
replace Igelman as concertmaster, and alongside him in the
second chair was the former concertmaster Bill Hardiman.

Among local principals were William Douglas, second violin; Lorna Hogensen, viola; Audrey Bush, bass; Allen Jensen,
flute; Louis Booth, oboe; Stewart Grow, trumpet; and Grace
Louise Webb, harp. Paul Gruppe, cello; Napoleon Cerminara,
clarinet; Norris Norkin, bassoon; Allen Fuchs, horn; John Swallow, trombone; and Walter Rothaar, tympani, were other first-

chair performers. Booth, Hogensen, Rothaar, and Webb were the only holdover principals from the 1946-47 season.

The first Abravanel season opened November 8, 1947, at the Salt Lake Tabernacle, and the new conductor lost no time in establishing himself as a master of the baton. Particularly was he impressive with his interpretation of the Beethoven Third Symphony, "Eroica." His ability to perform the "big works" with supreme authority not only became evident at this moment in his career but remained perhaps the most impressive component in his well-endowed baton for thirty-two years.

For the remainder of the program, Abravanel presented the Utah Symphony in its first performance of the Richard Strauss "Don Juan" and added the Prelude to Wagner's "Die Meistersinger" and Samuel Barber's "Adagio for Strings." It was a most convincing debut.

Meanwhile, the symphony board cast a wary eye in the direction of a diminishing financial reserve. Only $43,000 remained in a "Symphony Progress Fund" that fell some $60,000 short of its goal of $150,000 to cover anticipated deficits over a three-year period. The board designated $25,000 from the fund to go to the 1947-48 season while renewing its efforts to fill the "progress fund" bin.

President Fred Smith went to his colleagues on the Utah State Institute of Fine Arts board of November 18 for help and came away with $8,000. He had informed the board that "orchestra finances have reached a crucial situation." He said the budget of $130,000 was balanced by estimated revenues of approximately $100,000, including $25,000 from the progress fund, leaving an anticipated deficit of $30,000. Unless funds could be secured from such sources as Centennial Commission surpluses or art institute appropriations, he added, the "orchestra operation would have to cease." The board then voted to allot $8,000 of its $10,000 appropriation for fiscal 1948 to the symphony.

Another contribution had come to the orchestra in the form of a rehearsal auditorium donated by the Salt Lake City Commission. Abravanel had met his symphony for the first time on October 27 at the city-operated Kiwanis-Felt building, a recreation center for boys and girls at First South and Second East. This old building carried an interesting history, having been a Masonic temple and then the "hippodrome," scene of promoter Hardy Downing's popular boxing cards.

Musically, the season was a solid success with something new and exciting on every program. Besides a first hearing of the Robertson "Punch and Judy," the audience at the second concert on November 22 was treated to a performance of the Brahms Second Symphony, in which Abravanel distinguished himself as an accomplished and sensitive exponent of the great romanticist.

The following week Abravanel took the Robertson piece with him on a guest-conducting jaunt to Houston. Both the conductor and the Utah work were big hits, and after ultimately refusing an attractive offer to return to the Texas metropolis and take over the orchestra, the maestro added that performance to the long list of experiences from which he built the Utah Symphony.

Aware of the absence of many major works on past programs of his new orchestra, Abravanel placed the Beethoven Violin Concerto on the list for the December 13 concert and secured the sensational young French virtuoso Ginette Neveu as soloist. The powerful young artist and orchestra collaborated in an unforgettable performance under a masterful baton. Heralded as one of the greatest new concert artists to come on the music scene in many seasons, the young woman performed only in Boston, New York, and Salt Lake City on her only American tour. Not long afterward, the concert world mourned her death in an airplane accident in Europe.

During the week before the Neveu concert, Robertson's "Trilogy" received its world premiere in Detroit; the event was to have a marked effect on plans for the next Utah Symphony program on January 3 at the Tabernacle. The renowned pianist Arthur Rubinstein was forced to cancel a scheduled appearance on that date, and Abravanel immediately programmed the Robertson work as a replacement.

This imaginative symphony in three movements received a good share of critical acclaim at its premiere and was repeated by Conductor Krueger and the Detroit Symphony Orchestra over the ABC radio network on December 14. Harvey Taylor, writing in the *Detroit Times*, noted: "Robertson has written a competently contrived and reasonably well-disciplined symphony. We particularly enjoyed the first movement which, despite angularities and certain awkwardnesses in writing for strings, nevertheless has tight, well-thought-out themes developed with busy counterpoint.... Robertson is a composer worth watching."

It was not surprising that the Utah premiere of the "Trilogy" drew the largest crowd of the season. It occupied the second half of the program and followed performances of the Bach Suite in D Major and the Mozart Symphony No. 40 in G Minor.

The season went on to produce one triumph after another. On a program at the end of January, Abravanel presented a contemporary American section consisting of Copland's "Appalachian Spring," "The White Peacock" by Griffes, the William Schuman "Side Show," and the world premiere of a "Dirge" by Walter Kaufman.

The Gates premiere in February was a liberal and well-received "Scenario" from "Promised Valley," with the composer conducting the orchestra and cast, including Dr. C. Lowell Lees as narrator; soloists Harold Brereton, baritone, and Sharon Monk, soprano; a seventy-voice "Promised Valley" chorus; and the Bryant Junior High School Chorus. The program also included the debut of concertmaster Posner as a soloist with the symphony in the Brahms Violin Concerto.

The season reached its climax on March 13 in the first local performance of the Beethoven Ninth Symphony, another of those "big works" in which the mastery of Abravanel becomes such a factor. His chorus was the Richard P. Condie-trained University of Utah A Cappella Choir; the soloists were Ruth Jensen Clawson, Annette Richardson Dinwoodey, Ray Brimhall, and Harold H. Bennett, all Utah artists. It was an electrifying event that brought shouts of approval from the audience.

For the final concert at Eastertime, on March 27, the maestro presented an all-request program that included the Tchaikovsky "Pathetique" Symphony No. 6 in B Minor, the "Good Friday" music from Wagner's "Parsifal," the Largo movement from Randall Thompson's E Minor Symphony, the Overture to Nicolai's "Merry Wives of Windsor," and Ravel's "Bolero."

It was a busy first season for Abravanel. Besides his guest appearance in Houston and the subscription series, he conducted his new orchestra in four Saturday morning youth concerts and in five out-of-town performances at Logan, Ogden, and Provo. A series of ten live radio broadcasts from the Granite High School auditorium and Kingsbury Hall under sponsorship of ZCMI and KSL radio added to the symphony's exposure over the region. Included in this series were some memorable concerto performances with two highly skilled Utah pianists, Reid Nibley and Gladys Gladstone, and cello principal Paul Gruppe as soloists.

Abravanel and the Utah Symphony also drew national attention at midseason with an appearance on the NBC network's "Orchestras of the Nation" series. The Robertson "Punch and Judy," Gates' "Promised Valley" suite, the Kaufman "Dirge," and Ravel's "Daphnis and Chloe" made up the program.

His first season a distinct success, the maestro involved himself in community affairs and the summer season. He was as concerned as anyone with the symphony's fiscal condition and did what he could about it. He was to find, however, that the financial problems were much more complex than those involving the performance of his ensemble.

In the matter of artistry and personnel, the orchestra was on a solid foundation. Its future was undeniably bright, if the money would come forth to support it. The symphony board had an outstanding product to sell but watched its most persuasive efforts fall woefully short of covering the orchestra's debt in the crisis year ahead.

CHAPTER 11

CRISIS ON THE HILL

At no other time in its forty-six years of existence has the Utah Symphony experienced a more crucial financial crisis than the one that carried the orchestra to the brink of disaster in the winter of 1948-49. Only through tenacious persistence and an unyielding refusal to quit or to accept a suggested liquidation did the symphony survive.

It took the full commitment of Abravanel, the local players in the orchestra, and such devoted benefactors as the Wallaces and Rosenblatts to keep the musicians playing. That the musicians went on to complete the season was some sort of miracle.

From the time the season opened, the symphony was in financial trouble, starting with a record budget of $137,500 that was based more on hope than promise. There was an item in the anticipated revenue on which the budget was based, for instance, that called for a state appropriation of $50,000 to cover a proposed series of network broadcasts. It never developed. Nor did the hoped-for collection of $22,000 in progress fund pledges or other attempts to secure state funds.

As it turned out, the symphony board would find that it could depend upon the state for no more than it had received in the past through the art institute. With the replacement of

Governor Herbert B. Maw by the ultraconservative J. Bracken Lee, any attempt to receive additional state support would be futile for the eight long years of the new governor's two-term administration.

Compounding the immediate problem was a deficit carried over from the previous season. Seymour Wells, prominent Salt Lake City accountant and treasurer of the art institute and the symphony, had presented a statement showing 1947-48 expenditures of $132,874.21 against income of $118,544.95, leaving a deficit of $14,329.26.

During the summer interim, Fred Smith brought to an end his eight years of impressive leadership, resigning as president on August 5 with a promise to continue his cooperation and support of the orchestra from his position as a member of the board. His significant contribution as a leader was the subject of a letter signed by the board along with Governor Maw and Salt Lake City Mayor Earl J. Glade. Written by secretary Martin at the request of the board, the letter read in part: "It is with profound regret that the Utah Symphony Board of Directors received your letter of resignation. During eight long, long years, we have had the pleasure of working together and seeing a humble instrument grow to an eloquence and power undreamed of. All of this time we have been mindful that yours has been the major contribution in time, labor and organizing skill.

"We have also been mindful that never in all this time has anything but consideration for the highest standards of performance been your chief objective. Standards have never been lowered or decisions influenced by any desire on your part for personal gain or public glory. Your unfailing courtesy and patience, your boundless tact have all commanded our admiration as well as strengthened our bonds of affection. For what you have done to advance the cause of music in Utah, there will always be a perpetual memory in the history of the state."

With Smith's resignation, vice-president Glenn Wallace became acting chairman of the board and on October 1 was elected president. Calvin W. Rawlings, an eminent local attorney and power in the Utah Democratic Party, was elected first vice-president with Judge Crockett as second vice-president.

Also during this period, an important affiliation of the Utah Symphony with the University of Utah was effected. Through the foresight of Dr. A. Ray Olpin, president of the university and a patron of the arts, along with Abravanel and the symphony management, the move brought about a strong tie between the school and the orchestra. As a result, the symphony secured new rehearsal quarters in one of the buildings formerly occupied by the military at Fort Douglas and now in possession of the university as an annex to its upper campus. In return, the orchestra's library became available for special duty in the university's music department, and leading symphony personnel, including Maestro Abravanel, became available for instructing instrumental students.

Orchestra members, meanwhile, had been in the pit at Stadium Bowl for productions of Shakespeare's "A Midsummer Night's Dream" and Jerome Kern's "Showboat." Produced by the University of Utah under the direction of Dr. C. Lowell Lees, with Abravanel directing the music, the two shows used the setting created for the Centennial "Promised Valley" production the year before. Their success stimulated plans for annual summer festivals, and, at the invitation of Dr. A. Ray Olpin, president of the university, the Utah Symphony became a part of the planning.

When the orchestra appeared for its first rehearsal on October 25 at its new quarters, several personnel changes had taken place. Perhaps most important was the appointment of Dr. David Austin Shand as assistant conductor. Dr. Shand, a Salt Lake native who had studied with Walter Piston (the noted contemporary American composer), Hugo Leichtentritt, and Nadia Boulanger at Harvard, had joined the first violin section of the symphony during the past season.

Notable newcomers included Herbert Blayman, the new clarinet principal in place of Napoleon Cerminara, who had joined the New York Philharmonic. Herbert Eisenberg occupied the first chair in the trumpet section, and Ken Kuchler had replaced Hardiman as the assistant concertmaster.

Just before the opening of the season, Dr. Shand produced a benefit concert for the symphony in the form of a testimonial for the immortal soprano Emma Lucy Gates Bowen at the Assembly Hall on Temple Square. Features of the evening were the Bach "Magnificat" and the "Denunciation Scene" from Verdi's "La Traviata." The proceeds, though not large, went to the Symphony Progress Fund.

With little evidence of the financial turmoil that was waiting down the road, the Utah Symphony moved ahead with an eventful season. Abravanel had programmed a number of major performances, including a share of world premieres. The opening concert on November 6 was dedicated to The Church of Jesus Christ of Latter-day Saints in appreciation for the use of the Tabernacle for the symphony's annual subscription series. Acknowledgement on behalf of the Church was made by President George Albert Smith in brief intermission remarks.

In honor of the symphony's new affiliation with the University of Utah, the program opened with the Brahms "Academic Festival" Overture.

Two weeks later Abravanel presented the world premiere of two works. Pianist Jacques Abrams was soloist in the first performance of Benjamin Britten's revised Piano Concerto following the premiere of Robertson's "Prelude, Scherzo and Ricercare."

Early in December, excitement ran high, and artistic excellence was accorded a tumultuous ovation at Kingsbury Hall in a symphony "special," its first performance of the Beethoven "Missa Solemnis," another of those "big works" that Abravanel handles so well. The triumph was shared by the orchestra, the University of Utah Chorus, and four local soloists, Blanche Christensen, soprano; Rachel Connor, contralto; Walter Richardson, tenor; and Harold H. Bennett, bass-baritone. The performance was so well-received by the packed house that it was later repeated on a series of live radio broadcasts and drew another capacity audience.

As in the performance of the Ninth Symphony the previous spring, Abravanel's authoritative interpretation underscored the production of this Beethoven masterpiece. Once again the maestro was in complete control with his masterful coordination of orchestra, chorus, and soloists, something that was to draw worldwide attention in performances and recordings of great choral and orchestral works in years to come. In praise of the event, Lowell Durham wrote in the *Tribune*: "First of all we have in Maurice Abravanel a conductor whose knowledge of both orchestra and chorus is beyond question. His powers of musical comprehension are tremendous. His feeling and understanding of Beethoven are especially keen. His interpretation of the 'Missa' is another triumph to add to those previously scored in performances of the same composer's 'Eroica' and Fifth Symphonies, as well as several of his concerti. It is imperative that we retain his services."

At about the same time the "Missa" went on stage, the symphony administration tested the financial winds on Capitol Hill. A committee waited on the State Board of Examiners, then consisting of Governor Maw, Secretary of State Heber Bennion, and Attorney General Grover Giles, and asked for an emergency appropriation of $10,000. The examiners sent the committee and its request on to the Legislature, which was scheduled to convene in January.

With a dire need to meet "current expenses," the symphony accepted a combined "loan" of $10,000 from Mrs. Wallace and Mr. Rosenblatt, with hopes of reimbursement from the Legislature. As it turned out, the donors were never repaid, nor was Mrs. Wallace for generous allocations of personal funds made to meet other emergencies during the season and thereafter.

The new money provided the orchestra with the "breathing room" it needed to go ahead with the season. It had performed at Logan, Cedar City, and St. George during December and looked forward to resuming its schedule after the holidays. Early in January, the symphony was joined by Grant Johannesen in the Brahms Piano Concerto No. 2 in B-flat and performed Arthur Shepherd's "Overture to a Drama" on the same program.

One week later Abravanel again presented the "Missa Solemnis" at Kingsbury Hall to open a seventeen-week radio series over KSL under ZCMI sponsorship. From then on the live concerts were presented on Thursday nights, most of them from Kingsbury Hall. The exceptions were single-broadcast performances originating in Logan and Provo and a program at South High School featuring Reginald Beales as soloist in the Bruch Violin Concerto. Among other soloists were pianists Johana Harris and Gladys Gladstone and Soprano Carol Olsen Welling. Mrs. Harris was the wife of the noted American composer, Roy Harris, then in residence at Utah State University in Logan.

When the symphony presented its sixth concert of the season at the Tabernacle on January 22, 1949, the financial crisis that was soon to make headlines was closing in. There was little evidence of the behind-the-scenes problems, however, in the music-making of Abravanel, the players, and the guest soloist, Joseph Szigeti, the renowned Hungarian violin virtuoso. Often looked upon as a "violinist's violinist," Szigeti was in exceptional form in the Beethoven Violin Concerto, the highlight of a program of interesting contrasts. The "Sinfonia in B-flat" by Johann Christian Bach and two works by French impressionists, "La Mer" by Debussy, and Ravel's "La Valse" completed the performance.

In the days that followed, the Utah Symphony literally hung by a thread. At one point a majority of the symphony board agreed to start liquidation proceedings on Friday, January 29, in the event the State Board of Examiners failed to grant a request for deficit funds needed to complete the season.

Mrs. Wallace opposed liquidation under any conditions and eventually stopped the proposed action by disregarding a directive to dissolve the orchestra. She joined, however, in the plea for help from the Board of Examiners, but without success. The three-man board, now consisting of Governor Lee, Secretary of State Bennion and a new attorney general, Clinton D. Vernon, again sent the board to the Legislature.

The actual turning point in the crisis, a selfless move that saved the orchestra from threatened dissolution, came on Friday, January 29, 1949, the appointed day on which the liquidation proceedings were to start. Upon learning of a directive for the board president and manager to appear before the players and inform them that the orchestra had ceased to exist, Abravanel took matters into his own hands. He told the musicians he would carry on rehearsals and concerts, regardless of orders, as long as a nucleus of players would continue their services, even without expectation of being paid.

Backing up the maestro with a courageous performance of his own, the union representative, personnel manager Ben Bullough, went against usual musicians federation procedures and stayed on his job in the first violin section. With no money in sight to fund the payroll, Bullough could have walked out, and the orchestra would have followed. Realizing that such a move would be the end of the symphony, however, he not only stayed with his conductor but urged the other players to do likewise.

The full orchestra responded and played the February 5 concert in the Tabernacle. At that point, however, imported players, with one or two exceptions, refused to perform without pay. This left most of the first chairs abandoned, but since Abravanel had declared he would perform so long as he had as many as thirty people, he went on to Ogden with his remaining musicians for afternoon and evening concerts the following Tuesday.

It required an extra rehearsal between performances to prepare a substitute for the Randall Thompson Symphony No. 2 in E Minor, which had been programmed for the evening performance and was scored for extra instruments, mainly in the brass sections. The imported players stayed away until the middle of February, when emergency contributions came forth to pay the players.

For three and a half weeks, from the time Abravanel took full charge on January 29, the steadfast musicians performed eight times a week, including regular rehearsals and concerts, without even a promise of being paid.

With the orchestra presenting such a united front, the notice of nonexistence was never delivered. Instead, on February 3, the symphony officials went before the joint appropriations committee of the Utah Legislature, and an almost constant vigil of nearly two weeks was set up in the legislative halls at the state capitol. Mrs. Wallace, who as president of the symphony had refused to accept liquidation as an answer to the organization's money problems, headed the move. Along with Abravanel, members of the board and other orchestra boosters worked around the clock during this period.

Symphony vice-president Rawlings presented the case before the appropriations committee, declaring that the orchestra could not survive without an emergency appropriation to cover the deficit of $35,000 and an additional $15,000 to finance the rest of the season. "Unless this money is forthcoming from the Legislature," he said, "the orchestra will go into bankruptcy. It will be forced to liquidate after the Saturday Night [February 5] concert."

Speaking in support of the request, composer Roy Harris warned the legislators of the "disastrous effect the orchestra's bankruptcy would have on the state." Chairman Rosenblatt of the symphony's finance committee said that the Legislature was the "last hope" for the orchestra, and Dr. Olpin, now a board member, said that the Utah Symphony offered a tremendous advantage for University of Utah students.

Rawlings also presented a request for an appropriation of $100,000 to cover deficits for the next two seasons but found no encouragement for such a move. It was presented in cooperation with proposals of the Utah State Institute of Fine Arts, which had grown out of studies made in late 1948.

A committee composed of board members Maud Hardman, Gail Plummer, and Gail Martin had proposed that the art institute "request a legislative appropriation for a building to house the Utah Symphony program and the Institute's art program," while at the same time expressing "little hope that such a program will succeed." Looking into the future, however, the committee held that "the Utah Symphony program is at present, and the state's art program could be in the future, among the most valuable assets and choicest ornaments that Salt Lake City possesses. By using the prestige of these programs, a building program best serving the needs of both state and the capitol city might be evolved."

On November 26, the institute board, then headed by Judge Crockett, agreed to submit a budget request of $355,000 to the governor for 1949-50 operations, including $250,000 for the Art Museum and $105,000 for the symphony. When the request was carried to Governor Lee by Chairman Crockett and board members George M. Gadsby and Thomas Taylor, however, they were told that the items could not be included in the budget because appropriations requests had already greatly exceeded the estimated revenues. At the suggestion of the governor, the institute then submitted the two items in separate bills.

Neither request received serious consideration, but the matter of an emergency appropriation for the symphony became a major issue of the legislative session. The appropriations committee had suggested that the request be taken directly to the floor of the Legislature, and the symphony board members girded themselves for an all-out effort.

With many members of the Legislature in attendance, the February 5 concert was a huge success, and the orchestra averted, for the time being, the threatened liquidation. Cellist Gaspar Cassado impressed the audience as guest soloist in the first local performances of Bloch's "Schelomo" for Cello and Orchestra and the Haydn Cello Concerto.

In the meantime, the symphony finance committee had been busy laying some groundwork with Governor Lee, the obvious key to the state treasury. A meeting, apparently held with the chief executive on Friday, February 4, led to some immediate action by the Legislature. Although not substantiated by the former governor, the meeting is well-remembered by Mitchell Melich, who at the time was a young Republican senator from Moab. Now a prominent attorney in Salt Lake City, he gives an interesting account of the gathering: "Brack Lee called me down to his office with Lon Hopkin [Alonzo F. Hopkin, Democratic senator from Rich County]. Lon was president of the Senate and I was the minority leader. When we got down to the governor's office, there was Morris Rosenblatt; Fred Smith of First Security Bank, who was a strong supporter of the symphony; and John Wallace. They told us that the symphony was not able to meet its payroll and that they needed an appropriation to cover the deficit.

"I, of course, didn't know these men very well, only by

reputation. I was a young man out of Moab practicing law, and my wife and I had read about these prominent businessmen in Salt Lake. During the conversation I said to them: 'I've followed your careers for some time, and I'm somewhat surprised that men of your prominence would allow the symphony to have this kind of deficit.' They got madder than hell at me. I guess they thought I had no business talking to them like that.

"The conversation went on, and, as I recall, Brack said if the Legislature would pass a bill appropriating these funds, he would approve it. The meeting broke up, and we left with the understanding that I would introduce a bill in the Senate appropriating state funds to cover the deficit of the Utah Symphony."

The following Monday a bill was introduced in the Senate by Senators Melich and J. Francis Fowles an Ogden Democrat. In its original form the measure called for a $50,000 appropria-tion, including $35,000 to cover the deficit and $15,000 to pro-vide funds for the rest of the season. Symphony supporters, however, indicated that if the state would pay the deficit, they would attempt to raise the other funds through subscriptions.

The Senate took up the bill immediately, and Senator Hop-kin moved to reduce the amount to $35,000 "on grounds that the state should meet the obligation already incurred, but should not encourage any more deficit spending." A comprom-ise of $40,000 offered by Senator P. S. Marthakis, a Salt Lake Democrat, was accepted, and the bill was given unanimous approval of the twenty senators in attendance, with three absent.

One day later, the $40,000 bill passed the House of Repre-sentatives by a margin of forty-six to twelve, but only after a debate in which the symphony organization came in for some sharp criticism from the downstate representatives, who cited "mismanagement." Representative George A. Hurst, a San Juan Republican, declared that "the state has better uses for its money than to spend it for entertainment for a few people."

With such a wide margin of legislative support, Melich says he "figured that when it got to the governor we would sign it," but such was not to be the case. The former senator recalls:

"After the bill got down to the governor's office, I had a call from Brack. I went down to his office and he said, 'Mitch, I'm going to veto that bill.' I said, 'Well, Governor, we had an understanding that if we passed it, you would sign it. We had a promise, an agreement, and I think you ought to keep it because we did what you agreed to.' I told him further that I was going to do everything I could to override the veto, but we were not able to. I learned later that Orval Adams [a prominent Salt Lake banker] had called Brack Lee and told him to veto it."

The aged ex-governor Lee, now well into his eighties, denies this, however; he insists that "nobody said a word to me about that bill at all until it was passed—until it hit my desk. I guess everyone was convinced I was going to sign it."

He maintains that the symphony vice-president Rawlings was the first to talk to him about the $40,000 bill. "Cal asked if I was going to sign the bill," he says. The former governor also admits seeing Rosenblatt, Smith, and Wallace, but says it was after the bill came to him.

Upholding Melich's recollection of the earlier meeting, however, is an article in the *Salt Lake Tribune* of February 12, 1949, the day after the veto, reporting that officers of the Utah Symphony had greeted the governor's action with "enormous surprise." Finance chairman Rosenblatt is quoted as saying that he was "amazed the governor should veto the bill through which he suggested we meet our deficit." To the reporter he further stated: "I recall the governor very clearly recognized the importance of the orchestra, and while against the policy of the Board of Examiners authorizing deficits while the Legislature was in session, the governor said if the bill were introduced and passed in both houses, he would not oppose it."

While it may be difficult, in light of this testimony, to understand the governor's veto, it would be equally difficult, knowing the nature of J. Bracken Lee, to explain why he might allow such a bill to become law, other than his likely promise to do so. On February 9 he had vetoed a bill that would have permitted Weber College to become a four-year institution, citing his "economy program."

Thus, when he vetoed the symphony bill two days later,

the governor underscored the economy message and gave the same reason as he did for disapproving the Weber College move. "In brief," he said, "the reason is that certain fundamental and essential functions of government must receive priority in the expenditure of our revenues, and that the state must live within its income."

Lee's veto took place on Friday, and over the weekend some members of the Senate came under heavy pressure to sustain the action. A problem they faced was the continued deep snow and heavy winter over the state, requiring legislative assistance in rescuing livestock. Also editorials in Monday morning editions of the *News* and the *Tribune* supported the veto.

The unusually long *News* editorial, entitled "Whirlwinds and Zephyrs That Make Them," was particularly supportive of the veto, while the *Tribune* noted in its headline that the "Governor's Veto Reaffirms His Economy Program." Among other things, the *News* held that state support of orchestras might be approved in Europe, where it had long been a tradition, but it had no place under America's free enterprise system.

On the other hand, there were those who claimed that American taxpayers were virtually subsidizing European orchestras through the foreign aid program while their own governments, for the most part, were all but turning their backs on symphony orchestras and other art endeavors at home. It would be some time yet before private and public interests would join in recognizing the symphony as a valued business as well as a cultural asset to the community.

When the Legislature returned on Monday, Melich and the symphony forces could muster only thirteen of the sixteen votes needed to override the veto, and the $40,000 went to other state causes. The ten sustaining votes came from outside the Salt Lake-Ogden area and included Senate president Hopkin.

Almost immediately talk of liquidating the Utah Symphony resurfaced, only to be silenced again by Glenn Wallace. A group of prominent business men offered to pay the orchestra's debts and finance the remainder of the season, if she would dissolve the organization. The intrepid symphony president flatly refused the proposal.

Also refused, largely because of opposition from the business community, was a proposal by Senator Hopkin and others to introduce another bill in the Legislature to cover back salaries for the musicians. As Mrs. Wallace reported to the Art Institute Board in March, the effort was turned down because "sponsors of the orchestra had been told by representatives of certain business groups that if the orchestra accepted increased financial aid from the state, assistance of private groups would be curtailed."

The mood was easily discernible. Obviously there was an element that would have liked to have sent the symphony packing. Perhaps the sentiment was best expressed in an offhand remark by the wife of one of the business community's leading spokesmen. During a social gathering and with her husband's approving smile, she told this writer, "If we want to *see* a symphony, we'll go to San Francisco to *see* a symphony."

Following the veto of the symphony appropriation, Abravanel and manager Cowan told the press that they had refused to accept any pay until the financial difficulty could be worked out; they also noted that the musicians had decided to stay on the job. Ben Bullough had again supported the maestro.

With all hopes of state assistance lost, the symphony board was called into special session and, instead of folding, moved forward in a spirit of solidarity to match that of the orchestra. According to secretary Martin's minutes of the meeting, Mrs. Wallace told the board that failure of the symphony legislation had left the organization "facing the need to raise money to continue the season—a task which did not seem impossible in view of all the favorable publicity and unknown strength the orchestra had developed during the legislative fight."

Martin further recorded that "many prominent citizens had volunteered to help in a fund-raising campaign, which Mrs. Wallace urged to be opened immediately."

When the immediate problem of back pay for the musicians came up, the Wallaces, John and Glenn, advanced $10,000 to meet the payroll. Not only did this generous act get the fund-raising drive underway, but it also lifted the morale of the entire organization.

Another significant entry on the minutes noted that "board members as well as the president commended Conductor Abravanel and members of the orchestra for their devotion to the highest interests of the community and to the progress of music during a trying crisis."

The orchestra, now intact, resolutely moved on through the remainder of the season, performing the Thompson Symphony and joining with Rudolph Firkusny, Czech war refugee and piano virtuoso, in the Brahms Piano Concerto No. 1 in D Minor on February 19. Then, with rumors circulating that its March 5 concert would be the last, the symphony attracted one of its larger crowds as it was joined by violinist Isaac Stern in a performance of the Tchaikovsky Violin Concerto.

By that time the orchestra payroll was up-to-date, and Mrs. Wallace completely dispelled the rumors by appearing before symphony subscribers at the intermission with assurances that the season would be completed. She said a general campaign was underway to raise funds to pay off the concert deficit and finance a 1949-50 season.

The season came to a close with an "all-request" program on March 19 with the Beethoven "Pastorale" Sixth Symphony as the principal work.

Despite all the financial problems, the orchestra had distinguished itself on two more special occasions aside from the subscription series. Late in February, Abravanel took his players to Pocatello, Idaho, where they performed two concerts in the Pocatello High School Auditorium and conducted a music clinic over a two-day period. Special demonstrations and instruction courses presented by orchestra principals at clinic sessions were cited as an unusual service for a major symphony to provide.

Two weeks later Abravanel and the orchestra filled an engagement on the National Broadcasting Company's "Pioneers of Music" Symphony series. Originating at Kingsbury Hall, the concert included works of Glinka, Smetana, Grieg, Albeniz, Villa-Lobos, and Gilbert.

It had been a long and arduous season—a run through the refiner's fire—but much had been learned, and the planning for the season ahead would soon reflect the influence of those lessons.

CHAPTER 12

PART-TIME OPERATION

After its harrowing experience during the winter of 1948-49, there was little else for the Utah Symphony to do but pull in its horns and perform from a smaller financial base. The result was a reduction of nearly 25 percent in the budget and the adoption of a part-time operation, a deep cut for a major symphony to absorb in one season.

At the first meeting following the closing concert of the crisis season, Mrs. Wallace reported that a final deficit of $55,000 had been reduced to $35,000 by the collection of $20,000 by the "industrial committee headed by John M. Wallace."

Faced with the initial task of paying off the debt, the administration opened negotiations for a new arrangement with the musicians. A pact placing the orchestra on a part-time rehearsal schedule was adopted during a board meeting on June 6, allowing approval of a $104,990 budget, some $32,500 below that of the previous season.

Under the new agreement, the players contracted to fill 112 services, including rehearsals and performances, over eighteen weeks. A big reduction in rehearsals was made possible by replacement of daily morning and afternoon sessions with an evening practice schedule. This permitted the musicians to hold daytime teaching positions and other jobs while continuing to play in the symphony.

Preparing the budget and working out the player agreement were the last official duties of Ruth Cowan as manager of the symphony. She submitted her resignation before the budget meeting, as she was returning to southern California to pursue other interests. She pointed out that she had in mind the three-year "Symphony Progress Fund" program when she took the position in 1946.

Although she received her immediate release, with an expression of regret and a vote of thanks "for devoted service," Miss Cowan remained through the month of June and helped with a "Symphony Carnival" at the Jerry Jones "Rainbow Randevu." The event, chaired by board member L. Howard Marcus, netted a profit to the symphony fund of $4,900. It was the first of three fund-raisers during the summer, with the others including a University of Utah student rally that produced $1,450 and a Stadium Bowl concert by pianists Jose and Ampara Iturbi that netted $3,015.

With the departure of Miss Cowan, the board, in the late summer of 1949, signed David S. Romney, a former mayor of Ogden and Bennett Paint and Glass Company executive, as the new manager of the Utah Symphony. He had been appointed to the board at the close of the 1948-49 season and, with the reelection of Mrs. Wallace as president in June, was elected as one of the two vice-presidents along with James L. White, prominent Salt Lake City financier.

University of Utah Summer Festival performances of "The Great Waltz" and Bizet's "Carmen" at the Stadium bowl were triumphs for directors Lees, Abravanel, and a heralded newcomer, ballet master and choreographer Willam Christensen. A native of Brigham City, whose uncle before him had established the Christensen Ballet School in Salt Lake City, Christensen had joined the team through the efforts of Abravanel and the support of university president Olpin. He and his brothers, Lew and Harold, had established the San Francisco Opera Ballet, and because of his experience in working with the San Francisco Symphony Orchestra and his Utah background, he was a natural to handle the important dance sequences in Summer Festival productions.

This was the beginning of the sensational rise of ballet in Utah and the Mountain West. Not long afterward, Christensen joined the University of Utah staff and founded the University Theater Ballet, which evolved into Civic Ballet and then into Ballet West. He first built a ballet corps through his classes and, encouraged by Abravanel and supported by President Olpin, started what has become the annual production of the "Nutcracker" Ballet. Thus was created an important new medium of artistic endeavor and entertainment on the local scene, as well as a new source of income for symphony players.

In August, the new symphony manager announced an eighteen-week season that included a subscription series of nine concerts—shorter by two weeks and one performance than the previous season. The starting date of November 30 was later than usual, allowing Abravanel an opportunity to fill an award-winning guest assignment.

The maestro had been extremely busy between seasons, starting with three more appearances on the "Standard Hour," this time conducting the Los Angeles Philharmonic. Music of Utah's Robertson and Gates, including the "Punch and Judy" and "Promised Valley" Suite, was performed as part of the series of evening concerts.

Abravanel then returned for the Summer Festival at the Stadium Bowl and later was able to accept an engagement as conductor of Marc Blitzstein's "Regina," a work based on the drama "The Little Foxes," on New York's Broadway. He trained and conducted the orchestra and cast through its pre-New York run in Boston and then took the show to Broadway, where he conducted until November 19. Through his efforts he received the "Tony" (Antoinette Perry) statue, theater's equivalent to the "Oscar," for his conducting.

When the Utah Symphony gathered for its first rehearsal of the new season, most of the imported players had abandoned ship, and the turnover in personnel was larger than usual. Tibor Zelig had come from Portland to replace Lenny Posner as concertmaster, and Harold Schneier was the new cello principal.

Joseph Wetzels, who had performed with the Britt Trio in concert with the orchestra at Kingsbury Hall some years before, was also new in the cello section.

Don Peterson had replaced Allen Fuchs in the first chair of the French horn section. Martin Zwick began a long stay as the principal clarinetist. Lorn Steinberger returned as lead trombonist, and Wesley M. Lindskoog was the new first trumpet.

Among other first-chair performers were Rose Watkins, second violin; Sam Pratt, flute; William Watilo, bassoon; and William Johnson, percussion. Rebecca Wagner had taken over on the harp.

Abravanel made the most of the new reduced rehearsal schedule and guided the symphony through an ambitious season. Besides the subscription series, it included three special programs to commemorate the University of Utah Centennial. The first of these was the symphony-choral event of the year, with Abravanel conducting the orchestra and combined University Choruses in the Verdi "Requiem." The experienced group of Utah soloists again consisted of Blanche Christensen, soprano; Rachel Connor, contralto; Walter Richardson, tenor; and Harold H. Bennett, bass-baritone.

Leading the list of guest soloists on the subscription series was the virtuoso pianist Arthur Rubinstein. Forced to cancel two seasons before, the fabulous keyboard artist performed not one but two major concerti on the program. He then gave his permission to use transcriptions of both performances on the orchestra's thirteen-week radio series without charge, donating his talent to boost the Utah Symphony.

One of the sensations of the season, the Rubinstein program included the Rachmaninoff "Rhapsody on a Theme of Paganini" and the Beethoven Piano Concerto No. 4 in G Major.

Other guest soloists included violinists Frances Magnes in the Brahms Violin Concerto and Nathan Milstein performing the Lalo "Symphonie Espagnole" and Bach Concerto in E Major. Appearing late in the season was the accomplished local pianist and teacher Frederic Dixon in the Franck "Symphonic Variations."

In one of the University of Utah Centennial programs, concertmaster Zelig distinguished himself as soloist in the world premiere of Robertson's Concerto for Violin and Orchestra. A violinist of skill and artistry, Zelig repeated the performance later on the subscription series at the Tabernacle on a program that included an appearance of Mrs. Wagner as harp soloist in the Debussy "Danses Sacree et Profane" for Harp and Strings and the performance of two other contemporary American works, "Over the Plains," by George Anthiel, and Saunders' "Saturday Night, a Barn Dance." Anthiel was in the audience; following the concert, he called the orchestra "one of the finest in the country." He further commented: "Sometimes the folks just don't know how good an orchestra they have, and I am telling you at no one's request but my own that you have a great orchestra here. I have had my Sixth Symphony premiered in New York, another work premiered in St.Louis and other compositions played the country over, but nothing has impressed me more than the way Mr. Abravanel and the orchestra played my work here tonight."

The orchestra again toured throughout the state. When it went to Provo at mid-season, three composers connected with Brigham Young University were honored in a performance of their works. Two of the compositions were by members of the faculty and included the familiar "Promised Valley Interlude" by Gates and Leon Dallin's "Film Overture." The third, "Suite Elegiaque," was a creation of Glen Dalby, a former student of Leroy Robertson at BYU and at the time a member of the Utah Symphony's horn section.

All three of the works were repeated later on a subscription concert at the Salt Lake Tabernacle in a "Utah section" that also included the "Prelude, Scherzo and Fugue" by Lowell M. Durham, a University of Utah graduate and member of the U of U music department.

One other concert to attract unusual attention was a Christmas "Pops" program that brought the first Utah performance of Prokofiev's "Peter and the Wolf," with Roscoe Grover, KSL's popular radio character "Uncle Roscoe," as narrator.

In all, it was an impressive season, despite the curtailed operation, with Abravanel exhibiting a talent for pulling rabbits out of the symphony hat. He knew that by staying close to his friends, the musicians in the orchestra, he could keep the organization tied together.

Top Left: *Grant Johannesen (shown here in 1954 photo) performed as soloist with the Utah Symphony more or less biennially and became Utah's internationally prominent pianist.*
Top Right: *Pianist Claudio Arrau was a frequent and popular soloist with the Utah Symphony for more than two decades.*
Middle Left: *Leonard Pennario's solo appearances with the Utah Symphony dated back to World War II years when the popular pianist on one occasion performed in his army uniform.*
Bottom Left: *Zino Francescatti was one of the world's most sought after violinists, appearing on several occasions with the Utah Symphony.*
Bottom Right: *Dr. Alexander Schreiner, Salt Lake Tabernacle organist; Utah Symphony organist and soloist.*

Top Left: *Pianist Arthur Rubinstein accepts enthusiastic acclaim of Tabernacle audience.*
Top Right: *Jose Iturbi rose to fame in Hollywood films and was a popular Utah Symphony piano soloist on several occasions.*
Middle Right: *Jan Peerce, Metropolitan Opera star, performed in conert and recordings with Utah Symphony.*
Bottom Left: *Eileen Farrell, possessor of one of the great soprano voices of all time, received enthusiastic applause at Utah Symphony concerts.*
Bottom Right: *Zara Nelsova was beloved by Utah audiences for her sensitive and moving cello solos.*

Top Left: *Nathan Milstein was one of the Utah Symphony's favorite violinists on many occasions. For many years the celebrated artist refused to fly, traveling by train instead.*

Top Right: *Gina Bachauer's solo appearances with the Utah Symphony grew into an enduring friendship and ultimately the orchestra's sponsorship of an international piano competition in her name.*

Bottom Left: *Andre Watts performed as piano soloist several times with the Utah Symphony. He was numbered among the world's most celebrated artists.*

Top Left: *Roberta Peters' instant Metropolitan Opera stardom won for her a place in Utah music lovers' hearts. She became one of the orchestra's most popular soloists at repeated appearances.*

Top Right: *Itzhak Perlman's phenomenal performances lofted him into world "superstar" status. His Utah Symphony solo appearances were almost a sure sell-out.*

Bottom Left: *The defected Soviet cellist, Mstislav Rostropovich, was a sensation at his two Utah Symphony solo performances.*

Bottom Right: *Robert Merrill, baritone star of the Metropolitan Opera was a hit with audiences in his Utah Symphony solo engagements.*

S. HUROK

Top Left: Van Cliburn, pianist who won Tchaikovsky Competition prize in Moscow and appeared as soloist with Utah Symphony on several occasions, always played to sold-out houses.

Top Right: Beverly Sills first performed with Utah Symphony while virtually unknown and credits Maurice Abravanel with giving her an important break. She recorded and performed several times with the orchestra.

Bottom Left: Gladys Gladstone Rosenberg was a frequent piano soloist with the Utah Symphony.

Bottom Right: Isaac Stern, for some years considered to be one of the world's top violinists, returned several times to perform with his friend, Maurice Abravanel, and the Utah Symphony.

Top Left: *Metropolitan Opera diva, Leontyne Price, thrilled a capacity Tabernacle audience at the Utah Symphony's 5,000th performance on February 1, 1986.*
Top Right: *The illustrious bel canto soprano, Joan Sutherland, and her distinguished husband-conductor, Richard Bonynge, filled the huge Mormon Tabernacle for their Utah Symphony appearance.*
Bottom Left: *Flutist Jean-Pierre Rampal was a relative newcomer in the Utah Symphony's list of celebrated guest artists.*

Top Left: *One of the legendary performers of his time, Yehudi Menuhim appeared several times with Abravanel and the Utah Symphony.*
Top Right: *JoAnn Ottley, soprano soloist with Utah Symphony for numerous concert, opera and recording performances.*
Bottom Left: *Gary Graffman, for many years in the fore-front of the world's piano artists, performed frequently with the Utah Symphony.*
Bottom Right: *Jack Benny, star of radio, TV and films, admires key to the city presented him by Salt Lake City Commissioner Conrad B. Harrison upon the comedian-violinist's arrival for Utah Symphony "Benny-fit" concert, November 14, 1964.*

NEW YORK TIMES

Top: *Princess Irene of Greece and Gina Bachauer performed as duo-pianists with Utah Symphony February 8, 1969.*
Bottom Left: *The youthful artistry and exuberance of pianist Barbara Pace is typical of Salute to Youth soloists.*
Bottom Right: *Eugene Watanabe is one of the approximately 150 soloists appearing at a "Salute to Youth" concert sponsored by the Deseret News for 25 years.*

CHAPTER **13**

SPIT AND BALING WIRE

Before he signed his first contract with the Utah Symphony, Maurice Abravanel was well aware of the job he had taken on. He knew of the work that would be required and the concessions and sacrifices that would have to be made to produce his kind of music. He also knew that what he developed would be his own orchestra, identified with his name. That is why he wanted the job in the first place.

The indomitable conductor proved early that it would take nothing short of a major earthquake to shake him out of his place, just as he had made it clear before coming to Utah that the most tempting offer meant nothing to him if it did not lead to the Beethoven Ninth Symphony.

Abravanel recalls that while he was awaiting word from Salt Lake City, his agent, Judson, tried to dissuade him from moving west by encouraging him to take the Radio City Music Hall position at twice the salary. The offer had come through Judson's office at $30,000 for the first year and annual raises thereafter. "You have the world at your feet," implored Judson.

"But I became a musician to do the Ninth Symphony and such things," answered Maurice. "Does this lead to the Ninth Symphony?"

"Oh no," returned the agent. "It leads you to recording contracts, to Hollywood contracts, to everything in the world, but not to the Ninth Symphony."

"Well," said the conductor, "I'm afraid I would have to spend all that money with a psychoanalyst after six months."

Abravanel knew what he was looking for and refused to let anything get in his way. On the evening before the symphony board decided to offer him a contract, he put his chances in jeopardy by indicating what he meant by taking full control of the programming.

He had arrived in town for the first time that morning and was whisked from the Union Pacific Station by his welcoming party, Ruth Cowan and R. W. (Dick) Harris, a board member and a local advertising executive. Explaining that his room at the Hotel Utah was not ready, they drove the prospective music director up City Creek Canyon, where he declared: "This is the place I want to stay, because there are mountains like I had in Lausanne where I was raised. There is something very nice about it, very friendly, a beautiful sky and all that fresh air. Not hot in the morning, not muggy, as in New York. I like it very much."

That evening on the roof of the Hotel Utah, Abravanel was again impressed with the mountains, the sky, "very good food and very nice people." His hosts were symphony executives Smith, Wallace, Rosenblatt, and Cowan. During the course of the evening, Maurice said he was told that he would be expected to play Ravel's "La Valse" very soon. Mrs. Wallace had heard him conduct it with the NBC Symphony on a coast-to-coast broadcast. The conductor, however, rejected the proposal on the grounds that there were too many neglected works that should be brought out first. (In due course, "La Valse" made its appearance.)

Later in the evening, Abravanel relates, Mrs. Wallace brought up the name of Jacques Thibaud, and a mutual friendship with the French violin virtuoso was discovered. Maurice remembers that Glenn informed him she had told Thibaud "he could come next year." Again Maurice frankly turned down the idea, for while he had a great regard for the violinist and knew him to be "marvelous" on certain works, he was not available for the Beethoven and Brahms concerti, which were first in line.

Abravanel was to sign a contract giving him full authority over the programming—no more program advisory committee—and the selection of guest artists. He would upset a few people, as he did the night before he won the job, but in the end his choices were accepted—and rightfully respected.

He raised some eyebrows when he first programmed the Stravinsky "Firebird." It was an electrifying performance and well-received, but when he attempted "The Rite of Spring" for the first time several years later, he lost half the regular Tabernacle audience. So noisy was the reception, however, that he repeated the concert ten days later to a near capacity house and received a standing ovation.

There was little music of substance the maestro did not throw at his players. Not long after the agreement was signed with the University of Utah, Abravanel inaugurated a contemporary music series at Kingsbury Hall, and the works of Milhaud, Schoenberg, Piston, Hindemith, and others became part of the Utah Symphony repertoire. Although it was a mighty step forward musically, there was more than a smattering of dissenters. Many of these were to find a balancing of the books in the presentation of Gershwin, Grofe, Gould, and even Copland, Gottschalk, and Goldmark at the Tabernacle.

As earlier noted, Maurice got to Beethoven's Ninth Symphony in his very first season. He came on with the "Missa Solemnis" the year following, and soon added the Verdi "Requiem." The Beethoven Third, Fifth, Sixth, and Seventh symphonies became program standards, with the Schubert C Major Symphony; the Franck D. Minor; the later Mozart and Haydn symphonies; Debussy's "Images," "Nocturnes," and "La Mer"; Ravel's "Daphnis and Chloe"; the works of Bach, Dvorak, Prokofiev, Tchaikovsky, Rachmaninoff, Richard Strauss, Wagner, and Berlioz. Everything had the Abravanel stamp of authority on it, but even with his treatment of the bigger works among those mentioned, none brought more accolades than his interpretation of the Gustav Mahler symphonies in performance and on recordings. In the music world he will be remembered as one of the world's great Mahler authorities.

With all his confidence in the ability of local musicians to produce, Maurice still had to mold them into an ensemble with credibility. He was careful but firm in his efforts to upgrade the output of his musicians, begging them to practice overtime in off hours and to secure finer instruments where needed to polish precision and to improve sonority.

His players became a part of his life, and he a part of theirs. The few who went through those days and are still with the symphony recall the mutual desire to perform well. Violinist Frances Darger remembers the positive attitude, the dedication, and the fierce pride that developed. "Today, the sniffles can keep you home," she says, "but in those days there was total commitment, and only when you were at death's door did you miss a rehearsal or a concert."

When the maestro came to the symphony in 1947, he signed at a salary of $15,000 a year, but during the crisis of 1949 he voluntarily cut his salary back to $12,000 and carried on. Not until 1952 was the original salary restored, and it was then that he prevailed upon the board to raise the minimum wage for orchestra members from $37.50 to $40 a week.

Many times Abravanel had to work around a stubborn union to accomplish his goals. From the beginning he wanted to audition everyone who wanted to be heard, but he was told that the union would not permit it and that he could hear only union members.

"Look," he said, "my goal is to have as few imported players as possible. I want to hear what there is here, even people without any experience whatsoever. I want to hear whoever wants to audition."

Finally the union agreed, with the condition that a union representative attend the audition. That was all right with the maestro, and Bullough, himself a violinist in the symphony, sat in. After thirty-five minutes, however, he left, convinced that Maurice was trying to encourage each prospect and that he was looking for the kind of people who would work and improve. At one time the maestro used only six or seven imported players, mainly in the first chairs.

After many of the imported players abandoned ship following the rough seas of 1948-49, Manager Cowan and Abravanel met with the union on July 8. One day later the following proposal was made in a letter from Cowan to Bullough, president, and James Foley, secretary, of the Salt Lake Federated Musicians: "The union is to have the right to approve imports as formerly. Mr. Maurice Abravanel desires a free hand in this regard (approval of imports), his present estimate is about 7 needed imports as follows: Concertmaster, first cello, trombone, clarinet, trumpet, probably 1st horn, and timpanist. We feel that there will be no disagreement in this matter in view of the fact that we all have the same objectives of using all possible local musicians."

This was the course Abravanel followed with the union through his years with the orchestra, gaining not only the trust of his players but eventually the full authority to fix and secure salary raises and pay scales. He went on to make the needed changes and one year later found himself faced with filling as many as five seats in the cello section, including the principal.

Harold Schneier had accepted another position; Eileen MacIntosh Turner and Glenna Carpenter Swallow had joined their husbands in positions out of state; Marian Robertson was on a Fulbright scholarship in France; and Gustave Buggert had found it too difficult to commute from Provo. Joseph Wetzels, once with the Denver Symphony under Saul Caston and his own Belgian Piano String Quartet, took the first chair. Others in the section included Joseph Clive, Helen Riser, Jean Perkins, Evelyn Hilgendorff, Norma McLeod, and Verda Stubbs.

One other significant change in personnel for the 1950-51 season occurred in the viola section, where Sally Peck, a brilliant young local musician, took over as the principal at the unselfish suggestion of Lorna Hogensen, who moved back a seat to make room. Peck, only sixteen when Abravanel arrived, was nineteen when she moved into the first chair.

Among his eighty players, Abravanel had two other teenagers, who had been accepted through the auditioning program and whose presence was duly noted in a special feature on the *Tribune* Sunday music page at mid-season. Richard Jones, a

seventeen-year-old East High School student, was in the clarinet section under his teacher and principal, Martin Zwick;
and Raymond Wood, an eighteen-year-old University of Utah
freshman, was playing the bass fiddle. Both were examples of
the maestro's recognition of talent and effort and of the influence on young musicians of the symphony and the outstanding instruction emanating from its ranks.

While the hiring of young players was a part of the "building" program, it also had its drawbacks. Several years later the
University of Utah Department of Music was to seek a curb on
the employment of its students by the symphony. After what he
termed "ten years" of "contemplation," Lowell M. Durham, then
dean of the University's College of Fine Arts, with the head of the
music department, Leroy Robertson, finally wrote to Abravanel
on January 10, 1958, about the matter. He asked that the maestro give "careful consideration" to two proposals (1) that "no
Freshman student at the University be signed to a Symphony
contract," and (2) that all University students in the orchestra be
required to play in the University of Utah Symphony Orchestra
as part of their contract with the Utah Symphony.

The contention was that Freshman students were failing
their courses because of the importance they placed on their
positions in the symphony. Too, it was argued that students in
the Utah Symphony, quite naturally the finest instrumentalists
on the Campus, generally felt little or no obligation to perform
for the school and that their limited participation was causing a
serious morale problem for the university orchestra.

This problem, one of the few to surface in the most fruitful
and valuable affiliation for both the university and the symphony, was successfully negotiated without direct imposition
of the restrictions. While continuing to perform under Abravanel, the students became more cooperative on the campus.

Each such experience offered additional evidence that the
maestro would use every means at his disposal to build his
orchestra for the good of the state, city, and region. But his "spit,
baling wire, and mirrors" operation did not belong to his
department alone. It was part of the entire orchestra operation.
Manager Romney had a one-chair office staff that had existed

for years. Elsie Shepard, whose duties as office manager for the Utah State Institute of Fine Arts and the Utah Symphony went beyond the orchestra's founding, was still at her post. For several years yet she would run the office, serve as secretary, pay the bills, and do the job of a general "handyman," as she often referred to her position.

One chore Elsie was relieved of, however, was the accounting and bookkeeping. For this the symphony had a prominent Salt Lake accountant, Seymour Wells, who contributed many hours of time to his appointed position as treasurer of the institute and the symphony. His close watch over the books and timely checks on expenditures in the scaled-down, part-time operation during the 1950s proved invaluable.

Every attempt was made to avoid large deficits while paying off the $35,000 deficit remaining after the 1948-49 season. During the next season, the orchestra took in $103,987 and spent $106,003 to record a deficit of $2,016. The following season, the deficit climbed to $6,164 on increased expenditures of $123,380 and income of $117,216. This was offset the following year when the operation resulted in a surplus of $6,783 on expenditures of $127,608 and income of $134,391, all due to a growth in earned income against a decrease in contributions from business and industrial firms, organizations, and individuals.

The contributions actually declined steadily from $31,144 in 1949-50 to $27,497 two seasons later. The orchestra, on the other hand, upped its earned income dramatically. By extending the touring schedule around the state, it increased the number of concerts from twenty-six in 1949-50 to thirty-five the following year and fifty-one in 1951-52, virtually double that of two seasons before. The unit cost fell from $4,077 to $2,502 over the three seasons, and the percentage ratio of earnings to contributions went from 58.8/41.2 to 71.3/28.7.

Public assistance decreased over the period, although Art Institute Chairman Crockett, who had become a Utah Supreme Court Justice, requested a $10,000 increase in the biennial budget of $30,000 submitted to Governor Lee in 1951. The governor, however, not only denied the increase but cut the agency's small two-year appropriation of $20,000 to $15,000, and the legislature went along.

This left the institute with but $7,500 per year, out of which its symphony was allocated $5,200 against the $7,885 meted out for each of the two previous years. It was as much as the orchestra could expect form the state while Lee was in office. He felt strongly that such contributions were "unconstitutional" and in the 1960s fussed and fumed in opposition from his position as mayor of Salt Lake City while the city commission approved annual appropriations of $5,000 to the Utah Symphony.

Making up for the loss were fund-raising activities among the women, and the women's committee, under Mrs. M. M. Wintrobe, presented $10,000 to the cause in 1951-52 as its part in the Symphony Progress Fund drive. It was one of the last seasons that group would operate as a "committee," however, as the Symphony Guild was to make its appearance in 1953. The Symphony Guild became an effective adjunct and supporter of the orchestra for thirty-three years and is worthy of its own chapter in symphony history.

Also occupied with fund-raising were the symphony officers and members of the board. Mrs. Wallace was particularly active from her position as president and teamed very closely with Manager Cowan in administering symphony operations. Not long after the manager resigned in the summer of 1950, however, Mrs. Wallace severed her connections with the Utah Symphony, ending nearly eleven years of solid support and active interest.

Responding to her resignation, members of the executive committee met on December 12 and voted unanimously to recommend to the board of directors that it refuse to accept the president's action and "importune her to continue as president until the end of the term.... the second Monday in April, 1951." She insisted on leaving; in later years she said she found it virtually impossible to carry on as an administrator with Mr. Romney as manager.

Judge Crockett was elected to fill the unexpired term of Mrs. Wallace, with Leland B. Flint and James L. White as vice-presidents. The new president was succeeded as chairman of the Art Institute Board by Mrs. Stuart P. Dobbs, an Ogden arts enthusiast, and continued as head of the symphony until April of 1952 when he turned the gavel over to Raymond J. Ashton, a prominent Salt Lake City architect.

In a recent interview, the retired Supreme Court Justice gave considerable weight to a statement made to him by Ruth Cowan to the effect that the "only real purpose" of the symphony board of directors was to "raise money." He further observed: "The board members, of course, were under the illusion that they had some other functions, but she wasn't very far from the truth from the standpoint of those who actually managed and promoted the orchestra. The main thing they wanted out of the board was to finance it. I can't disagree with that. I have often thought it was true."

Obviously symphony manager Romney had the same feeling, and for several years a "caretaker" operation seemed to do little more than "mark time" in the front office. Musically, however, the operation was a different story. Abravanel and the orchestra accepted the challenge of a limited rehearsal schedule and turned the decade into the "Fabulous Fifties." They opened up the world of symphonic music, including the great choral masterpieces, and drew from every age and idiom. No music was too rich, too meaty, too old, or too new for Abravanel's audiences. The maestro mixed traditional and contemporary, the known and the unknown. Sometimes he programmed a full evening of established but unfamiliar works in "first" performances or filled a concert with Utah compositions and world premieres. When appropriate, a serving of "pops" variety fare filled the bill.

Typical of Abravanel's adroit and artistic programming was the season of 1950-51. He had persuaded the noted American dramatic soprano and Wagnerian artist, Helen Traubel, to leave her newly entered night-club career and appear as guest artist in the season opener at the Tabernacle. The concert was a huge success, with the first half including the Respighi-Bach "Passacaglia in C Minor" and Richard Strauss's "Till Eulenspiegel." After intermission the emphasis was on Wagner, all "firsts" on the symphony schedule. The conductor's mastery of dynamics brought life to the "Rhine Journey," "Funeral March," and Traubel's stirring "Immolation" from "Gotterdammerung." Earlier Traubel had been heard in arias of Wagner and Gluck.

With such a beginning, the season went on to include two performances of Bach's "St. Matthew Passion" at Kingsbury Hall in cooperation with the University of Utah Choruses prepared by John Marlowe Nielson and Newell Weight. Muriel Maxwell, a California mezzo-soprano, and five Utah singers, Blanche Christensen, Walter Richardson, Kenly Whitelock, Harold H. Bennett, and Marvin Sorensen, were the soloists.

When Vladimir Horowitz, the fabulous keyboard artist, appeared with the symphony for the first time, Abravanel sandwiched the "Iberia" section of Debussy's "Images" between the Haydn "Drum Roll" Symphony No. 103 and the Tchaikovsky Piano Concerto. In another concert he presented Milhaud's "Suite Provencale" along with the Mendelssohn Violin Concerto, with Concertmaster Zelig as soloist, and the Franck Symphony in D Minor.

On still another occasion the maestro went to a program that was all new to his subscribers. The memorable evening included the Hindemith "Mathis der Mahler"; the Mahler Fourth Symphony, with Blanche Christensen as soloist; and the Adagio and Hallelujah sections of William Grant Still's "Afro-American" Symphony. In the *Salt Lake Tribune* the next day, Lowell M. Durham said it was "one of the most ambitious programs" yet attempted by Abravanel and the new symphony and wrote of the Hindemith: "It was given a thrilling performance, from the initial bars to the thrilling chorale climax in brass choir. The first two movements came off as well as you would hear them anywhere.... The working-out section of the finale is a challenge to the world's most renowned orchestras, with its ultra-high E-string work for violins, technically tough cello passages and rapid-tonguing demands of the winds. Yet the young ensemble met the challenge surprisingly well."

This, incidentally, was another of those years when snow piled high and funds ran low for the symphony and a saving feature was Kennecott Copper Corporation's sponsorship of a radio series over 50,000-watt KSL that put $20,000 into the orchestra's coffers. As somewhat of a gesture of appreciation, a concert was presented on a wintry night in Bingham for miners, townspeople, and students, and the result put the Utah Symphony on the front page of the Sunday arts section of the *New York Times* once more. Jack Goodman made the trip just as he had with Janssen and the symphony to Vernal in 1947.

It seems that Maurice Abravanel and a Kennecott official had engaged in a gin-rummy session, and Maurice was bemoaning the fact that the orchestra was in the red. At the close of the game, the Kennecott executive told the baton master: "If your orchestra can play music as well as you can play gin, come round to the office tomorrow—we're hunting for a radio program."

The radio series and the Bingham Canyon concert resulted, but the mine officials were skeptical about a performance in the mining town. "Abravanel knows music, but we know miners," they said.

The bosses were amazed at the speed with which 300 tickets were snapped up, and they had to provide more, especially when the workers learned there was only standing room left in the 960-seat Bingham High School Auditorium.

The orchestra made the trip by bus in a gale-force wind and had barely arrived when the snow joined in, sixteen inches of it before the storm subsided. The blizzard cut off some ticket-holders in nearby Lark, Highland Boy, and Copperfield, but the hall was jammed with Binghamites, and the mild menu of Smetana ("The Moldau"), Humperdinck ("Hansel and Gretel Overture"), Liszt ("Les Preludes"), and Weber ("Invitation to the Dance") received foot-stomping approval.

Mine superintendent L. F. Pett said to the audience at the end of the concert: "I think it's safe to say we can expect more concerts in the future. Please drive carefully on the canyon road going home—we want to make sure you're alive to attend them. As for the orchestra, we'll make sure they'll come back—we've called for a snow plow to clear the road for them to Salt Lake."

As he approached the end of the season, the maestro presented Paul Creston's "Frontiers" and the "Corral Nocturne" and "Hoedown" from Copland's "Rodeo" on a program that included the Sibelius Second Symphony and Glazunov Violin Concerto, with Ricardo Odnoposoff, South American violinist, as soloist. And for the closing concert he started with Mozart's "Eine Kleine Nachtmusik" and the Beethoven Second Symphony, then finished with Rossini's "La Gazza Ladra" Overture and a dazzling first performance of Stravinsky's "Firebird." So noisy and long was the reception that Abravanel responded with Gould's "American Salute" as an encore. There was never anything dull about Maurice's programming or performance.

When called upon for the climactic performance of the biennial convention of the National Federation of Music Clubs in Salt Lake City during May of 1951, Abravanel and the symphony responded with—what else?—the Beethoven Ninth Symphony, again with the University Choruses. The soloists were four Utahns, soprano Ruth Jensen Clawson, contralto Annette Richardson Dinwoodey, tenor Ray Brimhall, and bass-baritone Harold H. Bennett.

The concert also included the Leroy Robertson Violin Concerto with Zelig as soloist and was broadcast nationwide over CBS radio under the sponsorship of the Standard Oil Company of California.

As Abravanel came out to start the performance, he faced the audience and in a most appropriate gesture personally dedicated the concert to President George Albert Smith of The Church of Jesus Christ of Latter-day Saints and to the beloved opera diva, Emma Lucy Gates Bowen, "two great friends of music who have passed on." Both had passed away during the previous season.

Between seasons, Concertmaster Zelig left for greener pastures and was replaced by Jerome Kasin. Walter Green took over the first bassoon chair, but both new players lasted but a year as Harold Wolf replaced Kasin and Douglas B. Craig supplanted Green. Wolf was to hold his position about as long as any concertmaster with the Utah Symphony, while Craig remains at his post with thirty-four years' continuous service.

Other newcomers that year were Eugene Foster, who replaced Sam Pratt as flute principal; Adine Bradley, successor to Sam's wife, Louise Pratt, with the harp; and William Sullivan, the new trumpet principal. One year later Harold Schneier returned to the first cello chair in place of the ailing Joseph Wetzels and remained three years before giving way to David Freed.

It would be difficult to chronicle all the events through which the Utah Symphony progressed under Abravanel as it became an orchestra possessed of a spirit unlike that of any other. Often it was said that the Utah Symphony "may not be the best of the major symphonies but none can match it in spirit."

During the '50s, hardly any composer was played more than Leroy Robertson, many of whose works received world premieres by the Utah Symphony under Abravanel. By 1969 Robertson shared the list of the orchestra's ten most-performed composers with Beethoven, Mozart, Brahms, Tchaikovsky, Wagner, Ravel, Debussy, J. S. Bach, and Richard Strauss; and perhaps no choral work, not even the Beethoven Ninth Symphony, had been performed more than Robertson's "Book of Mormon" Oratorio.

At the persuasion and encouragement of Abravanel, this great Mormon epic was finally completed in 1952, and on February 18, 1953, it received its world premiere in the Tabernacle. Joining the symphony under Abravanel were the University of Utah choruses, trained by John Marlowe Nielson, Kenly Whitelock, Richard P. Condie, and Dr. Shand; and the East High School Girls Chorus under Lorraine Bowman. The difficult role of Samuel, the Lamanite prophet, was created by Desire Ligeti, a powerful bass-baritone secured by Abravanel for the production. Other soloists were Harold H. Bennett, Melba Egbert, Naomi Farr, and Kenly Whitelock.

Before the season was over, the oratorio had been repeated in Ogden, with the same cast, as well as over the Kennecott Symphony Hour on radio and again in the Tabernacle on April 6, the anniversary date of the founding of The Church of Jesus Christ of Latter-day Saints. It was recorded several times, once on the Vanguard label and more recently on CBS Masterworks with the Tabernacle Choir. Other cities, including Logan and Provo, eventually heard the oratorio, and on April 6, 1954, it was repeated in the Tabernacle.

The Robertson oratorio continued to appear on the schedule and was almost a fixture for the Church anniversary each April 6. Col. Arthur Kent, formerly at the Metropolitan Opera and at that time stationed at Fort Douglas, and Roy Samuelson, a Utah baritone, in order succeeded Ligeti as Samuel.

Other works by the Utah composer appeared on the repertoire each season. Besides the Violin Concerto, the Piano Rhapsody was revived with Foldes as soloist, and the "Trilogy" made its periodic appearance. "Passacaglia," given its world premiere in Athens in the summer of 1955, received its first home performance on December 10 of the same year. During the following season, on February 20, 1957, as the feature of an all-American program, Robertson's orchestration of "American Serenade for Strings," from his American Serenade for String Quartet, was given its world premiere at the Tabernacle.

Still another world premiere was yet to come in the performance during the 1956-57 season of the Robertson Cello Concerto with Zara Nelsova as soloist.

Meanwhile, there were works of other local composers to draw Abravanel's attention and consequently take their place on the schedule. One night in December, 1953, while the maestro was guest conducting in Houston, Crawford Gates was on the podium for his own symphony No. 1, a premiere of the complete work from which he had earlier performed the first movement. Assistant conductor David Shand handled the remainder of the program, which included a performance of Mozart's "Sinfonie Concertante," with concertmaster Harold Wolf and violist Sally Peck as soloists.

The following season, Glen Dalby took a bow from his chair in the French horn section in response to an ovation for "Opus 18" from his "Aztec Ceremonial." It preceded by two weeks a performance of "Lament," by Carlos Alexander, who had been directing operations of the Utah Opera Theater, on a program that found Gladys Gladstone as soloist in the Mendelssohn G Minor Piano Concerto. During the following season Abravanel performed a work by Dr. George H. Durham, the "New England Pastorale."

Alexander Schreiner's versatility as a virtuoso at the organ and as a composer had long been evident, and when he composed his Concerto for Organ and Orchestra, Abravanel premiered it with the composer at the console on February 22, 1956. Schreiner had also performed with the symphony in the Walter Piston "Prelude and Allegro for Organ and Strings" and Handel's Concerto in D Minor for Organ and Orchestra; later he joined the ensemble in a presentation of the Saint-Saens "Organ" Symphony No. 3 in C Minor.

Meanwhile, the introduction of exciting, unfamiliar scores to symphony audiences continued at a steady pace. When Abravanel first performed the Prokofiev Fifth Symphony, Dr. Durham observed in the *Tribune*: "The marvelous thing about the whole performance.... is the fact that we have an organization and a musical director who can bring us first rate performances of works of such dimension and difficulty."

Stravinsky's "Petrouchka" and "L'Histoire du Soldat," the latter in a Kingsbury Hall "special" that included Milhaud's "La Creation du Monde" and the Schoenberg "Transfigured Night," were among "modern" scores given good exposure. Another was Samuel Barber's "Concerto for Orchestra"; and when Arthur Shepherd was beckoned from Cleveland to conduct his "Horizons"—Four Western Pieces for Orchestra, Abravanel performed the Mozart Symphony No. 40 in G Minor and Hindemith's "Symphonic Metamorphosis on Themes of Weber" on the same program.

The maestro's variety was remarkable, as was his ability to perform the bigger works as well as the small in spite of fiscal austerity. He added to the Mahler repertoire with "Das Lied von Der Erde," presenting Soprano Nell Tangemann and Tenor Raymond Manton as soloists, and the big Second ("Resurrection") Symphony. He also brought in Nan Merriman for the solo part in de Falla's "El Amor Brujo."

On the 200th anniversary of Mozart's birth, January 27, 1956, Abravanel opened a Mozart cycle at Kingsbury Hall with a performance of the "Requiem." John Marlow Nielson's University Chorale and a corps of Utah soloists, Blanche Christensen, Beryl Jensen, Glade Peterson, and Arthur Kent, were in the cast.

Given strong support by university president A. Ray Olpin, the cycle included two other concerts, with concertmaster Wolf and Gladys Gladstone as soloists, and a production of the "Marriage of Figaro" on the Kingsbury stage.

In his fifth season, on February 23, 1952, Maurice performed the Honegger oratorio, "King David," for the first time, using Blanche Christensen, Annette Richardson Dinwoodey, and Marvin Sorensen as soloists and Harold Folland as narrator. Five years later he presented the same composer's "Joan of Arc at the Stake" in a magnificent production and cast headed by the stage and screen star Dorothy McGuire in the title role. Other spoken parts were dispatched by Folland, Ron Ross, John Nicolaysen, and Lila Eccles Brimhall; the soloists were Christensen, Jean Preston, Lota Lamoreaux, Dale Blackburn, and Don Watts.

Between the Honegger works was a production of Haydn's "Creation" with Christensen, Kent, and Blackburn in the solo roles.

Throughout the decade, Abravanel was a sought-after guest conductor, but he kept his acceptances well within bounds and in compliance with his heavy schedule at home. He conducted the Pittsburgh Symphony in Denver in 1951 and accepted regular appearances with the Los Angeles Philharmonic and San Francisco Symphony on the "Standard Hour." On one occasion Grant Johannesen was with him in San Francisco on a program that included the Beethoven Third Piano Concerto and three movements of the Brahms Second Symphony.

Early in 1953 he conducted the Seattle Symphony at a time when that orchestra was seeking a new conductor, prompting a Seattle critic to comment: "If the Seattle Symphony board is seeking a permanent conductor, it now has an example of what to look for. All it has to do is find another Maurice Abravanel—or perhaps woo Abravanel from his Utah Symphony Orchestra post."

Answering this at the beginning of the next season, the Salt Lake Area Chamber of Commerce presented the maestro with the Distinguished Citizen Award, after which Maurice conducted in Vancouver, British Columbia. He returned through Ogden and conducted a concert with the eighty-five piece Weber College Orchestra.

The Houston Symphony and Grant Park Symphony in Chicago were among other guest assignments before he accepted an invitation to return to the Berlin Philharmonic in the early summer of 1959. There he presented a program of "new" music, including the "Passacaglia" of Leroy Robertson. Before returning home, he went to Vienna for recording sessions for Westminster with the Vienna State Opera Orchestra.

The remainder of the summer, as had been the case for several years, he spent at the Music Academy of the West in Santa Barbara, California, where he had become the music director.

At home, Abravanel continued to engage soloists to fit his planned repertoire for each season. For the 1951-52 season he was able to get approval from the board for Jascha Heifetz at a fee of $3,500 and Arthur Rubinstein and Oscar Levant at $2,500 each. Heifetz performed the Beethoven, Brahms, and Sibelius violin concerti in different appearances over three seasons.

Grant Johannesen was an annual attraction for several years and generously responded with two performances on each program. In one concert he played the Saint-Saens Piano Concerto No. 4 and D'Indy's "Symphony on a French Mountain Air"; one year later he was heard in de Falla's "Nights in the Gardens of Spain" and the Grieg Piano Concerto. On another occasion he performed the Mozart Piano Concerto No. 21 in C Major and the Ravel Concerto in G and in another concert paired the Schubert "Wanderer Fantasie" and the Ravel Concerto for the Left Hand.

Yehudi Menuhin appeared as soloist for the first time with the symphony at the close of the 1954-55 season in the Brahms Violin Concerto. Then, as an added feature, Abravanel presented a Salute to Israel one week later on March 19 in the Tabernacle as a part of the Jewish Tercentenary Festival. His program included the Bloch Concerto Grosso No. 1 for Strings and Piano with Gladys Gladstone at the keyboard; Copland's "El Salon Mexico" and the "Hoedown" from "Rodeo"; Kurt Weill's "Three Walt Whitman Songs," sung by Arthur Kent; Gershwin's "Porgy and Bess" Suite; and Irving Berlin's "God Bless America." The program was recorded and televised for presentation on "Voice of America."

One of the significant events of the 1950s, one that would permanently effect the affiliation of ballet and symphony, took place in the late fall and winter of 1955. It was the birth of the "Nutcracker" in Utah.

For four years Willam Christensen, ballet's "Mr. C," had been building a corps de ballet for his University Ballet Theater, and he and Abravanel had looked for the day that full-scale ballet production would come to life at Kingsbury Hall. Christensen had already successfully produced the Tchaikovsky "Nutcracker" in 1944 in San Francisco, and Abravanel encouraged a try on the local stage. They looked to Christmas holidays but were told that productions at that time were doomed to failure because of so many other Yuletide activities.

After prevailing on Dr. Olpin, the University president, however, it was decided to go ahead, and the jackhammers invaded Kingsbury Hall. An orchestra pit was sunk into Kingsbury's concrete, much to the chagrin of the management, while orchestra and ballet prepared for the opening.

The venture, with Sally Bailey and Conrad Ludlow of the San Francisco Opera/Ballet as principals, was a success before the first curtain went up. Every performance was sold out, and a matinee had to be added to help meet the demand for tickets. So it has been and so it remains today, a popular holiday event that provided the real base for the development of what became Civic Ballet and is now Ballet West, a monument to "Mr. C."

Christensen had come to Salt Lake City permanently in 1951 after directing the dance sequences at the summer festival in the Stadium Bowl for three seasons. With an established symphony to provide the essential music support, he could see a future for his artistic profession. He had worked with Abravanel and Lees and was impressed with the possibilities. Maurice had been particularly successful in securing outstanding performers for the summer productions, and local singers and dancers had supplied an array of talent that sustained a professional product.

Few of the festival performances exceeded the excellence that marked the "Faust" production of 1950 with Norman Scott, Jon Craig, Dorothy Sarnoff, and a brilliant Civic Ballet. It had followed a revival of "Promised Valley" with Scott, Dorothy Kimball Keddington, and Theodore Uppman.

Abravanel also brought in the great Wagnerian "Heldentenor" Lauritz Melchior for a special night at the stadium, and the guest attended and performed at a fund-raising "soiree" at the Salt Lake Country Club. The next summer, Benny Goodman came with his clarinet, performing a Mozart concerto with the symphony and adding a jazz session with pianist Paul Smith and drummer Alvin Stoller at the other Country Club "soiree."

Patricia Morison came from Broadway to perform in "Kiss Me Kate" and "The King and I," and Robert Rounseville, John Druary, Kitty Carlisle, Elaine Malbin, and David Atkinson were among other prominent singers to appear. Christensen, meanwhile, brought Sally Bailey from the San Francisco Ballet to perform several times. She had thus already won over a Utah audience when she appeared as the prima ballerina in the first "Nutcracker" in 1955.

It was in the summer of 1953 that Abravanel first introduced a brilliant young soprano, Beverly Sills, to Stadium Bowl audiences in "Naughty Marietta" and "La Traviata." She returned again the next summer for "Aida" to follow up an "Oklahoma" production with Laurel Hurley, who with Sills later reached the Metropolitan Opera stage.

It was thus that Abravanel helped to launch the sensational career of Sills and others, including two other sopranos and a tenor who went on to become "Met" stars: Grace Bumbry, Martina Arroyo, and William Olvis.

Olvis was the first to appear in April 1957, leading a strong cast in Abravanel's first production and recording of Handel's "Judas Maccabaeus" at the Assembly Hall. A capacity audience heard the public performance with the symphony; the University of Utah Collegium Musicum, directed by Dr. Shand; and soloists. The recording session for the Handel Society followed, and the results won the praise of critics from coast to coast.

Herbert Kupferberg in the *New York Herald-Tribune* hailed the effort as one in which "Maurice Abravanel blows the dust off this ancient masterpiece with a breath of life," and the *New York Times* in a one-column review and two-column picture lauded the Handel Society for "rendering another significant service." The society was praised for its enterprise in rounding up "excellent, if not yet famous, forces with which to perform the oratorio" and in finding the "Utah chorus and closely related Utah Symphony Orchestra, with the latter's regular director, Maurice Abravanel, an expert conductor, to hold the forces together." The *San Francisco Chronicle* added: "This is—orchestrally and chorally—a marvelously clear and beautiful performance."

Bumbry and Arroyo also made their first appearance under Abravanel's guidance in concert and recording sessions, the first to be produced for the Westminster label. Bumbry joined a cast that included Blanche Christensen, Cohleen Bischoff, Dale Blackburn, Don Watts, and Warren Woods, with the University choruses and the Utah Symphony in Handel's "Israel in Egypt."

One year later, "Judas Maccabaeus" was brought back with Arroyo and Bumbry, Richard Storrs, Marvin Sorensen, and Don Watts, and in 1960 Abravanel brought back the two sopranos and Norman Treigle to join Sorensen in Mendelssohn's "Elijah."

By that time Herold L. (Huck) Gregory had been two years on the scene as executive director and manager of the Utah Symphony and was a force in the emergence of the orchestra on records.

Gregory had been presiding over the East German Mission of The Church of Jesus Christ of Latter-day Saints with his thespian wife, Mary Ethel Eccles, and their children since 1953. When he returned in 1957, he found the symphony job waiting for him. He virtually traded places with the manager, David Romney, who left to preside over the Church's Western States Mission in Denver. The symphony offices were then located in the Bennett Glass and Paint offices at 55 West First South. Gregory, with little more than an introduction to the desk, files, and books by the departing manager, literally walked in as Romney walked out.

It was a good acquisition for the symphony and one that has proved to be a boon for twenty-nine years. Gregory was well-prepared for his role, having worked in banking in his hometown of Farmington with postgraduate study at the University of Utah in accounting, marketing, business law, economics, banking, finance, investments, and taxation to go with his degree in radio speech with emphasis in music.

With an immediate goal of filling the concert hall, Huck turned three straight years of declining ticket sales abruptly around, and box-office revenues began a steady increase. In every season in which he was the chief operating officer, with but one insignificant exception, the symphony finished "in the black"; and in every season but two, the ticket revenues showed an increase. With Abravanel and Gregory working as a team, the Utah Symphony steadily pulled away from being a part-time operation on its way to becoming a world-class orchestra with a year-round schedule.

Huck recognized early in his symphony career that his major contribution lay in filling the halls, increasing concert bookings, finding new ways to expand orchestra services, building the image of the Utah Symphony, and looking after myriads of details so that Abravanel could concentrate on the artistic end of the operation. Huck's was a never-ending job stretching from early morning breakfast meetings to late evening concerts—always with too small a staff—and he never stopped coming up with new ways to promote Utah's outstanding symphony orchestra.

Huck's management style was unique in that he deliberately chose to remain in the background and focus the spotlight on the musicians, their conductor, and board members and other unpaid volunteers. He liked to view himself as the glue holding it all together as he exploited the talent and dedication of the musicians, the genius of Abravanel, and, in later years, the unbounded enthusiasm and phenomenal fund-raising prowess of Wendell Ashton.

CHAPTER 14

AN ERA OF RECORDINGS

Shortly after joining the Utah Symphony as its manager, Huck Gregory overheard a patron remark, "The Utah Symphony is okay for a small-town orchestra, but by no stretch of the imagination can it be compared to our great orchestras in the East."

The tone and content of this and other pompous comments were clearly intended to impress the local yokels who had presumably never been to the big city and heard a "real" orchestra.

Huck was not impressed. He had spent six of the previous eight years in Berlin, where he had held season tickets to the Berlin Philharmonic and had also attended concerts of the Berlin Radio Orchestra and visiting orchestras, including the Philadelphia Orchestra.

Huck knew that musician for musician the Utah Symphony was not the equal of, for example, the Berlin, London, New York, Boston, or Philadelphia orchestras, but he also knew that on some occasions the Utah Symphony's level of performance actually matched or exceeded that of the acknowledged world leaders, and he set about to make local music lovers aware of that fact.

An effective aid in this educational process was the emergence of the Utah Symphony's recordings. Glowing reviews of music critics appeared in the leading journals of the land, and it was no longer appropriate to relegate the Utah Symphony to a subordinate rank among America's major orchestras.

A *High Fidelity* reviewer subsequently described a Utah Symphony recording as "an interpretation of awesome, inspired magnificence." He added, "No praise could be too high for the work of the Utah Symphony, which on this occasion successfully challenges comparison with the London Symphony in top form."

A London critic wrote, "By any standards the Utah orchestra is a first-class ensemble. Make no mistake, this is a great orchestra."

As Maurice Abravanel was wont to explain, one cannot make a valid comparison between a recording and a live performance. In earlier years it was necessary to record a complete side of a disc without stopping, but today it is possible to snip out errors or mediocre passages and splice in a backup performance so that the end result is a nearly perfect recording. With a live performance, on the other hand, what you hear is what you get.

Not surprisingly, local patrons who heard what are commonly called "flubs" or "clams" in the symphony's live performances erroneously assumed that such things never happened in the so-called "great" orchestras; their only basis for comparison was a fastidious recording from which all imperfections had been eliminated. Once the Utah Symphony began recording, its performances on records were judged on equal footing with other recording orchestras. Local patrons as well as national and international critics began to see that the Utah Symphony's finished product often compared favorably with that of even the most prestigious orchestras elsewhere.

Thus the Utah Symphony recordings opened up new horizons. They would eventually stir feelings of envy among orchestras much larger and better endowed than the Utah Symphony, and they would also become one of the primary factors responsible for international tours. Out of America's hinterlands were emerging recordings that astounded even the most skeptical listeners at home and abroad.

Enhancement of the orchestra's image was only one of the benefits derived from recordings. At a time when symphony members were employed less than six months out of the year, recording sessions provided welcome additional employment for them. It was obvious that musicians of first-rate professional caliber could not be expected to stay in Utah for what amounted to a part-time job in their chosen field.

A bonus benefit was the fact that recording demands a greater precision and concentration than a routine rehearsal or concert. Microphones are objective and unforgiving, and the Utah Symphony's recording program undoubtedly helped improve the artistic quality of the orchestra.

How the symphony's recordings came about is a saga in itself, and the uncontested hero thereof is Maurice Abravanel, a man of great determination, vision, and indomitable spirit who refused to accept an outdated, inequitable status quo.

In April 1952 Abravanel persuaded the Handel Society to record "Judas Maccabaeus" with the Utah Symphony; an *Esquire* reviewer called the performance "the greatest Handel recording ever made." The *Christian Science Monitor* reported: "The Utah Symphony Orchestra plays superbly under Maurice Abravanel."

It must have been providential that a conductor with a great love for orchestral-choral music would be drawn to a community and state in which choral music is held in such high esteem. Abravanel has often said that some of the most sublime music expressions are to be found in the orchestral-choral masterpieces.

It is not surprising, therefore, that the first recording made under his baton was one of the universally acclaimed masterpieces of orchestral-choral literature. The combined choruses of the University of Utah were marshaled for the choral parts as they would be for many future performances. The individual choirs and choruses would prepare the music separately and then come under the direction of another director who would further rehearse them. Ardean Watts was one of the most effective directors in this role, as evidenced by the fact that his 1960 combined choirs participated in the first award-winning recording, Honegger's "King David."

In later years the combined choruses would give way to the newly formed University Civic Chorale, whose name was subsequently changed to Utah Chorale and later, on September 1, 1984, the Utah Symphony Chorus, still loosely associated with the University of Utah but a separate nonprofit organization. Its principal directors have been Newell Weight, John Marlowe Nielson, and Ed Thompson.

The world premiere performance of Leroy Robertson's monumental "Book of Mormon Oratorio" on February 18, 1953, was taped and subsequently released as an LP album through a joint venture between Allen-Duff Associates and the Utah Symphony. Later, the master tape and all recording rights were sold to a Los Angeles firm that released an identical pressing under the Century label.

But not until December 1957 did the Utah Symphony's commercial recording program come into full bloom, with the Westminster Recording Company based in New York. Maurice Abravanel set up the recordings and conceived and arranged for a landmark recording concept that made the project possible.

Abravanel realized that probably no major recording company would record a relatively unknown orchestra in what was considered to be America's vast cultural wasteland. The formula under which the handful of recording orchestras operated was that the record company would pick up the entire cost, including a handsome fee to the symphony involved, which usually covered musician's salaries and benefits and then some. In addition, the companies advertised their recordings on a grand scale. Abravanel correctly reasoned that an RCA, Columbia, or Decca would not spend a fortune building up its celebrated recording orchestra and then go to the expense and effort to record Brand X Orchestra out in Utah in direct competition with itself.

Westminster was a logical choice for the Utah Symphony's first venture into the fiercely competitive commercial recording field. It was not one of the industry giants, but the quality of its products was unsurpassed. While Westminster was prepared to pick up all production, manufacturing, and distribution costs against a royalty to the Utah Symphony, the company would not pay orchestra salaries for the sessions.

Under the prevailing American Federation of Musicians agreements, payments to musicians for recording sessions were based on a national scale. It didn't (and still doesn't) matter if the orchestra was from Cleveland, Philadelphia, or Utah— the base scale was the same.

In contrast, salaries paid to orchestral musicians for their regular rehearsals and concerts have long been determined through the local collective bargaining process resulting in a master agreement between the local musicians' union and the local symphony. Thus, in the case of the Utah Symphony, the national recording scale was about three times as much as the minimum paid to one of its musicians for the same amount of time worked under the local master agreement.

Maurice Abravanel perceived that this disparity was patently unfair to musicians in any but the handful of giant recording orchestras, notwithstanding it was the avowed purpose of the union to provide employment under equitable conditions for all of its members. How, he reasoned, could Utah Symphony musicians possibly compete against this virtual monopoly?

Having raised the question, Maestro Abravanel also answered it. He devised a plan under which Utah Symphony musicians would receive for the recording sessions a payment equal to that earned for the same time spent in a rehearsal or concert (about one-third of the national recording scale). The Utah Symphony management would advance the cost of the musicians' salaries and fringe benefits. Royalties received from the sale of the recordings would be paid to the musicians up to the national scale, once the management had recouped the amount it had advanced.

This Solomonic arrangement was presented to Herman D. Kenin, then president of the American Federation of Musicians, who told Mr. Abravanel that not only was the plan fair and equitable in every respect but also that it should be made available to any symphony orchestra.

Kenin attached one specific requirement: Inasmuch as the plan was a departure from the established federation policy, every musician must separately petition the local symphony management in writing, indicating his or her willingness to participate. It could not be a one-page petition signed by all orchestra members; instead, it had to be a separate sheet for each musician so as to avoid peer pressure.

The petitions were easily obtained from every Utah Symphony musician, and the program was off and running. As expected, there were grumblings from musicians in some other orchestras that were not recording, but the complaints went nowhere. In the first place, the plan had the personal blessing of the federation president, and in the second place it was available to any orchestra that wanted to participate. It was reported that here and there other orchestras tried to initiate such a program, but always a few musicians refused to go along, believing it was not in their personal interests.

The first Westminster recordings were made in the Assembly Hall on Temple Square in December 1957. The Tabernacle was not used because the LDS Church authorities felt that this might not sit well with Columbia Records, with whom the Tabernacle Choir had been recording for several years. While physical facilities of the Assembly Hall posed some problems, the acoustics were superb, and the finished product was outstanding.

That first recording project was three-pronged. The major work recorded was Handel's "Israel in Egypt," which Maurice Abravanel, the Utah Symphony, the combined choirs of the University of Utah, and the soloists had performed on the previous Saturday evening next door in the Tabernacle.

Another disc comprised three Gerswhin works: the Piano Concerto in F, with Reid Nibley as soloist; "An American in Paris"; and "Rhapsody in Blue." Recording these works was a somewhat daring undertaking since they already were available on more than twenty other discs.

The first session also included the Saint-Saens "Organ Symphony," with Alexander Schreiner as soloist on the Assembly Hall organ.

As intended, the new recordings made a real splash and raised eyebrows wherever they were sold or played. Interestingly, ten years after they were made, the Gershwin recordings sold over 10,000 copies in one year in West Germany alone.

The first Westminster recordings were followed by even more ambitious sessions in December 1958, also in the Assembly Hall. In this group was a re-recording of Handel's "Judas Maccabaeus," along with works ranging from Copland to Tchaikovsky, with Grofe, Grieg, Franck, and Gershwin in between. The Gershwin, by the way, was a premiere recording of an original suite from "Porgy and Bess" made by the composer himself and brought forward by George's lyricist and brother and close friend of Maurice Abravanel, Ira Gershwin.

More recordings were scheduled with Westminster the following season, only to have them canceled when it was learned that the company had gone into receivership. Sadly, the Utah Symphony collected only about ten cents on the dollar in royalties due. It took ten years for the symphony management to recoup its original investment and begin distributing excess royalties among the participating musicians. This continued until about 1978, when the old Westminster recordings were no longer being issued or reissued.

Fortunately, the enterprising Maurice Abravanel was able to persuade Vanguard Recording Society of New York to take up where Westminster had left off. The first Vanguard recordings were made in April 1961 on the University of Utah campus in what was known then as the Music Building, formerly the Student Union Building and now the Gardner Music Hall.

One of the first Vanguard albums was a re-recording of Leroy Robertson's "Book of Mormon Oratorio," this time a studio recording instead of the taping of a live performance. The quality of the finished product was only fair but was nonetheless an improvement over its predecessors. The sale of the albums was less than stellar as well.

Also in that first group of Vanguard recordings was a two-record album of the complete music from Tchaikovsky's "Nutcracker Ballet." The album made the New York Herald Tribune's list of thirteen best orchestral recordings released anywhere during that year. The recording continues to sell year after year.

The third title recorded in April 1961 was the Mass of St. Cecilia by Scarlatti, which somehow failed to make the charts.

So elated were the people at Vanguard that they returned eight months later, in December 1961, to record eight discs. This time, LDS Church officials gave permission to record the Honegger "King David" in the Salt Lake Tabernacle. The other works were recorded again at the University.

The longstanding and productive relationship between Vanguard Records, Maurice Abravanel, and the Utah Symphony proved to be one of the most significant developments in the orchestra's history. In 1963 they recorded the Mahler Eighth Symphony ("Symphony of a Thousand"), which led to recording the Mahler Seventh in 1964. The Seventh won the admiration and plaudits of the International Gustav Mahler Gesellschaft in Vienna, which conferred honorary membership upon Maurice Abravanel and hailed his recording as the best ever.

The Utah Symphony went on to record all nine of Mahler's symphonies at a time when this composing giant was not yet in vogue. They also recorded the Adagio from the Mahler Tenth Symphony, which was the first authentic recording of the great work.

The Vanguard collaboration came to a halt following the sessions in April 1969, when the company was struggling to overcome a sales slump in the classical records market. They had just recorded two Mahler symphonies (No. 3 and No. 9) and the Berlioz Requiem, which was the first to be recorded in what was called "surround sound."

By this time, the recording prowess of Maurice Abravanel and his Utah Symphony was well-known, and Vox Records was persuaded to begin recording the Utah Symphony in December 1970. Spanning three seasons, the Vox collaboration yielded recordings of all six Tchaikovsky symphonies and tone poems plus works by a variety of British and American composers.

Between the first and second recording sessions of Vox, the cooperative formula devised by Maurice Abravanel in 1957 came under attack from other orchestras around the country who, for whatever reasons, found this ingenious departure from "the book" inappropriate and unjustified. By this time, Mr.

Kenin had passed on and the federation was presided over by a new pharaoh "who knew not Joseph."

Additionally, the plan had run its course with the musicians of the Utah Symphony. By 1972 their season employment had expanded to the point where additional services for recording sessions were not as inviting as they had been. Also, by this time orchestra salaries under the master agreement had increased to the point where there was little likelihood that record royalties would ever exceed the advances made by the management to cover recording salaries and benefits. In practical terms, there was little hope for surplus royalties being paid to the participating musicians as they had been in the beginning.

Under a ten-year projection made in connection with the Ford Foundation's matching endowment grant, the length of the contract season for the musicians was to increase by approximately two weeks each year, reaching a full fifty-two week season in 1976. During those years of expansion, it was not always possible to use fully all of the services for which the musicians were to be paid. In view of this and the foregoing factors, the Utah Symphony musicians were credited against their annual guarantee for the full national recording scale in connection with the sessions for Vox in May 1972, and the cooperative plan became a thing of the past.

The Utah Symphony's association with Vox Records continued through May 1973 and would probably have extended beyond that season had it not been for a suggestion from the president of Vox, George de Mendelssohn-Bartholdy. He asked Abravanel to consider recording the rest of the Mahler symphonies. The maestro, however, felt it would be inappropriate to record the remaining Mahlers with Vox without at least giving Vanguard an opportunity to do them.

Seymour Solomon, who had in the meantime had serious health problems, was enthralled with the idea of completing the Mahler cycle on Vanguard's label, and in May 1974 he and his engineer flew with their equipment to Salt Lake City and recorded the Mahler First, Fifth, and Sixth Symphonies along with the Adagio from the Tenth Symphony.

The door now being wide open, between January and December 1975 the Utah Symphony recorded for Angel, Vox, CRI, and Orion. The Vox sessions in May yielded four discs devoted entirely to the music of Edvard Grieg, including the Piano Concerto, with Utah's Grant Johannesen as soloist.

In May 1976 Vanguard again returned to Utah to record a four-record album comprising the four symphonies and three shorter works of Brahms.

Six months later Maurice Abravanel returned from a trip to Paris, suffering from chest pains, and underwent triple by-pass heart surgery. It appeared that the recording sessions with the maestro at the helm might be at an end, but within another six months, in May of 1977, he was back with his musicians. They recorded for Vanguard the seven symphonies of Sibelius, including some that Abravanel had never heard, let alone conducted. This would almost have to be some kind of record for the medical annals, particularly when one considers that Maurice went on in September of that same year to conduct all the concerts in a four-week, four-country European tour.

It began to appear that Angel Records would be the successor to Vanguard and Vox as principal collaborators. Angel had recorded the Harris "Folk Song Symphony" in May 1975 and returned in May 1977 for a recording of the Bloch Sacred Service, which was underwritten by one of the orchestra's most avid fans and benefactors, Dean Eggertsen.

In May 1978 Angel returned to record four discs with Maurice Abravanel and the Utah Symphony. Commitments had already been made with Capitol Records for the following year, but a shuffling of that company's top management led to an unceremonious cancellation of the recording dates.

The last recording to be made under the baton of Maurice Abravanel was a work he had championed over the years, Leroy Robertson's "Oratorio from the Book of Mormon," this time with the Mormon Tabernacle Choir for the CBS Records label. This recording took place in the Tabernacle the week following a performance in the same building in May 1978. During the same month Abravanel and the Utah Symphony recorded a new work called "Colloquy," by Ussachevsky.

Another ambitious recording project involving eight sessions in the summer of 1979 was planned with Vanguard but later canceled because of Abravanel's decision in April of that year to retire from active conducting on the advice of his doctors. In a valiant effort to save the project, Gregory and Solomon considered every reasonable substitute conductor for the sessions, even making telephone calls to London and Australia, but to no avail.

Maurice Abravanel would have been the first to decry an end to Utah Symphony recordings, having invested so much of his time and effort to establishing them in the first place and having generously given of himself by conducting them all without fee.

There being services available, and inasmuch as the orchestra had now moved into its new home, Symphony Hall, the Utah Symphony decided to join hands with the *Salt Lake Tribune* to record an album of popular favorites, "Tops in Pops," under its new assistant conductor, Robert Henderson, in July 1980.

With Abravanel's successor, Varujan Kojian, on board, the Utah Symphony embarked on another productive relationship with a small but artistically superior company in Los Angeles, Varese Sarabande Records, which recorded albums in June, September, and October 1981 and in March 1982.

Of his efforts that first season, *Stereo Review* reported, "Conductor Varujan Kojian is off to a most auspicious start with a Berlioz Symphonie Fantastique that is outstanding musically and an audiophile's dream sonically. Their performance ranks with the best of its recorded predecessors, including those led by Pierre Monteux and Jean Martinon and Leonard Bernstein's with the Orchestre National de France."

Alongside Kojian's recordings of the standard repertoire, Varese Sarabande also involved him and the Utah Symphony in recordings of outstanding film scores such as "Robin Hood," "Star Wars," and so on.

In between, the Utah Symphony, under its associate conductor, Charles Ketcham, did a world premiere recording of Richard Adler's "Wilderness Suite" for RCA under a grant from American Telephone and Telegraph in February 1983.

Joseph Silverstein succeeded Varujan Kojian as music director and conductor in 1983, and by November of that year the Utah Symphony had entered into a four-year agreement to record for a Minneapolis firm, Pro Arte Records. Their first project was a recording of the Mendelssohn Violin Concerto with Silverstein appearing as conductor and soloist, together with three Mendelssohn overtures. *Stereo Review* chose this recording as the "Best of the Month," calling the performance "just about ideal," favorably comparing it to a recording by Sir Thomas Beecham and predicting that the disc would "give all those gilt-edged versions a real run for the money."

Also in 1983 was a Varese Sarabande recording of music from Crawford Gates's "Promised Valley," conducted by the composer himself.

By 1985 Silverstein and the Utah Symphony had produced three more albums for Pro Arte, bringing the total to four, and the recording tradition appeared to be alive and well in Salt Lake City.

It is estimated that between 1957 and 1985 more than two million Utah Symphony recordings were sold throughout the United States and Canada and in Western Europe, Asia, and South America. In all, some 120 discs were recorded, several of which were released and re-released both domestically and internationally.

In addition to the 120 albums bearing the Utah Symphony name, members of the Utah Symphony billed as the Columbia Symphony participated in recordings of the Tabernacle Choir on several occasions.

Top: *Utah Symphony headquarters at Bennett's, 55 West 1st South, Salt Lake City, Utah, 1949-1979.*
Bottom: *Ardean Watts conducting the Utah Symphony in one of its many student assembly concerts.*

Top: *Photo of a portion of the orchestra at the Utah Symphony's first concert for inmates of the Utah State Prison.*
Bottom: *Utah Symphony and Mormon Tabernacle Choir at the dedication of O. C. Tanner Amphitheatre at Springdale, Utah, near Zion National Park, June 11, 1976, as part of seven-concert U. S. Bicentennial series marking the first collaboration of the two groups. Concerts were conducted by Maurice Abravanel, Jerold Ottley and Crawford Gates.*

Top: *Utah Symphony, Ardean Watts conducting, in Second Annual Salt Lake Arts Festival free concert on Main Street, June 14, 1978.*
Bottom: *Utah Symphony performing at benefit dinner concert at Salt Lake City's ZCMI Mall.*

Top: *Spectacular setting for Utah Symphony summer concerts at Snowbird, Utah.*
Bottom: *Val A. Browning Center for the Performing Arts on the Weber State College campus. The Utah Symphony has given its Ogden series concerts in this facility's Austad Auditorium since 1965. Prior thereto the orchestra played in the Ogden High School Auditorium.*

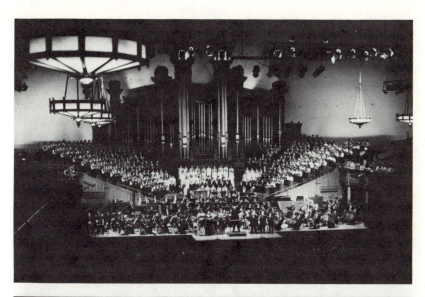

Top: *Maurice Abravanel conducting Mahler Eighth Symphony at Utah Symphony's 1977-78 season finale in Salt Lake Tabernacle. Appearing with the orchestra were Utah Chorale, U of U Combined Choruses, Utah Boys' Choir, South High Girls' Choir and seven soloists.*
Bottom: *Utah Symphony and Mormon Tabernacle Choir under Maurice Abravanel performing Leroy Robertson's "Oratorio from the Book of Mormon," May 25, 26, 1978, in the Salt Lake Tabernacle.*

ROLF W. KAY

Maestro Maurice Abravanel concludes his distinguished conducting career at the Utah Symphony's season finale performance of the Verdi Requiem with Utah Chorale and solosits in the Salt Lake Tabernacle, Saturday, April 21, 1979. The concert also marked the end of the orchestra's last season in the Tabernacle which had served as its "home" for 32 years.

Top: *Honoring Utah Symphony's opening concerts, Sept. 14-15, 1979, in new $12 million Symphony Hall, Utah Gov. Scott M. Matheson proclaims Utah Symphony Week. (l-r) Herold L. Gregory, Utah Symphony executive director; Gov. Matheson; Obert C. Tanner, Utah Bicentennial Committee chairman; Wendell J. Ashton, Utah Symphony president.*
Bottom: *At the opening of Symphony Hall, Obert C. Tanner (l.), chairman, Utah Committee for the American Bicentennial, greets President Gordon B. Hinckley, First Presidency of the LDS Church, as Utah Gov. Scott M. Matheson and Maurice Abravanel look on.*

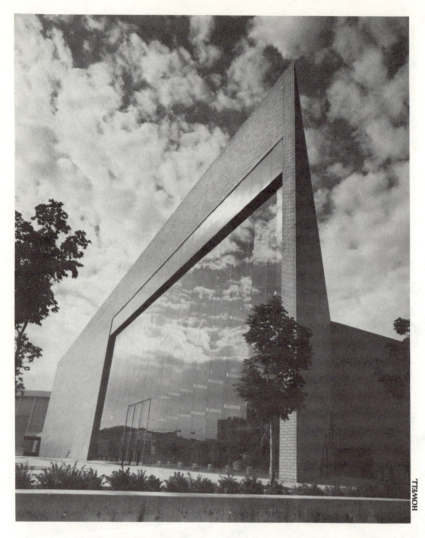

Gleaming, new Symphony Hall became the home of the Utah Symphony in 1979 following 32 years of concerts in the venerable Mormon Tabernacle.

Top: *Formal photograph of Utah Symphony under Joseph Silverstein at Symphony Hall, the orchestra's home since 1979.*
Bottom: *Utah Symphony at Symphony Hall, Salt Lake City, Utah.*

CHAPTER 15

MOUNTAIN WEST BY BUS

Mention the Lewis Brothers
Stages—buses—to a Utah Symphony musician and just about
anything can happen. Each one may react differently as
memories and reminiscences crowd in, but none will deny that
the Lewis buses have been almost as involved with their lives in
the symphony as anything outside of their instruments.

Many of them can describe in detail the interior of every
bus Lewis has operated for nearly forty-five years. They have
practically lived in them for days at a time. On hundreds of
occasions, the busloads of players left (and still leave) Salt Lake
City two at a time, bound for destinations within the state and
beyond, even outside the Mountain West, to perform scheduled
concerts.

What the eighty to eight-five musicians and Maurice
Abravanel did for thirty-two years in the acoustically-opulent
Salt Lake Tabernacle, of course, provided the foundation for
their musical outreach. There they performed their season
subscription concerts, and from there they extended their
season, to eight concerts in Ogden and three in Logan. There,
too, they recorded performances for radio syndication (from
Los Angeles and Sacramento to Pittsburgh and Washington,

D.C.) and for records. And there they found valued sponsors to finance youth concerts, "pops" concerts, and the "Salute to Youth" for young artists.

As early as the 1940s, the Youth Concerts were given some support by the Kearns-Tribune Corporation, and by 1950-51 the annual amount contributed was $3,200. The following year the AG Stores, an organization of grocers, came into the picture as a cosponsor supplying approximately $3,400 of the $4,900 package. The *Salt Lake Tribune* was the lone sponsor in 1953-54, providing $4,900 for the orchestra's coffers, after which AG took over for more than ten years.

The Kearns-Tribune organization has remained a backer of the symphony, underwriting a number of orchestra-sponsored events, including the appearance of such touring ensembles as the New York Philharmonic, the Philadelphia Orchestra, and the Chicago Symphony.

One of the longer symphony-sponsor affiliations, the AG Stores Youth Concert series was a satisfying experience that regularly filled the Tabernacle with young people of the area. In the 1960s a "Family Night," was added and the annual contribution reached $6,500. General manager Donald P. Lloyd and advertising manager Claude Purles of AG, along with Abravanel and the symphony management, brought Vernon J. LeeMaster, supervisor of music in the Salt Lake City schools, into the cooperative effort. Don Lloyd and his wife, Helen, became fast friends of the Abravanels and joined the symphony movement. Helen has long been a prominent figure in the Symphony Guild, and Don, as a member of the symphony board, was instrumental in securing Joseph Silverstein as conductor through his work on the search committee.

For a quarter of a century, the *Deseret News* has sponsored the "Salute to Youth" concerts, a creation of Abravanel for the purpose of giving exposure and honor to promising young musicians whose performances merited an appearance with the Utah Symphony.

Early in the 1950s, Violinist LaVar Krantz won honors at the Utah State Fair; Abravanel responded by giving him a solo spot with the orchestra and then installed the young musician in the first chair of the second violin section. The following year Percy Kalt, violinist, and Kay Hicks, a promising young Salt Lake pianist, were winners at the state fair and were invited to perform with the symphony. Kalt played the Bach Concerto in E Major; Miss Hicks performed a movement of the Mozart Piano Concerto in A Major.

It was not until Maurice put the spotlight on young David Brown, a Salt Lake City pianist who had won a national award for his playing, however, that the "Salute to Youth" series, as such, became a reality. Feeling that the teenage keyboard artist was as deserving of tribute as the many athletes amply honored for feats at every level, the maestro presented Mr. Brown with the symphony in the Brahms Piano Concerto No. 1 in D Minor at the Tabernacle on November 25, 1960. Annually, from that point on, several young musicians have appeared with the symphony on the Deseret News Salute to Youth Night.

As an "alumnus" of that program, Eugene Watanabe, a fourteen-year-old virtuoso, won the Music Teachers National Association Competition in 1985 and in the summer appeared with the Utah Symphony at Sundance in an amazing "double." After playing the Mozart Piano Concerto No. 21 in C Major with the orchestra, Eugene turned to the violin and, with Ricklin Nobis at the piano, performed the Mozart Sonata No. 6.

The "UTOCO Pops" concerts were sponsored by the Utah Oil Refining Company before it became American Oil; they brought annual contributions that reached $10,000 in 1960. Initiated as a Salt Lake Tabernacle feature, they were expanded to include performances at Provo, Ogden, and Logan. Meanwhile, Utah Power and Light Company sponsored two annual concerts for children at the Bear River High School auditorium at Garland and at Orem, American Fork, or Pleasant Grove. Sponsors of single concerts along the way were Safeway Stores (Family Night) in 1960-61 and Prudential Federal Savings (Salute to Youth) in 1962-63.

Such was the fare that awaited Abravanel and his players when they returned from bus trips far and wide. They were busy at home, it is true, but as one talented publicist on the symphony staff wrote in the 1970s, "Maestro Abravanel and the

Symphony aren't content to hoard their artistry like musical chattel within the Tabernacle walls, to parcel it out sparingly. Of more than 1,400 Utah Symphony concerts in the past 25 years, a third were school or youth concerts, many of them presented in gymnasiums and auditoriums throughout the Intermountain West without charge. Subsidies from the state of Utah keep the program strong, a program that every three years touches virtually all state high school students and thousands of elementary school people in Idaho, Montana, Wyoming, Colorado and Arizona as well as Utah.

"Scarcely one in 12 of the Symphony's non-school concerts is performed in Salt Lake County, evidence of the ensemble's commitment to a 'regional' orchestra concept. Bus seats are as familiar to the musicians as their orchestral chairs.... Among cities like Los Angeles, Seattle, New York and Washington on the Utah Symphony itinerary fall towns like Nampa, Idaho, and Roosevelt, Utah.

"In 1969, the southern Utah town of Loa (population 369) had a visitor, one that touched the families of farmers and ranchers and storekeepers and businessmen alike with new understanding. Many in the town had never heard live classical music. They heard it that day, as few orchestras in the world can play it, when Maestro Maurice Abravanel and the Utah Symphony came calling. In a town of 369, more than 900 came to hear the music.

"This is the thrust of the Utah Symphony, according to Maestro Abravanel, who gave it direction—to reach new ears, to instill new love for the great art and the personal experience of music. They do it, these 85 musicians and their eminent conductor, through a determination to serve as a 'regional' orchestra, and to reach young people in as many schools as they can, to show them what music offers."

Not often did the Utah Symphony go beyond its state borders by bus until the late 1960s, but there were a few jaunts into Idaho and Wyoming ahead of that time. Lewis Brothers had been carrying the players throughout Utah to as far south as St. George on the west, and Moab on the east, and Logan and Garland on the north. Then, on March 18, 1954, the troupe went to Twin Falls, Idaho, where a pianist, Willetta Warberg, had been located. Before her home folk, she joined the symphony under Abravanel as soloist in the Franck "Symphonic Variations." Later, in 1956-57, Pocatello and Rexburg were included in a "concert tour" of Southeastern Idaho.

On only one or two overnight trips inside or outside the state did Abravanel ride the bus. He was soon to find that transportation was needed at the stopovers and that meetings and visits with music people and official personnel merely delayed the bus departures. So, in order to avoid exorbitant costs of "taxis" and the like employed by a previous conductor, it became the order for manager Huck Gregory to drive the maestro and Lucy, who always accompanied her husband on such trips, in his own car. Thus, the business as well as the musical end of the organization were available to the parties involved.

Idaho potato country in the Snake River Valley has known its moments in Utah Symphony history, with Idaho Falls quite often the focal point. There in the Civic Auditorium on November 12, 1958, Paul Whiteman made his debut as conductor of the symphony in a four-concert Idaho-Utah engagement.

Huck Gregory chauffeured the giant of the "big band" era and watched the proceedings with interest. He recalls that Ardean Watts had made the trip to play the Gershwin "Rhapsody in Blue" on the program. The talented and versatile Watts, who served for years as assistant conductor under Abravanel, had become official pianist with the departure of Reid Nibley for study in Europe. Apparently Ardean made quite a hit. Whiteman told Gregory: "That cat plays that thing better than anyone I have heard in all the performances I've conducted."

Huck found Whiteman, with his size and distinctive features, "the most visible person I've ever known." He tells of stopping with his guest at a small cafe in Malad, Idaho, on the way home from Idaho Falls and finding there was no chance the noted band man could go unrecognized. The waitress's eyes widened, and she asked, "Are you Paul Whiteman" The affirmative answer "turned the place on its ear," Gregory says with a laugh.

Whiteman, incidentally, conducted the symphony in Ogden before finally getting back to Salt Lake City for the Symphony Ball on November 14 and a concert in the Tabernacle the following night.

During the next season, on February 6, 1959, the Utah Symphony headed south, this time to cover a first booking in Las Vegas, Nevada, performing an afternoon youth concert ahead of the main event.

Two performances of the "Nutcracker" with the Civic Ballet took the orchestra back to Idaho Falls on November 25, 1960, and, on a cold and snowy January 6, 1962, the symphony traveled to Rock Springs, Wyoming. The bus ride almost came to an end in a blizzard on Parley's Summit during the return trip.

That season the Utah Symphony performed fifty-three concerts, up only slightly from the forty-seven in 1956-57, excluding the usual thirteen radio broadcasts sponsored by Kennecott Copper and eleven "Nutcracker" performances at Kingsbury Hall. By 1966-67, when the orchestra made its first overseas trip to Greece, the concert total was up to eighty, but the radio broadcasts were gone, and the "Nutcracker" added only seven services for the players. Obviously the time had come to expand some horizons. The buses had not crossed the Utah state line all season—airplanes, yes, but not buses.

Enter Shirl Swenson and Uncle Sam. Swenson, a retired Air Force Colonel, joined the symphony staff in early 1967 as a public relations and booking agent, with special emphasis on securing Title I and III funds for school concerts through the government's Health, Education, and Welfare Department. The Seattle Symphony had toured extensively through Alaska on the program, receiving substantial grants for the concerts.

When schools found they could put the funds to use in other areas, however, the money was no longer available to the symphony, and Swenson's job took on a new twist. He talked with Abravanel about concert bookings; the maestro told him to sign "as many as you can, I'll never say 'Uncle.'"

Shirl headed in every direction in its turn, booking concerts as he went, and the results began to show immediately. That fall he sent the maestro and symphony by bus to seven cities in

Idaho. Before the season was over, they had played 105 concerts and performed for twenty-two presentations by the Utah Civic Ballet and twelve University of Utah Opera performances. Besides going to Boise, Caldwell, Nampa, Burley, Rexburg, Idaho Falls, and Pocatello, Idaho, the orchestra traveled by bus to Las Vegas for concerts at the University of Nevada and up to forty performances in Utah outside the Salt Lake Valley. Monticello, Hurricane, Cedar City, and Roosevelt were included.

The next season's touring schedule started in the northwest again, leading to a total of 107 concerts with thirty-five ballet performances and ten operas. The buses wound their way to Ontario, Oregon; Missoula, Montana; and Pocatello, Boise, Caldwell, Nampa, Moscow, Rexburg, and Idaho Falls, Idaho, over a two-week period in October after the first subscription concert in the Tabernacle.

Another tour went to Fort Lewis College in Durango, Colorado, for two concerts, and visits to Moab, Blanding, and Price, Utah. In the spring, Swenson sent the performers to Grand Junction, Gunnison, and Alamosa, Colorado; Wingate, Gallup, Silver City, Las Cruces, Portales, and Los Alamos, New Mexico; and El Paso, Texas, with a stopover at Moab on the return trip.

For Shirl it was not just a matter of booking the symphony, but assuring a guarantee to supplement national Endowment of the Arts funds. His method was to first approach the mayor. One of his first was in Price, where he suggested ten committees to secure $200 each. They became the Boosters of Utah Symphony—BUS—with the slogan "Don't Miss the BUS."

Each year the schedule became more crowded as Swenson stopped at almost every town in ten western states. Once, the orchestra accused him of booking a "mirage" when he sent the players to China Lake, a "dry lake" north of Edwards Air Force Base near Los Angeles County's Antelope Valley. It turned out to be an actual concert site, but the troupers had to drive to Barstow for lodgings.

In the 1970s, Shirl built the bookings to where the orchestra was playing 175 concerts in the weeks alloted. One night his telephone rang. He picked it up and heard someone say "Uncle" and then hang up.

A minute later the phone rang again. It was Abravanel, laughing but adding that he was saying "Uncle." There wasn't the time to handle any more concerts, he said, and he implored Shirl to hold the line on the number of bookings. That's the way it stayed until more weeks were added to the players' contracts and the way cleared to add more concerts.

Playing the Mountain West by bus has not been easy for the maestro and his musicians, but has been part of their dedication. In the fall of 1959, the orchestra moved to a new rehearsal hall in the remodeled University of Utah Music Hall, and the players made their way to the bus depot on West Temple near Fourth South, with no parking places. Later the old Christian Science Church at Sixth East and South Temple became available as the rehearsal hall. For some years, the buses picked up the players at this site, and parking was available for their cars. As an interim, the old Immanuel Baptist Church at Fourth East and Second South served for rehearsals, and the players went back to the bus depot. Now they board the buses at the newer depot at Fifth West and Fifth South, where they can park their cars, and travel over 20,000 miles a year, not including international tours, playing to a combined audience of over a quarter of a million people.

CHAPTER **16**

COMING OF AGE

$$T$$he Utah Symphony was coming to the end of its twenty-fifth anniversary season in the spring of 1965 when there began a series of developments that would have a profound effect upon its entire future. International tours to the music capitals of the world and unprecedented new sources of income were soon to bring about major changes in the course the orchestra would follow from that point on.

The first international tour in 1966 to Greece, Yugoslavia, Austria, West Germany, and England was one of the most momentous events in the Utah Symphony's history. Beginning at the same time, a Ford Foundation matching endowment grant was to provide a financial base on which the symphony would "come of age" among the world's great orchestras.

Both were mammoth projects in the symphony's development, and each required a major fund-raising effort—tasks made to order for two masters of the art, T. Bowring Woodbury and Wendell J. Ashton. Close friends, prominent in banking and advertising and in public affairs, they were new in administrative leadership of the Utah Symphony and, with the new assignments, willingly accepted the challenge. Seizing each opportunity as it appeared, they blew aside skeptics and doubters in a campaign that in time would see the symphony shed its part-time operation and adopt a full-time fifty-two-week season.

They were fortunate, however, to find the orchestra and its business operation well-geared for the venture—virtually in orbit and waiting for the thrust of the Woodbury-Ashton afterburner. The combination of Maurice Abravanel and Huck Gregory had produced some remarkable advances in the front office, while the maestro and his players were scoring new triumphs in concert halls and on records.

The symphony's total income grew from $153,956 in 1957-58 to $387,647 in 1964-65, and there were no deficits. Reflecting this growth was a steady increase in ticket sales for the Tabernacle subscription series. Huck Gregory came up with the orchestra's first newsletter, "Sympho-News," for which he established a mailing list that gave it wide distribution. These innovations, with other promotions and expansions of the subscription series from nine to thirteen concerts, boosted annual box-office revenues from $41,000 to $84,000 over the eight-year course. By 1964-65, the sale of season tickets alone had reached $60,000, and Gregory had implemented the "recycling," or resale, of unused tickets, creating what has become an important source of income and a courtesy to symphony patrons.

Front office costs were held to a minimum with small staffs efficiently handling the work. Gregory, Elsie Shepherd, and part-timer Harold Gottfredson (current property manager and a longtime member of the trombone section of the orchestra) handled the business end of the operation in 1957-58. Elsie retired in 1958, and by 1965 the staff had grown to six members—Gregory, administrative assistant Gladys Shalberg, program editor Gilbert Scharffs, publicity director Mitzi Glauser, and two box-office attendants. Glauser had taken over the public-relations operation the David W. Evans Advertising Agency had so graciously furnished for several years through one of its executives, Jimmy Hodgson, a former sports writer who eventually went on to head the Evans firm.

It was not until 1966 that Shirl Swenson joined the staff, and in 1967 Carleen Landes, now the artistic manager, returned to handle a myriad of duties, including those of office manager and assistance at the box office. A granddaughter of Alfred Press and a niece of Ross Beckstead, former symphony players, Carleen had worked in the office under David Romney from 1949 to 1953. Fourteen years later she found a career with the orchestra. She acts as orchestra coordinator and assistant to the music director, Joseph Silverstein, and performs other duties in her present office.

Abravanel, meanwhile, left little to be desired in the steady development of artistic excellence in ensemble performance. Indicative of the esteem in which the maestro and his players were held on the home front were the messages of Governor George D. Clyde and LDS Church President David O. McKay marking the opening of the symphony's twenty-fifth anniversary season on October 14, 1964. The governor designated the symphony as "one of our great cultural ambassadors," while President McKay, in recognizing its "significant contributions to the cultural life of our community and state," added: "We share with all Utahns sincere pride in the national and international acclaim that the orchestra's musical efforts have brought to Utah and its people.

"To Maurice Abravanel, the Utah Symphony's tireless and dedicated music director and conductor, I extend warm congratulations and best wishes. Many have contributed both in personal effort and financial support to the development of the Utah Symphony, but it is Mr. Abravanel whose vision and determination have made of the Orchestra an organization that is respected everywhere."

Presented "In Memorium of Fred E. Smith" (the first president of the symphony, who died in 1963), the season opener included the world premiere of Crawford Gates's "Portrait of a Great Leader." The work, dedicated to President McKay, was commissioned by the Utah Symphony through a grant from Joseph Rosenblatt, a constant benefactor of the orchestra.

Gates said he was "impressed.... by Mr. Rosenblatt's statement to the effect that President McKay was held in such high esteem, respect and affection by members of all faiths as to suggest the appropriateness of matching this view with an appropriate portrait of dignity and meaning." This he did with a composition in four movements entitled, in order, "The Mantle of a Prophet," "The Landsman of Huntsville," "The Poet of Human Charity," and "The Seer of Human Triumph."

Another new creation by Gates, his Symphony No. 3, was among five works premiered by Abravanel and the symphony in a University of Utah contemporary music festival at the end of the season in Kingsbury Hall. Also included on the program were three other Utah compositions, "The Pearl," a ballet suite by William Fowler of the university faculty scored with guitar played by the composer; Laurence Lyon's "Festival Prelude"; Robert Cundick's "A Full House" Suite, with Reid Nibley at the piano; and Henry Lazarof's "Odes for Orchestra."

Unfortunately, the concert was injected with somewhat of a sour note for the writers and performers before it ever started. On the day of the event, April 10, 1965, *Deseret News* music critic Harold Lundstrom suggested in his column that the whole menu might be "garbage." He was anything but encouraging to the would-be concertgoer as he conjectured: "Even if you are free tonight, will the 2,000 chairs up at Kingsbury hall be as they were Monday evening [a concert by the Beaux Arts Trio of New York]? It will depend on whether you prefer hearing five compositions never heard before or numbers last Monday you knew.

"There will probably be some listener tonight at the University of Utah Contemporary Festival who will turn to his wife and say, 'You don't want to stay and hear all this garbage, do you, dear'? Another at intermission may say, 'Can't we go now? Why should I have to feel so uncomfortably bored at the end of a long day?' In a word—there is no accounting for musical tastes."

By way of contrast, James Fitzpatrick, writing in the *Salt Lake Tribune* the next morning, asserted that the "cause of contemporary music—Western style—advanced" as a result of the concert. He found the Lazarof to be a "densely textured and meticulously scored" work that "varied from shimmering incandescence to rigorous assertion with style, grace and wit."

The Gates symphony he regarded as the "most ambitious and most severe of the works on the program," containing "passages of extraordinary tenderness and beauty."

The silver anniversary season also took note of Leroy Robertson's retirement from the University of Utah music faculty, the orchestra performing on February 5 his "Saguaro" Overture. Based on the Arizona State University "Alma Mater" by Miles Dresskill, the work had been commissioned by Dr. G. Homer Durham, then president of Arizona State University, and premiered by the Phoenix Symphony the previous October 19.

A first local performance of Mahler's Symphony No. 7 ("Song of the Night") and an evening of French choral works, Honegger's "Judith" and Milhaud's "Pacem in terris," were among other season highlights. Netania Davrath, Blanche Christensen, JoAnn Ottley, Val Stuart, and Marvin Sorensen were soloists with the symphony and University of Utah chorus in the Honegger. Florence Kopleff and Roy Samuelson performed solo roles in the Milhaud.

Of particular significance, as it turned out, was the return of Gina Bachauer, the renowned virtuoso pianist from Greece, in March for one more of several appearances with Abravanel and the symphony. After a brilliant performance of the Rachmaninoff Piano Concerto No. 2 in C Minor on an all-Russian program that also included the Shostakovich Fifth Symphony, the guest initiated a Utah Symphony trip to Athens. Highly impressed over the years with the skill and spirit of the symphony under Abravanel, she almost single-handedly secured an invitation for the Utah organization to the Athens Festival.

When the invitation arrived, it received little serious consideration from the old guard around symphony headquarters. Even Abravanel and Gregory thought it was a most gracious gesture but felt that such a trip was entirely out of reach.

But by then Woodbury and Ashton had taken charge of the administrative chores, and they immediately envisioned in such a tour the opportunity to put the Utah Symphony "on the map." Needless to say, the invitation was accepted.

A succession of changes in the presidency had resulted in T. Bowring Woodbury's acceptance of the post on March 29,

1965, after less than a year on the board. The rapid turnover in leadership started on July 16, 1963, when an ailing Ray Ashton resigned after eleven years as president. He was succeeded by O. Preston Robinson, then publisher of the *Deseret News,* who served for a season. New assignments forced his resignation, and in March of 1964 he relinquished the gavel to Jack Gallivan, publisher of the *Salt Lake Tribune,* who served until Woodbury took over a year later.

"By" Woodbury, as he was known far and wide, followed a natural course into his activity with the Utah Symphony organization. Besides being drawn to such civic affairs through his talents as a motivator and fund-raiser, he had a genuine interest in the arts, which he shared with his wife, "Bubbles," the former Beulah Blood. Music had been a companion since his college days in the late 1920s and early '30s. He is remembered by old-timers at such haunts as the Coconut Grove, Lagoon, and Saltair as a popular dance-band leader.

Early in his business career, he joined Culver Aircraft as sales manager in Hawaii and became president of the firm in Wichita, Kansas. There he became a member of the Wichita Symphony Orchestra board of directors and was instrumental in arranging an appearance of the Mormon Tabernacle Choir with that orchestra in 1958. Shortly before that concert, however, By and Bubbles had left to preside over the British Mission of The Church of Jesus Christ of Latter-day Saints in London. With their release, having disposed of the business in Wichita, the Woodburys returned to Salt Lake City, where By affiliated with Zions First National Bank in an executive role.

Woodbury's first and perhaps most productive move, so far as the future of the symphony was concerned, was to persuade his close friend Wendell J. Ashton to become his "general" vice-president and head an impressive V-P corps that included Donald P. Lloyd, Neal A. Maxwell, David Lawrence McKay, and the Symphony Guild president, Mrs. Yvonne Willey.

Ashton, who was soon to succeed a stricken leader and serve as symphony president for nineteen years, found himself in almost the strangest position he had ever been in. Never, to this point, had there been any room in his busy life for symphony music. He had absolutely no interest in symphony concerts and assiduously avoided them while encouraging his first wife, Marian Reynolds Ashton, a devotee of the symphony, to attend with her mother. Wendell's entertainment world was wrapped up in a package marked "Sports," and not until Abravanel and his players became a major concern in the Ashton portfolio was the symphony allowed to enter.

It was shortly after Marian succumbed to a six-year fight with cancer in 1963 that Ashton and Woodbury first joined in a fund-raising crusade. Wendell, out of love and respect for his deceased wife, had accepted the chairmanship of the American Cancer Society's 1964 annual statewide campaign for funds. In organizing the program, he secured the services of By Woodbury to head the drive in Salt Lake City, but little did he know what the price would be. Wendell had no way of knowing that Woodbury, most impressed with his friend's ability to collect money for the cancer society, would soon be after him to return the favor.

Not long afterward Wendell married Belva Barlow, secretary to Dean Henry Eyring at the University of Utah and a former staff member of United States Senator Arthur V. Watkins in Washington, D.C. He had settled into his role as a busy advertising executive and was engaged in other civic affairs when his friend By asked him to join him in the symphony administration. But Wendell wanted no part of it, and in his search for a way out, he sought the aid of his new bride. He knew of her feeling that he had too many civic responsibilities for a man with five of his six children still at home.

To his surprise, however, Belva said: "Wendell, I think this is one position you ought to take." Along with some added ammunition from Woodbury, who had reached her first, she suggested to Wendell that most of his activities were "Church-related" and that the proffered assignment would give him an opportunity to broaden his contacts and interests.

Her husband knew she was right. He had served the LDS Church as a missionary to England, a stake president, and in various other capacities. Much of his fund-raising activity had been for the Church, although he had also worked on campaigns for the Boy Scouts of America, the United Fund, and the University of Utah. His varied career was spent largely in positions with Church institutions, the one major exception being his years as an executive with Gillham Advertising Agency under his friend Marion Nelson. Prior to that, he had been managing editor of the Church-owned *Deseret News*, and when he left Gillham's it was to organize and serve as the first director of public communications for the Church. He then returned to the *Deseret News* as its publisher, and in 1985 he left both the *News* and the Utah Symphony to become a mission president for the Church in England.

The orchestra could have had no better combination than Woodbury and Ashton at the administrative helm when the Athens and Ford Foundation challenges emerged. Woodbury had only six months to function in his new role, but he used every available hour in building the momentum and supplying the vision that started both projects on their way to a successful conclusion. It was as much because of his friend By's vision and foresight as it was Belva's logic that Ashton accepted the position of first vice-president. "I admired By Woodbury because he thought big," he says. "He really had a big vision."

Woodbury's "big vision" at the time was a Utah Symphony winging over Europe with triumphant stops in the capitals of five countries. It would take $150,000, nearly twice the symphony contributions of the season before, to finance the tour, but Woodbury and Ashton knew it could be done.

Hardly had the tour reached the planning stage and the drive for funds initiated, however, when Woodbury suffered a massive stroke. Ashton assumed the role of acting president and moved ahead while his friend fought for his life. The stricken administrator furnished what motivating spirit he could muster between his physical therapy treatments, but the main burden soon fell upon the shoulders of Ashton and the board. They set about raising the $150,000, and in the spring of 1966 they targeted the U.S. State Department for a key contribution of $50,000. To that point, the largest gift had been a $17,500 check from the LDS Church.

Knowing he had little chance as a Republican facing a

Democratic administration, Ashton asked board member and prominent Democrat Calvin W. Rawlings to handle the bid for government funds. Rawlings accepted and started the ball rolling with a call to Senator Frank E. Moss, another powerful Utah Democrat with seven years' experience in Congress. The senator took up the quest, helped arrange an application for $50,000 from the National Endowment for the Arts, and enlisted the aid of Vice-President Hubert H. Humphrey.

Shortly thereafter Humphrey gave assurance that the grant had been approved, and the symphony honored Senator Moss at a public reception, presenting him with a beautiful plaque for his efforts. The whole thing was premature, however, as Humphrey had no authority. Standing in the way all along had been the National Endowment chairman, Roy Larsen of Time-Life, Inc., who had the final say in the matter. In no uncertain terms, he had let it be known that the Utah Symphony was near the bottom of his list of recognized American orchestras and thereby soundly rejected the funding.

With President Lyndon B. Johnson offering the last hope, Senator Moss put his plaque under his arm and headed for the White House. He also took with him Utah's immensely popular Democratic governor, Calvin L. Rampton, a long-time acquaintance of the president; Rampton was in Washington on another matter. As Rampton recalls the incident in his memoirs, "Moss laid the plaque on the President's desk and said: 'Lyndon, how would you suggest I approach this matter when I have to give this back' The President looked at his fellow Democrat and said, 'I'll call Larsen.' We got the $50,000."

Senator Moss doesn't remember the circumstance as being quite that dramatic, but his friend Cal's recollection is vivid. Both agree that the final order came from the White House, and, as the senator was to learn, President Johnson didn't stop with Larsen, but called Secretary of State Dean Rusk as well. A day or two after his visit with the president, Moss was called to Rusk's office and was asked by the secretary of state just what the symphony needed to assure its tour. Moss said $50,000, so Rusk arranged for that amount. Later, when the money was delivered, Moss was informed it was in checks from three different agencies, prompting Cal Rawlings to remark, "Man alive, did he ever scrape the barrel to get that money!"

What had been done to get the federal grant was typical of the entire campaign for the tour funds. Ashton threw himself into the project and, in the absence of Woodbury, not only commanded the crusade but made many personal contacts with effective results.

During the 1965-66 season, his first in a symphony role—acting vice-president, no less—he had "taken the plunge" by attending concerts in the Tabernacle with Belva and became impressed with the "spirit" emanating from the music of Abravanel and his players. He was very much in the planning, also, for the evening on March 16, 1966, marking the thousandth concert (backed by 5,000 rehearsals) of the Utah Symphony since its inaugural performance on May 8, 1940. The brilliant all-Beethoven program, with Isaac Stern as soloist in the Violin Concerto, climaxed "Utah Symphony Day" in Utah, as proclaimed by Governor Rampton.

Six months later, on September 1, one week before he was to lead the overseas tour, Wendell Ashton was elected by the board to be the eighth president of the Utah Symphony. "He took the occasion," as reported in the *Salt Lake Tribune*, "to say the symphony will be 'eternally grateful' to Gina Bachauer, Greek concert pianist, and Christopher Athas, Salt Lake City businessman, for their part in arranging the orchestra's forthcoming European tour." On the following Sunday, the touring party was honored at a forenoon "farewell" brunch in the pleasant gardens of board member Obert. C. Tanner and his wife, Grace, generous symphony sponsors.

It was a gala occasion, and one centered around Abravanel and the members of the orchestra, at least five of whom were teenagers. Mitch Morrison, a sixteen-year-old East High School student, was the newest of the lot. He had joined the bassoon section, where he was regarded as the youngest symphony bassoonist and contra-bassoonist in the United States. Christopher McKellar, viola and cellist Becky Sollender, both eighteen, and two nineteen-year-olds, Edward Allen, French horn, and James Rose, bass, were the other youngsters. Still with the orchestra are McKellar, now the viola principal, and Morrison, who has become associate principal in the bassoon section.

The tour itself was a magnificent success, starting with a first visit to Carnegie Hall on a stopover in New York City. Honors were heaped upon Abravanel and his eighty-four players there and at each of ten European centers. Doubters such as the National Endowment's Larsen were soon to learn there were music ambassadors in the hinterlands who could win friends for America. One of the first western orchestras to tour internationally, the Utah Symphony proved a worthy representative of its city, state, and nation. Although the San Francisco Symphony Orchestra first made a transcontinental tour in 1947, its initial trip outside the country was in 1968 to Japan, and not until 1973 did it visit Europe.

The brilliantly conceived and well-planned stop in New York City proved to be far more than a routine springboard for the three-and-a-half week jaunt ahead. Besides enhancing its enviable position in the world of symphonic music, the orchestra took on a greater dimension in its role in the development and promotion of Utah business and industry.

Throughout the week ahead of the Carnegie Hall concert, a regiment known as "Rampton's Raiders" (on this occasion 300 in number) had been promoting Utah to New York financial, industrial, and business leaders. Exhibits, fashion shows, and luncheons for food editors, travel editors, and businessmen were the order of each day at the Waldorf-Astoria Hotel.

Most of the food served in the hotel through this period had been transported from Utah. For a lavish buffet preceding the concert on Friday night, September 9, Utah turkey, beef, fish, vegetables, enormous peaches, and even ice cream were flown in to feed 900 guests. Ashton had secured Lee S. Bickmore, president of National Biscuit Company and a product of Paradise in Utah's Cache Country, to host the event. His chief aide was G. Stanley McAllister of New York's Lord and Taylor, another transplanted Utahn who proved tremendously effective in the effort. He was largely responsible for a big committee of former Utah residents who filled Carnegie Hall for the concert and was a power in the entire preparation campaign. The work of coordination, meanwhile, was in the capable hands of Winnifred Bowers, a former Salt Laker with a great love for the Utah Symphony.

Attending both the Waldorf reception and the concert were U. S. ambassador to the United Nations, Arthur J. Goldberg; ambassador at large, W. Averill Harriman; the Greek ambassador to the United Nations, Alexis S. Liatis; and New York City mayor John Lindsay.

Abravanel gave the New York audience the same ambitious program his orchestra was to perform along the tour in Europe. It consisted of the Bernstein Overture to "Candide"; the Symphony No. 6 of Vaughan Williams; Prokofiev's Piano Concerto No. 3, with Grant Johannesen as soloist; and the Stravinsky "Firebird" Suite. The "Pastoral" from Leroy Robertson's "Book of Mormon Oratorio" was presented as an encore.

The response of the critics was most satisfying, to say the least, with Harold Schonberg in the *New York Times* finding the orchestra to be an "enthusiastic and well-drilled organization" whose playing was "rhythmically accurate, vigorous and full of the special quality that occurs when visitors are in Carnegie Hall, playing their hearts out to make a good impression." Abravanel, he wrote, "is obviously a superior conductor, more interested in music than in himself." The critic also praised Johannesen as "one of America's best pianists," who was fully "up to the ferocious technical demands" of the Prokofiev.

Writing in the *New Yorker* magazine, Winthrop Sargeant found the Utah Symphony to be "the kind of orchestra that has been built to achieve a high standard of performance entirely through the methodical efforts of a great conductor." He then added: "He [Abravanel] had drilled his orchestra to the point where it sometimes sounds almost like one of the top symphonic organizations of the country. Its personality is responsive, accurate and wonderfully disciplined."

After New York City, the tour had all the marks of the hurriedly planned affair it was. A great experience for Abravanel, the eighty-four players, and the fifty-five orchestra spouses and fans who accompanied the tour, it was nevertheless somewhat handicapped by the short time available for preparation. Accommodations were not always the best, but the transportation, aboard a chartered Trans-World Airlines Boeing 707, was comfortable.

One casualty, before leaving New York, was the orchestra's bass drum. In its case, it could only get through the hatch opening, where it stopped because of fuselage curvature in the baggage compartment. Back to Salt Lake City it went by air freight, leaving the problem to be dealt with ahead. As manager Gregory put it, "Everyone should share the experience of borrowing a bass drum in four different languages and six different countries."

Next stop for the Utah Symphony, following the New York sendoff, was Athens, Greece, where on the three nights of September 13, 14, and 15, it performed before crowds totaling more than 15,000 in the famous old Herod Atticus amphitheatre at the foot of the Acropolis. Throughout the three days the travelers were virtual guests of the royal family of Greece. King Constantine II himself gave a reception for the symphony party at intermission the first night, and Princesses Sophie, now queen of Spain, and Irene entertained in a hotel reception on another occasion.

Abravanel started with his New York program, which this time presented Bachauer at the keyboard in the Prokofiev Concerto. It was a memorable experience to be matched only by the emotional high-point of the third evening. David Oistrakh, the great Russian violinist, joined the maestro and the symphony on the final program for a performance of Russian composer Shostakovich's Violin Concerto, and the demonstration from the audience was astounding. One photograph and caption in a Greek newspaper the following morning told the story as conductor and soloist faced the audience appearing "speechless, sentimentally touched and motionless from last evening's exciting event at Herod Atticus, which reached climactic enthusiasm."

From Athens the orchestra flew to Salonika, the birthplace of Abravanel. There the maestro was feted during a two-day stop in a climate that was so humid one of the percussionists told Wendell Ashton it was "like playing his drum at the bottom of a river."

Next came performances in Belgrade and Ljubljana, Yugoslavia; Vienna, Austria; and four German centers, Stuttgart, Kassel, Wuppertal, and Berlin, before the tour turned in the direction of home and a September 29 concert in London.

Even more than Salonika, the concert in Berlin was a sentimental "homecoming" for Abravanel. Critics took note of his earlier successes there and were obviously impressed with what was now "his own orchestral instrument, which he himself has developed."

One writer in the *Berlin Daily* made particular note of the "stormy applause in Philharmonic Hall" and of an orchestra that "maintains a high standard, especially in regard to ensemble spirit." He also observed that "many ladies (how could it be different among the Mormons) played harmoniously along with the men." A day later in the same newspaper, another critic wrote: "Snobs, who have until now been of the opinion that good music is only being made in Berlin and perhaps Vienna, had to lay down their weapons. The traveling stars under their 63-year-old conductor, Maurice Abravanel.... made music with great perfection, virtuosity and candid pleasure of playing."

The program, regarded by the *Morgenpost* as "clever and fittingly-chosen," was the same performed back in Carnegie hall, with Grant Johannesen again soloist in the Prokofiev in Piano Concerto. He had rejoined the orchestra at Belgrade and appeared as soloist in all concerts in Yugoslavia, Austria, and Germany.

Obviously accustomed to orchestras with very few, if any, female players, the *Morgenpost*, like the *Berlin Daily*, noted the "many young girls," and the "Telegraf" the "many women" in the Utah Symphony, all a part of ensemble playing, "startling because of the high degree of precision in spite of the difficult score." Held responsible for the "highly technical level of accomplishment" was Abravanel, who "radiated encouragement and certainty." Said *Morgenpost* in this regard, "It is easy to understand why the orchestra plays with such youthful passion under his leadership."

Near disaster overtook the weary travelers in London, where entanglement with customs red tape delayed the start of the concert a full three hours. Apparently the instruments had arrived from Holland without the necessary clearance documents, so while the players were on hand for the performance at Fairfield Hall in Croydon, their instruments were locked up by authorities ninety miles away in Harwich. By the time the scheduled 7:45 P.M. concert started at 10:45, the original crowd of fifteen hundred had dwindled to eight hundred.

Yet the event turned out to be one of the great triumphs of the tour. To a man, the critics of the *London Times*, the *Daily Mail*, the *Daily Telegraph*, and the *Manchester Guardian* agreed, as they poured out the highest praise on the orchestra, that the concert was fully "worth the wait."

Two days after the arrival of the symphony back home on Sunday, October 2, a *Salt Lake Tribune* editorial keyed on the London experience in summing up the tour. It said: "Let the orchestra's achievements be recorded, not in the light of Utah enthusiasm, but through the eyes of the critic of the *London Times* who, after a three-hour wait because instruments were tied up in customs, wrote—'The orchestra was worth waiting for.... [it] achieved a high standard of playing as remarkable for its polished ensemble and rhythmic precision as for the general quality of its tone which is rounded, fully resonant and of great flexibility—'.

"This was typical of the response in concert after concert, all of which helps give remote and sparsely populated Utah a global image of cultural attainment which is beyond price.

"Utah is in the symphony's debt, and in the debt of a superb conductor, Maurice Abravanel, and Utahns will shortly have an opportunity to repay that debt by matching a million dollar grant from the Ford Foundation which will insure further development and achievement for the symphony.

"Meeting the challenge of a million dollars of additional support over a five-year period will not be easy. But Utah's music-loving people surely now owe that to the symphony which has so firmly established nationally and internationally this state's reputation for a high level of artistic value and attainment."

After a two-day stopover at Albuquerque, New Mexico, to open the new Fine Arts Auditorium at the University of New Mexico, the symphony arrived home to the cheers of an excited crowd headed by Governor Rampton and other dignitaries. One thirty-foot sign, prepared and displayed under direction of By Woodbury, said it all: "Welcome Home, Utah's Ambassadors of Music."

With the successful first international tour now a pleasant memory, Ashton turned his attention to the Ford Foundation campaign while Abravanel and his players faced a twenty-sixth season opening on October 13. Two works from the tour repertoire, the Brahms Symphony No. 4 in E Minor and the Stravinsky "Firebird," were on the program with the Brahms "Academic Festival" Overture and Barber's "Adagio for Strings." Shouts of "Bravo" greeted each performance and were reminiscent of the receptions in Europe.

At a reception following the concert, the sponsoring Symphony Guild, through its president, Mrs. David L. (Blanche) Freed, presented Abravanel with his portrait in oil by the noted artist Alvin Gittins. The first of two paintings of the maestro by Gittins, it has found a permanent home in Kingsbury Hall.

The preliminary drawings of the Ford Foundation plan were first brought to Utah during the 1965-66 season by George Kuyper, former manager of the Chicago Symphony and more recently the Los Angeles Philharmonic. He had explained to Huck Gregory on the telephone that the Ford Foundation was considering some kind of assistance to America's professional orchestras. His assignment was to visit several symphony organizations to determine just what kind of assistance would be meaningful and appropriate.

In a schedule of in-depth interviews with the symphony president, Woodbury, and others involved in the local movement, Kuyper left Abravanel until the last. Huck Gregory, who had discussed the matter only briefly with the visitor, joined the interchange of views and at the suggestion of Abravanel chauffeured the party on a leisurely drive up Emigration Canyon, over Little Mountain, and down Parley's Canyon. After discussing various funding possibilities, Abravanel suggested a Ford grant of a million and a half dollars, with the symphony required to raise an amount of one million dollars in matching funds. It became the pattern for the program ultimately established by the Ford Foundation for its $85 million endowment grant program announced in the summer of 1966.

There were to be other surveys, however, before the final program would be announced. From the information gathered, the foundation concluded that America's symphony orchestras were indeed in need of help in facing some serious problems. They found that the nation was in danger of losing many of its fine, seasoned, professional musicians who in increasing numbers were leaving the symphonic field to go into far more lucrative occupations and professions. They also found there was a continual siphoning off of key players from orchestras in smaller communities to the giant symphonies in great metropolitan centers. Clearly, some decisive action was needed in order to forestall these trends.

At about this time, the Utah Symphony itself had arrived at the crossroads. Almost from the minute Abravanel assumed the reins as music director and conductor, he sensed that Utah would never have a truly fine symphony orchestra unless it provided sufficient employment to attract and hold serious musicians. Still several years away from that point, the community orchestra he had taken over in 1947 nevertheless had been expanded until its regular season was now twenty-eight weeks plus recording sessions and other special services. Some of the musicians still felt they were moonlighting from their regular jobs and were not so sure they wanted full-time with the symphony.

When the Ford Foundation created the matching endowment grant program, the Utah Symphony was one of sixty-eight American orchestras with annual budgets of $100,000 or more invited to apply. The grant offer stipulated that matching was all-or-nothing. Any applicant that failed to match the grant amount dollar for dollar could keep its collections but would forfeit the Ford grant.

There were other well-conceived provisions in the program. For example, the Foundation, feeling that any given orchestra might extend itself so completely to match its endowment grant that it would neglect its regular annual fund-raising for operations, required each orchestra to raise at least the same amount in operating funds each season during the five-year matching period. But the Ford officials saw the great strain most applicants would be under and announced that each might apply for nonmatching or developmental grants to help carry them through the matching period.

For a project of such magnitude, an organization commensurate with the challenge was sought by Ashton and his associates. Board member Obert C. Tanner was named general chairman, and after discussing terms of the application in a series of meetings with such leaders as Wendell Ashton, John W. Gallivan, Abravanel, Governor Rampton, Huck Gregory, and others, he suggested that the matter be given a community and state airing.

At the governor's call, a meeting of Utah business, civic, education, religious, professional, and labor leaders was held at the Alta Club in Salt Lake City on December 30, 1965. From that meeting came the eventual decision to apply for a matching grant of one million dollars and $500,000 in nonmatching funds, $100,000 a year for five years.

Against the backdrop it had created, the Ford Foundation announced in midsummer of 1966 that it would establish a ten-year trust in the amount of $85 million to aid America's professional symphony orchestras. Later it approved the Utah Symphony application as it had been presented, and Tanner and his committee once more approached the state's leading citizens. In a presentation dated December 29, 1966, one year following the Alta Club meeting and three months after conclusion of the Athens tour, Tanner, Ashton, and company defined the situation in this succinct manner: "It is important to note that the whole amount of $1,000,000 in matching funds must be raised by local support in the five-year period ending July 1, 1971, or the grant will not be forthcoming.

"If we undertake the project we would then have a $2,000,000 trust fund from which the orchestra would receive only the interest for a period of 10 years starting last July. After

10 years the $1,000,000 Ford principal amount as well as our own $1,000,000 in matching funds, together with such increased worth as may have been attained, would be available to the symphony for whatever purposes it desires. . . .

"President McKay and Governor Rampton are extremely desirous that our state undertake the job of raising $1,000,000 in five years and have asked E. M. Naughton, president and general manager of Utah Power & Light Company, if he would head a campaign to raise the money. He has said he is perfectly willing to attempt it provided the people in Utah are behind and will support the project.

"The question then is: Do you favor the project and will you support it?"

A good many citizens expressed doubts that Salt Lake City and Utah could ever raise a million dollars in five years. To be sure, it was never a foregone conclusion that it could be done, but the answer to the question was, "Go for it!"

Chapters could be written on the fund-raising effort alone, but it was O. C. Tanner's vision and the decisiveness of Ashton and his untiring quest for the matching money that is generally credited with the success of an effort that yielded a total of $1,058,000 by June 30, 1971. The symphony president found lots of help, with Naughton and his committee in the forefront as they covered the state for funds.

Not until April 13, 1967, was Naughton permitted to hold his first formal committee meeting, and by that time he reported pledges of $300,000. Nearly two years later, on February 26, 1969, Naughton and Abravanel carried the campaign to a Rotary Club meeting in Ogden, where the chairman reported that 90 percent of the goal in pledges and contributions had been reached. The pleas for funds produced an amount in excess of the goal set for the Ogden area, adding once more to that city's important role in the success of the Utah Symphony.

Once a bus stop for one or two performances a season on the Utah Symphony schedule, Ogden became a vital force in the orchestra's operations with its own annual subscription series soon after Abravanel moved to Utah. In the fall of 1949, principally through the efforts of Mrs. A. C. (Beverly) Lund, and Ginny

Mathei, and a small dedicated group, the first series was presented at the Ogden High School Auditorium. The cost of the concerts was $400, and three hundred people attended. The number of annual concerts grew to eight at one point, but now it is five, as explained by today's average cost of $10,920 per concert, with an average attendance of seventeen hundred. The cost of the symphony alone is $7,500 per performance, placing a strain on the organization's budget. Fund raising, too, is difficult in light of the fact that some sources, particularly those headquartered in Salt Lake City, are solicited by the orchestra's board.

Many in that first group of interested workers were members of the Welfare League (later the Junior League). They took over in 1950 and became a factor in the early establishment and growth of the orchestra. The effective organization handled symphony affairs in Ogden for six years, after which a broader-based Ogden Symphony Guild came into existence. In 1979 the name was changed to the Ogden Symphony Association, and with the added sponsorship of Ballet West, the organization became the Ogden Symphony-Ballet Association. In addition to the symphony subscription series, now at the Weber State College Val A. Browning Center for the Performing Arts, the organization's season includes three performances of the "Nutcracker" and two presentations of each of three other Ballet West productions, plus a free summer "pops" concert and four Utah Symphony chamber concerts.

Maintaining the operation of the Ogden association's front office over the years have been Eve Gibbons and, in more recent times, Jean Pell. Mrs. Lund continued her interest with the organization until her untimely death in 1961. Mrs. Harmon (Gwen) Williams and succeeding presidents have kept an alliance with the Utah Symphony as automatic members of the board. One of these, Thomas J. Moore, supervisor of arts in Weber County Schools, served as a member of the search committee to find a successor for Abravanel upon his retirement in 1979.

Ogden and every other center in the state was to benefit from the Ford Foundation matching endowment grant as its tremendous impact on the future and destiny of the Utah Symphony became apparent. Throughout the period, the symphony received its $100,000 in non-matching funds each year, and the question arose as to how these funds should most appropriately be used.

There was no doubt that the money was intended for increased orchestra salaries, but it was not certain as to how and when. Maestro Abravanel put the matter squarely in the lap of the musicians inasmuch as they were the ones most directly affected. That they handed it back to the conductor with full confidence was not surprising.

Perhaps the most treasured document in the maestro's file is a memo to him form "The Orchestra Committee" dated January 21, 1966. It reads: "If the Utah Symphony receives a monetary gift from the Ford Foundation in the fall of 1966, we feel that the best interests of the Symphony will be served if you dispose of the money in any way you see fit. We are in complete agreement on this subject."

The memo is signed by Art Peterson, Carol Edison (Nelson), James Loveless, Jack Ashton, and Douglas Craig. It was one more sincere demonstration of the trust the players had placed in their conductor almost since the first time they responded to his baton.

Accompanying that memo, incidentally, was another signed by the same committee that relieved Abravanel of any concern about future rehearsal plans in connection with expansion of services. "We fully support a change to daytime rehearsals at any time you feel such a move is practical," it assured the conductor. "We represent the feelings of the orchestra members in this matter."

Ahead, however, were events that would further broaden the scope of symphony operations and bring the musicians face to face with the tough decisions forced by increasing demands upon their time for orchestra services. The growth in activities was clearly defined in the rapidly advancing symphony budget, which jumped from $338,000 in 1965-66 to $669,000 in 1966-67, the first year of Ford Foundation grants and the year of the first international tour. By 1970-71 the figure was up to $1,203,000 including a five-week Latin American tour and reflecting the success of a tour of the West Coast, the second of two that carried the symphony closer to full-time status.

The first major domestic tour was put together in 1968 by Ashton and Abravanel as an out-and-out industrial development project for Governor Rampton and the state of Utah. Greatly impressed with the impact of the symphony's 1966 tour, and particularly so with the "Utah Week" festivities in New York City, the governor figured that a trip to the four major West Coast cities of Seattle, San Francisco, Los Angeles, and Portland might be even more productive. He started by approaching Abravanel.

"Maurice," he said, "would you object to our using the Utah Symphony for crass commercial purposes such as industrial development?"

"Not only would we not object, but we would be flattered," came the reply.

Thus was initiated the orchestra's first major domestic tour—the first by air to western cities. The Rampton and Ashton administrations organized a two-pronged attack on the four metropolitan centers with the state paying all touring costs above and beyond musician's salaries, less revenues from ticket sales.

Rampton's industrial development team set up invitational reception luncheons or dinners ahead of each concert. The governor was convinced that a community's cultural offerings were as important as its economic and tax climate when it came to attracting industry. Consequently, he appeared in person with the business sector, while his industrial attraction tool—the Utah Symphony—told the Utah story in musical dimensions.

Even a special session of the Utah Legislature couldn't keep the chief executive off the four-day tour. Back and forth aboard his Utah Air National Guard plane he commuted between his office and the Pacific Coast.

But even on the most successful and best-planned tours, not everything goes quite according to expectations. Given a whirlwind start in Seattle on Friday, June 21, the governor returned following a luncheon reception for some legislative business. On Saturday he found time for a golf game at the Salt Lake Country Club before going on to Los Angeles for a reception at the Palladium and the symphony concert at the Hollywood Bowl that night. He had arranged with his wife to have his formal duds ready to be picked up on the fly at his home across the street from the country club in order to save time.

When Cal opened the bag to change clothes on the plane, he discovered that Lucybeth had grabbed the one containing the tuxedo and shirt belonging to son Vince. No way could the portly governor get into his slender boy's outfit. What could he do? Walk into a reception looking as though he had just come from the golf course?

Fortunately, on board was Big Bill Bruhn, a member of the industrial development team, former mayor of Panguitch and at that time Rampton's director of community relations. His dark coat, the golf slacks, a white shirt, and a black bow tie did the job. Needless to say, there were no such problems connected with the appearances in San Francisco and Portland the following Monday and Tuesday.

Meanwhile, the symphony played to large crowds and won standing ovations at every stop. More than twenty-one thousand people, half of them at Hollywood Bowl, heard five concerts. It was the largest crowd the Hollywood Bowl would see all season, even though the performance played more than two weeks ahead of the normal opening on July 9.

Largely responsible for the incredible turnouts were committees of former Utahns along the route who staged the concerts and raised some $18,000 on their own to handle the promotions. As he had done through Bickmore and McAllister at the Waldorf-Astoria reception in New York City, Wendell Ashton had selected effective promoters on the West Coast. In Los Angeles, Daken K. Broadhead led the campaign, putting a crowd of approximately eleven thousand in an auditorium that seated average audiences of five thousand during its summer season. D. Forrest and Gerda Greene headed a committee that sold out the Opera House in San Francisco. Equally effective at the Seattle Opera House and Portland Civic Auditorium were former Utahns Clark M. Wood and Dr. Donald C. Wood and their respective troops.

Once more Abravanel avoided the ordinary in his programming. He and his eighty-eight traveling musicians gave the huge crowd at Hollywood Bowl a memorable performance of Mahler's magnificent "Resurrection" Symphony No. 2 with soprano Jean Preston and contralto Lili Chookasian as soloists. Preston, a former Salt Lake City resident, had been used in other Abravanel productions, always excelling with dependable musicianship and intelligent and artistic vocal production. She was an excellent choice, as well, in the Mahler Symphony No. 4 on the four other programs, in which Utah was further represented by Grant Johannesen at the piano in the Prokofiev Concerto No. 3. Ned Rorem's modern work "Lions" opened the Los Angeles performance, and Ravel's "Daphnis and Chloe" Suite No. 2 was the closing work in the other four cities.

Hewell Tircuit, writing in the *San Francisco Chronicle,* reported that "as an unprecedented gesture" to the large and warm audience, the orchestra "gave a round of applause" for their listeners. He then added: "The real compliment to the city, however, was a decent program," and he noted that "the major key to success such as the Utah Symphony had. . . . is that they played something worth hearing."

Another San Francisco critic, Alexander Fried, in the *Examiner,* found the Utah Symphony to be a "big-scaled, excellent orchestra" and observed that "the French horns had a surety that gave the San Francisco horn section some reason for envy."

At Hollywood Bowl the orchestra was joined in the Mahler by a 135-voice Southern California Mormon Choir, prepared by H. Frederick Davis, who once had his own choir in Salt Lake City. With the other performers it received the cheers and a standing ovation from the huge crowd, which Harold Lundstrom, who made the tour for the *Deseret News,* called "record-breaking."

The en-route concert at Santa Barbara on the Sunday evening following the Los Angeles appearance was in response to a request from that city's Music Academy of the West, where Abravanel had served as music director for fourteen summers.

It was a warm homecoming for the maestro, and a performance that brought an assertion from Ronald D. Scofield of the *Santa Barbara News-Press* to the effect that "the Utah Symphony stands as an orchestra of great vitality, fine proficiency, with the potential for artistic growth and perfectibility that cannot be denied and deserves the highest commendation."

So successful was the 1968 tour that Columbia Artists Management, Inc., the world's largest booking agency, contacted the symphony management and proposed a sweep through other cities in West Coast states in 1970. Herbert O. Fox, vice-president of CAMI for western operations, was impressed with the possibilities of such a tour as he sat in the audience at the Hollywood Bowl concert, and he was reduced to tears by the Mahler work.

The result was a three-and-a-half-week bus trip that took the orchestra within sixty miles of the Canadian border at Everett, Washington, on the north to within twenty miles of the Mexican border at Brawley, California, on the south, crisscrossing the four coastal states in the process. One of the tours booked by Shirl Swenson, this one included two concerts in Idaho, five in Washington, three in Oregon, and thirteen in California—twenty-three in all. One of those California stops, incidentally, was the China Lake "mirage."

This second West Coast tour was of historical significance if only because of its impact on the musicians themselves. The journey had brought to a head the concern of the players about their future with the orchestra.

As they neared the end of their odyssey, the ramifications of an extended season and its inherent touring and other demands became apparent. For a considerable number of musicians it meant leaving their "real jobs" as schoolteachers and business people. They fretted over the chances of jeopardizing their futures by playing in a Utah Symphony for substandard salaries. Also to be considered were the increasing tours that took them away from their families and friends for extended periods.

In Southern California the musicians met on Friday, April 17, 1970, and drafted a letter to Wendell Ashton as president of the symphony, expressing their displeasure with the direction the orchestra seemed to be taking. Signed by seventy-nine orchestra "regulars," the letter openly doubted that Utah could ever field a truly full-time symphony in which the players could earn a living wage. Reading from the letter we find the concerns: "We concerned members of the Utah Symphony feel it necessary to inquire as to the philosophy that will determine the future of the orchestra. The magnificent achievement of the Maestro in building this organization has been greatly helped by the unique stability of the membership which has resulted in less turnover than in any other orchestra of comparable stature. The orchestra has been highly stable for many years because the personnel has been able to find meaningful employment in addition to that provided by the Symphony. This stability of the orchestra may of necessity come to a conclusion because of the trend in recent years to do extensive touring and maximum numbers of services per week. If the present demands are increased but fall short of providing a fully adequate, sole source of employment, many members (teachers, housewives, students and people involved in business) who have dedicated years to the growth and development of the orchestra, will find it necessary to terminate their employment with the Symphony. This state of affairs would result in replacement with musicians most likely to be hired from out of the area.

"We would like to pose the question as to whether the Symphony Board is financially prepared to support an orchestra composed largely of imports. And secondly, is the Board desirous of having such an orchestra represent the State of Utah?....

"If in the near future a full-time, fully professional orchestra is the ultimate aim of the Board and Management, then the local musicians should be able to make a decision on the matter before their other employment is put in jeopardy—employment which in effect for many years has subsidized the individual musician's opportunity to make a living wage."

The letter goes on to request that a complete accounting of expenditures, including player salaries and operating expenses, and of operating capital projected earnings be made available to the musicians. It suggested means of creating new audiences on home ground and expressed a need "to explore the questions we have presented" through a suggested meeting of a committee of players with the symphony board. The committee, with violinist John Chatelain as "honorary chairman," was designed to represent each area of employment outside of symphony work.

Shortly after arriving home, a nine-member orchestra committee sought and received an audience with symphony president Wendell Ashton. Huck Gregory and Shirl Swenson were also present at the meeting, but Maurice Abravanel was notably not invited. The musicians obviously wanted an opportunity to test the validity of their independent observations and concerns.

To Wendell, the meeting presented the one most critical moment in his nineteen years of administering the affairs of the Utah Symphony. After facing again the questions of the players and pondering the situation, he finally told the delegation that the goal of the management and administration was to attain full-time status for the symphony. "The only promise I will give you," he said, "is that we will keep working the way we have to raise the funds."

Ashton then took the letter to the symphony board, a move that called forth a resolution to the effect that Utah indeed would one day have a full-time, fully professional, major orchestra that could compete with other orchestras on an equal footing. Of course, the resolution recognized that the orchestra could probably never enjoy the same level of funding and public support as some others because of Utah's limited population and resources.

The musicians went along with the board's conclusions and within a year were within thirteen-and-a-half weeks of the goal. In 1965-66 the minimum salary levels were $80 a week for a total of twenty-four symphony weeks, or $1,920 for the entire season. The Ford Foundation nonmatching grants and expanding orchestra activities made it possible by 1971 to lengthen the season to thirty-eight-and-a-half weeks. This brought the total annual salary to $6,930, or $180 per week—still

not enough to sustain a musician with a family, but nevertheless enough to be considered the principal source of income
for a majority of the players.

Perhaps as instrumental as any move in the steady
progress toward the ultimate fifty-two-week season, finally
reached in 1980, was the initiation of new state funding for
school concerts. Its accomplishment once more brought
Governor Rampton into the picture as a champion for the
symphony.

The 1968 West Coast industrial development tour had
been completed and a new season about to get underway when
the governor received a visit from Ashton, Abravanel, and
Gregory. The maestro came directly to the proposition: Was the
governor satisfied with a very good part-time community
orchestra for the state of Utah, or was it his desire to have a
full-time professional world-class symphony orchestra?

It didn't take Rampton long to assure his visitors that he
would not be satisfied with anything but a first-class operation
for his constituency. He started out by getting the Legislature to
approve an added amount of $70,000 in the education depart-
ment budget for extended school concerts. When this was
increased to $100,000 the next time around, the lawmakers put
on the condition that previous nominal costs assessed the
schools for the concerts be eliminated. From that time the
orchestra has toured the school districts of the state with free
performances. In doing so, however, its education appropriation has increased to $437,400 in the 1985-86 season.

Concurrent with the steady growth in this fund was a
rising allotment from the Utah Arts Council's annual appropriation for all of the arts. Amounting to only $4,500 in 1955-56, this
fund reached $13,000 in 1959-60 and remained there until it
doubled to $26,100 in 1966-67. From then on it grew to the
$100,000 mark in 1977-78 and today is $146,500. Added to the
education appropriation, it gives the orchestra a total of
$583,900 in state funds to help support an overall budget of
nearly $5,000,000.

Top: *Sen. Frank E. Moss presents appreciation plaque to Vice President Hubert H. Humphrey for his assistance in obtaining funding for first international tour, 1966.*
Bottom: *A Carnegie Hall debut launched the Utah Symphony on its first international tour in 1966 and opened that venerable hall's 75th anniversary season.*

Top: *Utah Symphony under Maurice Abravanel during the orchestra's Vienna debut, September 22, 1966, in the Grosser Musikvereinssaal, home of the Vienna Philharmonic.*
Bottom: *A breathtaking and historic moment as Maurice Abravanel and the Utah Symphony debut at their first concert on foreign soil at the Herod Atticus Amphitheatre at the base of the Acropolis in Athens, Greece, September 13, 1966.*

Top: *Wendell J. Ashton (l.) observes as Utah Gov. Calvin L. Rampton signs Utah Symphony Week proclamation.*
Bottom: *Utah Symphony musicians board chartered jet during 1968 West Coast tour.*

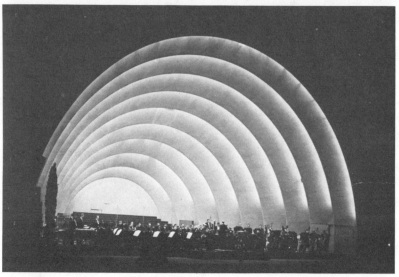

Top: *President Spencer W. Kimball (right) of the Church of Jesus Christ of Latter-day Saints greets Maestro Maurice Abravanel following Utah Symphony concert at New York's Carnegie Hall in May 1975.*
Bottom: *Utah Symphony conducted by Maurice Abravanel in the orchestra's Hollywood Bowl debut, June 22, 1968.*

Top: *Maurice and Lucy Abravanel enplane for first leg of 5-week Latin American concert tour, 1971.*
Bottom: *William Sullivan, Utah Symphony trumpeter, inhales oxygen to assist breathing at La Paz, Bolivia, (elevation 11,910 ft.) concert as Sheldon Hyde, personnel manager and second trumpet (r.) looks on.*

South American concert-goers surround Maurice Abravanel seeking
autographs of souvenir programs and Utah Symphony recordings, 1971.

Top: *Mrs. Maurice (Lucy) Abravanel (l.), wife of Utah Symphony conductor, greets Nicaragua President and Mrs. Anastas Somoza (r.) at reception following Managua concert, July 1, 1971. Wendell J. Ashton and wife, Belva, are in background (rear).*
Bottom: *Maestro Maurice Abravanel (second from right) greets Bolivian president and wife at La Paz concert June 24, 1971, as U. S. Ambassador looks on.*

Top: *Utah Symphony members outside of the Kennedy Center, Washington, D. C., on first leg of the orchestra's third international tour in May-June, 1975.*
Bottom: *Maurice Abravanel conducting the Utah Symphony at Royal Festival Hall, London, England, June 2, 1975.*

Top: *National Tourist Organization of Greece Director Michael P. Mavraganis (2nd from left) officially invites Gov. Scott M. Matheson (r.), Maurice Abravanel (l.) and Wendell J. Ashton (3rd from left) to attend Utah Symphony's 1977 Athens Festival performances.*

Bottom: *Maurice Abravanel (r.) and Lucy Abravanel (second from left) have audience with Queen Sofia and her daughter in Madrid, Spain. Sept.-Oct. 1977 4th International Tour.*

Top: *(L.-r.) Gerald Uhlfelder, Buenos Aires concert manager; Wendell J. Ashton, Utah Symphony president; and Shirl H. Swenson, orchestra manager, discuss details of 1971 Latin American concert tour.*
Bottom: *Anatole Heller, Parisian booking agent, (l.), confers with Harold Gottfredson, Utah Symphony bass trombonist and stage manager, during 1977 European concert tour.*

CHAPTER 17

INTERNATIONAL ORCHESTRA

With two successful major tours—in 1966 to Europe and in 1968 to the West Coast— providing the impetus, the Utah Symphony was soon to make a practice of visiting distant capitals of the world. Wendell Ashton was so impressed with the orchestra's new travel-enhanced image that he persuaded board and management to adopt a policy of planning an international tour every four or five years. This resulted in the mounting of four concert excursions to foreign lands in a twelve-year period.

The symphony president knew that such tours were important if only to impress upon local patrons and supporters the stature of their orchestra. Maurice Abravanel had come to the same conclusion many years earlier about recordings of the orchestra. As they developed, the touring and recording programs complemented each other.

Upon reaching its decision calling for periodic tours, the management was directed to begin working on plans for a trip in 1971 directed mainly toward Central and South America. As it developed, the five-week tour of twenty-six concerts also included stops in Washington, D.C., New York City, and the Virgin Islands in the Caribbean.

Financing was not nearly the problem it had been in bringing to life the 1966 European expedition. Abravanel, who was in a constant stew over the funding before leaving for Athens, was able to concentrate entirely upon preparing his ensemble for performances all the way from Salt Lake City to Buenos Aires and back. There would be no reason this time for him to make any such rash offers to his president as he made in 1966.

It will be recalled that in the beginning Maurice beheld the Athens trip as little more than a dream. In one unguarded moment, according to Ashton, the maestro said, "Wendell, if you raise the money for that European tour, I'll let you baptize me into the Church." Wendell then assured him, "Maurice, I won't forget."

When the tour was over and Wendell told Abravanel he was "ready to collect," Maurice merely answered, "What will Lucy say?" and that was that.

Ashton had great respect for Lucy Abravanel's concern for a healthy balance in symphony influence and support. "She didn't want the Mormon influence to prevail," he recalls, "and this has been a good thing."

"Through this sort of understanding," he said, "the Utah Symphony has been a great bridge between all the religious persuasions; between political loyalties, business, and labor; and between many rival factions. I'll never forget visiting with Vernon Romney at the state capitol when he was attorney general. He said, 'There's nothing like the Utah Symphony in this state. Everybody loves it—the Democrats up here, and the Republicans. The Mormons and non-Mormons, they all love the Utah Symphony.'"

This unity of purpose enjoyed by the orchestra was particularly helpful in fund-raising campaigns. It came into play in the financing of the 1971 international tour, which required a backup of $200,000.

Taking advantage of a lesson learned from the 1966 tour, the orchestra's management determined it should never again attempt such a project with less than a year to plan it. Nothing could be made final in the planning of that first tour until the federal grant was secured just four or five months before the departure for Athens. By that time it was virtually impossible to obtain adequate facilities in some of the cities.

By contrast, most of the costs of the 1971 tour were underwritten more than a year before the orchestra was to leave Salt Lake City. Oddly enough, one of two principal contributors to this favorable situation, a carefully guarded reserve fund then amounting to $100,000, had been passed over in the 1966 campaign. As it turned out, not one cent of the fund was used for the 1971 trip either, but in the beginning it provided a solid backing on which the tour could be properly planned.

The all-important reserve fund had been created nearly ten years before as a result of two events that netted a total of $40,000. One was a Utah Symphony-sponsored appearance of the New York Philharmonic under Leonard Bernstein at the Salt Lake Tabernacle on Wednesday, September 7, 1960. It was a very warm night, coming right after the hottest August on record—including three consecutive weeks in which the daily temperatures neared 100 degrees—but the house was full and the net profit was $20,000.

A like amount was realized from the other event, a spectacular first performance by the young American pianist, Van Cliburn, heralded winner of Russia's Tchaikovsky Piano Competition, with Abravanel and the Utah Symphony at the Tabernacle on Wednesday, December 7, 1960. This was actually a delayed appearance of the pianist in Utah brought on by an obstinate board member who had insisted that Huck Gregory negotiate for a reduction in Cliburn's fee—60 percent of the gross receipts—when he was available two years before. It was a mistake. The availability was snatched up overnight. After all, this was the red-headed young Texan who had received the internationally publicized bear hug from Soviet premier Nikita Kruschev after receiving his award, and who had been honored with a ticker-tape parade in New York City. When he finally came to Salt Lake City, his fee was 65 percent of the house with an added minimum guarantee.

What to do with the $40,000 became a matter to be discussed at length by Gregory and Abravanel, with much consideration given to player salary increases. The players had long since resolved that they would not ask for an increase in pay so long as Abravanel was their conductor, and the maestro now faced a new challenge. It was decided, however, that it would be unwise so late in the season to put this one-time "windfall" into salaries.

Soon afterward Gregory unilaterally put the $40,000 into a reserve fund for the symphony. Along the way, he whisked other unplanned profits into the deposit; and by 1970, when the Latin American tour began taking shape, the fund was nearly $100,000. Its existence had become known, and Ashton suggested that the reserves be committed to the tour in case the necessary funds could not be raised elsewhere. In the end, the campaign spearheaded by the president's luncheon and breakfast appeals allowed the reserve fund to remain untouched.

Replacing the reserves, much of the tour's local funding came from a new program instituted by Ashton and his fellow administrators for the sole purpose, at the time, of financing the Latin American tour. Sponsors were secured for specific events and for various reasons, one of them contributing $8,000 to finance a concert in La Paz, Bolivia, where local financing was out of the question. The donation was most appropriate in light of the fact that one of the principal purposes of the tour was to promote goodwill.

So successful was the sponsorship appeal on this occasion that it was soon to become a permanent part of the symphony's fund-raising program. As acknowledged in the elaborate souvenir program for the Latin American tour, printed in English, Spanish, and Portuguese, that first list of donors included C. Comstock Clayton, the grand marshal of the tour; Dean Eggertsen, a close friend and generous contributor to the symphony, both personally and through the S. B. Eggertsen Foundation; Sidney M. Horman, prominent Salt Lake builder and developer; and Mr. and Mrs. Charles W. Goff.

Also on the list were the Boyles Brothers Drilling Company, the National Lead Company, the F. W. Woolworth Company, the Kresge Foundation, two sponsoring groups of former Utah residents in Washington and New York City, and the Mormon

Tabernacle Choir, all indicating the breadth of the contributing forces. The choir had more than once been a tour contributor through fund-raising concerts.

Assistance was sought from an organization called the Partners for the Alliance, an association of business and civic leaders in Salt Lake City greatly interested in this country's neighbors "south of the border." The group was unable to contribute funding, but they did provide air transportation for Shirl Swenson, the symphony's tour manager, to fly over the entire proposed tour route. The result was a month-long visit at the end of 1969, in which Swenson made a thorough inspection covering all phases of the excursion. He returned with a recommendation that Conciertos Gerard, an impresario agency located in Buenos Aires, be engaged to handle the booking, and that Tintec Tur take over the travel arrangements.

It was a move that paid off handsomely. Where only three of sixteen airplane departures on the Athens tour were on time, for instance, only three of more than thirty during the five weeks in Latin America were late. No concerts were missed because of delays, but several "near-misses" were chalked up to a cargo plane bearing the instruments.

Overall, transportation for the 1971 tour posed a far different set of problems than the Athens-European trip five years earlier. On that jaunt, the musicians, their luggage, and their instruments (except for that bass drum) all fit snuggly into a Boeing 707 chartered from Trans-World Airlines for the Salt Lake City/New York, New York/Athens and London/Albuquerque flights. On all overland legs of the tour, the instruments and music were transported by a German-based truck that met the orchestra in Salonika. Shipment across the English channel was by boat.

While the flight from Salt Lake City to Washington, D.C., and New York City to set up the Latin-American tour was by chartered aircraft, from there on the musicians flew via regularly scheduled airlines, and the instruments traveled on a chartered freight carrier. This separation presented some uneasy situations from the beginning.

Before leaving Salt Lake City, the orchestra manager arranged with Bill Edde of the now defunct local charter, Edde Airlines, to provide transportation for the instruments. He in turn engaged a line that serviced Central and South America, completely unaware that the company was in trouble.

A short two weeks or so before the tour departure, Huck Gregory received a call from Florida; he was informed that the president of the firm Edde had contacted was in an Ecuador jail on charges of smuggling a million dollars worth of heroin and gold. Gregory and Shirl Swenson did some checking and found it was not one million but two million dollars in contraband goods. They had visions of the plane and the orchestra's instruments impounded in some South American airport and canceled the agreement.

Edde immediately went into action again, and when the symphony left New York for the Virgin Islands, an old cigar-shaped, World War II vintage C-46 was there to airlift the instruments. With no apologies, it made the trip, although sometimes at great wonderment. Flying well behind the orchestra's Boeing 727, the cargo plane reached St. Thomas just an hour before the concert, the first of several close calls. Thanks to continued effort on the part of Bill Edde through Murdock Travel, involving daily telephone conferences with Shirl Swenson, who was with the orchestra on tour, the vintage C-46 was finally replaced by a more modern DC-6B at Buenos Aires. Even the newer plane was not immune to problems, however. Another "near miss" came in La Paz, Bolivia, which the instrument plane reached in the nick of time. It had made a forced landing in Chile when its oil line froze while crossing the Andes.

The bookings set up an itinerary covering nineteen cities in eleven countries, with twenty-two concerts over a one-month period, from June 3 through July 2. The only real opportunities for rest came in a two-day stop in Caracas, Venezuela; a two-day layover (with no concerts) in Trinidad; and three days of concerts at the famous Teatro Colon in Buenos Aires, Argentina.

As with the 1966 visit to Europe, the Latin American tour was launched on the East Coast, this time from two great centers, Constitution Hall in Washington, D.C., and, again, from New York City's Carnegie Hall. Very much in evidence once more was the invaluable assistance furnished by committees of former Utahns and their strong leadership. In the nation's capital, Wendell Ashton had secured Jesse R. "Bob" Smith, legal counsel for the Armstrong Tile and Linoleum Company, to chair the effort; and in New York City, Robert Sears, vice-president of Phillips Petroleum, with Winnifred Bowers, once more coordinating the movement. These groups promoted the concerts, sold tickets, solicited sponsorships and contributions, and generally took care of all details for the two events.

Abravanel's programming in Washington set the tone for the entire tour and drew a noisy reception from the capacity house. After opening with an American work, the Symphony No. 3 by Indiana-born Ned Rorem, he turned to the "Varaciones Concertantes" of one of South America's leading composers, Alberto Ginastera, a native of Buenos Aires. The closing work was the Brahms Symphony No. 1 in C Minor.

Heard in place of the Ginastera at Carnegie Hall the following night was the Ravel Piano Concerto for the Left Hand, a work not a part of the general tour repertoire, with Grant Johannesen at the keyboard.

Five other American works were performed along the route, including Samuel Barber's "Adagio for Strings," the Overture to "Candide" by Leonard Bernstein, Aaron Copland's "El Salon Mexico," "An American in Paris" by George Gershwin, and the "Punch and Judy" Overture by Leroy Robertson. Another South American composer, Brazil's Heitor Villa-Lobos, was represented by his "Little Train to Caipira."

Completing the list of fourteen compositions from which the programs were drawn were the Beethoven "Eroica" Symphony No. 3 in E-flat major; Ernst Bloch's "Schelomo" for Cello and Orchestra, with principal cellist Christian Tiemeyer as soloist, the Mozart "Haffner" Symphony No. 35 in D Major; the Rimsky-Korsakov Symphonic Suite, "Scheherazade"; and the Tchaikovsky Symphony No. 5 in E Minor.

Although encores were common in response to enthusiastic receptions throughout the tour, it was an unexpected demonstration at the final performance in Buenos Aires that kept the orchestra playing the longest. Warned that the blase Sunday afternoon crowd was a literal "sleeper," Abravanel and his musicians were a bit apprehensive, even with a program of Mozart, Ginastera, and Brahms. There was no need to be concerned, however, as the resulting tumult forced a pair of encores before the party could pack up and get on its way. The prolonged applause was to be rivaled only at the Palacio de Bellas Artes in Mexico City, the tour finale, where the audience cheered the playing of Bernstein, Copland, Gershwin, and Tchaikovsky.

The tour was tiring for the musicians, and at times the living facilities were not the best. There were compensations, however, such as the two-day holiday in Trinidad. There a scheduled concert had been canceled just before the tour started, but the itinerary remained unchanged. The layover followed appearances at St. Thomas and St. Croix in the Virgin Islands and a pair of concerts in Caracas, where the travelers enjoyed luxury accommodations. Just ahead lay the only real travel problem and the worst hotel accommodations of the tour, the low point of the entire trip.

With no scheduled airline service from Trinidad to the next concert site in Brasilia, Brazil, the symphony reached an agreement with Pan American for a charter flight to Belem, an uninviting city at the mouth of the Amazon River, on the north coast of Brazil near the equator. Only a few rooms were left in an undesirable hotel, and some of the party bunched up in rooms. Others, including Huck Gregory, bedded down on the floor of the lounge off the hotel lobby. The tour manager, Shirl Swenson, with the concertmaster, Oscar Chausow, and wife, Leyah, all unable to tolerate the filthy conditions of their rooms, spent the night walking around the town. Needless to say, the travelers were happy to get on their way the next morning, but the unsavory experience left its mark with many in the form of an abdominal disorder and diarrhea that developed on the plane and persisted during much of the day in Brasilia.

Nevertheless, the orchestra performed with distinction before a crowd that included a large number of government and military dignitaries from several countries. Four other stops in Brazil carried the symphony to Rio de Janeiro, Sao Paulo, Curitiba, and Porto Alegre. Next came six performances in Argentina, including an opener in Corrientes, three in Buenos Aires, and one each in Cordoba and Mendoza.

Perhaps the most anxious moments on the trip were experienced in Mendoza, where the touring party was met at the airport by an armed military escort and taken directly to the concert hall. During the concert, a flatbed truck full of soldiers waited outside the Teatro Municipal, apparently guarding against any political action. Following the performance, another military escort was provided to the airport, where the symphony and company flew off to Santiago, Chile, en route to the next concert in La Paz, Bolivia.

If the Latin American tour found its climax in Buenos Aires, it reached its high point in La Paz, where the altitude is nearly twelve thousand feet, and the airport is a thousand feet above that on a plateau outside the city. As a protection in the rarefied atmosphere, oxygen masks were made ready off the concert stage. Mormon missionaries met the plane and supervised the handling of the luggage while warning the visitors against overexertion in such high country.

All along the route, the LDS missionaries had been evident with a number of services, but not quite the kind that was to occupy two of them in La Paz. Wherever it had been desired, the national anthem of the country visited was played at the beginning of the concert, but Bolivia had not responded with a request.

The office of the U. S. Ambassador in Bolivia, however, insisted that the Utah Symphony play the Bolivian national anthem, only to find that the music was not readily available. By some frantic behind-the-scenes footwork, the music was delivered to the orchestra's librarian, Robert Lentz, only minutes before the musicians boarded busses at the hotel to be taken to the concert.

To the dismay of all, it was discovered that on the photocopied orchestral parts many of the staff lines were nonexistent, although most of the notes were clear enough.

After a futile search for a native Bolivian who knew the national anthem, two LDS missionaries were found who could hum the tune while part leaders filled in the notes and music staves. Miraculously, the symphony's rendition of the national anthem was a resounding success.

The missionaries went back to dispersing souvenir programs, a chore they and their counterparts handled in many of the concert cities, and the orchestra gave a rousing performance of the national anthem. The effect was to change what could well have been a hostile atmosphere into a friendly one, a coup in itself.

This concert, performed in a gymnasium, was financed by a sponsor's generous contribution back in Salt Lake City. The donation, incidentally, also made it possible for the proceeds, over and above costs, to be turned over to the government to help construct schools in Bolivia. As it turned out, the revenue from the concert, combined with local labor and handmade materials, financed the construction of two one-room schools, which were dedicated a year later.

From La Paz the tour went on to wind up with successful, artistic triumphs in Lima, Peru; Medellin, Colombia; Panama City; San Jose, Costa Rica; Managua, Nicaragua; and Mexico City.

Wendell Ashton had such success with the sponsorships as a way to raise funds on the Latin American tour that he went on to make them his principal way to raise money for the symphony. By 1975 such sponsorships were bringing in some $230,000 a year, and from 1981 to 1985, Ashton had built this fund to between $800,000 and $1,000,000 yearly.

He went on to push for more international tours and in 1975 took the Utah Symphony back to England for a week of concerts, one of them in London's Royal Festival Hall on the banks of the Thames. It had been a disappointment to him that the orchestra had missed this great concert hall in 1966.

The seeds of the 1975 tour were sown when Lord Thomson of Fleet visited Salt Lake City on a speaking assignment and became acquainted with the ever-alert Utah Symphony president. The legendary newspaper baron, who began with one newspaper in Toronto and parlayed that into an empire of publishing, including the London Times and other prestigious dailies, soon found himself in a discussion of symphony orchestras. He was made aware of the symphony's desire to perform in the Royal Festival hall and left Ashton with a promise to look into the possibilities. Not long afterward Wendell was advised that a date was set in the Royal Festival Hall for early June 1975.

In all, the tour included six concerts in England covering a week's time, from May 27 through June 2, and three performances in the East Coast cities of Washington, D.C.; Red Bank, New Jersey; and New York City, May 20 through 23. This time the symphony played its first concert in Washington's Kennedy Center, a glittering success before a prestigious audience. Committees again handled arrangements here and at Carnegie Hall. The Red Bank concert at the Monmouth Art Center Auditorium was booked as a one-night stand by the Community Concerts arm of Columbia Artists Management, Inc.

For all three concerts on the East Coast, Abravanel carried a program made up of Copland's "Billy the Kid," the Vaughan Williams Symphony No. 8 in D Minor, and Prokofiev's Symphony No. 7. Completing the repertoire for the six concerts in England were Satie's "Les Aventures de Mercure," the Brahms First and Beethoven Seventh Symphonies, Barber's "Adagio for Strings," and Richard Strauss's "Death and Transfiguration."

Although the tour eventually became an unqualified success, there was a time in New York City when the orchestra wondered if their chartered Pan American would ever get under way. The players and others in the traveling party had hurried directly to the airport from Carnegie Hall by bus, but the trucks carrying the luggage became lost en route and arrived very late. Meanwhile, the ground crew ignored the advice of the symphony's property and stage manger, Harold Gottfredson, who had had firsthand experience with Boeing 707s twice before. They threw in the suitcases and small items without waiting first to load the large, padded instrument crates and later found it necessary to remove some seats in the forward section of the cabin and secure the larger items in that area.

Not until nearly daylight was the plane ready for boarding. By the time the weary passengers had taken their seats, however, fair weather had changed to fog and the takeoff was again delayed. To ease the situation somewhat, breakfast was served but then quickly cleared away as the fog lifted and the plane departed. When the tired, unhappy musicians finally arrived in Glasgow, Scotland, the festive reception committee awaiting them had long since given up and gone home.

Three comfortable buses carried the orchestra to Newcastle, where it became the first American symphony to perform since Eugene Ormandy and the Philadelphia Orchestra visited there twenty-five years before. Following the concert at City Hall, Abravanel and his musicians played successive days in Middlesbrough, Huddersfield, Hempstead, and Portsmouth before catching their breath with a free evening in London. They rehearsed during the day, however, at the Royal Festival Hall, scene of the tour finale.

The London concert was a brilliant affair, capped by a performance of the Vaughan Williams Eighth Symphony with the widow of the composer, a close friend and admirer of Maurice Abravanel, in the audience. The *London Times* said of the performance, "Mr. Abravanel's straightforward unadorned methods produced results of considerable fire and conviction."

Wendell Ashton, who accompanied all of the major tours, observed that this one "differed from the orchestra's two previous trips abroad in one important repsect.... This time the reputation had already been established." In the 1966 and 1971 tours, he said, the symphony was building the reputation it was now carrying.

In Hemel Hempstead, near London, one newspaper called the Utah Symphony performance "a musical milestone," while another reported: "The first foreign orchestra to play in the Pavilion won a standing ovation, a chorus of stamping feet and shouts of 'more' last night. The audience loved what they heard. It was Beethoven's Symphony No. 7 which won the Utah Symphony the heart of Hemel Hempstead. The response was deafening. Five times Mr. Abravanel was called back to the stage for an encore."

And in London, after accompanying the orchestra on its entire tour of England, Eric Caller, known as "Newcastle's Mr. Music," commented: "In all my experience I have never met a group so friendly, gracious and warm. I do not know their secret, but there is something about these people that is different from anything I have encountered."

Not always, however, was there complete harmony within the symphony organization. There were sure to be increasing labor and management differences, one of which erupted into a contest of considerable significance at the end of the journey to England. It had to do with an extra day given the musicians in London before flying home after the Royal Festival Hall performance. It turned out to be a holiday with a discordant finish.

Before leaving Salt Lake City, Gregory and Swenson decided that the musicians should have an extra day after the strenuous schedule of one-night stands to enjoy the city and see the sights. The symphony would pick up the cost of hotels and an extra per diem allowance. But that was not enough, for while many of the players appreciated the package as presented, some insisted they must also be paid for the extra day on tour.

Unfortunately, the problem was not resolved before the tour started, it being agreed to work it out at the end of the journey. By that time, however, the musicians' union had dug in its heels and demanded the pay. An arbitrator, governor-to-be Scott M. Matheson, then counsel for the Union Pacific Railroad, was selected, and after a lengthy deliberation and consultation with attorneys on both sides, he held for the union. His conclusion was that, under the contract, the symphony was not justified in keeping the musicians away from their homes without paying them.

It was a victory for the union that marked a pivotal moment in the labor history of the Utah Symphony. Since then, as Abravanel predicted when the issue was not settled in the beginning, the players' demands have steadily increased and their influence on overall operations has been keenly felt.

Hardly had the symphony returned from its 1975 tour when the plans were underway for a trip back to Athens and fourteen other cities on the European continent in the fall of 1977. In a way it was an extension of the 1975 tour to England, since an attempt had been made to lengthen that trip to the continent. Competition from other touring American orchestras at the time, however, made such an extension impossible. Consequently, when another invitation to the Athens Festival arrived, it was snapped up, and the symphony once more hauled out its traveling togs.

On this occasion the Utah Symphony went directly to Athens, for the first time passing up the East Coast, because of the comparatively recent visit in 1975. The tour was booked by the Paris impresario Anatole Heller on September 19, 20, and 21. A return performance in Salonika was then followed by concerts in Austria, West Germany, and Spain, winding up with two appearances in Barcelona on October 13 and 14.

Heller was highly respected in the concert world and on this occasion proved himself to be a master at his trade. Everything about the tour was first class, with accommodations for the musicians perhaps more consistently excellent than on any other trip abroad.

The second visit to Athens was certainly as warm as the one in 1966, and perhaps even more so. There was a buffet reception at the U. S. Embassy for the entire Utah Symphony party, and the U. S. diplomatic community was most visible throughout the visit and elsewhere along the tour route.

Since the 1966 Athens tour, the great Greek pianist and strong friend of the Utah Symphony, Gina Bachauer, had passed away, and it was most fitting that the opening concert was dedicated to her memory. Also honored with a moment of silence at the beginning of the program was another late Greek artist, the fabulous soprano Maria Callas, who passed away only hours before the symphony arrived in Athens.

A Greek pianist, Vasso Devetzi, and contralto Maureen Forrester appeared as soloists in the first two concerts, the third being all-orchestral. Devetzi was at the keyboard for the

Rachmaninoff Piano Concerto No. 2, a solo role occupied throughout the remainder of the tour by pianist Claude Kahn.

Two Salt Lake City music critics on the tour, William S. Goodfellow of the *Deseret News* and David L. Beck of the *Salt Lake Tribune*, were tremendously impressed with the orchestra's reception in Athens and throughout the excursion, attesting to the high reputation attained by Abravanel and his musicians abroad as well as at home.

Goodfellow, for instance, reported "another tremendous ovation" from Augsburg, West Germany, with this added note: "It was the latest in what has been so far a succession of audience triumphs since the orchestra's tour began in Athens last week." He went on to report the presence of a "standing room only" crowd at Linz, Austria, the night before in the magnificent Brucknerhalle on the bank of the Danube River. There, after playing the Bruckner "Die Nullte" Symphony, Abravanel "held up the score for its own ovation" while expressing to the audience an appreciation for the great privilege afforded him and the musicians in the performance of Bruckner in that auditorium.

It was the first time both Salt Lake City newspapers had sent their top music writers to cover an entire tour. In 1966, Norman R. Bowen, city editor of the *News*, and James Fitzpatrick, music editor of the *Tribune*, were official representatives of their papers. Only former sports editor Hack Miller, then a staff writer with the *Deseret News*, was along on the Latin American tour, and Dell Van Orden, a *Deseret News* staff writer, was the lone Salt Lake newspaperman on the 1975 trip to England.

From Greece the symphony had flown to Linz for its single concert in Austria. In attendance was United States ambassador to Austria, Milton A. Wolf, who had come from Vienna for the event. Following the performance he gave a buffet reception for the orchestra and special guests. There in a brief toast he remarked, "This is one of the finest symphony orchestras I have ever heard. Mr. Abravanel and members of the Utah Symphony, tonight you have made us proud to be Americans."

From Linz the symphony started an exhausting string of one-night stands in West Germany. For nine days in a row the players bussed from city to city, giving a concert in each, starting in Augsburg and moving on to the huge Meistersinger-halle in Nuernberg, then to Mainz, Hoechst, Karlsruhe, Duesseldorf, Witten, Heidelberg, and Marburg.

Five concerts in Spain wound up the tour, with the first two in Madrid, where the queen and former Princess Sofie of the Greek royal family was in attendance. She had been in Athens for the orchestra's visit in 1966 but since had become the queen of Spain. After a concert in Liria, near Valencia, and two in Barcelona, the symphony headed for home and the beginning of its next-to-last season in the Salt Lake Tabernacle.

Programming for the tour was typically Abravanel—respectful, imaginative, and exciting. The Mahler Symphony No. 1 was the major work in Greece and Spain, but nowhere else on the tour. Through Austria and Germany the principal works were the Brahms Second Symphony; the Schumann "Spring" Symphony No. 1; the Beethoven Seventh Symphony; the Richard Strauss "Death and Transfiguration"; and the Rachmaninoff Piano Concerto No. 2, with Kahn as soloist. Usually opening the concerts were the Bach Suite in D or the Barber "Adagio for Strings."

This was the last international tour for the symphony with its master architect and builder at the helm. When the next trip to Europe was organized in 1981, Abravanel had retired.

Three Utah Symphony presidents, (l-r) Wendell J. Ashton, Raymond J. Ashton and J. Allan Crockett, mark the orchestra's 1,000th performance March 16, 1966.

Top: (l-r) Jon M. Huntsman, Utah Symphony Board chairman, 1985 to present. T. Bowring Woodbury, Utah Symphony Board president, 1965-66. Bottom: (l-r) John W. Gallivan, Utah Symphony Board president, 1964-65; general chairman, bicentennial arts complex construction committee. O. Preston Robinson, president of Utah Symphony, 1963-64.

BUSATH PHOTOGRAPHY

RAMON WINEGAR

Top: *(l-r) Deedee Corradini, vice chairman, Utah Symphony Board, 1985 to present. Donald P. Lloyd, Utah Symphony Board member; president of Associated Food Stores, sponsors of children's concerts for 20 years; symphony benefactor.*
Bottom: *Alonzo W. Watson, Jr., member, Utah Symphony Executive Committee, and Vice President (Legal Affairs).*

Top: *(l-r) Barbara L. Tanner, Guild president, board member and chairman, Utah Symphony Gina Bachauer International Piano Competition. Haven J. Barlow, Utah Symphony board member and president, Utah State Senate.* **Bottom:** *M. Walker Wallace has served as Utah Symphony and Utah Arts Council board member, and for many years as Utah Symphony treasurer.*

ROLF W. KAY

Top: *(l-r) David S. Romney, managing director of Utah Symphony, 1949-1957. Herold L. (Huck) Gregory, executive director of Utah Symphony, 1957-1986.* **Bottom:** *W. Boyd Christensen, executive vice president, Utah Symphony, 1981-82 season.*

ROLF W. KAY

Top: *(l-r) Paul R. Chummers, Utah Symphony executive director, appointed August 1, 1986. Robert J. Darling, consultant and acting executive director of Utah Symphony, 1985-86.*
Bottom: *Stephen W. Swaner, executive vice-president of Utah Symphony, 1982-85.*

CHAPTER 18

THE SYMPHONY GUILD

While the administration and board of directors historically have raised funds to finance the Utah Symphony, not all of this most important function has been retained inside the central organization. Always existing alongside has been a women's division with a principal purpose of collecting money for the orchestra.

Even the efforts of the first women's groups, modest as they were, went mainly into fund-raising and ticket-selling, but it was not until the Symphony Guild was established in 1953 that the operation began to flourish. Its broad base of activities induced wider participation and thereby increased contacts.

Quite naturally the social amenities and other symphony-oriented services associated with the guild functions became a part of the program. Any impression that this was a "punch-and-cookie" organization, however, was eventually put to rest in light of the many hours of work contributed by members in behalf of the Utah Symphony.

In the very beginning of its operation, the orchestra board, through the efforts of Glenn Wallace, enlisted the services of Salt Lake Junior League members in campaigns to promote interests in the inaugural concert and in the first season of 1940-41. It was not until the following year that a "women's committee" of the Utah State Symphony Orchestra was organized, with Mrs. Martin C. Lindem as president.

Organization of the Women's Committee was first proposed to the symphony executive committee on January 23, 1941, with the committee "to operate permanently for the purpose of increasing interest and participation in symphony membership campaigns. Named vice-presidents with Mrs. Lindem were Mrs. Fred Smith, Mrs. J. A. Hale, Mrs. Arthur P. (Virginia) Freber, and Mrs. Charles W. Yard. Mrs. Samuel Carter, a member of the symphony board, served as chairman of children's concerts, and Mrs. Lucille Hayes was "out-of-town" chairman.

Through the early years the committee met in the homes of members for "music study" and to plan their fund-raising activities. They gave a number of parties to promote their cause, and with the arrival of Maurice and Lucy Abravanel in 1947 they added other members and stepped up operations.

Pre-concert symposiums were initiated by the group, and in 1949 the violin virtuoso Isaac Stern joined the women in the University of Utah Union Building, discussing with them the Tchaikovsky Violin Concerto before performing it with the symphony. The organization figured prominently in arrangements for the two summer soirees at the Salt Lake Country Club, featuring Lauritz Melchior, the noted Wagnerian tenor, in 1950, and the classic-jazz clarinetist Benny Goodman in 1951.

At the close of one of its final seasons as a women's committee of the symphony board, the organization concentrated on the Progress Fund Drive, and on March 31, 1952, symphony manager Dave Romney reported to the combined boards of the Utah State Institute of Fine Arts and the Utah Symphony that the "women's committee in the Progress Fund Drive under Mrs. M. M. [Becky] Wintrobe collected over $10,000, with some other small contributions still expected."

When Margaret Beecher (the wife of prominent architect Harold K. Beecher) returned from Denver in 1953 with the format for organizing a symphony guild, a new mission shaped itself for the women. Margaret had been in charge of a "Music

Festival" after the opening concert of the 1952-53 season honoring the members of the symphony and the Abravanels. Held in the Starlite Gardens atop the Hotel Utah, the event was a late buffet and dance with over four hundred guests attending. She was later a guest of the Denver Symphony Guild, from which she received information leading to the creation of the Utah Symphony Guild.

"The Guild," as a title, has long been recognized as a property of women organized as an adjunct to every kind of endeavor in the performing arts. Most widely known perhaps is New York's Metropolitan Opera Guild with a membership that reaches westward to the Pacific and northward into Canada.

In Salt Lake City, the ballet, opera, and most theater organizations have added a guild to that of the symphony. One may presume that so many such societies would stretch thin the available membership, but these many efforts merely complement each other in promoting the arts.

On her return from Denver, Mrs. Beecher met with Lucy Abravanel and Becky Almond, and the guild was born. Becky became the first president with a panel of vice-presidents, including Mrs. Beecher, Mrs. Thomas A. (Ruth Jensen) Clawson, Mrs. Folke A. (Katherine) Myrin, and Mrs. R.W. Madsen, and a long list of minor officers and committee chairwomen. The University of Utah Union Building, now the David P. Gardner Building, remained the site of symposiums two days before each symphony concert. Among the speakers were guest artists, leading Utah musical figures, and symphony personnel.

Guild members, volunteers all, covered symphony operations with their services, working in the ticket office, raising money, entertaining visiting artists, and organizing fund-raising activities. At one time, guild funds were invested in a local business, and the profit, with the added help of Gerald Daynes of Daynes Music Company, covered the cost of a set of chimes presented by the guild to the symphony.

Few of its members will deny that to no other person did the guild mean so much as it did to Lucy Abravanel. Beloved and respected by all who knew her, she was a constant strength as she helped to hold the organization together on more than one occasion. As Mary (Mrs. Edward W.) Muir, president of the guild from 1963 to 1965, said in a comment so representative of many others: "She was vital to the life of the guild—a real strength. The organization may have foundered many times if it had not been for Lucy. She was a remarkable lady and a beautiful liaison between the presidents of the guild and her husband, Maurice, who regarded the guild as a vital arm to symphony fund-raising."

When Lucy died at the age of eighty-two in the spring of 1985, it remained for Maurice to extol her virtues and emphasize her important role in successes of the symphony. To the press he remarked: "Nobody realized how much Lucy worked for the symphony and the arts in this community while keeping strictly in the background. She was fiercely independent, and nobody on this planet could make her do anything that she did not believe in or could stop her from doing anything she thought she needed to do or say.

"In particular, when our entire recording program was collapsing for purely technical reasons, and where I, myself, had given up the idea of continuing, it was she, with her blessed stubbornness, who forced me to find a way to continue. It is no exaggeration to say that without her the recording program should have stopped before we completed the hundred-odd recordings for which music lovers all over the world hold this orchestra in particular affection.

"She was a most loving wife, totally loyal, and gave me total support every minute of the way; but also because the Utah Symphony was my life, she subdued any personal ideas to the interests of the symphony. That she did for thirty-two years."

It was Lucy who once joked about holding down third place behind the symphony and the cigar in her husband's affections. Later, when he discarded the cigar, she was happy to be "second." But there was no doubt of their mutual affection and loyalty to each other. Her position was well described in this excerpt from a *Deseret News* editorial: "He didn't drive; she served as his chauffeur. She was his bookkeeper, social secretary, hostess and gourmet cook at innumerable dinner gatherings. Her home served as a meeting place and bridge between people of different cultures, faiths, economic backgrounds and political persuasions.

"She was supportive, always at the maestro's concerts, traveled with him on tour, took care of him, and generally was what he called a 'tower of strength'. But she carefully stayed out of the limelight. In fact, she so successfully avoided being any part of her husband's fame that the public outside of those around the symphony were generally unaware of her.

"Yet Lucy Abravanel remained a woman in her own right. Those who knew her found her astute, clever, witty and dignified. A New York music critic close to the Abravanels once wrote about her as being 'busy, level-headed, and very French.'

"Raised in Paris, she always remained, first and foremost, a Parisienne. But she spent her life in the mountains of Utah, helping her husband bring great music to the state."

Although the guild was organized in 1953, its first membership tea was not held until 1954 at the home of Mrs. James L. White on Military Way. More than 270 women paid annual dues of three dollars to join the organization.

In her role as one of the guild's founders and first president, Becky Almond furthered her long service to the arts in the community. Following her career as a concert pianist of note, she taught piano and figured strongly in music organizations. During her two-year term of office, the guild continued its post-concert soirees, presenting two in 1954-55— one for the opening event, with pianist Jose Iturbi as guest, and one after the final concert, with violinist Yehudi Menuhin in attendance.

Margaret Beecher, herself an accomplished pianist and a teacher of the instrument for fifteen years, succeeded Becky as president of the guild and, among other projects, promoted a formal symphony benefit that included attendance at an art film on the life of Richard Wagner at the Tower Theater. A bomb scare emptied the audience onto Ninth South near Ninth East, on a snowy winter night, until the house could be checked and the movie resumed.

It was the first of two such alerts to be experienced by the guild, the second coming during the 1967-68 term of Oma (Mrs. W. Stanford) Wagstaff. A gala Symphony Ball crowd was dumped out into Main Street in front of the Terrace Ballroom, many down the emergency exits, while a search was made of the hall.

The guild's first Symphony Ball was staged during the administration of Judy (Mrs. Charles A.) Boynton, third president, on November 14, 1958, with Virginia (Mrs. Rulon W.) Clark as chairman. Featured guest was Paul Whiteman, who conducted the symphony for a grand march and dance that became a tradition at annual renewals of the event.

It was the guild, through the efforts of Helen (Mrs. Donald P.) Lloyd, that brought Jack Benny and his violin to the Salt Lake Tabernacle on November 14, 1964, for a performance with Abravanel and the Utah Symphony. A highly successful fund-raising effort, the project, as might well be expected in the company of such a comedian, had its share of addenda. Helen Lloyd, for instance, during her term as president of the guild from 1959 to 1961 attempted to secure Benny for a benefit concert. It was not until Mary (Mrs. Edward W.) Muir had taken over in 1963, however, that the fiddling humorist agreed to come. Then, much to their embarrassment and the smiles of their guest, the two women ran out of gas while bringing Benny into town from the airport.

There is also a footnote about the guild's being able to book the noted tightwad for peanuts. Contrary to a reputation emerging from his famous comedy routine, Benny asked only an advance of around $700, from which he paid all expenses, including his manager and a sizable entourage. Huck Gregory, who handled the funds for the event, recalls that after Benny had returned home he sent a check to cover the leftover "change."

When Katherine (Mrs. Folke A.) Myrin became president of the guild in 1961, she persuaded Vernal to sponsor the symphony in concert. As was the case back in the Werner Janssen season, the response was exceptional. The hosts not only sold tickets throughout the Uintah Basin but entertained the orchestra as well.

Jack Benny was not the only celebrity to visit during Mary Muir's term. Grant Johannesen returned from a triumphant concert tour to Russia and was honored by the guild in his hometown. Mary was followed by Yvonne (Mrs. Richard H.) Willey, daughter of a former symphony president, Raymond J. Ashton. Yvonne carried on the program for a year and then turned the gavel over to Blanche (Mrs. David L.) Freed when she moved away after serving one year. Blanche promptly gave up a trip to the American Symphony Orchestra League convention, attended annually by the reigning guild president, and used the money to pay for the first Gittins portrait of Maurice Abravanel. Following its presentation to the maestro, it was hung at Kingsbury Hall, where it has remained since.

After several years on the spring schedule, the Symphony Ball was changed back to a fall date by Janice (Mrs. Robert, Jr.) Hinckley in 1968; Helen (Mrs. George A.) Stahlke followed by adding a new dimension to fund-raising with a "pyramid" organization. Women were invited to luncheons in foursomes with each woman paying one dollar. Then each woman in turn set up similar functions of their own, and so on. The plan brought many dollars to the symphony fund.

Nellie (Mrs. Glen M.) Hatch will long remember two exceptional symphony balls that brought in proceeds of about $25,000 each during her 1972-74 term as president. She then joined other guild members in an all-out campaign for votes as her successor, Dorothy (Mrs. Wilford M.) Burton, led a drive that helped to produce a successful Symphony Hall bond election in 1975.

Guild membership broadened considerably and contributions from the Symphony Ball increased significantly during the term of Barbara (Mrs. Norman C.) Tanner in 1976-78. Sponsors were secured to foot the ball expenses for the first time, and the profit for the symphony went to $40,000.

In the following two years, Barbara (Mrs. John M.) Scowcroft engineered a restructuring of the guild's bylaws and board of directors. She also worked with presidents of the opera and ballet guilds to bring some needed coordination and continuity to the programs. During this period the guild also sponsored an appreciation dinner for Maurice Abravanel upon his retirement as music director of the Utah Symphony, an event chaired by Lucybeth Rampton.

As the Symphony Hall was nearing completion in 1979, Barbara and other members of the guild donned white gloves and spent the better part of a week affixing 18,000 beads of Bohemian crystal to six 16-by-16-foot brass chandeliers that now grace the concert hall. The gloves were to prevent finger-prints from dimming the luster of the crystals, as the volunteers, following blueprints, painstakingly hung the strings of crystals and prisms on the chandeliers imported from Austria and Czechoslovakia.

The first president to be elected under the restructured organization, Jean (Mrs. Thomas C.) Moseley instituted evening symposiums to accommodate a larger number of members, after which Josephine (Mrs. Melvin R.) Davis served through an observation of the symphony's 4,000th concert. Dorotha (Mrs. Charles R.) Smart concentrated on a docent program for Sym-phony Hall during her years as president in 1982-83. During that season Dorotha directed a Symphony Ball ("Mardi Gras") that produced $60,000 for the symphony treasury.

When Carol (Mrs. William L.) Nixon assumed the guild's first chair, she found the symphony with a new conductor and facing a strike. Fortunately the player problems were resolved in time for the "Silverstein Season" opener, and the guild was among the leaders in rallying around the new music director, Joseph Silverstein, and his wife, Adrienne. Upon her arrival, Adrienne was installed in a position of honor as a member of the guild, and since then another charming and congenial symphony companionship has made its presence felt.

Meanwhile, further revision and refinement of the guild's bylaws, largely on the advice of national consultants, was directed by Carol during an administration that preceded her selection as director of the Utah Arts Council. Her successor, Beverly (Mrs. Dale G.) Johnson, found the way cleared for a number of developments. She published the guild's first direc-tory, listing a membership of nearly four hundred, including thirteen members "at large" who volunteer as friends of the symphony as it visits their towns in Utah, Wyoming, and Idaho. Beverly also initiated a guild newsletter and made the most of three fund-raising events. Included were a gourmet food event,

"The Taste of the Towne"; a fashion show; and "The Viennese Ball" (the annual symphony ball) which netted $73,000. In all, the fund-raisers brought in $100,000, exceeding by $5,000 the guild's financial commitment to the orchestra for the season.

By the time Gloris (Mrs. Charles) Goff became president and took her place on the symphony board in 1985, the guild had reached proportions far beyond the dreams of early organizers. Its well-defined purposes were now to "foster, promote and facilitate the operation of the Utah Symphony Orchestra financially, socially and educationally" as an "organization separate and apart from the Utah Symphony board or any other board."

Membership dues had been established at $20 a year, providing a healthy financial base. The meeting schedule called for five evening "Meet the Artist" programs and the annual membership tea in the same September spot on the calendar it had occupied for thirty-two years.

To lend continuity to the guild program, the organization had long since placed the chairmanship of the annual symphony ball with its incoming vice-president and president-elect. Consequently, during the Gloris Goff year, the "Crystal Ball" arrangements were under the direction of Joyce Ann (Mrs. Robert D.) DeForest, who succeeded to the presidency in the summer of 1986. Elected vice-president and symphony ball chairman, the president-elect for the 1987-88 season, was Joann (Mrs. Edwin) Svikhart.

The "Crystal Ball," meanwhile, netted $96,000, the principal item in a record one-year contribution of $118,000 by the guild to the symphony's coffers.

The symphony store in Symphony Hall, featuring symphony T-shirts, sweatshirts, and other orchestra-related items, has become one of many projects developed by guild members to expand fund-raising and promotion. Among other ventures on the schedule are the Docent program, the Youth Guild, and the tour guide activity for Symphony Hall.

In the last analysis, there is no brighter role in Utah Symphony history than that filled by the women "in the trenches" with their countless hours of volunteer service.

Without a question, the worth of "The Guild" to the Utah
Symphony is inestimable.

CHAPTER 19

NEW HOME FOR
THE SYMPHONY

While away on its fourth international concert tour in the fall of 1977, the Utah Symphony had more than the firsthand experience of sights and sounds and hospitable crowds in Europe to be excited about. Back in Salt Lake City, a new home for the orchestra, a symphony hall of its own, was rising in the middle of town.

The triumphant troupe of musicians arrived back in Utah just in time to help lay the cornerstone for the emerging edifice. With music by Handel, Mozart, Sibelius, Copland, Weinberger, and Gould, Abravanel and the players added a significant touch to the ceremonies on a clear day in late October.

Here, a short half-block from the Salt Lake Tabernacle, a home it had occupied since 1946, the Utah Symphony was to find an all-inclusive permanent residence. A lounge and practice rooms for the musicians, space for instruments, offices for the music director-conductor and assistants, a permanent box office, headquarters for the administration and management, and a "green room" to be known as the "Abravanel Room" would be among the features of the new hall.

Ground had been broken for the edifice in the cold and snow on March 10, 1977, just seven months before the cornerstone was put in place. Except for turning the first shovelful of dirt, the historic ceremonies were held next door in the Salt Palace, which for eight years had been awaiting the arrival of a symphony hall partner it had lost along the way.

There in the assembly hall, Obert C. Tanner, the master figure in the overall project as chairman of the Utah American Revolution Bicentennial Commission, marked "this Center for the Arts" as his commission's "crowning achievement."

A member of the symphony board since 1963, Tanner had used this new role to achieve a goal that had been long in becoming a reality. Armed with the solid support of Governor Rampton and his administration, the forward thrust of Wendell J. Ashton, and the organizational skills and determination of John W. Gallivan, he had seen his prime project reach the construction stage.

Gallivan had figured prominently with many others in developing the Salt Palace complex, which had been sheared of its music-hall wing before contracts were ever signed. He knew of that agony and had joined forces to recover the loss.

As earlier noted in this history, a civic auditorium and an all-purpose music hall of some kind had been in the back of many minds around Salt Lake City for a long period of time. It was not until the early 1960s, however, that the thinking became serious. Interested planners, spurred by the efforts to secure supportive legislation, engaged in a study focused on a civic auditorium complex, regarded as a missing link in the chain of community needs for the metropolitan Salt Lake area.

Out of the movement, and the legislation, came a Salt Lake County civic auditorium board to spearhead the planning, location, and construction of a center for sports, exhibitions, and the arts. All was included in the original planning, bringing on a successful countywide bond election to ensure the project. Immediately involved was the purchase of property at the selected location between South Temple and Second South, West Temple and Second West, a two-block business area of twenty acres. Much of the area was owned by The Church of Jesus Christ of Latter-day Saints, and all of it eventually took the form of a gift when the county was given a perpetual lease to the ground at one dollar a year. The gesture greatly eased the problems of those concerned with acquiring the site and saved a few million dollars along the way.

When the Salt Palace was dedicated on Sunday afternoon, July 13, 1969, by President N. Eldon Tanner of the LDS First Presidency, the complex had shed the proposed music hall. Bids on the original plans had exceeded the available funds by some $4 million, so on November 29, 1966, the auditorium for the performing arts was eliminated from the project.

It was not the first "Salt Palace" in Salt Lake City. There are those who still remember the glittering rock-salt-covered entertainment and amusement center by that name at State Street and Ninth South. Built in 1899, it burned down in 1910.

Now a new and modern sports arena and exhibit hall had been raised in the center of the city. Its construction, viewed in a *Deseret News* music column nearly twenty years before as a necessary precursor to the building of a music hall, had been accomplished. All of that prompted this author and writer of that column to comment from a position as Salt Lake City Commissioner during dedicatory ceremonies: "It is our ambition now to get the other third of the complex—the music hall. Our hearts are set on it and we surely will achieve it."

During the next ten years, great men of vision, devotion, and determination fulfilled that promise and listened while one of them, President Tanner, dedicated the Symphony Hall on September 14, 1979. And with that, a mission placed in the hands of Obert Tanner by Governor Rampton during a casual conversation on a day in April 1972 had been accomplished.

In his book detailing the creation of the Bicentennial Center for the Arts, Tanner recalls the chance meeting with the governor in which he replied in the negative when asked if he had any free time. He quickly changed his tune, however, when Rampton offered in explanation, "I thought you might be willing to help get a symphony hall." "That's different," said Tanner, and he quickly accepted a call to serve as chairman of the Utah American Revolution Bicentennial Commission.

The eminent author, educator, lawyer, and businessman, already with an impressive record as a philanthropist and civic leader, was soon head over heels in his new task. He found that a Rampton remark indicating that the job "wouldn't take over about four hours a week" could well become "the greatest understatement in his three terms as governor."

A man of letters—he had earned eleven degrees—Tanner had just retired from the University of Utah, where he had been a philosophy professor for many years, teaching courses in social ethics and the philosophy of democracy. He had left the school with plans for writing two or three books to add to his impressive list of literary achievements. He was also about to begin a sizable expansion of his O. C. Tanner Company, a jewelry firm he had started in 1927. This project he eventually completed, and the store, at its new location on South Temple Street, has come to be regarded even by his competitors as the most beautiful store of its kind in the world.

Add to these careers a law degree, through which he remains a member of the bar, and one begins to get the idea of the man's capacity and his scope for performance and activity. That capacity, incidentally, had already been noted in Tanner's civic service. His new challenge to produce a symphony hall through a Bicentennial commission program was not his first in the field of orchestral development in Utah.

It was some years following his return to Utah from Stanford University in California, where he had been on the faculty for five years, that Tanner accepted a position on the Utah Symphony board. Since then he has served in a number of capacities, among them chairman of the Ford Foundation matching grant project. Meanwhile, he and his wife, the former Grace Adams of southern Utah's Parowan, have kept their purse open for the benefit of the symphony. They were on the first list of symphony performance sponsors in 1971-72; their funds helped obtain matching grants for the orchestra, and the Tanners have continued periodically in this role since. In the summer of 1981 their gift of $200,000 started a retirement fund for the musicians and staff, and in 1983 they established, at a much greater outlay, the biennial Gift of Music concert, a free Utah Symphony-Tabernacle Choir presentation in the Tabernacle.

Tanner's first and perhaps most important move in his new assignment was to secure the services of symphony president Wendell J. Ashton as vice-chairman of the Utah Bicentennial Commission. Ashton's heart was as much set on the acquisition of a concert hall as Tanner's, and his dedication to the cause was such as to carry the project over some rough spots along the way.

Some time after Joseph Fielding Smith had become president of The Church of Jesus Christ of Latter-day Saints in January of 1970, Wendell and Huck Gregory, at the invitation of the First Presidency, had visited with him and his first counselor, President Harold B. Lee, at Church headquarters. There the two symphony administrators heard of the Church's concern for the future of the Salt Lake Tabernacle.

In the role of spokesman for the First Presidency at the meeting, President Lee first let it be known that the Church was proud of the Utah Symphony and was proud to have the orchestra perform in the Tabernacle. He then assured his visitors that as long as no other facility was available to adequately house the symphony concerts, the orchestra would be welcome to perform in the historic structure.

President Lee went on to explain, however, that the Tabernacle, now over one hundred years old, was taxed more than ever with Church activities and visiting tourists. He expressed the desire of the Church to preserve the building, particularly to meet the growing religious demands for which it was erected. As one welcome change, he cited the fact that the United States presidents and major presidential candidates who had always appeared there were now being seen and heard at the Salt Palace. The Church official emphasized that the Church would look with extreme favor on any effort to secure a new home for the symphony, but it would not initiate such a project since it did not want to exert undue influence.

It now being obvious that almost everyone with an interest in the Utah Symphony was anxious to help locate the orchestra in its own residence, the Bicentennial program became an encouraging potential path to that end. Most reassuring, meanwhile, was the knowledge that the Tabernacle, as it had been for twenty-five seasons to that point, would continue to be available rent free until the goal was reached.

The Bicentennial Commission's path to its crowning achievement—the Symphony Hall—contained some frustrating twists and turns before it took a straight and reliable course. First to be encountered was a curve set up in the halls of Congress. A possibility had surfaced that the federal lawmakers might appropriate $1.25 billion to be divided equally among the fifty states to be used as they saw fit in celebrating the bicentennial year of 1976. The idea had reached a point where a National Bicentennial Commission appointed by Congress had sent the firm of Booz, Allen and Hamilton to determine if a required feasibility study had progressed to a point where Utah would be eligible for its $25 million share of the fund. In the end, however, it mattered little. In 1973 Congress dropped its grandiose idea and decided that each state and community should plan and finance its own bicentennial celebration. In place of the $25 million, it made a token amount of $45,000 available for each state, provided it was matched with state money.

Governor Rampton and the Utah legislature not only matched that figure but went well beyond in appropriating $8 million to the Bicentennial Commission, with $6.5 million to be used for a concert hall, also with a provision that the amount be matched by other than state funds. The other $1.5 million was to be spent outside of Salt Lake County and eventually went into more than three hundred projects.

After exhausting other routes, during which time the Legislature fixed a deadline of December 31, 1975, for matching the state's offer, Obert Tanner and his commission followed their path to the Salt Lake County Commission. As a last resort, commissioners William E. Dunn, Ralph McClure, and Pete Kutulas agreed to place a countywide $8,675,000 general obligation bond issue before the voters on December 16, two weeks before the matching-fund deadline.

Virtually a year-long crusade, the Symphony Hall bond campaign and its preparation was an arduous affair that became the principal occupation of the twenty-five-member

Tanner commission and two resourceful and enterprising overseers.

Jack Gallivan was an ardent campaigner who had received his share of special election lumps along the way. A prominent member of the Catholic community, publisher of the *Salt Lake Tribune*, and a highly respected community leader, he was a strong supporter of the Utah Symphony and recognized it as an invaluable asset to the city and the state. He had been its president in 1964-65 and was still on the board as an advisor to the president.

Among Gallivan's disappointments at the polls had been the denial of two propositions in which he was intensely interested. One was an attempt to merge Salt Lake City and Salt Lake County into a single government, and the other, in 1968, was a bitterly fought campaign to permit sale of liquor by the drink in the state of Utah. One of his principal opponents in the latter was Wendell Ashton, who now saw Gallivan as the logical man to be general chairman of the Symphony Hall bond election. He suggested the appointment, and upon a direct invitation from Governor Rampton, Gallivan agreed to head up the all-important campaign.

In the meantime, Tanner had seen the need of an experienced campaign manager to work with the chairman. For this job he found Richard Eyre, a Utahn then living in Washington, D.C., where he was head of a firm consulting in political campaigns. He had already made his mark at home by managing Jake Garn's successful campaign for the United States Senate in 1974. To secure his services, Tanner not only personally paid a substantial salary but offered at his own expense to move the Eyre family to Salt Lake City and to give the prospective campaign manager an attractive bonus on the success of the election. It was enough to bring the needed Eyre expertise into the program.

During the critical campaign year of 1975, meanwhile, some most significant changes came into the ultimate planning for Utah's Bicentennial Center for the Arts. A general understanding had developed that the facility would house the symphony, ballet, opera, and related music presentations. This thinking started to change, however, when Dr. Cyril M. Harris of Columbia University, a recognized leader in the field of acoustics, was invited to become involved in the project as acoustical consultant. Asserting that multi-purpose halls had never been completely successful and were never likely to be, he declined. He went on to say he would be very interested in working on a symphony hall if some other place, such as an old theater, could be restored for the other performing arts.

In a coincidental move, the Bicentennial Commission chairman, at his own expense, had sent Rick Eyre on a tour of concert halls throughout the United States. In his book about the bicentennial project, Tanner reports that the visits included one to St. Louis, where Eyre became impressed with the successful restoration of a vintage theater. With this in mind, according to the author, the campaign manager on returning home happened to glance at the Capitol Theatre on Second South and saw the possibility of remodeling the structure for ballet and opera purposes. Tanner credits Eyre with first conceiving this idea, leading to that important part of the Bicentennial arts program and to the ultimate construction of a hall designed principally for symphony performances.

The two performance halls, together with the art museum adjacent to Symphony Hall, made up the proposed $18 million Bicentennial Arts Center complex that was dependent upon the passage of the proposed bond issue. It was a challenging assignment for Gallivan and Eyre and company, particularly in light of the normally discouraging odds they faced. The voters in the county had in 1973 turned back a $49.5 million bond issue that included a music hall, and with business in a recession in 1975, more than 93 percent of the bond attempts placed before voters throughout the country had failed.

In a study of bond elections in the county, however, Eyre had found they attracted a low turnout and that consequently they were controlled by a small percentage of voters. His deduction was that the thousands of pro-symphony residents in the valley could control this election if they were contacted and persuaded to vote. His reasoning was accepted by Gallivan, and the vigorous, skillfully organized campaign concentrated on people and areas favorable to the arts. The result, in a comparatively heavy vote for a bond election, was a decisive victory for the Bicentennial arts project, 32,932 votes for the bond program and 25,716 against.

From then on it was full steam ahead for Symphony Hall. Gallivan, instead of retiring from the picture after a coveted victory, became chairman of the planning and construction committee. With him were O. Thayne Acord, chairman of the Salt Palace board, symphony president Ashton, Frank A. Nelson, Jr., and two architects, George S. Nicolatus, a vice-president with First Security Corporation, and Glen R. Swenson, head of the state building board.

Theirs was a most successful accomplishment in bringing together the elements that produced a magnificent building with exceptional acoustics. Dr. Harris, having changed the course of planning at the critical point, accepted a position as acoustical consultant, and his expertise is credited with producing an orchestral sound chamber to rank among the finest in the world.

Designed by the Salt Lake City architectural firm of Fowler, Ferguson, Kingston and Ruben, the hall is perhaps most characteristic of the Avery Fish Hall in New York's Lincoln Center, home of the New York Philharmonic. In form, according to its creators, it also bears characteristics of the fine symphony halls such as the Symphony Hall in Boston, Vienna's Grosser Musikvereinssaal, and the Concertgebouw in Amsterdam.

Several factors came into play in providing the acoustical excellence of the golden-toned and golden-hued auditorium. Strictly a concert hall in design, it is without a proscenium curtain and the other components of a conventional stage. Thus the orchestra platform in effect becomes an extension of the main body of the hall, contributing to the quality of sound created by its rectangular "shoebox" shape and carefully planned size and dimensions—approximately 160 feet long, 90 feet wide, and 55 feet high. The seating capacity of 2,802 provides space for 1,828 in the orchestra section, 406 on the first tier, 298 on the second, and 270 on the third; that is considered to be the maximum for acoustical perfection.

Generous symphony donors and sponsors soon provided the appointments and special features to give the new concert hall an elegance complementary to the design and fine musical properties of the building. To enhance the approach to Symphony Hall, a 136-foot-long fountain created a wall of water to be reflected with the Salt Lake City skyline in the huge glass face of the structure. Contributed by Obert and Grace Tanner, the fountain was one of many presented by these philanthropists to lend a living artistry to public buildings and areas in the city.

To help adorn the four-story lobby inside the glass doors, the Tanners provided twenty-four-karat gold leaf for the grand staircase and a large concrete wall. This feature was extended into the concert hall as a contribution of the benevolent and humanitarian rags-to-riches Salt Lake merchant, Maurice Warshaw and his wife, Inez.

A blonde hardwood ceiling of white oak in the lobby is a gift of the Union Pacific Railroad Foundation, and, as previously recorded, the chandeliers inside the orchestra hall, to which the crystals had been fitted by members of the Symphony Guild, were paid for by the C. Comstock Clayton Foundation. A concert grand piano for the use of the Utah Symphony was donated by Zion's Cooperative Mercantile Institution (ZCMI) through the efforts of Oakley S. Evans, president, and the musicians' chairs were gifts of Mrs. Morris S. Rosenblatt in memory of her late husband.

Even the business offices and musicians quarters, which, like the lobby, are isolated from the concert hall, were objects of symphony givers. The decor design of the business offices, for instance, was a contribution of Stephen L. Richins of the Richins Organization. Nearby, the conductor's office and dressing room and the guest artist dressing rooms were furnished by Mr. and Mrs. M. Walker Wallace. Behind the performance area, the furnishings of the new conductor's room and the musicians' lounge were added gifts of Obert and Grace Tanner.

Finally, the "Abravanel Room," with its furnishings, decorations, and Mason and Hamlin baby grand piano, was a gift of

Salt Lake City businessman Monte C. Nelson and his family in memory of their daughter and sister Nancy Jolene.

When the Symphony Hall was finally ready for its grand opening and dedication on September 14, 1979, the man to whom the magnificent edifice would stand as a monument was not on hand to lead the orchestra he had built. Maurice Abravanel had retired and would never conduct in the place that had been his dream for many years.

In his stead there remains a second portrait by the master painter, Alvin Gittins, a gift of the Ogden Symphony-Ballet Association. It hangs in the grand lobby almost as the very conscience of the symphony this master of the baton had molded into greatness.

Top Left: *George S. and Dolores Dore' Eccles, unexcelled Utah Symphony benefactors.*
Top and Middle Right: *C. Comstock Clayton and Mabel Clayton generously supported Utah Symphony through the C. Comstock Clayton Foundation.*
Bottom Left: *(L.-r.) Mrs. and Mr. Norman C. Tanner, symphony sponsors. Mrs. Tanner also served as general chairman of the Utah Symphony Gina Bachauer International Piano Competition.*
Bottom Right: *Joseph Rosenblatt, industrialist, philanthropist, Utah Symphony sponsor and board member.*

Top: *Grace A. and Dr. Obert C. Tanner standing before Symphony Hall lobby plaque honoring American Revolution Bicentennial. Dr. Tanner chaired Utah's Bicentennial Commission in 1976 which spearheaded construction of Symphony Hall and renovation of the Capitol Theatre.*
Below Left: *Donald P. and Helen Lloyd, Utah Symphony patrons. Mrs. Lloyd was Utah Symphony Guild president. Mr. Lloyd was president, Associated Food Stores, 20-year sponsors of children's concerts; also Utah Symphony Board member.*
Below Right: *Dean E. Eggertsen (r.), trustee of S. B. Eggertsen, confers with Maurice Abravanel during 1975 European concert tour. Eggertsen undertook to endow the conductor's podium.*

Top Left: *Maurice and Inez Warshaw, longstanding Utah Symphony patrons and sponsors.*
Top Right: *Spence and Jill Clark, major sponsors of Utah Symphony concerts and other activites.*
Middle Left: *John and Marilyn Dahlstrom, major sponsors of the Utah Symphony.*
Middle Right: *Monte C. and Viola Nelson, Utah Symphony benefactors.*
Bottom Left: *Howard and Kay Ruff, Utah Symphony benefactors.*
Bottom Right: *For 20 years Bennett's (represented here by Sen. Wallace F. Bennett) provided office space for Utah Symphony at 55 West 1st South, Salt Lake City.*

Top: *John M. and Glenn Walker Wallace have provided major funding at crucial junctures of the Utah Symphony.*
Below Left: *Dr. A. Ray Olpin, president University of Utah; ardent supporter and board member, Utah Symphony, 1946-1964.*
Photo credit: Photo Archives, Special Collections Dept., U of U Libraries.
Below Right: *The Church of Jesus Christ of Latter-day Saints provided a home for the Utah Symphony without charge for 32 years in the Tabernacle as well as the building site for Symphony Hall. Over the years the Church has been a major donor.*

CHAPTER 20

THE MAESTRO RETIRES

When Maurice Abravanel retired from his post as music director and conductor of the Utah Symphony on April 21, 1979, he put away his baton for the last time. Just as an athlete might obey his physician's order and hang up his shoes for good, so the maestro responded to his doctor's advice to step down from the podium.

The final decision had been two-and-a-half years in the making. Heart surgery in November 1976 had interrupted Abravanel's physical presence with his orchestra for the first time in twenty-nine years. Now he was faced with bidding farewell to his beloved players and turning them over to a new leader.

As his many friends and host of followers were well aware, Maurice could not go on forever. Moreover, no one was more conscious of this than were Maurice and Lucy Abravanel after the maestro had conducted the symphony to a flying start in his thirtieth anniversary season.

He had come to that season after a particularly outstanding 1975-76 series that audiences were still savoring. It started with a remarkably imaginative contemporary program including the Chadwick "Jubilee" Overture, a world premiere of

Tabernacle organist Robert Cundick's Concerto for Organ and Strings with the composer at the console, the Roy Harris Symphony No. 3, and the Shostakovich Symphony No. 5.

The list of guest artists was a box-office bonanza. Pianist Arthur Rubinstein, in his final performance with the Utah Symphony, performed the Brahms Piano Concerto No. 1 in D Minor. Itzhak Perlman, the noted violin virtuoso, joined Abravanel and the orchestra in the Mozart Violin Concerto No. 4 in D Major, and pianist Van Cliburn appeared in the MacDowell Piano Concerto No. 2 in D Major. The sensational Russian cellist, Mstislav Rostropovich was scheduled for a spring performance but because of illness gave way to Gregor Piatigorsky, then in the twilight of his career, in a performance of the Dvorak Cello Concerto.

Choral works involving Newell Weight's Utah Chorale included an evening with Haydn's "The Creation," with soprano JoAnn Ottley and baritone Robert Peterson as soloists, and a program that featured two works recorded by the full company on Angel records, the "Symphony of Psalms" by Stravinsky, and Randall Thompson's "Testament of Freedom" for male chorus and orchestra. Also on the regular series was the Mahler Symphony No. 7 ("Song of the Night").

Robertson's "Trilogy" was revived on the first of two concerts on the University of Utah Contemporary Music Festival on February 20. It followed two world premieres, the Vladimir Ussachevsky "Colloquy for Symphony Orchestra, Electronic Tape and Various Chairs" and a piano concerto by Ramiro Cortes, a Dallas, Texas, composer in residence at the University of Utah. The composer conducted, while Sally Peterson, the 1972 "Miss Utah" and Julliard School of Music graduate, performed at the keyboard.

In all, 144 performances were presented during the season, with 22 of them in subscription series at Salt Lake City and Ogden. The other 122 were presented in cities and towns through the state and in four separate tours that carried the orchestra from Holland, Michigan, on the east to Hayward, California, on the west, a total of 32 concerts. Shirl Swenson was still booking Abravanel and the symphony across the country, and the California tour was an annual affair.

The symphony took winter trips to six northern California cities following an opening performance at Reno, Nevada; it also played in Helena, Great Falls, and Butte, Montana; and in Idaho Falls, Rexburg, Boise, and Pocatello, Idaho. The first midwestern tour, in April 1976, to ten cities started in Michigan; then it worked westward through Naperville and Quincy, Illinois; Ames and Burlington, Iowa; Madison and Stevens Point, Wisconsin; Columbia, Missouri; and Iola, Kansas. It closed at Rapid City, South Dakota, with a concert in the Black Hills. A regional tour to Boulder, Colorado, and six towns in Wyoming in May ended the interstate traveling for the season.

The Bicentennial summer of 1976 produced a historic event in Utah music that marked with appropriate grandeur the celebration of 200 years of American independence. For the first time in 31 years the Utah Symphony and the Salt Lake Mormon Tabernacle Choir appeared together, presenting a series of seven Bicentennial concerts.

Opening at the Salt Lake Tabernacle on May 29, the program began with Crawford Gates conducting "A New Morning," his Symphony No. 4 for Orchestra and Choir. Jerold Ottley then took the podium for a performance of Howard Hanson's "Song of Democracy," and Abravanel finished off with the Bernstein "Chichester Psalms" and the "Battle Hymn of the Republic."

Repeat performances of the program, sponsored by Utah's American Revolution Bicentennial Commission, were heard in Logan, Ogden, Provo, Zion National Park, and Manti before a return to the Salt Lake Tabernacle for the final performance on June 15.

Abravanel opened the 1976-77 season with two all-orchestral concerts and a performance on October 30 with Grant Johannesen in the Prokofiev Piano Concerto No. 3, after which he and Lucy made a fateful visit to France. It was to be an utterly frustrating and disappointing experience.

Maurice had been invited to conduct a performance of Darius Milhaud's gigantic "Oresteia" in Paris. Written between

1913 and 1922 to Paul Claudel's translation of a trilogy by Aeschylus on the tragedy of Orestes, the huge operatic work had never been done in its entirety in a single performance. The "Les Chorephores" middle section was performed in Paris in 1919, and the first part, "Agamemnon," was done there in 1927. The huge "Les Eumenides" third section, a three-act opera in itself, was given a complete performance in Brussels in 1949, a production that was a great satisfaction to Milhaud. He wrote in his autobiography that the work is "so difficult I never expected to hear it performed in my lifetime."

When Milhaud died in 1974, Abravanel was known to have become the composer's favorite conductor of his works, and it had been his personal request that Maurice do the "Oresteia" in Paris. Now the invitation had come, and Maurice prepared himself to fulfill the request in a scheduled November 1976 performance. It was such a gargantuan undertaking, with the course of the work running three and a half hours and requiring an orchestra of 120 musicians, large choruses, and many soloists, that Abravanel seemed to be about the only conductor capable of pulling it off.

But the intended grand premiere production was not to be. For though he had put forth the effort to learn the huge and difficult score and had prepared himself well for the historic event, Maurice found the obstacles in Paris to be insurmountable. At his first rehearsal it was clear there would be some problems. Discipline among the players was poor. Some of the key musicians the conductor had been promised were not available because they were said to be needed for a production Leonard Bernstein was conducting at about the same time. In the end, the situation became so difficult that Abravanel, for the first time in his long conducting career, threw down the score and told the concert sponsors there was no way he could continue. Then he walked out.

It was a deeply traumatic moment for one so dedicated to his craft, and it was bound to take its toll physically. As he and Lucy prepared to leave Paris, the maestro felt some chest pains and other discomfort in his chest. Again on arrival in New York City he complained of the same problems.

When he reached Salt Lake City Maurice was examined by his physician, who forthwith ordered him to the hospital. There on November 29 he underwent surgery for a triple coronary bypass.

A shock to the orchestra and to its world of devotees, the cardiotomy slowed Utah Symphony operations, but not for long. Motivated by some medical predictions of a short life ahead, particularly for a man of seventy-three years, Maurice determined he would upset the forecasts. His recovery soon indicated an early return, and in less than three months he was back on the podium. And, as noted in the minutes of the Utah Symphony executive committee meeting on February 18, 1977, "Although not conducting during this period, Mr. Abravanel had nevertheless functioned as music director making artistic decisions, etc., for all except one week following his operation."

While Maurice was immobilized, the conducting chores fell upon his associate conductor, Ardean Watts, who handled the situation with amazing composure and skill. Ardean had been before the orchestra on many occasions, but never with Abravanel flat on his back and the full load on his shoulders. He had the full confidence of the maestro, who had selected him because of his remarkable ability to do so many things, and to do them well.

Born in the little south-central Utah town of Kanosh, Ardean spent much of his early life in Idaho, attending school there and in Utah before furthering his music education at the Academy of Music in Vienna, Austria. A most versatile musician of unerring technical facility, he had joined the Utah Symphony in 1956 as its official pianist and had distinguished himself in orchestra, choral, opera, ballet, and musical comedy conducting. For years he doubled with the orchestra as official pianist and associate conductor, and he often appeared at the piano, harpsichord, or celeste when the instrument was needed.

Credited with founding the Utah Opera Company, Watts served as its executive musical and stage director and for a number of seasons was music director and conductor of Ballet

West. He has been described by critics as "a one-man music factory" who is "nothing short of spectacular."

While Abravanel was in Paris, Gunther Schuller, talented American composer, conductor, and educator, appeared with the Utah Symphony in guest-conducting role that would bring him back in 1981 and again in 1985. The principal work on the program of contemporary music was Schuller's own Violin Concerto, with Zvi Zeitlin as soloist.

Watts then took over, and on December 4, five days after Abravanel's heart surgery, he conducted a moving performance of Ernest Bloch's "Sacred Service" at the Tabernacle, with the symphony joined by the Utah Chorale and baritone Douglas Lawrence as the cantor and Rabbi Abner Bergman as the minister. The Prelude and "Liebestod" from Wagner's "Tristan and Isolde" and the Richard Strauss tone poem "Death and Transfiguration" filled the first half of the concert.

It was a busy time for Ardean, who conducted everything up until February 19, with the exception of a concert on January 12 when Guido Ajmone-Marsan appeared as guest conductor in a program of Barber's "Adagio for Strings," Mozart's Symphony No. 34, and the Dvorak Symphony No. 8.

On one evening of rare musical collaboration, soprano JoAnn Ottley appeared with Watts and the symphony on February 4 in the Berlioz song cycle, "Les Nuits d'ete," and two Verdi arias. For Ottley it was the first of four performances with the symphony over the remainder of the season. The wife of Jerold Ottley, conductor of the Tabernacle Choir, JoAnn had become the most sought-after lyric soprano in the area, following in the steps of such artists as Blanche Christensen and Jean Preston. An excellent singer possessed of fine musicianship and superb and consistent quality all along her wide range to the high tessitura, she had caught the ear of Abravanel when he needed s soprano in an emergency for a recording session. Once that happened she became almost as well acquainted with the Utah Symphony as with the Tabernacle Choir.

When Abravanel returned to the Tabernacle podium on February 19, JoAnn Ottley was there. She sang the solo role in the Mahler Fourth Symphony in G Major on an all-Mahler program that also included the First Symphony in D Major. And in the final event of the season subscription series, Ottley was the soprano soloist with Christina Krooskos, contralto; Louis Welcher, tenor; Philip Frohnmayer, baritone; and the Utah Chorale in the Bach B Minor Mass, another Abravanel triumph. The principal instrumentalists were Alexander Schreiner at the organ and Ardean Watts at the harpsichord.

Ottley still wasn't through. On June 8 Maurice turned once more to the Beethoven Ninth Symphony for "The Brotherhood of Man" concert at the Tabernacle honoring the Salt Lake International Center on its dedication, an event presented under full sponsorship of Adnan M. Khashoggi, Saudi-Arabian billionaire, through the Triad Foundation. JoAnn again was soprano soloist, this time with Lani Lee Poulson, Ray L. Arbizu, and Robert Peterson.

Meanwhile, Watts found it necessary to keep his baton warm. He had conducted a special Lincoln's Birthday concert at the Tabernacle on February 12, just before Maurice returned, with Governor Scott M. Matheson as narrator in "A Lincoln Portrait," by Copland. His next subscription concert assignment came at Ogden on April 7 with only a five-minute warning that he would be replacing the maestro.

The situation arose at the intermission of a subscription concert after Maurice had conducted a performance of the Tchaikovsky "Pathetique" Symphony No. 6 in B Minor. As announced to the audience by Shirl Swenson, Abravanel had "overtaxed himself" and was unable to proceed with the closing work on the program. In addition to the tiring Tchaikovsky opener that evening, he had been through a difficult rehearsal earlier in the day at the Salt Lake Tabernacle.

Watts was studying in a nearby building when he got the word to change quickly into concert dress and take over. He did so and conducted the Rachmaninoff Piano Concerto No. 3, with the Soviet virtuoso, Lazar Berman, as soloist.

Under his contract, Ardean was "on call" at all times in the event Maurice was not able to perform, but not until after the maestro's heart surgery did the possibility of such emergencies become a serious matter. Watts had chauffeured Abravanel to and from rehearsals for twelve years, and the two had formed a close alliance. The assistant conductor knew of the music director's precarious health problems and was now present, nearby, at all times with his formal attire within arm's reach.

On this occasion Berman first angrily rebelled and threatened not to go on without Abravanel. Realizing the seriousness of the situation, however, he agreed to perform and at the close was so pleased he locked Watts in a real Russian bear hug and spent the rest of the evening at a reception extolling the Watts performance.

Ardean conducted the full concert the following night in Salt Lake City and again made an excellent showing. David L. Beck, the *Salt Lake Tribune* critic, gave the performance some particularly high marks and, with regard to the associate conductor, wrote: "The Utah Symphony and the community owe Mr. Watts a great deal this season for holding things together, working even harder than usual during the convalescence of Maurice Abravanel. . . . But the Berman concerts may have been his finest moment."

Maurice observed the completion of his thirtieth anniversary season on May 24, 1977, with a special concert in the Tabernacle. Joining in the celebration with arias from operas of Mozart, Rossini, and Donizetti was Beverly Sills, the celebrated diva who was a promising young soprano when introduced to Utah years before by Abravanel in summer festivals at the University of Utah Stadium Bowl. The brilliant affair was followed by a dinner in honor of the maestro at which Maurice and Lucy were presented with a brand new automobile, an Oldsmobile Delta 88 Royale paid for by Joseph Rosenblatt and his sister-in-law, Mrs. Morris Rosenblatt. Lucy could now get rid of her worn-out Buick and chauffeur her husband around town in the nice new car. Maurice never took to driving an automobile.

So well did the maestro rally from his surgery that, in addition to his concert schedule, he was able to conduct ten recording sessions during which the Utah Symphony recorded for Vanguard all of the Sibelius symphonies. As already noted, he accompanied the orchestra on the four-week European tour in the fall, after which he turned his attention to another demanding season.

There was no attempt on Abravanel's part to cut back on the symphony schedule. Rather he seemed to intensify the effort to reach a fifty-two-week season for his players and to increase the musical output for their listeners. The touring continued on a regional basis and beyond, with two trips in the spring of 1977 taking the symphony to Southern California and Las Vegas for four concerts and to the Northwest for twenty concerts. That jaunt reached Vancouver, British Columbia, after a start through northern California, and wound its way through Oregon, Washington, Montana, and Wyoming.

Abravanel's last two seasons as music director and conductor of the Utah Symphony were the orchestra's final years in the Salt Lake Tabernacle. It all came out even, a total of thirty-two years for the maestro's Utah career and thirty-two years of symphony in the historic pioneer gathering place of The Church of Jesus Christ of Latter-day Saints. The great hall was made available a year before the arrival of Abravanel, but one season had been spent at Highland High School to permit some needed refurbishing of the hundred-year-old building.

In appreciation for the long association with the Tabernacle, Abravanel and the orchestra were joined on June 10, 1978, by some old friends and popular performers in a "Tribute to the Tabernacle" program. Metropolitan Opera baritone Robert Merrill occupied the vocal role, and pianist Grant Johannesen came home once more for the solo spot in the Beethoven "Emperor" Concerto No. 5. Providing the variety were the Osmonds, Utah's favorites of the national teen set.

During the season before that event, the late Gina Bachauer had been honored in a memorial concert of Tchaikovsky works. Van Cliburn was guest soloist in the Piano Concerto No. 1, leading off another season of virtuoso guest performers. Rostropovich finally appeared with the symphony, stunning his listeners in the Prokofiev "Sinfonia Concertante" for Cello and Orchestra on an all-Prokofiev program. Violinists Perlman, in the Mendelssohn Concerto, and Isaac Stern, playing the Mozart

Concerto No. 5 and the Prokofiev No. 1 in a single evening, were on the schedule, as was the diminutive Spanish keyboard master Alicia de Larrocha, in an all-Beethoven evening, performing the Piano Concerto No. 4 in G Major.

Perhaps the high points in the season, however, were two prodigious Mahler productions that required extra forces and greater effort from Maurice and the orchestra, choruses, and soloists. On December 9 the maestro followed the Adagietto from the Mahler Fifth Symphony with the triumphant "Resurrection" Symphony No. 2 with Newell Weight's Utah Chorale and JoAnn Ottley and Christina Krooskos as soloists.

For the season finale on April 15, Abravanel produced the gigantic Mahler Eighth Symphony, the "Symphony of a Thousand," a work he had recorded for Vanguard in 1964. The maestro augmented the orchestra to 112 pieces, including a mandolin played by Kenneth Kuchler, the assistant concertmaster, for this performance. Particularly noticeable was the buildup in the brass section, with seven horns, seven trombones, and eight trumpets in place of the usual three. Combined into the choir were Newell Weight's Utah Chorale and the University of Utah's a cappella chorus, the University Chamber Chorus, directed by Dr. Bernell Hales; the University Masterworks Chorus, directed by Louis Welcher; and the Utah Boys' Choir and South High School Girls' Chorus, both under the direction of Richard Torgerson. The battery of seven vocal soloists was made up of JoAnn Ottley and Jean Hieronymi, sopranos; Mariana Paunova and Nina Hinson, contraltos; Louis Welcher, tenor; Hervey Hicks, baritone; and John Trout, bass.

As had been proved so many times before, nothing was too big for Maurice, and once more he pulled off an incredible performance. In the midst of the prolonged, resounding reception, the maestro, as he had with the Bruckner "Nullte" in the Brucknerhalle in Linz, Austria, seven months before, held up the Mahler score to share the ovation.

A part of the vocal cast returned six weeks later on May 25 and 26 to join with the Utah Symphony and the Salt Lake Tabernacle Choir in one of their rare collaborations. This time it was a performance of Robertson's "Book of Mormon Oratorio," with Maurice Abravanel conducting, the production later to be recorded by CBS Masterworks. Handling the youth chorus assignments were Torgerson's Boys Choir and South High girls unit. Hervey Hicks was heard in the difficult role of the prophet Samuel. Other soloists included Don Becker, John Prather, and JoAnn Ottley. To open the concert, the choir and symphony presented the "Ode of Supplication," a new work by a rising Utah composer, Robert P. Manookin, with Ottley and baritone Clayne Robison as soloists.

Guest conductors took some of the strain off Abravanel during the 1978-79 season, but not enough to keep it from being the maestro's last with "his orchestra." There had been some hope that the new Symphony Hall would be ready during that season, but this, too, was not to be, and he finished his career in the Tabernacle.

The impressive young American conductor James DePreist, who had debuted with the symphony the previous January as a baton guest, was back on October 28. Peter Eros took over the podium on December 8 and conducted the Vaughan Williams "A Sea Symphony" with the Utah Chorale and soloists Ottley and Hicks. Sarah Caldwell, perhaps the most prominent female conductor of the day, filled a January 19 date, and Ardean Watts conducted on February 23.

One of the principal personnel changes had seen J. Ryan Selberg replace Christian Tiemeyer as the principal cellist. Tiemeyer had turned his hand to conducting and with Watts shared the podium in five Utah Symphony summer concerts at the Snowbird winter and summer resort in Little Cottonwood canyon. Selberg distinguished himself as he shared the solo spotlight with concertmaster Oscar Chausow and viola principal Christopher McKellar in a performance of the Richard Strauss "Don Quixote" under Abravanel on November 11. Another orchestra principal, clarinetist Christie Lundquist, was soloist in the Thea Musgrave Clarinet Concerto on the Caldwell program, a University of Utah Contemporary Music Festival concert. The Watts program was also on the contemporary music festival schedule, and the concert included music of Hovhaness, Shostakovich (the Symphony No. 15), and George

Crumb. Abravanel's Mahler concert for the season, meanwhile, had been the Symphony No. 3 on January 13 with the combined Utah Chorale and University Masterworks Choir, and with Paunova as contralto soloist.

An interesting departure from the regular schedule occurred on March 2, when the Honolulu Symphony under Donald Johanos appeared at the Tabernacle in an exchange arrangement that sent the Utah Symphony to the Hawaiian capital. Johanos conducted his ensemble in "The Birds" by Respighi and the Ginastera "Variaciones Concertantes." The following night he whipped up a "Hawaiian Pops" concert, complete with a corps of Hula artists, as the Capitol Theater.

It was about this time that Maurice began to think seriously, with Lucy's encouragement, of following the doctor's orders about retirement. On the morning of March 23, 1979, he called the symphony's executive director, his close associate for twenty-two years, Huck Gregory, to say he was not feeling well and could not conduct the concert scheduled that evening in the Tabernacle. He had conducted the performance in Ogden the night before, with Andre Watts as soloist in the Brahms Piano Concerto No. 2, but he was too ill to repeat it on the subscription series in Salt Lake City. Before he called Gregory, Maurice had already spoken to Ardean Watts about taking over. The associate conductor agreed to fill in and, in addition, conducted a California tour scheduled the following week.

Hardly had the symphony returned from its trip to the West Coast when, just twelve days after finding it inadvisable to conduct the March 23 concert, the maestro gave his final notice. He was scheduled to conduct the usual Ogden and Salt Lake City concerts on April 6 and 7 with Judith Blegen as soprano soloist. Blegen had been a product of the Music Academy of the West in Santa Barbara under Abravanel, so there was no doubt he was looking forward to working with her. Once again, however, on Wednesday, April 4, he called Wendell Ashton and Huck Gregory and told them he was turning over the rehearsal of that day to Ardean Watts and could not conduct the upcoming Friday and Saturday concerts. Abravanel then advised the administration and management of the symphony that he had decided to retire as music director effective immediately.

Naturally every attempt was made to get the maestro to postpone his decision. Ashton and Gregory assured him he could conduct as much or as little as he liked, but to stay on for his own good and that of the symphony. Maurice would not be dissuaded, however, and he insisted on resigning the post. During the afternoon, while on the way home, Wendell Ashton stopped at the Abravanels' and urged Maurice to conduct the Blegen concerts and the final program of the year, the Verdi "Requiem," at the Tabernacle on April 21. The maestro refused to appear that weekend but agreed is was logical for him to finish out the season by conducting the last concert.

Meanwhile, when Ardean showed up to conduct the rehearsal on April 4, the musicians rebelled. So difficult was the situation for Watts that he summoned Gregory and Shirl Swenson to meet with the players at the rehearsal hall in the old Immanuel Baptist Church at Second South and Fourth East.

The orchestra members were concerned that Watts was being groomed to slip into the slot of music director if and when Abravanel should retire or become incapacitated. They wanted others to be considered. They were assured that such was not the case and went on with the rehearsals and the weekend concerts, feeling they had made their point. Almost to the very last performer, the musicians expressed a high personal regard for Watts as a colleague and friend and great respect for his loyalty and superb musicianship, but they said they simply did not enjoy playing under his direction. Consequently, because of Ardean's extra conducting occasioned by the maestro's increasing inability to function, there was a growing discontent among the players insofar as the conducting was concerned.

By the time the musicians faced Watts for the Saturday concert, they knew of Abravanel's resignation. They were also aware of an action by the administration that was reassuring as to the selection of a new music director and conductor. That very morning Wendell Ashton had called an emergency meeting of the full Utah Symphony board at the rehearsal hall. There he announced the resignation of Maurice Abravanel and the appointment of a search committee to find his replacement. Dr. R. J. Snow, a University of Utah vice-president with an impressive reputation in such projects, was secured as chairman. Others included Mrs. Norman C. (Barbara) Tanner, president of the Symphony Guild; Board Member M. Walker Wallace; Mrs. David L. (Blanche) Freed; Clarinetist Christie Lundquist, representing the orchestra; Lowell M. Durham; and Thomas J. Moore, president of the Ogden Symphony Guild and vice-president on the symphony board. Huck Gregory was appointed secretary with Carleen Landes as his assistant.

Two weeks later Abravanel returned to the Tabernacle for the first time in two-and-a-half months to conduct the season finale, Verdi's "Requiem." With him were his music-making friends and associates of many occasions, his Utah Symphony, Newell Weight and his Utah Chorale, and four soloists, JoAnn Ottley, Mariana Paunova, Glade Peterson, and Hervey Hicks.

A most fitting description of the emotion-packed final concert is that of Abravanel's close friend and confidant, chauffeur, symphony business consultant, and associate, Huck Gregory. From his memoirs we take the following: "As expected by those close to the unfolding drama, the season finale in the Tabernacle on the evening of April 21, 1979, became and remains one of the great moments in Utah Symphony's history. The Requiem performance was exquisite in its interpretation. The Utah Chorale was at its best. Almost without exception the soloists sang beautifully. It was a truly moving performance.

"Thunderous applause greeted the performers at the conclusion of the concert. After graciously acknowledging it, the conductor and soloists made their way through the orchestra to the archway leading backstage. As the applause continued, they emerged through the same archway and threaded their way through the orchestra, this time accompanied also by the director of the Chorale, who shared the accolade. Orchestra and Chorale were invited to stand as usual and receive their crescendo of applause. Again the conductor, soloists and Chorale director left the stage, and again they returned to reenact the acknowledgement from the audience, then left the stage.

"Finally the Maestro emerged through the archway and made his way to the podium for a solo bow. He signalled the musicians to rise, but they refused. It is doubtful that there was ever a more emotional, prolonged ovation in the venerable Tabernacle than the one given by a grateful capacity audience in a fond farewell to the man who had done so much for the cause of great music and the arts in Utah and had in the process endeared himself to so many music lovers and non-music lovers. They simply would not let him go. At length he stepped off the podium and made his way backstage as the sustained applause told him of the people's love and appreciation to him and tears streamed down the cheeks of a great many in attendance that evening. The man who came to Utah to conduct ten concerts of a fledgling Utah Symphony in 1947 and built the orchestra into one of the most highly respected ensembles in the nation had conducted for the last time."

During the ovation, as noted by William Goodfellow in the *Deseret News*, Abravanel "held the score aloft for its share of the accolade," following up his action at the close of the Mahler Eighth Symphony in the season finale the year before. The music critic referred to the "cheering and foot-stomping for the conductor, now at 76 winding up 32 years of dedicated service to the orchestra and community he adopted as his own in 1947." He noted that it was Abravanel's "first appearance in two-and-a-half months, coming only two weeks after his decision to retire following Saturday's concert for reasons of health," then added: "But to anyone apprehensive about the implications of that, it must be pointed out that there seemed on this occasion no visible diminution of his powers. Indeed, with few exceptions, his presence inspired singers and musicians alike to a level of achievement seldom encountered in these quarters, and in a piece that in the course of its 90-minute timespan asks a lot of everyone."

With the close of that monumental evening, the Utah Symphony had come, and abruptly so, to the end of an era. Soon it would be in its new home, the Symphony Hall, with a new music director and conductor, and no longer with part-time players but with a full-time year-round world-class orchestra—the legacy of Maurice Abravanel.

CHAPTER 21

THE KOJIAN YEARS

After thirty-two years of depending on Maurice Abravanel for its musical operations, the Utah Symphony found itself saddled with a number of unanticipated problems when he retired in the spring of 1979. There was, of course, the necessity of finding a new music director, but for the management and the administration there were more immediate decisions to be made.

The first item facing the management was a scheduled recording program as ambitious as any the symphony had attempted. The Vanguard Recording Society was set to record all of the Beethoven symphonies with the Utah Symphony under Abravanel during the summer. Huck Gregory tried desperately to save the project, conferring with Seymour Solomon, president of Vanguard, in the matter of securing a substitute conductor. In the final analysis, however, Seymour was interested in recording with Maurice and no one else, so the entire recording project was scrapped.

Another problem arose when Ardean Watts, after conducting the orchestra through its usual post-season schedule, submitted his resignation as associate conductor. Without mounting a major search for his successor, some twenty prospective candidates were considered, and seven were given an opportunity to audition by conducting improvised orchestra rehearsals. Since the recording project had been canceled, the symphony decided to use the previously scheduled orchestra services for the audition rehearsals. The musicians presented an evaluation report on each of them to the orchestra committee, which came up with the names of two strong candidates.

After reviewing the evaluations with the orchestra committee, Gregory and Swenson submitted their recommendation to the executive committee, which engaged Robert Henderson on June 20 as assistant conductor for one year. Later to become associate conductor, Henderson had just started his career with the baton when he came to Salt Lake City. He was perhaps better known for his mastery of the French horn, having performed with the San Francisco Symphony Orchestra, the American Ballet Theater Orchestra, the Los Angeles Philharmonic, and the London Philharmonic. He was one of the busiest free-lance French horn players in Hollywood at the time he made his debut as a conductor with the Los Angeles Philharmonic in the Hollywood Bowl in 1979.

The new assistant conductor had his hands full with the Utah Symphony from the time he signed his contract. He was the only Utah-based conductor available to the symphony for nearly a year, and through the transition season of 1979-80, he found himself on the podium for more than eighty school concerts and a full schedule of regional and state tour concerts. In addition, he was pressed into service for several subscription concerts in Ogden and Salt Lake City.

With the summer schedule at Snowbird, Ogden, and Salt Lake City now in competent hands, the symphony management and administration turned their attention to the Symphony Hall inaugural and dedication concert in September and to engaging a conductor for the event. There was hope on some fronts that Abravanel might be persuaded to return for that special evening, but fearing the consequence if he were forced to bow out at the last minute for health reasons, he declined an offer to take the assignment.

As expected, the search was difficult in light of the short notice, but fortunately Stanislaw Skrowaczewski, who had resigned that spring from the Minnesota Orchestra after eighteen years as its music director and conductor, was found to be available and willing to come. Having left his position to devote more time to guest conducting and composing, he was not available for a permanent role with the Utah Symphony, but he did agree to conduct the gala opening concerts on September 14 and 15.

Skrowaczewski's conducting, the Utah Symphony, and the acoustics of the new hall were all spoken of in superlatives after performances of the Bartok "Concerto for Orchestra" and the Brahms Symphony No. 4 in E Minor in the two concerts sponsored by Obert and Grace Tanner. Prior to the performance on the first night, the dedicatory prayer was offered, as at the Salt Palace ten years before, by President N. Eldon Tanner of the First Presidency of The Church of Jesus Christ of Latter-day Saints. He dedicated the new hall in place of President Spencer W. Kimball, who was recuperating from surgery.

Meanwhile, the search for a new music director for the symphony progressed, and by the middle of the summer the field had narrowed to some sixteen candidates. To get to this point, according to a report of chairman R. J. Snow to the symphony executive committee on July 17, files of more than one hundred prospective candidates had been examined by all members of the search committee and the secretary. In the search, the committee enlisted the aid of the American Symphony Orchestra League in various ways, worked with orchestra managers and artists' agents, inquired of musicians in other orchestras, and sought recommendations and evaluations from leading music critics.

One candidate, Varoujan Kodjian (the spelling later changed to Varujan Kojian), visited Salt Lake City late in the summer and met with the committee and alone with symphony president Wendell Ashton. Here began an association that eventually won him the post, although in the beginning there was a conscious effort on the part of the committee not to be swept off its feet by such a charming and charismatic personality. Yet subconsciously there appeared to be a unanimous feeling that Kojian might very well be a likely music director.

As the search continued, an effort was made to schedule the leading candidates as guest conductors on the 1979-80 subscription series of fourteen concerts. Two of the performances had already been committed to Ardean Watts, while others already signed were Henri Lazarof, Roger Wagner, and James DePreist. Of these, only DePreist was on the search committee's list of finalists. He had appeared as guest conductor during each of the two previous seasons and had won the respect and admiration of Abravanel and the musicians. In fact, had the maestro been consulted, he may have suggested DePreist be engaged as music director. A black man with a reputation as an excellent and sympathetic conductor, he later took a position as music director of the Oregon Symphony Orchestra, formerly the Portland Symphony, which he still holds. It should be pointed out that Maurice had said he did not want to be part of the search process, and apparently his advice was never sought.

Other candidates eventually engaged as guest conductors included Kojian; Maurice Peress of Kansas City; Kenneth Schermerhorn, then conductor of the Milwaukee Symphony; Christopher Keene, conductor of the Syracuse Symphony; Daniel Lewis of Pasadena; Antonio de Almeida, a Paris-born musician with a European conducting background; Lawrence Smith, then at Portland; and Uri Segal of the Stuttgart Radio Orchestra.

As were the members of the search committee, Wendell Ashton was particularly anxious to fill Abravanel's shoes with a strong and reliable music director, one he could relate to as he had Maurice. Through his desire to reach the commendable and lofty goal he had set for the Utah Symphony over the years, he now faced the first season in Symphony Hall with a budget of $2,914,131, more than twice what it had been five years earlier. This he had backed with a persistent and productive fundraising effort through private sponsorships and contributions and public grants that enabled him to keep his promise to the musicians—a year-round season of orchestra services with an acceptable salary.

By that time the orchestra was at eighty-four members. The managerial staff had grown to thirteen, headed by Gregory as executive director and chief of operations; with Shirl Swenson as manager; Carleen Landes, artistic manager; Betty Kay, marketing manager; Douglas Neiswender, accounting manager; Gloy Barwick, box office manager; Ray L. White, development director; and Veronica Bettinson, development assistant.

The musicians, incidentally, were not alone in feeling the loss of Abravanel. Ashton had developed a great friendship with Maurice and Lucy, and through the association with the maestro and his music he had come to love the classics—Beethoven, Brahms, Bach, Mozart, Wagner, and even the works of Mahler. Gregory, too, for twenty-three years had virtually lived with Abravanel as they consulted together on symphony business and was aware of a noticeable change in operations without his presence.

Ashton has often spoken of his admiration of Abravanel as being "as much for him as an individual as for him as a musician." He recalls that Maurice was always aware of the struggle to get money for the orchestra and that "he would never take an increase."

"I remember," said Wendell, "we forced a raise or two on him and he didn't want to take it. He wanted it to be spread among the musicians. I just couldn't believe how selfless he was. And it was such a boost for the morale and the spirit of the orchestra. I remember after that first concert in Carnegie Hall [in 1966] I was told 'there may be orchestras that are more finely tuned so far as the techniques are concerned, but no orchestra plays with more spirit than the Utah Symphony.'"

As to his relationship with Abravanel in symphony operations, Wendell observed: "Good symphonies are a two-prong job. You've got to have good musicians with a good director. With that you've got to have the money. I just concentrated on raising the money and Maurice concentrated on the music."

Those comments fit in well with those of Ruth Cowan, the orchestra manager thirty-three years before, when she remarked to Judge Crockett that the job of a symphony board of directors was to raise money. "That's right," said Ashton, "it's true today."

Through the funding secured under Ashton's direction, the administration was able to negotiate a three-year contract with the musicians in 1977 that provided for a forty-two-week season with expansion to fifty-two weeks in 1979-80. The agreement provided that there be no increase in the minimum weekly salary guarantee of $330 for three years. Instead, the musicians received two weeks of paid vacation and a significantly expanded work opportunity through the lengthened season.

One year into the contract, however, in 1978, Maurice proposed an increase in the minimum salary to $350 a week and to lengthen the season by three weeks. As usual, he discussed the matter with Huck Gregory who, after a financial study, carried the recommendation to the executive committee and received approval for the increase and expansion.

During the contract negotiations, it was brought out that Abravanel had fired only three musicians in thirty years, all for very good reasons. With this the management held off proposed tenure for the musicians and worked out a provision that little more than two years later would have a marked effect upon the relations between a new music director and his players. In essence, it locked a player with five or more years with the orchestra into his position for another two-and-a-half years, unless given notice of pending termination before March 1 of the first contract year. More specifically, the notice would provide that "on or before March 1 of the following year their contract for the next season will not be renewed unless they correct certain inadequacies during the interim period." As will be noted, any five-year player receiving notice could count on a year and a half of service before termination of contract. All of this provided a way to ease the release of long-standing musicians by giving them time to seek other employment. Of more importance, they were given an opportunity to remain in the orchestra by making satisfactory improvements in their performance.

Only two viable candidates for the position of music director of the Utah Symphony, Peress and Schermerhorn, had performed at Symphony Hall when Kojian came as guest conductor on October 26 and 27, 1979. He had already conducted the same program at Ogden on October 25, and his bandwagon was rolling. He chose the Beethoven Fourth Symphony and Shostakovich Fifth Symphony for the three programs; he could have found no better vehicle.

The Ogden Symphony Guild was a large and influential organization in the orchestra's operation with eight subscription concerts and several other services on its schedule. Its voice in the final selection of a music director was certain to be heard with respect, particularly after one devotee called Ashton after the concert and told him, "We don't need to look any further. You've got your conductor in this young fellow, Kojian."

The sensational reception at Ogden carried over into Symphony Hall, where the audiences were electrified by Kojian's performance. The administration and search committee were besieged by symphony buffs and players alike to sign him.

Salt Lake critics added their acclaim, giving the Kojian debut performance particularly high marks. William S. Goodfellow, in the *Desert News*, called it a "resounding success," stating that it was "the season's most unexpectedly satisfactory performance to date, and an impressive local debut for Varoujian Kodjian." Further on he commented: "Playing in both pieces was brilliant and alert, with greater attention to matters dynamic than has often been the case.... I find a welcome solidity of conception and a musicianly control that served him well at nearly every point" of the program.

In the *Salt Lake Tribune*, Paul Wetzel wrote: "Rarely, if ever, had this orchestra played with such grace and power. Mr. Kodjian made of this ensemble an instrument which produced music of artful line and classic proportion. This was a proud night for Mr. Kodjian and for the musicians of the Utah Symphony."

The same glowing response that greeted the candidate in northern Utah followed him on a concert tour with the orchestra down Interstate-15. His army of fans grew with each stop in southern Utah, including Cedar City and St. George, and on into Nevada. He rode the bus, gallantly brushing aside an invitation to ride in a private car, and fraternized with the players. At the

Halloween concert in Las Vegas, Kojian came on stage wearing a funny mask, much to the delight of all present. Almost to a player, the orchestra seemed to favor his immediate appointment, a sentiment that was further enhanced when he arose early the next morning and went to the airport to bid farewell to the musicians as they boarded the plane for the return flight to Salt Lake City.

It is not surprising that in less than three weeks after that whirlwind campaign, Kojian was signed to a three-year contract as music director of the Utah Symphony. The clamor to keep him in Utah had reached a climax on the evening of Tuesday, November 20, right after the orchestra's annual Salute to Youth concert. While a special session of the full symphony board waited in the Abravanel Room, the search committee in another area unanimously recommended that Kojian be engaged immediately. With equal solidarity, the board accepted the proposal.

As a matter of record, no one particularly wanted to abort the search procedure at that point, but in the final analysis there appeared to be a good chance that the candidate of their choice would not be available if they waited to complete the process. Both the board and the committee were well aware of reports that Kojian was being considered for the music director's post in Portland, Oregon, and Louisville, Kentucky.

On the very next morning after the meetings, Wendell Ashton boarded a plane for Washington, D.C. There in the lobby of the terminal building at Washington National Airport, he met with Varujan, his brother Miran, and Agnes Eisenberger, his personal manager with the Colbert Management. He quickly signed the new conductor for three years, effective July 1, 1980.

For Kojian, who had exchanged the violin for the baton in his list of priorities some seven or eight years earlier, this was the ideal position. A brilliant violinist and student of Jascha Heifetz at the University of Southern California, Varujan took a position in 1965 as assistant concertmaster with the Los Angeles Philharmonic under Zubin Mehta. He then became assistant conductor as well, and Mehta was so impressed with his work on the podium that he not only encouraged his young assistant to study conducting as a career but also offered to pay for his lessons. As a result, Kojian left Los Angeles in 1971 to enter the Vienna State Music Academy. There he studied with Hans Swarowsky for two years and determined to make his way with the baton.

Born in Beirut, Lebanon, of Armenian parents, Kojian was introduced to the violin by his father at an early age. His rapid progress put him at the Paris National Conservatory of Music in 1950. After six years he moved on to America, where he entered the Curtis Institute of Music in Philadelphia. From there in 1960, Kojian was accepted in the Heifetz Master Class at Southern California.

After returning from Vienna in 1972, Kojian signed on as associate conductor of the Seattle Symphony, and one year later he became the principal guest conductor of the Swedish Royal Opera in Stockholm. He gave up the Seattle post in 1975 to devote his time to conducting, teaching, and coaching in Stockholm, still hoping for a position as music director of a reputable symphony orchestra.

With the signing of his contract, the new Utah music director flew to Stockholm and began to wind down his final season in the Swedish capital. Part of his time, however, was to be spent on the telephone discussing personnel matters back in Utah. When he returned to Salt Lake City the following April, all was not quite as it had been five months before. The jubilant courtship and blissful marriage of conductor and symphony had already shown signs of decay. The honeymoon was nearing an abrupt end, and in little more than two years' time the official announcement would come that the Kojian contract would not be renewed—on the termination of the three-year period, the divorce would become final.

It all began while Kojian was in Stockholm and before he started on the first year of his contract. He apparently was not aware of the clause in the musicians' contract concerning notice of termination for unsatisfactory performance. Nor did he know, of course, that the deadline for such notices would arrive on March 1, 1980.

On the other hand, there were those in Salt Lake City who were very close to the orchestra's principal product of good music and who were very conscious of the deadline. They felt that Kojian should be alerted to the situation and given a chance to respond. Among them was the retired Maestro Abravanel, who thought it would be unfair for a new music director to take over and find he could make no changes in personnel for two and a half years.

The staff, meanwhile, had adopted something of a "hands off" attitude, feeling the matter belonged to Kojian alone. But with the pressure mounting, Huck Gregory was persuaded to call the new conductor and advise him of the deadline. As he recalls, the music director told him he had noticed some weak spots in the ensemble during the ten days spent with the musicians in October. He said Kojian reasoned it would be wise to give notice to those who were of questionable artistic skill, particularly since none of them were being fired but only told they needed to improve. He then came up with a list of seven musicians to receive such tentative nonrenewal notices. Another seven players were told that while they were not on notice, they needed to improve their playing. This second list was developed in consultation with the new assistant conductor, who, in turn, had conferred with members of the orchestra in identifying players with performance deficiencies.

With Kojian in Sweden, it fell to Gregory to call in the fourteen musicians before the March 1 deadline and advise them one at a time of the music director's decision. He then followed up with letters of confirmation.

In retrospect, the whole thing was a costly and damaging episode for the new music director, and for that matter, for his assistant conductor and the unwitting bearer of the notice.

It seemed an unfortunate blunder to give the seven notices and the additional warnings even before the conductor had come on the job in person. Blunder or not, it started him on the way to an early end of his direct association with the Utah Symphony. In a recent conversation, Kojian indicated to this writer that at the time there seemed to be a good possibility the musicians would gain the final say in hiring and firing. If that should be the case, he reasoned, in order to make any personnel changes whatever in the foreseeable future it was necessary to issue tentative nonrenewal notices immediately as a last resort. In an interview with William Goodfellow published in the *Deseret News* on April 3, 1980, he is quoted as saying that "there is no secret" about his serving notice to seven players and that "I wish them to prove themselves better. . . . I don't feel they were giving their best."

He then went on to say that it was not an instantaneous decision and that he had "many performances with them."

"I spoke with other people," he continued, "and there were different reasons for different players, but in the end the decision was mine. . . . None of them has been fired. There were two resignations, but that was their decision. The door is open, none is asked to leave, and I am praying none will have to be dismissed."

The effect of the action, however innocent the intention, was to break up the newly formed friendship between the music director and the orchestra and to reinforce efforts of the musicians to win control of hiring and firing. On January 2 they had submitted through their Local 104, American Federation of Musicians, to the symphony management a twenty-six page master contract proposal outlining a number of demands. Principally they sought establishment of audition and review committees of nine players each, one to control the filling of vacancies as they came up in the symphony, and the other to have final authority in the upholding or rejecting of a dismissal or nonrenewal decision with regard to any orchestra member.

Other proposals called for a restriction in orchestra services, elimination of part-time status, and higher pay, particularly in the form of fringe benefits. It was the first time since 1949 that the union had asked for a salary increase, having left the matter with Abravanel in the past.

Negotiations dragged on for nearly ten months, during which time certain of the musicians used the press and media as well as personal contacts to argue their point of view, while the board and management adopted and followed a decision to remain silent. Agreement on both sides was finally reached at the end of a thirty-day "play and talk" period, with the musicians yielding on most of their demands.

John Crawford, an executive with Mountain Fuel Supply Company and a Utah Symphony Board vice-president, headed the symphony's negotiating team. He reported to the symphony executive committee on October 23, 1980, that the negotiating committee had met all of the requirements of the board, with two minor adjustments in the final hours: (1) a two-year instead of three-year contract, and (2) an agreement that there would be no new nonrenewal notices given in the first year of the contract and thereafter no more than four in any season. Also agreed upon was a gradual conversion of all "B" (part-time) contracts to "A" (full-time) contracts over a six-year period.

In the meantime, the 1979-80 season had run its course with two fewer guest conductors than originally scheduled. After a new music director had been hired, Daniel Lewis and James DePreist found it no longer possible to fill their conducting assignments on January 25 and 26 and on February 6 and 7, respectively. Robert Henderson filled in on both occasions and in the process established himself even more as a competent conductor.

In setting up the season program, the symphony management had signed no conductor for a pair of subscription concerts on April 4 and 5 for which the Beethoven Ninth Symphony had been scheduled. While an effort had been made to fill this slot, the thinking had been that such a project could well be undertaken by the new conductor, if one were signed. With Kojian under contract, it was a simple matter to put the Beethoven in his hands.

For the audience, it was a triumphant return for the conductor. As usual, the orchestra performed well and the Utah Chorale distinguished itself in the choral sections. The soloists—Cohleen Bischoff, Cynthia Pannell, Louis Welcher, and Clayne Robison—received the acclaim of the critics.

Behind the scenes, however, the cheering had stopped. A disenchantment with the new music director was quite apparent, not alone among the players but among the critics as well. In contrast to the accolades six months before, the *Tribune*'s

Wetzel wrote: "The program's major work ended up an exercise in theatricality and bombast." And Goodfellow's comments in the *News* were equally deflating.

"I only hope that in time Kojian will display greater interpretive maturity in music of this sort," he wrote, "as well as a keen ear for orchestral sound with which he won us all over in the beginning."

When Kojian returned to Salt Lake City in the fall of 1980 for his first full season with the Utah Symphony, a certain coolness had developed between conductor and players. As the season wore on, the breach tended to widen.

No sooner had Kojian signed with the Utah Symphony than the number of guest-conducting appearances around the country picked up markedly. As a result, he traveled widely throughout North America and beyond, conducting in all but a few instances major symphony orchestras. In January 1980, not long after signing his Utah Symphony contract, he flew from Sweden to conduct the Chicago Symphony, and the following May he was guest conductor of the New York Philharmonic. Then, from November 1980 to November 1982, he filled more than a dozen bookings. There were three added visits to Chicago, one of which included two concerts at Orchestra Hall and a tour as guest conductor. He again conducted the New York Philharmonic; he performed with the Los Angeles Philharmonic, the Rochester Philharmonic, the San Francisco Symphony, the Philadelphia Orchestra, the St. Louis Symphony, and the Grand Rapids Symphony; and he twice went halfway around the world to lead the Hong Kong orchestra.

Ironically, his phenomenal success as a much-sought-after guest conductor contributed in large measures to the disenchantment of his Utah Symphony musicians, who noticed he was absent much of the time while Henderson handled school concerts and tours. Whether valid or not, the perception grew among the musicians that Kojian was more concerned with his guest-conducting appearances than he was with preparing himself and the Utah Symphony for concerts at home. Some musicians began to wonder about Kojian's qualifications, casting doubt upon his skills as a conductor and claiming him to be unprepared and absent much of the time. This should not be too surprising when one considers that Kojian's predecessor had shunned guest-conducting invitations for the greater part of his career and, as a result, was at home "tending the store" an unprecedented nine months of the year.

In all, it was Kojian's unfortunate beginning that led to his short stay with the Utah Symphony. With two strikes against him from the nonrenewal notices to seven players, he added to his problems by not giving himself and his time completely to the orchestra.

The combination of problems created a situation that (along with a life-style that was not in tune with the prevailing life-style of the Salt Lake community) ultimately resulted in the decision to terminate Mr. Kojian's services as music director.

Nor was it all the fault of the new music director. The orchestra administration, along with well-meaning influential admirers and symphony fans, had placed him on a pedestal without giving him a chance to prove himself.

No one openly questioned the musicianship and artistry of Kojian. His potential in this regard was obvious. But for him, or for anyone taking up the Utah Symphony baton at this time, the requirements and the devotion necessary to follow successfully in Abravanel's footsteps was almost insurmountable. Maurice had come to Salt Lake City with a formidable background, and for thirty-two years his first obligation was to his orchestra and its development as a virtuoso ensemble. Throughout that period he had the complete respect and trust of his players. He had taken them to world capitals with honor and had won praise for them far and wide with recordings of distinction. The Maestro left few, if any, of the known symphonic works for his successors to bring forth. No major work escaped his attention. Typical was the giant "Symphony of a Thousand," by Mahler, the No. 8 in E Flat, which Abravanel and the orchestra not only performed twice in the Salt Lake Tabernacle but also recorded for Vanguard. It was the first recording of the work anywhere, resulting in lavish critical acclaim such as that of Robert Angles in *Records and Recording* out of London: "The overall success of this performance.... undoubtedly rests with Abravanel; it will be a long time before I hear anything to match the glory he conjures from the final pages of the Eighth, setting the seal upon a great Mahler performance that marks a major event in the history of the gramophone."

Maurice had left the podium to the cheers and tears of his host of admirers. In his possession was an autographed score of Aaron Copland's "Appalachian Spring" on which the composer had penned, "To my dear friend, Maurice, an exemplary model for all of us to follow."

And on top of all the accolades had come the ultimate recognition of Maurice Abravanel as a master musician and fighter for the cause of orchestras. At Dallas, Texas, on June 19, 1981, just two years after his retirement, he was presented with the "Gold Baton," an award reserved for highest achievement by the American Symphony Orchestra League. Its inscription is a tribute "To Maurice Abravanel, orchestra builder, orchestra advocate, for a lifetime of singular devotion to the advancement of all orchestras."

Abravanel's young successor, in the meantime had not fared so well. The critics noticed a difference in his performances, and not until his final season did they find his work near the equal of his audition concert in October of 1979. When he opened the 1980-81 season with the Mahler Fifth and Schubert Fifth symphonies, William Goodfellow noted in the *Deseret News*: "His first concerts here last fall were impressive; so much so that they won for him the job of music director of the Utah Symphony. Then Varujan Kojian returned the following April to lead the orchestra in the Beethoven Ninth Symphony that for all its electricity struck me as generally superficial and too much hurried by half."

He went on to regard the Mahler performance as "lacking" in feeling, but added: "If this exposure failed to match the high standards the conductor set for himself last October, neither was it as unsettling as the rat race he presided over a few months later."

By now the musicians were on a fifty-two-week schedule with the expansion of orchestra services. Notable among personnel changes was the acquisition of Robert Stephenson from the Savannah, Georgia, Symphony to replace Darrel Stubbs as principal oboist. Kojian said he was still seeking a harpist and co-principal in the horn section, two positions eventually filled by Sarah Bullen and Jeffry Kirschen. Also being sought was a new concertmaster to replace Oscar Chausow. Since this became a longer search than anticipated, the reliable Ken Kuchler was temporarily installed in the first chair.

Kuchler thus became closely associated with Kojian and was a loyal supporter through the problems that developed later on. He recalls advising Varujan to go out to the schools with the orchestra and thereby become acquainted with people in the community and state.

"He had Henderson doing the school concerts," Kuchler remembers. "In the eyes of the kids, Henderson was associated with the symphony. They didn't even know who Kojian was. I don't think he understood what Abravanel did."

It seems clear that Varujan's problem with the musicians contributed most to an eventual agreement that his three-year contract not be renewed. That decision was not reached, however, until the close of his second season, in June 1982.

Plans for a European tour were under way when Abravanel resigned in April 1979, more than two years before the trip was scheduled. The European tour manager, Hans Ulrich Schmid, had been assured that a new music director would be signed for the Utah Symphony in time for the tour, but he needed something more definite for booking the concerts and proposed that Witold Rowicki, the respected Polish baton master, be engaged for the tour.

Before answering Schmid's proposal, the Symphony signed Kojian, only to find Schmid even more insistent that Rowicki be the conductor. A noted impresario operating out of Hannover, Germany, the tour manager knew the concert situation in Europe well and said that since Kojian was not known outside of Sweden, there was no possibility he could be used for the concerts the agent had booked. The symphony finally agreed, and Rowicki was engaged to conduct nine concerts.

Schmid had scheduled the orchestra through Hannover, Kassel, Stuttgart, Heidenheim, Waldshut, Frankfurt, Duesseldorf, and Berlin, Germany, with a performance in Courtrai, Belgium, between Frankfurt and Duesseldorf. He tried to book concerts in Holland and Denmark to augment the tour, and on failing to do so, he granted permission for the symphony manager, Shirl Swenson, to see what he could do about it. Swenson came up with two performances at Tivoli in Copenhagen to open the tour on May 17 and 18 and a concert in Utrecht, Holland, between Courtrai and Duesseldorf. Schmid then provided a brilliant closing for the journey by booking the symphony into the Grieg Festival at Bergen, Norway, for two performances on June 2 and 3.

While the symphony management yielded to Schmid in the selection of a conductor for the Germany-Belgium section of the tour, it held the line in the matter of repertoire. Rowicki obviously was not aware of the orchestra's experience with the more formidable symphonic works and wanted to go to light pieces unbecoming of a major symphony. It was only through an exercise in diplomacy and patience that all arrived at two presentable programs. One included the Shostakovich Symphony No. 5, Paul Creston's "Invocation and Dance." and a suite from Smetana's "Bartered Bride." The other included the Prokofiev "Classical" Symphony; "Medea's Meditation and Dance of Vengeance," by Samuel Barber; and the Moussorgsky-Ravel "Pictures at an Exhibition." At Hannover, Rowicki substituted the Mendelssohn First Piano Concerto for the Barber, with Karl Engel at the piano.

Although replaced in nine concerts by the Polish guest conductor, Kojian was very much in evidence on the tour. He conducted the first pair of concerts in Denmark and the last two in Norway, as well as the performance at Utrecht. Bob Henderson was injected into the picture for the side trip to Heidenheim, where he directed a "pops" program of sorts.

Before leaving for Copenhagen, the symphony flew Rowicki from Warsaw to Salt Lake City for a series of ten rehearsals, five for each program. The management then had him conduct two "send-off" concerts a week apart at Symphony Hall. Ticket sales were disappointing, however, contributing to a project deficit that had to be made up with sponsorships and other contributions.

Transportation arrangements were turned over to Scandinavian Airways System, which agreed to fly the instruments to Europe at no cost to the orchestra in exchange for using SAS planes for the musicians. Only once was Scandinavian Air not available. The party departed from Salt Lake International Airport aboard a Western Airlines plane, flying to Los Angeles. There it boarded an SAS 747 for the hop over the Arctic to Denmark.

For his concerts in Copenhagen, Kojian stayed with Rowicki's programming. He then left the tour, rejoining it to direct the program in Utrecht.

One of the more enthusiastic audiences on the tour met the orchestra in Heidenheim. Crowded into a school auditorium with a capacity of fewer than nine hundred, the listeners drew a number of encores from associate conductor Henderson and his players. The performance also turned out to be a special experience for three or four of the musicians who were filling in just for the tour. For the final encore, Henderson called for Sousa's "Stars and Stripes Forever" from memory, which proved quite a surprise for the temporary players who had never played it, nor even heard it, before.

From a strictly musical standpoint, the concert at Duesseldorf on Saturday, May 30, was perhaps the most successful of the tour. Rowicki had taken a rest while the orchestra was in Holland, and he was now ready to wind up his end of the journey with this performance and the one in Berlin. He took advantage of a fine sound chamber and left the audience ecstatic with the results. It was the same hall in which the orchestra had performed in 1977, but it had been completely renovated and was now "in the round." There was a magnificence to the sound that reminded the entire company of home and Symphony Hall.

The previous evening, Friday, May 29, Kojian had conducted an enthusiastically received concert in Utrecht. The audience, however, was small for this large city a mere twenty miles from Amsterdam. It was not a surprising circumstance, however, when it became known that the famed Concertgebouw would not have filled the hall except on a subscription series. Ticket revenues fell far short of covering even the impresario costs, but there were compensations.

There had been no concert scheduled between Courtrai on Wednesday, May 27, and Duesseldorf on Saturday, May 30, and Utrecht offered an opportunity to appear in the Netherlands for the first time. More important, it attracted Dutch-American sponsors who helped finance the tour and set up a "Utah Day" in Amsterdam. The affair featured a symphony-sponsored luncheon on the day of the Utrecht concert that brought Utah and Netherlands government and civic leaders together.

Much as he and Calvin Rampton had done at the Waldorf Astoria Hotel in New York City in the fall of 1966, Wendell Ashton and Rampton's successor, Governor Scott M. Matheson, promoted the State of Utah on this occasion. The governor and his wife, Norma, joined the tour at this point and remained to the conclusion with a much more elaborate Utah promotion in Bergen, Norway, the following Wednesday, June 3.

The two highly successful affairs were largely the work of the symphony's director of development, Ray L. White, an effective fund-raising specialist and promotions expert. He had flown to Amsterdam in advance of that occasion and then had gone directly to Bergen to set up the arrangements there.

Matheson had assumed the governorship in 1977, and he and Norma immediately took up where Cal and Lucybeth Rampton had left off in supporting the symphony and other arts institutions in Utah. As guests of Wendell and Belva Ashton, who accompanied each of the symphony tours, they welcomed the opportunity to become better acquainted with the orchestra and the scope of its operations.

On the final day of the tour in Bergen, the governor asked for an opportunity to speak to the musicians before they began their rehearsal. He praised them highly for the excellent job they were doing as musical ambassadors of the State of Utah and for their exceptional professionalism. To Shirl Swenson and Huck Gregory he commented, "I never realized it before; this is a really professional organization. Everything is well-organized and thoroughly professional."

Later in the day, more than eighty Norway community leaders were entertained during "Utah Day" festivities that were more than enough to brighten up a gray, rainy day. Flown in for a luncheon were Utah products such as Cache Valley cheese, Norbest turkeys, and Snelgrove ice cream. Even Utah celery and other vegetables were served as the affair carried over to a reception following the closing concert for 400 musicians and guests.

The two concerts were distinct successes and closed the tour on a high and memorable level of musical excellence. Kojian programmed the "Peer Gynt" of Saeverud, the Barber Intermezzo from "Vanessa," Copland's "El Salon Mexico," and the Grieg Piano Concerto with Carl Engel as soloist for the first performance. A complete sellout, the closing night was a particular triumph for conductor and orchestra, performing works of Prokofiev, Creston, and Shostakovich.

Soon after the return of the orchestra to Salt Lake City from its latest success, Shirl Swenson, in his report to the board of directors, called it the "smoothest tour in the Utah Symphony's history with no serious complaints from the musicians." The Musicians' Local 104 president, Hepworth, followed by observing that the reason there were no complaints was due to the fact that "the planning and execution of the tour was excellent in every detail."

It was another journey in which the orchestra left a string of highly favorable impressions with discriminating European audiences. Typical perhaps was the response of Grieg Festival officials to Shirl Swenson after the first concert in Bergen. Although they had carried some reservations as to the quality of the orchestra as a festival participant, the officials were so excited after the performance that they asked Shirl, "When can you come back again?"

"But," said Shirl, "I thought you never brought any artists back for repeat performances."

"We never have in the past," they stated, "but we'll take the Utah Symphony any time you come our way."

With the conclusion of the 1981 tour, Kojian was off to New York, first to conduct the Rochester Philharmonic and then to serve his first summer as music director of the Chautauqua Institution, a position not unlike the one Abravanel had held for years as music director of the Music Academy of the West at Santa Barbara.

From that point through the 1981-82 season, the relationship between the new music director and the orchestra steadily deteriorated. Kojian's life-style had also become a topic for discussion. It had caused a large segment of the community to seek the termination of his services. It is possible that this objection to Mr. Kojian would not have caused the nonrenewal of his contract had the conductor been more attentive to his musical responsibilities. However, the two forces resulted in a situation that caused the board of directors to take action. The players were generally unhappy with the way things were going. By the end of the season they had solidified their position against the conductor and were a most potent force against renewal of his contract.

When the symphony board met on April 22, 1982, the problem could no longer be ignored. In response to pressures from orchestra members and others, the administration approved appointment of an ad hoc music director review committee to conduct an inquiry. Named to head the committee as chairman was Kem C. Gardner, who had gained prominence as a real-estate developer and who, as a board member, was head of the management committee. With him were Dr. Burtis R. Evans, a local physician and chairman of the audit committee; Don A. Stringham, an attorney and chairman of the development committee; symphony treasurer M. Walker Wallace; R. J. Snow; Barbara L. Tanner; and W. Boyd Christensen, who had been installed five months earlier as executive vice-president of the symphony, who served as secretary.

Over the next two months, the review committee conducted a series of hearings that produced information substantiating the dissatisfaction of all but a few orchestra members with the conductor.

At the same time, however, there were witnesses with formidable backgrounds in music who defended Kojian's credibility as a musician and artist. Maurice Abravanel, for instance, regarded as "unquestionable" the conductor's potential as a musician of exceptional talent. Ramiro Cortes, composer in residence at the University of Utah, and Lowell M. Durham testified that Kojian had "great potential" and that he "needs more time to demonstrate what he can do." Ken Kuchler was one member of the orchestra who appeared in support of his music director, and Tom Moore, president of the Ogden Symphony Ballet Association and a member of the search committee that recommended engagement of Kojian, brought a message of strong support from his organization.

Player representatives had taken the time to quiz the players about their impressions, and the results produced a substantial effect on the proceedings as well as later action of the symphony board. Lynn Larsen, a member of the French horn section and president of the orchestra committee, reported results of a questionnaire to which 77 percent of the musicians had responded. It showed that 82.5 percent were not satisfied with Kojian as music director and conductor and that only 9.5 percent were satisfied. The remaining 8 percent were undecided. John Chatelain, second violin principal, representing thirteen of the orchestra's sixteen first-chair performers, said all thirteen were dissatisfied with the conductor as a musician or leader.

An interesting observation about these statistics and the general feeling he had found within the orchestra came later from Ross Thoresen, a management-labor relations authority and the symphony board's vice-president for personnel. A witness at one of the hearings, he noted that comments of the musicians suggested a "morale problem," and that Kojian was "so deeply in trouble with the musicians" that he could not extricate himself.

With the conclusion of the inquiry, the committee found itself with no clear-cut decision, although a majority favored in some form or another the renewal of Kojian's contract. Only Evans and Stringham were firmly against retaining the music director. Gardner, however, brought about a meeting of the minds by suggesting that Kojian's third season be probationary and that his future with the Utah Symphony depend on how convincing his improvement might be. The suggestion was adopted for recommendation to the board, but it was not to be the committee's final decision.

Obviously concerned about Wendell Ashton's reaction to the committee's action, Gardner invited the symphony president to hear the recommendation at a special meeting. Wendell rejected the proposal as entirely unacceptable, and the committee resumed its deliberations. It finally decided on a four-to-three vote to recommend that "the president be authorized with the executive vice-president to make a decision as to the renewal of Maestro Kojian's contract."

It was not surprising that Ashton would assume a major role in decision-making as it concerned disposition of the Kojian affair. For sixteen years he had been the primary figure in the financial promotion and growth of the Utah Symphony from a part-time operation to a full-time, internationally known institution. He had injected himself into the management of the organization and, although a search committee had recommended the hiring of Kojian, it was Ashton who had taken the lead in engaging him. Wendell Ashton had sped off to the east coast to get Kojian's signature and then rolled out the red carpet for the new music director. But unfortunately the carpet seemed to roll right up behind Varujan as Wendell became keenly aware of the deterioration in his relationship with the orchestra. To the symphony president, the situation had reached a point where the only satisfactory solution would be a change in musical leadership. He did not want to sidestep such a responsibility.

Wendell had not always endeared himself to those people he encountered as a fund-raiser and operations watchdog for the symphony, and his experience in the Kojian case would be no different. But even though his methods may have evoked some displeasure at times, he sincerely did what he had to do in what he felt was the best interests of the organization.

With his roots and his interest so deeply imbedded in the multimillion dollar symphony operation, Ashton was determined to rid it of existing discord. As he observed at a meeting of the executive committee on June 30 at the Alta Club, "the problem with the musicians' discontent has been growing and will not just go away."

The executive committee went on to approve the review committee's recommendation, leaving the final decision to the entire board at its meeting on July 7 at the Hilton Hotel. It was a meeting that would see the recommendation of two committees discarded as the board decided on a vote of thirty-one to seven not to renew Kojian's contract.

Ashton recalls that "we went to the board with a plan" for Kojian to finish out his contract and then resign. Board member and former governor Cal Rampton, however, questioned the legality of the executive committee to place authority to make the final decision with the president and executive vice-president. Wendell says he remembers that Rampton then said: "If you are going to terminate, why don't you pull the mustard plaster off in one jerk and not try to peel it off gradually?" It set the course to the final action.

Kojian still had a season to go, and he made it the finest of the three he spent with the orchestra as music director. Critical acclaim followed each performance, beginning with the Beethoven "Eroica" Symphony at the season opener on September 18, 1982. Paul Wetzel of the *Tribune*, in referring to the decision not to renew the conductor's contract, wrote: "The controversy which has surrounded that decision was evident when the conductor strode onto the stage and received prolonged applause and a standing ovation from his most ardent supporters."

Wetzel praised the performance, particularly that of the Beethoven, which he found to be "rich in emotional and musical understanding." In closing he noted that "to some this concert probably had become a sort of trial of Kojian and an opportunity for his vindication. It was he, after all, who suggested after the board's decision that he be judged by his performances, and he publicly invited his detractors to do just that."

Summing up after a production of the Mahler "Resurrection" Symphony No. 2 in the final subscription concert on April 30, 1983, *Deseret News* critic William Goodfellow said the performance "deserves to be ranked among the best, and not just from an executional standpoint."

"What a pleasure," commented Goodfellow, "to consistently hear strings that were together, and steadily intoned well-focused brass, not to mention the controlled dynamics that have been a conspicuous part of his [Kojian's] last few programs in particular.

"No less impressive, however, was this conductor's growth interpretively, at least as a Mahler conductor.... [It was] an evening that very nearly became a 'resurrection' of sorts for the conductor, at least judging by the prolonged ovation that followed."

After June 30, 1983, Kojian was no longer under contract with the Utah Symphony, but he kept his musical base in Salt Lake City. He continued with his summer assignment at Chautauqua until he resigned at the end of the 1985 season. At that time, he signed as music director of the Santa Barbara Symphony Orchestra. One of his principal posts is still as music director of Ballet West, where he conducts the musicians who were so influential in ending his stay with the Utah Symphony.

His following in Salt Lake City and in Ogden, where he appears with the ballet company several times a season, remains strong, and he is still sought after as a guest conductor, which isn't particularly surprising. After all, it was no less than *Stereo Review* that placed him in prime company when it wrote of his first recording with the Utah Symphony: "Conductor Varujan Kojian is off to a most auspicious start with a Berlioz Symphonie Fantastique that is outstanding musically and an audiophile's dream sonically. Their performance ranks with the best of its recorded predecessors, including those led by Pierre Monteux and Jean Martinon and Leonard Bernstein's with the Orchestra National de France."

After once settling the Kojian case, the symphony soon opened its quest for a new music director and conductor. On August 10, 1982, the executive committee appointed a search committee to be headed by Donald P. Lloyd. Others were Mrs. W. Robert White, Mrs. John M. [Barbara] Scowcroft, Alan F. Frank, Ross Thoresen, Provo Symphony Association president

Robert G. Allen, and Mrs. David [Bonnie] Bennett, representing the members of the orchestra, with Huck Gregory as secretary.

Meanwhile, there had been changes on both the musical and management fronts. The associate conductor, Henderson, left well ahead of Kojian, resigning on May 11, 1982; he was replaced by Charles Ketcham on July 7. And in the front office, young Stephen W. Swaner had taken over as executive vice-president the same day Boyd Christensen's resignation was accepted on October 5.

The executive office had surfaced with board approval of Christensen's appointment on December 9, 1981. It was established on advice of an audit committee consisting of Burtis Evans; B. Z. Kastler; the former executive officer of Mountain Fuel Supply Company; and Wendell Ashton.

Originally from Utah, Christensen had returned to Salt Lake City from the midwest, where he had once been an executive with Allstate Insurance Company in Chicago. He accepted the assignment to oversee the symphony's multimillion dollar operation, but in less than ten months he resigned to give full time to his position as general manager of the Utah Associated Municipal Power Systems.

Swaner was Wendell Ashton's personal choice to replace Christensen. A Utah native and graduate of the University of Utah with emphasis in the fields of psychology and economics, the new executive left a position as managing associate with Korn Ferry International, an executive search firm in Los Angeles, to join the symphony organization.

While Swaner was getting acquainted with his new office, Don Lloyd and his search committee sifted through a list of 163 candidates for the position of music director. As the field rapidly narrowed, two names came to the front. One of them, Joseph Silverstein, was assistant conductor and concertmaster of the Boston Symphony. The other, Gerard Schwartz, music director of the Los Angeles Chamber Orchestra and an equally prestigious chamber group in New York City, was considered one of the real "comers" among young American conductors.

Both of the front-runners visited Salt Lake City and impressed the committee with their qualifications. Neither auditioned before the Utah Symphony, but each was heard by committee members in performance on his own ground. Lloyd found both to be impressive conductors, attending first a Schwartz concert in New York and then a performance by Silverstein before the Baltimore Symphony in one of his many appearances as principal guest conductor of that orchestra.

Bonnie Bennett also visited Baltimore, where she not only attended a Silverstein rehearsal and concert but also visited with members of the Baltimore Symphony. And finally, Lowell Durham, who had been recruited by the committee to assist in evaluating the candidates, was on hand when Silverstein conducted the Baltimore Symphony at the Kennedy Center in Washington, D.C. He recalls being so impressed that he phoned in his recommendation immediately after the concert and suggested that the candidate from Boston be signed.

It was not until some time later, however, that the committee decided to recommend the engagement of Silverstein. After the board had approved the recommendation on January 19, a delegation composed of Ashton, Lloyd, and Swaner signed the new music director to a three-year contract effective September 1, 1983.

CHAPTER 22

AHEAD WITH SILVERSTEIN

While the Utah Symphony administration was changing the musical leadership of the orchestra, an important event was added to the organization's music schedule. The Utah Symphony Gina Bachauer International Piano Competition came under the symphony's wing in the spring of 1982.

Making such a move possible was the emergence of George S. Eccles, a longstanding board member, and his wife, Delores Dore Eccles, as sponsors of the biennial program. This affiliation was to prove a boon to the symphony in succeeding years, as Mrs. Eccles carried on after the death of her husband which occurred near the time of the 1982 competition. In addition to sponsorships to the Bachauer competition totaling $125,000, the George S. and Dolores Dore Eccles Foundation has contributed nearly three-quarters of a million dollars to symphony endowments and sponsorships.

The Bachauer competition received its start on the Brigham Young University campus in Provo during June 1976 as the Brigham Young University Summer Piano Festival and International Piano Competition. A year later, it was given the name of the Gina Bachauer International Competition in honor of the revered Greek piano virtuoso who had died in Athens in 1976. Then, in 1978, the competing finalists were heard in a complete piano concerto with the Utah Symphony as the orchestra brought a new dimension to the contest.

The competition remained on the Brigham Young University campus as an annual event through 1980, after which, at the invitation of the operating committee, it moved to Symphony Hall in Salt Lake City under the Utah Symphony management and added the symphony's name to its official designation. There, in June of 1982, the competition became a biennial event under the capable chairmanship and direction of Barbara L. Tanner.

Using the experience of five previous contests, Mrs. Tanner's extensive organization, a prestigious panel of jurors, and the orchestra built upon the rising excellence of the competition. The list of applicants reached record proportions, requiring increased preselection efforts to determine a final list of some seventy competitors.

In the end, Michael Gurt of Ypsilanti, Michigan, joined the winner's circle with five previous first-place winners—Douglas Humphreys of Idaho Falls, Idaho; Christopher Giles of Los Angeles; Arthur Greene of Lenox, Massachusetts; and Panayis Lyras and Duane Hulbert of New York City.

By the time Barbara Tanner and her committee began making final plans for the 1984 event, the competition had become one of only four such contests in the United States to be admitted as an official member of the International Federation of Music Competitions of Geneva, Switzerland. Membership to the seventy-two-member organization had been accepted in 1983.

Emerging from a field of sixty-seven contestants, David Buechner, a twenty-four-year-old New York pianist out of the Juilliard School of Music, won the seventh competition in 1984. He performed the Gershwin Concerto in F with the Utah Symphony under Lawrence Leighton Smith in the final round and claimed the commemorative gold medal. With it came a Steinway grand piano presented by Gerald "Skip" Daynes of Daynes Music Company, a New York recital debut at Alice Tully

Hall, and other concert engagements, including an appearance with the Utah Symphony on its subscription series. Daynes had been responsible for competition winners' receiving grand pianos since 1978.

Not to be overlooked in the origination and careful planning and construction of the now-prestigious competition is the contribution of its founder, Paul C. Pollei. Known as an "international ambassador for piano music," this Salt Lake City native and member of the Brigham Young University piano faculty founded the contest in 1976 and remains a strong influence in its operation.

Under the continued brilliant organization of chairman Barbara Tanner, the competition in June 1986 had more international appeal than ever. With her on the executive committee were Pollei, as the director-founder; Rebecca Felton, associate chairman; and Jay L. Beck, associate director.

The eighth winner of the competition, receiver of the Steinway Model L grand piano from Daynes Music, was Alec Chien, a thirty-three-year-old native of Hong Kong. His other awards included the Alice Tully Hall recital debut, $3,000 in cash, an appearance with the Utah Symphony and numerous other concert and recital engagements, the coveted commemorative gold medal, and a cash award of $250 to apply against the cost of shipping the piano. The $3,000 cash award, incidentally, was contributed by Alec Sherman, one of the jurors and the husband of the late Gina Bachauer.

The value of the competition to the Utah Symphony may be found in the added exposure of the orchestra nationwide and new prestige among major orchestras. Following the 1982 keyboard contest, the top three medal winners were presented in a two-hour video concert with the symphony under Varujan Kojian that was presented nationwide before an estimated audience of 30 million viewers over PBS. Produced by the University of Utah's KUED-TV, the project was repeated from the winning Buechner performance in 1984, and in 1986 has been made ready by KUED-TV from the performances of Chien; silver medalist Thomas Duis, 27, of West Germany; and bronze medalist Benedetto Lupo, 22, of Italy, with the Utah Symphony under Joseph Silverstein.

Back in 1982, when Silverstein's name surfaced before the orchestra's search committee, it was not the first contact between the Boston Symphony concertmaster and the Utah Symphony. In 1979, when the orchestra began looking for someone to replace Maurice Abravanel as music director, Silverstein was invited to become a candidate for the position.

After informing the committee that his situation was such that he did not want to "uproot the family" and "could not consider a major change" at that time, the prospective conductor again concentrated on his demanding role in Boston.

Within a year, however, in the spring of 1980, Silverstein visited Salt Lake City on tour with the Boston Symphony. He recalls being most impressed, "as was the whole orchestra," with Symphony Hall, as well as being "very taken with the city." A fitness enthusiast, he remembers: "It was a nice clear March day and I ran in the morning, all the way out to the University of Utah campus and back. I was impressed with the whole ambience of the city."

He had found through his jaunt to the east bench, as had Maurice Abravanel from vantage points in City Creek Canyon and the Hotel Utah Roof Garden thirty-three years before, that Salt Lake City was a desirable new location very much to his liking.

Little more than two years after that visit, Silverstein was contemplating his future and was ready to seek the music directorship of the Utah Symphony that again was open to qualified candidates.

"I had been with the Boston Symphony for twenty-seven years," Silverstein reflects, "and I was trying to decide whether I was going to finish my career in that post or leave the orchestra and pursue the guest conducting and solo appearances which were becoming so frequent that I had to refuse a number of them. The day-to-day routine of the orchestra also was beginning to wear on me, and I felt that as concertmaster of the Boston Symphony Orchestra I had to be there most all of the time and not be flitting about conducting other orchestras. My loyalty to the symphony was in direct conflict with my desire to have a certain amount of personal expression as a conductor and as a soloist."

At this time Silverstein determined to resign from the Boston Symphony Orchestra upon completion of his thirtieth season. Hardly had he made the decision, however, when he became aware of the opening with the Utah Symphony. A letter to Maurice Abravanel, whom he had known from his summers in Tanglewood, stated well the violinist's desires and position: "If there is a change contemplated, I should like to be considered even in an 'interim' capacity should that be needed. At the time you retired, I was asked to submit my resume, but my personal situation at that time didn't permit me to entertain such a possibility. At this point, however, Adrienne and I are in a much freer position without children's schooling, and we are contemplating a change of 'life-style' with happy expectations. My career in Boston is almost 30 years old and my guest conducting/solo activities have grown to the point where my schedule here is really a bit confining. The challenge of being the artistic and 'spiritual' leader of a fine orchestra is my ultimate goal (while continuing to play, of course) and if the Salt Lake position is open, I'd like a chance to fill it!"

The letter brought a call from Maurice and then from Don Lloyd, who invited Silverstein to submit his resume and other materials and to meet with the search committee. On December 3 and 4, 1982, the candidate met with the committee and the orchestra, but it was not until six weeks later that he was next contacted and told he had been selected. By that time Silverstein had made commitments with the Boston Symphony that somewhat limited his first season in his new position.

Because of his awareness of the past and a schedule based upon his availability in 1983-84, the new conductor asked that he be an "artistic director" and that the three-year contract not be made final until he had "lived with the orchestra for a month."

Joseph Silverstein had been playing in orchestras since he was eighteen and had conducted in a limited role since he was twenty-one. He knew the value and the necessity of close ties between the podium and the players on one hand and the audience on the other. "I felt the orchestra had to have a chance to live with me for a month," he said, "not only subscription concerts, but children's concerts, and that the public had to have a chance to see me in action just to really sense what I was all about."

Born into a musical environment in Detroit on March 21, 1932, young Joe found a violin under his chin almost as soon as he was able to hold one. His first teacher was his father, who had come from his native Poland as a child and studied violin with Franz Kniesel, himself a former concertmaster of the Boston Symphony, at what was then the Institute of Music Arts, later the Juilliard School of Music, in New York City. From there the elder Silverstein moved to Detroit, taught music in the public schools, and conducted the All-City Junior Band.

The young violinist's mother, an amateur pianist with a great interest in the arts, was widowed when her husband died at the age of forty-six in an automobile accident. When she succumbed to cancer at the age of forty-nine, her son was left with a rich musical legacy.

After the beginnings with his father, Silverstein went on to study the violin, first with Josef Gingold, and then with Efrem Zimbalist at the Curtis School of Music in Philadelphia. Another of his teachers was Mischa Mischakoff, leading to a chair in the Mischakoff String Quartet during the summers at Chautauqua.

In 1950, at the age of eighteen, Joseph joined the Houston Symphony, where he played for three years before moving to the Philadelphia Orchestra for the 1953-54 season. He followed this with a single season as concertmaster and assistant conductor of the Denver Symphony under Saul Caston. His next move, in 1955, was to the Boston Symphony, where he became concertmaster in 1961 and assistant conductor in 1971.

Meanwhile, performing with his violin, Silverstein won the silver medal at the 1959 Queen Elisabeth of Belgium Competition and the 1960 Walter M. Naumburg Award. His solo performances with orchestras throughout the United States and Europe perhaps outnumber his many guest conducting appearances and include ensembles in Geneva, Jerusalem, Brussels, Denver, Detroit, Los Angeles, New York, Indianapolis, Philadelphia, and Rochester.

It was from an appearance before the Phoenix Symphony that Silverstein flew to Salt Lake City early in June 1983 for his first concerts with the Utah Symphony in a "Meet the Maestro" series. The debut came in Provo on the night of June 7, three days after the first rehearsal with his orchestra (he had conducted in Phoenix on June 3) and just ahead of performances at Symphony Hall the following two nights.

For his introduction, the new music director chose an all-Brahms program, with which he scored well on all fronts. He opened with the "Academic Festival Overture," then went to the "Variations on a Theme of Haydn," and finished with the Symphony No. 4. Terry Orme of the *Salt Lake Tribune* observed: "Mr. Silverstein is a conductor who only occasionally is given to flamboyant gestures and dramatics. . . . He practices his art with efficient economy. . . . It appears the relationship between symphony and conductor is off on the right foot."

In the *Deseret News*, William Goodfellow wrote that with the coming of Silverstein, "it was plain that a new sensibility is in charge." He found that from the beginning of the "Academic Festival Overture" the performance "offered as much to chew on interpretively as it did sonically."

"This was not just an improved sound but a transformed one," the critic wrote, "sporting not only warmth and precision but the finest string playing I have yet heard from the orchestra."

Goodfellow also noted that "as conductors go, Silverstein himself cuts a fairly unprepossessing figure on the podium. . . . His work is generally direct and to the point."

Buoyed by the positive response to his performances, Silverstein went on to a recital in Detroit and dates in Greensboro, North Carolina, and Baltimore, Maryland, playing and conducting at both places before finishing out the summer at the Berkshire Music Festival.

When he returned to Salt Lake City on September 1, expecting to begin rehearsals for the "Silverstein Season," he found the musicians picketing Symphony Hall. They had called the first strike in the forty-three-year history of the Utah Symphony. And, although "frustrated, dismayed, and unhappy," all the conductor could do was look on and hope for a quick end to the conflict.

There were others as disturbed as Silverstein and the symphony management over the work stoppage. The producers of the first biennial Obert and Grace Tanner-sponsored "Gift of Music," a performance of the Verdi "Requiem" with the combined Utah Symphony and Mormon Tabernacle Choir, were a bit anxious about their September 16 date. Ballet West would need a prepared orchestra for its opening on September 28, and the Utah Opera Company was nearing rehearsals for its production of Verdi's "Aida" at the Capitol on October 27.

Late in August, the symphony management had presented the players a new three-year contract proposal calling for a one-year wage freeze, with an 11-percent increase over the following two years. The proposal also provided for a one-year moratorium on the conversion of so-called "B" (part-time) players to full-time, a process to be completed by 1986.

On Wednesday night, August 31, however, the musicians, on a vote of seventy-four to five, rejected the proposed pact, and they took to the picket line the following morning. In place of the rejected pact, they presented a set of demands covering wages, working conditions, conversion of part-time contracts, and the hiring of an orchestra manager.

Wendell Ashton's response was one of disappointment, branding as "unrealistic" the union's rejection of what he called a "generous" offer by the symphony's executive committee. Obviously his executive vice-president and chief operating officer, Steve Swaner, had expected approval of the contract. Soon after presenting it to the musicians, he left on a symphony-sponsored ten-day Mediterranean cruise.

In Swaner's absence, Ross Thoresen, the board's human resources advisor and professional labor relations counselor, became the management's chief negotiator in sessions with union representatives Lynn Larsen, a French horn player; Larry Zalkind, principal trombonist; and William Sullivan, Local 104 president.

By the evening of Monday, September 5, the two sides had agreed upon a new three-year contract. Accepted by the executive committee and ratified by the musicians on a vote of seventy-six to three, it called for an increase in the minimum weekly salary from $450 to $465 on April 1, 1984, with semiannual raises to a goal of $520. Equally important was the continued, gradual conversion of part-time "B" players to full-time "A" status on the payroll and the placement of two orchestra members on the symphony's board of directors.

The settlement not only brought a sigh of relief but a commendation from Wendell Ashton to the union negotiators for their "statesmanship in not pressing for more money now when we are coming out of a recession." He said of the contract that "there is little change in the dollar total from our original proposal" and called the pact "a great victory for the symphony, the state and all concerned."

Silverstein regarded the settlement as "most amicable" and joined Ashton in praising the negotiators, noting particularly the contribution of Thoresen. "If anyone comes out as a hero, it is he," said the conductor.

A major issue in the 1983 contract negotiation was the establishment of a retirement program for the musicians. This time around, however, the concern centered not so much on the need for a retirement fund per se as on the form that such program was to take.

During the summer of 1981, Obert C. and Grace A. Tanner had invited all symphony employees to the O. C. Tanner Company dining room for a luncheon, at which they announced their generous gift of $200,000 to start a retirement fund for the musicians and staff. To this The Church of Jesus Christ of Latter-day Saints added $100,000, and the state, through the efforts of Governor Scott M. Matheson, allocated another $25,000.

Creation of the $325,000 fund came as a surprise to the musicians and caused some apprehension among them that the long-awaited retirement program was being set up without their consultation. The musicians and their union representatives had hoped that the contributed funds would be used to purchase defined benefits upon retirement, whereas the board, symphony management, and donors themselves viewed the funds as an endowment from which the earnings would provide retirement benefits.

It became one of those issues in which each side was waiting for the other to make the next move, and it was not until 1983 that the matter was finally resolved. In the interim, the funds were placed in an interest-bearing, segregated account awaiting a general agreement as to what form the new program would take.

At considerable expense and effort, the musicians, through their union, had developed an elaborate pension plan that they felt best served their needs. As the 1983 contract negotiations wound down, it was agreed that the retirement endowment earnings could be funneled through this plan according to a fixed formula. A simpler plan was adopted simultaneously for the benefit of staff employees.

In initiating the new retirement program, the administration increased the retirement endowment fund by transferring into it from the regular endowment fund the $100,000 proceeds that had been realized from a 1980 benefit concert featuring Danny Kaye. Also, half of the proceeds from Silverstein's "Meet the Maestro" concert at Symphony Hall on June 7, 1983, a total of $11,238, went into the fund. Total contributions to the retirement endowment fund reached $536,238 on May 5, 1984, when a second Danny Kaye benefit concert yielded another $100,000.

All but overlooked in the establishment of a pension plan was the fact that the symphony had been paying on the musicians' behalf into an American Federation of Musicians-Employee Pension and Welfare Fund for nearly twenty years.

Enrollment of the orchestra members in the AFM-EPW Fund had been approved by the symphony board on May 29, 1964, during the presidency of J. W. Gallivan. Under this program, the symphony began paying into the union-administered pension fund on behalf of each player an amount equal to 5 percent of the current annual salary. Excluded from this formula were recording payrolls on which the symphony was already required to pay an amount equal to 8 percent of the total payroll into the fund.

In an effort to provide some kind of severance pay, during the 1980 contract negotiations the symphony agreed to pay a musician upon termination of employment any accrued, unused sick leave. It was subsequently realized, however, that this created a monstrous unfunded liability, and the provision was eliminated in 1983 in deference to more manageable retirement plans.

Even though a long-overdue retirement program was established in 1983, it was recognized that such a program would provide only minimal benefits for a musician or staff member who, for whatever reason, would leave the symphony before meaningful retirement benefits could be accrued. To fill this need, a length-of-service plan was developed under which long-term employees leaving the symphony within ten years would receive a supplemental payment.

As a result of their 1983 strike, the Utah Symphony musicians lost the pay they would have received for the three canceled orchestra services that had been scheduled for September 1, 2, and 3. Silverstein was able to meet with his players, however, for four rehearsals before the opening "New Audience" concert on Thursday, September 8. This concert, on the evening before the official subscription series inaugural, was the first of a series designed to lure new listeners into Symphony Hall.

Regular subscribers, for the most part, were still to be fully sold on the new music director and, with the critics, held in reserve their judgment on the "Silverstein Season." As *Deseret News* critic Goodfellow had commented back on June 5 on announcement of the season programs: "The era of the blockbuster.... is over for a while in Utah. Large scale pieces are either absent or have been left to others."

Goodfellow looked upon the season as one of "conservative music," with Silverstein exercising caution at being "on trial." He concluded that "the symphony may not have latched onto the most daring music director in the world."

Writing in the *News* on September 9 after the season opener, however, the critic had nothing but praise for Silverstein and the orchestra. Both Goodfellow and the *Tribune*'s Paul Wetzel echoed their comments of the previous June as they lauded the quality of sound and interpretive skills exhibited in performances of the Brahms "Second Symphony"; the

Mozart "Violin Concerto No. 4"; with Silverstein as soloist; and Vaughan Williams's "A Lark Descending."

"Where the conductor really came into his own," wrote Goodfellow, "was the Brahms, a performance of this symphony whose strength and nobility impressed from the first—as did the sound of the orchestra. As the sound seemed to have been built from the ground up, so did the interpretation, a resoundingly committed view as remarkable for its depth as for its grandeur."

Wetzel was particularly impressed with the final two movements of the symphony, asserting that "it was here that Mr. Silverstein's interpretation really soared." And in his reference to the sound, he held that "there was more body in the lower strings than has been characteristic of this orchestra for a long time."

For Silverstein, the reception marked a most satisfactory beginning for his self-imposed trial before his new orchestra. With each concert, his position became more secure. As noted in his own impressions: "It seemed as though things were going to work out all right. After polling the orchestra, the search committee and the executive committee, they voted to make the appointment permanent. I felt it was important for me to put my head on that chopping block. I know I was heavily criticized by some New York managers for that. They felt I had entered into a public beauty contest.

"I wasn't worried about the city, about the audience, or about the orchestra. I was concerned about how they were going to receive me. I'm not a flamboyant personality on the podium. I have a certain kind of musicianship. I have certain convictions about what the role of a music director should be, but, as we know, chemistry is a very strange thing—it can work and then it can go sour in a hurry. So I was anxious for all concerned to have a say in the final decision, and I think it started us off on the right foot."

Silverstein began his career in Utah with an orchestra that had experienced few personnel changes for several years. Particularly noticeable, largely as a result of steady improvement in the salary structure and working conditions, was a marked decline in turnovers among the principals. The one notable exception was the role of concertmaster, where new faces continued to appear as they had for more than forty years.

Andres Cardenes had been concertmaster for one season when Silverstein arrived. The new conductor promptly scheduled the violinist to perform the Bartok Violin Concerto on the 1983-84 subscription series and the Dvorak Concerto the following season. The second of three concertmasters to be engaged over a four-year period, Cardenes joined the orchestra in 1982, replacing William Preucil, who had accepted a similar position with the Atlanta Symphony after one season under Kojian. It was Preucil who had come in 1981 to take over from Ken Kuchler, who went back to his associate concertmaster chair after a season and more as acting concertmaster. Cardenes, incidentally, stayed only until the summer of 1985, when he became concertmaster of the San Diego Symphony. He in turn was replaced by Ralph Matson, who had left his post as associate concertmaster of the Minnesota Symphony to join his former teacher Joseph Silverstein.

One other change among the principals took place in 1982 when Gary Ofenloch left the Boston Pops Orchestra to replace Gene Pokorny on the tuba. Before that, and soon after the symphony's first season in its new hall, Larry Zalkind succeeded Stephen (Ben) Ivey as trombone principal, and Ronald Holdman became the timpanist in place of Robert Lentz. In this group, too, is Jeffry Kirschen, a co-principal with Don Peterson in the French horn section. Rather ironically, it was while his fellow musicians were out on strike on September 3 and 4 of 1983 that Kirschen was in Atlanta, Georgia, winning first place in the professional division of the American Horn Competition.

Virtually commuting between his eastern commitments and Utah through his first season, the new director was able to conduct eight of the fifteen concerts on the subscription series. Associate conductor Charles Ketcham was on the podium for a program that included the Bruckner Symphony No. 4, and Varujan Kojian was there to close the season, conducting an all-Beethoven evening with Andre Watts at the piano in the "Emperor" Concerto. Other guests included such baton personalities as Walter Hendl, Uri Segal, Yoel Levi, Uri Mayer, and Murry Sidlin.

The following season, his ties at Boston and Baltimore now severed, Silverstein conducted all but four subscription series concerts, two of which were turned over to Ketcham. Guest conductors included David Atherton and Gunther Schuller, who caused a sensation with a "Ragtime" session midway through the concert. Known as a ragtime enthusiast, the noted conductor gathered the symphony's first-chair performers around him in a rare encounter with the music of Scott Joplin, Artie Matthews, Ubie Blake, and James Europe.

The year 1985 became a critical period in the expanding operations of the Utah Symphony, starting early with the planning of the 1985-86 season. After agreeing to lengthen the subscription series to nineteen concerts, the administration and Silverstein discussed programming and a need for making the season as attractive as possible. It marked the first time the board had injected itself into matters dealing with repertoire since the days of Hans Heniot in the 1940s.

While Silverstein and the orchestra were earning critical acclaim for artistic production, the line of "conservative music" noted by *News* critic Goodfellow back in June 1983 was tuning out listeners, and, as expected, some members of the board were getting the message.

When a season of "Music from the Romantic Era" was announced in March, Silverstein quickly pointed out that it would "take us in a different direction than we have followed in the past year and a half." Enthusiastic over the prospects, he further explained in a message carried in the symphony newsletter "Encore": "After our survey of a number of American works and the worldwide concentration on the music of Bach and Handel, it seems an ideal time to search out the treasures of the period which falls in between the Baroque and the Contemporary, namely the Romantic era. There is no musical period that offers a richer opportunity for musical self-indulgence than the Romantic period. My mouth waters at the prospect of performing a number of compositions by Brahms, Mendelssohn, Schumann, Dvorak, Tchaikovsky, and Berlioz, and let's not forget Wagner."

The 1984-85 season closed on a high note with the viola virtuoso Pinchas Zukerman as soloist in the Teleman Viola Concerto and the Berlioz "Harold in Italy," and management reported that earned income, endowment earnings, and contributions had overbalanced the expenses.

But the summer program, the busiest in Utah Symphony history, was a complete financial disaster, throwing the organization into its new season with a deficit of over a half-million dollars. Expensive outdoor concert ventures in Murray, Deer Valley, Sundance, and other locations drew small audiences. One such scheduled undertaking at Bear Lake West was canceled when ticket sales and staging came to naught, and the orchestra returned without playing a note.

In June, Silverstein presented an ambitious Bach/Handel Tricentennial Festival chamber orchestra series at Symphony Hall and Snowbird that, despite its musical excellence, was a loser at the box office. More successful was the regular Snowbird/Symphony Hall series in June, July, and August, but it just wasn't a good summer for the Utah Symphony's purse.

In a way, it was a rude baptism for a new symphony administration which would find the summer months a financial burden. Regarded as "off season" to a degree, this out-of-doors, vacation period could sustain fewer concerts than the regular season, yet in spite of reduced income, fixed costs such as salaries for musicians and staff were still there.

In the spring of 1985, Wendell J. Ashton left the Utah Symphony to accept a call to become president of the LDS Church's London, England, Mission. Ashton left the symphony organization in a position far advanced from that in which he found it in 1965, and he had accomplished most of the goals he had set for himself along the way. He kept his word with the musicians made in 1970 when he told them of his goal to attain full-time status for the orchestra. To do that, he led a constant fund-raising crusade that saw the operating budget of the symphony grow from $388,000 in his first season of 1965-66 to $4,700,000 in 1984-85.

Always on the lookout for sources of money, Wendell found new donors and symphony enthusiasts. His well-conceived program of enlisting sponsorships for symphony concerts and other undertakings became the backbone of the financial structure and helped to bolster prospects for building a formidable endowment fund.

Wendell's final task as president was to ascend the podium during an "Executives at Pops" concert at Symphony Hall on the night of May 18 and wave the orchestra through Sousa's "Stars and Stripes Forever." He had come a long way with the symphonic music he had had little use for when he took the administrative reins twenty years before.

As Silverstein handed the baton to his boss for the brief encounter, he noted that "for all these years Wendell has been supplying the gasoline for this machine but has never had a chance to drive it."

In a parting climax to the memorable occasion, the Salt Lake Area Chamber of Commerce presented its coveted "Giant of the City" award to the retiring president for outstanding service to his community.

Two days after the Saturday night concert, Jon M. Huntsman, chairman and president of Huntsman Chemical Corporation, succeeded Ashton and became chairman and chief executive officer of the Utah Symphony board of directors. Also elected by the board in the reorganization were six vice-chairmen: Rodney H. Brady, president and chief executive officer of Bonneville International and former president of Weber State College; Spencer F. Eccles, chairman and president of First Security Corporation; David E. Salisbury, prominent attorney, business leader, and a member of the symphony's executive committee; Barbara L. Tanner, former president of the Utah Symphony Guild and chairman of the Utah Symphony Gina Bachauer International Piano Competition; M. Walker Wallace, chairman of Wallace Associates, with a long record of service on the board and its executive committee; and Alonzo W. Watson, Jr., prominent attorney and former president of Westminster College, who had served on the board and executive committee as vice-president in charge of legal affairs for the symphony.

Assuming the title of president was Stephen W. Swaner, who had served two years as executive vice-president and who continued as chief operating officer.

A few weeks after he became chairman, Huntsman reported to the executive committee and later to the full board that he had had time to analyze the overall situation of the Utah Symphony and his own personal situation and found a need to restructure the board leadership. Under his plan, he would continue to serve as chief executive officer but would delegate the day-to-day decisions to a vice-chairman, Deedee Corradini, while concentrating his efforts almost exclusively on the urgent matter of fund-raising. His plan was approved by the full board on September 10, 1985.

The new symphony leadership assumed responsibility for an orchestra with a 1985-86 operating budget of $5.6 million and an operating deficit in the previous season of between $500,000 and $600,000. Fortunately, endowment earnings more than covered the deficit, but only because investments yielded 18 percent over the same period due to nonrecurring shifts in investment policies.

Supporting the busiest symphony orchestra in the country has become an awesome challenge to an administration no longer with the dominating fund-raising skills of Wendell Ashton. The American Symphony Orchestra League's latest survey in 1983-84 showed that the Utah Symphony logged 251 performances that season, counting subscription series in Salt Lake City and Ogden, youth concerts, school appearances, ballet and opera services, tours, recording sessions, and other engagements. Closest to that figure was 241 performances of the Boston Symphony, with 186 San Francisco Symphony concerts a distant third.

Management of the multi-million dollar operation involving 251 performances a season now demands a staff of nineteen in place of the two, a manager and a secretary, who were in the office when Huck Gregory took charge in 1957. But then, notes Huck, the budget, too, has grown more than thirty times from its $170,000 over that twenty-eight-year period.

The musician's payroll, now covering a roster of eighty-five full-time players, demands 60 percent of the operating budget. Players' salaries claim 52 percent of the outlay, while another 8 percent pays for salaries of the music director and associate conductor and the fees for guest conductors and artists.

"We have not recovered from the added cost of phasing the "B" [part-time] players into full-time," remarked Steve Swaner as he noted the projected $220,000 shortage in the 1985-86 budget.

That was just before the erstwhile president and chief operating officer resigned from his position effective November 1. His development director, Edward F. John, had already left the staff on October 8.

Before leaving their respective posts, Swaner and John were pushing hard for development of the orchestra's endowment fund. Both had agreed that the symphony's ability to meet its future financial problems is tied in no small way to this capital reserve. They felt a need to build the fund to a point where its earnings are sufficient to cover the growth of the budget.

Brought into Utah Symphony operating with no experience in that field, Swaner said he regarded the producing of symphony concerts "much the same as a manufacturing firm producing goods for another market."

He was soon to find, however, that the raising of funds to cover the costs not met by earned income was something different and "most difficult." It posed a particular problem in his budget-making, bringing up the question "How do you budget an unknown amount of gifts?" He felt the best answer might lie in an endowment fund double or even triple its present size.

Starting with the $2,000,000 Ford Foundation grant and matching funds, the endowment has grown to $5.4 million. Of this amount, however, $700,000 belongs to employee retirement, and its earnings are restricted for that purpose. Income from another $1.2 million is also restricted until the 1986-87 season. This amount is the result of a $150,000 Mellon Fund grant made in 1978 with the provision that it be matched by three times that amount and that the $600,000 principal and its earnings not be touched for eight years. With interest rates what they have been in recent years, it is not surprising that the untouched fund has doubled in size.

Ed John points out that while most major symphonies realize from 11 percent to 17 percent (some as much as 40 percent) of their income from endowment fund earnings, the Utah Symphony return is 7 percent. He noted that the Cincinnati Symphony realized 41 percent of its budget from endowment fund interest, Oregon 31 percent, and Pittsburgh 23 percent. Although the release of the Mellon Fund money could increase the Utah endowment return a point or two, the potential could be much more with some sizable donations, he observed.

John, a native of Salt Lake City who, like Swaner, had gained experience in other markets, had joined the symphony administration as a professional fund-raiser and taken over as director of development sometime after Ray White left to join Sinclair Oil Company in 1981. He regarded the fund-raising priorities as three-fold, the first being audience development to increase earned income by filling the seats and expanding the number of programs. The others included the endowment fund with its planned gifts and income from wills and trusts, and the annual contributions and sponsorships.

Earned income concerns developed over a decline in subscription sales during a five-year period from 90 percent of available season tickets in 1980 to 70 percent in 1985. Only 43 percent of the orchestra's total revenues now come from ticket sales, with another 13 percent coming from recording fees and state, federal, and local grants, a total earned income return of 60 percent.

To take up the slack, management and the administration turned to fund-raising with greater attention on the entire state and region while continuing to draw on local sources. They were fully aware that 97 percent of contributions derive from the metropolitan Salt Lake area, with major donors carrying much of the burden.

Typical are the charitable foundations of Obert and Grace Tanner, George and Dolores Eccles and Union Pacific. The Church of Jesus Christ of Latter-day Saints, now working through its business affiliations, has aided immensely in carrying the orchestra with its "in kind" and dollar giving.

Other major contributors over the years have been John M. and Glenn Walker Wallace; Salt Lake developer S. Spence Clark and wife, Jill; Donald P. and Helen Lloyd; Mrs. Mabel S. Clayton and the C. Comstock Clayton Foundation administered by Calvin H. Behle; the Marriner S. Eccles Foundation; Dean E. Eggertsen of the S. B. Eggertsen Foundation; Norman C. and Barbara L. Tanner; the Financial Foundation; Mr. and Mrs. John A. Dahlstrom; Mr. and Mrs. Howard J. Ruff; Kennecott Minerals Company; First Security Bank; Mr. and Mrs. Bill Daniels; Mr. and Mrs. Edgar B. Stern, Jr.; the Skaggs Drug Centers; Mountain Bell; Mountain Fuel Supply Company; and Utah Power and Light Company.

In-kind contributions of considerable proportions, largely with respect to the Bachauer Competition, have come from KUTV, Inc.; Western Air Lines; and the Hotel Utah. Add to these the generous contributions from the Salt Lake City and County Commissions, the University of Utah, and the Utah Symphony Guild, and the concentration of Utah Symphony support in Salt Lake Valley becomes clear.

In addition to direct contributions to the Utah Symphony, the Tanner Foundation's "Gift of Music" stands out for its generosity in the field of great symphony-choral production. The second such biennial event, presented free to the public, was made available to Salt Lake Tabernacle capacity audiences on the evenings of November 15 and 16, 1985, with the celebrated guest conductor Michael Tilson Thomas directing the orchestra and Tabernacle Choir in the music of three American composers, Aaron Copland, George Gershwin, and Howard Hanson.

It was on the eve of those concerts, November 14, that Copland observed his eighty-fifth birthday, and his "Canticle of Freedom," a selection from his settings of "Old American Songs," and four motets well represented his creative genius. Gershwin was on the program through his Second Piano Rhapsody with the conductor at the keyboard; and Hanson, through the hymn from his "Song of Democracy." The Copland works were recorded by CBS Masterworks the following week.

Meanwhile, the "new direction" taken by Silverstein and the Utah Symphony appeared to be a right move from the very first subscription concert of the new season. For the event the conductor programmed the Berlioz "Symphonie Fantastique" as the major work and came away with a presentation the critics described as "stunning." Weber's "Oberon" Overture and the "Pelleas and Melisande" Suite by Faure completed the program.

"The orchestra certainly emerged shining," was the comment of Anne Mathews in the *Salt Lake Tribune*. "With music director Joseph Silverstein conducting, they achieved a vigour, a warmth, and a precision.... One of Silverstein's strengths is that he avoids histrionics. There is no wasted movement when he conducts and he never detracts from the performance in the way many of the more flamboyant conductors do."

It was the beginning of another 250-plus performance season anchored by subscription series in Salt Lake, Ogden, and, for the first time, Provo.

In Salt Lake City, the season-ticket buyer was offered a choice between the extended nineteen-concert series and shorter groupings of twelve or seven programs. Purchasers of the full season found themselves with a twenty-concert season, the added prize being a free ticket for nineteen-concert subscribers only to the orchestra's 5,000th performance on February 1 in the Salt Lake Tabernacle with soprano Leontyne Price as guest soloist.

Also available at Symphony Hall were the six-concert chamber series with Silverstein and Ketcham dividing baton chores; the visiting orchestra series, presenting the Israel Symphony, the Los Angeles Philharmonic, and the Philadelphia Orchestra; the youth series of three performances; and a "preview" series of three concerts.

As he turned into his third season with the Utah Symphony, Silverstein had been given an extended contract through the 1987-88 season. Very much aware of the symphony's financial needs, he decided to make the best of the situation. Among other things, he canceled a scheduled performance of Holst's "The Planets" in October because of the cost of bringing in the extra players the work requires.

Silverstein put himself down to conduct eleven concerts on the subscription series, including the milestone 5,000th performance and the closing presentation of the Beethoven Ninth Symphony in April. He assigned two concerts to his associate conductor, Ketcham, and signed Kojian to return, this time for the Mendelssohn Symphony No. 4 and the Schostakovich Symphony No. 5 in March. Other guest conductors included Jorge Mester, George Cleve, Yoav Talmi, Catherine Comet, Yoel Levi, and Kazuyoshi Akiyama.

While the music director has changes in mind, they all lie in the future, both for musical and financial reasons. He sounds like a coach who feels his team is not playing up to its potential.

"At this point," he says, "I don't think the Utah Symphony under my direction and with the present personnel is playing as well as it can. When I feel that we are playing as well as we can together, then I'll consider making personnel changes. But at the moment I think the instrument, as it stands today, can produce a better result, and I've addressed myself to that."

Silverstein agrees with the management that the endowment fund holds the key to the future. He is convinced it will take nothing short of a big increase in that fund to allow an enlargement of the orchestra and to make other changes.

"The income from such an endowment fund," he believes, "would take the heat off the annual fund-raising to a degree where we could make plans five or ten years down the road. At the moment, we don't have a really finite long-range plan because we are working so hard in terms of shoring up the finances."

While he feels he is doing all he can to help the situation, the music director does not want to be actively involved in fund-raising, but rather, in summary, wants to be "actively involved in making a case for the orchestra as an important force within the city — something that people will be able to hang onto as an indication of the civility of this area, of its goals and of its spiritual quality."

Fast in the sights of the music director is a larger ensemble to provide "more flexibility," perhaps the addition of as many as twelve players. But, again, he knows this goal must be shelved until financing catches up with the increased payrolls and other added expenses linked to fifty-two weeks of concerts a year.

It appears he will have the opportunity, however, to make his first international tour with the orchestra. If plans fall into place, the late summer journey of 1986 will find the Utah Symphony revisiting Yugoslavia, Austria, and West Germany while adding the German Democratic Republic and Liechtenstein to its long list of foreign concert stops.

The first concert of the tour will be in West Berlin and the second in East Berlin. As far as is known, this will be the first time that any American orchestra has performed on both sides of the Berlin Wall during the same tour.

It is no secret that the impending tour was on shaky ground in the spring and early summer of 1986, what with European travel threatened by terrorists. But as fears diminished, the symphony organization flashed the green light.

Somewhat influencing the decision, too, was a stabilizing of the administration's front office and the fiscal picture at the close of the subscription season. Not long after assuming the chairmanship in 1985, Jon Huntsman had secured the temporary services of Robert J. Darling as acting executive director. President of J. F. Ward Associates, a Salt-Lake-City/based international management-consulting firm of thirty years' experience, Darling had been serving on the symphony's strategic planning committee.

So successful was the arrangement that Huntsman could only express pleasure in June 1986 at the progress made during the interim without a permanent executive director.

"With Acting Executive Director Darling's steady hand at the wheel, and Board Vice Chairman Deedee Corradini's unflagging attention," he said, "the Utah Symphony has cut costs, increased revenues, located new contribution sources for broader-based support, and increased participation of the board. The best news is that for this season, the orchestra is projecting an overall balanced budget."

That budget, incidentally, for the approaching 1986-87 season had been fixed at $5,270,000, a sharp reduction from the $5,600,000 budget for 1985-86.

Huntsman's optimistic projection had coincided with the announced appointment of Paul R. Chummers, at that time manager of the Chicago Symphony, as executive director of the Utah Symphony. The announcement culminated a seven-month search by a committee headed by Deedee Corradini, who spoke for the fourteen-member panel: "We feel Paul Chummers is one of the top people in symphony management. His sixteen years of orchestra management experience and his extensive business background will be of great benefit to the Utah Symphony."

Until he came on board with the Utah orchestra on August 1, 1986, Chummers had been manager of the Chicago Symphony for seven years and had served one of those seasons, 1984-85, as acting general manager. Before joining the Chicago organization, he had been assistant managing director of the Minnesota Orchestra for seven years.

Still as busy as any symphony orchestra in the nation, the Utah Symphony continued its full schedule through the spring and summer of 1986. In early summer, such popular guests as Roberta Peters, Mitch Miller, Norman Leyden and the world championship Vocal Majority barbershop chorus joined the orchestra in special performances.

During August, before turning its full attention to a pair "Bon Voyage" concert on September 5 and 6 and the European tour, the summer series wound up with concerts under the direction of guest Newton Wayland and the orchestra's assistant conductor, Charles Ketcham.

For Ketcham, it marked the end of his stay with the Utah Symphony. His replacement, Christopher Wilkins, was standing in the wings as Silverstein and the orchestra prepared for a 1986-87 season of nineteen subscription concerts.

Wilkins came from the Cleveland Orchestra, where for three years he served as Exxon/Arts Endowment Conductor, filling the position of assistant conductor as holder of the Elizabeth Ring and William Gwinn Mather Endowed Chair.

The new assistant conductor undoubtedly will make his appearance during the forthcoming subscription series, as Silverstein has two openings for conductors on the schedule. One of them features the music director himself in the Elgar Violin Concerto, and the other presents harpist Sarah Bullen in the Ginastera Harp Concerto.

Silverstein is scheduled to conduct eleven concerts, including the orchestra and Utah Symphony Chorus in the Brahms Requiem in November and "The Seasons" by Haydn in May. Guest conductors will include pianist Leon Fleisher, who will also be at the piano in the Ravel Piano Concerto for the Left Hand; James DePreist with Bachauer competition winner Alec Chien at the piano, Theo Alcantara, Hugh Wolff, Uri Segal, David Zinman, and Sergiu Comissiona.

It is a new plateau that Silverstein and the Utah Symphony occupy today—a plateau to which the orchestra has climbed through the devoted and dedicated leadership of the likes of Maurice Abravanel and Wendell Ashton. Ahead now stands the challenge of maintaining the great achievements that lie in the wake of 5,000 performances. Surely the furtherance of those goals becomes the specific task of the future.

On the musical side, it becomes a matter of constant striving for musical excellence. The growing pains have long since subsided, and "spit, baling wire, and mirrors" are no longer required to hold the operation together.

But financial problems remain a challenge as they have through the forty-five years since a loyal band of founders first gave life to the orchestra. As then, today's board of directors finds itself struggling to cover a deficit. To what extent it gains from the experience of the past could well determine the symphony's future.

Top: *(l-r) Maurice Abravanel, Wendell J. Ashton and Willam F. Christensen cut cake honoring Ballet West's "First Family" at reception April 17, 1984, as Herold L. Gregory and Bruce Marks look on. It was also Utah Symphony's 4500th performance.*

Bottom: *Current members of the Utah Symphony with at least 30 years' total service as of 1 February 1986, the date of the orchestra's 5,000th concert: (seated, left to right) Normal Lee Madsen Belnap, Katherine Peterson, Evelyn Loveless, Maestro Maurice Abravanel, Dorothy Freed, Frances Darger; (standing, left to right) Ralph Gochnour, Douglas Craig, Kenneth Kuchler, Richard Dickson, Don C. Peterson, Harold Gottfredson, John Chatelain.*

INDEX

AFM-EPW Fund, 386
Abrams, Jacques, 170
Abravanel, Lucy, photos 279, 281,
    283; death 310-311; 154, 155, 243,
    308, 309, 353
Abravanel, Maurice, photos 83, 87,
    144, 148, 230, 233, 234, 235, 276,
    278, 279, 280, 281, 283, 329, 402;
    appointed conductor 149; bio
    157-165; arrival 160, 308;
    foregoing pay 173; heart ailment
    226-227; birthplace visit 260; no
    salary demands 288;
    appreciation dinner 313;
    retirement 333, 347; Paris
    debacle 335-336; bypass surgery
    227, 336, 337; resignation 344-345;
    farewell concert 346-7; Gold
    Baton 363; other vi, vii, ix, 3, 86,
    112, 126, 142, 149-185, 195-227,
    240-243, 251, 262-273, 299, 300,
    313, 327, 350, 353-4, 358-364, 380,
    401
Abravanel Room, 326
Acord, O. Thayne, 325
acoustics, 125, 126, 127, 325
Adams, Orval, 177
Adler, Larry, 119-120
Adler, "Wilderness Suite" 227
Ahearn, Elsie, 62, 67
Aitken, Webster, 103
Ajmone-Marsan, Guido, 338
Akiyama, Kazuyoshi, 398
Albeniz, 180
Alcantara, Theo, 401
Aldrich, Nelson W., 98
Alexander, "Lament" 208

Allen-Duff Associates, 220
Allen, Edward, 256
Allen, Robert G., 374
Allen, Roy L., 62
Almond, Becky, photo 82; debut 33;
    68, 69, 70, 309, 311
amateur musicians, 9
American Federation of Musicians
    (see Musicians Union)
American Symphony Orchestra
    League, 363
American Theatre, 28
Andrews, Morris, 35
Angel Records, 226
Antheil, "Over the Plains" 185
arbitration, 297
Arbizu, Ray L., 339
Arnold, Edward, 138
Arrau, Claudio, photo 186; 119
Arrington, Leonard J., viii
Arroyo, Martina, 213, 214
articles of incorporation, 49
artistic decisions, 106, 197
Ashton, Belva B., photo 281; 253,
    256, 367
Ashton, Jack, 267
Ashton, Raymond J., photo 301;
    203, 252, 313
Ashton, Wendell J., photos 277, 281,
    283, 284, 301, 402; bio 253; enters
    picture 247-248; elected
    president 256; signs Kojian 356;
    departs 391-392; other vi, vii, 215,
    251, 259, 264, 265, 268, 271, 273,
    285, 294, 295, 296, 318, 321, 323,
    344, 345, 351, 352, 353, 354, 367,
    371, 374, 375, 384, 393, 401

Asper, Frank W., 35, 47, 54
Assembly Hall, 66
assessments, orchestra, 37, 38
associate conductor search, 350
Associated Food Stores, 50, 240
Athens Festival, 127
Atherton, David, 380
Atkinson, David, 213
auditions, 105, 136, 198, 359
Austin, Milton N., 67

B contract musicians, 359, 360, 384,
    385, 394
Babcock, Maude May, 72
Bach, J. C. "Sinfonia" 172
Bach, J. S., 197, 207, 353; B Minor
    Mass 339; Bach/Handel
    Tricentennial 391; Bach-
    Respighi "Passacaglia" 138; Saint
    Matthew Passion 204; Suite in D,
    164, 300; Toccata and Fugue
    135; Bach Violin Concerto, E
    Major, 184, 241
Bachauer, Gina, photo 188; 251,
    256, 259, 298, 341
    Bachauer, Gina, Int'l Piano
    Competition (see Utah
    Symphony Gina Bachauer Int'l
    Piano Competition)
Bailey, Sally, 212, 213
Bakaleinikoff, Vladimir, 120, 134
Baker, Grant, 110
Baker, Ralph, 35
Ballet Russe, 114, 116, 119
Ballet West, 25, 183, 266, 373, 384
Bamberger, Clarence, 94
Bamberger, Gov. Simon, 42
Barber, Adagio for Strings, 162, 262,
    291, 295, 300, 338; Concerto for
    Orchestra 209, 351; "Medea's
    Meditation and Dance of
    Vengeance" 365; "Vanessa" 368
Barlow, Haven J., photo 304
Barratt Hall, 29
Bartok, Violin Concerto 389
Barwick, Gloy, 353
baseball game, 34
bass drum, 259

Bassett, Sybella Clayton, 45, 47, 48,
    51, 54
Beales, Reginald, photo 80; vi, vii,
    53-105, 172
Beales, "Pastoral" 69, 73
Beck, David L., 299
Beck, Jay L., 379
Becker, Don, 343
Beckstead, Ross, 119, 137, 249
Beecham, Sir Thomas, photo 81;
    109, 111, 114
Beecher, Mrs. Harold K. (Margaret),
    viii, 308, 309, 311
Beeley, Mrs. A. L. (Glenn), 72, 100
Beesley, Dell, 35
Beesley, Ebeneezer, 9, 12
Beesley, Fred, 35, 41, 43, 44, 48
Beesley Music Co., 63
Beethoven, Ludwig van, xi, 14, 207,
    353; Beethoven, G Major
    Romance, 78; "Missa Solemnis"
    156, 170-172, 197; Piano
    Concerto No. 3, 56, 69, 78; Piano
    Concerto No. 4, 184, 342; Piano
    Concerto No. 5 "Emperor" 24,
    32, 33, 341, 389; Symphony No. 1,
    13; Symphony No. 2, 53;
    Symphony No. 3 "Eroica" xi, 31,
    107, 162, 171, 197, 291, 372;
    Symphony No. 4, 355;
    Symphony No. 5, 30, 31, 139, 171,
    197; Symphony No. 6 "Pastorale"
    31, 180, 197; Symphony No. 7, 96,
    99, 156, 197, 295, 296; Symphony
    No. 9, 164, 195, 197, 206, 207, 339,
    360, 363, 398; Violin Concerto
    163, 172, 211
Belgian String Quartet, 112
Bell, Mrs. J., 13
Belnap, Norma Lee Madsen, photo
    402
Benevolent Protective Order of Elks
    (see Elks' Lodge)
Bennett, Harold H., photo 84; 164,
    170, 184, 204, 206, 207
Bennett, Mrs. David (Bonnie), 374,
    375
Bennett, Sen. Wallace F., photo 330
Bennett's Glass and Paint, photo

229; 214
Bennion, Dr. Adam S., 76, 77, 78, 99, 111, 112
Bennion, Heber, 171, 172
Benny, Jack, photo 192; 312
Benzell, Mimi, 141
Bergman, Rabbi Abner, 338
Berkhoel-Siegel, Mrs. Agatha, 33
Berlin, "God Bless America" 211
Berlioz, 197, 390; "Harold in Italy" 391; Requiem 224; Song Cycle 338; "Symphonie Fantastique" 227, 373, 397
Berman, Lazar, 339, 340
Bernstein, Leonard, 152, 336; "Candide" Overture 258, 291; "Chichester Psalms" 335
Berry, Charles G., 27, 35, 43
Best, Alfred, 25, 33
Bettinson, Veronica, 353
Bicentennial (see Utah American Revolution Bicentennial)
Bicentennial Center for the Arts, 318, 319, 323, 325
Bickmore, Lee S., 257
Bird, Elzy J., 72
Bischoff, Cohleen, 214, 360
Bixby, Lela, 68
Bizet, "Carmen" 182; "L'Arlesienne" Suite No. 2, 30, 64
Blackburn, Dale, 210, 214
Blayman, Herbert, 169
Bleak, Howard, 97, 110, 137
Blegen, Judith, 344, 345
blizzard, 205, 244
Bloch, Concerto Grosso 211; "Sacred Service" 226, 338; "Schelomo" 175, 291
Blood, Gov. Henry H., 71, 75
Board of Examiners, 171, 172, 177
Boccherini Minuet, 17
Bolivian President, photo 281
bond election, 324, 325
Bonynge, Richard, photo 191
Booth, Louis, 67, 68, 97, 117, 137, 161, 162
Boothby, Lydia White, 45, 48
Borodin, "Polovetsian Dances" 114; Symphony No. 2, 138

Boston Symphony, 126
Bowen, Emma Lucy Gates (Mrs. Albert E.), photo 85; 53, 54, 170, 206
Bowers, Winnifred, 258
Bowery on Temply Square, 4
Bowman, Lorraine, 207
Boynton, Mrs. Charles A. (Judy), 312
Bradley, Adine, 56, 206
Brady, Dr. Rodney H., 392
Brahms, Johannes, 207, 226, 353; "Academic Festival Overture" 170, 262, 383; Haydn Variations 383; "Hungarian Dances" 45; Piano Concerto No. 1, 180, 241, 334; Piano Concerto No. 2, 171, 344; Requiem 401; Symphony No. 1, 107, 137, 291, 295; Symphony No. 2, 156, 300, 387; Symphony No. 4, 138, 262, 351, 383; Violin Concerto 184, 211
Brereton, Harold, 164
Brico, Antonia, 150
Brimhall, Lila Eccles, 210
Brimhall, Ray, 164, 206
Britt, Horace, 114
Britt String Trio, 114
Britten, Piano Concerto, 170
broadcasts, 137, 139, 165, 167, 171, 180, 205, 206, 207, 211, 244, 379
Broadhead, Daken K., 269
Brodine, Russell, 137
Brotherhood of Man concert, 339
Brown, C. M., 55
Brown, David, 241
Brown, Deane Wakeley, ix, 66
Brown, E. T. (Ted), 54
Browning Center for the Performing Arts, photo 232; 266
Brox, Adloph, 35
Bruch Violin Concerto, 35, 45, 66
Bruckner, Anton, "Die Nullte" 299, 342; Symphony No. 4, 389
Bruckner, Moritz, 48
Bruckner, Sam, 35
Bryant Jr. High Chorus, 164
Budge, Helen, 68, 69
budgets, 100, 101, 102, 132, 143, 167, 181, 248, 267, 352, 391, 393, 399

Buechner, David, 378
Buggert, Gustave, 199
Bullen, Sarah, 364, 400
Bullough, Ben, 53, 173, 179, 198
Bumbry, Grace, 213, 214
Burgin, Richard, 134
Burton, Mrs. Wilford M. (Dorothy), 313
Bush, Audrey, 161
Bush, Earl, 67
business support, 54

CBS Broadcast, 137
CBS Masterworks, 207, 226, 228, 343, 396
CRI Records, 226
Caldwell, Sarah, 343
Callas, Maria, 298
Caller, Eric, 297
Cameron, Dr. Basil, 61
Cannon, Marian, 43
Cannon, Tracy Y., 69, 72, 78, 92, 106
Capitol Records, 226
Cardenes, Andres, 389
Careless, George, 7, 11
Careless Orchestra, 8
Carl, Mrs. Sigrid Pedersen, 32, 33
Carlisle, Kitty, 213
Carnegie Hall, photo 275
Carter, Mrs. Samuel J., 78, 104, 308
Cassado, Gaspar, 175
Castelnuovo-Tedesco, 138
Cates, L. S., 54
Cerminara, Napoleon, 161, 169
cessation of operations, 35, 39, 43, 46, 51, 55, 56, 173, 178
Century Records, 220
Chadwick, George, 18; "Jubilee" Overture 333
chamber concerts, 391, 397
Chamber of Commerce, 52
Champ, Mrs. F. P. (Frances Winton), 69, 72
Chapman, Rachel, 114
Chapple, Stanley, 150
Chatelain, John, photo 402; 273, 370
Chausow, Oscar, 292, 343, 364
Chien, Alec, 379, 401
Child, Stanley, N., 72

children's concerts, photo 87; 49, 50, 107, 134, 240, 242
Choir, Mormon Tabernacle (see Mormon Tabernacle Choir)
Chookasian, Lili, 270
Chopin, 68; Piano Concerto No. 1, 114; Piano Concerto No. 2, 69, 117
Choral Society, 12, 14
Christensen Ballet School, 36
Christensen, Blanche, photo 84; 170, 184, 204, 209, 210, 214, 251, 338
Christensen, Christian, 25
Christensen Dancing Academy, 25, 49
Christensen, Harold, 182
Christensen, Heber, 67
Christensen, L. P., 20
Christensen, Lew, 182
Christensen, W. Boyd, photo 305; 369, 374
Christensen, Willam F., photo 402; vii, 25, 86, 107, 115, 182, 212, 213
Christian Science Church, 246
Chummers, Paul R., photo 306; 399, 400
Church of Jesus Christ of Latter-day Saints, The, permitted Sunday concert 33; contributed Symphony Hall property 318; use of Tabernacle 321, 331; other 4, 5, 7, 11, 41, 51, 123, 124, 125, 127, 128, 137, 170, 206, 207, 254, 341, 385, 395
civic auditorium, 120, 318
Civic Ballet, 183, 212, 244
Clark, Pres. J. Reuben, Jr., 123, 124, 135
Clark, Mrs. Rulon W. (Virginia), photo 85; 312
Clark, Spence and Jill, photo 330; 395
Clawson, Spencer, Jr., 24
Clawson, Mrs. Thomas A. (Ruth Jensen), photo 85; 68, 164, 206, 309
Clayton, C. Comstock, photo 328; 228, 326, 328, 395

Clayton, Mabel, photo 328; 395
Clayton, Shepherd Lawrence, 48, 53
Cleve, George, 398
Cliburn, Van, photo 190; 287, 334, 341
Clive, Joseph C., 119, 199
Clive, William C., 13
Clyde, Gov. George D., 249
Clyde, W. W., 72
Coates, Albert, 109, 110, 114
Cohn, Edna, 33
Coleman, Martha, 68
collective bargaining (see labor negotiations)
Colonial Theatre, 22, 25
Columbia Artists Management, 271
Columbia Symphony, 228
Columbia Theatre, 38
Comet, Catherine, 398
Comissiona, Sergiu, 401
Commercial Club, 52
compensation, 6, 7, 15, 35, 49, 100, 103, 116, 135, 155, 173, 179, 180, 195, 198, 199, 211, 221, 225, 267, 272, 273, 274, 288, 297, 354, 384, 385, 387, 393, 398
concert length, 19, 24, 32
Condie, Richard P., 68, 118, 164, 207
conductor evaluation, 369, 370
conductor search committee, 149, 152, 153, 346, 351, 355, 356, 373, 374, 375
Connors, Rachel, photo 84; 170, 184
Consolidated Music Hall, 36
contemporary music, 197
contract negotiations (see labor negotiations)
contributed services, 28, 29, 38
contributions, 201, 352, (see also fund raising)
Coop, Squire, 31, 41
cooperative recordings, 224, 225
Copland, Aaron, photo 148; 197, 223, 317; "A Lincoln Portrait" 339; "Appalachian Spring" 363; "Billy the Kid" 295; "Canticle of Freedom" 396; "Corral Nocturne" 205; "El Salon Mexico" 211, 291, 368; Old

American Songs 296; "Rodeo" 11, 206, 211
Coppin, John, 137
Cornwall, J. Spencer, 118
Corradini, Deedee, photo 303; 393, 399, 400
Cortes, Ramiro, 370; Piano Concerto 334
Cowan, Ruth, 136, 150, 151, 182, 196, 199, 203, 353
Craig, Douglas, photo 402; 206, 267
Craig, Jon, 212
Crawford, John, 360
Creston, "Frontiers" 205; "Invocation and Dance" 365, 368
crisis, financial, 162, 165, 167, 170, 172, 198, 401
Crockett, Judge J. Allan, photo 301; vii, ix, 108, 111, 123, 124, 152, 153, 168, 174, 175, 201, 202, 203, 354
Croxall's Band, 11
Crumb, George, 344
Cundick, Robert, "A Full House" Suite 250; Concerto for Organ and Strings 334

Dahlstrom, Mr. and Mrs. John A. (Marilyn), photo 330; 396
Dalby, Glen, "Aztec Ceremonial" 208; "Suite Elegiaque" 185
Dalby, Max, 106, 109
Dallin, "Film Overture" 185
Damrosch, Walter, 34
Daniels, Mr. and Mrs. Bill, 396
Darger, Frances Johnson, photo 402; 109, 141, 198
Darling, Robert J., photo 306; 399
Davis, H. Frederick, 270
Davis, Mrs. Melvin R. (Josephine), 314
Davrath, Netania, 251
Daynes, Gerald R. "Skip" 309, 378
Daynes Music Co., 378-379
Daynes, Royal W., 35
de Almeida, Antonio, 352
Debussy, Claude, 207, "Clair de Lune" 139; "Danses Sacree et Profane" 185; "Images" 197; "La Mer" 172, 197; "Nocturnes" 197;

"Petite Suite" 47, 54, 73
de Falla, (see Falla)
deficit, 17, 21, 22, 23, 36, 52, 115,
    116, 143, 162, 165, 168, 174, 176,
    181, 201, 365, 367, 391, 393, 401
DeForest, Mrs. Robert D. (Joyce
    Ann), 315
de Larrocha, Alicia, 342
Delius, "Hassan" 111; "On Hearing
    the First Cucko in the Spring"
    114
DePreist, James, 343, 352, 360, 401
depression, 59
de Rimanoczy, Jean, 119
Deseret Philharmonic Society, 5
De Sokotum, 28
Detroit Symphony, 114
Devetzi, Vasso, 298
Dewsnup, Maurine, 69
Diche, H. F., 94
Dickson, Richard, photo 402
D'Indy, Symphony on a French
    Mountain Air 211
Dinwoodey, Annette Richardson,
    photo 85; 164, 206, 210
Dixon, Frederic, 184
Dobbs, Mrs. Stuart, P., 203
Docent Program, 315
Done, Bernard C., 62
Donizetti arias, 340
Douglas, William, 77, 161
Downes, Olin, 132
Druary, John, 213
Duis, Thomas, 379
Dunbar, William C., 6
Dunn, Commissioner William E.,
    322
Dupre, Organ Concerto 139
Durham, Dr. G. Homer, 251
Durham, Dr. George H., "New
    England Pastorale" 208
Durham, Dr. Lowell M., photo 81;
    vii, 138, 200, 346, 370, 375
Dvorak, Antonin, 197, 390; Cello
    Concerto 334; "New World"
    Symphony 96, 139; Slavonic
    Dances 45; Symphony No. 8,
    338; Violin Concerto 389

earned income, 201
East High School Girls Chorus, 207
Easton, R. C., 13
Eberhardt, Alex, 50, 94
Echaniz, Jose, 109, 116
Eccles, George S. and Dolores Dore,
    photo 328; 377, 395
Eccles, Marriner S., Foundation,
    395
Eccles, Spencer F., 392
Egbert, Melba, 207
Eggertsen, Dean E., photo 329; 226,
    288, 395
Eggertsen, S. B., Foundation, 395
Eggleston, Elizabeth, 21
Ehlers, Alice, 119
Eisenberg, Herbert, 169
Eisenberger, Agnes, 356
eight-thirty town, 19
Electoral Orchestra of Mannheim,
    xii
Elgar, 42, "Pomp and
    Circumstance" 18; Violin
    Concerto 400
Elks Club (or Lodge), 52, 53, 54
Elman, Mischa, 116
Empress Theatre, 29, 33
endowment, 101, 128, 393, 394, 395,
    398
Engel, Karl, 365, 368
England Tour, 294-297
Epperson, Emery, 53
"Esmeralda" 11
European Tours, photo 284, cover;
    129, 251, 254, 262, 298, 299, 300,
    341, 364, 399
Evans, Dr. Burtis R., viii, 369, 370,
    374
Evans, David W., 6, 248
Evans, Isaac B., 32, 35
Evans, J. A., 9
Evans, Jessie, 68
Evans, Mr., 19
Evans, Oakley S., 326
Evans, Richard L., 139
Exchange Club, 53
Executives at Pops, 392
Eyre, Richard, 323, 324

Falla, "El Amor Brujo" 209; "Nights in the Gardens of Spain" 211
Family Night, 240
Farr, Naomi, 207
Farrell, Eileen, photo 187
Faure, "Pelleas and Melisande" 397
federal funding, 244, 255
Federal Music Project (see also WPA), 18, 59, 91
Felton, Rebecca, 379
female musicians, 48, 56
Fiedler, Arthur, photo 145
film track recordings, 227
financial crisis (see crisis, financial)
Firkusny, Rudolph, 180
first concert, photo 79; 9, 101
First Security Bank, 396
Fisher, Robert, 56, 68, 97, 119
Fisher, Mrs. Robert S., 108
Fitzpatrick, Eddie, 45
Fitzpatrick, John F., 78, 105, 106
Five Thousandth Concert, 397
Flashman, W. J., 18, 31 32, 35
Fleisher, Leon, 401
Flint, Leland B., 202
Foldes, Andor, 116, 117, 208
Folland, Harold, 210
Folland, Helen Budge, 68, 69
Ford Foundation, The, 128, 227, 247, 261-267, 394
Forrester, Maureen, 298
Forstat, Milton, 119
Fort Douglas, 169
Foss, Lukas, 150
Foster, Eugene, 206
Fowler, Ferguson, Kingston and Ruben, 325
Fowler, "The Pearl" 250
Fowles, J. Francis, 176
Fox, Alice, 117
Fox, Herbert O., 271
Fox, Sidney S., 78
Francescatti, Zino, photo 186
Franck, 223, "Symphonic Variations" 184; Symphony in D Minor 197, 204
Frank, Alan F., 373
Freber, Anton (see Anton Pedersen), 10

Freber, Arthur P., vi, 30-53, 97, 110
Freber, Mrs. Arthur P. (Virginia), 106, 308
Freed, David B. (musician), vii, 142
Freed, Mrs. David L. (Blanche), viii, 262, 313, 346
Freed, Mrs. David B. (Dorothy Trimble), photo 402; vii, 109, 142, 143
French, Ralph, 137
Frey and Braggiotti, 107, 108
Friedman, "Slavic Rhapsody" 68
Frohnmayer, Philip, 339
Fuchs, Allen, 161, 184
full-time musicians, 136, 272, 273, 384, 391
fund raising, 36, 37, 52, 73, 74, 102, 131, 132, 133, 134, 143, 162, 175, 179, 180, 182, 202, 203, 255, 256, 264, 266, 286, 307, 308, 315, 352, 353, 371, 391, 392, 393, 394, 398

Gadsby, George M., 77, 78, 108, 175
Gallivan, John W., photo 301; 252, 264, 318, 323, 324, 325, 386
Gardner, Kem C., 269-371
Gardner Music Hall, 223
Garff, Rep. Thelma, 72
Garrett, Ruby Stringham, viii
Gates, B. Cecil, 46, 47, 54, "Festival Overture" 31, 32; "Scherzo" 69; Symphony 98
Gates, Dr. Crawford, photos 148, 230; 208, "Promised Valley" 135, 160, 161, 164, 165, 169, 183, 185, 213, 228; "Portrait of a Great Leader" 249; Symphony No. 1, 208; Symphony No. 3, 250
Gates, Emma Lucy (see Emma Lucy Gates Bowen)
"Genesis" Suite 138, 139
Gentle, Alice, 50, 51
George, Florence, 119
Gershwin, George, 223, "An American in Paris" 222, 291; Piano Concerto in F, 222, 378; "Porgy and Bess" 211, 223; "Rhapsody in Blue" 107, 108, 222, 243; Second Piano

Rhapsody, 396
Gershwin, Ira, 223
Gewandhaus-Orchester, xii
Giannini, Dusolina, 119
Gibbons, Eve, 266
Gift of Music (see Tanner Gift of
    Music)
Gilbert, 180
Giles, Christopher, 378
Giles, Grover, Attorney General, 171
Giles, Henry, 6
Giles, Prof. Thomas, 42
Ginastera, Harp Concerto 400;
    "Variaciones Concertantes" 291,
    344
Gittins, Alvin, 262
Glade, Earl J., Mayor, 78, 104, 168
Gladstone, Gladys (see Gladys
    Gladstone Rosenberg)
Glauser, Mitzi, 248
Glazunov, Violin Concerto 206
Glinka, 180
Gluck, 204, "Iphigenie en Aulide"
    73
Gochnour, Ralph, photo 402
Godard, "On the Mountain" 64
Goff, Mr. and Mrs. Charles (Gloris),
    288, 315
Goddard, H. S., 13, 18
Goldberg, Arthur J., U. S.
    Ambassador to U.N., 258
Goldmark, 41, 197
Goodall, Donald B., 78
Goodfellow, William, 299, 347
Goodman, Benny, 213, 308
Goodman, Jack, vii, viii, 139
Gordon, Max, 152
Gordon, Rabbi Sam, 152
Gorin, Igor, 115, 119
Goshen, Reverend Elmer I., 19, 20,
    21, 27, 43, 45, 48, 52
Gottfredson, Harold, photos 284,
    402; 248
Gottschalk, 197
Gould, Morton, 197, 317; "American
    Salute" 206
Gounod, "Faust" 212
government support, 74, 118, 242
Graffman, Gary, photo 192

Graham, Fred C., 25, 51
Grainger, Percy, 120
Grand Prix du Disque, 127
Grant, Pres. Heber J., 47
Green, Walter, 206
Greene, Arthur, 378
Greene, Mr. and Mrs. D. Forrest
    (Gerda), 269
Greenwald, J. A., 53
Greenwell, Darrell J., 60
Gregory, Herold L. "Huck" photos
    235, 305; appointed manager,
    214-217; vii, viii, 127, 217, 227,
    243, 248, 251, 259, 262, 264, 273,
    287-297, 321, 344-349, 353, 354,
    358, 367, 374, 393, 402
Grieg, Edvard, 10, 56, 180, 223,
    "Norwegian Dances" 17, 45;
    "Peer Gynt" 45; Piano Concerto
    23, 29, 69, 115, 226, 368
Grimshaw, Jonathan, 5
Grofe, Ferde, 197, 223
Groneman, George, 35, 43, 45, 67, 97
Grover, Uncle Roscoe, 185
Grow, Stewart, 161
Gruppe, Paul, 161, 165
guarantors, 49, 108
guest conducting (Kojian), 361, 362
guest conductors, 343
Guilmant, Concerto for Organ and
    Orchestra, 73
Gurt, Michael, 278

Hadley, "Angelus" 73
Haigh, Bertram, 103
Hainke, Rudolph, 66, 68, 77
Hale, Mrs. J. A., 106, 308
Hales, Dr. Bernell, 342
Hallen, Rhapsodie in F Major 29
Handel, G. F., 5, 56, 317; "The
    Faithful Shepherd" 111; "Israel
    in Egypt" 214, 222; "Judas
    Maccabaeus" 213, 214, 219, 223;
    Organ Concerto 209; Viola
    Concerto 138; "Water Music" 96
Handel and Haydn Society, 8
Handel Society, 213, 214
Hanson, "Song of Democracy" 335,
    396

Hardiman, Frances Osborne, 119
Hardiman, William M., 110, 119,
  161, 169
Harding, Ann, 136
Hardman, Maud, 174
Harline, Leigh, 138, "Centennial
  Suite" 139
Harriman, W. Averill, 258
Harris, Dr. Cyril M., 324, 325
Harris, Johana, 172
Harris, R. W. "Dick" 196
Harris, Roy, 174, "Folk Song
  Symphony" 226; Symphony No.
  3, 334
Harrison, Conrad B., photo 192
Harrison, Guy Fraser, 150, 153
Hartman, Mr. and Mrs. Prof., 12, 13
Hatch, George C., 131, 132
Hatch, Mrs. Glen M. (Nellie), 313
Hawaiian Pops, 344
Hawkins, Clarence J., 27, 35, 41
Haydn, Franz Joseph, xi, 5, 197;
  Cello Concerto 175; "The
  Creation" 118, 210, 334; "Drum
  Roll" Symphony No. 103, 204;
  "London" Symphony 74; "The
  Seasons" 401
Hayes, Mrs. Lucille, 308
Heaps, Seldon, 69
Heifetz, Jascha, 211
Held, John, Band, 16
Held's Boy Scout Band, 46
Heller, Anatole, photo 284; 298
Henderson, Robert E., photo 146;
  227, 350, 360, 361, 364, 365, 374
Hendl, Walter, 150, 153, 380
Heniot, Hans, photo 80; 95-119, 380
Heppley, Oscar R., 56, 103, 110, 112,
  118, 153
Hepworth, Loel, 368
Herod Atticus Amphitheatre,
  photos, cover and 276
Hewlett, Margaret Stewart, 68
Hicks, Hervey, 342, 343, 346
Hicks, Kay, 241
Hieronymi, Jean, 342
Higgins, Arnold, 37
Highland High School Auditorium,
  124, 341

Hilgendorff, Evelyn, 199
Hill, Mrs. Maxine Bleak, vii
Hills, Mrs. Della Daynes, 32
Hinchcliff, Lester, 33
Hinckley, Pres. Gordon B., photo
  235
Hinckley, Mrs. Robert Jr. (Janice),
  313
Hindemith, Paul, 197, "Mathis der
  Mahler" 204; "Symphonic
  Metamorphosis" 209
Hinson, Nina, 342
Hoberman, Arthur, 137
Hodgson, Jimmy, 248
Hodgson, Leslie J., 72
Hofmann, Josef, 34
Hogensen, Lorna, 109, 137, 161, 162,
  199
Hogensen, William, 109
Holdman, Ronald, 389
Hollis, Eva, 99
Hollywood Bowl, photo 278
Holst, "The Planets" 397
Honegger, Arthur, "Joan of Arc at
  the Stake" 210; "Judith" 251;
  "King David" 127, 210, 220, 224
Honolulu Symphony, 344
Hoover, President Herbert, 60
Hopkin, Sen. Alonzo F., 175, 176,
  178, 179
Horenstein, Jascha, 150
Horman, Sidney M., 288
Horne, Alice Merrill, 71, 76
Horowitz, Vladimir, 204
Hotel Utah, 396
Hovhaness, Alan, 343
Howard, E. O., 94
Howard, John C., 50, 94
Howe, Maurice, 72
Hulbert, Duane, 378
Humperdinck, "Hansel and Gretel"
  21, 205
Humphrey, Vice Pres. Hubert H.,
  photo 275; 255
Huntsman, Jon M., photo 301; 392,
  393, 399
Hurley, Laurel, 213
Hurst, Rep. George A., 176
Hyde, John, 5

Hyde, Sheldon F., photo 279; vii, 46
Hyde, Orson, 46

Igelman, Otis, 137, 141
Immanuel Baptist Church, 345
Import musicians, 136, 141, 142, 154, 161, 198, 199 (see also local musicians)
instruments impounded, 261
instrument plane, 289, 290, 366
International Gustav Mahler Society, 224
international tours, 247, 285
investments, 20
Ippolitov-Ivanov, "Caucasian Sketches" 32
Irene, Princess of Greece, photo 193
Irvine, Gayle, 97
Israel Symphony, 397
Iturbi, Ampara, 182
Iturbi, Jose, photo 187; 182, 311
Ivey, Stephen "Ben" 389

Janssen, Werner, photo 82; 134, 143, 150, 151; "Music George Washington Knew" 139
Jepperson, Florence (Madsen), 25 33
Jenkins, Mable Borg, 68
Jensen, Allen, 161
Jesperson, Chris, 56
jet-set conductor, 142
Johannesen, Grant, photo 186; 68, 69, 116, 117, 138, 139, 171, 211, 226, 258, 260, 270, 291, 312, 335, 341
Johanos, Donald, 344
John, Edward F., viii, 393, 394, 395
Johnson, Mrs. Dale G. (Beverly), viii, 314
Johnson, Pres. Lyndon B., 255
Johnson, William, 184
Jones, Ernie, 62, 97
Jones, Richard, 199
Jones, Thomas Clyde, 67
Jordan, Capt. Joe, 114
Jorgensen, Oge, 35, 97, 109
Jorgensen, Paul, 109

Jorgensen, Thorvald, 35, 56, 109
Jorgensen, Val, 56, 109
Josie, Charles, 67
Judson, Arthur, 135, 151
Junior League, 95

KSL Radio, 139
KUTV Inc., 396
Kahn, Claude, 299, 300
Kalt, Fred, 67
Kalt, Percy, photo 85; 241
Kasin, Jerome, 206
Kastler, B. Z., 374
Kaufman, "Dirge" 165
Kay, Betty L., 353
Kaye, Danny, photo 145; 386
Keddington, Dorothy Kimball, 69, 213
Keene, Christopher, 352
Keler, "Wander-Ziel Lustspiel" 13
Kennah, Sylvia, 67
Kenin, Herman D., 221, 222, 225
Kennecott Copper, 204, 205, 244, 396
Kennedy Center, photo 282
Kent, Charles, 17
Kent, Arthur, 208-211
Kern, "Showboat" 169
Ketcham, Charles, photo 146; 227, 374, 389, 390, 397, 398, 400
Khashoggi, Adnan M., 339
Kimball, Edward P., 49, 51, 52
Kimball, Ranch S., 116
Kimball, Pres. Spencer W., photo 278; 351
King Constantine II, 259
King, Otto, 30
Kingsbury Hall, photo 79; 3, 107, 119, pit 212
Kipnis, Alexander, 96, 102
Kirschen, Jeffry, 364, 389
Kiwanis Club, 53
Kiwanis-Felt Bldg., 162, 163
Klingler, Albert, 137
Knights of Pythias Band, 11
Kojian, Miran, 356
Kojian, Varujan, photo 144; bio 356; vii, 227, 228, 349-373, 389
Kopleff, Florence, 251

Korngold, 138
Krantz, LaVar, 240
Krooskos, Christina, 339, 342
Kuchler, Kenneth, photo 402; vii,
    106, 169, 342, 364, 370, 389
Kullmer, Ann, 150, 153
Kutulas, Commissioner Pete, 322
Kuyper, George, 262

LDS Missionaries, 293, 294
labor negotiations, 6, 7, 354, 359,
    360, 384
ladies in orchestra (see female
    members)
Ladies Orchestra, 11
Lalo, "Symphonie Espagnole" 107,
    184
Lamoreaux, Lota, 210
Landes, Carleen, viii, 248, 249, 346,
    353
Lange, 153
Larsen, Lynn, 370, 384
Larsen, Mary Olive, 10
Larsen, Roy, 255, 257
Latin American tour, photos 279,
    280; 128, 268, 284, 285, 288
Latter-day Saint converts, 5
Lawrence, Douglas, 338
Lawson, William, 67
Lazarof, Henry, 352,"Odes for
    Orchestra" 250
Leary, Dean W. H., 72, 92
LeeMaster, Vernon J. 112, 240
Lee, Pres. Harold B., 321
Lee, Gov. J. Bracken, photo 84; vii,
    168, 172, 175-178, 201, 202
Lees, Dr. C. Lowell, 164, 169, 182
Legislature, (see Utah State
    Legislature)
length of concerts, 19, 24, 32
length of season, 183, 272-274, 353,
    354, 386-391
length of service payment, 386, 387
Lentz, Robert, 283, 389
letter, orchestra members', 272
Levant, Oscar, 126, 211
Levi, Yoel, 380, 398
Levitzki, Mischa, Valse in A Major,
    53

Levy, Lottie, 17
Lewis Bros. Stages, 239, 242
Lewis, Daniel, 352, 360
Leyden, Norman, 400
Liatis, Alexis S., Greek Ambassador,
    258
Ligeti, Desire, 207, 208
Lincoln, Frances, 13
Lindem, Mrs. Martin C., 106, 108,
    153, 308
Lindsay, Mayor John, 258
Lindsay, John S., 7
Lindskoog, Wesley M., 184
Lions Club, 53
Liszt, Franz, 68, "Hungarian
    Fantasy" 33; "Hungarian
    Rhapsody" 69; "Les Preludes"
    21, 109, 205; Piano Concerto No.
    1, 45, 53, 74
Lloyd, Donald P., photos 303, 329;
    vii, 240, 252, 329, 373-375, 396
Lloyd, Mrs. Donald P. (Helen),
    photo 329; viii, 240, 312, 396
Loa, 242
loans, 171
local musicians, 136, 142, 154, 156,
    161, 198, 199 (see also import
    players)
London Philharmonic, xii
Los Angeles Philharmonic, 397
Loveless, Evelyn, photo 402
Loveless, James, 267
loyalty, 156
Ludlow, Conrad, 212
Lund, Anthony C. "Tony" 42
Lund, Mrs. Anthony C. (Beverly), 72,
    265, 266
Lund, Judy Farnsworth, 72, 92
Lundquist, Christie, 343, 346
Lupo, Benedetto, 379
Lyon, "Festival Prelude" 250
Lyon, Jack, viii
Lyras, Panayis, 378

MacDowell, Piano Concerto No. 2,
    334; Suite for Orchestra, 51
Madsen, Florence Jepperson, 25, 33
Madsen, Norma Lee (Belnap),
    photo 402

Madsen, Mrs. R. W., 309
Magnes, Frances, 184
Mahler, Gustav, 353, "Das Lied von
    der Erde" 209; Symphonies 197,
    224, 225; Symphony No. 1, 225,
    300, 339; Symphony No. 2
    "Resurrection" 209, 270, 342,
    372; Symphony No. 3, 224, 344;
    Symphony No. 4, 204, 270, 339;
    Symphony No. 5, 225, 342, 363;
    Symphony No. 6, 225;
    Symphony No. 7 "Song of the
    Night" 224, 251, 334; Symphony
    No. 8 "Symphony of a
    Thousand" 233 (photo), 224, 342,
    347, 362; Symphony No. 9, 224;
    Symphony No. 10 Adagio, 225
Malbin, Elaine, 213
Malko, Nicolai, 114, 116, 119, 150
Mancini, Henry, photo 145
Manookin, "Ode of Supplication"
    343
Manton, Raymond, 209
Marcus, L. Howard, 182
Marks, Bruce, photo 402
Marthakis, Sen. P. S., 176
Martin, Gail, photo 81; vi, 60, 69-78,
    92-118, 153, 168, 174
Martin, George Jay, 53

master agreement, 384
Mathei, Ginny, 265, 266
Matheson, Norma, 367
Matheson, Gov. Scott M., photos
    235, 283; 297, 339, 367, 385
Matson, Ralph, 389
Maw, Gov. Herbert B., 101, 168, 171
Maxwell, Muriel, 204
Maxwell, Dr. Neal A., 252
Mayer, Uri, 380
McAllister, G. Stanley, 257
McClellan, J. J., 16, 21-28; "Mass for
    Orchestra and Choir" 21
McClure, Commissioner Ralph,
    322
McCune School of Music, 46
McCune, Mr. and Mrs. Alfred W.,
    47
McGuire, Dorothy, 210
McKay, David Lawrence, 252

McKay, Pres. David O., 125, 249,
    265
McKellar, Christopher, 256, 257,
    343
McLeod, Norma, 199
Melchior, Lauritz, 213, 308
Melich, Mitchell, vii, 175-178
Mellon Fund, 394
memberships, 35, 73, 102
memorial funds, 101, 108
Memory Grove, 68
Mendelssohn, 5, 390; "A
    Midsummer Night's Dream" 30,
    139; "Elijah" 41, 214; Piano
    Concertos 208, 365; Symphony
    No. 3 "Scottish" 18, 41;
    Symphony No. 4 "Italian" 111,
    398; Violin Concerto 138, 204,
    228, 341
Mendelssohn-Bartholdy, George
    de (Vox), 225
Menuhin, Yehudi, photo 192; 138,
    211, 311
Merrill, Harrison R., 72
Merrill, Robert, photo 189; 341
Merriman, Nan, 209
Mester, Jorge, 398
Midgley, Fred, 27
Midgley, LeRoy, 35, 62, 97
Milhaud, Darius, 138, 197, "La
    Creation du Monde" 209;
    "Pacem in Terris" 251; "Suite
    Provencale" 204; "Oresteia"
    335-336
military service, 41, 43, 106-113
Millennial Star, 5
Miller, E. Hugh, 53
Miller, Hack, 299
Miller, Mitch, 400
Milstein, Nathan, photo 188; 184
Moffat, D. D., 54, 77, 78
Monk, Sharon, 164
Montes, Monna, 115
Monteux, Pierre, photo 144; 109
Moore, Thomas J., 266, 346, 370
Morison, Patricia, 213
Mormon pioneers, xii
Mormon Tabernacle Choir, photos
    230, 233; 6, 13, 16, 25, 41, 42, 118,

125, 127, 139, 228, 288, 335, 338, 342, 384, 396
Morris, William N., 62, 67
Morrison, Mitch, 256, 257
Moseley, Mrs. Thomas C. (Jean), 314
Moses, "Nanon" 13
Moss, Senator Frank E., photo 275; vii, 255
Mountain Bell, 396
Mountain Fuel Supply Co., 396
Moussorgsky-Ravel, "Pictures at an Exhibition" 365
Mozart, Wolfgang Amadeus, xi, 197, 207, 317, 353, 340, "Eine kleine Nachtmusik" 206; "Magic Flute" 24; "Marriage of Figaro" 210; Piano Concerto No. 21, 211, 241; Requiem, 209; "Sinfonie Concertante" 114, 208; Symphony No. 34, 338; Symphony No. 35 "Haffner" 114, 291; Symphony No. 39, 55; Symphony No. 40 G Minor 107, 164, 209; Violin Concerto No. 4, 334, 388; Violin Concerto No. 5, 341-342
Muir, Mrs. Edward W. (Mary Margaret), viii, 310, 312
Munsel, Patrice, 113
Music Academy of the West, 211, 369
Musgrave, Clarinet Concerto 343
Music Building, 223
Music Project, v, 101
Musicians Union, 26, 78, 103, 105, 142, 173, 198, 199, 221, 222, 297, 359, 368, 384, 385
Musikvereinssaal, photo 276
Myrin, Mrs. Folke A. (Katherine) 309, 312

national anthem (see Star Spangled Banner)
National Endowment for the Arts, 71, 255
National Federation of Music Clubs, 206
National Broadcasting Company, 165
Naughton, E. M., 265
Nauvoo Band, 4
Nauvoo, Legion 4
negotiations (see labor negotiations)
Neiswender, Douglas A., viii, 353
Nelson, Beth, 56
Nelson, Carol Edison, 267
Nelson, Frank A., 325
Nelson, Monte C. and Viola, photo 330; 327
Nelsova, Zara, photo 187; 208
Neveu, Ginnette, 163
New Audience Series, 387
New York Philharmonic, xii, 126, 240, 287
New York Symphony, 34
Nibley, Reid, photo 85; 165, 250
Nicolai "Merry Wives of Windsor" 17, 45, 53, 165
Nicolatus, George S., 325
Nicolaysen, John, 210
Nielson, John Marlowe, photo 147; 204, 207, 209, 220
Nixon, Mrs. William L. (Carol), 314
Nobis, Ricklin, 241
nonrenewals, 354, 357, 358, 359, 362
Noren, Ireva, viii
Norkin, Norris, 161
number of concerts, 66, 67, 70, 201
number of musicians (see orchestra size)
Nutcracker Ballet, photo 86; 107, 115, 212, 213, 244

Odeon Ballroom, 25
Odnoposoff, Ricardo, 206
Ofenloch, Gary, 389
Ogden Symphony/Ballet Assn., 232, 266, 370
Ogden Symphony Guild, 265, 266, 346, 355
Ogden Tabernacle Choir, 33
Oistrakh, David, 259
Olpin, Pres. A. Ray, photo 331; 169, 174, 182, 183, 209, 212

Olvis, William, 213
Opera House Orchestra and Silver Band, 11
orchestra committee, 267
orchestra letter, 272
orchestra size, 22, 35, 37, 45, 53, 55, 56, 63, 64, 100, 103, 106, 108, 110, 134, 136, 173, 257, 342, 353, 393, 398
Orion Records, 226
Ormandy, Eugene, 296
Ormanson, John, 67
Orpheum Theatre, 11, 21
Orpheus Club choruses, 9, 25
Osmonds, 341
Ottley, Dr. Jerold, photos 147, 230; 335, 338
Ottley, JoAnn, photo 192; 251, 334, 338, 342, 343, 346
O'Connor, W. J., 77, 78, 100

Pace, Barbara, photo 193
Paderewski, Ignance, 18, 28
Pannell, Cynthia, 360
Pantages Theatre, 36
Paris Conservatory Orchestra, xii
Partners for the Alliance, 288
part-time musicians, 181, 262, 272, 273, 274, 359, 360, 384 (see also B Contract musicians)
Parrish, John, 68
Parry, Caroline, 72, 92
Paunova, Mariana, 342, 344, 346
payment to musicians (see compensation)
Peck, Sally, 199, 208
Pedersen, Prof. Anton, 9-15, 25-30
Peerce, Jan, photo 187
Pell, Mrs. Jean, viii, 266
Pelletier, Wilfred, 150, 153
Pennario, Leonard, photo 186; 115
pension fund (see retirement fund)
Peress, Maurice, 352, 354
Perkins, Jean, 199
Perlman, Itzhak, photo 189; 334, 341
permanent orchestra, 8, 98
Pernel, Orrea, 107
Peters, Roberta, photo 189; 400

Peterson, Art, 267
Peterson, Don, photo 402; vii, 109, 110, 116, 184, 389
Peterson, Glade, 209, 346
Peterson, Katherine, photo 402
Peterson, Robert, 334, 339
Peterson, Sally, 334
Peterson, William, 56, 115
Pett, L. F., 205
Philadelphia Orchestra, 126, 240, 296, 397
Philharmonic Society, 8
Piatigorsky, Gregor, 334
Piston, Walter, 197, "Prelude and Allegro for Organ and Orchestra" 209
plan, long range, 132, 133, 225
Plummer, Gail, photo 82; 115, 116, 174
Pokorny, Gene, 389
Pollei, Dr. Paul C., 379
Poole, Valter, 150, 153
Posner, Leonard, 161, 183
Poulson, Lani Lee, 339
Poznanski, Mischa, 119
Prather, John, 343
Pratt, Louise, 206
Pratt, Sam, 184, 206
Press, Alfred, 67
Preston, Jean, photo 85; 210, 270, 338
Preucil, William, 389
Price, Leontyne, photo 191; 397
Primrose, William, 138
Princess Sophie, 259, 300
Pro Arte Records, 228
professional musicians, 8, 9, 103, 131, 272, 273, 274
program length (see concert length)
programming, 203, 380, 387, 396, 397
Progress Fund, 131, 143, 162, 182, 202, 308
Prokofiev, 197, "Classical Symphony" 365, 368; "Peter and the Wolf" 185; Piano Concerto No. 3, 258, 259, 260, 270, 335; "Sinfonia Concertante" 341;

Symphony No. 5, 209;
Symphony No. 7, 295; Violin
Concerto No. 1, 342
Puccini, "Madame Butterfly" 32
Purles, Claude, 240
Pyper, B. T., 52, 54
Pyper, George D., 6, 13, 16, 21

RCA Records, 227
Rachmaninoff, 68, 197, Paganini
Variations, 184; Piano Concerto
No. 2, 69, 138, 251, 299, 300;
Piano Concerto No. 3, 339
Rampal, Jean-Pierre, photo 191
Rampton, Gov. Calvin L., photo
277; vii, 255, 256, 262, 264, 265,
268, 269, 277, 318, 319, 322, 323,
367, 372
Rampton, Lucybeth, 313
Ransom, Haze, 67
Ravel, 207, "Bolero" 165; "Daphnis
and Chloe" 165, 197, 270; "La
Valse" 172, 196; Piano Concerto
in G, 211; Piano Concerto for
Left Hand, 211, 291 401
Rawlings, Calvin W., 168, 174, 177,
255
recording royalties (see royalties)
recordings, photo 280; 207, 217-
228, 334, 338, 340, 343, 349, 362,
363, 373, 396
recruitment, musicians, 5, 37
recycling tickets, 248
Reece, Joseph William, 67
Reed, John, 109
Rees, Will, 35
regional touring, 242, 244, 245, 341
Reichhold Award, 160
relief players, 67
repertoire (see programming)
reserve fund, 17, 20, 22, 286, 287,
288
Respighi-Bach, "Passacaglia" 203;
"Pines of Rome" 138; "The
Birds" 344
resumption of operations, 45, 47
retirement fund, 128, 385, 386, 394
Reynolds, Theron, 63, 97
Rice, John D., 78

Richards Street Auditorium, 34
Richardson, Walter, 170, 184, 204
Richins, Stephen L., 326
Rimanoczy, 134
Rimsky-Korsakov, "Russian Easter"
Overture 138; "Scheherazade"
291
Riser, Helen, 48, 56, 199
Robbins, Mrs. Burtis F., 76, 78, 100,
104
Robertson, Dr. Leroy J., photo 148;
61, 117, 160, 161, 200, 206, 251,
"American Serenade for
Strings" 208; Book of Mormon
Oratorio 129, 207, 208, 220, 223,
226, 233, 258, 342; Cello
Concerto 208; "Passacaglia" 208;
Piano Rhapsody 117, 160, 208;
Prelude, Scherzo and Ricercare
170; "Punch and Judy" 161, 163,
165, 183, 291; "Trilogy" 160, 161,
163, 164, 208, 334; Violin
Concerto 185, 206, 208
Robertson, Marian, 199
Robinson, Dr. O. Preston, photo
301; 252
Robison, Clayne, 343, 360
Romney, David S., photo 305; 182,
200, 202, 203, 214, 249, 308
Roosevelt, Pres. Franklin Delano,
60
Rorem, "Lions" 270; Symphony No.
3, 291
Rose, James, 256
Rosenberg, Gladys Gladstone,
photo 190; 165, 172, 208, 209,
211
Rosenblatt, Joseph, photo 328; 249,
340
Rosenblatt, Morris, photo 148; 123,
152, 153, 171-177, 196
Rosenblatt, Mrs. Morris (Mollie),
326, 340
Ross, Ron, 210
Rossini arias, 340, "La Gazza
Ladra" 206
Rostropovich, Mstislav, photo 189;
334, 341
Rotary Club, 53, 107

Rothaar, Walter, 137, 161, 162
Rounseville, Robert, 213
Rowicki, Witold, 364, 365, 366
Royal Festival Hall, photo 282
Royal Italian Band, 17
royalties, 221, 225
Roylance, Kenneth, 56
Rubinstein, Anton, Piano Concerto, 34
Rubinstein, Arthur, photo 187; 163, 184, 211, 334
Ruff, Howard and Kay, photo 330; 396
Rules and Regulations, 77, 78
Rusk, Dean, Secretary of State, 255

Sadleir, Beulah Huish, 68
Saeverud, "Peer Gynt" 368
Saint-Saens, "Algerian Suite" 114; Cello Concerto 30; Introduction and Rondo Cappriccioso 55; Intermezzo 64; Organ Concerto 209, 222; Piano Concerto No. 4, 211
Salisbury, David E., 392
Salt Lake Art Center, 324
Salt Lake Arts Festival, photo 231
Salt Lake City Commission, 396
Salt Lake County, 108, 322, 396
Salt Lake Junior League, 307
Salt Lake Oratorio Society, 31
Salt Lake Orchestral Society, 56
Salt Lake Philharmonic, 11, 27, 33, 39
Salt Lake Public Library, viii
Salt Lake Symphony Orchestra Assn., 9
Salt Lake Symphony Orchestra, 12, 14-17, 27, 53, 55, 56
Salt Lake Tabernacle Choir (see Mormon Tabernacle Choir)
Salt Lake Tabernacle, photo 87, 233; 16, 25, 50, 51, 73, 87, 120-127, 135, 137, 224, 233, 234, 341, 346, 397
Salt Lake Theatre, 5, 6, 8, 16, 17, 21, 25, 33
Salt Lake Theatre Orchestra, 6, 7
Salt Lake Tribune, 227, 240
Salt Palace, 120, 127, 319, 325

Salute to Israel, 211
Salute to Youth, photo 193; 240, 241
Sample, James, 109, 113, 119, 121, 132-134
Samuelson, Roy, 208, 251
San Carlo Opera, 119
Sanderson, Homer L., 62
Sargeant, Winthrop, 258
Sarnoff, Dorothy, 212
Satie, "Les Aventures de Mercure" 295
Sauer, "Springtime in the Rockies" 21
Saunders, "Saturday Night" 185
Saxe, Adolph, 13
Sayre, Fern, 118
Scarlatti, Alessandro, xi, Mass of St. Cecelia 224
Scharffs, Gilbert W., 248
Schermerhorn, Kenneth, 352, 354
Schiller, Judge H. M., 153
Schmid, Hans Ulrich, 364
Schmitz, E. Robert, 74
Schneier, Harold, 183, 199, 206
Schoenberg, Arnold, 138, 197; "Transfigured Night" 209
Schonberg, Harold, 258
school concerts, photo 229; 49, 65-69, 74, 102-104, 118, 242, 274
Schramm, Mrs. F. C., 32-37, 44
Schreiner, Alexander, photo 186; 73, 138, 208, 222; Organ Concerto 209
Schubert, 14; C Major Symphony "The Great" 31, 32, 197; Minuet 64; "Unfinished" Symphony 13, 17, 29, 32, 45, 55, 138; "Wanderer Fantasie" 211
Schuller, Gunther, photo 148; 338, 380
Schumann-Heink, Mme. Ernestine, 34
Schumann, 390; Symphony No. 1, 300
Schwartz, Gerard, 374, 375
Scott, Norman, 212, 213
Scowcroft, Mrs. John M. (Barbara), 313, 373
Seager, Austin, 118

search committee (see conductor search committee)
season length (see length of season)
Sebastian, George, 150, 153
Seder, Jules, 110
Seegmiller, David, 68
Segal, Uri, 352, 380, 401
Selberg, J. Ryan, 343
Setaro, Signor, 17
severance pay (see length of service pay)
Shakespeare, "A Midsummer Night's Dream" 169
Shalberg, Gladys, 248
Shand, Dr. David Austin, photo 146; 169, 207, 208, 213
Shepard, Elsie, 201, 248
Shepherd, 53, 54
    Shepherd, Albert, 45, 55, 56
    Shepherd, Arthur, 15-29, 45, 97, 209; "Horizons" 18, 209; "Overture Joyeuse" 18; "Overture to a Drama" 171
Shepherd, Charles, 29, 35, 41-56, 94
Shelton, Robert, 67
Sheranian, Rose N., 68
Sherman, Alec, 379
Shostakovitch, Symphony No. 5, 251, 334, 355, 368, 398; Symphony No. 15, 343; Violin Concerto 259
Sibelius, 100, 317; "Finlandia" 96; Symphony No. 2, 206; Violin Concerto 211
Sidlin, Murry, 380
Sills, Beverly, photo 190; 213, 340
Silver Band and Opera House Orchestra, 11
Silverstein, Adrienne, 314
Silverstein, Joseph, photos 144, 237, arrival 314; bio 380-382; contract extended 397; first appearance 382, 383; first season 383; new title 388; signed 374-375; vii, 3, 117, 228, 240, 249, 379, 385, 396, 401
Simms, Walter, 13
Sinclair, Marguerite, 68
Sinding, Christian, 10

Skaggs Drug Centers, 396
Skelton, George E., 17
Skrowaczewski, Stanislaw, photo 145; 351
Smallens, 153
Smart, Mrs. Charles R. (Dorotha), 314
Smetana, 99, 180; "The Bartered Bride" 365; "Die Moldau" 96, 205
Smiley, Beryl Jensen, 209
Smith, Charles L., 77, 78, 104
Smith, Fred E., photo 81; first president 24; vi, 50, 76-78, 92-106, 114, 121, 123, 131-136, 141, 149-153, 162, 168, 175, 177, 196, 249
Smith, Mrs. Fred E., 308
Smith, Pres. George Albert, 123, 125, 170, 206
Smith, Jesse R. "Bob" 291
Smith, Jessie Evans, 68
Smith, Pres. Joseph Fielding, 321
Smith, Lawrence Leighton, 352, 378
Smith, Paul, 213
Snow, Irving, 35
Snow, Dr. R. J., 346, 351, 369
Snowbird, photo 232; 343, 391
Social Hall, 5
Sofia, Queen of Spain, photo 283
Sollender, Becky, 256
Solloway, Gloria, 137
Solomon, Seymour, 127, 225, 227, 349
Somoza, Pres. and Mrs. Anastas, photo 281
Sorensen, Marvin, 204, 210, 214, 251
Sousa, "Stars and Stripes Forever" 366, 392
South American tour (see Latin American tour)
Southern California Mormon Choir, 270
South High Girls' Choir, photo 233; 342, 343
Spencer, John D., 9, 10, 20, 21
Spohr, George, 12
sponsorships, 288, 294, 352

stage hands, 7
Stahlke, Mrs. George A. (Helen), 313
"Star Spangled Banner, The" 6, 42,
    111, 293, 294
state appropriations, 74, 75, 167,
    174-176, 201, 202, 274, 385
Statehood, Utah's, 16
Steinberger, Lorn, 137, 184
Stephens, Prof. Evan, 13, 16
Stephenson, Robert, 363
Stern, Mr. and Mrs. Edgar B., Jr.
    (Polly), 396
Stern, Isaac, photo 190; 180, 308,
    341
Stevens, P. C., 44, 49, 50
Stewart, LeConte, 72, 77
Still, "Afro-American" Symphony
    204
Stokowski, Leopold, 126
Stoller, Alvin, 213
Storrs, Richard, 214
Strauss, Johann, 99, "Blue Danube"
    53, 68; "Die Fledermaus" photo
    86; "Emperor" Waltz 96;
    "Southern Roses" Waltz 18;
    "The Two Hussars" 18
Strauss, Richard, 197, 207; "Death
    and Transfiguration" 295, 300,
    338; "Don Juan" 162; "Don
    Quixote" 343; "Till
    Eulenspiegel" 138, 203
Stravinsky, 138; "Firebird" 197, 206,
    258, 262; "L'Histoire du Soldat"
    209; "Petrouchka" 209; "Rite of
    Spring" 197; "Symphony of
    Psalms" 334
strike, 383, 387
Stringham, Don A., 369, 370
Stuart, Val, 251
Stubbs, Darrel, 364
Stubbs, Verda, 199
subscription sales, 106, 108, 137,
    248, 395, 397
Sullivan, William, photo 279; 206,
    384
summer concerts, photo 232; 343,
    391
Summer Festivals, 133, 169, 182,
    183, 212

Sundgaard, Arnold, 161
Sunset Concerts, 108, 113, 118, 120
Sutherland, Joan, photo 191
Svendsen, Johan, 10
Svikhardt, Mrs. Edwin (Joann), 315
Swallow, Glenna Carpenter, 199
Swallow, John, 161
,Swan, Howard, 4
Swaner, Stephen W., photo 306; vii,
    374, 375, 384, 392, 394, 395
Sweeten, Claude, 35
Swenson, Glen R., 325
Swenson, Shirl H., photo 284; viii,
    244, 245, 271, 273, 284, 288, 290,
    292, 297, 334, 345, 353, 365, 367,
    368
Sympho-News, 248
Symphony Ball, 244
Symphony Hall, photos 235, 236,
    237; 120, 127, 314, 315, 317-327,
    350, 351
Symphony Office, photo 229
Szigeti, Joseph, 172

Tabernacle Choir (see Mormon
    Tabernacle Choir)
Tabernacle, Salt Lake (see Salt Lake
    Tabernacle)
Talmage, John, viii, 99
Talmi, Yoav, 398
Tangemann, Nell, 209
Tanner Amphitheatre, photo 230
Tanner Gift of Music, 320, 384, 396
Tanner, Grace A., photo 329; 256,
    326, 351, 384, 385, 395
Tanner, Pres. N. Eldon, 319, 351
Tanner, Norman C., photo 328; 396
Tanner, Mrs. Norman C. (Barbara),
    photos 304, 328; 313, 346, 369,
    378, 392, 396
Tanner, Obert C., photos 235, 329;
    vii, 128, 256, 264, 265, 318-329,
    351, 384, 385, 395
Tansman, 138
Taste of the Towne, 315
Taylor, Thomas, 175
Tchaikovsky, 197, 207, 223, 224, 390;
    "Nutcracker" 45, 54, 107, 115,
    138, 223, (see also "Nutcracker"

Ballet); Piano Concerto 21, 47, 115, 204, 341; "Romeo and Juliet" 138; Symphony No. 5, 110, 138, 291; Symphony No. 6 "Pathetique" 51, 107, 165, 339; Violin Concerto, 180, 308
Telemann, Violin Concerto, 391
Temianka, Henri, 103
Templeton, Alec, 108, 118
tenure, 354
theatre orchestras, 46
Thibaud, Jacques, 196
Thomas, Charles J., 5-12
Thomas, Michael Tilson, 396
Thomas, "Mignon" 53
Thomas, W. Jack, 78
Thompson, Dr. Ed, photo 147; 220
Thompson, Shirley Anne, 68
Thompson, Symphony No. 2, 165, 173; "Testament of Freedom" 334
Thomson, Lord, of Fleet, 294
Thoresen, Ross, 370, 373, 384, 385
Tibbals, Allen H., 77
Tibbett, Lawrence, 54
ticket sales, 391, (see also subscription sales)
Tiemeyer, Christian, 291, 343
tithing-office pay, 7
"Tops in Pops" 227
Torgerson, Richard, 342
tours, 65, 69, 70, 104, 107, 133, 137, 139, 140, 141, 165, 171, 180, 210, 239, 244, 268, 285, 334, 335, (see also regional tours)
travel, 21, 65, 69
Treigle, Norman, 214
Triad Foundation, 339
Trimble, Dorothy (see Dorothy Freed)
Trout, John, 342
Tullidge, Edward, W., 6, 8
Turner, MacIntosh, 199
Twenty-fifth Anniversary, 247, 249

U. S. Bicentennial, photo 230
U. S. State Department, 254
Uhlfelder, Gerald, photo 284
Union Pacific Foundation, 326, 395

University Chamber Chorus, 342
University Chorale, 209
University Civic Chorale, 220
University Masterworks Chorus, 342, 344
University of Utah, 3, 169, 396; A Cappella Choir 164; Ballet Company 107; centennial 184; chorus(es) 127, 170, 184, 204, 206, 207, 219, 222, 233, 251; Collegium Musicum 213; Contemporary Music Festival 250, 343; Stadium Bowl 118, 340; Music Hall 246; Theatre Ballet 25, 183; Summer Festivals (see Summer Festivals)
Uppman, Theodore, 213
Ussachevsky, "Colloquy" 226, 334
Ussher, Dr. Bruno David, 60
Utah American Revolution Bicentennial, photo 235; 318, 322, 335
Utah Art Center, 74, 75, 102, 120
Utah Art Institute (see Utah State Institute of Fine Arts)
Utah Arts Council, 274
Utah Boys' Choir, photo 233; 342, 343
Utah Centennial, 133-139, 160, 161, 169
Utah Chorale, 220, 334-346, 360
Utah Federation of Music Clubs, 48
Utah Historical Society, ix
Utah Opera Company, photo 86; 337, 384
Utah Opera Theatre, 208
Utah Power & Light Co., 396
Utah State Board of Examiners, (see Board of Examiners)
Utah State Institute of Fine Arts, 70, 71, 76, 91, 105, 162, 174, 201, 203, 308
Utah State Legislature, 75, 171-178, 202, 274, 322
Utah State Prison, photo 230
Utah State Sinfonietta, 64, 65
Utah State Symphony Orchestra, xii, 35, 91, 134
Utah Symphony, photos 83, 237;

name changed to, 134
Utah Symphony Board, 273
Utah Symphony Chorus, 220, 401
Utah Symphony Gina Bachauer
   International Piano
   Competition, 377-379
Utah Symphony Guild, 33, 202, 307-
   316, 396
Utah Symphony musicians, photo
   282
Utah Symphony Orchestra
   Association, 24, 76
Utah Symphony Orchestra Council,
   131
UTOCO Pops, 241

Vanguard Recording Society, 127,
   223-227, 340, 349
Van Orden, Dell, 299
Van Vactor, David, 150, 153
Varese Sarabande Records, 227, 228
Vaughan Williams, "A Lark
   Ascending" 388; "A Sea
   Symphony" 343; Symphony No.
   6, 258; Symphony No. 8, 295, 296
Verdi, arias 338, "Aida" 384; "Il
   Trovatore" 16; "Masked Ball" 54;
   Requiem 184, 197, 234, 345, 346
Vernon, Clinton D., 172
Vienna Philharmonic, xii
Villa-Lobos, 180, "Little Train to
   Caipira" 291
Vivaldi, 56
Vocal Majority, 400
Voice of America, 211
volunteer musicians, 8
volunteers, 108
Von Rhoden, Baroness Elspeth, 55
Vox Records, 224, 225, 226
Vrionides, Christos, 109

WPA Orchestra, photo 79; vi, 35, 59,
   60, 62, 66, 70, 75, 92, 102, 112
Wade, Morris, 137
Wagner, Rebecca, 184, 185
Wagner, Richard, 197, 207, 311, 353,
   390; "Lohengrin" 29, 139; "Der
   Ring des Niebelungen" 204; "Die
   Meistersinger" 162; "Parsifal"

165; "Tannhauser" 29, 54;
   "Tristan and Isolde" 138, 338
Wagner, Roger, 352
Wagstaff, Mrs. W. Stanford (Oma),
   311
Walker, Angelena Hague, 93, 95
Walker Brothers, 8
Walker, Matt, 94
Wallace, John M., photo 331, 395
Wallace, Mrs. John M. (Glenn
   Walker), photo 80, 331; vi, vii, 8,
   47, 49, 72-78, 92-108, 150-153,
   168-181, 196, 202, 307, 395
Wallace, M. Walker, photo 304; 326,
   346, 369, 392
Walsh, Mrs. Renata Freber, 31, 32
Walton, Beth, 48
War Services Center, 111
Warberg, Willetta, 243
Warner, Roland, 67, 97
Warshaw, Maurice and Inez, photo
   330; 326
Watanabe, Eugene, photo 193; 241
Watilo, William, 184
Watkins, Rose, 184
Watson, Alonzo W., Jr., photo 303,
   392
Watts, Andre, photo 188; 344, 389
Watts, Ardean W., photos 146, 229,
   231; vii, 219, 243, 337-352
Watts, Don, photo 85; 210, 214
Wayland, Newton, 400
Webb, Grace Louise, 106, 137, 161,
   162
Weber, "Invitation to the Dance"
   21, 205; "Oberon" Overture 397
Weight, Dr. Newell B., photo 147;
   204, 220, 334, 342, 346
Weihe, Willard E., 12, 25
Weill, Kurt, 150, 151; Three Walt
   Whitman Songs 211
Weinberger, 317
Weissmann, Frieder, 151
Welcher, Louis, 339, 342, 360
Welling, Carol Olsen, 172
Wells, Seymour, 168, 201
West Coast Tours, photo 277;
   268-274
Westerhout, "Ronde d'amour" 17, 18

Western Air Lines, 396
Westminster Recordng Company, 220-223
Wetzels, Joseph, 112, 184, 199, 206
Wheelwright, Lorin F., 69, 78
Wheeter, Lloyd, 94
Whisonant, Lawrence, 114
White, Clyde, 67
White, James L., 182, 202
White, Mrs. James L., 311
White, Dr. John T., 21
White, Ray L., viii, 353, 367, 395
White, Mrs. W. Robert (Georgia), 373
Whitelock, Kenly, 204, 207
Whiteman, Paul, 243, 244, 312
Whitney, H. G., 20, 21, 55
Widtsoe, Dr. John A., 42, 43
Wilhousky, (arr) "Battle Hymn" 335
Wilkes Theatre, 47
Wilkins, Christopher, 400
Willardsen, Armont, 69
Willey, Mrs. Richard H. (Yvonne), 252, 313
Williams, Mrs. Harmon (Gwen), viii, 266
Wilson, Guy C., 46
Winter Quarters, Nebraska, 4
Wintrobe, Mrs. M. M. (Becky), 202, 308
Wolf, Harold, 206, 208
Wolf, Milton A., U. S. Ambassador, 299
Wolff, Hugh, 401
women in the orchestra (see female musicians)
Women's Symphony Committee, 106, 202, 308
Wood, Clark M., 270
Wood, Dr. Donald C., 270
Wood, Raymond, 200
Wood, Warren, 214
Woodbury, T. Bowring "By", photo 301; 247-254, 262
Woodbury, Mrs. T. Bowring "Bubbles" vii
Wooston, Paul, 110
Works Progress Administration (see WPA)

Yard, Mrs. Charles W., 106, 308
year-round operations (see length of season)
Young, Brigham, 6, 8, 33, 54
Young, Dow, 35
Young, R. N., 53

ZCMI, 326
ZCMI Mall, photo 231
Zalkind, Larry, 384, 389
Zeitlin, Zvi, 338
Zelig, Tibor, 183, 184, 204, 206
Zimmerman, A. S., 12
Zinman, David, 401
Zukerman, Pinchas, 391
Zwick, Martin, 184, 200

BANISH
BAD HABITS
FOREVER

BANISH
BAD HABITS
FOREVER

Effective ways to take
control of your life

Vera Peiffer

PIATKUS

Visit the Piatkus website!

Piatkus publishes a wide range of best-selling fiction and non-fiction, including books on health, mind, body & spirit, sex, self-help, cookery, biography and the paranormal.

If you want to:

- read descriptions of our popular titles
- buy our books over the internet
- take advantage of our special offers
- enter our monthly competition
- learn more about your favourite Piatkus authors

VISIT OUR WEBSITE AT: www.piatkus.co.uk

First published in 2005 by
Piatkus Books Limited
5 Windmill Street
London WIT 2JA
e-mail: info@piatkus.co.uk

The moral right of the author has been asserted

A catalogue record for this book is available from the British Library

ISBN 0 7499 2618 X

Text design by Paul Saunders

This book has been printed on paper manufactured with respect for the environment using wood from managed sustainable resources

Typeset by
Palimpsest Book Production Ltd, Polmont, Stirlingshire

Printed and bound in Italy by
Legoprint SpA, Trento

For my friend
Madeleine Langford Bland
who has made the most amazing changes.

Contents

Introduction   1

PART 1 Understanding Habits   5

1. Assessing your own habits   6
2. What makes you tick?   23
3. How good habits can help   34
4. How do you structure your life?   46
5. Developing resources   53
6. Spring-clean your attitude   73
7. Preventing a relapse   86

PART 2 Kicking the Habit – The Manual   89

Introduction   90

8. Valuing yourself versus self-neglect   92
   Skipping meals   95
   Saying yes when you need to say no   99
   Not taking breaks   103
   Summary   107

9. Balance versus overindulgence   108
   Phone-a-holism   112
   TV addiction   116
   Sweet fixation   120
   Retail cravings   124
   Overeating   129

Problem drinking   133
Smoking   137
Internet mania   141
Summary   145

10. Confidence versus panic modes   146
Not opening bills   150
Procrastination   153
Checking and rechecking   157
Clutter chaos   161
Perfectionism   166
Summary   170

11. Respect versus attitude hiccups   171
Time-keeping   175
Telling fibs   177
Temper tantrums   181
Gossiping   184
Laziness   188
Summary   192

12. Relaxation versus stress   194
Overworking   197
Popping pills   204
Worrying   209
Fiddling   213
Summary   217

Conclusion   218

Further reading   220
Useful addresses   221
Index   223

We are what we repeatedly do.
Excellence, then, is not an act, but a habit.

ARISTOTLE

Introduction

You may have picked this book up and bought it because your eye was caught by a mention on the back cover of the very habit you're having problems with. And maybe you've come home, and are just now thinking of putting the book aside and reading it some time later – because your habit isn't really *that* bad, and actually, you haven't got the time and energy to do something about it just now, so . . .

Stop. Hold it there. Take just one moment to think about the repercussions of your habit as it is now. Do you already feel guilty or embarrassed when you think about your habit? Do your relationships suffer because of your habit? Or is your health compromised already, even though this is only noticeable to yourself and not yet to other people? In other words, is your habit starting to take over your life? If it is, you had better start doing something about it while it is still under your control!

Habits are unconscious patterns which can turn your life upside down if they start dictating what gets or doesn't get done in your daily life. If you are unable to carry out your work or keep up relationships with family and friends because you spend hours watching soaps or keep popping out to go shopping even though your credit cards are already maxed out, your habit has become a problem.

The good news is that problem habits can be turned around and made into good habits which can become a real asset in your life. But, you may ask, what's in it for you? Why should you go to all the trouble of establishing good habits and getting rid of the bad ones? Isn't it OK if you coast along on a huge overdraft or a bingeing habit? Who cares? Well, no one will, unless you do.

Refusing to deal with a bad habit will eventually have a negative ripple effect on other areas of your life. To keep the bad habit going, something has to give. This can be your health, your relationship, your work or your bank account; often, it is all four. In other words, if you hang on to your bad habits, it is almost inevitable that you will gradually become less and less successful in other areas of your life. A problem habit will always take its toll in one way or another.

On the other hand, working on turning problem habits into good habits has many advantages, not least of which is that you will feel better about yourself and achieve your goals in life with much less effort. Good habits also become tools you can use to shape a successful future for yourself and improve relationships with the people you deal with every day.

Banish Bad Habits Forever shows you smart ways of establishing good habits and using them to combat problem habits. You will read about how to find out what triggers your habit so that you recognise the danger zones within yourself that can trip you up. You'll discover how you can take back the control you lost by building up new resources that help shift your attitude and your behaviours in a way that benefits you and everyone around you. The aim of the book is to help you grow stronger, healthier and more confident so that you become happier within and about yourself.

The book also offers an extensive manual of problem habits and how to overcome them. This section contains numerous case histories of people who turned their lives around by using good habits, visualisation and affirmations, all of which enabled them to regain control and make a fresh start.

How to use this book

The most tempting way to use this book is, of course, to delve straight into your problem habit in Part 2. And that's fine. Make sure, though, that you also read the introductory part of the appropriate section your problem habit comes under. That way you can find out which facet of your personality you need to improve to achieve lasting results.

However, if you want to get rid of your problem habit for good rather than only temporarily, you really should read the other chapters! It's important to delve a bit deeper, as knowing what makes you tick is an invaluable tool for your personal development and success in life. (Another way of delving deeper is to consult a specialist if you need to, as I recommend for certain issues listed in the book. The 'Useful addresses' section on page 221 will help you find one.)

I would love to tell you that you can change your habits quickly. The truth is, it will require some effort, determination and willingness to look at yourself. But I promise you that it's worth it! As you work your way through the first parts of the book, you will already notice some positive changes, such as greater self-awareness and a more upbeat attitude. So by all means, start at the back – just remember that the front sections are there for a good reason.

Success is within your reach, and this book gives you the know-how to achieve a better future for yourself.

PART 1

Understanding Habits

CHAPTER 1

Assessing your own habits

If you have ever found yourself checking your e-mails every five minutes . . . if your sweet tooth is constantly getting the better of you . . . if you are prey to regular temper tantrums – then you'll know all about habits.

A habit is a routine which links a particular situation with a fixed response. Just as you might always brush your teeth before going to bed or always ring your family when you have arrived safely at your destination, a problem habit also occurs regularly and reliably whenever a particular situation presents itself. The only difference is that brushing your teeth and ringing your family are activities that benefit you, whereas not opening your credit card statements or spending hours in a chatroom rather than working are eventually going to land you in serious trouble.

It may sound bizarre, but just because a habit is making your life hell is no guarantee that you'll be able to give it up easily. And, even more bizarrely, just because a habit is making your life hell doesn't even mean that you will *want* to give it up.

It's human nature to be a mass of contradictions. A convicted felon who has been to prison for grievous bodily harm can be tender and caring with his cat, and an overweight woman can give excellent slimming advice to others and help her clients lose weight successfully. We humans are quite complex creatures, and we need to take that into account when we want to change aspects of ourselves. There is no quick fix for the more difficult problem habits, but I'll do my best to make it as easy as possible for you, so read on!

The advantages of good habits

You may think that this section is a waste of time because you already know that good habits are better than bad ones. Stay with me for a moment, though, because there is more to it than meets the eye.

Bad habits can be tenacious, so you might find it useful to do a hard sell on yourself about why you need good habits and why it is crucial to leave your bad habits behind. Think what you will gain if you work on establishing good habits:

- Greater self-respect

- Greater respect from others

- Increased confidence

- Greater freedom from fear

- Better relationships with your partner, family, friends, work colleagues and possibly even your bank manager!

- Better career prospects

- Fewer worries

- No guilty conscience any more

- More money available to spend on those things that are really important.

So far, so good. On the surface, it appears obvious that you'll be better off if you leave your bad habits behind. But if this is so obvious, how come you haven't done it yet? Why have you forked out the money and bought this book?

A-ha! moment 1 Just because something is obvious doesn't mean you are going to act on it.

I am sure you can rattle off a number of reasons why you should change your habit, and yet you haven't even started doing so. Why is that?

What you are looking at here is the dichotomy between your rational mind and your feelings – a division that represents one of life's great challenges. It has happened to all of us on one occasion or another. We want to get fitter and decide to do half an hour's exercise at home with a video every other night, but when the time comes, the video cassette mysteriously seems to become too heavy to lift and put in the appropriate slot, and somehow we end up on the phone to a friend rather than jumping up and down in front of the TV. And afterwards we feel bad, but it seems too late to start exercising now and we postpone it until tomorrow when we will *definitely* do it . . .

A-ha! moment 2 Just because you have all the right reasons to change doesn't mean you will go ahead with the change.

So what can you do to convince yourself to do that half-hour of fitness training? Basically, you need to sell yourself the idea of doing some exercise right now, and it's got to be a very persuasive sell. You have to answer the question 'What's in it for me?' in a way that is convincing enough for you to a) put the video into the machine, b) press the start button on the remote and c) start moving your body.

The process that leads to this glorious result is not the same one that you underwent when you sat on your friend's sofa with a glass of wine in your hand and suddenly felt how uncomfortably tight your trousers were around your belly or thighs (surely they shrank in the last wash?). At the time, you thought, or even said out loud, 'That's it! This can't go on! I need to exercise more and eat less!'

Have you ever noticed how at that very moment you seem automatically to reach for the bottle to pour another glass of wine and slouch a bit lower down into the sofa? You see, this is your unconscious mind's way of saying YOU MUST BE JOKING. While your conscious mind tries to implement a new rule, the emotional part of you goes on strike. It's all too much – too much like hard work, that is.

A-ha! moment 3 Unless you convince the emotional part of your mind about a new plan, nothing will change.

So what is the answer?

The solution is simple. *Bribe yourself.* It works for kids, and it will work for you. You might think that this is cheating, but it's a tried and tested method!

The answer to the question 'What's in it for me?' is *not* that you will be fitter, slimmer and more attractive in about six months' time if you stick to your new regime. The mere thought of that far-distant aim and all the horrible work you will need to put in to achieve it will be enough to put you off for good.

The correct answer that will actually get results is that, if you do half an hour now, you'll get to eat something nice afterwards. Or that you get to watch your favourite soap afterwards. Or that you can have a long gossipy conversation with a friend on the phone afterwards. (Note the repeated use of the term 'afterwards', this being the operative word here!)

Forget the future, forget next week, forget even tomorrow. The here and now is the only thing that counts, and provided your half-hour is followed by a treat, your chances of getting on with your routine tomorrow are seriously increased. And tomorrow, all you have to do is bribe yourself again.

A-ha! moment 4 Sometimes short-term plans are more effective than long-term ones.

A-ha! moment 5 Simple works best.

You now probably think that I have taken complete leave of my senses. How can I suggest to you to use food as a reward when you need to exercise to lose weight? Am I not simply encouraging you to swap one bad habit for another?

Actually, no, I'm not. For one thing, after your half-hour of exercise your metabolism is nicely revved up and will burn off any food you eat afterwards (that word again!) much faster. Also, just because you have set up the reward of a bar of chocolate for afterwards does not necessarily mean that you will actually eat all of it or even want it.

You see, the reason why successful people get to grips with their bad habits and others don't is that successful people get *started* with changing and others don't. And even if I only do five minutes' exercise with my video and you do none, I'm still ahead of you in the game.

A-ha! moment 6 Even a minor change is better than no change at all.

There is no need for complex strategies and you don't have to read a shed-load of books (except this one, of course!) to understand what you need to do. Simply ask yourself the question 'What do I know deep down inside I have to do?' The answer is there, because we all know what needs doing when we are stuck in a rut. Why not trust your inner knowledge for a change? Why make things more complicated for yourself by trying to come up with the perfect solution or the ideal time to implement a change? You *know* what you have to do, and you can do something about it today. And please hear me right: I'm not saying you can *try* to do something about it today. Trying, as we all know, is a noisy way of doing nothing. What I'm saying is that you can *do* something *today*. All it takes is a good old-fashioned bribe. How simple is that?

A-ha! moment 7 The best way of taking care of the future is to take care of today.

Thinking about the future at this stage is a luxury you can't afford as yet. During your first week of changing, any day-dreaming about the fabulous results you are hoping for will stop you from doing the work to get these results. It's only after the first week of having actively tackled your bad habit that you get to use positive visualisations as a reward. When you first start, it's time to do, not time to dream.

Habits are tenacious and they are stronger than you unless you know how to deal with them. The number one solution is therefore positive action *today*, followed by a reward. Not more and not less. It's breathtaking in its simplicity, don't you think?

What constitutes a problem habit?

Whether a habit constitutes a problem or not is a very subjective matter. What bothers one person only slightly can be a major problem for the next person. We all have our personal tolerance levels, and it simply depends on where your cut-off point is on your tolerance scale.

Generally, a problem habit can be defined as any routine that has spiralled out of control.

Case study

Sarah is the full-time mum of a two-year-old and a self-confessed catalogue addict. 'At any time, I have at least 15 catalogues in the house,' she confesses. 'The big attraction is that you don't have to travel, you are not jostled in a crowd of fellow customers, and you can look at the catalogues at any time of the day or night.'

All Sarah's catalogues are carefully annotated, corners turned down and Post-It notes stuck to the relevant pages. She says that she gets the buzz of three shopping rushes from her catalogues: once when she browses the catalogue, then when she phones to order and finally when the package arrives.

Parcels normally arrive when Sarah's husband is at work. She always makes sure she disposes of the packaging and other 'evidence' of her shopping spree before he gets home.

This all sounds quite fun, doesn't it? And it is probably all right, as long as Sarah's husband earns lots of money and doesn't mind her spending lots of it. And it also seems all right because it gives Sarah so much pleasure and excitement. So is this a problem habit or not?

The clue here lies in the fact that Sarah does not feel 100 per cent comfortable about her constant shopping. She makes sure she gets rid of the cartons and packaging before her husband can see that new goods have arrived. She obviously has a guilty conscience when she keeps on spending money on things that, as she herself admits, are often unnecessary and don't even go with the style of her house or with her existing wardrobe. 'Catalogues sell you a lifestyle and a dream, and it gives me a real high to leaf through one of these glossy, designery catalogues. I can just see myself in those clothes. It's like I'm reinventing myself,' she explains.

So does Sarah have a problem? The answer lies in how Sarah herself feels about her habit. When asked, she describes her habit as 'naughty' but does not seem overly concerned about it.

If, however, her husband pulled her up on her constant spending and it came to rows over it, it would be a different matter. Or if Sarah were single and got into debts which she was unable to repay, her habit would become a problem.

To see to what extent your habit is a problem, answer the questions in the following tests. Test 1 is for you if you can't stop yourself from doing something which you shouldn't, and Test 2 is for those who can't do something they know they should do.

TEST 1

Answer the following questions if your habit is about doing something you don't really want to do, such as overeating or binge shopping:

1. Have you ever tried to stop your habit but were unable to do so?

2. Do you feel guilty even *before* you indulge in your habit, but still can't stop yourself?

3. Do you feel bad after having indulged in your habit?

4. Is your habit negatively affecting your finances, health or life in general?

5. Have other people pointed out to you that you seem to have a problem?

6. Are you trying to hide your habit?

7. Have your relationships with other people suffered because of your habit?

8. Are your thoughts dominated by your habit?

9. Do you become grumpy when something prevents you from indulging in your habit?

10. Has this habit been with you for more than six months?

TEST 2

Answer the following questions if your habit is about *not* doing something you need to do, such as taking breaks or refusing unreasonable requests:

1. Do you find it impossible to imagine yourself overcoming your reluctance to do what is necessary? Close your eyes and try to imagine yourself actually doing out the thing that you think you can't do to check.

2. Does thinking about the task scare you?

3. Have you started avoiding certain situations because your inability to do what needs doing makes you feel inadequate?

4. Have you had unkind or critical remarks from others concerning your inability to do what needs doing?

5. Is your reluctance/inability to do what needs doing sabotaging your finances, health or life in general?

6. Do you become weepy or angry when someone tries to push you into doing what you are trying to avoid?

7. Are you ashamed to admit that you are unable to carry out this particular task?

8. Do you feel bad about yourself when the opportunity has passed and you didn't do what needed doing?

9. Have you lost self-respect because you are unable to do what needs doing?

10. Have you had this problem for more than six months?

Both tests score in the same way.

1–2 'Yes' answers

You still have control over your habit. It may be a bit of a nuisance but not a fullblown problem as yet.

3–5 'Yes' answers

Your habit is taking over too much space in your head and in your life. You are on the verge of losing control and need to do something urgently to stop matters from deteriorating further.

6–10 'Yes' answers

Alarm bells! Good job you bought this book. Start doing the relevant exercises in Part 2 once you have finished reading Part 1.

A-ha! moment 8 Answering the questions in the tests won't make you change or want to change – it will only show you the extent of your problem. Action is still required!

If you ended up with less than three 'yes' answers, don't break your arm patting yourself on the back. Make sure you do the exercises in Part 2 to avoid developing a problem habit.

If you ended up with ten 'yes' answers, don't haul yourself over the coals, inviting as it may be. The good news is that if you realise you have a problem, you are more likely to do something about it. As long as you hide from yourself and others the fact that you cannot cope with your habit, change is impossible. Being pro-active and initiating a change is an admission of discontent with the way things are. If, however, you pretend that everything is hunky-dory, the door to improvement stays firmly bolted shut.

It is useful if you can look at your problem habit in a factual way. It may have been triggered by someone else's unhelpful actions in the past or it might have been created by a mistake you once made, but it doesn't have to be a punishment or burden for life.

There is one very important thing you need to understand about habits: they always serve a purpose which aims to be of benefit to you. Strange as it may seem, your problem habit is trying to do something *for* you.

Think about it this way. If you 'treat' yourself with a packet of biscuits every time you have had problems with your boss at the office, your habit is *comforting* you, isn't it? Or if you've worked very hard all day long and are finally taking a break, and a cigarette is always part of that break, then smoking is a *reward*. Or if you categorically refuse to join an evening class even though the topic interests you, your fear *protects* you from failing in class. In other words, your problem habit is trying to do something *for* you.

A-ha! moment 9 Problem habits try to comfort, reward or protect you.

The problem is that *the way* they are trying to comfort, reward or protect you is not good for you. Nevertheless, this doesn't devalue the good intention behind the habit!

The wake-up call

The reason a problem habit can be ignored for a long time is that we don't pay much attention to it until it has accumulated to such an extent that it cannot be overlooked any more. Habits can creep up on you and they can even seem a bit of a joke to start with.

Case study

Tania went out with her girlfriends once a week on a Friday evening, and they would usually go for a meal before they went on to a pub. Tania had always had a sweet tooth, but one night she felt that her pudding portion was really not big enough, so she ordered a second one. The girls were giggling and joking and egging her on. Everyone was having a bit of a laugh about it.

At their meeting the following week, Tania's friends announced to the waiter that their friend would be having a double portion of dessert, and Tania went along with it quite happily. It was all just good fun, and so it went on for a few more weeks.

Tania was aware that the sugar made her tired and cranky, but she began to crave it more and more and began eating more sweet things during the week. Her wake-up call came when she realised that two pairs of her favourite trousers didn't fit her any more. First she wouldn't believe it and thought – as so many of us fool ourselves into thinking – that they had shrunk in the wash, but when she finally stepped onto the scales and found that she had put on five pounds, she realised that she needed to do something about her sweet tooth.

Wake-up calls come in all shapes and sizes. The two main variations of the theme are either when the problem has become so big that it cannot be ignored any longer, or when some outside event triggers an intuitive realisation that you need to change.

Tania's example illustrates the first variety. The following story illustrates how an intuitive realisation can also bring about positive change.

Case study

Janet had been married for eight years and felt that she loved her husband. But even though her husband was a 'nice person', she never really felt herself when she was with him. She tried all sorts of things to improve her relationship, but nothing seemed to work, so she spent more and more time away from home, going to the gym, doing voluntary jobs after work and anything else to escape.

She had always considered it her duty to stay in the marriage and do everything she could to make it work. 'That's how I was brought up,' she explained. 'You don't just leave a marriage because you can't be yourself with your husband.'

One day, Janet opened the property section of her local paper and suddenly realised that she didn't have to stay. All she needed to do was find a room to rent. Once she'd had this realisation, she acted quickly and moved out of the marital home the same week. 'If I hadn't had that sudden realisation, I'm sure my marriage would have gone on indefinitely, with me getting more and more discontented,' she said.

In Janet's case, a spontaneous insight acted as the catalyst for change. It suddenly became possible to take a step that was 'not allowed' before that moment in time. Her upbringing had always forbidden her to do what she wanted to do.

When you compare the two different types of wake-up calls, you find that they are different in one major respect: one initiates a forced change, the other one leads to a spontaneous change which can be carried out with inner conviction and relative ease. Tania felt herself *forced* to change her eating habits because her clothes simply wouldn't fit any more, whereas Janet was galvanised into voluntary and dedicated action through her *spontaneous* insight which made a difficult decision relatively easy for her.

> **A-ha! moment 10** Changing a habit does not have to be difficult.

Later in the book, we will be looking at how you can promote a voluntary change and make the transition run smoothly and comparatively effortlessly.

Life flashpoints that put you at risk

There are certain situations and periods in life that can contribute to turning an occasional habit into a chronic problem. Check whether any of the following situations apply to you and whether they have possibly created or exacerbated your habit.

Relationship problems

When there is tension between partners, whether expressed or unexpressed, and this tension is not dealt with, your emotional equilibrium will be disturbed. This disturbance can be a subtle thing that you are only vaguely aware of. It's like a noise playing at the back of your head which you cannot get rid of, and which gradually becomes a nuisance. We sort of 'know' that something is wrong but we don't really want to look at it because if we did, we'd have to do something about it – and that could become unpleasant.

It is also possible that one partner is willing and able to speak about the strained atmosphere, but the other partner is in denial about it. This leads to frustration which can in turn breed a problem habit, not just in the outspoken person but also in their partner who needs to keep denying that anything is wrong. This can happen both in private relationships and in relations at work.

Life changes

I'm using the term 'life changes' to describe anything that puts your life on a different footing. Life changes are events such as getting married, moving house, having a baby, starting your first job, being made redundant, or starting puberty or the menopause. All these events change not only the way you see yourself but also how you fit into the society around you. Anything that alters the way you have been living has the potential to become a stressor and throw you off balance.

Life changes are generally linked with a need to readjust a number of factors in your life. A classic example is having a new baby. The lie-ins you used to have at the weekend are no more, and there are no spontaneous weekends away or evenings out because everything has to be planned in advance with military precision. For a teenager just starting puberty, a whole new set of emotions and physical symptoms will need to be adapted to. This can also be true for some women who enter the menopause.

These life changes and the side-effects they bring with them can be a burden, even if the change is a positive one. A promotion at work is of course great, but it can also trigger stress and worries about whether you will be able to live up to the higher salary and extra responsibilities.

A-ha! moment 10 Even happy events can cause stress.

Family problems

These can be created either by a life change or by illness or death in the family. If there is a change in one person's life, it affects the whole family. If a member of the family becomes morose and unresponsive, it creates stress for everyone else around. The same is true if a family member becomes seriously ill or dies – everyone in the family is affected by this event, and this includes the extended family.

Problems occur because family dynamics have to change to accommodate the depressed or ill person. Tensions develop and people who used to get on suddenly begin to snap at each other, simply because of the general atmosphere and mounting pressures on them. Having to adapt takes energy, and if this ability to adapt is overstretched, bad habits can develop more easily than in times of contentment.

Boredom and under-challenge

The devil finds mischief for idle hands – how very true this saying is! Just as stress and overwork of any description can lead to unhelpful habits, so can boredom and a lack of challenge. I know couples whose good relationship deteriorated when the wife gave up work and stayed at home, or when the husband retired.

Meaning is essential in your life. It can be your work, your children or whatever you personally want to bestow with meaning. There is *no* meaning in watching all the soaps every day because this activity does not test or challenge you, let alone further your personal development.

Don't get me wrong – I'm not saying that you must work until you drop. What I'm saying is that even when you don't do anything at all, it has to have some meaning. If you don't do anything because you need a rest or because you enjoy relaxing, that's fine. When your relaxing and not doing anything makes you ill-tempered and lazy, it is no longer OK.

Laziness is possibly one of the worst habits to have because it causes havoc around you. Laziness is the closest you'll ever come to a near-death experience, but without the light at the end of the tunnel. Lifting yourself out of a state of paralysing stupor is one of the great challenges in life, and in Part 2 you will see how you can get yourself moving again.

Now that you've begun to get a handle on what your problem habits might be, let's delve a little deeper.

CHAPTER **2**

What makes you tick?

Your current problem habit could be the best thing that has ever happened to you, although you might not think so at the moment! In this chapter we'll find out how to *see* that, by discovering what really makes you tick.

Chances are you are pretty annoyed about yourself and your inability to stop doing or start doing a particular thing. You probably feel like a weakling and a sad failure and are likely to give yourself a hard time about it. But blaming yourself or others is neither constructive nor will it get results. On the contrary, the more you put yourself under pressure, the less likely it is that you will gain control over your habit.

If you feel trapped by your habit, you need to take a good look at yourself to see what you are doing or not doing to contribute to it. You may have to look at aspects of your personality that you would rather not acknowledge, but I promise you, it's not as bad as you think. Fear of finding out something truly awful about ourselves often stops us from looking closely at who we are. When we finally overcome our reluctance and examine our underlying motives for doing or not doing something, it can be surprising to discover the human and very understandable reasons behind the problem.

When you look around at your circle of friends or members of your family, you will be able to compare yourself and your problem habit with other people's 'performance'. If you are someone who can't stop worrying, you may be quite envious of friends who have a much more laid-back view of things to come. If you are struggling with your smoking habit and your brother gave up a few weeks ago and hasn't picked up a cigarette since, you may wonder what it is he has that you haven't got.

People are certainly quite different in their approaches to problems. Whether you are successful in building up a good new habit or not will largely depend on your outlook. The right attitude can truly move mountains! What you believe to be true will determine how you deal with life and how you deal with challenges. Note, though, that just because you *believe* something to be true does not mean that it really *is* true!

Have a look at the next questionnaire to find out what your attitude is. Give yourself a point for every time you agree with a statement.

QUESTIONNAIRE

☐ I'm the way I am, and that's that.

☐ I'm probably too stupid to change my problem habit.

☐ Life is hard.

☐ It's self-indulgent to want to be happier.

☐ I need to be hard on myself or I won't do anything right.

☐ My self-criticisms are mostly justified.

☐ Nothing I do can ever be good enough.

☐ When others give me a hard time, it's because I deserve it.

☐ I'm an unlucky person, always have been, always will be.

☐ There's no point in me trying to change anything. It won't make a difference.

☐ Other people can change, but I can't.

☐ I'm too frightened to consider changing myself and my habits.

☐ If I can only change by getting someone to help me, it doesn't count.

☐ I don't deserve to be happier.

How many points did you score?

Anything between 1 and 14 points will hold you back from achieving a successful change! Each of the above statements is a block on the way towards a good result. If you have more than six blocks, they build into a nice solid wall right in front of you, so it is really worth looking at how you can change your attitude. Life truly can be a lot easier once you take a different view of things.

Let's go through the statements in turn and find out what they say about you.

'I'm the way I am, and that's that.'

On the surface, a very convenient attitude. You won't have to change, and the others will just have to lump it or leave it. It can make you a lonely person, though, if others decide to leave it rather than put up with it.

Start thinking where you have learnt to believe that change is impossible.

'I'm probably too stupid to change my habit.'

'My self-criticisms are mostly justified.'

'Nothing I do can ever be good enough.'

These attitudes are learnt responses. No child thinks that they are too stupid without having been told or shown that they are not good enough.

Start thinking about the origins of your self-criticism. Where did you learn to believe that you are not good enough?

'Life is hard.'

'I'm an unlucky person, always have been, always will be.'

'There's no point in me trying to change anything. It won't make a difference.'

These are sweeping statements that lack observation. When you look at your life, you will be able to find memories of times when life was easier and when things went well for you.

Start thinking where you learnt to believe that you have no control over your life.

'It's self-indulgent to want to be happier.'

While there is no point in constantly bemoaning your fate, it is not at all self-indulgent to look at and change what is making you unhappy in life. Your own happiness is all-important if you want to make others happy, so working on your own content-ment is actually very altruistic!

Start thinking where you learnt to believe that your feelings don't count.

'I need to be hard on myself or I won't do anything right.'

'If I can only change by getting someone to help me, it doesn't count.'

Where does this self-punishing regime come from? This is a learnt behaviour of over-strict parents, teachers or other adults. Alternatively, it can also be the consequence of a past failure you are still struggling to forgive yourself for.

Start thinking where you learnt to believe that you need to make up for a past shortcoming or failure.

'When others give me a hard time, it's because I deserve it.'

'Other people can change, but I can't.'

Where does this glorification of others come from? Why are others better than you are, and why are they always right? This is a child's belief in which adults are high up on a pedestal. Remember, though, that the great are only great because we are on our knees.

Start thinking about what fears stop you from taking charge of your life.

'I'm too frightened to consider changing myself and my habits.'

Fears can be based on facts or they can exist only in your mind. If you were shouted down last time you uttered a dissenting view to your husband, that is a fact. If you are afraid of having left the cooker on and check it five times before you leave the house every day, then your fear is irrational.

Start thinking whether there is a factual basis to your fear.

'I don't deserve to be happier.'

If all the other statements are unhelpful, this one is the weightiest and most destructive one. It comes from a sense of deep self-loathing and depression.

Start thinking where you learnt to believe so strongly that you are worthless.

You will notice that the 'start thinking' advice asks you to reflect on *where you learnt to believe* a particular thing. This is because many of the beliefs we hold today about ourselves or the world around us were initiated by past experiences, sometimes going back as far as childhood.

Case study

Peter was the son of working parents who had little time for him. Both his father and mother were following careers and working long hours so that Peter spent a lot of time with neighbours after school. An attempt at having *au pair* students in to supervise his schoolwork and cook him meals didn't work out.

The parents then sent him off to a boarding school, where he had more company but felt quite lonely. He felt that he didn't belong anywhere and became very worried about losing his possessions. Later in life, he found it impossible to throw anything away and began hoarding things, which caused problems because it became difficult for him to find anywhere to sit in his flat: everything was covered with papers, books, clothes and kitchen and bathroom utensils.

Peter's case is a difficult one because the connections between past events and present behaviour are not very obvious. In many cases, though, it is possible to put two and two together and link up past events with the present actions and behaviours they have caused.

You learn to believe that you need to cope with everything on your own when your parents are absent, too busy or have too many problems of their own. It can also happen when you have an unsupportive partner or if friends are unavailable when you need them in a crisis.

You learn to believe that you are not good enough when you were criticised or put down a lot or if you give yourself a hard time over a past failure. It can also happen if you have a partner who is undemonstrative, unfaithful or unsupportive.

You learn to believe that you have no control over your life when you were left to fend for yourself as a child without getting any help from adults. It can also happen if you have been ill or unwell for a while or if you were bullied or ostracised by others.

You learn to believe that your feelings don't count if you felt abandoned, ignored or criticised when in distress. In this context, it doesn't matter whether this happened in your child-hood or during your adult years.

You learn to believe that you need to make up for a past shortcoming or failure if you have, for example, failed an exam or done an injustice to someone in the past.

You learn to believe that you are worthless when you have been emotionally, verbally, physically or sexually abused. This is very serious and you may have to seek professional help to get out of the trap of self-abuse, addiction or self-neglect.

No matter where the origins of your problem habit lie, you will benefit from developing new resources. These can help you change the detrimental patterns that were established through an emotional link with past events or present unhappy rela-tionships or circumstances

Later on in the book, we will be looking at how you can develop new resources and establish good habits to help you overcome life patterns that are holding you back.

But before we look at solutions, let's find out a bit more about the possibilities of self-sabotage.

No more blame games

You may have found a few instances of past memories where you were treated unfairly, where you felt neglected or unsupported or where you failed at something that was important to you. It can be quite tempting to blame the person or persons responsible for your current problems, but that is not going to help you solve matters.

Don't get me wrong: you may have every reason to be angry at the injustice that has been done to you, especially if you have been abused in any way. You may also be right in being annoyed at yourself for, say, having failed an important exam because you left the revision to the last minute or because you were hung over when you went into the exam. What I'm saying is that it is not good enough to abdicate all responsibility for your problem habit just because someone else made your life a misery at one time. Neither is it productive to harp on about past mistakes you made and keep on saying 'if only'. That is not going to do anything to change your present situation.

If you need to let off steam, let go of guilt or shame, the best place is person-centred counselling (in which the counsellor actively helps a client with issues), analytical hypnotherapy (which aims to discover the root cause of a client's problem) – or simply the bottom end of your garden, where you can let rip a good rant. Other than that, have you considered speaking to the person who has treated you badly? This can be difficult and scary, but often it helps resolve matters one way or another. If you find this impossible to do or if the person concerned is already dead, you can still bring the matter to a conclusion, but you might have to get professional help to accomplish it.

Recognising where you learnt to acquire certain detrimental beliefs about yourself is useful in that it puts your problem into a context that highlights literally where you are coming from.

Knowing where a negative belief originates can be helpful in reversing unwanted behaviours, as we will see later in this book. In the rest of Part 1, you will also learn to distance yourself from your past in a calm and peaceful way.

Are you making the problem worse?

You may think that surely it is not in your interest to aggravate your problem habit and that you would never do so on purpose. That is true, and yet, you may have the best of intentions but still trip yourself up and make your problem worse by trying to get rid of it.

Case study

In a recent initial consultation, a mother brought her 24-year-old daughter in. The mother had told me on the phone that her daughter lacked confidence. They came in and sat down, and I started off by asking the daughter a few questions. The young woman answered the first few questions quite readily but seemed unsure what her problem was. She became a bit nervous when I offered a few suggestions to help her find areas in her life where she was less than happy with her own performance. She was still undecided and hesitant and seemed unable to formulate a clear statement of where her difficulties lay.

Now her mother started suggesting, in a very calm and tactful way, that the daughter might have a problem in groups of people and with authority figures. The daughter dismissed this out of hand and asked her mother not to say any more because this confused her further.

Mother: 'I'm only trying to help.'

Daughter: 'Well, don't. I can't think.'

Mother: 'But Vera needs to know where the problem lies, and you always told me you didn't get on with the people at work.'

> Daughter: 'Mum, don't talk. Stop talking, you're confusing me.'
> Mother: 'I'm only trying to help. You need to find ways of helping yourself if you want to become happier.'
> The daughter now burst into tears and wept hysterically.

This is an example of good intentions gone wrong. The mother genuinely wanted to help her daughter, and her concern and love came across very clearly in the warmth of her voice when she addressed her daughter. And yet, she was making matters worse. The daughter had actually asked her mother very clearly to stop talking, but the mother ignored this request. The mother's attempts at justifying her intervention resulted in the daughter becoming even more confused and anxious and being unable to think at all.

One typical way of sabotaging yourself when trying to change a habit is to try hard.

A-ha! moment 11 Trying hard creates stress.
Stress reinforces a bad habit.

When you try hard, your body starts tensing up; when you try extra hard, your body seizes up. The tighter the muscles, the less oxygen gets to the brain and the more difficult it becomes to think. The more tension you hold in your body, the more stress you experience and the harder it becomes to let go of the problem habit.

A-ha! moment 12 You don't force out a problem habit, you let it go!

When you exert force, the ensuing stress makes you want to carry out the bad habit even more. The answer, therefore, lies with an attitude of focus and relaxation, and these two things start in your head. The quality of your thoughts really and truly determines the quality of your life. Negative self-talk leads to bad feelings and they, in turn, prevent us from resolving problems. 'Thought hygiene' is therefore one of the main pillars of success, and in Chapters 4 to 6 we'll be looking at how it's done.

CHAPTER 3

How good habits can help

When a habit is giving you problems, you may want to abolish it, get rid of it and erase it from your behaviour.

Forcing a bad habit out with sheer willpower takes a lot of energy, though, and it will make your life unpleasant for a while to come. It can be done and it has been done, but for most people it is a constant struggle of fighting the habit and making progress, only to lose the battle a while later and falling back into the old unwanted routine.

To avoid this yo-yo effect, it makes sense to strengthen your willpower and build up independent good habits and resources to make your life more successful. This might mean that you have to work on adding a few new positive behaviours. These are not only an asset in their own right, but they can also help reduce negative behaviours and reactions at the same time. It is possible to not do anything about a problem habit and only start building up a related good new habit, and this is often enough to make the problem habit disappear.

In the following sections, we'll be looking at how you can establish some essential good habits and new resources to help you overcome problem habits. There will be lots of practical exercises to do and tips on how to initiate positive change and prevent relapses.

Establishing basic good habits

For a solid foundation of essential well-being in life, it is first of all necessary to set up some basic good habits. Without these, positive changes cannot happen. These basic habits are linked with feelings of self-worth, balance and respect for your own needs. We will look in more detail at all those separate issues in Part 2, but just now, it is important that you do a general MOT on your attitude towards yourself.

None of the basic habits needs to be arduous, lengthy or complicated to do. What I'm asking of you here is to give yourself a physical foundation to build all other progress on. You can adapt the following habits and tailor them to your particular circumstances, but each of them needs to be carried out in at least a small way, to give you a basis to work from.

There are seven basic good habits that will make a great difference to your life if you can follow them reasonably regularly. Here they are!

1. Drink water regularly

If you are dehydrated, your body cannot work efficiently. The nerve impulses that transmit messages to and from the brain are dependent on a good conductor, and your bowels, kidneys and liver need lubrication with water to function properly and flush out toxins.

So what does that have to do with changing my habits?

Without enough water in your system, you can't think straight and your liver cannot do its best work. If you are dehydrated, you are 'liverish', tense and irritable, and are more likely to stay stuck on a mental and emotional level. This will make it extremely hard to shift your problem habit!

One and a half to two litres of water is a must.

Is there an alternative?

Not really. Water cannot be replaced by any other fluid. Tea, coffee, alcohol and sugary fizzy drinks actually dehydrate the body even more. Weak herbal teas are a possibility, but nothing beats water. Make it still mineral or filtered water.

Do not simply drink water from the tap. Invest in a carbon water filter jug to get rid of the chlorine and other nasties in tap water. Chlorine is bleach and many people are sensitive to it.

Any tips?

If you can't stand the taste of still water, drink it with a straw. If you cannot manage one and a half to two litres, start with one glass and build up over a couple of weeks. Keeping a bottle of mineral water on your desk at work or on the kitchen counter can help remind you to take a drink. You'll be surprised how many physical problems disappear.

2. Move your body regularly

And I don't mean from the sofa to the armchair! Make it a rule to do at least 15 minutes of exercise every other day. This will help the lymph in your body move around and keep the blood 'clean', as lymph filters the blood. It can only do so if you move, as the lymph system has no internal pump like blood which is propelled through the body by the heart.

So what does that have to do with changing my habits?

Exercise is a mood enhancer. The more you move your body in a non-stressful way, the better you feel. And if you want to change a problem habit, you'll need to be in a good mood and feel positive. This is going to make it easier to tackle change. It's best to exercise for at least 15 minutes a day, three times a week. No need to go for the burn – just move briskly.

Is there an alternative?

Well, there are a number of different ways of moving the body, and, no, flicking the remote to switch channels is not one of them! If you can't go to a gym, exercise at home. Go for a brisk walk, buy an exercise video (and follow it), or get a mini trampoline. Walking up and down your stairs a few times will give you extra benefit. All you need to do is get your breathing rate up just enough to be different from your normal breathing rate. No need to be puffing and panting at the end of it for your exercise to count.

Any tips?

Do your minimum of 15 minutes' exercise in one go. It doesn't count if you do a bit here and a bit there – this is not going to get any results. Start slowly and build up gradually if you are unfit.

3. Get enough sleep

Your life might be hectic and your job stressful, but you need to keep a grip on your sleeping hours. It is at night that the body repairs itself and recharges its batteries. If you are running on empty because you don't get enough sleep, your immune system is impaired and you are more likely to get ill. You are also more likely to feel anxious and stressed if your body's recharging hours at night are cut short.

So what does that have to do with changing my habits?

Quite a few problem habits are due to stress. If you can cut down on unnecessary stress, such as not sleeping enough, your problem habit can be changed much more easily.

Is there an alternative?

No. Uppers and alcoholic drinks make matters worse.

Any tips?

If you suffer from insomnia, see a hypnotherapist, and also have a kinesiologist check out whether you have an allergy which might contribute to your sleeping problem. You may also be short of calcium or iron.

If you find it difficult to go to bed earlier, bring your bedtime forward gradually in 15-minute increments to give the body time to adjust.

4. Take it outside

Once a day, go outside and stand somewhere safe. Close your eyes and spend a few moments concentrating on yourself and getting centred. Breathe calmly and listen to the sounds your breathing is making. Now imagine how all your everyday thoughts and worries are drifting up and out of your head and floating away like little white clouds, leaving you feeling calm and peaceful and relaxed. Do this three times a week.

So what does that have to do with changing my habits?

Taking some time out to empty your mind of hectic worry thoughts and mind clutter will help you see things in perspective. Consider this habit a mini-meditation session.

Is there an alternative?

Yes. If standing outside your door means stepping into a busy high street and looking like a weirdo planted there with your eyes closed, stand by an open window instead or go into your garden at home. (Obviously, use your discretion if rain, snow or wind storms are raging outside!)

If you find it hard to concentrate on the imagery of the clouds, do some 'palming' instead. This is part of the Bates Method, a natural way of improving your vision, but I find that it also works very well for calming down the mind. Sit down by an open window and rest your elbows on the table. Close your eyes and put your palms over your eyes, with your fingers over-lapping on your forehead. A few minutes of this will calm and relax you very efficiently.

Any tips?

Try to go outside at least once a day, even if you have no time to do the visualisation exercise. Fresh air really does blow away the cobwebs!

5. Put on some music

Music has a profound effect on the way you feel. It can change your mood in a matter of seconds – calm you, lift you up or comfort you. (Remember how important it was to you when you were a teenager?) Treat yourself to a short session of music, ideally with your headphones on, and concentrate on the music completely. Don't do anything else while you are listening – make this 'out' time, just for yourself. Do this at least twice a week for ten minutes.

So what does that have to do with changing my habits?

Music can make you feel more optimistic by lifting your mood, and when you feel positive, it becomes easier to make any necessary changes in your life.

Is there an alternative?

Yes. Making music yourself by singing along to something on the radio, humming a tune, dancing to music or playing an instrument all have the same effect.

Any tips?

Don't listen to heavy metal or dramatic classical music with the volume turned up while you are driving. Research shows that this can cause stress and lead to accidents.

6. Learn something new

To keep your mind flexible, nothing beats learning a new skill. This does not have to be something useful – it can just be something that you find interesting. The further removed this skill is from your everyday life, the better. Make it something fun and make sure you make lots of mistakes to start with while you are learning, so that your teacher doesn't feel redundant!

Learn something new every time you feel stuck or bored or when you catch yourself taking yourself too seriously.

So what does that have to do with changing my habits?

By learning new things, you are flexing your mental muscles, and it is exactly these muscles that you need to overcome problem habits. Learning new skills also increases your creativity and overall confidence.

Is there an alternative?

Yes. It is not necessary to go to evening classes to learn a new skill. How about finally reading the manual for your video recorder so that you can set it yourself and not have to bribe your six-year-old to do it for you? And there's nothing stopping you taking up a craft (knitting is experiencing a surge in popularity), trying your hand at writing poetry or redesigning your garden with the help of advice from websites and books.

Any tips?

This is a time to be outrageous and learn something unusual. Go for it!

7. Be nice

A really good way to de-stress and come out of your shell is to take an interest in other people. Take the time to find out how your friends are and what they are up to. Look for the positive in other people. Pay compliments, write cards, send flowers, be in touch with them. People respond well to kind gestures, and their happiness will make you feel good, too.

So what does that have to do with changing my habits?

When your life seems to reel out of control, your focus can turn in on yourself and you start getting that 'me against the world' feeling. If you want to change a habit, you need to feel supported, and the best way of getting this support is by encouraging others, by nurturing your friendships and by exuding positive vibes.

Are there alternatives?

Yes. Another good way of connecting up with others is to help them. Doing some work as a volunteer for a charitable organisation or helping someone who needs help are also good ways of increasing your self-esteem.

Any tips?

If you are already overworked, don't add to your burden by taking on yet another task like voluntary work. Stick to the compliments, cards and flowers instead. Even returning private phone calls promptly could be useful!

You're the boss!

Problem habits can easily make you feel incompetent, helpless and very, very frustrated. At best, the habit is a nuisance; at worst, it can hold up your career and severely compromise your relationships with friends and family. If your attempts to change a bad habit are unsuccessful, you can even become quite depressed over it.

Case study

Sandra (36) was getting desperate. She was a chocoholic who seemed unable to tame her habit. She knew it wasn't good for her to eat a big bar of chocolate a day – if not more. Not only was she putting on weight, but eating all that chocolate also made her kidneys hurt. Although Sandra had been suffering from kidney problems in the past and had even been off sick with it, she felt unable to control her cravings. 'It's like I have a split personality,' she explained to me. 'I know I shouldn't have chocolate, but there is a part of me that is stronger than my rational thoughts. It's like I'm standing next to myself, saying "Don't do it" while I'm stuffing myself with chocolate, but it makes no difference. I know it's wrong, but I do it anyway.'

Sandra drew the line when she realised that her mood swings caused by sugar withdrawal would cost her her relationship with her partner Pete. He had finally put his foot down when she pleaded with him in the middle of the night to go and buy her some chocolate from a 24-hour garage a few miles away. 'When he refused, I just lost it. I screamed at him like a mad woman. I ended up getting into the car myself and driving out to the garage. The next morning, Pete told me I had to get help with my addiction because he wasn't going to put up with this any more.'

I was able to help Sandra with health kinesiology and visualisation techniques to give up chocolate, and her health and relationship improved greatly as her mood swings and cravings disappeared.

With any problem habit, it is essential to take back control. Make sure you get into this good habit of taking charge. There is *always* a solution; there is *always* a way of overcoming even the worst of habits. Your attitude now becomes all-important. If you keep telling yourself 'I can't do it', that is exactly what will happen – you won't be able to overcome your problem. Remember that everything you think, every thought that goes through your head, has an impact on the results you are getting.

Try the following experiment. Think to yourself 'I'm a weak and pathetic person. I am completely useless' and repeat these sentences a few times in your mind. Now check how you feel. You will notice that your whole body reacts to these negative statements by tensing up and feeling uncomfortable.

Now think the opposite. Think 'I'm a strong and confident person and I can achieve anything I want to achieve.' Again, think this sentence several times over and check how you feel. You will notice how your body reacts – it will relax, and you'll find yourself suffused with a pleasant feeling of well-being.

What is happening here is that the negative words made your body tense up and weaken as your mood deteriorated. This happens even if you don't believe what you are thinking! Positive thoughts, on the other hand, result in a lightening of mood and physical relaxation, and those are great foundation stones for tackling a difficult issue and resolving it.

Take the trouble to 'listen' to your thoughts every once in a while. I find that some people don't even know that they are constantly thinking negatively!

Words don't just have an effect on the body; they also influence your general performance. If you keep telling yourself that you are useless and a failure for not overcoming your problem habit, it will make you feel weak both physically and emotionally, with the result that it becomes even less likely that you will succeed in conquering it.

In order to increase your chances of success, first of all you will have to change the way you think about yourself in relation to the problem. Victim mode has to make way for taking back the reins. The only reason you're not in control is that you are not *taking* control.

A simple change you can make is to state to yourself 'I am the boss!' Notice how your body posture changes when you think this sentence a few times – you stand up straighter, your feet are firmly planted on the floor and your chin goes up a little. In other words, your posture shows determination and decisiveness, and this gives you the edge over your habit.

If your negative thinking is ingrained, your next thought will now be 'That can't possibly help me with my problem habit!' Take control immediately by replacing this weakening thought with a more positive one: 'I can and will change for the better.' Feel your shoulders square and notice how your mood lifts a little.

A-ha! moment 13 In order to be the boss, *think* like the boss.

The reason it is necessary to put yourself back in charge by changing your thinking is that this is the only way you can win. Faint heart never won fair lady, and faint heart certainly never made any progress in life either. Do not be content with what you have if what you have is a bad habit. You can have more fun in life, enjoy better relationships and rid yourself of a great deal of unnecessary stress if you take the trouble to change your thinking to positive.

You don't even have to *believe* that you are the boss, as long as you consistently think the sentence. Eventually, your attitude will change for the better. By regularly repeating your positive phrase like a mantra, it is sinking in on a subconscious level. Once it is subconsciously established, you begin to feel more confident and self-assured, so that your positive thought becomes true.

Your subconscious mind is that part of you that runs all your autopilot programmes. All the involuntary bodily functions such as your heartbeat, digestion, temperature control and so on are functions of the subconscious mind. You can control these consciously by breathing faster or slower to make your heart beat faster or slower, but normally we let all these body processes work automatically.

Another area that is ruled by the subconscious is our emotions. Emotions happen spontaneously and are not under our voluntary control. That is why it is so hard to carry out good advice such as 'Forget him, he's not worth it' after a relationship break-up. Much as we would like to suffer less and forget that person, our emotions of despair, anger or hurt pop up anyway, often when we least expect them.

It is this same automatic emotional reaction that stops us from opening our bank statements or throwing away useless clutter that we have been hoarding. Even though *consciously* we know it would be sensible to see what's happening in our account and even though we *consciously* know that we'd live more comfortably if we decluttered our home, a *subconscious* feeling of fear stops us.

To stop our feelings from governing our lives, we need to take back control by *consciously* feeding new information into our subconscious mind. This information needs to be strong and confident, so only positive thoughts will do. By converting negative thoughts into positive ones, you are multiplying your chances of success a hundredfold.

CHAPTER 4

How do you structure your life?

Habits give life a structure; in fact, habits are structure. Generally speaking, a structure is useful because it allows you to do things in a certain order. Provided this order is well thought through and appropriate to your current situation, it can save you time and helps you meet deadlines more comfortably. If, for example, your habitual structure at work is to come in, prioritise what needs doing by making a list, then do the most pressing things first and leave less important things for later, you are likely to get your job done efficiently. In this case, the structure you set up for yourself can be said to work. Once you have a structure in place and then continue using it so that it becomes automatic, the structure becomes a habit.

Problems occur when you have either not thought your structure through carefully enough to start with or your structure is emotionally imposed.

When it comes to jobs and projects, no matter whether they are paid work or things you need to do at home, a structure is absolutely essential. An ordered way of going about tidying up your flat, planning your day with your kids or organising your firm's annual conference is essential if you want to get good results within a specific time frame. Whether we like it or not, most of our activities are governed by the clock, and this limits the number of options we have when it comes to organising these activities.

If we haven't thought our structure through properly, it won't work as we want it to. Or it won't work at all because it will never happen. Hanging on to the same ineffective structure, we are creating stress for ourselves and other people, and we are also creating a problem habit.

Case study

Clare's motto was 'rushing is uncool', and she was late for virtually everything. Whether she was meeting a friend, going to a parents' evening or keeping a dental appointment, she was always late. She never left enough time for travel and took her friends for granted. Some of her friends sighed and put up with having always to wait for Clare for at least half an hour; others were clearly irritated. Clare hated letting them down, but she just couldn't change. Her wake-up call finally came when she missed her return flight from holiday because she arrived at the airport two hours late. She was stranded for two days in the airport lounge with her young son and no money.

Clare has no structure. She lives her life basically ignoring the time frame within which she needs to accomplish a task. Her attitude is that there shouldn't be a time frame in the first place. And because clocks are unimportant, there is no need to plan or create a structure of how to arrive anywhere at a particular time.

For Clare to progress, she will need to work on developing new resources. In her case, the main resources she needs are respect (for others), honesty (about the problems her lateness creates), consistency (in combating her problem habit) and pro-activity (to set up a time structure that will enable her to arrive on time).

Clare's case illustrates someone not thinking things through properly. Our next case shows how emotions can underlie a problem habit.

Case study

Nadia had been trying to lose weight for the past ten years, but without success. She had tried every diet under the sun, been to Weight Watchers, tried to fast and tried to cut down on her portions, but in every single instance, she had managed to sabotage her own efforts. 'I've got a very stressful job as a nurse, and eating is really my big passion in life,' she explained. 'The longest I ever stuck with sensible eating is five days. Sometimes it's even less time before I go for the biscuits and double-decker sandwiches again. Every time I'm upset, annoyed or frustrated because of something that happened at work, I go straight for the biscuit tin. Vegetables and fruit don't stand a chance – they just don't have the same comfort value as something stodgy.'

Nadia's problem habit is clearly emotion-driven. The moment she gets unpleasant feelings, she goes for comfort by eating filling foods. She has over the years established a structure of linking up good feelings with certain foods. There is one problem, though. The comfort lasts only while she is eating. As soon as she has finished, she begins to feel guilty for having stuffed herself and all her inner self-talk becomes very negative. She feels bad about her binge, which creates stress, upset, annoyance and frustration, and we know what Nadia does when she get upset and frustrated . . . !

To combat her problem habit, Nadia will have to work on a number of resources which will help her establish a better structure. She'll do better with her sensible eating once she has worked on her perseverance. Also, developing a sense of humour will be beneficial to deal better with stress at work, and some motivation could also help her see through her better eating regime.

Other habits that are emotion-driven have had their structure set up a long time ago. In Chapter 2 (page 28) we have already looked at how the past can influence our habits today. Now we can look a bit more closely at how your past experiences have possibly shaped a structure that has become an automatic, habitual response.

Case study

John always had the same problem in relationships. Everything went well for a few months, then he began to criticise his girlfriend and start arguments with her. 'I don't really know why I'm doing this,' he says. 'There's nothing wrong with my girlfriend, but in both my last relationships, the girls left because they said I was constantly picking fights. I know I'm doing this, but I can't stop myself. What's the matter with me?'

John's current relationship was already heading in the same direction, the only difference being that John was madly in love with this girlfriend and was therefore very willing to look at what was going on inside him.

John's habit of ruining relationships has the underlying structure that links a certain time frame with a sabotage act. When a certain number of months have elapsed in the relationship, John starts to become super-critical of his girlfriend. The fact that this pattern has repeated itself several times already indicates that it has become a habitual response. But what set up this habit in the first place?

Analytical hypnotherapy revealed the answer. When John was six years old, his mother left the family and the shock had stayed with John throughout his life. Even though he entered into new relationships with the best of intentions, he could not stop destroying them. The fear of being left was so great that it was safer for him to sabotage the relationships because then the girlfriend's leaving would not come as such a shock.

Working through his past trauma helped John release the emotions around the originating event so that he could show his love more openly and remain settled in his relationship with his girlfriend.

If you want to work on your problem habit, you will need to find out what structure is underlying it. You may find that your habit is emotion-driven or simply the result of ineffective planning, but it could also be a combination of both. Being out of sync emotionally does not make for effective organisation!

We may think we know what the underlying pattern of our habit is, but sometimes we don't see the whole picture. It is therefore useful to observe closely what happens just before we go into an automatic response which we don't like.

Exercise

- Keep a diary for ten days and write down when you notice your problem habit occurring.

- Note down how pronounced your habit is on that day.

- Note down the degree to which it upsets you. Grade your upset 0 to 10, with 10 denoting 'extremely upset'.

- Also note down *what preceded* your habitual reaction. Did something upset you, frustrate you or make you feel guilty, for example?

Once you have completed your ten-day diary, look at the structure that emerges.

Clare's structure looks like this:
Trigger: no knowledge/interest in time-keeping → disorganised departure time → constant lateness

Nadia's structure looks like this:
Trigger: negative emotions → binge eating

John's structure looks like this:
Trigger: greater closeness → bad mood → rowing → split up

You can see here that it is not only negative emotions that can trigger a bad habit, but also positive ones as in John's case, where a feeling commonly considered to be 'good' is perceived by the individual as being threatening. If you find that in your case, a positive emotion or action results in a negative response, you need to ask yourself where you learnt to believe that this positive emotion is dangerous.

Case study

Mandy came to see me with enormous stress problems. It quickly became clear that Mandy hated herself. Whenever she made a mistake or did something which, to her exacting standards, wasn't good enough, she berated herself in the most insulting terms. She also found it impossible to relax. Whenever she sat down to try to get a bit of rest, her mind was immediately flooded with negative thoughts about herself and all the unhappy memories of past events. To escape these unpleasant thoughts, Mandy had to get up and do some work. This meant that she was virtually unable to take a break until she eventually went to bed and got a few hours' sleep.

Mandy's structure is:
Trigger: feeling tired → sitting down → negative thoughts and memories → fidgeting → having to get up again and work

As it turned out, Mandy had been berated by teachers at school and by her father when she was younger. This had formed the view in her mind that she was a useless person who didn't deserve any rest. Working and doing constantly was the only way she could make up for her perceived inferiority as a human being.

You can see in this case study how powerful the hold of childhood events can be. Her father's words had become Mandy's thoughts and were being replayed in her mind, tyrannising her every waking hour of the day.

What structure did you find for your problem habit? Is your trigger a purely structural one which can be remedied by creating a more efficient order in your life? Is your problem habit set in motion by positive or negative feelings? Or is your problem the result of both an organisational *and* an emotional trigger? Hang on to your findings for now and read on to see how these triggers can be corrected and turned into positive outcomes.

CHAPTER 5

Developing resources

So if good habits are an essential ingredient for success and happiness in life, how can you build them? The answer is that you need to either develop new resources or use existing resources better.

A resource is any mental or emotional skill that can help with creating constructive behaviours and greater success in relationships. What follows is a list of resources which you might find helpful in developing positive habits.

Patience

It is important to be patient with yourself and others when something doesn't work out immediately. Impatience can adversely influence an outcome.

Flexibility

Flexibility is a great asset when unexpected glitches happen or a project proves to be unachievable via the designated route.

Rather than banging your head against a brick wall, a flexible attitude will get you around the impasse with less hassle.

Tolerance

Tolerance means accepting a person or a situation, even if they are less than perfect. It allows you to deal with situations which, without tolerance, you would have to leave or reject.

Inventiveness

This is one of the greatest assets you can have. If you can come up with ideas in a difficult situation, you can often save the day. Inventiveness is the ability to listen to your hunches and take them seriously.

Love

Respecting yourself is a great asset and absolutely essential if you need to get through a lengthy period of change. If you can stand by yourself, despite unsuccessful attempts, you will eventually succeed. Accepting and respecting yourself is a prerequisite of loving others. If you can love others without neglecting yourself, your relationships will blossom.

Perseverance

If you can persevere when the going gets tough, you will greatly increase your chances of coming out a winner. To persevere, it is essential to keep focused on a successful outcome and approach your goal in little steps.

Humour

Lots of difficult life situations are made more bearable if you can laugh about them. If you are in the process of fighting a problem habit and it turns out to be more challenging than you thought it would be, laughing about yourself can take the sting out of the struggle.

Motivation

Being able to pursue an aim with relish makes the job easier. Motivation is dependent on whether a task catches your imagination and whether it can fire up your enthusiasm. Motivation is one of the most important assets when you want to make changes for one main reason – it gets you started!

Honesty

Being honest about your problem habit is already half the battle. Once you have admitted that your habit is beyond your control, you can move forward to a solution.

Consistency

When a habit has become a problem, it needs to be dealt with in a consistent way. It is not very effective if you say 'no' to someone once but then let them talk you into saying 'yes'. Once you have made up your mind, you need to stick to your guns.

Pro-activity

All the positive thinking in the world won't get things done. When you want to change aspects of yourself or your life, action has to follow thought.

So how can you develop these new resources? Let's find out which resources you already have and which ones you need to work on acquiring.

Patience

- Does your impatience overtake you at every opportunity?

- Do you frequently hassle other drivers (flashing, tailgating and so forth) when you are on the road?

- Do you get irritable when you yourself cannot perform a task as quickly or efficiently as you would like?

- Does your impatience make you feel stressed?

- Do you easily lose your temper with your family or when you are at work?

If you have answered 'no' five times, you already have this resource. Move on to the next resource.

If you have any 'yes' answers, use the following exercises and tips to help you improve.

Exercise

For the next week, slow down the speed at which you talk. You don't have to slow down to a funereal pace – just speak more clearly and distinctly and a little slower than you would normally.

TIP Stop three times a day to remind yourself that you need to speak more slowly. If possible, set an alarm or pin up a discreet reminder to yourself where you will see it. Or send yourself an e-mail last thing in the evening to remind yourself the next day.

In the following week, slow down the speed at which you move. Continue to speak more slowly, but now begin to move in a more fluid and deliberate way. This means making your head, arm and hand movements less 'staccato' by moving them more deliberately and linking movements together in a softer way.

Slowing down the body has a relaxing and focusing quality and makes you less stressed and less impatient.

TIP Doing t'ai chi can be very helpful, as it will teach you to pay great attention to your movements.

Flexibility

- Do you believe that there is only ever *one* right way of doing things?

- Does it throw you when a friend turns up unannounced, or if an ad hoc meeting is called at work?

- Does it irritate you or make you nervous when an appointment has to be changed?

- Does it throw you when you are asked to change an aspect of a project you are working on?

If you have answered 'no' five times, you are already very flexible. Move on to the next resource.

If you have any 'yes' answers, use the following exercise and tip to help you improve.

Exercise

For the next week, take a slightly different route to work every day. If you are not working, devise a daily 15-minute walk which takes you along a different route. For the following two weeks, change your route to work or for your walk again and ask directions of someone you see on the street on three different occasions.

TIP If you find it too scary to address strangers to ask them directions, start off by saying hello audibly to people you know by sight only, for example a neighbour, a cashier at the supermarket or someone you sometimes see at work but who you are not working with directly.

Tolerance

- Are there people at work or in your private circle who have a way about them (the way they speak, sniff, hum, eat etc) that drives you nuts, even though nobody else seems to be bothered?

- Do you feel that fat/thin, black/white, young/old, Christian/Muslim people are better than other body shapes, skin colours, age groups or religions?

If you have answered 'no' to both questions, you are probably reasonably tolerant. Move on to the next resource.

If you have any 'yes' answers, use the following exercise to help you improve.

Exercise

If you have answered 'yes' to the first question, think about three reasons why this person is doing what they are doing, without using insulting or belittling language. Consider that they may be displaying their (to you) unacceptable behaviour for reasons other than trying to annoy their fellow human beings. Write down the three reasons on a piece of paper to make sure your explanations are factual rather than sarcastic.

If it is someone you know who irritates you with their mannerism, have a conversation of at least 15 minutes with them to make an effort to find out more about them and get to know them better. In this conversation, you are *not allowed* to mention or ask about their mannerism. The reason for your conversation is to check whether any of your assumptions about their mannerism are correct.

If you have answered 'yes' to the second question, check out what exactly your assumptions are concerning that group of people. Write down your assumptions on a piece of paper. For example:

Thin people are
– anorexic
– stressed
– on a stupid diet and don't eat enough
– vain

Now think about a person in that group who does not fit in with your assumptions. Do you know a thin person who is eating plenty of food and not particularly concerned about their appearance? If you do, start talking to another thin

continues

person over the next few weeks to find out whether your assumptions are confirmed or not. You are *not allowed* to mention or ask about their weight or appearance. By the time you have carried out this exercise, you will have become a bit more tolerant, even if you find that your assumptions were partly correct for some of the people.

Inventiveness

- Do you tend to trust your instincts?

- Do you act on your intuitive thoughts and find them correct most of the time?

- Do you usually find your way out of a difficult situation through your own efforts?

- Are you someone with lots of ideas?

If you have answered 'yes' at least three times, you are doing well on the inventiveness front. Move on to the next resource.

If you have no 'yes' answers, use the following exercises to help you improve.

Exercise

The trick with inventiveness is to take the little voice at the back of your head seriously rather than dismissing it by thinking 'Aw, that'll never work!'. Begin to train your

continues

intuition by thinking of an everyday situation such as finding a parking space for your car, getting a seat on the bus/train, guessing what the time is. The situation should be one that recurs regularly and that you can check easily. With your eyes closed, concentrate on the situation and imagine you are capable of remote viewing.

If you try to guess what the time is, imagine looking at the clock where you will check the time in a moment. Where do you see the hands on the clock in your mind's eye? If you try to guess whether you will get a parking space, imagine the car park where you are planning to go and look around it in your mind's eye to see whether there are any spaces and where they are.

Carry out this exercise every day for a couple of weeks, focusing on one particular situation, and notice how many times you are accurate in your predictions. If your predictions are accurate just over 55 per cent of the time, you are doing well. If your estimate of time is within 5 minutes of the actual time, then this is a good result.

This exercise opens the door to increased inventiveness and more spontaneous ideas.

Exercise

If you managed to estimate the correct time within 5 minutes, you may also be able to set your inner clock. Imagine setting your inner clock to a particular hour the next morning to wake you up. If you normally use an alarm

continues

clock, set your inner clock time to before your alarm normally goes off.

To do this exercise, close your eyes and imagine the time when you want to wake up. You can either see the numbers or imagine the hands of the clock in the relevant positions. Now imagine a sign with the word 'alarm' flashing on that clock.

Check the next morning how near the actual clock time you are when you wake up.

The more you can concentrate on the image of the clock with the flashing alarm sign, the more effectively you'll be able to do this exercise. If you come within 5 minutes of the set time, you are doing very well.

Love

- Do you like yourself even though you can see your own shortcomings?

- Do you eat well on a regular basis, and permit yourself a break or rest when you need it?

- Do you know about the likes and dislikes of people close to you? Would you be able to give them a birthday present that you could be sure they liked?

- Have you had at least three long-term friendships (longer than five years if you are over 25) in your life up until now?

If you have answered 'yes' at least three times, you are doing well with closeness to others and self-love. Move on to the next resource.

If you have any 'no' answers, use the following exercises and tip to help you improve.

Exercise

Do the following exercise if you answered 'no' to the first two questions.

In order to like and respect yourself more, concentrate on your good points.

- Write down any achievements you have accomplished throughout your life to date. Write this in the third person, as if you were an outsider writing about someone else. Write, for example, 'She worked hard and consequently did well in her A-levels.'
- Write down any obstacles you had to overcome in life to arrive at where you are today. Write this, too, in the third person.
- Evaluate, as an outside observer, how this person is doing. Which character traits are admirable? Which personality traits are lovable?
- Make a list of the good qualities you found and pin them up where you can see your list to remind yourself daily of your positive points.

If you can concentrate on your good qualities, you begin to develop self-respect, and this is the basis for self-love.

Do the following exercise if you answered 'no' to the last two questions.

- Pick one person close to you and make it your task for the next two months to find out more about their likes and dislikes. Spend more time with them. Ask them over, ask them out if they are friends. Tell them about yourself

continues

and ask them about themselves. Have at least two meetings with them. Pay close attention to what they are telling you. *Listen carefully.* What have you learnt about them after the conversation?

If you can cultivate an attitude of honest attention to someone else, you are laying the foundation stone for a lasting friendship, and out of this, love can develop.

TIP Make sure you always thank those around you for their help, support and thoughtful actions towards you.

Perseverance

- Do you start lots of things but don't finish them?

- Do you give up quickly when things don't go as expected?

- Are you easily put off a project when you do not get the support from others that you expected?

If you have answered 'no' three times, your perseverance is good. Move on to the next resource. If you have any 'yes' answers, use the following exercise and tip to help you improve.

Exercise

Set yourself a simple task such as tidying up a cupboard, filing some paperwork or sorting out a drawer at home. Alternatively, pick any reasonably straightforward task that

continues

you have been avoiding for a while. Plan some time when you will carry out this task, then go and do it. Make sure you pick a time when you are least likely to be disturbed. If you can't avoid being disturbed, do it anyway!

A-ha! moment 14 Don't wait for the right time – it may never come!

If you can't avoid being disturbed and you have sleeping problems anyway, you may choose to do your task in the middle of the night – at least something useful will get done while you are awake, rather than tossing and turning in bed.

If you carry out your task during the day, put the answering machine on, turn your TV off and turn some music on instead.

Do not stop before you have finished your task. Reward yourself afterwards.

By repeating this exercise with other tasks that need doing, you can gradually increase your staying power.

TIP Make sure the first few tasks are quick to do. Build up your resource of perseverance gradually, and don't put yourself off by choosing a very lengthy task to start with.

A-ha! moment 15 Reading about all these exercises is good, but only *doing* them will build your resources.

Humour

- Are you able to laugh about yourself?

- Are you able to see the funny side of things when something goes wrong?

- Can you have a really good laugh when you watch something funny on TV or hear a good joke?

- Do you laugh a lot?

If you have answered 'yes' at least three times, you possess a good sense of fun and you can move on to the next resource.

If you have more than one 'no' answer, use the following exercise and tip to introduce more laughter into your life – and help you feel lighter and more carefree.

Exercise

Stop a moment and think what it is that makes you laugh. Is there any particular film or programme on TV that can set you off? Is there anyone among your friends or family who has a way of making you laugh? If there is nothing or no one who can make you laugh, is there anything that can make you smile?

I'd prefer it if you could find something that can bring out a laugh in you, but if laughter is not available at the moment, a big smile will do!

Spend some time twice a week with whoever or whatever makes you laugh or smile. Do this for the next four weeks to rediscover the less serious side of life.

TIP If you are stuck for lighthearted friends, simply smile more, whether you feel like it or not. Pulling up the corners of your mouth into a smile activates a positive feeling within you and makes other people smile back at you. The harder you work, the more time you need to make for laughter. Keep a balance between serious work and fun play.

Motivation

- Do you find it hard to get going on a new project?

- Do you have to force yourself to do things that should really be a breeze?

- Do you have lots of plans but never get started?

- Would you rather be bored and miserable than busy?

- Do you feel too tired to muster enthusiasm for anything?

If you have answered 'no' at least four times, you are doing OK for motivation. Move on to the next resource.

If you have any 'yes' answers, use the following exercise and tip to help you improve.

Exercise

Think about something you need to tackle but cannot muster any enthusiasm to do. Divide the task into a few smaller, more manageable steps and decide on a reward once you have done the first step.

For example, if your desk is a mess, your first step could be to put any rubbish in the bin and put things, unsorted, into tidy piles. This will clear some of the chaos. A reward could now be to go and have a cup of tea. The second step could then be to start sorting through the piles of documents on the table and make new piles of papers that all belong

continues

together. Then give yourself another short break and reward, and so on.

The main thing is to break an unpleasant task into smaller bits and reward yourself a few times until you have done the whole job.

TIP Do at least one step of the task per day. If you space it out further, you'll lose the impetus.

If you are too tired to be motivated, only do half of what you think you should do. If you find that tiredness is an ongoing problem, take a multivitamin-and-mineral supplement, at twice the recommended dose.

Honesty

- Are there certain areas of your life that you avoid looking at?

- Are there certain aspects of yourself that you would rather ignore?

- If something bothers you, will you pretend to others that everything is OK?

- Do you find it impossible to say 'no' to a request that will seriously inconvenience you?

- Are you afraid people won't like you any more if you say what you want?

If you have answered 'no' at least four times, you find it easy to say what you want and to be honest about things that aren't quite right in your life. Move on to the next resource.

If you have any 'yes' answers, use the following exercise to help you improve.

> ## Exercise
>
> Recognising that you need to check out a problem area before you can sort it out, take some time to look at those issues in your life or about yourself that you have avoided so far. Now answer the following question. Imagine someone else was struggling with these issues; what advice would you give them?
>
> Can you take some of your own advice and put it to the test? If there are reasons why you can't, what are the underlying issues that you need to tackle first?

Consistency

- Do you tend to set up rules and then break them when you are working on a project/dealing with your kids or other people?

- Do you find it hard to come up with a clear concept of how to tackle a job/deal with your kids/deal with other people?

- Are you easily swayed by other people's dissenting opinion so that you give up what you wanted to do even though you know you are right?

- If someone moans a lot, will you give up your stance on a matter, even though you know you should stick by what you said first?

If you have answered 'no' at least four times, you are a consistent person. Move on to the next resource.

If you have any 'yes' answers, use the following exercises and tip to help you improve.

Exercises

Pick an area of your life where you have been inconsistent. To start off, choose something that is not too difficult to be firm about. Now set yourself a limited time span within which you will work on being consistent about your actions.

For example, if you keep on surfing the internet instead of doing your chores, set some clear rules whereby the internet becomes the *reward* after having done one or several chores. Your rules could be that there are certain times of day which are reserved for work, so no surfing before, say, 4 PM. Another rule could be that your surf time is limited to, say, one hour. (If this is one of your rules, place an alarm clock by you and set it. And there is no extra time just because a phone call interrupted your surfing!)

Make a concerted effort to see these rules through for a couple of weeks. Even if you cannot be 100 per cent consistent, it will nevertheless help you improve.

If others can scare or pester you into becoming inconsistent, tackle this problem with a very simple but effective method. Once you have explained to the other person what you are planning on doing, and if the other person disagrees, say, 'I can see you don't agree with me on this point, but I still feel that this is the best course of action.' Then proceed to do what you said you were going to do.

continues

If someone – often a child – is moaning about a course of action you are suggesting, explain your reasons simply and briefly, then get on with doing what you said you were going to do. If it is important to get compliance, it is perfectly OK to bribe the kids with a reward if they toe the line.

TIP Never ever part with a reward *before* the kids have done what they were supposed to do. And do not reward yourself unless you have followed the rules you set yourself. No results, no reward!

Pro-activity

- Do you have good ideas but are at a loss as to how to start implementing them on a practical level?

- Do you know the right thing to do but don't do it?

- Do you feel guilty but still unable to do what needs doing?

- Are you afraid of making a mistake if you tackle an issue and therefore avoid taking action?

- Are you overwhelmed by the size of your problem and therefore avoid taking action to resolve it?

If you have answered 'no' at least four times, you are a pro-active person and don't need to work particularly on this resource.

If you have any 'yes' answers, use the following exercise to help you improve.

Exercise

If you are inventive in theory but cannot convert your thoughts into reality, think about what advice you would give someone else who had the same idea but was struggling to carry it out.

Pick a real-life situation that is relevant to you at the moment. If you are still stuck, think of someone you know who is a successful, pro-active person and think how they would do it.

- Ask yourself whether you really don't know how to translate your ideas into reality or if you are just worried that you might make mistakes or a wrong decision.
- If you know what to do but don't do it, is this because you are afraid? If you are afraid, what can you do about your fear? The project now is no longer to start your project, but to prepare yourself better so that your fears are allayed and you have the confidence to go ahead.

From all the above resources, pick one or two that are most relevant to you and start working on them.

CHAPTER 6

Spring-clean your attitude

Attitude is everything. You don't need public schooling, a university education, money or friends in high places to change for the better. What you need is the right attitude. With a bit of luck, you were born with a positive outlook on life, or your parents were and taught you how to tackle life's ups and downs with optimism and determination. If not, don't worry – it is possible to learn to be constructive and pro-active.

In order to improve your life and turn around problem habits, it is necessary to cultivate a 'can do' stance. This means that thoughts like 'I can't change', 'I can't change this' and 'change is hard' need to be converted into their opposite. After all, if I promised you a sizeable amount of money, or, in other words, if you had a very tempting incentive, you would find ways of doing what you think you are incapable of doing at the moment, wouldn't you?

Well, since I *won't* be offering you a sizeable sum of money, we'll have to find alternative ways of helping you change.

So let's say you want to start building up one of the resources from the last chapter in order to establish a good new habit, but you simply can't get started with the exercises that are necessary to produce the positive change you want. Your logical mind is saying that this is a good idea, but your gut feeling is pulling in the exact opposite direction. Your head says 'go ahead – this will be useful', but your gut feeling pulls on the handbrake. And somehow, your gut feelings always seem to win . . . even though the subconscious doubt and fear don't make a lot of sense half the time, it doesn't stop them from being unreasonably persistent nevertheless.

This constant tug-of-war between reason and fears is very stressful, and when you are stressed, you are not exactly in the best position to make progress.

What are you thinking?

In order to change your attitude, you need to find out first of all what is actually going through your head. What are you thinking? How are you stopping yourself from taking the necessary steps to become happier and have a better life?

It's time to check what thoughts are going through your head. You have already heightened your awareness of what triggers your problem habit. Now, it's time to start observing what thought prevents you from starting to do the right thing.

Preparation

Think about your current situation. Imagine you are about to do something that will be helpful to you, but something inside you won't let you get on with it.

What is the thought that intervenes and stops you?

Here are a few examples.
You want to start tidying up your flat, but just as you are about

to get out of your chair and start, you think, 'Oh, I can't be bothered. It's going to take forever to do this properly!' And you sit down again.

You want to start looking through your latest bank statements to find out what your financial situation is, but as you are about to gather the necessary paperwork, you think, 'There's no point. I'm no good with money anyway,' or, 'I don't really want to look – I might get a nasty shock.' And you drop the paperwork back in the drawer.

If, on the other hand, you can't stop yourself from doing something which you shouldn't be doing if you want to make progress, you might find that your interfering thoughts go something like this.

Say you want to stop checking your e-mails every five minutes and you have manfully, or womanfully, stayed away from the room with the computer. But now this little thought creeps in: 'I wouldn't want to miss anything important. I had better go have a look, just in case . . . ' and before you know it, you are back at the computer.

You want to stop snacking between meals, but you find yourself thinking, 'Oh, *one* piece of toast is no big deal. After all, I've had a hard day at work today. I deserve a little reward.' And before you can stop yourself, a slice of white bread – which you know is not exactly the healthiest thing to be eating – has gone in the toaster.

Exercise

Do it! Step 1

It is not necessary to wait until the situation arises in reality to find out what thought precedes the inappropriate action. You can simply sit down, close your eyes and imagine you are in the trigger situation.

What is the sabotaging thought that goes through your mind and makes you do what you don't want to do?

What is the sabotaging thought that pops into your mind and stops you from doing what you need to do?

A sabotaging thought is your subconscious mind in action.

Do it! Step 2

We have already looked at some of the beneficial effects of bad habits in Chapter 2. Your subconscious mind is always trying to do something positive for you by trying to comfort, reward or protect you. The only problem with your subconscious mind's good intention can be that you don't like the way in which it is comforting, rewarding or protecting you.

You therefore need to find out what the good intention is that is underlying your problem habit. Are you twiddling your hair all the time because you feel stressed or overwhelmed, and the twiddling comforts you and helps you relax? Are you avoiding speaking at meetings because this protects you from saying the wrong thing and looking like a fool to the others? Or are you unable to stop raiding the fridge after work because, somewhere deep down inside, you need to reward yourself for all the hassle you had with the customers today?

continues

Do it! Step 3

Once you have found out whether your problem habit serves to comfort, reward or protect you, you can start thinking about more positive alternatives which will achieve the same benefit.

Rather than twiddling your hair, can you do a simple breathing exercise to help you unwind after a stressful or unsettling event, and get your comfort that way?

Rather than avoiding speaking at meetings, could you try to make one suggestion at a small meeting with colleagues you know well?

Rather than emptying the fridge into your stomach, could you let go of pent-up emotions with a workout and then reward yourself with some quality food?

Once you have established the answers to the three Do it! Steps, you are ready to activate your findings. The following exercise will help you do this, and will also train three crucial resources: inventiveness, love and pro-activity.

Exercise

- Close your eyes and imagine you could make your sabotaging thought into a person who stands in front of you and stops you from doing what you want to do/makes you do what you don't want to do.
- Give that person a voice, a face and a name. If you give your person some outrageous clothes and a funny name, you'll also be training your sense of humour!
- Thank the person for their good intention.

continues

- Explain to them how they can help you in a more constructive way to be comforted, protected or rewarded.
- Agree on a trial period of one week during which they can encourage you to do the right thing.
- Shake hands on the deal.

Now test-run the new agreement in reality. Hear the new messages from your subconscious during the problem situation and notice how it makes you feel stronger and more confident.

Mind magic

It is true to say that what the mind can perceive, the mind can achieve, and this has less to do with willpower than you might think. You already know that the subconscious mind is the seat of all automatic physical responses and the seat of our emotions. This means that if your problem habit is emotion-driven, you need to access the subconscious level of your mind in order to bring about change. Logical thinking and logical solutions won't do the trick, simply because the problem is not located on the rational level. Logically, you know that biting your nails looks gross and makes your hands look unattractive, but no matter how often you tell yourself to stop, it won't make a difference because the problem is emotion-driven. Whenever you get stressed or worried, your hand automatically goes up to your mouth, and before you know it (and often you don't even notice it consciously), one or several fingernails are bitten down again. And even if you *do* notice yourself doing it, you can often only interrupt it for a moment before your hand finds its way back to your mouth.

To really get rid of an unwanted habit, you need to employ a few new strategies which involve the subconscious level of your mind. Only when you deal with the emotional side of the problem will you get lasting success, and the emotional component of your personality is located in the subconscious.

Influencing your subconscious is easier than you may think. You can do so either with words or with pictures, and ideally with both.

- First of all, sit down for a moment. Think which good habit you want to establish or which problem habit you want to eradicate. Be clear what you want to work on.

- To access your subconscious mind, all you have to do now is close your eyes. This will help the body become still and the mind to be more inwardly focused.

- Now make a positive statement, also known as affirmation, concerning your target habit. Phrase it positively and in the present tense. With nail-biting, for example, this could be, 'I can stay calm and relaxed at all times and allow my hands to rest comfortably.'

- With your eyes still closed, repeat your affirmation several times in your mind with feeling. Really *feel* the calmness and relaxation and *feel* what it is like to have your hands rest comfortably in your lap while you are thinking your positive thought.

- Repeat the affirmation regularly, at least ten times in a row and at least twice a day *with feeling*.

What you are actually doing with these positive thoughts is establishing a new subconscious pattern. By feeding positive affirmations into the subconscious, you are helping your mood to lift, your body to relax. In addition, you are influencing your automatic responses to become more positive and constructive. When you find yourself remaining calmer in stressful situations as in our example, you will be able to deal with the stress much better and preserve your fingernails, which will make you feel quite proud of yourself on top of everything else. Certainly worth putting the effort in for, don't you think?

But there is also a second way in which you can further promote positive change on the subconscious level, and that is with pictures. Visualisation is a powerful process which can help you move mountains when it comes to habits.

The principles are similar to those for affirmations.

- Make yourself comfortable and close your eyes.

- Now imagine having achieved what you want to achieve. Imagine having established the good new habit. Make a picture of the successful outcome. If you want to value yourself more, imagine in great detail how you do something nice for yourself. If you want, for example, to stop nail-biting, imagine your hands with perfectly manicured nails and feel the sense of happiness and pride inside that comes with the achievement.

- Make sure that your visualisation is entirely positive. Don't build any flaws into it to make it more realistic. The job here is to impress the successful outcome onto your subconscious mind. Only if your image is as brilliant and perfect as possible will it change your feelings to happy and expectant and positive. This is essential if your problem habit is emotion-driven.

- Use your visualisation at least three times a day until you see some progress. It doesn't have to take long to do – half a minute is usually enough, provided you really concentrate on your image so that you can *feel* the uplifting feelings.

It makes sense to use both affirmations and visualisation when you work on habits. That way you fill your subconscious mind not only with the right words but also with visual images to promote positive change.

Ditching the jitters

It is especially essential to get the body to relax before you concentrate on your affirmations and mind images if feelings of fear or insecurity are involved in your problem habit. But also if you come off an addiction habit such as sweet cravings, overeating, drinking or smoking, it can be extremely useful to know how to relax physically.

As you already know, it is the subconscious mind which runs the autonomic nervous system, meaning all those bodily functions which we don't normally influence consciously. If we get frightened, the autonomic nervous system *automatically* releases adrenaline which, among other things, gets the heartbeat to increase and muscles to tense up. These automatic physical responses are a godsend because they are far too complex and numerous for us to monitor and activate on a conscious level.

It is a problem, though, if the body adopts a pattern of stress-arousal every time a particular situation arises. If you get anxious whenever you are being called in to your boss's office, even though you don't know what your boss wants, a negative body-mind link becomes established that can become a habitual response.

Case study

Dawn is working as a dental nurse for a dentist who she describes as 'a lovely, lovely lady', and yet, every Monday morning when Dawn is getting ready for her start-of-the-week meeting with her boss, she feels sick. 'It doesn't make sense,' says Dawn. 'All we do is talk through what needs doing in the coming week, and it's all perfectly pleasant. Why do I get all worked up about it? I don't understand.'

This is a good example of how the conscious, reasoning mind is quite helpless when it comes to problems that stem from the subconscious level of the mind. It therefore makes little sense to use willpower to overcome the subconscious problem because willpower is a function of the *conscious* mind, and this is not where the problem lies!

To get body and mind to slow down and calm down, you can do a very simple breathing exercise.

Preparation

- Sit down for a moment and make sure your waistband isn't too tight. If necessary, open a button or loosen your belt one notch.

- Place a hand over your navel and imagine that you have a balloon inside the area underneath your hand. This balloon needs to be pumped up by your inbreath.

- Take a breath in and allow the belly under your hand to fill up with air so that your hand is being pushed up by your expanding belly.

- Breathe out again and imagine that the balloon deflates again under your hand.

TIP If you find it difficult to let your belly expand while breathing in, start off by sucking your belly in quite strongly *before* you breathe in. When next you breathe in, the belly has nowhere else to go but *out*. Do this a few times and you will get the hang of belly-breathing quite quickly.

Exercise

- Sit or lie down comfortably and loosen any tight clothing.
- Breathe in through your belly to the count of five.
- Breathe out, letting the belly deflate, to the count of seven.
- Repeat ten times.

This exercise will not only start to relax your body, but also helps calm down racing thoughts and dampens down cravings. It's ideal in situations where you normally get nervous, frightened or fidgety.

Another good way to feel more centred and strong is to use imagery. The scenario you choose for your visualisation is not important, as long as it has relaxing and soothing connotations for you. For some people, it is a beach, for others it is a garden or a cosy room. In the following, I'll give you an image that you can get started with, but feel free to adapt it to your own needs and preferences.

Exercise

- Lie or sit down comfortably and loosen any tight clothing.
- Close your eyes and listen to your breathing for a few in and out breaths.
- Imagine a golden sparkling stream of energy particles entering your feet, cleaning and energising them, filling them with vibrant energy.

continues

Imagine the golden sparkling energy particles *slowly* flowing into your lower legs. Watch in your mind's eye how the level of golden particles rises up to your knees and feel the energy in your lower legs.

- Allow the energy levels to rise *slowly* further up into your upper legs, then gradually up into your abdomen and chest cavity.
- Now imagine the energy rising all the way up into your shoulders, cleansing, refreshing and energising the entire trunk of your body.
- Now the golden flow of energy slowly spills down into your arms and down into your hands and fingers, until your arms are entirely filled with sparkling energy particles.
- Now let the level rise all the way up your neck and throat into your head, filling the inside of your head with life-giving energy.

Stay with this vibrating energy inside your entire body for a few more movements and then open your eyes.

If you are overtired or exhausted because you can't stop rushing, add on the next exercise.

Exercise

- Lie or sit down comfortably and loosen tight clothing.
- Close your eyes and listen to the sound of your breathing. Also concentrate on your chest and belly rising with each inbreath.

continues

- Imagine yourself sitting on the grassy bank of a little brook that is flowing past you. Listen to the little splashing and gurgling sounds the water makes as it is flowing and eddying along.
- See how clear and clean the water is. You can see the pebbles on the bottom quite clearly. Some little fish are darting in and out of the shallower bits of the riverbed, and warm sunshine is making the water's surface sparkle and shine. As you are sitting on the grassy bank, your breathing is getting really easy. You can feel the softness of the grass beneath you and you can hear some birds singing in nearby trees. Everything is very peaceful, and you are just relaxing, watching the water of the brook flow past.

  You are beginning to really relax now because there's nothing else for you to do. Nobody else there for miles and miles, just you relaxing, watching the water, listening to the sounds around you and feeling the soft grass under your hand as you gently touch it. There's nothing to do, nothing to think, nothing to decide. You are just there, part of nature, feeling peaceful and relaxed.

- Finish the exercise in this way:

  Slowly bring your mind back into your room, into your chair. Reorientate yourself in the here and now, and open your eyes. Remain still for another five minutes, and feel the relaxation in your body and mind.

CHAPTER 7

Preventing a relapse

Once you have built up and established good new habits, life becomes easier and stress levels tumble. For some people, this is a once-and-for-all development, and the good habits become so ingrained that they become second nature. Someone who used to bite their nails and now has beautifully manicured hands will normally stick with their new attitude towards their own appearance for the rest of their life. Someone who used to arrive late for everything and has mended their ways will normally stick to their reformed attitude.

And yet, sometimes we are thrown off course, and this is when we are in danger of reverting to our old ways. This is not a disaster, but it does need immediate attention.

Situations that trigger a relapse are usually similar to the ones that caused the problem habit in the first place. It is therefore wise to make yourself aware of the situations where you used to be unable to resist reverting to your problem habit, and mentally flag them up as potential pitfalls. If you used to find smoking particularly irresistible when in company, you need to be aware that parties, weddings and other gatherings may prompt the same stress in you and possibly trigger cravings for a cigarette.

Typical situations that can propel you back into the Never-Neverland of bad habits are sudden shocks, bad news concerning yourself or someone close to you, overwork, boredom, PMT, illness (your own or that of someone close to you), or marital or relationship problems.

In order to safeguard against a relapse, write down the answers to the following questions on a separate piece of paper.

- What were the problems your habit got you into?

- Why did you develop the problem habit in the first place?

- What were the danger situations that tempted you to slip into your problem habit?

- What was the positive thought that got you over the danger situation without succumbing to your habit?

Pin this up where you can see it or make it into a bookmark and put it between these two pages. At the very first sign of slipping back into old ways, look at your notice or turn to your bookmark and refresh your memory.

So far we've had a good grounding in how to discover your problem habits and what to do about them. Part 2 explores this process in far more detail. Now let's get on with kicking problem habits permanently!

PART 2

Kicking the Habit
– The Manual

Introduction

In this part of the book, you'll find an array of problem habits grouped around a good habit you need to work on. In Part 1, we looked at basic good habits that are essential as a foundation stone for any changes you want to make in life. We are now going to expand on these to see how you can achieve more specific good habits which will help you become more confident, centred and strong.

If you want to be successful in your personal life and career, you need to cultivate a set of good habits that can become second nature to you. Once these positive habits are in place, you will find that life becomes a lot simpler, less frustrating and more rewarding. Good habits also help you preserve energy, so that those tasks which you would normally have considered to be difficult or a chore become simple and can be carried out effortlessly.

Not only are good habits an asset in themselves, but they are also ideal tools for turning around habits that are holding you back. I'd even go as far as saying that if you succeed in establishing the following good habits with the help of a few new resources, you will start seeing problem habits disappear by at least 50 per cent!

At the start of each of the following sections you'll find a specific exercise or project to help you build up your good habit. This is then followed by help with overcoming any of the problem habits that are linked with a lack of the main good habit of that section.

Throughout this part of the book, you will be using your skills of influencing your subconscious mind to achieve your aims of building positive habits and overcoming negative ones.

CHAPTER 8

Valuing yourself versus self-neglect

There is no point in doing anything in life unless you think you're worth it. Why bother improving your relationships unless you think you deserve to have good relationships? Why bother finding a better job unless you think you're worth it? Why, come to that, bother getting up in the morning unless you think you are entitled to lead a happy and fulfilled life?

A lot of our day-to-day thinking revolves around how we appear to other people, what others expect of us and how our performance is rated by others. We are very focused on what others think of us, but we rarely stop to consider what we think of ourselves. And yet, it is our own opinion about ourselves that ultimately decides how happy we are within ourselves.

If we dislike ourselves, no glittering accolades from others, no shooting-star career and not even our dream partner will ever be able to make up for the lack of self-love. If you do not value yourself, you live your life for others, constantly seeking other people's approval to bolster your self-esteem. If you do not value yourself, you make yourself dependent on the moods of others and on their whimsical judgements of you and your efforts. This leaves you without peace of mind.

Valuing yourself gives you inner substance that carries and supports you in everything you do. You may never have learnt to appreciate yourself because you were brought up in an environment which didn't teach you self-love, but you can still learn it. All that is needed is your willingness to tackle the problem now.

The benefit of valuing yourself is good self-esteem, which will help you become motivated and pro-active – invaluable assets in life!

Happy, successful people look after themselves and make sure they eat regularly and well, and take breaks. They have the self-respect to decline unreasonable demands. You can spot people who value themselves easily:

- They speak up for themselves when necessary.

- They consider themselves to be on the same level as everyone else.

- They are able to say 'no' if they are faced with a demand which they cannot or do not want to comply with.

- They appear well-groomed, even when they are in an informal setting.

- They don't boast, but they also don't hide their light under a bushel. At work, they will point out to their boss what they have achieved.

Affirmations

To affirm yourself, you need to say to yourself:

- I deserve to look after myself and provide myself with what I need.
- I am as good as everyone else, no matter what their position in society.
- I have the right to stand up for myself because I'm worth it.

Visualisation

Build an image around the situation that leads you to neglect yourself. For generally enhancing your feelings of self-worth, use the following imagery:

- With your eyes closed, imagine yourself as an outsider, looking at yourself.
- Staying in the outsider's shoes, walk up to your alter ego and hold both their hands in yours.
- Look them in the eyes and say one of the affirmations to them, addressing them directly.
- Now give them a long warm hug and tell them that they are great.

Example: You lack self-esteem and your name is Susan. Imagine becoming an outsider who is looking at Susan and say to her, 'Susan, you deserve to look after yourself. You are just as good as everyone else!' Then give Susan a

continues

long warm hug and tell her 'You're great! I'm very happy that we are friends.'

- Now change sides. Be yourself and feel the other person take your hands, look you in the eyes and say the positive things to you. Hear it, feel it and allow yourself to believe it as they hug you and tell you they are glad to be your friend.

TIPS

- If ever you are in doubt about whether you deserve to have the good things in life, imagine what your answer would be if you had to answer your best friend's doubts about the same matter.
- It would enhance your life and your chances of happiness immeasurably if you could stop having double standards. It is not OK to put yourself above everyone else as a human being, but it is equally not OK to degrade yourself, even if you do so only in thought, as being worth less than others.

Skipping meals

Hm, a funny one this. I was just about to skip breakfast to start writing this chapter. Not a good idea, though. I'll tell you why after I have had my bacon and eggs . . .

I'm back! You see, I'm busy and you are probably busy, but skipping meals is *not* an option, especially when you lead a hectic life. Your brain and the rest of your body need fuel to produce energy for you to walk, talk and think. Your body also needs food to keep all the body processes going. So not eating is the same thing as not putting petrol in the tank of your car and still expecting it to run. You wouldn't dream of doing that, would you?

You may think you are saving time by not eating, but you aren't. If you don't provide fuel for your brain, it cannot function properly and you'll fail to think clearly. The mistakes you make as a consequence then have to be ironed out. This is not only time-consuming, but can also be quite embarrassing if your mistake affects other people!

Another misconception is that it will help you lose weight if you eat nothing or very little. Some people (women!) think they can kill two birds with one stone by skipping meals: save time and shed a few pounds as a bonus. The facts are that *if* you lose some weight, you'll put it on double quick once you start eating again, and in most cases, you put on more than you lost. What this means is that by not eating, you gain weight in the long run. However, most people don't even lose weight by skipping meals! The reason for this is that you need fuel – that is, food – to digest and to lose weight. Without food, no weight loss!

Also, think of what it says about you if you keep skipping meals. Are you really going to put everyone else and everything else before your own fundamental needs? Do you really rate yourself so low that you are not worth being fed regularly? Why do you put yourself last? (You should know the answer to this question already if you have worked through the section on attitude on page 73. If not, go back to it and do it right now.)

If you really like yourself so little that you won't even feed yourself, then use the following affirmations and visualisation and *pretend* you think you are important enough to supply your body with food. Eventually, if you tell yourself often enough, you will be able to accept that you are more worthwhile than you thought.

Affirmations

- I eat regularly because I'm worth it!
- I feed my body and brain regularly so that I can work more efficiently.
- As I eat the right foods regularly, I can lose my excess pounds one by one.
- Eating regularly is a sign of intelligence, and I am very intelligent!
- Eating regularly provides me with enjoyable and necessary breaks from work.

Pick the affirmation/s you like best. You can also use several and combine them differently. Repeat your affirmation/s at least ten times in a row, three times a day, for a couple of weeks.

Visualisation

Close your eyes and imagine yourself sitting down, eating and properly chewing what you are eating. See or feel a big smile on your face as you really enjoy your food.

If you want to lose weight, see all the right foods on your plate.

If you are worried about losing precious work time, see yourself eat in peace and quiet and then work effortlessly and efficiently, finishing a lot of work in a short time.

TIPS

- Always sit down when you are eating. Eating over the sink is so out these days!

- Always put food on a plate, even if it is only a biscuit.
- If you want to lose weight, put your food on a small plate. That way it looks like more.
- Eat slowly and don't do anything else while you are eating. This will help you digest the food better and that, in turn, helps you lose weight more easily.
- Concentrate on the flavour of the food.
- It is better to eat at a silly hour than not to eat at all. Just try to avoid eating proteins such as meat or beans before you go to bed, and eat little if it is late. Proteins take a long time to digest, so they are better eaten in the morning or at lunchtime.

Case study

Claudia came to see me because she had been having problems with her stress levels ever since she started her new job as a management consultant. Apart from feeling under siege all day long, she also struggled with recurring bouts of cystitis. 'Before I started in this job, I worked in marketing. That was very demanding, too, but nothing compared to my current position. Sometimes, I feel like I don't know whether I'm coming or going!'

On asking her to go into more detail about her current situation, I found out that Claudia was very ambitious and anxious to prove her worth in the new job. Even though she was entitled to a lunch break, she often skipped it, and more importantly, she also often skipped going to the toilet to pass water. When she did go, she rushed into the cubicle and hardly ever allowed her bladder to empty completely before rushing back to her desk. This meant that her bladder never really discharged all the urine, which led to an irritation of the bladder and consequently recurring bouts of cystitis.

Claudia learnt to look after herself better by doing palming (page 39), a breathing exercise (page 82) and a visualisation. She imagined herself calm and relaxed as she tackled her work as a consultant, moving calmly as she took phone calls and speaking to people in a relaxed and confident way. She also started to use her lunch break for eating rather than working and began to drink more water. Her stress levels reduced drastically, and as she became calmer, felt more in control and was able to pass water without rushing, her cystitis soon disappeared.

Saying 'yes' when you need to say 'no'

I know that this is a tricky one. It can be difficult to decide where to draw the line. This is where it is very helpful if you are used to listening to your own needs and have a good understanding of what makes you tick. Hopefully, by this stage, you will have worked through the various exercises in Part 1 of the book, in particular the ones in Chapter 5, which target developing resources.

When do you really need to say 'no'? There are no hard and fast rules, but you need to know your boundaries. What situations or demands will you definitely not tolerate? Which situations or special circumstances will warrant you making an exception? Your gauge will always have to be the level of your discomfort. If you genuinely don't mind carrying out a request that someone else would call unreasonable, then it's perfectly OK to say 'yes' to it and do it. If, however, it makes you feel resentful, then you will have to respect your own boundaries and say 'no', politely but firmly (see Tips at the end of this section).

Sometimes it can be necessary to compromise and to say 'yes' even though a 'no' would be more appropriate. This can occur when a family member or a close friend needs your help because they are in an emergency situation. Maybe they are ill or cannot carry out a particularly important task because they are prevented through no fault of their own. If, in a genuine emergency, you decide to extend your boundaries, make sure the other person understands clearly that this is an *exception*. If you are helping out at your own cost, losing your time to relax or jeopardising your well-being, you owe it to yourself to say that this needs to be a one-off.

Where you should always be extremely cautious about saying 'yes' is when it comes to money lending. Anything that, to you, is a big sum, has to be thought through very carefully. *Never* say 'yes' straight away, whether it is a loan or a business proposition. Take into account the other person's track record when it comes to paying back debts, to you or anyone else. Lending someone money who cannot handle money is like giving a drink to an alcoholic. They'll promise you anything you want to hear until you have given them what they want. At that point, they will switch off from you, and all you'll ever get back are promises and excuses 'explaining' why they can't pay you back at the moment.

The same is true for relationships that don't work. Do you keep saying 'yes' to your partner even though the last few times you did, you were taken advantage of? Are you, yet again, taking someone back who hasn't changed? You know the old saying, don't you? If someone takes advantage of you a first time, it's their fault. If they take advantage of you a second time, it's *your* fault.

Most people who say 'yes' when they ought to say 'no' are trying to help. The trick is to find out whether you are really helping or whether you are giving someone else an easy ride at your expense.

Affirmations

- I deserve to be treated with consideration and respect, and I ensure that others do so.
- I have a right to my own boundaries.

continues

- I look after myself. I can say 'no' in a calm, polite and effective way.
- It is perfectly OK to say 'no'. Everyone else is allowed to do so, and so am I.

Pick the affirmation/s you like best. You can also use several and combine them differently. Repeat your affirmation/s at least ten times in a row, three times a day, for a couple of weeks.

Visualisation

Pick a recent situation where you said 'yes' instead of 'no'. Close your eyes, rerun the memory and practise in your head how to decline the demand in a calm and self-assured way should it be made again.

While you imagine yourself saying all the right words, feel yourself standing straight, shoulders squared, with good eye contact and a firm voice.

Alternatively, if you need to prepare yourself for an upcoming situation where you already know you will be asked to do something you don't want to do, practise with your eyes closed how to deal with it confidently.

TIPS

- Don't get stuck. Just because you said 'yes' to something in the past doesn't mean you are committed to doing it for life.
- Talk about your feelings when saying 'no'. If you say 'I don't feel right about this', it is much harder for someone to argue with you.

- Sandwich the 'no' between a compliment and an alternative. For example, 'This looks really interesting but I'm afraid I'm tied up at the moment. I'm sure Marion would appreciate being given this responsibility.'
- Buy time if a straight 'no' is too difficult. Say something like 'This isn't a good time. I'll let you know if I can spend time on it later.'
- Don't be vague. 'I don't really have time to do this' is not a clear statement of refusal because the word 'really' implies that there is some leeway. It's better to say 'I'm sorry but I just can't do this' and suggest an alternative.
- You do not have to give a reason why you won't or can't say 'yes', but it softens the blow for the other person if you do.
- There is no need to apologise profusely for saying 'no'. A brief 'I'm sorry' is absolutely adequate.

Case study

Sam (34) was a father of two boys aged seven and ten. He was in a managerial position at work and got on well with his colleagues and staff, but he felt that he had no control over his children at home.

Whenever the boys were unruly or did anything that Sam considered to be naughty, he told them he was 'disappointed'. When the kids still didn't toe the line, he sulked and was in a bad mood. He also expected his sons to do helpful things without being asked to do them, but this didn't happen.

Sam realised that this was not working but he could not stop himself from automatically responding with a sulk.

Sam had never really stepped into the role of father properly. He treated his children as if they were employees who should know what they were supposed to do, and if they misbehaved, he blamed them for it. Sam needed to learn to be the 'boss' with his sons, give clear instructions and insist on them being carried out in a firm but pleasant way.

Sam practised a few key situations in his imagination and soon got the hang of it. He visualised arriving home with his sons in the car. He wanted his elder son to get out of the car and open the garage door for him. He imagined addressing his son directly and instructing him to do this: 'Jeremy, can you please open the garage door for me?' Jeremy now had the chance to get it right and be thanked afterwards for having been helpful.

When the boys had a fight in the car, Sam learnt to raise his voice slightly and say very clearly that he wanted them to be quiet and stop arguing.

He started to feel more confident and in control, telling his kids what he wanted them to do; and the boys became more relaxed and less troublesome because they knew what was expected of them, and learnt to listen when they got a clear 'no' from their father.

Not taking breaks

It's a basic truth that no one can turn in their personal bests all the time, and no one can work all the time without taking breaks. And when I say no one, that includes *you*!

A-ha! moment 16 Switching off and taking breaks is crucial to high-level performance.

It is a common misconception that wanting to switch off is selfish, but the fact is that taking breaks is the only way you can keep up a demanding schedule. Just as elite athletes interweave training with periods of rest, and just as weight-training work-outs take place only every other day, so your emotional and mental 'muscles' need the time to recuperate. In this context, it doesn't matter whether your work consists of looking after your family or running a multinational corporation. You simply cannot constantly fire on all cylinders without taking breaks.

Taking some time out in a busy day should theoretically be an organisational matter, but in reality it is a very emotional one. When it is your job to look after your family, you may feel guilty when your children are getting on your nerves and you want some time on your own. For some women, the mere thought of wanting a few hours away from their children makes them feel really bad about themselves as mothers. And a similar thing is true for professional men and women who work very hard, either because the company demands it of them or because they demand it of themselves.

The emotion that is driving you through a relentless schedule is usually fear – fear of being seen as not good enough, fear of failure and fear of being swamped by an overwhelming workload. Once you take away the emotional content of your unwillingness to take a break, it usually becomes quite easy to organise yourself slightly differently and introduce some breathers into your busy day.

Breaks do not have to be long. Even a five-minute rest can work wonders. Try it out now!

Exercise

Sit down quietly and put your hands in your lap. Lean your head back and close your eyes for approximately five minutes, letting your everyday thoughts drift away. What happens now is that your body and mind start de-stressing, and this helps recharge your batteries. It also helps calm your emotions and makes you feel more focused and centred. So if you find it really hard to take time off, do a few of these five-minute breaks over a working day.

You will also need longer breaks during the year. Yes, I'm talking about holidays! A holiday is anything that takes you out of your everyday environment and away from your

continues

everyday chores. It doesn't have to be exotic, expensive or far away; it just has to be away from home. The relaxation effect of a holiday comes from being free of daily routines and chores, and it is often only when you are on holiday that you realise how much you needed it.

Affirmations

- I have a right to enjoy breaks in my daily schedule.
- I work hard and I deserve to take little enjoyable breaks throughout the day.
- I now start listening to my body and give it the rest it needs to function optimally.
- I can really enjoy little breaks throughout the day and luxuriate in the thought that I look after myself.

Pick the affirmation/s you like best. You can also use several and combine them differently. Repeat your affirmation/s at least ten times in a row, three times a day, for a couple of weeks.

Visualisation

This is an easy one! By doing *any* visualisation, you are already taking a break. Pick any scenario that appeals to you and that has a soothing, relaxing effect on you. Close your eyes and imagine a leisurely walk along a sun-drenched beach. Imagine lying in a blissfully comfortable recliner in a beautiful garden, or sitting in a meadow covered in flowers somewhere on a hillside, looking out over a marvellous landscape.

TIPS

- Plan your big breaks well ahead. For holidays, enter time off into your diary at the start of the year or, better still, in autumn of the previous year.
- Work in timed bouts. After 90 minutes at the latest, leave what you are doing and walk away from it for ten to 15 minutes. The brain thrives on variety, and just going to make a cup of tea will refresh the old brain cells.
- Do anything important at a time of day when you are at your best. For most people, this is in the morning.
- Make a list in the morning of all the things that need doing and build in breaks as one of the things to do.

Well, I suppose I had better own up here. Not taking breaks is one of my bad habits. If you have a lot to do, it seems such a waste of time to interrupt your work, and it is particularly tempting to work nonstop when you are working from home and the office is next door to your living room.

A few years ago, I was so inundated with work – helping clients, writing books and running my Positive Thinking correspondence course – that I was quite exhausted by the end of the year. I knew I had to rethink how I was going to run my working days so that I wouldn't get ill.

I decided to mark some weeks as holiday weeks in the coming year rather than leaving it to chance when I could take some time off from my busy schedule. I also divided time more clearly into work time and time off. I designated half a day a week for a cinema visit or any other entertainment and gave up my Harley Street practice, which I was running two days a week. This cut down on commuting to and from London's West End, which made a huge difference to the quality of my life.

I now have quieter days working only from home and feel a lot better for it.

Summary

If you don't respect yourself, no one else will. Treat yourself as you would treat your best friend – with care and attention! This will not only make you more successful in everything you do, it will also keep you healthier and more contented. Remember that you have to live with yourself 24/7, so make sure it is a positive experience.

CHAPTER 9

Balance versus overindulgence

When we are intent on pursuing an aim or just unthinkingly living day to day, we can easily get into a rut. We are doing the same things all the time, in the same way, irrespective of whether this works or not. It's easier to get a takeaway than to cook a proper meal; it's more important to further your career than to get a reasonable number of hours of sleep; it's simpler to stay at home and be bored than to make the effort to go out.

Or is it? If your life runs along the same lines, day in, day out, you can often find yourself facing an imbalance. If you eat only junk food, what happens to nutrients your body needs? If you spend hours at work, what happens to carefree fun? If you keep cancelling dates with friends, what happens to your friendships and your need for closeness and belonging?

We are often not aware of this imbalance, but only of an inner sense of discontent and a feeling of being stuck. The question is: what has happened to the other side of life, the complementary opposite? The missing link usually lies in a lack of awareness. We are so wrapped up in what we are doing that we lose the big picture.

Here are some areas in life that need to be in a good balance for you to be relaxed and comfortable within yourself:

- Work and play

- Solitude and company

- Security and adventure

- Rest and physical activity.

If you only ever get *one* of the two opposites, there is an imbalance.

You may want to ask yourself what the right proportion between the two opposites needs to be. Many people assume that only 50:50 will work, but this is not so.

Each one of us has our own personal preferences towards one end of the spectrum. You may be someone who enjoys the security and cosiness of a quiet life. There is nothing wrong with this, but make sure that you also do a few things out of the ordinary. You'll be relieved to hear that this doesn't mean having to climb Everest or joining your local bungee jumping group. For someone who likes to put their feet up in the evening in front of the telly, having a day out one weekend or finally inviting an old friend over for dinner can be quite an adventure, and that's fine.

You will know how much you need to do to counterbalance your daily routine. Trust your instinct!

The benefit of balance is that life doesn't become dull or exhausting.

Happy, successful people enjoy a variety in life without overindulging or becoming obsessed and one-sided. You can spot balanced people because:

- They enjoy themselves without getting obsessed.

- They are not addicted to substances or activities.

- They have a healthy respect for their well-being and are generally moderate in their eating and drinking.

- They know when they have had enough and act on this knowledge.

- They can balance things out if ever they go over the top by making up for their overindulgence later.

- They are able to enjoy both calmness and excitement, routine and adventure.

Affirmations

- I can find my own inner balance which allows me to feel comfortable within myself.
- I can learn to listen to my own needs and act on them. I can provide myself with the right contrasts to make my life happy and exciting.
- Only I can know how to find my inner balance. I trust my intuition completely.

Pick the affirmation/s you like best. You can also use several and combine them differently. Repeat your affirmation/s at least ten times in a row, three times a day, for a couple of weeks.

Visualisation

It is always best to build an image around your specific problem situation and see yourself dealing with it in a balanced way.

continues

For generally improving your sense of balance in life, imagine the following with your eyes closed:

- You are standing, looking down in front of you. Right in front of your feet, there is a line on the floor that stretches straight ahead of you for as far as you can see.
- Imagine dancing along this line, veering with your dance steps into the area left of the line, and then dance over into the area to the right of the line. Keep the line in the middle as your reference point while you are dancing.
- Become more daring by drifting further away from the line, but make sure you spend approximately the same amount of time on each side.

TIPS

- In order to keep a balanced work schedule, allocate 'work units' to specific tasks. If, for example, you need to drive out to see a client, give it 2 work unit points. If the client comes to your office, give it 1 work unit point because you don't have to travel. Each work unit point will then require the counterbalance of leisure activities like, for example, a five- or ten-minute break. Make these leisure activities compulsory.
- If you have overindulged, have a retribution activity ready. Say you have overeaten. Just ensure that you do more exercise that day or the next, or if you have been on the phone chatting for ages, start doing a cleaning or tidying job that is long overdue.

Case study

Roger wanted to get to grips with his addiction to television. Rationally, he knew he was wasting his time by sitting slumped in front of the box for hours on end, and he even admitted that most of the programmes didn't really interest him at all. 'But even though I'm bored, I just can't tear myself away from the box. There are so many more interesting things I could do instead of watching television. I feel really pathetic!'

Roger was in his late fifties when he came to see me. He was a company director, quite well off, with grown-up children who came to visit occasionally. He had a good relationship with his grandchildren, whom he babysat at times. As one of the top people in the firm, he was able to be flexible about what time to go in to work, and it didn't matter if he arrived late because he had been watching television all night long. 'I can't seem to motivate myself to get out of that armchair,' he confessed in his first session.

What Roger really wanted more than anything else was to have a partner. He had been divorced for many years but was concerned that, at his age, he would be unable to find someone else, and certainly not if he kept sitting in front of the television.

As Roger was a very visual person, he responded very well to mental images. His visualisation included seeing himself with a new partner, spending time together travelling and going out for dinners. Even food shopping in the supermarket became an exciting prospect with a partner by his side.

Roger began to find it easier and easier to leave the television screen switched off. Instead, he joined a salsa class, where he was spoilt for choice in ladies who were interested in him.

Phone-a-holism

Does one of your ears already have a permanent imprint on it from your mobile? Have the arm muscles on one of your arms overdeveloped through lifting the telephone receiver to your ear 24/7? Do you become severely ill-tempered when you can't phone your friends because you've run out of credit? Or have you contracted repetitive strain injury in your thumb from texting all the time?

Just as with other portable gadgets, phoning can become an obsession, especially if you are a very sociable person. It is one thing if you need your mobile for business calls but quite another when you use it mainly to chat with friends.

There are two indicators that will tell you whether you are having a problem with phoning. One is when you are on the phone to the exclusion of other things that you know you should be doing. The other indication that you are in trouble is if you have to start worrying about the bills you are running up.

You may think that all you are doing is keeping in touch with friends, and in this light, this isn't a problem. But look a bit more closely at your phone habit:

- Are you ringing the same person more than once a week or even every day?

- Are there quite a few friends whom you are ringing more than once a day?

- Is phoning a substitute for a social life?

- Are people closest to you, like your partner or your family, unable to get through to you because you are constantly on the phone?

- Is your work begining to suffer because you are constantly on the phone?

- Is your phone on overnight even though you don't expect any truly urgent calls?

- Do you make or receive phone calls mainly to gossip or discuss television programmes?

- Do you struggle to find the money to pay your phone bills?

- Are you in debt because of your high phone bills?

When a habit starts ruling your life or begins to put you into a quandary because you neglect important things by chatting on the phone, you have a problem that needs to be addressed.

Affirmations

- I now allow myself to turn my attention to my work/my family/my partner/the really important matters in my life. I enjoy being calmer and more focused with every day that goes by.
- I enjoy changing my life around and meeting up with my friends in person.

Pick the affirmation/s you like best. You can also use both and combine them differently. Repeat your affirmation/s at least ten times in a row, three times a day, for a couple of weeks.

Visualisation

Concentrate on images where you see your friends face to face. With eyes closed, visualise meeting up with your best friend and having an intimate one-to-one chat. See yourself going out with a bunch of friends, having a brilliant time.

If finances are a problem because of your long phone calls, imagine all the things you could do or buy if your phone bill were half of what it is now.

TIPS

- Keep most of your news to yourself until you actually see your friends in person. This will make you look forward to the meeting even more.

- Change your mobile contract to a tariff that restricts your speaking time.
- Turn off your mobile before you go to bed or, if your problems relate to a landline, put the answering machine on and turn the volume off.
- Make it a rule not to answer the phone in certain situations. Have an evening cut-off time, do not answer the phone when you have guests over, and switch the phone off when you are relaxing.
- Put your phone bill next to the phone if you are tempted to have another two-hour talkathon, to remind yourself that you are adding to your debts if you go on for too long.
- Set an alarm to limit your time on the phone.

Case study

Lucinda, who's 20, is a student and shares a house with three friends who are attending the same university. Lucinda describes herself as 'extremely chatty'. She spends hours on the phone every day, and when she is not talking, she is sending texts from her mobile.

Lucinda's wake-up moment came when she wanted to go on holiday but found she was drained of spare cash because of her phone habit. Her mobile phone bill was up to £100 most months, and even the landline topped £150 a quarter. Whenever her flat-mates wanted to use the phone, Lucinda was on it, and their families and friends would complain about the constantly engaged tone. Her constant phoning also incensed her boyfriend, who finally left her because of it. 'He felt that the phone was more important to me than he was,' Lucinda sighed ruefully.

In order to go on her holiday, Lucinda needed to sort out her finances and get a grip on her problem habit. She put a stack of glossy holiday brochures by the phone as an incentive, and to remind her what she was saving for. She also had to set herself a budget for her phone calls and had to stick to it by working out how much calls cost. Whenever she made a call on her landline, she set an alarm to limit herself to a reduced speaking time. She also changed her mobile tariff to a lower limit. When at home, she mostly turned her mobile off, leaving a message to say she could be reached on her landline. When she went out, she mostly left her mobile at home. 'That way, I can concentrate more on the people I'm with, which gives me plenty of free talking time!'

Lucinda chose to say the affirmation 'I'm taking control of my finances now and it is easy! I'm looking forward to my well-deserved holiday.'

Her visualisation was simple. All Lucinda had to do was see herself in her holiday resort, enjoying herself, eating exotic food, quaffing a delicious cocktail at the pool bar and soaking up the sun.

With all the practical changes and her new mental attitude, Lucinda cut down her phone bills by two-thirds and was able to treat herself to a very nice holiday with her savings.

TV addiction

I have not had a television for years, and I'll tell you why. Despite the fact that there was rarely anything on that I wanted to watch, I used to have it on a lot. I love pictures, I love pictures that move, and I like colours. Television is ideal for me because it flicks on at the press of a button, and it has lots of colourful, moving images flitting across the screen. When I realised that I spent more time getting annoyed about the poor quality of the programmes than enjoying the viewing, I decided that enough was enough, and I gave my TV set away.

I now read more and listen to the radio regularly. With the introduction of digital radio, some very interesting stations have appeared and I love listening to actors reading novels and poems. It helps me make colourful, moving picture in my mind much better than television ever could.

If you are someone who can view programmes selectively and switch the box off afterwards, good for you! That is the best way of using your television. But so many of us drift off into the next programme without having had the intention of watching it. Sometimes this can lead to a very pleasant surprise, but most of the time it's just the same old stuff that we don't really want to watch but leave on anyway. The pictures on the screen become moving wallpaper while we sit, inert, in front of the box, consuming meaningless or even annoying programmes.

Not only does this mindless staring at the screen make you feel tired, it can also cause stress and lead to insomnia. Even though the radiation from the screen dulls your senses and makes you lethargic, it also disturbs your body's electromagnetic field. While you are looking at the screen, the radiation overexcites your brain so that, even if you have nodded off in front of the box, you find it hard to sleep deeply afterwards once you have gone to bed.

Eating in front of the television is another no-no. If you are having your dinner, you shovel down your pizza, ready meal or, meat and (hopefully) veg without tasting anything or chewing what is in your mouth. You are usually hunched over a plate on a tray, bending your back so that your stomach is all squished together, which further undermines your digestion. There is no real harm in doing this occasionally, but if it becomes a way of life, it will play havoc with your health.

The real problem, however, lies in an addiction to certain programmes – and soaps are the most common of all. In severe cases, people arrange their entire life around the broadcast time of their favourite soap. Invitations are refused and social arrangements postponed because they collide with the next episode. Phone bills rocket as a whole group of friends need to discuss the implications of the latest episode and try to second-guess what will happen next. Quality time with partners is ruthlessly curtailed because it gets in the way of the next episode.

This is when you start to lose touch with reality. You are beginning to live in your head as you become involved in the fictitious life of people who you think you know, but who don't really exist.

Affirmation

- Get a life!

Visualisation

Fill your mind with the words 'exciting', 'thrilling' and 'inspiring'. Keep thinking the words over and over and watch which ideas, thoughts and images come into your mind. Do any of these images link up with a real-life activity that you can get involved in? If no ideas will come, think back and remember one time when your life was exciting, thrilling or inspiring. Can your memories help you experience these uplifting feelings again by inspiring you to take on new projects?

TIPS

- Have you had complaints from your friends or partner about your preference of TV over their company? Take these complaints seriously or you could lose the friendships.
- Wean yourself off the box by allocating certain days of the week to activities other than watching television.
- Force your hand by making arrangements to go out at least once a week so that you have something fun planned that will prevent you from slouching in front of the box yet again.

Case study

Lorna (43) is the mother of two-year-old Liam and lives out in the suburbs with her partner Simon. When pregnant with Liam, she spent a lot of her time watching television and became hooked on one of the soaps. She got into the habit of watching her favourite soap four times a week, but once Liam was born, there was no time any more to watch it during the day, so Lorna videoed the programmes to watch later instead. 'Initially, watching television was a great way of unwinding from the day's stresses, but at some stage it started taking over,' Lorna explained.

Her partner Simon got back from work around 8 PM each evening. At that stage, Lorna was putting Liam to bed, and after that, she was engrossed in watching a couple of the recorded episodes rather than speaking to Simon.

Lorna's wake-up call came when she forgot to video a programme for Simon but had recorded her soap instead. She realised that she was spending time watching other people's lives rather than taking part in her own, and this finally kicked her into action.

Whenever she felt like setting the video, she called a friend instead or ran herself a bubble bath. She also had to tell all her friends that she was trying to kick her soap habit. This was necessary because her friends had started using Lorna to catch up on the latest developments in the soap or to discuss the latest episode with her.

Lorna's affirmation was 'I have a full and exciting life and I'm going to live it now!' Her visualisation consisted of imagining all the alternatives to watching TV. With her eyes closed, she kept filling her mind with the words 'exciting and rewarding' and simply waited for her subconscious mind to throw up some ideas. 'My substitute good habits may not be exciting to the next person, but they are to me,' Lorna said. 'I've started cooking again, making meals from scratch, and making something special for when Simon comes home. That way, we eat together and have time to talk about what has been happening during the day. We now have our evenings back, which is so much nicer than when I was just glued to the box!'

Sweet fixation

When I was coming back from my holiday in Tunisia, my partner Carl pointed out a lady whose T-shirt said: ' Just give me chocolate and nobody will get hurt.' Entirely my sentiment! I find chocolate one of the hardest foods to resist in life.

Most of us don't feel too pleased with ourselves when we have had a chocolate or sweet binge, mainly because we think of the calories we have just consumed and what that will mean for our weight and shape. If you are a parent, you may also try to discourage your children from eating too many sweets out of concern that it will rot their teeth. All these are justified concerns, but the health implications are far more dire than most people realise.

If you eat lots of sweets and consume fizzy soft drinks on a regular basis, you are on your way to developing insulin resistance and diabetes. Insulin is a hormone produced by the pancreas. Hormones are the chemical messengers between cells, and for the body to function well, all of them have to be at their normal levels so that they can communicate correctly with one another. If your insulin levels are too high or too low, this communication breaks down.

Insulin's major function is to regulate blood sugar levels. It 'escorts' sugar into cells, where it is used as fuel, helping keep blood sugar levels on an even keel. It also protects the brain from receiving too much sugar, which damages cells.

If you eat lots of sweets, cells become so filled up that they can no longer take up any more sugar molecules. The cells then protect against further sugar overload by reducing the numbers of so-called receptors for insulin. A good way of picturing this process is to imagine that each cell has little 'doors' in it – the receptors – that can only be opened by insulin. If these doors are now bricked up, the insulin cannot unload any more sugar into the cell. There is now an overload of sugar in the body, so your pancreas goes berserk and produces more insulin to get rid of the sugar. This results in too much insulin in the bloodstream, and the cells start locking even more of their insulin receptors. The excess sugar begins to be dumped into fat storage. When the fat cells are also full, the sugar has nowhere else to go and so it remains in the bloodstream. This is type 2 diabetes.

People who are addicted to sugary food and drinks are often also addicted to refined carbohydrates, and will eat far too much bread, pasta, cakes, biscuits and other wheat products.

Check whether you have an addiction to sweets by answering the following questions:

- Do you always end up eating more sweets than you intended?

- Have you tried several times to give up sweets but were unable to do so?

- Do you build your day around eating sweets?

- Do you still eat the sweets even though they regularly make you feel unwell afterwards?

- Do you get moody when you can't have sweets?

If you have answered 'yes' to most of these questions, you are likely to have built up an intolerance to sweets.

Affirmations

- With every day, I'm leaving my craving behind more easily and moving forward to a calmer, healthier life.
- The sweetness of sugary food and drinks is becoming nauseating to me.

Pick the affirmation/s you like best. You can also use both and combine them differently. Repeat your affirmation/s at least ten times in a row, three times a day, for a couple of weeks.

Visualisation

Imagine you can see inside your body and imagine the right foods – try fruits, vegetables, lean meats or beans – going into the bloodstream. Imagine the insulin receptor doors in the cells reopening and watch the sugar molecules in the cells being used up for energising the body, making your limbs move and your brain work.

TIPS

- Have protein for breakfast, such as scrambled egg, bacon or beans on oat, rye or wholemeal toast; two hardboiled eggs; or cottage cheese on a bagel.
- You *must* eat breakfast to get over your sugar cravings.
- Keep a diary of what you eat and how you feel.
- Reduce sugar intake as much as possible. Remember that this goes for food *and* drinks.
- Make sure you eat three meals a day, ideally all with good-quality protein such as lean chicken, eggs, cheese or beans.
- If you must eat pudding, use a small spoon and eat slowly, savouring every bit. That way, you'll feel fuller sooner, so you eat less. Or, choose a healthy option like fruit.

Case study

Lynda is a 25-year-old marketing assistant with a particularly sweet tooth. Not a day went by without her having a sizeable amount of chocolate. When the cravings got hold of her, she would go to the egg compartment of her fridge where, instead of real eggs, she kept Cadbury Creme eggs. Sometimes she would devour a whole cake in one go or would skip a main course and have a double portion of dessert. Whenever she went into town, she would inevitably end up in a chocolate shop, where she would buy a bag of luxury chocolates or special fudge to eat on the way home.

As a consequence of her high sugar consumption, Lynda had put on weight and had problems getting into her clothes. Her eczema was out of control and she had to have numerous fillings in her teeth. I explained to her that her excessive sugar intake was aggravating her skin complaint, and as this was what bothered her most, Lynda decided to work on overcoming her problem habit.

We worked out a couple of affirmations for her. Lynda chose the thoughts 'I now allow my body to recover and my skin to heal. I am beginning to prefer the crisp clean taste of healthy foods to the sickly sweet smell and taste of chocolate.'

To help her come off sweets more easily, I devised an aversion visualisation for Lynda. She was to imagine that she was bringing a piece of chocolate up to her mouth, but even as her hand was getting near her face, she imagined a sickly sweet smell in her nose which was quite disgusting. She then imagined that she was putting the chocolate in her mouth, where she immediately became aware of a sickly sweet taste which spread through her whole mouth, and was so nauseating that she had to spit out the chocolate and rinse out her mouth with water to make the last remains of the awful taste and smell disappear.

This visualisation proved to be highly effective. In the event, Lynda found it quite easy to stay away from sweet things. Just in case she got a craving, she had plenty of fruit around which she could tuck into as a substitute. She also changed her route home to avoid sweet shops. Four weeks into her new lifestyle, Easter came around and Lynda was given an Easter egg made from her favourite chocolate. When Lynda bit into the Easter egg, she found – surprise surprise – that it tasted 'nauseatingly sickly', and that she couldn't eat it. 'That gave me the final impetus to kick my sweet habit for good,' she said. Her eczema improved dramatically and she lost half a stone in weight.

Retail cravings

Shopping has become a national pastime. It has ousted the cup of tea as prime comfort, distraction, reward and relaxation method – but it is much, much more expensive.

The easy availability of credit cards is what's driving this explosion in shopaholism. It is so much easier to hand over a piece of plastic than it is to count out banknotes at a till. Suddenly, you are within reach of a lifestyle that you cannot afford on real money but are capable of entertaining on credit cards. And unless you keep strict control of your spending, the rude awakening follows without fail. Even in 20-year-olds, this can easily go into four-figure sums.

Shopping is not unlike alcoholism. You don't particularly feel like you have a problem, and you are convinced that you could stop any time you want; it's just that you don't want to stop right now. And anyway, there is this amazing bargain which you couldn't possibly miss out on . . . And so it goes on.

Despite soaring credit card debts, shopping addicts stick their heads in the sand and continue to shop because they simply cannot stop. 'Shop until you drop' does not apply to shopaholics, because even if they drop, they can still order stuff over the internet. This is how important shopping can become – your whole life revolves around the next bargain.

If you find shoe, clothes or gadget shops totally irresistible, and can't pass one without popping in with your plastic at the ready, I have a remedy for you. It will cost you a bit of money but I personally consider it worth every penny. Here's what you need to do.

Book a two-week holiday in Tunisia or Morocco and spend at least three hours a day in the markets, where they sell clothes, shoes, handbags, jewellery and leather goods. Three hours every day, mind you! The cure will only work if you do it for several hours every day of your holiday.

This is what happens when you enter a North African market. A shopkeeper from the shop nearest you approaches with a big smile, arms spread out wide in a warm welcome. He speaks your language, no matter where you are from. He takes you by the arm and leads you into his shop where there may be nothing you would ever consider buying, but that doesn't make any difference to our shopkeeper. He is here to do his job, which is to sell you something, no matter whether you want it or not. Before you have politely disentangled yourself from his friendly armlock, he will have put a gold necklace around your neck and led you in front of a mirror where you will be encouraged in the most charming and persuasive way to say how wonderful and exquisite this piece of jewellery is. By now, you may have repeated four or five times that you do not wish to purchase any jewellery, but this won't stop the sales pitch.

The shopkeeper now enters the bartering stage. He will encourage you to tell him how much this gold chain would be where you come from. In order to please the shopkeeper and not hurt his feelings, you may now be tempted to give him a realistic but not too low value appraisal of his gold necklace. Big mistake! Now he has you where he wants you. He is going to give you an (according to him) ridiculously low price which will bowl you over! At this stage, you have said a few more times that you don't want a gold necklace, but you have still failed to impress this fact on him as he is now in full flow.

In desperation, you make your way to the door, saying 'thank you' ten times and handing back the necklace, and as you are approaching the outside of his shop, he runs after you, citing you lower and lower prices, but you escape in the end out into the street. (But this is only if you can say 'no'. If you can't, you will have bought whatever he wants you to buy just to get out of the shop!)

You are happy, you are relieved, you are ecstatic – you made it! And you didn't buy anything! You start walking along the street with a spring in your step when you suddenly see another shopkeeper a few yards further down the road who approaches you with a big smile and open arms . . .

Three days of this, and you will be cured of wanting to shop. I admit it's a bit of a radical cure, a kind of aversion therapy so to speak, but it has a long-term effect. It is one thing to be encouraged to shop, but quite another to be virtually forced. I know people who bought a rug in Tunisia because they felt it was the only way they would be let out of the shop again after two hours!

Affirmations

- I now take control of my finances and enjoy the satisfaction of using/wearing all the things I bought in the past.
- Thanks to good choices I made in the past, I now have enough exquisite clothes/shoes to wear which look fabulous on me.
- I enjoy saving up for a very special thing/purchase/holiday (name what you are saving up for).

Pick the affirmation/s you like best. You can also use several and combine them differently. Repeat your affirmation/s at least ten times in a row, three times a day, for a couple of weeks.

Visualisation

If you have chosen to save for something special with money you would normally spend on shopping, fill your mind with images of having achieved your special aim.

TIPS

- Know your weak times in the week. If you tend to use the late opening times on a Thursday for shopping binges, arrange to see a friend that evening instead.
- Leave all your credit cards at home when you go out.
- Pay for things only with your current account debit card and cheque book.
- Get all your latest credit card statements out and check how much you can pay off monthly on each of them.
- Consider consolidating your debts by getting a loan and then cutting up your credit cards.

Case study

At the tender age of 24, Clarissa had managed to amass debts to the tune of £22,000. She had spent freely on her credit cards, buying designer clothes and shoes and living it up with her girl-friends in upmarket London restaurants and clubs. She still owed her boyfriend her share of the rent, which came to £3,000. But none of this stopped her from spending more on luxury articles for herself.

She was now under pressure from her boyfriend to repay her debts to him. On her credit cards, she repaid only the minimum amount every month, so didn't really make any inroads into reducing the monies she owed. At the same time, she accumulated further debts through the interest accruing on the borrowed money.

Clarissa had manoeuvred herself into a position where she had lost control of her finances and was unable to sort out the mess by herself. After paying the minimum amount off her credit cards and her share of the household bills, she had no money left over at the end of the month, mainly because she continued to spend money on going out. When her boyfriend threatened to cut his losses and leave, it finally made her sit up and take notice of her overspending habit.

First of all, I sent Clarissa to her bank, which had been helpful in the past. The customer adviser sat down with Clarissa and went through all her credit card statements to get a clear picture of what needed doing. At the same time, he also totted up what Clarissa's monthly spending on clothes and entertainment were and how much she was bringing in from her telesales marketing job. He helped Clarissa consolidate her debts and cut the bills coming in to just one, so all this was now sorted out.

But none of this would work unless Clarissa actually stopped spending on luxury goods and expensive nights out, and that was what Clarissa was struggling with most. Her boyfriend offered to take her out more often, and they went for walks in the park and to little neighbourhood restaurants. They also spent more time together preparing and cooking nicer meals at home, and for half a year, things improved. Clarissa missed her bling-bling lifestyle, but stuck to her new regime and started to pay back some of her debts.

But when things didn't work out with her boyfriend in the end and Clarissa found she couldn't afford to keep up the flat on her own, she decided to move to London. The glitter of city lights was too much, and Clarissa fell back into her old ways. She replaced her credit cards, gave in to her urge for luxury goods, and was soon spending as much as she had before.

Rescue came in the form of Clarissa's mother. The ex-boyfriend had told her about Clarissa's financial mess, so this resourceful woman decided to intervene. She gave her daughter a good talking-to and checked up on her every few days to see that she was sticking to her agreement of going back to a more frugal lifestyle. She also persuaded Clarissa to take on an extra job in the evenings working in a wine bar to make some extra money. By making this move, she was in an environment she liked but was unable to spend any money while there. This gave Clarissa extra strength to stick to her good intentions and start repaying her debts again. She knows that it will take several years for her to be completely debt-free, but her resolve is strengthened and hopefully she will see her project through to the end this time.

Overeating

You used to only see grossly overweight people only in America, but the epidemic has spread. More and more people in the UK and Europe are now not only overweight but obese, which means the extra weight they are carrying is a health hazard.

Fast food with a high fat and sugar content is the main culprit. It is not a problem if you eat it only occasionally – say, not more than once a month – but eat it more often than that and it *can* become a problem.

The documentary *Super Size Me* by the American director and producer Morgan Spurlock showed what happens when you eat fast food three times a day for a month. Before his experiment, Morgan had himself checked out by a number of specialist doctors and a nutritionist. He was declared an ideal weight, very fit and in excellent shape. After only two weeks of eating three fast food meals a day, he began to develop pains in his chest and was advised by his supervising doctor to go to the emergency department of his local hospital *immediately* if the pains became worse. Worried about the amount of sugar he was consuming every day, Morgan's nutritionist begged him to at least stop drinking coke every day and replace it with water. He also gained weight, and felt lethargic and depressed. In addition, his girlfriend stated that his sexual performance wasn't what it used to be!

After four weeks, Morgan had gained an extra 15 per cent of his body weight and was quite ill. He still looked slim, but his health had deteriorated to such an extent that it took him eight months to get his weight back down again and his liver and heart to work as efficiently as before. This is a terrific film to watch if you want to fast-forward to the disastrous consequences that result when you eat too much sugary and fatty food!

There is no need to be thin. You don't even have to be slim, but if you want a good-quality life, you need to strive to achieve a reasonable weight for your body build. Eating sensibly and eating the right food is not just about weight, it is also about emotions. Feeling down can make you want to overeat, but overeating itself can also make you feel depressed (as Morgan Spurlock found).

If you eat to comfort or reward yourself, do the exercise on page 76 and negotiate a better deal with your subconscious mind. Build up your resources to give yourself more options in life and make you more resilient to stress, and find an eating regime that works for you. It is best not to exclude any particular foods unless you are intolerant to them. Cutting out certain foods only makes you want them more. Just cutting down on the amount you eat and improving the quality and kind of food will do the trick for most people.

Affirmations

- I can eat smaller amounts of food and still feel completely satisfied.
- My stomach feels much smaller and I find it impossible to eat as much as I used to.
- With every day I'm losing the excess pounds one by one, and it is really easy.

continues

Pick the affirmation/s you like best. You can also use several and combine them differently. Repeat your affirmation/s at least ten times in a row, three times a day, for a couple of weeks.

Visualisation

First, imagine yourself in front of a small plate with a modest portion, eating it with relish. Now imagine the food going down into your stomach and filling it quite quickly so that no more can go in. Next, imagine yourself in front of a full-length mirror, having lost the excess weight and looking so much healthier and slimmer. Feel the sense of pride in yourself and your achievement.

TIPS

- Never go food shopping when you are hungry. Grab a piece of fruit or a handful of nuts and raisins to snack on if you're in a rush to go shopping and haven't had time to eat.
- Healthy foods are mostly located at the back of supermarkets. Go straight there and use a basket or small trolley so that it is full by the time you pass by the unhealthy foods.
- Avoid the aisle with sweets and biscuits entirely.
- Always write a shopping list and stick to it.

Case study

Loren (29) was 5 foot 3 inches tall and had weighed around 12 stone most of her life. She wasn't particularly happy with her weight but decided to concentrate on her job, and ended up not doing anything about it. At the age of 20, Loren met Darren, and they soon moved in together. As both had demanding jobs, they ate out frequently, and the pounds began to pile on. When Loren became pregnant four years later, she put on even more weight. Her diet was the same as always: pizza, pasta, lots of bread with jam, crisps, chocolate. These eating habits went right back to childhood when she had constantly craved sweets and did hardly any exercise. At school she had regularly got out of PE lessons by saying she was ill.

When her daughter Daisy was born, Loren weighed nearly 14 stone, with a body mass index (BMI) of 33.7. She was obese and had to wear a size 20. She had no confidence and didn't even want to go out any more because she felt unattractive and depressed.

Loren's wake-up call came when she saw a photo of herself with Daisy. 'My first thought was that I should never have allowed Darren to take the photograph. Then I just felt awful and couldn't believe I'd let myself go so much,' Loren says.

She decided then and there that something needed to be done about her weight. 'I didn't want to be a fat mum and an embarrassment to Daisy once she started school.' Loren decided to join the postal programme offered by Weight Watchers. Her husband fully supported her. Even though he had no problem with Loren being the size she was, he could see it was making her unhappy and so encouraged her to join.

Loren joined an eight-week programme and she was given a book listing the points ratings of various foods along with a series of recipes. Instead of going to weekly classes to weigh in, Loren had to post off cards every week to report how much weight she had lost.

Even though the first week wasn't easy and Loren felt hungry at times, she was greatly encouraged when she found she had lost 4 pounds. 'Being at home with Daisy all the time made things a bit harder because the fridge was always there, tempting me!'

Gradually, Loren started eating better-quality food, reduced her fat intake and started introducing lean meats and vegetables, so the whole family was now eating healthier foods.

She was still not keen on exercise but decided to take Daisy for longer walks in her pushchair to help speed up the weight loss. 'When I got down to 12 stone after eight weeks, I could really feel the difference,' Loren reports. 'I had so much more energy and was thrilled that I could fit into my size 16 jeans again.'

Loren decided to renew her membership and continued to lose weight steadily until she had finally reached 10 stone – her target weight.

Problem drinking

With so many things in life, the trick is knowing when to stop. Everyone has their own specific cut-off point, but do you know where yours is? Can you refuse another cocktail or glass of wine at the point where your body can't cope with any more? Are you still in control of how much alcohol you consume on a daily or weekly basis?

Alcohol turns to sugar in the body and if you have a sugar intolerance, this may well be linked with your inability to control your alcohol consumption. Sugar craving is often a sign of sugar intolerance, as we've seen. When you eat chocolate or something sweet, you get a high from the sugar hit, but the sugar is then used up in the body and you start to feel cranky because of the drop in blood sugar levels. So to feel better again, you need your next hit of sugar – or alcohol. It takes a lot of determination to escape this vicious circle, and when you are drunk, this determination is simply not available to you. You feel happy, relaxed and a bit muzzy, and nothing really matters, and so you stay stuck.

Many people these days feel that the only way to relax and have a good time is through alcohol. They are too insecure to be relaxed without it; their life seems too dreary without drinking; their nightmares from the past threaten to overwhelm them without the godsent stupor of too much alcohol. Or they are simply sugar intolerant.

Whatever your personal reason for losing control over the amount of alcohol you drink, you will probably need some outside help to sort it out. The affirmations and visualisation that follow can give you support and additional help, but this is a formidable problem habit that needs long-term attention of a practical nature. Alcohol is everywhere, it is easy to buy and it is a social thing to drink when you are with others. It is outside the scope of this book to deal with actual alcoholism, but the affirmations and visualisation can still be valuable in supporting you while getting professional help. If, however, you have just gone off the track with your drinking and need to get a handle on your habit, you should find that you achieve good results with the following positive thinking methods.

What I would like you to do, though, is to check whether you are still in control, because that is something you need to know. Ask yourself the following questions:

- Do you drink every day?

- Do you think that you drink too much?

- Do you feel ill regularly after drinking but still continue to drink?

- Do you have blanks where you don't remember what happened during a drinking session? Has this happened more than once?

- Do you get maudlin when you drink? What are you really sad about?

- Do you get aggressive when you drink? What are you really angry about?

- Do you do or say things while drinking that embarrass you afterwards when you hear about them?

Even if you answer 'yes' to a few of these questions, you may not be an alcoholic, but you are certainly having a problem with alcohol. Check through the section on sweets (page 120) to see whether you have a sugar intolerance and do the exercise on page 76 to find out whether your drinking is protecting you from, or rewarding or comforting you for, something that is going on in your life at present or some old unfinished business from the past. These are good initial steps to show that you are taking the situation seriously. Health kinesiology can help you with sugar cravings and if you feel you need to deal with emotional baggage, go to see an analytical hypnotherapist, a counsellor or a psychotherapist.

Affirmations

- I can learn to stand strong and stay sober.
- Staying sober puts me back in control of my life.
- I can learn to live as a free person.

Pick the affirmation/s you like best. You can also use several and combine them differently. Repeat your affirmation/s at least ten times in a row, three times a day, for a couple of weeks.

Visualisation

With your eyes closed, imagine your liver and see it pitted and ragged and irritated. See it as having dull outer skin. Imagine lots of clean, clear water coming down into the liver, cleaning and refreshing all the cells, repairing the tissue so that it looks plump and shiny and is working efficiently again.

TIPS

- Avoid the places where you normally drink too much.
- Avoid the people with whom you normally drink too much.
- Get rid of any alcohol you have in the house.
- Get help from someone who specialises in alcohol problems.
- Take a different way home to avoid your local off-licence.
- Drink lots of water to flush through your liver and kidneys.

Working on sorting out an excessive alcohol habit is not easy, and if you are struggling to contain your consumption, it is likely that you have a serious addiction and suffer from alcoholism. It is very important to tackle the problem. In extreme cases, it can cost you your life if you don't.

My stepbrother was such an extreme case. He was brought up in a family where the mother marked her displeasure by throwing crockery across the room. After his parents divorced, he stayed with his mother while his brother went with the father, who moved to a different town.

A sensitive child grew into a sensitive man who was intelligent and competent but very easily hurt. He achieved good positions in his profession, but changed jobs a lot. Whenever he felt unjustly criticised, he would get very upset and hand in his notice. Whether the criticisms were justified or not no one was ever quite clear about, but a steady pattern of leaving jobs began to emerge.

He had got married after university and was father to three children, and somewhere along the way he had started drinking. He was drinking secretly, but his family found the stashes of empty bottles. When confronted, he denied that he had a problem. He always claimed that he could stop any time, only he didn't want to stop right now.

He started losing jobs because he was drunk at work. He had finally used up all his connections and goodwill from friends, and had reached the situation where absolutely no one was willing to offer him another job. He was now unemployed and unemployable.

He began to drink throughout the day. His wife needed to start working again and accepted a very demanding job with disabled children. She returned home in the evenings to find that her husband hadn't lifted a finger. Exhausted, she had to tidy up, clean and do the shopping.

Her husband continued to deny that he had a problem. He was rushed to hospital twice with severe liver damage and told that, unless he stopped drinking, he would die.

Finally, at the end of her tether and supported by her children, his wife decided to divorce him. She made sure that he found a flat and kept in regular touch with him.

The last time I saw my stepbrother, he had a distended belly and his skin was yellow. He smelled of alcohol. In fact, his whole flat smelled of it. We spoke for a little while and then I left.

Three months later, he was dead.

Smoking

It is amazing how you can become addicted to something that tastes so disgusting when you first try it. In my hypnotherapy practice, I have not met a single person who, as a teenager, liked their first cigarette, and yet they all forced themselves to have a second and third one. Where there is a will, there is a way! Why doesn't the same principle apply when it comes to eating vegetables? Maybe if all the adults said that vegetables are really bad for you and eating them was a disgusting habit, we'd have kids munching celery sticks behind the bicycle shed. Then again, maybe not . . .

Being addicted to cigarettes is like being in a bad relationship. You know you shouldn't be in it, but you make all sorts of excuses why the relationship is not as bad as it may look and why you couldn't possibly leave at the moment. You are living in a world of make-believe where you refuse to take responsibility for what is a problem by denying there is a problem in the first place. You are enjoying your cigarette, you are enjoying the nicotine hit, you couldn't possibly go through a day without it. You can't even remember what it feels like to take a deep breath or get up the stairs without puffing and panting, but you have to have the next fag when you get to the top to reward yourself for having done something to keep fit.

The reality is that it is not the smoking that relaxes you but rather the deep breaths you take when you inhale. A cigarette is also often an excuse to take a break, which of course is pleasurable in itself, so often people associate smoking with relaxing. 'A cigarette helps me think', 'smoking is a nice thing to share when you are chatting', 'I always smoke when I'm on the phone', 'I enjoy a cigarette after dinner'. All these are associations that smokers make that are linked to everyday activities. Subconsciously, smoking has been categorised as a pleasure-enhancer. You can see why it is hard to give it up!

Giving up smoking becomes easier if you start making negative associations with it. For most people, it is not enough to think about the health implications of smoking. Dying of a smoking-related disease is unreal to most people; it is too far away from them to act as a deterrent. What is more powerful is if someone close to you dies because they have smoked for years. This can be a very convincing wake-up call.

If you can remember the first cigarettes you ever smoked, it can be very useful to recall their unpleasant taste and smell. Even if you only pretend that cigarettes are disgusting, you begin to form a new negative subconscious association with your smoking habit which is helpful if you want to give up.

And, by the way, if you think that your smoking isn't so bad because you only smoke at weekends or when you go out, be advised that this is even worse. Binge smoking 20 cigarettes over four hours on a Saturday night is far more dangerous than smoking the same number over the course of a day. The amount of nicotine getting into the bloodstream is much higher, and puts incredible pressure on your lungs and heart!

Affirmations

- I deserve good health and do everything I can to promote it.
- I am strong and confident and refuse to be ruled by rolled-up, dried leaves.
- With every day, the taste and smell of burning tobacco becomes more distasteful to me.

Pick the affirmation/s you like best. You can also use several and combine them differently. Repeat your affirmation/s at least ten times in a row, three times a day, for a couple of weeks.

Visualisation

With your eyes closed, imagine the cancer-causing poisonous cigarette fumes destroying the lining of your nose and clogging up your lungs. Imagine the foulest possible taste in your mouth, like cow dung or dog mess, and a disgusting stench like sewage in your nose as you inhale.

TIPS

- 'Forget' your cigarettes when you go out.
- Buy smaller packets of cigarettes.
- Reduce the number of cigarettes you smoke every day by two. Do this for two weeks, then reduce the daily number by a further two.

- Drink lots of water to help the body flush out the toxins from the cigarettes.

Case study

Carl (53) began smoking at the age of 14. Most of the boys in his class smoked, and during lunchtime everyone would leave the school premises to puff away, always on the lookout in case they got caught by the prefects (who were probably smoking themselves). At that time, it was not only socially acceptable but practically expected of you to smoke, especially if you were a boy. 'It was like a rite of passage,' Carl remembers. 'When you were turning from boy to man, smoking was the thing to do.'

'When I went to my brother's wedding, relatives would offer me cigarettes. When I said I didn't smoke, they seemed surprised, as if it was strange I didn't smoke. So I thought – maybe I should be smoking, so I did.'

At the age of 16, Carl went to art college, where he encountered a more casual, bohemian way of life, but one that was still tied to smoking. The students joined the lecturers in the pub for lunch, and cigarettes were passed around while everyone was drinking – these two things went together. The more you drank and smoked, the more of a man you were.

'After college, I worked in television and the newspaper industry, both of which are professions which involve a lot of drinking and smoking,' Carl says. 'By that time, I was on 40 a day, sometimes even more.'

Carl moved to London while his parents were still in the north of England. His father, who had been a smoker himself, was diagnosed with throat cancer, which rapidly spread to his lungs. He died after nine months of illness.

'It wasn't actually my father dying of a smoking-related disease that made me stop. It was the way my mother looked at me when I was smoking after my father's death. She never asked me to stop, but I could see that she was thinking 'I lost my husband to smoking, and soon I'll be losing you as well.' That made me stop, and I haven't smoked since.'

Internet mania

The internet has become a type of interactive TV for some people. They have it on all the time and surf or visit chatrooms for hours at a time.

There is no doubt that the internet is an outstanding tool for digging out information. When I'm researching for a new book, I use the internet quite frequently, as I find it excellent as a source of information on certain health conditions or the latest literature on topics I'm discussing in my book.

What is worrying, though, is to see how easy it is to get prescription drugs over the internet. Every morning I'm inundated with spam adverts for pharmaceutical drugs. They are all filtered out by my spam filter, but you can still recognise the contents of the messages by their headlines, offering anti-depressants, pain killers, anti-anxiety and weight loss drugs without prescription.

Another worrying trend is the proliferation of websites geared towards helping you diagnose your medical condition. Some of them are good, but some of them are very superficial. They can make it relatively easy to get the wrong end of the stick. For instance, a friend of mine became convinced that she had cervical cancer after she started bleeding intermittently between her periods. She looked on the internet and found irregular bleeding diagnosed as cervical cancer. When she finally went to her doctor, he explained to her that her bleeding was due to having missed a couple of her contraceptive pills. The information on the website had been correct – intermittent bleeding *can* be a sign of cancer – but there are other causes for bleeding that the website had not mentioned.

One reason so many of us consult websites on health issues

is that doctors are often unable to spend time with their patients when they come with a problem. Driven by a crazy workload and stressed out by poor working conditions, doctors do not have the time to explain things or even just listen in more detail to what their patients are telling them. Patients often have a bare five minutes in the doctor's surgery before being sent off with a prescription or some basic advice. No wonder people look elsewhere for explanations and information.

As my regular readers know, I'm not a great friend of pharmaceutical drugs at the best of times, even if your doctor prescribes them to you. They are chemicals which are alien to the body and can trigger a host of side-effects which are often worse than the original complaint you are taking the drugs for. When you buy prescription drugs over the internet, you are unlikely to get information about these side-effects. Also, some of the drugs interfere with other drugs you might already be taking or even with herbal remedies you are currently on.

This is why trying to self-diagnose without further background knowledge can be risky. Go to your doctor if you like to go down the orthodox route and ask for tests, or go to an alternative practitioner if you prefer a holistic approach when sorting out your health problems. Let them check you out and then use the internet to look up the finer details. And remember that there are very good practitioners in both the orthodox and the alternative field, just as there are incompetent doctors and incompetent alternative practitioners. So ideally, go to someone recommended by a person whose opinion you trust.

It's not just over health issues that the internet can become a problem habit, however. Internet shopping can be just as much of a lure as all those gleaming shops on the high street (see page 124), and then there are the thousands of discussion forums and chatrooms. Any of the activities associated with these facilities, the writing and answering of e-mails, the suspense associated with replies and the fast turnaround time for replies, no matter where your correspondent lives, are all very alluring and can keep you glued to your computer screen for hours. This creates bizarre situations where we haven't spoken with close friends for weeks, even though they live around the corner, but where we correspond daily with someone who lives on the other side of the world. The skill is to enjoy what the internet has to offer but not allow it to take over your life.

Affirmations

- I can find a healthy balance between internet-time and real-life pleasures.
- The internet enriches my life but isn't my life.
- I resolve always to check my health diagnosis from the internet with a real-life expert.

Pick the affirmation/s you like best. You can also use several and combine them differently. Repeat your affirmation/s at least ten times in a row, three times a day, for a couple of weeks.

Visualisation

If you are worried about a health issue, skip the visualisation. Instead, get your phone book out and make an appointment with someone who has the professional knowledge and experience to diagnose and treat the symptoms that are worrying you.

If you have lost touch with your friends because you are addicted to mailing your web-friends, relax for a moment with your eyes closed and fill your mind with the words

continues

'fun' and 'excitement'. Check what ideas of real-life activities pop into your mind. Once you have stayed with your fun activity in your imagination and visualised it in as much detail as possible, open your eyes and start turning your visualisation into reality.

Case study

Lynette, who is 30, worked in advertising as a secretary and shared a flat with her sister. She was a true e-mail junkie – forever checking her messages, no matter how busy she was at work, and also checking them at home every five minutes. She also loved the internet, and in particular shopping. 'It's so easy,' she said. 'Just typing in your credit card details makes it feel like you're not really spending.'

Lynette's habit had an iron grip on her, to such an extent that she had to remortgage her flat to pay the debts she had run up shopping on the internet. She couldn't visit a friend without using their computer to check e-mail orders, and when her sister moved in with her, bringing her laptop, Lynette surfed for even longer. At least half an hour was taken up before and after work, checking for e-mail confirmations of her shopping, e-mailing friends and surfing for more bargains. Her worst nightmare was when the computer crashed occasionally. This would make her edgy and anxious because she was deprived of her 'fix' for a while.

Lynette's wake-up call came when her new boyfriend started teasing her about her preference for spending nights shopping online rather than giving him her full attention. 'And when my sister found out about my huge credit card bill, she gave me such an earful that it finally sank in,' Lynette said. 'My internet and e-mail hobby had become an obsession and a really bad habit.'

Radical measures were called for. Lynette agreed to cut up all her credit cards, bar one which she kept for real emergencies. She put the card in a sealed envelope and put it at the back of the top of her wardrobe, which she could reach only by using steps. She then changed her internet account to one that limited her surfing. Instead of e-mailing her friends, she arranged to meet up with them. Even though Lynette couldn't give up online shopping altogether, she now started using her current account card only, which automatically limited her spending. This way, she halved her time and her spending on the internet and improved her social life at the same time.

Lynette's affirmation was 'I now take control of my finances and improve my social life.' Her visualisation was to see herself meeting her friends and wearing the new clothes she had bought in the past. This visualisation worked well for Lynette because she found that she had bought so many pieces of clothing that she had already forgotten she had them. Some of them she hadn't even worn once since buying them, so this made them practically new for her.

Summary

On a number of occasions I have heard Californians taking delight in English grey skies, simply because they get fed up with the eternal sunshine in their country. Just another point to prove that you can have too much of a good thing, even if it is something as enviable as good weather! The same thing is true for other good things in life. Indulgence is fine, but overindulgence is a problem. Make sure you have a good mix of indulgence and restraint. It will help you get more true enjoyment out of the indulgence, which you do deserve every once in a while.

CHAPTER 10

Confidence versus panic modes

S ome people are born confident, and they retain their confidence, no matter what happens in their life. Other people are more hesitant and shy, never quite ready to say clearly what they want and much more dependent on positive feedback from other people. Sometimes children copy their parents' behaviour; but confident parents sometimes have shy children, and timid parents produce confident children. A lot will depend on the individual personality and the overall atmosphere at home during childhood.

Confidence is, in essence, the absence of fear and the presence of a sense of happy expectation. Confidence is *not* a devil-may-care attitude of reckless action which disregards your own and other people's feelings. It comes from inner calmness, a focused sense of purpose and a feeling of self-worth. A truly confident person does not have to shout, whine or manipulate.

A confident state of mind makes life a lot easier because things are straightforward – there are no hidden agendas. You know who you are, you know your strengths and your weaknesses, you have nothing to hide and you speak freely and easily. You are relaxed and polite. If anything is wrong in your life, you work on setting it right; if things go well, you enjoy them.

Confidence, in other words, is the presence of all the resources you have learnt about already: patience, flexibility, tolerance, inventiveness, love, perseverance, humour, motivation, honesty, consistency and pro-activity.

The benefit of confidence is that you get more of what you want in a stress-free way.

Happy, successful people deal with life in a calm, self-assured way and don't let others down. You can spot confident people quite easily because:

- They know who they are.

- They are themselves, no matter who they are with.

- They tackle difficult situations calmly.

- They know what they want in life.

- They make eye contact easily.

- They walk with purpose.

- They don't need to be the centre of attention but can handle it if they are.

Affirmations

- I can be/learn to be calm and collected, whatever happens in my life.
- With every day, my confidence is building to more and more comfortable levels.
- I can feel my confidence grow stronger and stronger, and I enjoy feeling in control.

continues

Pick the affirmation/s you like best. You can also use several and combine them differently. Repeat your affirmation/s at least ten times in a row, three times a day, for a couple of weeks.

Visualisation

Depending on the situations where you feel panicky rather than calm, build a mental image of success around that scary situation.

For building up confidence generally, use the following imagery regularly:

- With your eyes closed, visualise yourself with a strong centre in the middle of your body, approximately where your stomach is. Imagine that this centre stabilises and grounds you.
- Feel your feet firmly planted on the ground, your arms hanging comfortably down from your shoulders, and your breathing free and easy. Your shoulders are squared and your head sits proudly on the top of your neck.
- Combine this image with thinking one or several of your affirmations.

TIPS

- If you don't feel confident, pretend. It'll get you through the situation without losing face.
- Train yourself to maintain good eye contact. It looks confident and you will come across as being more decisive and sure of yourself.
- If you don't know what to say, smile!

- It's OK to leave a break in the conversation. You don't have to fill the silence.

Case study

Cherry (29) was very nervous about going out on her first date with a man she had met through a dating agency. She had been in a long-term relationship before, but hadn't needed to date at the time because she had met him on a working holiday, and things had developed from there. Before that, she felt she hadn't done too well when meeting men for the first time. She had always been very shy and didn't know what to say or how to behave during the date.

Cherry was now ready for another relationship but panicked at the prospect of having to meet someone new. 'I don't know what to wear, what to say or how to behave,' she said. 'I feel a bit silly, but I just don't have enough experience. I still remember those two first dates that didn't go well because I was so unconfident and shy.'

Cherry and I started off by looking at the practical side of things and clarified what would be best to wear and where to meet with her date. I gave her a few tips about safe topics of conversation and advised her to keep her first date relatively short – not more than an hour. However, the real work we needed to do was on Cherry's confidence. Her two unsuccessful first dates were firmly imprinted in her mind and made her feel very insecure about meeting her new man. She was convinced that she would fail again.

In order to build up Cherry's confidence and help her leave the past behind, she learnt to relax with a general visualisation (see page 83). We then thought up a few positive affirmations for her which she needed to repeat to herself several times a day. Cherry chose to use the statements 'I am confident as I calmly look forward to my date. I can have a good time, whatever the outcome.'

We then coupled the affirmations with a specific visualisation exercise where Cherry imagined herself walking into the venue, smiling confidently and greeting her date. She then imagined having a relaxed conversation with her date, laughing and chatting and feeling utterly at ease. This visualisation was her homework for a week to come.

Her date went very well. 'It was just as I had imagined in the exercise,' a beaming Cherry reported. 'We got on really well and I really liked him. And what's best: he wants to see me again!'

Not opening bills

Hearing mail drop through the letterbox can cause panic feelings in some of us. Maybe we are waiting for the answer to a job application or dreading our credit card sins finally coming home to roost.

If you are very scared of what you might read, you usually put all the letters in a neat pile somewhere in the kitchen – unopened. This just isn't the right time to face the music, but you'll definitely open those letters tomorrow, provided you feel strong enough, have time and are in the right mood for it . . . But that right time somehow just never seems to come.

Theoretically, we should just open the letters, check what the damage is and make plans to repay our debts; that is the logical course of events. In reality, the whole matter is a very emotional affair, especially when you know deep down inside that you have overspent and now have to deal with the consequences. Some people can grit their teeth and get on with sorting out their finances, but if your fears are too great, they can paralyse you. The mixture of fear, guilt and denial is very powerful and feeds on itself, and the longer you leave opening the bills, the more powerful the grip of those emotions is.

This ostrich policy of not facing the facts can lead to further complications when reminders and final notices join the stack of unopened letters and result in problems with your credit rating or withdrawal of services because you haven't paid up.

Just as some university students send a friend to have a look on the board to find out what their results are, so it can be easier to let a level-headed friend open your letters for you and tot up how much you owe. Better still, get someone to help you sort out your debts who is in a position to advise you professionally. Most banks will be happy to support you in your attempt to clear your debts and will talk through the options carefully with you.

The best way to ward off the nasty shock of debt revelation is to have a clear plan for a solution *before* you open the letters. Again, you might want to talk things through with a friend or financial adviser rather than trying to figure it all out by yourself. Talking about your problem with someone who is able to offer workable solutions helps make your financial problems less of a drama. It still won't be nice to have to face the facts, but at least you'll have a solution at the ready that will help you tackle the debts straightaway.

Affirmation

- I now take control of my finances. I'm relieved to know that everything can be sorted out.
- I can be strong and confident and look at my finances while staying calm and focused.
- It's OK to open the letters and look.

Pick the affirmation/s you like best. You can also use several and combine them differently. Repeat your affirmation/s at least ten times in a row, three times a day, for a couple of weeks.

Visualisation

With your eyes closed, imagine yourself sitting at a table, opening the envelopes calmly and methodically, pad of paper by your side, writing down the amounts for each bill carefully, totting it all up and reaching for the phone to make arrangements to sort out the debts.

TIPS

- Get advice from someone who understands about finances.
- Have a friend there when you open the bills, if you feel that would help you. You do not have to tell them what your debts are.
- Make sure you deal with the cause of your debts, not just with repayment (see also Chapter 9, page 124).

Case study

Harry (35) earned his living as a handyman and was probably the greatest chaos producer I had ever met. He was charming, but totally and utterly disorganised. He was always late paying any bills or submitting any forms because by the time payments were due, he had usually lost the relevant paperwork amid the chaos of his bachelor flat. He was also quite unconcerned about letters in general and didn't open most of them until a week later. It wasn't that Harry lacked the time, but he definitely lacked interest. 'I hate them things [letters],' he confessed.

This changed when he found a letter containing a sizeable cheque which was over a year old. This meant he was now unable to cash the cheque, and the company he had done the work for had in the meantime gone bankrupt.

Harry realised that he was losing out if he didn't get his act together. Although he felt that any bills were 'hassle' and any reminders represented an even bigger hassle, he recognised that if he got himself better organised, his life would be simpler.

The underlying problem with Harry turned out to be quite different from what I had initially expected. Harry had problems with reading. Not only was he practically illiterate, but he also needed glasses.

Once he got his eyes seen to and had attended literacy classes, he felt more in control and began to be more interested in opening letters and dealing with them. 'I won't be missing any more payments now!' he assured me.

Procrastination

Making decisions, big or small, can be hard. But why is it that some people can plunge headfirst into a problem and come out on top, while others thrash around indecisively for an answer they later regret? The fact is that some people are born with the ability to tune into their inner wisdom and instinctively 'feel' their way to the right solution, whereas others find it difficult to trust their intuition.

There are a number of stumbling blocks that prevent people from going with their intuitive feelings. For one thing, many of us don't trust our inner instincts, particularly if it is an important decision we have to make. We are so used to thinking rationally about problems that we have forgotten how to listen to that inner voice. Intuition is simply not considered a 'proper' tool for making decisions because it is based on feelings which can often not be substantiated rationally. You just have this strong thought in your mind that captures your attention, or a gut feeling which won't let go of you. This emotional reaction is so far removed from reasoned arguments that we are prone to dismiss it. And yet, your intuitive reaction to a person or a situation is there for a good reason, and if you have the courage and confidence to not just listen to your intuition but also act on it, you can start to turn your life around into something much more fulfilling.

Our intuition will often come up with unusual or even daring ideas that can be quite frightening. Even though they make you feel elated in the first instance, they can plunge you into great fears as soon as you actually start considering carrying them out. What if it all goes wrong? What if you can't do it? Many people fall at these first hurdles, even though, in theory, the intuitive idea appeals to them. The trick is to make sure you *can* do it. At this point in time, you need to throw yourself into serious and rapid research. Can you afford it? If not, how can you get the money together? Do you have the necessary skills? If not, where and how can you acquire them? Is there anyone out there who is successfully doing what you are intending to do? Can you get in touch with them and learn from them? Get your facts together and make this a priority. Find out as much as you can, especially if you are thinking of starting a project that involves a great outlay of money.

When you need to make a major decision, it is very important to let your *own* feelings decide. To decide something because you feel sorry for someone else is not going to help you be happier in your own life, and it often doesn't help the other person either. Remember that the happier you are, the happier you can make others.

A-ha! moment 17 If you live life with the handbrake on, it won't make anyone happy.

And one more thing – there are no right or wrong decisions, no matter what anyone tells you. You may have used your family and friends as a sounding board, and that is fine. But be very clear that, in the end, *you* will have to live with your decision, not them. All of a sudden, everyone is an expert, and if you ask ten people, you'll get 11 different opinions. This can be more confusing than helpful, so think carefully before you approach others for advice. Make sure they are confident, positive people who are successful themselves. Don't listen to anyone who spends their days in front of the television and has other people do the running for them. It is also often better to speak to people who are uninvolved in your life and who can advise you in an objective way.

Affirmations

- I stop faffing about and start living life like I mean it.
- I now take my own needs seriously and follow my intuition.
- I can learn to make decisions easily and effortlessly by trusting my intuition.

Pick the affirmation/s you like best. You can also use several and combine them differently. Repeat your affirmation/s at least ten times in a row, three times a day, for a couple of weeks.

Visualisation

Imagine your intuition as a wise old man or woman inside you who has the wisdom of your entire life and all the generations that have gone before you. This wise old man or woman has a quiet voice, though, so you need to listen carefully. With your eyes closed, imagine this wise old man or woman in as much detail as you can and give them a name. Put your question to them concerning the issue that needs a decision and listen to the answer you receive from them.

TIPS

- It's OK if your decision doesn't work out. Often, something good comes from a decision that seems to have gone wrong.
- Choose carefully whom you speak to in the run-up to turning your decision into reality.
- Check out facts and figures thoroughly before you commit yourself financially.
- Act on your decision as soon as you can.

The following case history is unusual in that the person concerned made several very important decisions in her life based on intuition and found that, in each case, she had made the right decision.

Case study

Yana (28) felt stuck in her old job. 'I could do it standing on my head,' she explained. 'It was no longer a challenge, and the point came where I knew I had to change and move on.' Yana didn't find it easy to leave her old job as it came with a good salary, and knowing the job inside out made her feel safe. 'But the urge to do something new was stronger than my love for comfort and security.'

Yana started applying for jobs in London and, to her delight, found a very good job there. As she lived too far away from London to be able to commute to work on a daily basis, she gave notice on her rented house and temporarily moved in with her father.

When a potential tenant came round for a viewing, Yana knew that there was something special about him. 'I couldn't put my finger on it, but Mike really captured my attention,' she remembered.

Mike took on the house and, a week later, Yana went around to collect her mail. They ended up talking nonstop for three hours and Yana found herself thinking that, if this was The One for her, she would never find out if she went off to London.

Mike asked her out for a drink and Yana found her first impression of him confirmed. 'I had an amazing first date with Mike,' she says. 'On the strength of this date, I decided to turn down my new job in London so that I could pursue our relationship.' However, Yana decided not to tell anyone. She didn't want other people to undermine her decision because she knew that she was taking a risk. Wisely, Yana also decided not to tell Mike about her decision, as she thought this might scare him off.

After their third date, Yana stayed over at his place – her old place – and never left. They are now happily married and run a design business together.

Checking and re-checking

Constant checking and re-checking is a stress reaction. If you feel overwhelmed by events in your life and everything gets on top of you, you can get into the habit of doubting that you can do anything right. As a consequence, you begin to doubt whether you have *really* turned off the cooker, whether you have *really* locked the door properly or whether you have *really* closed all the windows, so you have to go back, often four or five times, to check.

Observing someone doing their checking and re-checking routine might give the impression that this is really odd, and to the sufferers themselves it can feel as if they are afflicted by a mental disorder, but it is really not that bad. Checking and re-checking wastes a lot of time because it means you can never go out on the spur of the moment. It is a great nuisance to be afflicted with this obsession, but it can be dealt with. It might need some simple professional help, but if you follow the advice in this section, you might be able to sort it out yourself.

There are various ways of overcoming this habit. Ideally, you'll have someone to help you with it, maybe a partner, flat-mate or close friend, or, if you still live with your parents, your mum or dad or one of your siblings.

If you are the person designated to help someone with this problem, you need to know that sufferers may experience great anxiety if they can't carry out the repeated checking. They fear that something terrible, possibly life-threatening, will happen unless they check several times. Often, the checks that have to be carried out have a ritualistic quality.

One way of getting out of the habit of constant checking is to go cold turkey. This can usually be done only with the help of another person who is very firm and absolutely adamant and will not allow you to check more than once. This is tough, but it does show the sufferer that nothing horrible happens if they don't check several times.

A less drastic solution, and one that you can carry out your-self if you have this habit, is to buy a little booklet, and every single time you check, say, that the cooker knobs are off, you write down exactly *which* knob you turned off and at exactly what time of day. So if you normally check five times, continue to do so – but you *must* write it down in detail.

After a week or so, you can try to reduce this to checking four times only, but you *must* continue to write everything down in detail, as during the first week. In addition, use your affirmation and visualisation, and after reducing the number of times you check, you will eventually get rid of the habit altogether.

If you can't sort it out yourself or don't have anyone else to help you, see a hypnotherapist or behavioural therapist to help you with the problem.

Affirmations

- I can stay calm and relaxed as I gain confidence and gradually reduce my checking.
- With every day I become calmer and more confident and trust that I am protected.

Pick the affirmation you like best. You can also use both and combine them differently. Repeat your affirmation/s at least ten times in a row, three times a day, for a couple of weeks.

Visualisation

The best visualisation for this particular habit is one that helps you relax and also makes you feel protected. With your eyes closed, listen to your breathing for a few moments while lying or sitting comfortably. Gently tense and relax the muscles in your feet, your lower legs, your thighs, your stomach muscles, your chest muscles, hands and arms and shoulders. Once completed, imagine yourself with a guardian angel standing behind you who puts his hands lightly on your shoulders to keep you safe.

TIP

If none of these solutions appeals to you, you can also overcome your checking habit by changing an aspect of it. If, for example, you check the cooker knobs with your right hand, start checking with your left hand.

Case study

Brigid (38) was mother to three boys and worked during the day as a childminder for another two children. In the evenings, she supplemented her income by working as a cleaner. In addition to all of this, Brigid was also doing a college course. In the end, she decided to give up her jobs to be able to spend more time with her own children.

'It was a relief not to be working all the hours God's given, but at the same time I also felt guilty. It was as if I had let down the children I had been looking after. I saw myself as a failure because I hadn't been able to juggle everything.', Brigid said.

Brigid began to feel down and not her usual self. After using her gas cooker, she started checking it five or six times to make sure she had turned off all the knobs. After a while, she started doing the same thing with other electrical appliances such as the iron. Then, over a period of three weeks, the number of times she was checking appliances doubled and then trebled.

Brigid had to check all the time because of a very strong fear that the house might explode if she didn't, but the reassurance gained from her checking lasted for only a minute. She lay awake at night worrying about whether everything was switched off properly. Her depression became worse.

After a further month, Brigid started obsessing about hygiene and worried that she might contaminate her family's food and give them food poisoning. She now started washing her hands after touching anything. This, too, made her feel better for only a little while.

Brigid ended up washing her hands with soap and very hot water up to 70 times a day. It got so bad that her hands were permanently red raw, and would crack and bleed.

Brigid's wake-up call came when her youngest son wanted a cuddle and Brigid found herself shouting at him 'Don't come near me!' because she was afraid of contaminating him with the bacteria on her hands. When she saw the look of hurt on her little boy's face, Brigid finally decided to do something about her problem.

She came for hypnotherapy sessions with me, at which she uncovered some unresolved childhood incidents which had made her feel bad about herself. Once these memories had been worked through, Brigid started to feel her depression lifting and her compulsions to wash her hands and check everything began to lessen and finally disappeared.

Clutter chaos

If you're at home, look around you. What do you see? Do you find the floor strewn with clothes and paperwork, chairs and tables littered with piles of magazines and newspapers, the bin overflowing and the sink full of dirty pans and dishes? Are there plastic bags full of stuff cluttering up the hallway and half-open wardrobe doors with towels and bedlinen spilling out?

If the overall feel of your home is that your possessions are taking over like Triffids, you are what I call a chaos clutterer – someone who has lost control over their domestic environment.

To see whether you come into my chaos clutterer category, answer the following questions:

- Do you have to step over things when you walk through your home?

- Can you only sit down on chairs or sofas if you shift things off the seats?

- Are you unable to invite anyone over because your place is such a mess?

- Are all the rooms in your home untidy and messy?

- Would it take you more than one day to try to tidy up your home?

- Are you so overwhelmed by the mess around you that you cannot face starting to clear up?

- Has this mess existed for a long time?

- Are you adding to the mess on a daily basis?

All these are signs that you are losing or have already lost control over your living environment. Once you let things slide for a while, it can become a mammoth task to sort it all out again, and the longer it all goes on, the greater the reluctance to tackle the problem.

Clutter chaos is partly an organisational problem, but it is also emotion-driven. For someone who is not very methodical, staying on top of tidying up can be a nightmare, simply because they don't have a workable tidying system that helps with the daily task of sorting, cleaning and disposing. And the reason they don't is that they find it difficult to pay attention to one thing at a time.

If you're like this, you may find yourself picking up one thing to put away, and then getting sidetracked by something else you see. A classic example is someone who goes up into the loft to bring down a suitcase and ends up spending a couple of hours under the roof looking through old photograph albums. This is quite OK occasionally, but then you don't go up in the loft every day. Problems occur if you constantly get distracted when you need to tidy up, because then nothing or only very little gets done. This, of course, makes tidying up frustrating, and when an activity yields such meagre results, you are not exactly enthusiastic to tackle the task again the next day.

Clutter chaos can be a sign of anxiety and depression. The fact that you need to decide what you want to throw away and what you want to keep can cause great anguish in those who feel insecure, and they will insist that nothing is moved from where they put it. Newspapers are only glanced at because of lack of time, but they cannot be thrown away because there might be interesting articles in them that can be read at some stage in the future. And so the piles begin to accumulate on the floor next to the armchair. If anyone attempts to move these piles to a different room, the hoarder panics or becomes very agitated.

The cluttering up of the living environment can also be a sign that you are physically too exhausted to keep on top of the tidying tasks. In this case, you need to ask yourself whether you are overworked, and what you can do to remedy the situation (see also Chapter 8, 'Saying "yes" when you need to say "no"', page 99). Tidying up is normally not a physically demanding task unless you need to move heavy items around, which is rarely the case. So if you feel too tired or weak to carry out this activity, you need to look for the reason why your body lacks the energy to do what needs doing.

You know you have a real problem when you keep things that belong in the recycling or refuse bin, such as foil wrapping, polystyrene packaging, used paper plates, cigarette butts or half-eaten, stale or mouldy food.

If you find it hard to sort out your house or flat, start with a very small de-cluttering job. You can, for example, just go around and empty the waste paper bins in all the rooms into a black bin liner which you then take outside. Another way of tackling the task is to concentrate on one little corner of a room and sort out this small area. That way, you are making the task more manageable and you also avoid becoming worried because too much in the room is changing in one go. It is a very satisfying feeling to see a small area of a room starting to look neater and tidier!

There is, of course, always the possibility that you are simply sloppy or plain lazy, in which case turn to page 188 in Chapter 11 for some ideas on how to remedy this!

Affirmations

- I stay calm and relaxed as I begin to sort out a little corner of my home.
- I can easily handle ten minutes of light de-cluttering, and I'm beginning to enjoy taking control again.
- I deserve a pleasant, spacious living environment and I take pleasure in improving it bit by bit.

Pick the affirmation/s you like best. You can also use several and combine them differently. Repeat your affirmation/s at least ten times in a row, three times a day, for a couple of weeks.

Visualisation

Before you close your eyes to start your visualisation, pick an area in one of your rooms where you want to start tidying up. Take a moment to look at that area, paying attention to all the items that are cluttering it up. As you look at each item in turn, note which can be thrown away and which need to be kept.

Close your eyes and take a few deep breaths. Feel the air going in through your nose and down into your lungs, lifting your chest up on each in breath. Feel how the gentle rhythm of your breathing is relaxing and calming you.

Imagine yourself walking calmly towards your chosen corner and slowly and systematically sorting out the items there, putting rubbish into a bag to throw away and tidying away things to be kept. Feel yourself moving calmly and easily, reaching for things with fluid and self-assured movements, and watch how the corner of the room improves as you are working away at your own comfortable pace.

TIPS

- Initially, keep short the time that you set aside for your tidying task.
- Make the task as pleasant as possible by playing some music that you like.
- Make it a rule that you put everything you pick up where it belongs before you pick up the next item.
- Do not stop before you have finished your little task. As you have made it brief, this shouldn't be too difficult.
- Be strict with yourself so that you don't keep items that should be discarded.

Case study

Suzannah (56) had moved into a new house which needed a lot of work done. Her husband worked away from home during the week, which meant that Suzannah was left to arrange for workmen to come and give estimates for new windows and various decorating jobs. She felt anxious about taking responsibility for all these matters, and the general state of disorganisation in the unfinished house added to her unease.

In addition, Suzannah also liked shopping for furniture, and even though the house was already full of nice pieces, she could never quite resist another little side table or pretty chair. After a year in the new property, none of the needed refurbishment had been carried out, and the house was brimming over with furniture and bits and pieces which cluttered up the place.

Suzannah's husband was not best pleased when he returned at weekends. There was nowhere to sit without being surrounded by a plethora of junk and bits and pieces, as well as a clutter of furniture on which his wife had spent a considerable amount of money.

Suzannah knew that she needed to stop shopping and start tidying, but by now the clutter had accumulated to such an extent that she found it difficult to even think about getting started on it.

In her sessions, we worked on increasing her confidence and putting the matter into perspective. Rather than being over-whelmed by the magnitude of work ahead of her, we cut the job down into smaller chunks which were more manageable for Suzannah. She picked a particular area in her living room that was close to where her husband liked to sit as an area to start tidying up. She found it quite easy to do this, much to her surprise, and her husband was pleased that Suzannah had taken on board his unhappiness about the cluttered state of the house.

Suzannah eventually worked her way through the house by tidying away lots of knick-knacks into boxes and moving them into the garage. She couldn't face getting rid of any of her furniture. Instead, she distributed it more evenly throughout the house, which made it look a lot more spacious and inviting.

The tidying-up process took longer than anticipated, but in the end, it all got done.

Perfectionism

The bad news first: it is impossible to be perfect. Now for the good news: it is impossible to be perfect. Hmm . . .

You see, if you are trying to get everything absolutely right absolutely all the time, you are putting yourself under enor-mous pressure. Attempting to be perfect makes you work too hard at everything and leaves you exhausted and frustrated, because no matter how many hours you put in, it won't be perfect, no matter how much you want it to be.

Trying to be perfect is a thankless task which will leave you miserable, without the satisfaction of having achieved your aim. Attempting to do something very well, on the other hand, is more likely to lead to satisfying results. You may even get a very nearly perfect result!

Why does trying to be perfect make your life a misery whereas trying to be very good doesn't? Why is it that trying to be perfect yields imperfect results whereas trying to be very good often yields exceptional or near-perfect results?

The answer lies in your attitude. Trying to be perfect is usually a matter of trying hard, and trying hard makes your body and mind seize up. You become emotionally tense and physically rigid, and things can't flow. You are too uptight to perform well, whether you have to accomplish a practical task or an intellectual one. If, however, you set yourself high standards but label your desired outcome 'very good', you are taking the edge off your effort. You stay flexible, inspiration flows, the body is relaxed and the brain-hand coordination works optimally. So it is OK to *see* something as perfect in your imagination, but your intention should always be to do something very well rather than perfectly.

Some people get totally blocked by their desire to be perfect. They are so afraid they'll fail that they cannot face starting a job. If you are blocked in this way, your only way forward is to have the courage to permit yourself to be imperfect. Once the burden of perfectionism is off your shoulders, it will free up your inner energy to get started.

Insisting on being perfect yourself or expecting perfectionism from others is a sign of insecurity. It means that you as a human being are only validated if you deliver 100 per cent – ninety-nine per cent won't do. And even if you should manage to produce a perfect result, the pressure doesn't stop because now you have to perform the same miracle again when you are tackling the next task.

If you are haunted by an obsession to be perfect, ask yourself where you have learnt that you are only worthwhile if you produce top results all the time. Was it your parents who made unreasonable demands on you? Was it a teacher at school who pushed you past bearable limits? Or is it your partner who won't accept you unless you do everything just so? Whoever gave you the idea that you are worth less when you are not at your best was probably pushed in a similar way by someone close to them in their past.

But self-worth should not be dependent on top performance, and neither should recognition by other people. As long as you put a good effort into what you are doing, you deserve to be recognised for this. If you do well, that's even better.

Affirmations

- I now release the need to strain and strive and allow myself to concentrate with ease on the task ahead.
- I can learn to approach my tasks in a happy and focused way and look forward to very good results.
- Very good is good enough. I'm a worthwhile person, and I am good enough.

Pick the affirmation/s you like best. You can also use several and combine them differently. Repeat your affirmation/s at least ten times in a row, three times a day, for a couple of weeks.

Visualisation

Close your eyes and allow yourself to relax comfortably while listening to your breathing. Think of the task ahead and see in your mind's eye how you are carrying it out in a focused and easy manner. See things working perfectly, feel yourself breathing easily and moving effortlessly. See the result, which is very good indeed.

TIPS

- Cultivate a sense of sloppiness. Look for some task that is not very important and try out what it feels like to do it deliberately sloppily.
- Seek out people who make you laugh. Find the lighter side of life by watching funny programmes or reading entertaining books that make you smile. Cartoons can be great for that!
- Be clear that going for 'very good' instead of 'perfect' does not mean you are lazy. It just means you know how to heighten your chances of success.

Case study

Gemma (21) had just finished university and wanted to set up her own business designing mirrors and producing coloured glassware. She had done some very good work in the past, but as she was highly critical of her own efforts, it always took her ages to make herself get started on a new piece.

She had approached a shop owner who was interested in selling some of her work, but they wanted some extra mirrors, too. Suddenly, Gemma became even more blocked than she had been. Other people were going to see her work displayed in the shop and would have to pay money to buy it! She froze and was unable to go ahead.

Gemma had had an overcritical mother who had taught her daughter that she had to work hard at all times if she wanted to achieve something in life, and that nothing she produced was ever quite good enough. Being a good daughter, Gemma had taken these teachings on board wholeheartedly, even though she greatly disliked her mother for it.

In order to get Gemma's business off the ground, we had to get her started. I asked her for her next session to bring a truly tasteless and unworkable choice of coloured glass which she was to put together to make a truly awful mirror which no one would want to buy.

According to my expectations, Gemma brought in some very nice colours which, she admitted, did not meet my stringent demands because they went very well together. For her next session, Gemma was to 'try harder' and produce with these unfortunately very pleasant colours a hideous mirror. And what happened? Lo and behold – Gemma returned with a little masterpiece which looked beautiful!

Giving Gemma permission to produce something which was not only not perfect but even awful had freed up her emotions to let her get on with what she was perfectly capable of doing – producing very good work indeed.

Summary

Panic feelings can be overcome, no matter how great your fears are at the moment. As you help yourself calm down with the affirmations and visualisation in this chapter, you can begin to take little inroads into a more confident attitude which will allow you to let go of your fears gradually and at your own pace. If others can do it, you can do it too!

CHAPTER 11

Respect versus attitude hiccups

R espect isn't just an attitude towards others; it's also how we feel about ourselves. And it works both ways. We have already looked at valuing yourself, which comes from and will generate respect for yourself. But out of this self-respect also comes respect for others, and it is this consideration for others that makes for happy and fulfilling friendships and relationships.

Respect is the recognition that other people have their own needs which might be different from ours. Respect is also an interest and a willingnesss to understand these different needs and to fulfil them where this is necessary and appropriate. Respect does *not* mean sweeping your own needs under the carpet just to make other people's lives easier.

Valuing yourself and having respect for your own needs will prevent you from neglecting yourself, and your confidence will enable you to express your own needs calmly and politely.

Respect cannot be gained by coercion, as true respect is free of fear. However, everyone needs to earn your respect. No adult person has the automatic right to be respected, and that includes your parents. You are not obliged to respect someone just because they are related to you, older than you or in a better social position than you. You are equally not obliged to respect someone just because they are a doctor, priest, lawyer or teacher. If you are treated without respect by someone, you don't have to like it and you don't have to accept it. Depending on the situation, you need to use your confidence and self-respect to demand, firmly but politely, better treatment, or you need to walk away.

The benefits of respect are that you create and maintain harmonious relationships with others.

Happy, successful people are reliable, so that others can trust them. They have a positive outlook and are pro-active, and they respect others. They have self-discipline, both professionally and in their private life. You can recognise respectful people easily because:

- They arrive at meetings on time without rushing.

- They never gossip about others behind their backs.

- They are polite and stay polite even when things go wrong, but they are not a pushover.

- They keep their promises.

- They listen when others speak and don't interrupt.

- They notice when someone needs help and act on it.

Affirmations

- I respect myself as much as I respect others.
- I go through my day with dignity and self-respect.
- I am reliable, confident and strong.

continues

Pick the affirmation/s you like best. You can also use several and combine them differently. Repeat your affirmation/s at least ten times in a row, three times a day, for a couple of weeks.

Visualisation

Make sure you build your visualisation around the situation in which you tend to let yourself or others down.

For generally enhancing your positive attitude of respect towards others, use the following imagery:

With your eyes closed, imagine yourself going through all the people you work with, from the cleaning lady, the receptionist and your colleagues, all the way to your boss, and visualise yourself thanking them for their work or help. Hear yourself in your mind saying the actual words.

If there is someone you don't like at all, you still need to speak to them in your mind. If there is nothing you can thank them for, wish them all the best.

Do not move on to the next person until you have done the thanking or wishing the best properly with the previous person.

Once you have thanked everyone, stand in front of them all and take a bow.

TIPS

- Do the visualisation last thing at night. It is an excellent way to close on a positive note, and it is much better to wish someone the best than to waste your time resenting them.
- Sounds whacky, but a good variation of this visualisation is

to thank all the organs in your body, not just when you are ill. It is a great stress buster, makes you feel calmer and speeds up the healing process if something isn't right in your body.

Case study

As is often the case, it's not the person who is causing the problem who ends up at my practice, but the one on the receiving end.

This was certainly true for Amanda (24), a young mum with two children aged three and four. She had married young and was happy in her marriage with a supportive husband, even though he had to work away from home frequently.

Amanda's problem was a neighbour, a mother of two whom she had made friends with when they first moved into the neighbourhood. 'I like Sharon,' Amanda said, 'and I don't mind helping out. When I realised that she had little kids, just like I did, I agreed to pick hers up in the morning and do the school run. The agreement was that we would take turns, but somehow I seem to have ended up doing most of the runs. Recently, Sharon even asked me to babysit her two while she was off into town for a beauty treatment. I feel like an unpaid nanny!'

Sharon was taking advantage of Amanda's good nature and inability to say 'no' – not very respectful treatment towards someone who is willing to help out. On the other hand, it was up to Amanda to refuse the requests, but she just didn't have the courage to do so. 'I'm worried that we will fall out if I say no,' she confessed.

I explained to Amanda that it was essential that she clarify the situation with Sharon. The way to look at it was to think that she was giving Sharon an opportunity to get it right.

Amanda picked the affirmation 'I have a right to expect others to do their fair share.' Armed with this new attitude, she approached Sharon and said in a friendly but firm way that she didn't want to do more than three school runs a week. To her surprise, Amanda apologised to her and started pulling her weight by taking over her fair share of school runs. Sharon admitted that she had had a bit of a guilty conscience because she had felt she had been taking advantage, but thought that Amanda didn't mind as she had never said anything.

Time-keeping

Remember Clare from Chapter 4? Clare was late for everything, and finally learnt her lesson the hard way when she was two hours late and missed her return flight back home from holiday. Having to get through two days in the airport lounge without any money and a four-year-old who whined incessantly finally drove the message home that she needed to change. She felt stupid and guilty about this fiasco, which was clearly her own fault.

When she finally got home, she started making some simple changes to her life and found that her stress levels became much lower as a result.

People who have problems getting to appointments on time often think this is because they are very laidback. In reality, they are always in a panic, rushing and arriving out of breath wherever they go. This clearly is as far away from being laidback as you can get!

Being late all the time can be either an attitude problem ('What do I care if others have to wait?') or a lack-of-planning problem which then makes you panic. If your time-keeping disasters are due to the latter, please go back to Chapter 10 and do the general exercises starting on page 148.

But really, at base, either reason for being perpetually late amounts to an attitude problem. One is disrespect towards others, the other disrespect towards your own problem-solving abilities. You think 'I just can't be on time', which is a very unhelpful negative affirmation to give yourself. Here's how to remedy this.

Affirmations

- I owe it to myself to arrive unhurried and relaxed wherever I go.
- Everyone's time is precious, and I respect myself and others by arriving in good time.
- I can stay calm and relaxed as I competently organise myself to arrive on time wherever I go.

Pick the affirmation that best applies to you. Repeat your affirmation at least ten times in a row, three times a day, for a couple of weeks.

Visualisation

Close your eyes and allow yourself to relax comfortably while listening to your breathing. In your mind's eye, watch yourself getting ready to go to an appointment. See yourself getting ready in a calm and focused way, travelling in peace and quiet, walking confidently without rushing, arriving in good time. See the pleasure on the face of the person you are meeting as you arrive punctually.

TIPS

- Set all the clocks in your house to ten minutes early.
- Pin up a wall calendar where you enter all your appointments. That way you can keep track of what's coming up.
- If an appointment is particularly important, set alarms on your mobile phone for the day of the appointment.

- Stick a note on your bedroom door to remind you of an important appointment.
- If you have to go somewhere you haven't gone before, make time a few days before the appointment to familiarise yourself with the route to the venue. Ask a friend for help if you have problems planning the route.

Telling fibs

Lying and telling fibs are habits that are all too human. We do it to flatter others, escape punishment or gloss over a problem.

Lies on job application forms have become so common that companies that check CVs are booming. Some insurance companies have introduced voice detection on phone lines to spot false claimants, and you can now enlist an agency to track whether someone has opened your e-mail and if it's been forwarded.

Even though lots of lies are harmless social lubricants that keep relationships smooth, others can have a negative impact on your health and happiness.

One of the areas where lying is quite common is that of sexually transmitted infections (STIs). Although the incidence of STIs is soaring, 55 per cent of people wouldn't tell their partner if they had an STI, according to the *Durex Report 2004*. Chlamydia has been quadrupling over the past nine years, and will continue to spread further as long as people are not honest with their partners.

But it is not just the big lies that lead to problems. It's also the small ones. How often do we lie when a friend asks us about their weight or how they look in a particular outfit? We want to encourage and support and reassure our friend that no, her bum does *not* look too big in those trousers, when really it does. Fibbing to friends by telling them their weight isn't a problem when you really think it is may seem kinder, but it could lead to obesity in the longer term, which is obviously not good for their health.

We may not be honest with our employers, our partners or family and friends, but we also hide the truth from ourselves. Many of us don't want to face up to our expanding hips and thighs and, rather than diet, prefer to modify where we shop instead, especially as many clothes shops now accommodate our size denial. There can be a huge difference between a size 10 in a 'young' high street store and that in a mid-market store where an older clientele shop. Although sizing is arbitrary to an extent, there is a clear marketing advantage to being a bit more generous with your cloth – weight-conscious women will flock to a store that allows them to buy trousers in a size 10 rather than have to admit they really need a 12 or even a 14 because they have put on weight.

However, some fibbing may be the result of lack of awareness rather than outright dishonesty. Although some people don't tell the truth about how much they eat, it is often that they are unaware of all the little snacks they consume throughout the day that pile on the calories. While some people are in denial about the amounts they eat, others are genuinely shocked when they keep a food and drink diary for a week.

It's worth your while to work on becoming more honest with yourself and with others. Lying is stressful. It takes a lot of energy to be consistent in your lying, and people who do it a lot often end up depressed and filled with self-disgust. Ultimately, lying is self-betrayal. It's much better to work on getting the life you really want, rather than going through the stress of pretending to be something you're not.

A word of advice, though: don't shock your loved ones by launching an instant 'honesty assault' on them. Start on yourself first by taking a long, hard look at where you can improve. And the next time a friend asks whether their bum 'looks big in these trousers', and it decidedly does, look, then frown, wiggle your head and say, 'Hm, they're *not ideal* for you . . . '

Being honest is not just being critical, though. If you think someone looks nice, make sure you tell them. Compliments are a positive way of being honest.

Affirmations

- I can gradually learn to be true to myself.
- It is OK for me to look at myself and see a flaw. Seeing it gives me the opportunity to right it.

Pick the affirmation you like best. You can also use both and combine them differently. Repeat your affirmation/s at least ten times in a row, three times a day, for a couple of weeks.

Visualisation

With your eyes closed, imagine looking at yourself as if you were an outside observer. Watch yourself go through a typical day and observe what you see. Is there anything you see that you don't like? If so, how would it have to change to be better? Once you have completed your visualisation, think about how you can improve on that facet of yourself.

TIPS

- When you start being honest with others, stay polite and avoid extreme language.
- Learn to distinguish between necessary lies and unnecessary ones.

- Learn to distinguish between harmless lies and harmful ones.
- Set yourself a goal. Pick one area of your life where it is relatively easy not to tell fibs and be assiduous about self-honesty in that respect.
- If you have something nice to say to someone, be honest about that as well and tell them!

Case study

Gloria (49) was a polite person. In fact, she was over-polite. Everything was always 'excellent' and 'superb' when she spoke to someone else. She was gushing most of the time, and when she wasn't, she was loudly commiserating with tales of mishaps that were brought to her door. On the inside, however, things were quite different. She felt bitter and resentful that people unloaded their emotional rubbish onto her. She felt that she had enough to cope with, as she was saddled with a job she didn't like and was single again after the failure of her 20-year marriage. She felt that she had been shortchanged by life, and that other people were adding to her own misery.

Gloria was unable to be honest with her friends, who only ever came by when they needed something, and she had also never been very honest with her husband. Her marriage hadn't been a happy one because her husband had not been a very demonstrative person, but Gloria had suffered in silence and never complained to him about this lack of affection. And she certainly had never complained to her friends about her dissatisfaction, until one day her husband upped and went off to live with someone else.

In her sessions with me, Gloria learnt to take her own needs more seriously. She began to become more confident and self-assured and was now able to tell her friends in a kind but firm way that she was not happy being used as an emotional dumping ground, and never being invited out for enjoyable things.

As a consequence of her new-found confidence, she lost a few friends but found that her other friendships improved a great deal. She started having fun in life and felt calmer and more contented.

Temper tantrums

Have you ever sat on a plane with a child behind you constantly kicking your seat? If you have, you'll know what it feels like when anger builds up. If you are wise, you turn around early on and ask the child (and the mother) nicely to please stop the kicking. If you are used to suppressing anger because your confidence levels are low, you will just sit there and fume, with anger building up until you get so hot and bothered that you explode.

Anger as such is not a bad thing. It is part of our range of emotions and serves as a valuable warning signal that tells us something is not right. It just depends on how well you handle the follow-up to the first signs of anger.

> **A-ha! moment 18** Anger is a feeling of powerlessness, a feeling that you have no control over the current situation.

To be genuinely charming and giving is a great quality. However, for many people, pleasing others becomes a survival strategy which makes them bury their true feelings if they are unpleasant, such as anger. By not admitting that you feel discontented, left out, afraid or used by others, you let go of your integrity and give your power away in order to make yourself acceptable. Basically, the more of a pleaser you are, the angrier you get.

The short-term gain of pleasing others is a feeling of being acceptable. In the long term, though, you lose self-confidence and forfeit the respect and trust of others who sense that you are not being genuine. The price we pay for denial of anger is depression or illness.

Even though an angry person appears to be very powerful and is often frightening to others around them, they display a lack of confidence through their temper tantrum. They are afraid that no one will listen to them unless they shout. They don't trust anyone to do what needs doing, so they put pressure on them with harsh, angry words.

If you want to get rid of your temper tantrums, have a good look at yourself. Where have you learnt to believe that you are helpless and that no one listens to what you want? Where have you learnt to believe that you can never trust others? If there is unfinished business in the past, ask a therapist or counsellor to help you finish it. If it is your current life situation that makes you angry, what can you do *right now* to start resolving it?

Anger, by the way, is not the same thing as violence. Anger is a normal human emotion which we should learn to recognise as a warning signal and deal with in a constructive way. Violence is abuse and should not be tolerated.

Affirmations

- I stay calm and collected when I need to sort out difficult situations.
- I have all the necessary skills to resolve challenges in my life in a calm and considerate way.
- There is always a solution to life's challenges. As I allow myself to calm down, I can find these solutions easily.
- It is OK to ask for help if I need it.

Pick the affirmation/s you like best. You can also use several and combine them differently. Repeat your affirmation/s at least ten times in a row, three times a day, for a couple of weeks.

Visualisation

Imagine yourself lying on soft green grass in a beautiful green valley. The sun is shining and everything around is very still and peaceful. There is no one else for miles and miles. Imagine that this valley is the hand of Mother Earth which is gently holding you, keeping you safe and protected.

TIPS

- When you find yourself *starting* to get worked up, concentrate on your breathing and do not say anything.
- If someone annoys you, turn your head very slightly away from them so that one of your ears is marginally out of 'earshot'. While they keep on annoying you with their talk, check which ear is better turned away – the right or the left.

If you are at the receiving end of a temper tantrum, leave the room and say that you will come back later, when they have calmed down.

Case study

Philip (24) was married to Barbara. Both had finished their training as teachers and had started work, in different schools. While Barbara loved teaching, Philip found it quite hard to deal with children. Being a perfectionist, he did not want to admit to anyone that he was not very comfortable being a teacher, so he struggled through his days, feeling miserable most of the time. He found it difficult to sleep at night and his mood deteriorated. He became tetchy towards Barbara and even snapped at friends on the phone.

Deep down inside, Philip felt that he had chosen the wrong profession, but he thought that it would be admitting failure if he gave up. He felt that he had invested too much time and effort in his training to start all over again in a different profession.

As his anxiety became worse over time, so did his temper. Barbara kept asking him what was wrong and even suggested that he might have problems at school, but he fiercely denied this. When he threw a plate during an argument, Barbara told him that he needed to sort himself out or she would leave him. This was when Philip finally started taking notice of what he was doing to others and sought help.

He was initially reluctant to cooperate, but I managed to persuade him that he would be able to enhance his performance (always an incentive to a perfectionist) if he could boost his confidence when in a class environment. We worked on a few childhood issues which had been holding him back from relaxing and experiencing feelings of self-esteem, and his temper tantrums gradually became less and less severe.

In the end, Philip himself suggested that he was in the wrong job and said that he wanted to retrain for a different profession.

Gossiping

There are few things as destructive as gossip. When you see two heads move together, and one person looking over their shoulder, it's bad news – not just for the person who is being talked about but also for the people doing the gossiping.

There is a saying that great people talk about ideas, average people talk about events and small people talk about others. Maybe this is the reason why tabloids sell so well and soaps are so popular. Both deal with other people's miseries, shortcomings and scandals in lurid ways, and human nature seems to be attracted by negative news. Soaps thrive on people wanting to discuss their characters' lives with others, speculating, judging and sounding off about their actions.

If you engage in gossip, you become a walking tabloid – cheap and sensationalist. Talking about others behind their back is false and dishonest, and it makes you an untrustworthy person. When you gossip yourself, you criticise someone behind their back, someone who is not there to defend themselves. When you listen to someone else gossiping, you can be sure that they will be talking about you the moment your back is turned. In other words, you become someone who is a loose cannon and will not attract relationships that are any better.

I have a neighbour who is just such a person. (I'm not gossiping here because you don't know her name!) I once met her in the street, where she addressed me with the announcement that the council was useless and incompetent. She had asked the council to come and have a look at our damaged street sign which she wanted it to repair. The two men who had come from the council to check what needed doing were approaching us at that very moment, and my neighbour turned round to them, sweet as pie, and said, 'These two gentlemen will sort things out for us.'

What was the point of having complained about them to me in the first place? Was she just trying to make herself appear important by having a go at them behind my back? Or was she, worse still, trying to show me how skilful she was at pulling the wool over these men's eyes? Whatever the reason, I wasn't impressed and try to avoid her now as much as I can.

The worst scenario is if you have to work with gossipers. It is difficult to stay out of it, and it makes a very negative atmosphere at work if you are surrounded by people who discuss others all day long. The problem is that gossiping is an aggressive activity, and this can be frightening to someone who does not wish to gossip. You want to be on the good side of a gossiper in order not to incur their disapproval, but this is not possible. The best way of dealing with the situation is to change jobs if you can. If you cannot do this, give as little information about yourself as you can unless you want it discussed by everyone else. You will also have to resign yourself to the fact that you will be an outsider if you refuse to join in the gossip.

A bad working atmosphere needs to be dealt with by management, but if management are not communicating with staff, problems can grow worse and eventually undermine morale and productivity.

Check whether you are causing problems for others by talking behind their back.

- Do you spend time every day discussing other people with friends or colleagues?

- Do criticise people behind their back without telling them that you don't approve of what they are doing?

- Do you you find that people often stop talking when you walk into a room?

- Do your friendships fall apart easily?

Gossiping can be a bad habit, but it is not necessarily linked with malice. However, if you want quality relationships in your life, I strongly recommend that you work on becoming more humble. It's not as if you are without faults yourself or have never made mistakes. Bear that in mind the next time you criticise someone else behind their back.

Affirmations

- I can learn to become more respectful towards others.
- I can speak to others directly and respect their dignity at the same time.
- I have the humility to admit that I will never know the whole story about other people, so I might as well respect their privacy.
- Pick the affirmation/s you like best. You can also use several and combine them differently. Repeat your affirmation/s at least ten times in a row, three times a day, for a couple of weeks.

Visualisation

This is one of the few habits for which I won't give you a visualisation. My recommendation to you is that you find an interest in life, a hobby of some sort, that will fill your head, so that your thoughts will be about things other than other people's lives.

TIPS

- When you speak about others, always speak as if they were standing next to you.
- Make it a good new habit to tell everyone else if someone has done something well, but never when they have done something badly.

Case study

Juliana (20) had no friends. At school, she had been in a clique that dominated the classroom. She had occupied a powerful position because she was big and strong and not averse to hitting others. She had been surrounded by 'friends' who agreed with everything she said. She maintained her power by spreading nasty rumours about those girls in her class who didn't toe the line as far as she was concerned.

Juliana had left school at 16 and started work as a shop assistant. She continued her gossiping, but this time she met her match. One colleague Juliana had gossiped about asked to have a private talk with her, and confronted her with what she heard Juliana had said about her. Juliana apologised and was a bit sheepish for a while, but after a couple of weeks she went back to her old ways. The manager called her into his office and had a talk with her about her attitude. She was given a verbal warning and asked to seek help with her attitude.

Juliana turned out to be a very hard-working client. I found out that, as a child, she had been remorselessly bullied by her elder brother. Her parents, who had sometimes witnessed her brother hitting her, never intervened or told the brother off. Juliana felt humiliated and abandoned, and the only way she could vent her anger was by bullying others.

Once we had worked through her anger and distress about things that had happened to her, Juliana became calmer and more relaxed, and her attitude changed for the better.

Laziness

Some people are born idle, but in many cases there is something else behind the unwillingness to get going, and it is important to differentiate between different forms of inactivity.

If you feel unable to get going, you may be suffering from exhaustion. That is not the same thing as laziness! If small tasks make you feel unduly tired, you need to check out whether your energy levels are too low. There are a variety of reasons why this could be the case. You may be simply overworked, or there could be a problem with your thyroid or your diet. If you have an allergy and continue to eat the allergenic food, it will make you tired and depressed because your body cannot function properly.

Another reason why you may feel tired and unable to do anything is anxiety. When your mind is racing with lots of fearful thoughts throughout the day, this will sap your energy and immobilise you. Once you have overcome your fears, energy levels can return to normal and you feel better able to lead a more active life.

But then there is also the possibility that you are bone idle. If this is the case, you will probably need someone else to help you get going. Ideally, there will be a compelling reason that will act as an incentive to help you pull yourself out of your laziness. It would be nice if this incentive were something pleasant rather than a dire necessity, but either of them works.

A-ha! moment 19 Sometimes life needs to give you a kick up the backside before you are prepared and able to change.

Here is a list of signs that tell you that something is not right:

- Having to do any task, even if it is a very simple one, puts you in a bad mood.

This can be a sign of being depressed or that you suffer from anxiety. Alternatively, you could also be overworked. Seek professional help.

- Just thinking about having to do something the next day, even if it is only easy everyday chores, puts you in a bad mood.

You may be depressed or suffer from anxiety. Alternatively, you are physically exhausted. Seek professional help.

- You have missed out on good opportunities in life because you couldn't get off your backside to fill in a form or make a phone call.

This could be a sign that you are lazy. You probably have other people running around for you, doing the things that are really your job to do, but then, it takes two to tango! Maybe I should congratulate you on having unpaid staff . . .

- More than one person has told you that you are lazy.

This may or may not be true. Check carefully whether it is depression that is preventing you from becoming active, or merely idleness.

- You think you are lazy but this is not enough to make you do anything about it.

Chances are that you really are lazy, otherwise you would want to make an effort to get out of your idleness – even if it is just a case of going to your doctor to have a check-up.

- You are not interested in anything except not being disturbed.

This can be a sign either of being depressed or being bone idle. If you find that unpleasant memories from the past or general negative thoughts go through your mind, you are depressed. If you are just hanging out in a semi-stupor, listening to extremely loud music, you are probably a teenager and will hopefully grow out of it soon. If you are over 25 and still hanging out in a stupor, listening to extremely loud music, you are a lazy layabout and need a kick up the butt.

Remember: if you are inactive because you are depressed, anxious or exhausted owing to overwork, see a therapist or counsellor to help you overcome emotional obstacles and physical deficiencies. If you are truly lazy, maybe you are lucky enough to have a friend or family member who is willing to help you become more active. This friend needs to be a strong personality who won't cave in when you moan and groan about having to do things.

Affirmations

For anxiety or depression:
- I am slowly releasing my inner tension and becoming more peaceful inside.

continues

For exhaustion:
- I now treat my body with the respect it deserves and allow myself some rest, followed by a small task.

For bone idleness:
- Today I prove to myself that I can do a small task for myself. I look forward to the satisfaction of having completed something by myself.

Visualisation

Anxiety, depression and overwork:
- Concentrate on your belly button. With eyes closed, imagine energy running down your front and up your back, over the midline of your head, down your nose, your throat and down to your belly button. Do this visualisation seven times in a row and imagine how your body relaxes and your mind calms down.

Bone idleness:
- Imagine your worst enemy being given total control over you and the only way you can escape their regime is to become active.

TIP
- Ask for help!

Case study
The worst case of laziness I have ever seen was shown in a television documentary a while ago. The couple in question had one daughter who was nearly as lazy as her mother.

The mother spent most of the day sitting down, either in her bed with her feet up, or on the sofa or in an armchair. She had a little bell next to wherever she sat which she would ring if she wanted anything.

Her husband went to work and, when he got home, had to do all the housework, the cooking and the shopping because his wife would not lift a finger, not even to make herself a cup of tea. Instead, she would furiously ring her bell and shout at her husband to get her this or that or the other. Even though her husband hated being bossed around like this and even though he shouted back at her, he nevertheless did as he was told.

All this began to change when the time management team came in. They realised that the wife wanted to lose weight and pointed out to her that she was not moving enough to shed the extra pounds. They then devised a plan whereby the wife had to start doing little chores around the house which were gradually increased to give her a workload equal to her husband's. At the same time, the husband was advised not to do any of the chores that had been allocated to the wife.

The transformation after a few weeks was amazing. Not only was the wife starting to lose weight, but her relationship with her husband had improved. She was in a much better mood and started enjoying getting things done around the house. Her husband was also much more contented, and their constant bickering and arguing had stopped. Their daughter became more active, too.

Summary

It might be simpler to do just as you please in life and not care how other people are affected, but the long-term repercussions of this attitude are serious. If you don't consider other people's feelings and needs, people will start mistrusting you and ultimately, they will try to avoid you.

You can improve your relationships with others considerably and feel much better within yourself if you work on your attitude. Go on, it's not that hard. It feels great having true friends and commanding genuine respect from the people you have to deal with every day. You can do it!

CHAPTER 12

Relaxation versus stress

P hysical relaxation allows the body to rest and gather new energy. We normally get this benefit at night when we are asleep, but depending on our circumstances and state of mind, we may at times need more than just a good night's rest.

If your life is currently very stressful, your body's energy levels will become depleted by the constant demands made on them. In this case, extra relaxation during the day is needed to allow the body to re-balance. This can take the form of a brief powernap or little breaks during the working day. A change of scenery can also be helpful, even if it is only a ten- or 15-minute walk outside your office building or in your neighbourhood.

Relaxation is important because a tense body not only creates a muddled brain, but also has a detrimental effect on your emotions. And if you have a problem habit that is linked with anxiety or fear, relaxation is a fundamental skill that you need to work on as a priority. Once you feel calmer and physically more relaxed, your emotions will be on a more even keel, and you can think clearly again.

Physical relaxation is inextricably linked to mental relaxation. If you need to perform mentally, retain new information and access your memory bank effortlessly, you can only do so when your body is relaxed. Physical tension prevents sufficient amounts of oxygen from getting to the brain, which in turn diminishes its ability to work properly.

The benefits of relaxation are better health, a clearer head, better decision-making and greater inner calm.

Happy, successful people are relaxed because they are confident and calm. This translates into a physical repose, rather than the need to be always fiddling about. You can recognise relaxed people easily because:

- They are unhurried in what they do.

- They can sit still for a long time, only occasionally shifting to adjust their seating position.

- They can allow their hands to rest comfortably and use them only for emphasis when they speak.

- They move calmly and purposefully.

Affirmations

- My whole body is beginning to relax comfortably as I become calmer.
- I am poised and move effortlessly and with dignity.
- My hands can rest comfortably as I relax.

Pick the affirmation/s you like best. You can also use several and combine them differently. Repeat your affirmation/s at least ten times in a row, three times a day, for a couple of weeks.

Visualisation

Your visualisation will work best if you build it around your particular problem area.

To generally enhance your ability to physically and mentally relax, use the following imagery:

With your eyes closed, imagine a soothing golden liquid flowing from the air above you into your body, from your head down your neck and into your shoulders, gently down into your arms and all the way down into your hands. Imagine the golden soothing liquid flowing from the air above your head through the top of your head down into the trunk of your body, relaxing and soothing all the muscles and organs in your body, making everything work in perfect harmony together. Imagine the golden liquid continuing down into your legs, flowing right down into your feet and toes, soothing and calming and relaxing every single muscle and fibre in your body.

TIPS

- At the end of a long day, soothe away your tensions with a chilled eye compress. Douse two cotton-wool pads with cold witch hazel (keep the bottle in the fridge), wring out gently and put one over each eye.
- Yawning relaxes your body. Open your mouth really wide and let it all out! If you are somewhere where you can't do your hippo impression, try a long deep sigh instead.

The following case history is a good example of how you can change habits even if they date back many years. Moral: it is never too late to make positive changes!

Case study

John (45) had recently remarried. His wife Deborah had brought a two-year-old daughter into the marriage and had just found out that she was pregnant with John's child. Although all these events were happy ones, they were also quite stressful and made John feel tired and strung-out. As a consequence, he found it difficult to sit still when he came home from work. He was forever jumping up and fiddling with something, unable to sit down and chill.

'I have always been a bit like that anyway,' he explained. 'Even as a child, my parents couldn't get me to sit still. Now, having a new family, matters have become worse. I find it really hard to do nothing. I know I drive everyone else nuts with my jumpiness, but I don't seem to be able to stop it. Deborah is great as she is a very patient person, but I should really look after her rather than her having to try to calm me down when I get home.'

Like most people who are a bit anxious and have a nervous disposition, John was very good (to his surprise!) at learning how to relax. He practised his relaxation visualisation (see page 196) religiously every evening when he came home from work, and he soon noticed how he was able to sit down for longer and longer periods without feeling compelled any more to jump up and do something.

Overworking

So many of us work hard these days, but how many of us can gauge when we're overdoing it? If you have already found yourself reflected in Chapter 8's section on 'Not taking breaks' (see page 103), you may want to consider the following questions:

- Are you always the last to leave work?

- Can you not sleep because work issues are still going around in your mind?

- Is work taking up more than 80 per cent of your waking hours?

Unlike some people who consider work the ultimate four-letter word, I consider work a good thing. Even working hard is a good thing, but you need to know where to draw the line. If there is nothing in your life except work, you are likely to be becoming blinkered, one-sided and uptight in your thinking.

If you have answered 'yes' to the three questions above, this has already started happening to you. Eating, sleeping and taking breaks, by the way, do not qualify as non-work activities. They are survival essentials, not alternatives to working!

Things that qualify as counterbalance to working are seeing friends (and not talking about work all the time when you're with them), going to the cinema, theatre, opera or any other performance which has nothing to do with work, playing an instrument, painting, swimming, dancing or any other hobby that has nothing to do with work but is purely for your amusement, entertainment or personal interest.

So how are you doing on that score? If you cannot find anything in your daily life that constitutes a counterbalance to your work, why is that? Are you short of ideas? Or do you feel unable to say 'no' if more demands are made on your time, even though you already have more than enough to do? Or is there some old hidden agenda that makes you feel you have to prove yourself over and over again? Or have you lost the sense of when you have had enough? Many of these issues are connected, but let's look at them in a bit more detail.

Being short of ideas for what you could do outside work is a sure sign that it is high time for you to find an interest other than work. It almost doesn't matter what you do, as long as it is not connected to work. Start small. Once a week for half an hour is not exactly a massive counterbalance to six days working ten hours a day, but it is a start.

Allow yourself three bouts of ten minutes each to think about what interest you want to build up outside work. Do your thinking while carrying out a trivial task or use the visualisation on page 200.

If you cannot think of anything during the first ten minutes, go and do something else for at least two hours. Then think again, but don't take more than ten minutes over it. If you have an idea, start pursuing it immediately by making enquiries, booking up or getting ready for starting in any way possible.

If you have still not thought of anything, do something else for another few hours and then make another attempt. If you still can't think of anything, you need to ring a friend and ask for suggestions.

If you cannot work up enthusiasm for anything you have thought of or that was suggested to you, simply do the next activity you find mentioned in your local newspaper – join a local running group, photography club, dowsing society, sky-diving set, drawing class . . . Or simply take the least offputting idea you have had. For ways of creating ideas, do the visualisation on page 200.

If you are overworking because you can't say 'no' to unreasonable demands being made on you, go back to Chapter 8, page 92, to build up your self-esteem.

If, however, you find you cannot rein in your inner slave-driver, you need to ask yourself where you learnt to believe that you are not good enough unless you work yourself half to death. What terrible thing have you done in the past that says you are not allowed to have any fun in life? What are you making up for by working non-stop? Go back through Chapter 2, starting on page 23, and check whether you are making the problem worse in any way.

If your problem is that you simply don't know when to stop, there is a simple solution. For one week, make a note of how many hours you work every day. Now make a clear rule about the maximum number of hours you want to work on an average day, and make this maximum number half an hour less than your average working day. If you have skipped meals and not taken breaks, fill this free half-hour with these essentials (see Chapter 8 for more on how not to neglect yourself). If you are already eating and resting between bouts of work, start filling the free time with something pleasurable. Do this for one week, then gradually reduce your working time further until at least 20 per cent of your waking hours are available for things other than work.

Affirmations

- I deserve to have fun and enjoy entertainment during my working week.
- My pleasure is just as important as my work.
- Every day I'm happily working towards my enjoyable entertainment.

Pick the affirmation/s that suits you best. You can also use several and combine them differently. Repeat your affirmation/s at least ten times in a row, three times a day, for a couple of weeks.

Visualisation

With your eyes closed, fill your mind with the words 'enjoyable entertainment' and see what ideas pop into your mind. Don't exclude anything just because it seems too outrageous or unaffordable. Imagine no limits to what you could choose to do, as long as it is something enjoyable. You

continues

can always cut an idea down to size or moderate it when you start thinking about actually putting it into practice. If it helps, start off by choosing a category first – for example, 'physical activities', 'group activities' or 'learning activities' – before you start your visualisation. This might help by narrowing down the choice to something that is particularly important to you.

TIPS

- Make yourself do something with your free time, even if to begin with it is only contemplating a flower or doing a breathing exercise.
- Be adamant and stick to your chosen activity for at least six sessions. It's OK to change it later, but give yourself a chance to try it out properly before you dismiss it.
- Having 20 per cent pleasurable non-work activity one day a week is better than 0 per cent, but strive for several fun intervals a week if you can.
- If you really cannot make the time for your fun activity one day, make up for it the next. Just dropping the fun activity is *not* an option.

Case study

Samantha (30), a single mother, felt exhausted most of the time. She had set up a business for 'pamper parties', which she ran from home via her website. This meant checking orders, meeting customers, sending out estimates and dealing with her beauticians. This could at times be quite demanding, and recently there had been problems with one particular girl whom she had to dismiss and find a replacement for within 24 hours. Besides running her business, she had to look after her three-year-old daughter, Estelle. During her occasional evenings out to the gym or to see friends, a neighbour looked after Estelle.

Mornings were Samantha's worst time of the day. It was all she could manage to peel herself out of bed. 'It isn't that I don't like my work or find it demanding looking after Estelle. It's just that I'm so tired. Even though I sleep soundly, I feel shattered when I wake up,' she said.

I checked with Samantha to see what a typical weekday looked like for her. The first thing she did once out of bed at around 7.30 AM, even before she showered, dressed or ate breakfast, was to go to her computer to check whether any new orders had come in for her business. Once at the computer, she then went on to do some admin work, typing letters and sending out quotes for customers. By that time, Estelle had already woken up and was gallivanting around the flat.

Next, Samantha would make something to eat for Estelle and sit with her, looking through the post that had come in. She would nibble on a piece of toast and drink a cup of tea while chatting to Estelle, and then drive Estelle to her infant school.

Once back in the house, Samantha started tidying and cleaning the flat and had another bite to eat by grabbing something from the fridge and eating it over the sink. Then it was back to the computer and the phone, dealing with any business matters that had come up, or food shopping. It was then time to collect Estelle. 'By the time I have given Estelle her dinner and a bath and put her to bed, I have not had a single minute of relaxation or "me-time",' Amanda sighed. 'I don't mind working, and I love my daughter to bits, but I also resent that there doesn't seem to be any time for me. If only I wasn't so tired!'

Amanda needed to make some adjustments to how she dealt with her work. She also had to delegate some tasks, something she had never considered doing before.

I pointed out to Amanda that she could create 'me-time' by getting someone else to do the cleaning for her. At first, Amanda was reluctant because it would cost money which, as a single mother and with a new business that still needed to get on its feet, she felt she didn't have. However, she promised that she would look into it and eventually managed to find a cleaner whom she felt she could afford.

This problem was solved, but a second problem occurred when it turned out that Amanda did not use her free time to relax or to do something for herself. Instead, she filled it with more work. 'I feel a bit guilty if I don't do anything or spend time on myself,' she said.

I see this attitude in many people who come to my workshops or for individual therapy. On the one hand, they feel resentful that they have no time to themselves. On the other hand, they feel guilty when they don't do anything 'productive'. Together we worked out an affirmation for Amanda to use: 'I can learn to respect my needs and gradually relax a little more when I have time to myself.'

Amanda's visualisation was to imagine she could watch a film in which she saw herself working all day. She then imagined going into the film and giving her film-self a gold star as a reward. She then imagined being the film-self and being presented with a gold star for her hard work. These images helped her feel more comfortable about relaxing, and she managed to start taking a bit of time off to relax in a chair and listen to some favourite music when she needed a break.

The hardest thing for Amanda was to stop going into her office immediately after getting up. It took her quite a while to retrain herself to go down and have a proper breakfast before she even switched on the computer, but she finally managed to establish this good habit. Allowing herself to rest more and look after her own needs gradually made her feel calmer, sleep more deeply and feel more awake during the day.

Popping pills

For many of us, life is hectic and the days are full of things that need doing and other things you want to do but have to cram into an already busy schedule. Executives of multinationals are affected in the same way as housewives and mothers.

The pace is fast and furious and you stop noticing what is happening to your body – until it starts to play up, that is. You suddenly realise that you are not sleeping very well or that you take ages to go to sleep in the evening. Or you start feeling anxious and overwrought, possibly even a bit depressed, without really knowing why. Or you start feeling tired and rundown because there is no let-up in your daily schedule. Everyone is affected in different ways and everyone has their own 'pain threshold' of stress they can tolerate before body or mind starts giving off warning signals.

Once you begin to notice these danger signs, you can do one of two things. You can either take notice of these signals, or you can wave them away impatiently and pop a pill. Either way of dealing with the problem has its advantages and disadvantages.

Popping a pill is easy and convenient. You can continue in your usual routine and let the drug take care of the side-effects of your lifestyle. With a bit of luck, the pill sorts out your phys-ical or mental problems. If you are overtired, the pills gee you up and make you feel awake again; if you feel down and depressed, they lift your mood; and if you can't sleep, they relax you sufficiently to allow you to drift off. Sounds good so far.

But there are disadvantages. If you stay on the pills over any length of time, your body begins to rely on them. And because you have switched off your warning signal, there is nothing there any more telling you that things are not as they should be.

So if you worked too hard before taking stimulants, you might now load on even more hours of work because you know that the drugs will even out what damage you do to your body's energy balance. If you felt very low before taking antidepressants, you are now off the hook and don't have to look at what was making you feel unhappy in the first place. If you were bored before taking recreational drugs such as LSD or ecstasy, you are now having a fabulous time tripping (unless you die in the process, of course), and never end up looking at what is missing in your life.

These disadvantages may not sound all that grave – until the pills start not to work any more, or to cause side-effects. If this happens, everything suddenly becomes 1,000 per cent worse than the original problem ever was. Depending on the chemistry of the pills you were taking, your body may be screaming, your mind confused and your general condition highly unpleasant. You may not be able to think straight, your bodily functions can change for the worse and you could struggle to do even simple things.

If, on the other hand, you decide to look at the underlying reasons *why* you are having the sleeping problem, the anxiety or depression, this has a number of disadvantages as well. It is time-consuming and often tedious to try and understand what is going wrong. You might even have to spend money to get someone to help you find out why you are below par. (Mind you, pills cost money as well, even if you get a prescription from your doctor.)

Another disadvantage of taking notice of your symptoms is that you might come to the conclusion that you need to make changes to your life, and that could cause havoc to you and everyone else around you. Couldn't it?

Perhaps – for a bit. But the major advantage of taking the warning signs seriously and looking at the underlying cause is that you will get things sorted out eventually, and your life will be considerably better than it was before.

The choice is yours – quick fix followed by agony, or agony followed by a solution. I know it's not easy, but you can always change your mind whichever route you take.

Affirmations

- It's OK to look at what needs changing. I can do this with a calm mind.
- I value my health and now start making the changes that help me heal.

If you are struggling to come off pills:
- I am strong and confident and can reduce the drugs gradually, and step by step I'm regaining control.

Visualisation

Before you do this visualisation, make sure you've been to the toilet and then drink a large glass of water slowly.

Now imagine, with your eyes closed, your entire body getting heavier and heavier, sinking down into your chair or bed, sinking lower as your whole body begins to relax and unwind, your arms and legs heavy as lead. Imagine the chemicals in the pills beginning to be flushed out of your system by the water you drank. See the chemicals dissolve and the organs in your body becoming cleaner and fresher. Feel your breathing increase in a slow and comfortable way and imagine how each breath releases further chemicals via the lungs and your nose, slowly emptying your body of any toxins.

Once you have finished your visualisation, drink another glass of water. Do this slowly.

TIPS

- If you need medical support during times of stress, opt for herbal remedies rather than chemicals. Invest in a visit to a herbalist to make sure you are taking the right combination of herbs for your condition.

- It can sometimes be necessary to take pharmaceutical drugs, but these should be reserved for emergency situations and should not be considered a long-term solution.
- Consider physical causes for your distress. Root canal and amalgam fillings can be at the bottom of unexplained physical and mental complaints. Go to a holistic dentist and make sure your fillings are not causing you problems.
- A life coach will be able to help you reorganise your life, should that be necessary.

Case study

Emma started taking ecstasy for the first time at the age of 15. Although she was scared and knew of the risks, she took it to impress her older boyfriend. That first pill had a very positive effect on her: within half an hour, she started feeling very happy, confident and beautiful and spent the night chatting away to people. Even the come-down wasn't as bad as she had expected – she merely felt tired and dehydrated. Even though her relationship with her boyfriend didn't last, she was determined to take the drug again because it had made her feel so good.

Emma started living for the weekends, when she went clubbing and took ecstasy. Sometimes she was given the drug for free, but most of the time she had to buy it with her own money which she earned in a part-time job.

By now, Emma had become devious, lying to her mother about where she was going and what she was spending her money on. Things escalated rapidly and soon she was taking up to four ecstasy pills a night. When she felt one was wearing off, she would panic and take another.

Emma began to suffer from memory lapses and once collapsed in a club and came round with blurred vision, convinced that she was going blind. She was beginning to wonder what the drug was doing to her body. Her friends at school noticed how gaunt she looked. Her weight was fluctuating wildly. Because ecstasy suppressed her appetite, Emma would go without food for two to three days; but then, when her appetite returned, she'd eat until she was sick. 'I remember sitting on the kitchen floor eating a whole loaf of sliced bread in about ten minutes, then throwing up because my body couldn't cope with the sudden binge,' she recalled.

Emma also started suffering from frightening mood swings. After nights out, she would sit crying in her bedroom, petrified that she would feel awful for ever.

Her wake-up call came when she took two ecstasy tablets at a party and felt extremely ill. Her heart was pounding, she felt faint and then she began vomiting blood. She was too scared to call anyone in case she got into trouble. She just sat in the bathroom and cried for hours. At that point, she promised herself that she would never take ecstasy again.

Coming off the drugs left her seriously depressed. Emma also had trouble sleeping. She comforted herself with the thought that if it all became too much, she could always kill herself.

Emma was also left with severe eating problems, and was bingeing more and more. Within a year, none of her clothes fitted her any more. She had gone from a size 12 to an 18.

She finally decided to see her doctor about her depression, hoping he would refer her to a counsellor. 'My doctor didn't seem interested in listening to me and simply wrote me a prescription for Prozac.' Emma was too afraid to tell him about her drug problems, which she was convinced had caused her depression, because she was very worried about her past drug use remaining in her medical records.

Emma didn't want to replace one mood-enhancing drug with another, so she decided to throw out the Prozac and find another way through.

In the end, she resolved to take up running in a bid to get her body and head back together. She started very slowly, just five minutes at a time in her local park, and slowly her appetite started to stabilise. She also started cutting back radically on alcohol. Over the next year, she lost 3 stone and started to feel her depression begin to lift. She still feels that ecstasy has done serious damage to her mental health and that bouts of depression will keep on recurring, but she feels able to deal with them now in a constructive way.

Worrying

A worrier always feels that they have a good reason to feel worried. Maybe it is to do with newspaper reports and media coverage of disasters and conflict that set the tone for our thinking, but for many, worrying is a learnt habit. If you think back, you'll probably discover that one of your parents was someone who worried a lot.

Worrying can be expressed openly or in an indirect way through behaviour or implication. Some people express their worries openly by outlining all the things that could be going wrong. 'Put on your jacket or you'll catch a cold', 'don't leave your job – you'll never know whether the next one is any better' and 'why is he late? I hope he hasn't had an accident!' are all ways of expressing a concern that something unpleasant might happen or has happened.

But the strange thing is that even though nothing ever seems to go wrong in reality, the worrier still can't stop being concerned about the next thing that doesn't go quite according to plan. It's like they are unable to learn from positive experience – they just continue to worry. Feeling anxious about the future becomes like a superstition, a mantra along the lines of 'if I worry beforehand, nothing bad will happen. I sacrifice my peace of mind, I show I care because I'm worried, and then nothing will go wrong.'

Another way of worrying is expressed in your behaviour. You get all worked up because you are expecting guests for the weekend and you are scrubbing an already clean house from top to bottom. You have a difficult client at work the next morning and you can't enjoy your evening or sleep at night because you can't stop thinking about all the things that could go wrong the next day. The worrying is happening in your head and is expressed via your actions and reactions.

Another type of worrying is the one that happens by implication, and this one is particularly hard on other people, especially children. My father used to do this when we were little. Whenever we fell over when rollerskating or running around and came crying to the house, he'd get angry and tell us off for not having been more careful. This was not what we needed at the time, but it was his way of showing that he had had a fright that something had happened to us and the worry that it could have been something worse. His anger was his expression of concern and was probably meant to warn us that we needed to be more careful.

No matter in which way you worry, bear in mind the following points:

- Whether you worry or not about someone else will not change what is happening to them.
- If you worry about a matter concerning yourself, it will be more likely to be to your disadvantage rather than to your advantage.
- If you don't worry about yourself or others, it doesn't mean you don't care.
- If you don't worry about yourself or others, you are not asking for trouble. You are asking for peace of mind, and that's OK.

Let's be clear about one thing, though: your active input into a successful outcome and positive results in your life is still required. It's no good having a positive attitude and being passive. You won't pass your exams unless you study for them.

You won't find the right job unless you make efforts to find it. If you are lazy, you have every reason to worry. If you have done your preparation, you are entitled to relax.

Affirmations

- I release my need to know in advance what is going to happen next and expect the best.
- I feel comfortable and relaxed as I allow good things and happy events to unfold in my life.
- I have the humility to admit that I don't know what's going to happen next, so I might as well relax.

Pick the affirmation/s you like best. You can also use several and combine them differently. Repeat your affirmation/s at least ten times in a row, three times a day, for a couple of weeks.

Visualisation

With your eyes closed, feel your worry in your head and anywhere else it is located in your body. Now imagine you could drift upwards out of your body, through the roof of your house and further up into the skies, and feel how you are leaving behind all the worries, just floating along in the blue skies, far removed from the troubles and problems of everyday life.

TIPS

- Make sure your worrying is not a side-effect of being overworked. If it is, deal with your workload (see page 197 in this chapter).

- A good way of disrupting constant worrying is to set aside particular times of day for worrying. Allocate five worry-minutes and worry properly and extensively during this time. Do not stop worrying before the time is up, but then stop. If you catch yourself worrying outside the allocated worry-minutes, remind yourself that this is not the time.

Case study

Sandra, at the age of 44, was driving her family nuts. She worried about everyone and everything all the time. She lacked confidence and was constantly on the lookout for bad news to confirm that her worrying was justified.

Her husband Frank was generally quite laidback, but even he found his wife fussing over the smallest things immensely trying. When friends came to stay, Sandra became very anxious in her attempt to have everything ready on time. When her 20-year-old son was half an hour late coming home, she'd be on the phone to her husband at work to tell him about this, seeking reassurance that nothing awful had happened. She would also go over conversations she had had with friends and neighbours, worrying that she might have said something to offend them. If she invited someone round and they could not make that date, she took it as a personal rejection, and nothing her husband could say would reassure her. Everything and anything was a problem.

The whole matter came to a head when Sandra realised that her daughter had started displaying similar symptoms of anxiety. Sandra was convinced that she had caused her daughter to develop into an unconfident young woman. It was at this point that Sandra decided to seek help.

In her hypnotherapy sessions, we worked on dealing with the underlying causes of Sandra's anxious nature. She had grown up in a house with a very timid mother and a domineering father who expected his two children and wife to jump to attention whenever he gave out orders. Nothing was ever good enough for him, and praise was meted out only on very rare occasions.

Once Sandra had let off steam about some incidents when she had been wrongly accused of being lazy, she started feeling better. As her confidence increased, her worry habit began to diminish. She felt better within herself and started developing self-respect. This meant that if she got a 'no' from someone, she could react in a calm manner. Gradually, she stopped expecting the worst to happen. Her family were just as relieved as she was when Sandra slowly began to feel more in control of her life.

Fiddling

My 20-year-old stepdaughter still sucks her thumb when she gets upset. She has been doing it since she was a baby, and her father wishes they had given her a dummy. 'At least that is something you can take away from them one day,' he has said more than once. The spontaneous gesture of tucking her thumb into her mouth is now so ingrained that she finds it very difficult to stop, even though she is serious about wanting to overcome the problem.

Sucking your thumb or twiddling your hair are comfort habits. When you are tired, bored or feeling emotional, you go for your 'dummy'. The physical sensations of soft hair between your fingers or latching onto the thumb in the mouth feel reassuring. Your subconscious mind at one time made a connection between these gestures and a feeling of comfort, and that is why these habits are not easy to break. It just doesn't make emotional sense to give up something that is reassuring when you need reassurance.

In many cases, the habit is established as a release from stress, boredom or sadness, but this does not mean that the habit subsides once the stressful period is over. Once your mind has made the 'comfort = fiddling' connection, the habit becomes automatic, and before you know it, you have been twiddling or sucking your thumb for quite a while.

The more aggressive habits of biting your nails, picking your skin or even pulling out hair are a bit different – these are signs of letting off steam. They are usually caused by emotional stress which you feel you cannot discharge in any other way. Maybe things at work are difficult but you cannot or will not speak to the person concerned, so instead, you bite your nails or pull out your hair. Maybe you are very worried about a situation in your life or even about something that happened in the past and you need to release the tension by attacking your own body. In my experience, there is often a facet of self-criticism, self-doubt or lack of confidence paired up with these habits.

Ideally, you will go and have the underlying issues sorted out with the help of a therapist. Alternatively, ask yourself the following questions:

- Do you feel that you have too many faults to be likeable?

- Do you feel guilty about something that has gone wrong for you in the past?

- Do you feel inadequate in the way you are dealing with present life issues?

- Are you feeling constantly stressed?

If you have said 'yes' to at least two of the above questions, go back to 'What makes you tick?' on page 23 to see if you can look at yourself or past events in a more constructive way so that your stress can be reduced.

Also, look at the following affirmations and let them help you change your attitude towards yourself.

Affirmations

- I can treat myself with respect while I work on improving myself.
- I am entitled to leave the past behind and begin to relax into greater self-acceptance.
- I now give myself a break and allow my hands to rest comfortably in my lap.
- I use my hands to stroke my hair/skin/nails gently and then I can relax and rest.

Pick the affirmation/s you like best. You can also use several and combine them differently. Repeat your affirmation/s at least ten times in a row, three times a day, for a couple of weeks.

Visualisation

Sit down and let your hands rest in your lap. With your eyes closed, be very aware of the feel of the air on your hands and of the pulse in your fingers. Imagine the pulse creating relaxation molecules that slowly pulse upwards into your lower arms, through your elbows and into your upper arms and shoulders. From there, the relaxation molecules cascade down into the trunk of your body, relaxing your stomach so that it can be very comfortable. Feel the tension leave your body and imagine every fibre and every cell of your body relaxing.

TIPS

- If you catch yourself twiddling, picking or biting, finish off the movement by stroking gently with the same hand over the area that you have just twiddled, picked or bitten. Then, with both hands, stroke your head gently from your hairline over the top of your head to the back of your head. Then let your hands rest in your lap for a count of ten.

- If you bite your nails, make sure you always have a nailfile on you. Make sure the rims of your nails are always smooth, as jagged edges will make it very tempting to bite them.

- If you suck your, let's say, right thumb and you catch yourself doing it, allow your right hand to drop down, gently gripping the elbow of your left arm, and with your left hand, gently hold on to your right elbow. Breathe deeply a few times while you are holding your elbows until you feel comfortable letting both your arms drop down.

Case study

Rosie (25) could not stop picking her skin. Whenever she had a scab anywhere, she would pick it, often until it bled. Her arms and legs were covered in scars, but she couldn't stop picking.

In Rosie's case, the picking was due to anxiety. Rosie wasn't quite clear why she felt anxious, only that she woke up in the morning feeling uptight and frightened. 'I don't seem to be able to let go of this inner tension,' she said. 'I don't have fun anymore, I'm just worrying constantly about silly things. It's rare these days that I feel relaxed at all. Even with good friends, I feel tense and anxious, without any apparent reason.'

Picking her scabs gave Rosie a little relief for a moment or two, but at the same time, she felt embarrassed and ashamed about her compulsion and kept her arms and legs covered all the time, even in summer.

Rosie needed to learn how to relax, so I taught her self-hypnosis. I gave her a CD with a general relaxation visualisation which she had to listen to at least once a day. This helped Rosie feel a little more in control, and her anxiety levels began to diminish. I also checked her for food allergies as these can often cause anxiety and even phobias. It turned out that Rosie had an intolerance to wheat, which she was eating a lot of. Sandwiches, pizzas, cakes and pasties were all part of her staple diet, and she was not happy at the prospect of having to stay away from all these comfort foods.

In the end, I persuaded her to give it a try for a week. Rosie came back for her next session and reported that she felt considerably better. After only two days off wheat, she had noticed how much calmer she felt in the mornings.

Summary

As a one-time hectic type myself, I can assure you that working on becoming more chilled out is worth it. Once you have learnt to take life in its stride, problems that used to upset you don't affect you half as much as they used to in the past. It is worth investing a little time every day to help your body and mind calm down, as this in turn will result in your stress habit fading away.

Conclusion

Habits save a lot of time. When you don't have to think about what you need to do next but do it automatically, your head is free to deal with other issues.

This is great – as long as the habit is a positive one. If your habit is detrimental to your health, well-being and relationships, it can cause enormous problems.

Habits run our lives, so it's worth keeping an eye on them. Building up good habits will prevent problem habits from developing in the first place, but life, of course, doesn't always run smoothly. When events get on top of you, your resolve can crumble and old bad habits surface again. It happens to the best of us, and it's nothing to be ashamed of.

If a problem habit is causing you distress or discontent, it's up to you to do something about it. It is your responsibility to get happier and to regain control over your life. No one can do it for you. If you need help, that's OK – get help. That, too, is your responsibility. Remember that unless you run your life, someone else will run it for you. That means you'll have to like what you get rather than get what you like.

Changing a habit for the better can be a lot easier than you think. Don't delay: start doing something about it *now*. You are not on your own if you decide to turn your life around. Others have achieved it, and you can achieve it too! The only thing you need to do is get started!

Further reading

Allen, D., *Getting Things Done: How to achieve stress-free productivity*, Piatkus, 2002

Batmanghelidj, F., *Your Body's Many Cries for Water*, Tagman Press, 2000

DesMaisons, K., *The Sugar Addicts Total Recovery Programme*, Simon & Schuster, 2000

Holford, P., *The Holford Low-GL Diet*, Piatkus Books, 2005

Johnson, V.E., *How to Help Someone Who Doesn't Want Help*, Beacon Press, 1989

Mathews Larson, J. *Seven Weeks to Sobriety,* Fawcett Books, 1997

Pedrick, C., *The OCD Workbook: Your guide to breaking free from obsessive-compulsive disorder*, New Harbinger Publications, 2000

Peiffer, V., *Inner Happiness*, Piatkus, 2003

Peiffer, V., *Positive Thinking*, Element Books, 1989

Peiffer, V., *Total Stress Relief,* Piatkus, 2004

Riley, G., *Eating Less: Take control of overeating*, Vermillion, 1999

Useful addresses

Counselling
British Association for Counselling and Psychotherapy
0870 44 35 252
www.counselling.co.uk

Health kinesiology
HK UK
08707 655 980
www.hk4health.com

Hypnotherapy
The Hypnotherapy Society
0845 602 4585
www.hypnotherapysociety.com

Obsessive-compulsive disorder
OCD Action
020 7226 4000
www.ocdaction.org.uk

Positive thinking
The Peiffer Foundation
020 8241 1962
www.vera-peiffer.com

Problems with alcohol
Alcoholics Anonymous
0845 769 7555

Problems with recreational drugs
Helpline Talk To Frank
0800 776600
www.talktofrank.com

Narcotics Anonymous
020 7730 0009

Index

abuse 29
adrenaline 81
adventure 109
advice 154–5
affirmations 79, 80–1, 116
  for anxiety 190–1
  for bad tempers 182
  for balance 110
  for break taking 105
  for checking and
    re-checking behaviours
    159
  for clutter chaos 164
  for confidence building
    147–8, 149
  for decision making 155
  for depression 190
  for drinking problems 134,
    135
  for exhaustion 191
  for fiddling behaviours
    214–15
  for financial matters 151
  for gossiping 186
  for honesty 179
  for internet addictions 143,
    144
  for laziness 191
  for overeating 130–1
  for overwork 200
  for perfectionism 168
  for phone-a-holism 114
  for pill popping 206
  for punctuality 176
  for relaxation 195
  for respect 172–3
  for self-valuing 94, 97, 100–1
  for shopping addictions 126
  for smoking 139
  for sugar addiction 122, 123
  for television addictions 118
  for worrying 211
alcohol problems 133–7
alcoholism 136–7
allergies 188, 217
anger 181–4
antidepressants 205, 208
anxiety
  affirmations for 190
  and checking and
    re-checking behaviour 158
  and clutter chaos 162–3
  combating 81–5
  tiredness due to 188, 189

visualisations for 191
see also worrying
assessing your habits 6–22
    defining bad habits 11–13
    risk factors for bad habits
        19–22
    testing for bad habits 13–16
    wake-up calls 17–19
attitudes
    hiccups 171–93
        bad tempers 181–4
        gossiping 184–8
        laziness 188–92
        lying 177–81
        time-keeping 175–7
    and perfectionism 167
    spring-cleaning your 73–87
autonomic nervous system 81

babies 20
bad tempers 181–4
balance 108–45
    affirmations for 110
    awareness of problems with
        108
    case studies 111–12
    and drinking problems
        133–7
    and internet addictions
        141–5
    and overeating 129–33
    and phone-a-holism 112–16
    points system for 111
    recognising 109–10
    and shopping addictions
        124–9
    and smoking 137–41
    and sugar addiction 120–4
    and television addiction
        116–20
    tips for maintaining 110
    visualisations for 110
bank statements 75
bartering 124–5
Bates method 39
behavioural therapy 158
bills, not opening 150–3
boarding school 28

bodily functions 44–5
boredom 21–2
bragging 93
breakfast 122
breaks 194
    not taking 103–6
breathing exercises 82–3
bribing yourself 9–10, 11
    see also rewarding yourself
bullying 187–8

'can do' stance 73
case studies
    alcoholism 136–7
    anxiety 81–2
    bad tempers 183–4
    balance 111–12
    catalogue addicts 12–13
    checking and re-checking
        behaviours 160–1
    chocoholics 42
    clutter chaos 165–6
    comfort eating 48–9, 51
    confidence 149–50
    fiddling 216–17
    financial control 152–3
    gossiping 187–8
    hoarding 28
    internet addictions 144–5
    laziness 191–2
    lying 180–1
    meal skipping 98–9
    overeating 131–3
    overworking 201–3
    perfectionism 169–70
    phone-a-holism 115–16
    pill popping 207–9
    punctuality 47–8, 51
    relationship problems
        49–50, 51
    relaxation 197
    respect 174–5
    saying no 102–3
    self-hatred 51–2
    shopping addictions 127–9
    smoking 140–1
    sugar addictions 17, 18,
        123–4

television addictions 119–20
wake-up calls 17–19
worrying 212–13
catalogue addicts 12–13
change
    beliefs about 24, 25–7
    bringing about 8–11, 17–19
chatrooms 142–3
checking and re-checking
  behaviours 157–61
chlamydia 177
chocoholics 42, 120, 123–4
cleanliness obsessions 160–1
clothes sizing 178
clutter 161–6
    see also hoarding; tidying up
comforting habits 16, 76–8
    comfort eating 48–9, 51
    comfort gestures 213–14
confidence 146–70, 180–1
    affirmations for 147–8, 149
    case studies 149–50
    and checking/re-checking
      behaviours 157–61
    and clutter chaos 161–6
    definition 146–7
    and not opening bills 150–3
    and perfectionism 166–70
    and procrastination 153–7
    tips for 148–9
    visualisations for 148,
      149–50
consistency 55, 69–71
control
    lack of 26, 29
    taking 41–4
counselling 135, 182
    person-centred 30
cravings 42, 83, 123, 133
creativity 54, 60–2, 77
credit cards 124, 127–9, 150
credit ratings 151
critical people 49
cystitis 98–9

dating agencies 149–50
debt 127–9, 150–3
decision making 153–7

defining habits 6
dehydration 35–6
dental fillings 207
dental health 120, 123
depression 27–8
    affirmations for 190–1
    and clutter chaos 162–3
    and recreational drug use
      208–9
    tiredness due to 189, 190
    visualisations for 191
    see also antidepressants
diabetes 120
    type 2 121
diet 117
    compulsive snacking 75
    fast food 129–30
    junk food 108
    overeating 75, 129–33
    skipping meals 95–9
    sugar addiction 17, 42,
      120–4, 132, 133
discontent 108
discussion forums 142–3
doing things for others 41
double standards 95
drinking problems 133–7
drug use 204–9

eating disorders 208
ecstasy 205, 207–9
eczema 123, 124
electromagnetic radiation 117
e-mails, compulsive checking
  75
emotions 8–10
    and clutter chaos 162–3
    and comfort eating 48–9,
      51
    and life structure 46, 48–52
    and the rational mind 8–9
    release of 214
    and the subconscious 45,
      78–9, 82
exhaustion
    affirmations for 191
    and clutter chaos 163
    and laziness 188, 189

and perfectionism 166
and pill popping 204
eye compresses 196
eye contact 148

family problems 21
fast food 129–30
  see also junk food
fear 45
  of change 27
  and failure to take breaks
    104
  and the rational mind 74,
    81–2
fiddling 213–17
fights, starting 49
financial matters
  not opening bills 150–3
  shopping addictions 12–13,
    124–9, 142, 144–5
flexibility 53–4, 57–8
food allergies 188, 217
food diaries 122, 178
function of habits 16
  see also comforting habits;
    protective habits
future 11

good habits
  advantages of 7–11, 34–45
  basic 35–41
  establishing 34–45, 90–1
gossiping 184–8
guilt 203

hair pulling 214
hair twiddling 213
happiness 27–8
health kinesiology 38, 42, 135
herbal remedies 206
here and now, focusing on 10,
  11
hoarding 28
  see also clutter
holidays 104–5
honesty 55, 68–9
  see also lying
humour 55, 65–6

hypnotherapy 30, 38
  for alcohol problems 135
  for checking and re-check-
    ing behaviours 158, 161
  and smoking 137
  for worrying 212–13
  see also self-hypnosis

imagery 83–5, 148
impatience 53, 56–7
inner voice 153
insecurity 167–8
insomnia 38
insulin resistance 120–1, 122
internet addictions 141–5
intimacy 109
intuition 153–7
inventiveness 54, 60–2, 77

junk food 108
  see also fast food

laziness 21–2, 188–92
learning 40
leisure 108, 111, 198–201
life changes 20
life flashpoints 19–22
life structure 46–52
  plotting your 50–1
  and your emotions 46,
    48–52
  and your organisational
    skills 46–8, 51, 52
loans 127
love 54, 62–4, 77
LSD 205
lying 177–81

management consultants
  98–9
marriages, unhappy 18, 180
medical websites 141–2, 143
mind, rational 8–9, 74, 81–2
mobile phones 112–16
money lending 100
mood enhancers 36–7
mood swings 42
Morocco 125

mothers
over-bearing 31–2
single 201–3
motivation
as resource 55, 67–8
understanding your 23–33
music 39–40

nail-biting 78, 79–80, 214–17
negative thinking 43–4
neglect, parental 28
nervous system, autonomic 81
nicotine 138
no, being able to say 93,
99–103

obesity 129, 132
other people
doing things for 41
pleasing 181
outdoors 38–9
overeating 75, 129–33
see also sugar addiction
overindulgence 108–45
drinking problems 133–7
internet addictions 141–5
overeating 129–33
phone-a-holism 112–16
retribution activities for
111
shopping addictions 124–9
smoking 137–41
sugar addictions 120–4
television addictions 116–20
overweight 129, 131–3, 177–9
overwork 190, 197–203, 211

pace of life 204
palming 39
panic modes 146–70
checking/re-checking
behaviours 157–61
clutter chaos 161–6
not opening bills 150–3
perfectionism 166–70
procrastination 153–7
parents
neglectful 28

overbearing 31–2
single 201–3
partners
meeting 149–50, 156–7
wanting 112
see also relationships
past experience
and anger 182
and checking/re-checking
behaviours 161
and drinking problems
135
and life structure 49–50
and worrying 212–13
patience 53, 56–7
perfectionism 166–70
perseverance 54, 64–5
phone-a-holism 112–16
physical exercise 8–10, 36–7,
109
physical relaxation 81–5
pill popping 204–9
pleasing others 181
positive thinking 43–4
powernaps 194
prescription drugs, obtaining
over the internet 141, 142
privacy 109
pro-activity 55, 71–8
procrastination 153–7
promotion 20
protective habits 16, 76–8
protein, dietary 98, 122
Prozac 208
psychotherapy 135
puberty 20
puddings 122
punctuality 47–8, 51, 175–7

rational mind 8–9, 74, 81–2
recreational drugs 205, 207–9
reinforcement, of bad habits
32
relapse prevention 86–7
relationships
learning to say no in 100
meeting partners 149–50,
156–7

problems 18, 19–20, 49–50, 51, 180
  unhappy marriages 18, 180
  wishing for 112
relaxation 51–2, 194–217
  affirmations for 195
  balancing 108
  case studies 197
  and fiddling behaviours 213–17
  music for 39–40
  outdoor trips for 38–9
  and overworking 197–203
  physical 81–5
  and pill popping 204–9
  recognising 195
  for the subconscious mind 79–81
  tips for 196
  valuing yourself with 98–9
  visualisations for 196, 197
  and worrying 209–13
resources
  consistency 55, 69–71
  definition 53
  developing your 53–74, 91
  flexibility 53–4, 57–8
  honesty 55, 68–9
  humour 55, 65–6
  inventiveness 54, 60–2
  love 54, 62–4
  motivation 55, 67–8
  patience 53, 56–7
  perseverance 54, 64–5
  pro-activity 55, 71–2
  tolerance 54, 58–60
respect 171–93
  and bad tempers 181–4
  characteristics of respectful people 172
  definition 171–2
  and gossip 184–8
  and laziness 188–92
  and lying 177–81
  self-respect 93, 171
  and time-keeping 175–7
rewarding yourself
  for breaking habits 9–10, 11
  encouraging consistency with 70–1
  encouraging motivation with 67–8
  the role of habits in 16, 76–8
risk factors, for bad habits 19–22

schools, boarding 28
security 109
self-beliefs, understanding your 23–33, 42–3
self-blame 30–1
self-criticism 24–33
self-esteem 93
self-hatred 27–8, 51–2
self-hypnosis 216–17
self-love 54, 62–4
self-neglect 92–107
self-punishment 26–7
self-respect 93, 171
self-sabotage 29–33, 49–50, 76–8
self-valuing 92–107
  affirmations for 94, 97
  and being able to say no 93, 99–103
  and meal skipping 95–9
  tips for 95
  visualisations for 94–5, 97
sexually transmitted infections (STIs) 177
shopping
  addictions 12–13, 124–9, 142, 144–5
  catalogue 12–13
  for food 131
  internet 142, 144–5
single parents 201–3
skin picking 214–17
sleep 37–8, 194
smoking 86–7, 137–41
  binge smoking 138–9
snacking, compulsive 75
soaps 117–18, 119, 184
Spurlock, Morgan 129–30
stimulants 204–5

STIs *see* sexually transmitted infections
stress 74, 79–80, 194–217
    and fiddling behaviours 213–17
    and life events 19–22
    and overworking 197–203
    and pill popping 204–9
    and reinforcement of bad habits 32
    and worrying 209–13
stressors 20
stuck, feelings of being 108, 156–7
subconscious mind 44–5, 76, 78–81
    accessing 79–81, 91
    and the autonomic nervous system 81
    and the emotions 45, 78–9, 82
sugar addiction 17, 42, 120–4, 132
    and drinking problems 133
sugar intolerance 121, 133, 135
Super Size Me (Documentary) 129–30

taking advantage 174–5
television, addiction to 111–12, 116–20
tempers 181–4
tension 32, 194
thoughts
    listening to your 43, 74–8
    negative 43–4
    positive 43–4
    racing 83
thumb sucking 213, 216
tidying up 74–5
    see also clutter
time-keeping 47–8, 51, 175–7
tolerance 54, 58–60
Tunisia 124–5

under-challenge 21–2

violence 182
visualisation 42, 80–1, 94–5, 112
    for anxiety 191
    for bad tempers 183
    for balance 110–11
    for break taking 105
    for checking and re-checking behaviours 159
    for clutter chaos 164
    for confidence building 148, 149–50
    for decision making 155
    for depression 191
    for drinking problems 134, 135
    for fiddling 215
    for financial matters 152
    for gossiping 187
    for honesty 179
    and imagery use 83–5, 148
    for internet addictions 143, 144
    for laziness 191
    for overeating 131
    for overwork 191, 200–1, 203
    for perfectionism 168
    for phone-a-holism 114
    for pill popping 206
    for punctuality 176
    for relaxation 196, 197
    for respect 173–4
    for self-valuing 94–5, 97, 101
    for shopping addictions 127
    for smoking 139
    for sugar addiction 122, 123
    for television addictions 118
    for worrying 211

wake-up calls 17–19
water consumption 35–6
    filtered water 36
weight gain 123, 129–30, 131–3, 178

weight loss 96, 124, 132–3,
192
Weight Watchers 132
wheat intolerances 217
work
balance at 108, 111
feeling stuck at 156–7

gossiping at 184
overwork 191, 197–203, 211
promotion 20
worrying 209–13
see also anxiety

yawning 196